CONSUMPTION ECONOMICS:
A Multidisciplinary Approach

CONSUMPTION ECONOMICS:

A Multidisciplinary Approach

MARGUERITE C. BURK
University of Minnesota

JOHN WILEY & SONS, INC.
New York · London · Sydney

Library of Congress Catalog Card Number: 67-31372
GB 471 12370X
Printed in the United States of America

To the memory of CLARA BROWN ARNY

PREFACE

This book is designed to introduce *both* college students in marketing economics, agricultural economics, and home economics *and* practitioners in marketing to the range of knowledge of consumption economics pertinent to marketing problems. It assumes that the reader already has elementary knowledge of economic principles and of market economies such as that of the United States.

More precisely, this book has been written with five objectives in mind.

1. It should provide an overall view and some detailed descriptions and analyses of consumption aspects of the United States market for consumer goods and services.

2. It should survey and integrate those sectors of knowledge of economics and other social sciences about consumer behavior and consumption trends and patterns which are relevant to marketing.

3. Applications of such knowledge to analysis of consumption aspects of marketing problems encountered by individual firms, industries, agriculture, and government agencies—at both the micro and macro levels—are to be described and demonstrated.

4. It should appraise the current supply of knowledge in terms of needs for such knowledge and possibilities of further developments in the near future.

5. Consumption trends and patterns of the United States should be compared and contrasted with those in selected developing countries.

Because the multidisciplinary approach and the emphasis of this book are unusual, knowledge of their sources may assist the reader in evaluating them. The development of this approach was shaped by my research experiences in the course of my former career as an agricultural economist in the U.S. Department of Agriculture and my current activities in teaching and research as a professor of agricultural economics and home economics at the University of Minnesota. Whereas I was primarily concerned with the macroeconomics of food consumption in the USDA, at Minnesota my perspective has broadened to include microeconomics of consumption and consumption of nonfood commodities and services. The problem-solving orientation of both agricultural economics and home economics has encouraged development of a multidisciplinary approach to consumption economics, supplementing economic knowledge with concepts, relationships, and methods from other social sciences.

The emphasis of this book on marketing aspects of consumption problems stems both from my experiences in studying consumer demand for agricultural commodities and from appraisal of the needs of students preparing for professional careers in business firms and government agencies. The selection of topics covered in this book and its orientation also reflect the views of marketing specialists in business and government regarding knowledge required for analysis of current and prospective consumption problems. Other limitations of coverage result from my own incomplete knowledge and the relatively primitive state of the sciences concerned with consumer behavior.

The reader will find much vaguely familiar material in this book, but he should beware of assuming such a degree of familiarity that he fails to notice the special meanings and interrelationships. Although he has been consuming goods and services all his life and has already studied some economics, the two sets of experiences do not add up to knowledge of consumption economics.

Most sections begin with a description of pertinent consumption trends or patterns. Explanations and examples of key concepts and relationships are provided, taken both from economics and other social sciences. A number of conceptual frameworks that integrate these concepts are described for use in solving major problems encountered by the government, business, and agriculture. A considerable variety of data and some relatively simple procedures are introduced in the process of analyzing consumption aspects of these problems and of some policies and programs related to them. Procedures described in appendices to Parts II and III should be supplemented with further statistical training by anyone intending to become an economic or market analyst.

Empirical research on a number of problems is reviewed and references to other studies are provided. Examples are taken from a wide range of consumer goods and services, but food examples predominate because of the greater variety of data and research available.

This book does not purport to cover advanced topics in modern theory of consumer behavior or demand theory, especially those requiring econometric development. Nor does it provide guidance to help the reader consume more wisely or in any specified way. Instead, the emphasis is on the kinds of knowledge about consumption problems needed by marketing people, in business firms, and government agencies as they study future trends in consumption, the whys of low consumption rates, and how business and legislative actions can affect consumption patterns.

After studying this book, the reader is likely to have a broad view of the types of knowledge involved in consumption economics, but he will not know all about the subject. Even persons who have worked as consumption economists for years freely admit the limitations of their knowledge of this very diffuse field. Also, the more one learns about a subject as complicated and multidisciplinary as consumption the more one becomes conscious of gaps in his knowledge and in the total available supply of pertinent knowledge.

Part I is a general introduction to knowledge of consumption economics and the structure and processes of consumption in the United States and selected developing countries. Part II focuses first on the behavior of individual consumers and then moves toward groups as the process of aggregation leads to macro problems and knowledge. Part III is concerned with macroeconomics of consumption, initially in terms of static situations and structures, then with dynamics of trends in consumption. Chapters 16 to 18 provide a variety of examples of consumption studies related to macroeconomic analyses of changes in consumer markets and in other aspects of national economies.

Parts I and II can be used by mature college students interested primarily in micro aspects of consumer behavior. Parts I and III provide an introduction to macroeconomics of consumption. But I have found that rapid reading of Part II is usually necessary to refresh students' memories of materials touched on in elementary economics and to provide a little understanding of behavioral aspects underlying macro structures and processes of consumption.

ACKNOWLEDGMENTS

Every mature individual in professional life is aware of his indebtedness to many people who have stimulated and influenced his intellectual development. Ordinarily, these are unrecorded, except in authors' prefaces or acknowledgments.

Therefore it seems fitting to acknowledge my indebtedness to:

(1) Frederick V. Waugh, Oscar C. Stine, James P. Cavin of the U.S. Department of Agriculture and my former colleagues in the Consumption Section of the U.S. Economic Research Service who challenged, encouraged, and assisted me in learning how to study trends and variations in United States food consumption.

(2) Janet Murray and Faith Clark of the U.S. Agricultural Research Service who urged me to study the contributions of social sciences other than economics to understanding consumer behavior.

(3) Sherwood O. Berg, Vernon W. Ruttan, and E. Fred Koller of the Institute of Agriculture, University of Minnesota, for their support during the difficult process of carrying on a substantial research and teaching program concurrently with the development of a more comprehensive understanding of consumption economics.

(4) Reuben L. Hill, Murray A. Straus, and Wallace A. Russell of the University of Minnesota and James A. Bayton of Howard University who guided my studies in sociology and psychology.

(5) The many students in my classes in consumption economics during the last six years who forced me to think more clearly and to put forth my ideas in a more orderly fashion.

(6) Especially to the memory of Clara Brown Arny, teacher of teachers (Professor Emeritus of Home Economics, University of Minnesota), for professional and personal inspiration and advice as I learned the new role and responsibilities of higher education, and for her tutoring in how to teach and write so as to expedite learning.

In addition, I wish to note the professional contributions of the reviewers for a number of my articles and early drafts of this book, including Herman Southworth, Harold Breimyer, Frederick Waugh, Gwen Bymers, Ruth Deacon, Marilyn Dunsing, Lois Lund, Sylvia Ogren, Kenneth Ogren, Barbara Miller, Dale Dahl, James Shaffer, and reviewers for the *Journal of Farm Economics* and John Wiley & Sons. I am particularly indebted to the editors of the *Journal of Farm Economics, Journal of Home Economics, AAUW Journal,* and *Economie Rurale* who have stimulated and encouraged me to develop areas of research for articles in their journals and permitted me to quote them extensively.

An integrating book such as this draws heavily on professional literature. Although full citations are provided in the bibliography and brief references in footnotes, I wish to give special acknowledgments of permissions to quote substantial sections to: the editor of the *Journal of Marketing* published by the American Marketing Association; Irwin Friend, director of the Wharton School of Finance and Commerce staff for the Study of Consumer Expenditures, Incomes, and Saving; Alfred L. Seelye, editor of *Marketing in Transition;* Prentice-Hall, Inc., for text sections and data from *Impacts of Monetary Policy* by the Committee for Economic Development's Commission on Money and Credit; and the MIT Press for sections from Charles Abrams' *Man's Struggle for Shelter in an Urbanizing World.*

MARGUERITE C. BURK

St. Paul, Minnesota
September 1967

CONTENTS

CONTENTS

CONSUMPTION ECONOMICS:

A Multidisciplinary Approach

PART I

WHAT IS CONSUMPTION ECONOMICS?

1

ON THE SCOPE AND CONTENT OF CONSUMPTION ECONOMICS

1.1 INTRODUCTION

What do different groups of people buy? Why do they buy what they buy? What will they buy next year, five years from now, in ten years? What kind of houses will Americans want in 1980? What will be the demand for processed food X in the New York City area in 1970? Will American consumers continue to increase their consumption of beef? Why do the people of India eat so little beef? What will happen to the United States demand for foreign cars in the next few years?

These are samples of questions that require knowledge of consumption economics. Consumption economics is the branch of economics that focuses on consumers' behavior as they allocate economic resources to satisfy their wants. Consumption economists make use of a generally accepted or *standard* body of economic theory about the behavior of individual consumers and some theory pertinent to total or aggregate consumption for large groups of people, as in a whole country. In addition, marketing researchers and economists carry on a great variety of empirical research. Both detailed, short-lived facts about who consumes what and longer-lived generalizations and basic understandings about consumption trends and variations emerge from this research. Also, consumption economists make use of theories and empirical knowledge developed in the behavioral sciences of psychology, sociology, social psychology, and anthropology.

1.2 CONSUMPTION ECONOMICS IN RELATION TO ECONOMICS, MARKETING, AND OTHER SOCIAL SCIENCES

Definitions of concepts are an essential part of knowledge of each scientific discipline. Therefore we begin the study of consumption economics with a brief review of several definitions.

1.2.1 The Subject Matter of Economics

To determine exactly what *economics* is, let us look at two definitions. Samuelson describes economics as "the study of how men and society *choose*, with or without the use of money, to employ *scarce* productive resources to produce various commodities over time and to distribute them for consumption, now and in the future, among various people and groups of society."[1]

Robbins defines economics as the "science which studies human behavior as a relationship between ends and scarce means which have alternative uses."[2] Robbins' care in defining economics to include both material and nonmaterial means and wants is particularly helpful because we want to include, for example, cultural and recreational aspects of consumption as well as the usual food, shelter, and clothing. Although Robbins' definition has to be interpreted rather freely to cover income and employment analysis, commonly studied under the title of "macroeconomics," it clarifies the meaning of the economics part of consumption economics.

1.2.2 Consumption

For economic and marketing analysis, *consumption* is sometimes defined in terms of the quantities of goods and services taken from the

[1] Page 6 of Samuelson, Paul A. *Economics: An Introductory Analysis.*

[2] Page 16, Robbins, Lionel. *An Essay on the Nature and Significance of Economic Science.*

market. This definition does not encompass the consumption of goods and services produced for one's own use, called "subsistence production" or "home production." Nor does it take into account the fact that consumer goods such as houses and refrigerators are not used up immediately after they are purchased or "taken from the market." We must include both the selection and use of goods and services by consumers as parts of consumption economics because of their importance to analysis of variations in consumption among different groups of people and to prediction of changes in consumption from one time to another.

1.2.3 Aspects of Consumption Studied by Social Scientists

A number of social science disciplines involve some aspects of the knowledge of consumer behavior, but the emphasis differs. Since consumption economics is a branch of economics, it is not surprising that many *general economists* study the same problems as the more specialized consumption economists. The line between the interests and research of the two groups of economists is very indistinct. Specialists in consumption economics usually are involved in developing special sets of data and try to explore the ramifications of consumption problems. Consumption economists tend to draw more heavily on related behavioral sciences in order to study all aspects of consumers' behavior in making and changing their choices. By using a wider range of knowledge, these economists seek to improve their explanations and predictions of trends in consumption.

Some people argue that consumption economics is really more of a multidisciplinary field than a subarea of standard economics. But it retains its ties to economics by its focus on economic behavior and economic phenomena, i.e., on the allocation of scarce resources and on the value of goods and services purchased by individual consumers and by groups of consumers.

Marketing-oriented microeconomics of consumption overlaps both consumer economics and family economics to some extent. *Consumer economics* usually emphasizes the study of the consumer in the economy and the information needed for individuals and families to be more expert or more efficient or more satisfied consumers. It is taught from the consumer point of view, not from the standpoint of marketing interests in consumption.

Family economics includes the economics of income-earning and saving as well as that which is related to consumption. It focuses on the economic problems encountered by families of different types, on factors entering into those problems and affecting family decision making, and on the results of such decisions over the family life cycle.

Consumption economics is sometimes confused with *welfare economics*, a macroeconomic area which has developed from the theory of consumer behavior. Welfare economics starts from the assumption that the welfare of an individual is determined by the satisfaction or utility he derives from goods and services. The second key assumption is that the welfare of society is the sum of the welfare of individuals in the society. Because welfare economics is essentially a separate branch of economics and has contributed little to the development of the aspects of consumption economics pertinent to marketing, we will touch upon it only tangentially in this book.

Obviously, many *marketing specialists* also study consumer behavior and trends in consumption. Here the emphasis has been primarily on finding answers to questions of individual business firms, such as (1) what are the potential sales for a specific product X with certain characteristics, and (2) what kinds of communications through advertising and other forms of promotion will be most effective in getting certain groups of consumers to buy product X or to increase their purchases? Also, marketing researchers for business firms do more than study the demand for the products of their firms. They often investigate the characteristics of alternative marketing channels, alternative locations of specific types of processing and distribution facilities, and so on. Relatively few marketing researchers have taken a broader, long-range view of trends in consumption of an entire country. Such research is clearly within the macro area of consumption economics.

Many *psychologists* and some *sociologists* have worked on problems related to consumer behavior. They have been concerned with the potential demand for different kinds of characteristics in established products and for new products being developed or considered for development by individual firms. A number of important ideas about consumer behavior which have evolved from the cooperation of psychologists with economists and marketing specialists will be discussed in later chapters.

1.3 MAIN CURRENTS IN THE DEVELOPMENT OF KNOWLEDGE IN CONSUMPTION ECONOMICS

Every field of knowledge develops from convergence of several currents of activity. Consumption economics has been evolving from professional work along the following lines: (1) microeconomic theory relating consumer behavior to price, income, and in recent years to other socioeconomic factors; (2) macroeconomic theory of market demand (in response to price) and of the consumption function (in response to income); (3) empirical economic studies; (4) developments in the applied areas of family and consumer economics and in marketing; and (5) some subareas of the behavioral sciences, especially social psychology and sociology.

1.3.1 Microeconomic Theory of Consumer Behavior

Economic theory of consumer behavior was synthesized by Alfred Marshall toward the end of the nineteenth century from ideas of the classical economists and the proponents of the theory of marginal utility, especially the Austrian economists. Bentham is the best known among the group of classical economists who emphasized the subjective aspects of human wants and the utility derived from satisfaction of those wants. Members of this group are often called "hedonists."

Marshall identified consumption with demand and was primarily concerned with the relationships between consumer choice making and the determination of market prices. Although Marshall touched briefly on the subject of changes in demand over a period of years, he and most economists in the first half of the twentieth century concentrated on demand schedules and demand curves to explain the quantity of a commodity which would be taken from the market at alternative prices and at a given but unspecified point in time.

The concept of utility is basic to the standard theory of consumer behavior, and most of the formal economics of consumption is built on it. As empirical economics and the science of psychology developed, the impossibility of measuring utility in cardinal numbers caused a cardinal utility explanation of consumer behavior to lose favor. An ordering approach, called indifference analysis, has gained much favor, especially since J. R. Hicks gave it new impetus by his 1939 exposition in *Value and Capital.*

Since World War II numerous economic theorists, among whom Samuelson has been prominent, have worked toward integration of the alternative approaches to consumer behavior in response to variations in price. Other economists have paid particular attention to problems of categorizing and adding up or aggregrating both consumers and their choices from among commodities. The complexity of the concept of income has been explored and several hypotheses about its relationship to consumer behavior have been formulated at the micro level. These hypotheses have been applied extensively to the study of the behavior of aggregates of consumers, that is, at the macro level.

As economists have researched the demand for nonfood goods and services, especially for durables such as automobiles, household equipment, and housing, the significance of changes in socioeconomic factors affecting consumption and of accumulated stocks of goods has become apparent and has encouraged development of economic dynamics. In other words, economic theory is being developed to explain (and hopefully to predict) how the purchases of automobiles by families in one year are affected by the ages of their old cars, by earlier events such as income in the preceding two or three years, and by their expectations regarding future income and price changes.

The early theory of consumer behavior seemed to place every consumer in the position of Robinson Crusoe on a desert island but without the presence of his man Friday. Probably this is the result of the facts that economists are generally highly specialized and that few pay attention to concurrent developments in other social sciences. But there have been some notable exceptions among empirical researchers. The potential effect of our neighbors' income and purchase patterns on our behavior as consumers is increasingly recognized. Necessary changes in basic economic theory at the micro level remain to be worked out.

Postwar studies of decision making by consumers and entrepreneurs have emphasized the concept of process. The scope of investigation has begun to broaden from the assumption of endless repetition of initial choices by consumers to the recognition that subsequent consumer choices are affected by what consumers learn about the attributes of the goods they have bought and used. Also, a few economists are beginning to try to fit individual choices into a more general framework of problem solving.

Thorstein Veblen was a very original thinker and institutional economist. His book on human behavior, *The Theory of the Leisure Class*, was published near the end of the nineteenth century and has become a significant part of American social heritage. Veblen argued that changes in consumption occur through imitation of consumption patterns of the leisure class which is noted for its conspicuous consumption. This remarkably unsuccessful professor but prolific writer was always interested in the process of growth and change. This interest was common among institutional economists but uncommon among the orthodox economists. Today we criticize many of the facts and interpretations of this critic of American life, but we recognize his enduring contributions to our understanding of patterns and changes in consumption.

1.3.2 Macroeconomic Theory Related to Consumption

The subdivision of economics into micro and macro theory is largely a post-World War II development. Before 1940 most economic theory pertinent to consumption by large groups of people, as for example, the entire population of the United States, was developed from the theory of behavior of an individual consumer by direct generalization. What the individual consumer would do in response to price alternatives or income changes was assumed to hold true for all consumers in a market or country. This assumption ignored differences among individuals and a variety of problems in summing or aggregating over many people and often over several slightly different products.

The prewar theory of market demand which described how the quantities of a commodity taken by all consumers from the market would vary at alternative prices was such a generalization. The market demand schedule was envisioned as the sum of the schedules of individuals in the market, without many complications. But the aggregation of incomes of individuals making up the market was gradually recognized to involve quite complex problems.

Keynes' theory of the consumption function[3] was based on his introspective view of how a consumer must react to variations in income. This theory became an important part of his macroeconomic theory of employment, prices, and income. His theory of the income-consumption relationship is now described as the *absolute-income hypothesis* since it referred to income in the period of actual consumption and was not related to other incomes. Since 1945 several other hypotheses have been put forth. These relate current consumption to earlier peak income, to the income position of other families in the community, to incomes expected by families at particular stages in the family life cycle, or to lifetime income expectations.

1.3.3 Empirical Studies by Economists

To meet the need for data on national product, income, and expenditures, a system of *national income and output accounting* has been set up in practically all economically developed countries. Estimates have been made regularly since the late 1930s by the Office of Business Economics of the U.S. Department of Commerce, largely on the bases of census and trade data on production and distribution of consumer goods and from a great variety of data pertinent to consumer services.[4] National aggregates of consumer expenditures for major categories of goods and services are published regularly by the U.S. Department of Commerce. The evolution of such data during the last 30 years has been encouraged by the National Bureau of Economic Research and by proponents of Keynesian theories of employment, income, and consumption. These annual expenditure data cover the whole population of the United States. (They are examples of what economists call "time series.") The official series go back to 1929. Studies based on these data are published from time to time in the *Survey of Current Business*, is-

[3] See Chapter 6 of this book. The theory was described in Book III of Keynes, John Maynard. *The General Theory of Employment, Interest and Money*.

[4] For description of data and concepts, refer to *U.S. Income and Output*, a 1958 supplement to the *Survey of Current Business*.

sued monthly by the U.S. Department of Commerce.

The *quantities of food and some other goods and services consumed* in the United States have been studied for many years by researchers in the Federal agencies. Questions about farm surpluses, the national food situation during emergency periods of droughts and wars, long-time trends in demand, and nutrient supplies led (*a*) to the gradual development of a great variety of time-series data pertaining to food consumption, and (*b*) to extensive analyses of such data in the U.S. Department of Agriculture. The time-series data on total and per capita consumption of major agricultural commodities, especially food, are published regularly by the U.S. Department of Agriculture. They will be used extensively in Part III of this book to demonstrate the macro concepts, relationships, and analytical procedures of consumption economics. The variety, comprehensiveness, and reliability of data on food consumption are much greater than for any other major group of consumer goods or services.

In recent years public problems with consumer services such as medical care and housing have stimulated development of new statistical data by the Federal Government. But much more research is needed before such data achieve quality and coverage matching current food statistics and consumption research.

The inception of modern *statistical demand analysis* or *price analysis* is usually traced to Henry L. Moore's research on economic cycles in which he tried to establish laws of the demand for agricultural products.[5] Since Moore's findings were published in 1914, tremendous statistical effort by many researchers has gone into the study of factors influencing the prices of specific commodities.

In some respects, consumption economics has profited from such efforts because price analysis required the development of consumption data and statistical techniques useful in the analysis of consumption trends and variations. But price analysts have rarely paid much attention to the socioeconomic factors which bring about changes in consumer tastes and preferences. Economists generally consider the formation of tastes and preferences to be the subject matter for sociologists or psychologists. Therefore economists working on analysis of changes in market demand treat "tastes and preferences" as already set or "given." They often attribute to changes in tastes and preferences the residual of the total change in consumer demand which is not explained by changes in prices, in incomes, or by random variation. Some specialists in demand analysis have also made significant contributions to the development of consumption analysis, for example, Henry Schultz, Warren Waite, Meyer Girshick, Frederick Waugh, John D. Black, Mordecai Ezekiel, O. C. Stine, Willard Cochrane, Lawrence Klein, and Herman Wold.

Although some economists consider price or demand analysis to be a part of consumption economics, it is not covered in this book for several reasons. A number of textbooks handle the subject matter quite competently. Price analysis is usually applied to problems with short time spans. In contrast, consumption economics pertains more to problems with longer time periods, in which consumer tastes and preferences and a variety of socioeconomic factors may change.

Consumer surveys have been conducted and studied for centuries.[6] In the seventeenth century Gregory King surveyed English consumers as part of his tax research. A trio of nineteenth century Europeans interested in problems of poverty started an extensive series of studies of family living expenses. Edouard Ducpétiaux collected data from Belgian families in the middle of the nineteenth century. Frédéric Le Play started as a mining engineer but shifted to the full-time study of the living conditions of European workers who were in the midst of the Industrial Revolution. Another mining engineer, Ernst Engel, became interested in social statistics and developed his famous law about the relationship of food consumption to income from analysis of the data collected by Ducpétiaux and Le Play.

In 1875 Carroll D. Wright, Commissioner of Labor Statistics in Massachusetts, published an outstanding study of incomes and expenditures of Massachusetts workingmen's families, including a great collection of data which has

[5] For an evaluation of Moore's contributions, see Stigler, George. "Henry L. Moore and Statistical Economics," pp. 343–373 of *Essays in the History of Economics.*

[6] For an excellent review of early surveys, see Stigler, George J. "The Early History of Empirical Studies of Consumer Behavior," pp. 198–233 of his *Essays in the History of Economics.*

been subjected to careful analysis. Wright's interest stemmed from concern with social reform, a concern shared by many succeeding investigators of family expenditures in the late nineteenth and twentieth centuries. Others were concerned with nutrition education (Atwater), standards of living (Ogburn and Zimmerman), comparison of costs of living (British Board of Trade), and development of price indices (U.S. Departments of Commerce and Labor). In contrast, few economists evidenced any particular interest in income-consumption relationships until greatly improved income data were developed in the 1920s and 1930s.

The Great Depression of the 1930s focused attention on income and consumption and led to the monumental Consumer Purchases Study (CPS) of 1935–36.[7] Before the flood of data started from that study, Zimmerman, an American sociologist, published a comprehensive review of theories and empirical studies related to consumer behavior in *Consumption and Standards of Living.*

Since the thirties, there have been a number of large-scale and hundreds of small-scale surveys. Many were made with government or university financing so their results have been published. Others have been part of commercial market research by private firms, relatively few of which have been published. The nationwide studies of consumer expenditures by the U.S. Bureau of Labor Statistics and the U.S. Department of Agriculture and those of food consumption by the latter department supply many of the data used in examples of consumption analyses in Parts II and III of this book.

Near the end of World War II, the Federal Reserve Board began financing surveys of consumer finances. These were first conducted by the U.S. Department of Agriculture, later by the Survey Research Center (SRC) at the University of Michigan. Currently, the SRC and the U.S. Bureau of the Census use alternative approaches in their surveys of consumer finances. The SRC psychologist and economist, George Katona, has provided strong leadership for those economists who view shifts in consumers' expectations and attitudes as highly significant in economic change. Such surveys have also attracted the interest of business research groups in some universities and in business organizations like the National Industrial Conference Board. Many of the surveys have provided data for the study of expenditures on durable goods.

[7] Many reports with data from the CPS were issued, mostly by the National Resources Committee, the U.S. Bureau of Labor Statistics, and the U.S. Bureau of Human Nutrition and Home Economics.

1.3.4 Developments in Other Applied Areas

A relatively small group of economists has been concerned about *family and consumer problems* and about the roles of families and consumers in the economy. Hazel Kyrk led the way with her doctoral dissertation, *A Theory of Consumption*, published in 1923. Many of the economists who have specialized in family economics did their graduate work under her direction. Kyrk's theory of consumption was essentially that consumption is significantly determined by the "standards of living" of individual families and of the whole society, which, in turn, are shaped by the same socioeconomic forces that form other institutions. Kyrk and other family and consumer economists have pointed out quite explicitly the problems faced by consumers in making choices in a complex industrial society.

The Great Depression of the 1930s and a variety of governmental programs to encourage economic recovery sharpened a latent conflict between producer and consumer interests. The areas of this conflict were clarified by those consumer economists who sought consumer representation in government and urged legislative and administrative action to protect unwary consumers from the economic wolves among business firms.

Another major objective of consumer economists reflects their common background in high school and college teaching. They seek to teach the workings of the marketing system to consumers and to help them discover and follow wiser buying and financial management practices. The latter objective is similar to one objective of home management specialists within home economics.

Marketing has contributed to the development of consumption economics in three important ways. *First,* marketing people have raised many questions requiring integration of current knowledge of consumption trends and patterns. To find answers, exploration of new areas is often necessary, including collection and analysis of new data. Examples of such questions are: Why does the per capita consumption of family flour continue to decline?

How much more can the consumption of premixes be expanded?

Second, marketing people have stimulated recognition (by consumption economists) that marketing services are increasingly significant components of the commodities and services consumers want. These marketing services include assembly, handling, processing, storage, and distribution of raw materials produced by agriculture, fisheries, mines, and forests. As incomes, degree of urbanization, and complexity of industry and technology increase, the decline in subsistence or home production and increased total consumer demand for goods and services raise the demand for the services of marketing agencies.

Third, marketing researchers have contributed data on consumer actions with respect to individual products and on relationships between such consumer behavior and specified socioeconomic characteristics. Such specific data are useful in the search for generalizations about behavior which are needed for further development of consumption economics.

1.3.5 Psychological and Sociological Research Related to Consumer Behavior

Theoretical economics is a deductive science based on rigid assumptions regarding man's rationality, complete knowledge, and independence. Modern psychology and sociology contradict these assumptions. Many theoretically oriented economists pay little attention to the empirically based knowledge of other social scientists, but economists and marketing people engaged in empirical work on consumption problems have been considerably influenced by psychological and sociological research. In Chapter 5 of Part II we will consider some of the major contributions of such research to the understanding of consumer behavior. Frequent use will be made of concepts and variables developed in these behavioral sciences and in anthropology throughout this book.

1.4 KINDS OF KNOWLEDGE INCLUDED IN CONSUMPTION ECONOMICS

Each subarea or area of knowledge has a somewhat specialized language which is used to communicate ideas precisely and which plays a vital part in further development of its knowledge. Philosophers of science tell us that the concepts of a science are like the words of everyday speech and that the definitions and statements of individual facts and laws correspond to our usual sentences. Scientific theories are usually made up of sets of such sentences.

1.4.1 Concepts and Relationships

To be more precise, the concepts of science are descriptive terms which convey to the student of each science the key attributes and relations of inanimate objects, organisms, and societies. For examples, relatively few Americans are *hungry* (an attribute), but *larger* (a relation) numbers are badly housed because they are *poor* (an attribute). Note how many terms or concepts in that sentence can be fully understood only if we place them in the context of a specified level of living and provide some definitions. By convention, we do not refer to the degree of hunger experienced only just before meals. But we need to identify whether we mean hunger in terms of shortages of food energy or so-called "hidden hunger," meaning malnutrition due to shortage of one or more important nutrients in the diets of the people concerned. These concepts belong to nutrition, but they also have economic importance.

The concept of poverty is really quite complex. The average American layman with no knowledge of consumption economics can readily conclude that an American family of several persons living in a city with no assets and an income of $1000 in 1965 was poor. But his application of the term "poor" to an elderly widower living on his own farm and having $1000 in net money income would be much less certain. Consumption economists use *operational* definitions for such concepts which state the conditions which must be met for proper application of the term *poverty.* To get at the meaning of poverty, it is necessary first to define the term *net money income,* which is used to give meaning to the concept. The next step is to measure income and other characteristics of families, such as age composition. Then these measures for particular families must be compared with the conditions established for application of the concept.

An individual concept is useful or significant only when it is connected with one or more other facts. Again, our philosophers of science tell us that connections among facts or relationships are *general facts* or *generalizations.* Very broad generalizations are *laws.* One of the few laws in consumption economics is Engel's law which states that the poorer a family is, the larger the share of its expenditures which will be allocated to food.

Scientists develop and test tentative *hypotheses* or generalizations about relationships among concepts or sets of observed phenomena, such as expenditures and incomes. They seek *laws* which make possible adequate explanations of sets of phenomena and prediction of future events. At this beginning stage in your study of consumption economics, you need to know only that concepts are formulated according to certain rules and that there are other rules which govern the confirmation of hypotheses and the construction of theories.

1.4.2 Standard Economic Knowledge about Consumption

In elementary economics the reader should have encountered such micro concepts of consumption economics as utility, demand schedules, tastes and preferences, marginal utility of money, and the equimarginal principle. We will review the meanings of such concepts in Part II and go further into economic theory built with these and other concepts. In Part III we will take up concepts and relationships that apply to large groups of people, forming part of the macroeconomics of consumption. In considering both the micro and macro dimensions of consumption, we will shift back and forth from the quantitative aspects, such as poundage of meat or number of houses, to the price and value of food or housing or recreation consumed. In fact, *price* and *value* are particularly important concepts in economics.

During the last 25 years, knowledge of the nature and significance of the temporal dimension of consumption economics has developed considerably. Most economists now agree that knowledge of the current income of families is frequently insufficient for prediction of many of their consumption rates or aspects of their level of living. We need to know about their relative income position—relative to their own past levels and to the incomes of others—and about their expectations regarding their future incomes in relation to expected changes in their family situation.

1.4.3 Processes and Structure

For years economists have talked about production, distribution, and consumption processes, but they have been much more interested in inputs and outputs of such processes than in the processes themselves. They have ascribed knowledge of the processes as coming under *technology*. Since World War II the upsurge of interest in tracing stages in the decision-making process and collaboration with psychologists has added to our understanding of both processes and structure. The concept of *process* refers to a sequence of interrelated actions directed toward some goal, purpose, or end. Implicit in this concept are ideas of a time sequence, subprocesses, and overlaps in processes in the sense that one process often contains components of others. We will regard each process as terminating in an *event* such as a purchase or some other observable action. The concept of *structure* contains the ideas of an organized whole and of interconnected and dependent elements. Structures have dimensions, by which we will mean measurable extents such as length, depth, breadth, or poundage.

The standard economics of consumer behavior relates behavior in the form of variations in purchases of a good (the events) directly to variations in price or income or level of total expenditure. In so doing, economists assume one-to-one relationships between both (*a*) certain services needed by a consumer (e.g., protection from cold) and the attributes of a particular good such as a wool suit, and (*b*) the attributes wanted in this good and those available in the products generally offered in the retail stores. Economists generally ignore the importance of consumer perception of attributes needed, sought, and actually provided by the purchased item. But marketing people are particularly concerned with the whole matter of formation and change in tastes and preferences through learning and changes in consumers' perception. Therefore this textbook summarizes knowledge drawn in part from the behavioral sciences about the process of consumer *use* of goods and services as well as about the process of consumer *choice* and knowledge of the socioeconomic factors related to these processes.

Moreover we will consider *structure* in a variety of ways. At a descriptive level, the concept of structure may refer to the packages or combinations of goods and services which groups of consumers buy. Or we may apply the term structure to the pattern of rates of expenditure or quantities consumed by differ-

ent population groups such as low-, medium-, and high-income families, or to different regional groupings. To develop a clearer picture of sectors of the total market and investigate the *whys* of variations and trends in consumption, we must think of the socioeconomic structure of consumption with these dimensions:

(1) Behavioral	Using concepts and measures from the behavioral sciences
(2) Economic and technical	Measures of quantity, value, and quality
(3) Temporal	Varying from the situation to the highly dynamic
(4) Aggregative	Ranging from the micro case of one individual to the macro level of world consumption

1.4.4 Procedures

An essential part of the knowledge in each subarea of economics is made up of the basic procedures used in measuring the particular economic phenomena, applying generalizations, and testing hypotheses. Some of the procedures used by professional researchers in consumption economics are not generally covered in modern elementary statistics courses, so it is desirable to discuss them along with the basic content in this text. However, more sophisticated methods than those presented in this book are usually employed by skilled researchers whenever the data pertinent to a particular problem are sufficiently well developed.

1.4.5 Coverage of Consumption Economics in This Book

Formal economic theory of consumer behavior is part of the subject matter of advanced courses in general economics. The presentation of the basic elements of standard theory in this book is at a rather elementary level for several reasons. Many students who need some knowledge of consumption economics have had only a year's work in general economics and insufficient mathematics for an intermediate exposition of the formal theory. The writing of every textbook requires choices among the total range of pertinent subjects. Much of the knowledge of consumption economics used by researchers who are specialists in the field is not covered in any textbook in economics or marketing or in earlier books on consumption economics. The general criterion for selection of content and emphasis in this introductory text on consumption economics was the significance of the subject matter to people preparing for professional work related to marketing. Therefore the treatment of the formal economic theory of choice is limited in order to devote more attention to the process of use, and to description and analysis of the consumption patterns of individuals and households, including study of socioeconomic factors other than price and income.

Similarly, intermediate courses in macroeconomic theory devote much attention to the modifications of the original Keynesian theory of the consumption function as they consider the interrelationships of variations in employment, income, consumption, and saving. Some courses also cover changes in consumer finances and consumer attitudes in relation to changes in the business cycle. There are special economics courses and texts in welfare economics in which alternative public policies regarding taxation, subsidies, and so on are appraised in terms of maximizing total welfare of all consumers. The subject of market demand is an essential part of price theory, so knowledge about it is readily available to interested students. In contrast, relatively little has been published in textbooks about the concepts, relationships, and procedures used by specialized researchers as they study changes in the macro structure of the consumption of major types of goods and services. Therefore this text will emphasize the following topics in the macroeconomics of consumption:

(*a*) A description of historical changes in aggregates and averages and in variations in consumption of major groups of commodities and selected items;

(*b*) The study of interrelationships among these historical changes;

(*c*) The study of these relationships to other social and economic phenomena;

(*d*) The drawing of some general conclusions concerning trends and relationships which may eventually develop into a new body of formal theory.

1.5 PROBLEMS AND CHALLENGES

In writing this text, I have assumed that consumption economics is still in an early stage of development. Therefore it is important to identify for the reader which of the areas in the field require much more knowledge to be developed. They are best identified by describing the difficulties now being encountered by economists and other social scientists working on specific aspects of consumption problems. Each difficulty poses a challenge for research by specialists now working in the field and by those readers who will become consumption economists or who will be concerned with consumption problems in their roles as marketing specialists, general economists, agricultural economists, or home economists.

1.5.1 Some of the Difficulties

Consumer actions and their results are often hard to measure, interpret, and predict. This country has millions of consumers each making dozens of decisions and performing many economic acts every week. Even with modern data-collecting and data-processing systems, obtaining key facts about the major categories of economic activities of consumers and reasons for them is a very costly and time-consuming process. In contrast, there are fewer producers of goods and services and the results of producer decisions and actions are measured in terms of dollars of profit.

Economists have often said that consumers seek to "allocate their resources to maximize satisfaction," but they have never been able to measure satisfaction or "utility," as it is often called. Usually economists avoid the problem by talking about each consumer's ordering or ranking of his preference for different goods, but they do not know how to compare the satisfaction or utility Consumer *A* derives from a $5.00 basket of groceries with that derived by Consumer *B* from an identical basket. Limited by this frame of reference, they have trouble in dealing with consumption problems of the real world.

Students of consumers' economic actions can and must obtain help from social sciences other than economics to interpret seemingly irrational decisions and abnormal behavior. Consider the term *satisfaction* we have just been using. Many economists think of it as the reward for fulfillment of consumers' wants, obviously a psychological phenomenon. But few, if any, present-day psychologists use the concept of satisfaction. There has been much controversy over this and other concepts referring to subjective feelings or emotions. Rather, psychologists are concerned with stimulus and response or with motivation, cognition, and learning. When consumption of a steak, for example, leads to gratification of the initiating biogenic need for food (having a biological base) and of the psychogenic need for steak as a status symbol, many psychologists say there is reinforcement of the stimulus-response pattern and learning occurs.

Research by sociologists, social psychologists, and anthropologists indicates that current economic decisions and actions of individuals are significantly conditioned by the earlier learning experiences of each individual in his subculture, a process called "cultural conditioning." Such conditioning frequently explains consumer behavior which seems irrational when evaluated within the sparse and abstract framework of standard economic theory.

1.5.2 The Tasks Ahead for Consumption Economics

Faced with these problems but aided by new data-collecting and data-processing procedures, increasing numbers of economists and marketing researchers are clarifying concepts, making careful observations, and developing generalizations from relationships between variations in consumption and observed variations in socioeconomic phenomena. Gradually a body of "protheory" will develop and be tested and reworked. Over the last 40 years substantial progress has been made. Until the midthirties, the development of consumption economics suffered from lack of data. In this country in recent years we have had more data for use in solving problems than the available numbers of adequately trained researchers have been able to analyze. The chaotic combination of masses of data, many problems, and relatively little economic theory has made the field of consumption economics appear far more diffuse and insignificant than its rapid development and substantial contributions to agriculture, business, and government policy and program determination merit.

1.5.3 Objectives of Consumption Economists

The reader's introduction to the subject of consumption economics will be facilitated if he keeps in mind these objectives of professional people working in the field:

(1) To contribute to solving current problems of agriculture, business, government, and the general public by developing knowledge of consumption in this country and others;
(2) To make clear the bases and procedures used in current analyses and projections of future trends and patterns of consumption so that their strengths and limitations can be generally recognized;
(3) To develop relationships among knowledge in this branch of economics and other areas within economics, other social sciences, and other disciplines.

1.5.4 The Growing Importance of Consumption Economics

Every student of economics is familiar with the elements of the demand and supply situation for particular commodities. Similarly, there are factors affecting the demand for and the supply of particular types of knowledge. As the United States has become more affluent and as severe postwar shortages in supplies of consumer goods and services have disappeared in Western Europe, interest in studying factors related to increasing the consumption of consumer items has grown. National surpluses of some farm commodities and the awareness of increased competition among different types of commodities and consumer services have raised the demand for knowledge of consumption economics. Producers of goods and services are also aware of the competition for upper-income families among (*a*) the desire for more leisure time, (*b*) additional income to buy higher quality goods, and (*c*) savings for retirement and for their children. Also, many people in the more affluent societies have become self-conscious about their affluence in the face of poverty in some sectors of their own countries and, perhaps even more so, in the less-developed countries.

Social scientists in many parts of the world have noted the fact that want-creation (the development of the desire to consume more products or products new to the subcultures) is a necessary condition for the acceleration of production in the developing countries. Economic development is not just a matter of production economics or new technology. Stimulation and direction of changes in consumption are highly significant. They require considerably more knowledge of consumer behavior within each culture and much more information about factors underlying consumption trends and variations than are available. In fact, the less developed the country, the less developed the data-collection system tends to be. Consumption economists are challenged to assist with their knowledge about the kinds of data needed, alternative ways of collecting the data, and uses of existing data along with new data in studying a wide range of economic and social problems. In addition, the experience of consumption economists in working with other social scientists on complex problems often qualifies them for leadership and coordinative roles in group efforts.

2

THE ROLE OF CONSUMPTION IN A MARKET ECONOMY

The need for a national war on poverty in the most affluent and highly productive economy in history raises some basic questions about the interrelationships between production and consumption. Many of the theories and facts required for a full-scale analysis of such questions are parts of the content of intermediate and advanced courses in economics. But some of the knowledge required for their analysis is an integral part of consumption economics.

Among the questions raised by the poverty-affluence paradox is the role of consumer demand in determination of prices and production at both the macro and micro levels of our economy. Another is the relationship of consumers' wants and attitudes to national income and family incomes. When concerns about supplying basic human needs receive national emphasis, it is important to examine carefully the concept of *need* and how to measure needs. Marketing people and specialists in economic development frequently raise questions regarding consumer needs and wants—what they are, how they can be changed into effective consumer demand, and what effect such shifts in demand may have on directions of growth for individual firms and whole economies.

This chapter will bring into focus some aspects of the economic theory pertinent to these questions, some views of marketing people, and some of the ideas and empirical work of consumption economists on determination of needs and wants.

2.1 ROLE OF PRICE IN DETERMINATION OF PRODUCTION AND CONSUMPTION

In your elementary course in economics you were introduced to ideas about the circular flow of income and expenditures in a modern competitive economy. Recall that the Gross National Product is determined by personal consumption expenditures combined with government and business expenditures and that the GNP determines net national product (along with the flow into capital formation). Net national product flows into personal income (and corporate savings). Disposable personal income is the residual after subtraction of taxes paid to federal, state, and local governments from total personal income.

2.1.1 Standard Economic Views of Price

Most of the economics you learned in elementary courses is based on assumptions regarding (*a*) unlimited wants of individuals, (*b*) scarce resources of individuals and economies, (*c*) free competition, (*d*) economizing drives of individual firms and consumers to maximize profits, incomes, and satisfaction or utility, and (*e*) a rather static situation. Such assumptions are useful in developing preliminary analyses of several fundamental questions, including the determination of production, the determination of distribution of output in the form of incomes to factors of production, and the distribution of output through the marketing system to consumers.

More advanced courses in economics consider the complications for production and distribution which arise when monopolistic elements enter in and when economic and social changes affect the rates of adjustment in different sectors of the economy as they strive toward an equilibrium of supply and demand. There is considerable variation between theorists and empiricists in views about the role of prices and how they are now determined in the United States.

Economists frequently tell laymen and students that prices of individual products are determined by the interaction of supply decisions of business firms selling products and the buying decisions of households buying them. Then they illustrate the process with supply and demand curves based on hypothetical schedules of individual and market demand and supply.

At a somewhat more sophisticated level, economists take into account the effects of the time dimension on the determination of price and the possibilities of changes in production and changes in demand. In the shorter run, standard economic theory holds that available supplies largely determine the price and consumption of a commodity. Production patterns and levels are relatively fixed over the short run, which may include one season or several years for some agricultural and business enterprises. In the case of perishable commodities, available market supplies must be consumed or wasted unless they can be stored temporarily. Less perishable commodities can be carried over for several months or even a year or two. The marketing of specific models of durable goods is limited by their style lives, not their physical lives, so the longer-run point of view is more applicable for them. In the short run, the purchasing power of consumers is also relatively fixed, although credit may be used to expand it or savings to contract it.

Over a period of several years or more, production can be increased and the combination of goods and services being produced in the country can be changed. The degree of change in production is, of course, limited by the availability and flexibility of resources for use in production of goods and services. Similarly, income or purchasing power can be altered either in the whole economy or for individuals. Over several years, the demand for particular products can be created either through the efforts of producers promoting their new products or through changes in social customs or institutions.

When economists use the assumptions of free competition and economizing entrepreneurs and consumers, they generally agree that prices serve as the director of the whole economic system. But there is considerable argument about the extent to which prices are now manipulated by groups in the economy. Waite and Cassady stated the conventional or standard view quite succinctly:

> Our economic order provides for the direction of production and consumption through the medium of prices. Prices determine what is to be produced, who is to consume particular products, and when these products are to be used. For the most part, the process takes place spontaneously; i.e., the formation of these prices and the effects of particular prices take place within the order itself and without direction by some outside authority such as the government. The order, in consequence, is often said to be automatically regulated. . . .[1]

As the condition of free competition is relaxed and modifications described as imperfect competition or monopolistic competition are taken into account, there is much less agreement about the role of prices. Some economists view product differentiation and sales efforts as conducive to monopoly and impeding the operations of prices. In contrast, many marketing people consider product differentiation and promotion activities as alternatives to price competition.

2.1.2 More Empirical Views

In the real world of marketing, Professor Huegy and other marketing researchers have found that many prices are determined on the basis of administrative judgments of business executives who take many factors into account as they weigh alternative marketing policies.[2] Many firms have large enough shares of their markets to have their decisions affect the prices of individual products. Knowing little about consumers' demand schedules, management tends to set prices so as to cover costs plus an allowance for profits. Marketing executives have found that consumer demand for products with somewhat different attributes and with different prices can be fostered, directed, and even created through vigorous sales promotion campaigns. Thus price policies are necessarily interrelated with policies regarding market development and product promotion because programs to implement the latter categories of policies add to costs. Moreover labor and government policies and actions limit or influence pricing decisions, as in the cases of steel,

[1] Page 13 of Waite, Warren C., and Cassady, Ralph, Jr. *The Consumer and the Economic Order.*

[2] Huegy, H. W. "Price Decisions and Marketing Policies," pp. 228–242 of Wales, Hugh G. (Editor), *Changing Perspectives in Marketing.*

aluminum, copper, and air transportation labor-management negotiations.

At higher levels of income, consumers are apparently less influenced by comparative prices and more influenced by other characteristics of particular goods and services. Both high- and low-income consumers respond to advertising, although no researcher has definitely measured how much. The 1966 Report of the National Commission on Food Marketing was quite critical of the high costs of selling efforts which were deemed to yield little value to consumers. Consumers have difficulty in interpreting advertising; in judging quantities and quality and relative costs because of packaging, labeling, and pricing practices; and in making product comparisons. The majority concluded:

> . . . Renewed emphasis on price competition would bring about further economies. The consumer is, indeed, a sovereign; but she is not as she is so often told, an all-knowing, all-powerful, and fully-served sovereign.[3]

2.2 ALTERNATIVE VIEWS OF THE IMPORTANCE OF CONSUMPTION IN THE DETERMINATION OF PRODUCTION AND INCOME

Economists with different backgrounds and perception often disagree on some aspects of the nature and stability of relationships of consumption to production and income. Much of the disagreement stems from lack of scientific research findings about these relationships in dynamic economies. In the process of macroeconomic analysis, John Maynard Keynes argued that the levels of income and employment are determined by the aggregate supply and demand functions; that consumption depends on income, on some institutional factors (described as "objective"), and on "subjective" factors influencing individuals. On the grounds that the relationship of consumption to income is quite stable and that consumption changes less than income, Keynes concentrated his attention on production and employment as determinants of income.[4] Thus he subordinated the role of current consumption expenditures which economists now consider to be particularly important in the determination of United States income being generated through current production.

2.2.1 Differences Related to Degree of Economic Development

In recent years the potential effects of increases in consumer demand on economic growth have led to theoretical and empirical studies, particularly for the so-called developing, i.e., less-developed, countries. Economic experiments have shown that raising food consumption rates of poorly fed people can raise their productivity. A number of American economists who have worked on consumption problems in the less-developed countries have identified the need for extending the want-horizon of many peasants in the traditional societies as a prerequisite to changes in their production patterns. Productivity in the agricultural sector must be raised in order to release agricultural workers to the industrial sector of the economy. Many writers seem to measure economic growth in terms of increases in industrial production and pay little attention to changes in production of food for subsistence use by the producers' families. We will consider such changes in the developing economies in Chapter 4.

The situation in the United States economy and society differs in degree from that just described because here we have a highly developed industrial economy, and our commercial agriculture is already very productive. Poor people in American agriculture have many of the same characteristics as the urban poor, such as limited human resources in the forms of skills, education, and social psychological characteristics needed for success in the competitive industrial and business environment. These problems are now beginning to attract substantial research efforts because of the general lack of pertinent scientific knowledge.

2.2.2 Katona's Psychological Economics

Based on studies of the Survey Research Center of the University of Michigan, Katona stresses the significance of consumers' confidence in the economy as an element in short-run changes in consumer buying, in addition to their purchasing power. Although statistical studies have shown that Keynes was right in believing that overall consumption has a fairly stable relationship to income, they also show that the proportion of incomes spent on spe-

[3] Page 101, *Food from Farmer to Consumer*, June 1966.

[4] Keynes, John Maynard. *The General Theory of Employment, Interest and Money*.

cific goods may vary widely in the short run. Many Americans have a considerable amount of income above that needed for basic necessities—described as "discretionary income"—as well as reserve funds and the possibility of obtaining credit. Because of their large stocks of durable goods, they can often choose to postpone purchases of major items.

Katona's ideas concerning the significance of consumer confidence in the American economy also rest on modern knowledge of psychology.[5] As the result of accumulated experiences, consumers have habits, attitudes, and motives which intervene between (*a*) the stimuli they receive in the form of observations of what other people are doing and their awareness of what they want, and (*b*) how they react to them. The response, then, depends on both the environment and the person. Katona argues that the "levels of income and financial assets function either as enabling conditions (if they are ample) or as constraints (if they are insufficient)."[6] Even if consumers have the income and the financial assets, they may not be willing to buy if their expectations for the future are running low. This applies, of course, primarily to durable goods and the postponable purchases for nondurables and services.

2.2.3 A Synthesized Marketing View

In studying consumption from a marketing point of view, we will be primarily concerned with the longer-run adjustments of supply and demand. Viewing the economy in a broad perspective, expectations concerning consumption do affect production. Production is the major factor determining income, and income affects consumption. In the micro view of individual firms, prospective demand determines production. When production schedules for differentiated products are set, sales promotion programs are laid out. Sales efforts undoubtedly have some effect on sales. Sales, in turn, influence the income of producers and their plans for future production.

Since postwar production in the United States has exceeded all earlier expectations, consumption is viewed much less frequently as mere utilization of what has been produced. The increasing need to orient production and marketing to consumer demand is widely recognized. Years ago there was considerable talk of consumer sovereignty under free competition. But post-World War II market research has indicated that producers must expend a great effort to hold their place in the market as well as to sell additional quantities of new commodities to consumers. Also, sociologists and psychologists have provided evidence that consumers respond to a variety of factors other than price and income as they decide whether to buy, what to buy, and when to buy.

Individual firms take a pragmatic view of the relationship between consumption and production. Each firm produces in accord with its expectations regarding the market for its products. It seeks to develop new products and must actively promote its products. Most firms start with an initial schedule of quantities to be produced and try to be flexible as to whether larger or smaller amounts than the initial schedule should be produced. If the new product does not sell according to expectations in the trial stage, the firm may step up its promotion campaign or cut back its production schedule. Or it may eliminate the product from its line. But if the product sells very well, additional production facilities may be brought into use and output stepped up considerably.

2.2.4 Relationship of Consumer Wants to Family Income

The relationship between (*a*) the levels of consumption and (*b*) the income-earning activity of individual families has been clarified by information assembled and analyzed by Morgan and his colleagues at the Michigan Survey Research Center. They concluded:

> . . . In this country, high levels of economic activity, a wide range of jobs open to women, and a short working week which makes a second job possible, allow people to affect their own incomes by the decisions they make. Higher incomes also make the choice of whether or not to live with relatives a genuine decision, rather than a matter of necessity, and one which will affect family income, even relative to budget standards.
>
> Such opportunities for rational decision-making mean that family income itself is the result in part of a series of voluntary family decisions, not solely a predetermined factor that affects spending behavior. Consumption may help determine income.
>
> In addition to the decisions which affect present income, the family also makes decisions which will affect future incomes of the parents or of the children. The future is affected by decisions about sav-

[5] Chapter 1 of Katona, George. *The Powerful Consumer.*

[6] *Ibid.*, page 54.

ing for retirement, moving to new jobs, whether to send the children to college, and how many children to have.[7]

Thus individual consumers may vary their income or purchasing power, as Morgan pointed out, in order to buy more in a particular period; or they may use credit. The wife may get a job, the husband may work longer hours or he may shift jobs, or he may "moonlight" by taking an extra part-time job. The use of credit to expand purchasing power in a particular period, of course, has some limitations. But most American families, at all levels of income above the very lowest, buy ahead of income at least part of the time.

2.3 RELATIONSHIP OF NEEDS TO CONSUMPTION AND PRODUCTION

Appraisal of the adequacy of supplies to meet consumer needs is required for deciding on public policies during times of national emergency, for welfare policies, and in determining how much aid to give to the less-developed countries. The first step in such an appraisal is to clarify the concept of human needs.

2.3.1 What Are Our Needs?

Some modern psychologists differentiate among needs, motives, urges, wishes, and drives. Others use the terms interchangeably. But psychologists agree that needs fall into two general categories, biogenic and psychogenic. Biogenic needs arise from physiological tension systems and include hunger, thirst, and sex. Psychogenic needs are based upon psychological tension systems and are influenced by an individual's relations with others. Psychologists think of needs in connection with need-arousal in the motivation process. Such need-arousal is said to push the individual into actions which he thinks are most likely to lead to fulfillment of his needs. When he is aware of the "need-push," he ordinarily perceives a number of alternative goal-objects which may serve his needs.[8]

Let us take food as an example. Food is the goal-object of the *biogenic* need hunger, but it also meets *psychogenic* needs. Biogenic needs for food have been defined by scientists in terms of *specific nutrients required for life and health,* not in terms of food. Recommendations regarding dietary requirements for the United States have been made by the National Research Council's (NRC) Food and Nutrition Board and are described as "recommended dietary allowances." These recommended allowances can be supplied by many combinations of foods. Choices among these combinations are determined by social and psychological factors as well as economic elements of price and purchasing power. Berelson and Steiner summarize pertinent scientific knowledge thus:

> . . . The acts that satisfy hunger, thirst, and sex take on important social significance. That is, they become the focal point for significant rites and rituals with symbolic meaning that transcends their biological functions: e.g., the family meal, the business lunch, the puberty rite, the marriage ceremony, the corner pub. . . . social and psychological factors often determine the specific form in which the primary motives get expressed—*what* will be eaten; *how often, by whom,* . . .[9]

Home economists have been constructing *food budgets* for many years. They take into account nutritional requirements, current food patterns of families at different income levels, and several levels of overall food costs. Professor Stigler in 1945 poked some fun and raised some fairly significant questions about the objectivity of such diets in an article in the *Journal of Farm Economics.*[10] He took into account three sets of facts: the recommended dietary allowances of the NRC for ten nutrients, nutrients available in various foods, and food prices. Using trial and error methods which approximated linear programming, he worked out a list of seven foods which would provide the recommended dietary allowances for these nutrients at about one-third to one-half the cost of the low-cost food budget developed by the U.S. Department of Agriculture. His subsistence diet included very large quantities of flour, cabbage, and dried navy beans. Critics of his article pointed out that he had failed to consider certain physiological factors, chemical factors, and the whole range of cul-

[7] Pages 23 and 24 of Morgan, James N., David, Martin H., Cohen, Wilbur J., and Brazer, Harvey E. *Income and Welfare in the United States.*

[8] See Bayton, James A. "Motivation, Cognition, Learning—Basic Factors in Consumer Behavior," *J. Marketing* 22:3:282–9, January 1958.

[9] Page 243 of Berelson, Bernard, and Steiner, Gary A. *Human Behavior: An Inventory of Scientific Findings.*

[10] Stigler, George J. "The Cost of Subsistence," *J. Farm Economics* **XXVII**:2:303–314, May 1945.

tural factors. In truth, you can lead a man to food, but you cannot make him eat.

2.3.2 Minimum Needs and Family Budgets

The concept of a minimum level of needs is greatly influenced by sociological and economic factors. There is no scientific base for estimating needs other than physiological requirements to maintain life. Therefore budget construction is an expression of some knowledgeable person's judgment of what people need, often under assumptions which are not specified.

Laymen and economists use the term "needs" to describe the quantities and qualities of the goal-objects, with the connotation of basic or minimal needs. The effects of varying judgment as to needs are highlighted by differences among budgets combining estimates of needs for many commodities. For the period 1918, 1919, and 1920, Miss Reid found the following budgets:[11]

Agency Sponsoring the Measure of Cost of Living	The "Level" of the Budget as Described	Dollar Cost in 1919 Prices
War Labor Board (Federal)	Minimum subsistence	$1593
United Mine Workers of America	"Health and decency"	$2104
National Industrial Conference Board	"Minimum American standard of living"	$1329 and $1466
California Civil Service Commission	"Minimum health and comfort"	$2079

Note the wide range of costs estimated for a standard "adequate" budget for families of "workers," according to different agencies. Such estimates probably raise more questions than they answer.

Interest in needs and budgets has ebbed and flowed over the centuries. In the nineteenth century there was considerable interest in developing budgets to measure the cost of living of wage earners and to study problems of poverty. In the World War I period, the rapid rise in prices aroused interest again. During the depression years of the 1930s, a number of federal agencies and many state and local agencies developed budgets as part of relief plans and administration. The Works Progress Administration published "Quantity Budgets for Basic Maintenance and Emergency Standards for Living."[12] During World War II there was extensive work in the Federal Government on minimum civilian requirements, which will be discussed in the next section. The U.S. Bureau of Labor Statistics (BLS) published in 1947 a "City Worker's Budget" in response to concern over wage and price increases.[13]

To appraise the sufficiency of family incomes, in comparison with the City Worker's Budget, Hurwitz assembled data for Indianapolis, Indiana, indicating a median income for single persons of $1650, considerably above the estimated cost of the budget, $1170. But 31 percent of single individuals in that city in 1945 had incomes below the budget level. For families of two or more members, incomes ranged from $700 to $1000 above the estimated cost for the budget, varying with the size of the family. But about one-fourth of the families had incomes below the budget level.[14]

The BLS budget for workers' families has aroused so much interest and been so useful that it has been updated from time to time. Welfare agencies in many cities have modeled local budget standards after the BLS budget. For example, the Community Council of Greater New York issues *A Family Budget Standard*.[15] Such budgets are adapted to the consumption patterns of people in the particular city and to the prices prevailing at the particular period for which the budget pertains. The New York Community Council research group reported:

> This comparison indicates that the income received by about two-thirds of all families of two or more persons in 1959 was above the 1962 cost of the budget standard for families of corresponding size. . . . (Page 8.)

[11] From page 176 of Hoyt, Elizabeth E., Reid, Margaret G., McConnell, Joseph L., and Hooks, Janet H. *American Income and Its Use*.

[12] See Brady, Dorothy S. "Family Budgets: A Historical Survey," pp. 41–45 of the U.S. Department of Labor, Bureau of Labor Statistics, *Workers' Budgets in the United States: City Families and Single Persons*, Bulletin No. 927.

[13] *Ibid.* From time to time, revised budgets are issued by the Bureau of Labor Statistics.

[14] *Ibid.*, pp. 46–48, Hurwitz, Abner. "Family Incomes and Cost of Family Budgets."

[15] Community Council of Greater New York, Research Department, The Budget Standard Service, *A Family Budget Standard*.

2.3.3 Estimates of National Needs

During World War II careful study of *civilian requirements* was one step in planning for production and for the allocation of available supplies of food and other goods and services. The determination of minimum requirements had to be based on assumptions concerning the length of time to be covered by such requirements and the degree of control to be maintained over the distribution of minimum supplies. Attention was paid to potential effects of reduced consumption on morale, to the availability of substitutes for particular items, and to the institutions surrounding the use of particular goods and services.

A number of methods were used to estimate minimum needs. The simplest was to take an arbitrary percentage of production or supply or consumption in a given year. A much preferred method was to use scientific requirements or scientific findings regarding physiological requirements, such as those for food nutrients. The minimum low-cost diet developed by the War Food Administration assumed equitable distribution of supplies, availability of purchasing power, and no excess consumption by some people. A third method was to rely on expert opinions regarding essentiality. Most of the estimates of requirements were based on careful examination of variations in consumption patterns among different groups in the population, rich and poor, urban and rural.

Determination of essentiality was the critical element in developing the minimum requirements. Specialists took account of the value of food items in meeting particular nutrient requirements, past consumption rates, the availability of substitutes, and demand and price relationships. Particular attention was paid to physiological needs of heavy workers and vulnerable groups, such as infants and pregnant and nursing women. Also considered were the costs of production in terms of acreage, manpower, and machinery; costs of processing and transportation; perishability; and consumer acceptability.

Since the war, the most comprehensive job of estimating America's needs was done by Dewhurst and his associates.[16] They developed a "standard of minimum need for the maintenance of health and decency" for each group of necessities. Then they determined the costs per capita or per household of supplying those needs for 1950 and 1960. Finally, they worked out estimates of the total costs of making up the deficiencies for all United States consumers with incomes too small in 1950 and 1960 to meet such minimum needs. In the case of food they were able to start with the recommended dietary allowances for the nutrients and the food plans developed by the Department of Agriculture. But for clothing, housing, and furnishings, the essential determinants of needs, as they saw them, are psychological and social, not merely physiological. Therefore they noted the judgment factor in such estimates. These experts concluded that the greatest gap in the United States between supplies and needs around 1960 would be in medical care (Table 34, page 107). But their estimates for medical care were projected from some cost estimates for a prepaid group plan in operation in St. Louis plus some allowances for capital costs of expanding hospital facilities (pages 344–5).

Estimates of needs are also used in international food planning. In 1964 the Department of Agriculture issued the *World Food Budget, 1970*.[17] Researchers in the U.S. Department of Agriculture used available data on supplies and distribution of foods in many countries of the world to develop estimates of food supplies and consumption in 1970 for most countries and all regions. The expected supplies of food energy; total, animal, and pulse protein;[18] and fat were compared with nutritional reference standards developed by the Consumer and Food Economics Research Division of the U.S. Agricultural Research Service to identify potential deficiencies per capita. Using population estimates for 1970, total deficiencies were calculated and then converted into estimates of the amounts of wheat, beans and peas, nonfat dry milk, and vegetable oil that would be needed to fill these gaps. These data have been used extensively in speeches around the country and in congressional hearings to indicate the need for USDA shipments of food to other countries, one means of utilizing the surpluses

[16] Dewhurst, J. Frederic and Associates. *America's Needs and Resources: A New Survey.*

[17] U.S. Department of Agriculture, Economic Research Service, Foreign Agricultural Economic Report No. 19.

[18] Pulses are dry beans and peas, sometimes called edible legumes.

of this country. We will examine their impact on food policy in Part III of this book.

Such efforts are criticized because of the lack of necessary scientific information on food requirements, inadequate data on food supplies, and because they do not take into account the great variations from the average rates of consumption in the countries. Professor Hoyt has criticized the frequent development of standards thus:

> . . . If, then, we ascribe undue importance to one set of "standards" and go to unnecessary cost in trying to secure them, we shall have fewer resources to meet another set of standards or desiderata for something else which may be more important still. For this reason it is best to play safe by not making an absolute requirement of anything that can not be scientifically verified, or at any rate that does not have the consensus of world-wide scientific opinion behind it.[19]

2.3.4 The Concept of Wants

Definitions of wants vary all the way from minimal needs to effective demand (what people can pay for) and to full desires of people. A committee of experts of the United Nations wrote this:

> Human needs and wants, however, range from common biological needs—as for food, water and protection against cold—to culturally defined motivations and wants which may differ from society to society or from individual to individual. Into the picture enters the whole field of desires and values for which man may be striving; desires for particular types of food, drink, housing and clothing appealing to the taste; for access to educational, cultural and recreational facilities; for opportunity to do the kind of work that is satisfying to the individual; for satisfactory working conditions; for security safeguards covering the risks of illness, unemployment and old age; etc. . . . Not all needs are recognized by individuals. For example, the diet that represents good nutrition is but poorly perceived. Furthermore, fulfillment of some needs or wants may mean less satisfaction of others.[20]

Economists have been writing about wants for years, chiefly on the basis of introspection. A variety of definitions and classifications has been set forth, depending on the value system of the classifier and on his purposes. Categories such as necessities as opposed to luxuries, primary vs. secondary wants, and the like have been used.

Thorstein Veblen at the turn of the century launched a sharp attack on conspicuous consumption based on his observations of the *nouveaux riches* in the United States. In part, the attack arose because of his belief that overconsuming by the leisure classes left smaller supplies of goods and services for the immigrants and other poor in the country. But also he saw more clearly perhaps than anyone else at the time that wants are social phenomena and the result of social conditioning. This conditioning process has both an emotional and a cognitive base. He viewed conspicuous consumption and waste as symbols of status by the leisure class.[21] Modern sociologists research extensively on the use of such symbols by all classes in our society.

In the 1930s Wyand wrote about "primary wants . . . that must be gratified to maintain normal life" and "secondary wants," those cultural wants that are important to happiness and general welfare.[22] Other consumption economists have devised other ways to classify human wants, but the subcategories for psychogenic or sociogenic wants lack scientific foundations.

Psychological, sociological, economic, marketing, and technological factors influencing consumer wants will be studied in later chapters. At this point we need only note that these factors bring about variations and changes in tastes and preferences of consumers. Contrary to the views of some popular writers, the individual consumer is not a mere puppet whose wants are completely formed by persuasion.

A central theme of Galbraith's *Affluent Society* was that American wants for public goods have been filled much less satisfactorily than have the wants for private goods. Among the public goods to which Galbraith referred are education, recreation, fresh air and open spaces, parks, forests, and highways and other facilities for mass transportation. Privately supplied goods are promoted in the public eye by their producers, whereas no one sponsors or pushes the cause of public goods with the exception of small public interest groups. (Data related

[19] Page 32 of Hoyt, Reid, et al., op. cit. "Desiderata" refers to goods and services desired.

[20] Page 5 of Report on *International Definition and Measurement of Standards and Levels of Living*, United Nations.

[21] *The Theory of the Leisure Class.*

[22] Pages 120 and 121 of Wyand, Charles S. *Economics of Consumption.*

to this argument will be reviewed in Chapter 3.)

An important economic concept in the field of wants is that of *demand*. By demand, economists mean the quantities of goods or services that will be taken from the market at a given price and under given economic conditions. There is much more public knowledge of the demand for farm products than for other goods and services because of research over many years by the U.S. Department of Agriculture. A number of sets of projections or tentative estimates of demand under specified conditions have been developed to meet needs of government agencies. These projections have indicated, for example, that our supplies of cereals and other starchy foods are likely to continue for some years to exceed domestic demand at prices even substantially lower than those now prevailing. But if prices of some of the livestock products were reduced from recent levels, somewhat larger quantities would be consumed than at current prices. Such price reductions have been politically unacceptable because of their serious impact on agricultural incomes. Meanwhile most American consumers have continued to be very well fed. In fact obesity is the most serious health problem in this country.

Laymen often speak of their *desires* for goods and services, referring apparently to their demand *if* they had the available purchasing power. A more precise concept is that of *standards of living*, by which we mean the combination of the desired levels of consumption of goods and services plus desired levels of attainment of the nonmaterial elements such as social environment. Professor Davis contrasts several concepts in this quotation:

> *Consumption* means the commodities, their uses, and services consumed; *living* includes consumption and much more, working conditions, cushions against major and minor shocks, freedoms of various kinds, and what I tentatively call "atmosphere." The *level* of consumption or living, as I see it, is that actually experienced, enjoyed, or suffered by the individual or group; the *standard* of consumption or living is the level that is urgently desired and striven for, special gratification attending substantial success and substantial failure yielding bitter frustration.[23]

[23] Pages 2 and 3 of Davis, Joseph S. "Standards and Content of Living," *Am. Econ. Rev.* **XXXV**: 1:1–15, March 1945.

3

LEVELS OF CONSUMPTION IN THE UNITED STATES, CURRENT AND PAST

This chapter summarizes a variety of information about the current situation of American consumers in total and of certain groups of consumers in particular. It also reviews historical trends in order to place the current picture in perspective. In the last section is a discussion of how findings about consumption trends and patterns are used by public agencies, business firms, and citizen consumers.

3.1 CONSUMPTION IN THE UNITED STATES IN THE 1960s

American consumers spent about $431 billion for goods and services in 1965. This was six times as much as the 1940 total when measured in current dollars. Even though there were 60 million more people to be fed, clothed, and housed, average outlays per capita quadrupled, reaching $2210. In addition to the $431 billion for current consumption, we spent about $28 billion for residential construction, $123 billion for civilian operations of our federal, state, and local governments, $2 billion for foreign economic aid, and $57 billion for national defense and space research.[1]

3.1.1 Current Expenditure Ratios

To judge better the current American level of living, consider the following relationships. In 1965 about 18 percent of our *income* was allocated to food, and we ate about 7 percent more food per capita than in 1940.[2] Food prices were fairly low in 1940, but 22 percent of our income went for food. Food is vital to life. Therefore the ratio of value of food to income or total consumption expenditures provides a basis for comparing our economic situation with that of other countries. In recent years the countries in the European Economic Community (the Common Market countries of Western Europe) have allocated about a third of their consumption expenditures to food. The Japanese ratio is about the same. But food takes somewhat more than half of total income in India.

Another way of assessing our present level of living is to examine how we divide up our personal expenditures for consumption in the United States. In 1965, almost 20 percent of our expenditures were for food, another 20 percent for housing and household operation, 8 percent for clothing and shoes, and 5 or 6 percent each for medical care, personal business, and recreation.[3] (See also Figure 3.1.)

3.1.2 Variations in Income and Consumption

Differences in level of current income considerably affect rates of consumption, although the rates are also influenced by past experiences with income, expectations for the future, and relative income position. Even in the United States in the 1960s, there is wide variation in the degree to which individual families share in our economic abundance, as evidenced by the need for a war on poverty. The distribution of families and single individuals maintaining households according to size of money

[1] Data derived from *The National Income and Product Accounts of the United States, 1929–1965.*

[2] U.S. Department of Agriculture, Economic Research Service, *U.S. Food Consumption*, Statis. Bulletin No. 364 and the Supplement for 1965.

[3] Op. cit.

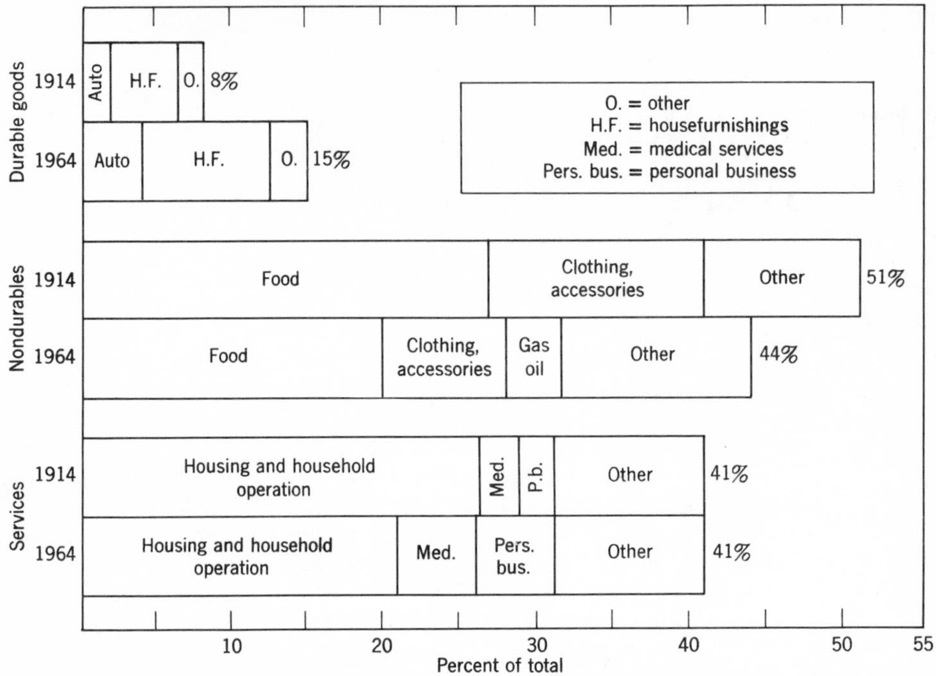

FIGURE 3.1 Percentage distribution of personal consumption expenditures, 1914 and 1964. (Based on data in Appendix 4–5 of Dewhurst and Associates, *America's Needs and Resources: A New Survey*, and in *The Survey of Current Business*, July 1966.)

income before taxes in the early 1960s was approximately:[4]

Under $3000	20 percent
$3000 to $4000	10 percent
$4000 to $10,000	50 percent
$10,000 or more	20 percent

In terms of real income, i.e., current money income adjusted for changes in the general price level, this distribution apparently continued during the following several years.

Wide differences between the expenditure patterns of low-income families and high-income families are revealed by the Survey of Consumer Expenditures and Income made by the U.S. Departments of Labor and Agriculture in 1960–1961.[5] As an example, note in Figure 3.2 the substantially larger proportions of total expenditures for current consumption spent for food and housing by urban families and single consumers with disposable money incomes of $2000 to $3000 compared with those in the $10,0000 to $15,000 income bracket. The high-income group compensated with larger proportions and much larger dollar outlays for transportation, clothing and services, and recreation, reading, and education.

Differences among income levels in quantity of food consumed are indicated by data from the U.S. Department of Agriculture.[6] In the spring of 1955 per person use of food commodities (measured in terms of their values at the farm level or at the ports) was about 15 percent lower among *urban* families with incomes below $2000 than among those having incomes of $4000 to $5000. Food use by high-income families (over $10,000) averaged 18 percent above the average for the $4000 to $5000 group. Farm families used more food per

[4] Based on 1963 data published by the U.S. Department of Commerce. Money incomes include wages, salaries, income from property, etc.

[5] U.S. Bureau of Labor Statistics, *Consumer Expenditures and Income. Total United States, Urban and Rural, 1960–61*, Survey of Consumer Expenditures 1960–61, BLS Report No. 237–93 (USDA Report CES-15).

[6] Appendix D of Burk, Marguerite C. *Measures and Procedures for Analysis of U.S. Food Consumption*, USDA, Economic Research Service, Agr. Handbook 206.

person than urban families at the same level of dollar income. Many farm families had subsistence or home-produced supplies from their own gardens, trees, and livestock.

Purchases of new houses vary considerably from one income level to another. In fact, income has been identified as the single most important factor in such purchases. Families whose heads are in the 25- to 45-year age bracket with a college education are much more likely to be buyers of new houses.[7] At each income level, the families with better educated heads tend to buy more expensive houses, according to data from 1959–1960.

[7] Page 23, Atkinson, L. Jay. "Factors Affecting the Purchase Value of New Houses," *Survey of Current Business* 46:8:20–36, August 1966.

The following sections will introduce in a more systematic fashion some of the types of knowledge currently available about the socioeconomic factors related to variations in consumption at one point in time.

3.1.3 United States Surveys for 1960–1961

Many types of surveys are used to collect information about people's incomes and how they spend their money. Government agencies, business groups, and private agencies sponsor sample surveys of families. The housewife or another knowledgeable member of the family

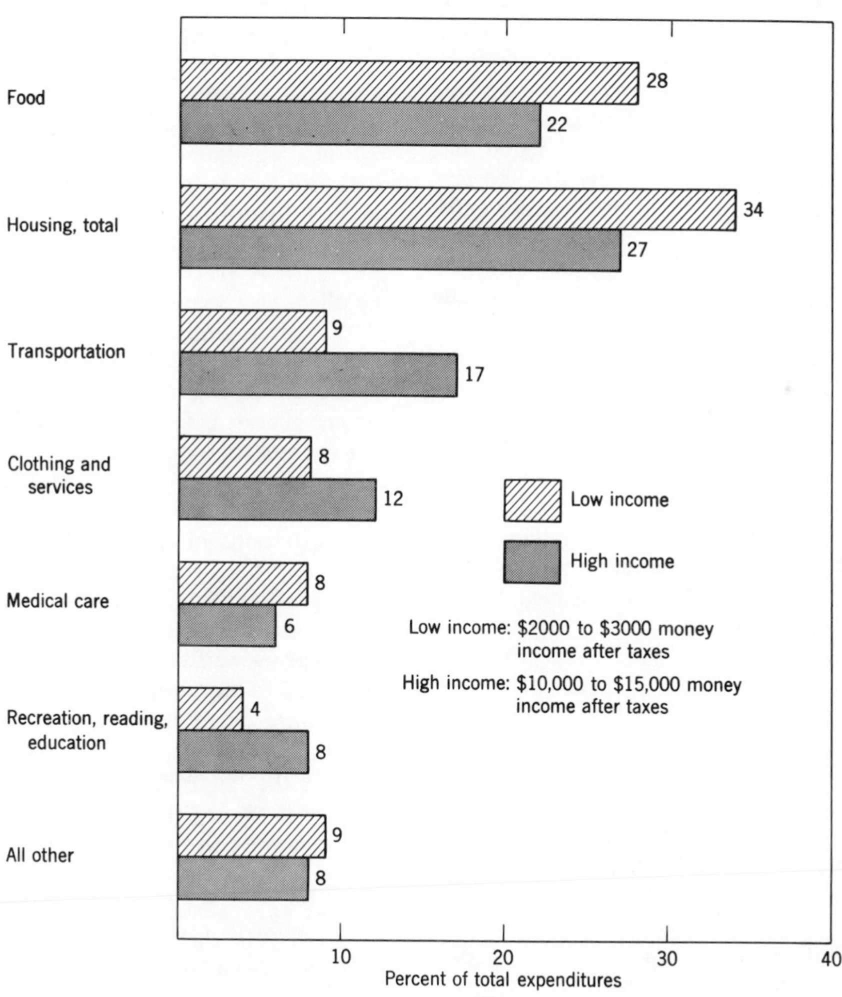

FIGURE 3.2 Proportion of total expenditures spent for major commodities and services by high- and low-income urban families and single consumers, United States, 1960–1961. (Data from Table 1 A of *Consumer Expenditures and Income, Urban United States, 1960–61*, BLS Report No. 237–38, April 1964.)

is interviewed to obtain estimates of income, savings, and expenditures. Sometimes the surveys pertain only to selected items—as is more common for private surveys. Other surveys cover the whole gamut of goods and services —as in the 1960–1961 survey by two agencies of the United States government (the BLS-USDA Survey of Consumer Expenditures and Income). For that very extensive study the U.S. Bureau of Labor Statistics (BLS) surveyed 9476 urban families and single consumers and cooperated with the U.S. Department of Agriculture (USDA) in interviewing 2285 rural nonfarm units. The USDA obtained data for 1961 from 1967 farm families and single consumers about incomes, expenses, and savings. These carefully gathered, current data confirmed the preliminary conclusions of earlier studies. It was found again that variations in expenditures are related to income, occupation, and age of the head of the family, region, degree of urbanization, and race. Moreover the effects of these factors are interrelated. For example, the occupation of the head of the family materially affects family income. Statistical analysis of the data can measure the effects of individual factors reasonably well. An overall view of their effects is provided by the data in Tables 3.1, 3.2, and 3.3, selected from reports of the 1960–1961 surveys.

3.1.4 Variations in Consumption with Degree of Urbanization

The BLS-USDA Survey of Consumer Expenditures and Income found significant differences in money income after taxes and in expenditures among families classified by *degree of urbanization* but less than earlier surveys had revealed. Urban incomes and current expenditures averaged 6 to 7 percent above the United States average for 1961. Farm money incomes were 21 percent below the average and expenditures were 29 percent lower than the overall United States average. Rural nonfarm families in metropolitan areas had incomes and expenditure patterns quite similar to those of urban families. Patterns for nonfarm families living in the more rural areas were more like farm income and expenditure patterns. The more important differences between urban and farm allocations among consumption categories are the much larger urban shares for shelter, and the somewhat larger farm shares for medical care and transportation (Table 3.1).

3.1.5 Variations with Income, Occupation, and Age

As you would expect, consumption expenditures by families and single consumers in the low-, medium-, and high-income groups differed greatly, as shown in Table 3.2. Note that on the average, the low-income group spent a little more than current income, whereas the $10,000 to $15,000 income group did some saving. The high-income group allocated a much smaller proportion of its total expenditures to food (22 percent) than did the $2000 to $3000 income group. But the dollar expenditures by the high-income group for food were almost three times as large. A similar relationship holds for shelter. In contrast, clothing, recreation, reading and education, and transportation were much more important parts of the total expenditures by the $10,000 to $15,000 income group of families than for the $2000 to $3000 group.

When the same sample of families and single consumers is reclassified by occupation, we find that incomes of families headed by earners in the "salaried, professional, and official" category averaged twice as high as for the unskilled wage earners. Note that 35 percent of the latter group was nonwhite compared with 3 percent of the former category. Reflecting differences in income, unskilled wage earners allocated significantly higher percentages of their consumption expenditures to food than did the salaried, professional, official group. This larger share for food was offset by smaller proportions spent for household operation, recreation, reading and education, and transportation by unskilled wage earners.

To show the general relationships between consumption patterns and age of the family head, the same sample cases were re-sorted into groups based on the age of the head of the family. From these groups were taken the data for the last three columns of Table 3.2. The family size of the oldest families (headed by a person 65 to 74 years of age) is half that in the youngest group of families shown in the table. Also, incomes of the oldest families averaged somewhat lower. The major differences in allocations of expenditures between the families with heads 25 to 34 years of age and those with heads in the oldest age category are: higher percentages allocated by the youngest families to housefurnishings and equipment, clothing and services, recreation, and transpor-

TABLE 5.1 Summary of Family Characteristics, Income, and Expenditures: All United States Families and Single Individuals, by Urbanization, 1961

		All U.S.				Standard Metropolitan Statistical Areas[a]					
						Inside			Outside		
Item	Unit	U.S.[a]	Urban[b]	Rural Non-farm[c]	Farm[d]	Total	Urban	Rural Non-farm	Total	Urban	Rural Non-farm
Percent of families	Pct.	100.0	72.6	21.1	6.3	63.7	57.5	5.6	36.3	15.1	15.5
Average											
Family size	No.	3.2	3.1	3.5	3.8	3.2	3.1	3.6	3.3	3.0	3.4
Net change in assets and liabilities	Dol.	229	219	176	519	243	243	220	206	128	161
Age of head	Yrs.	49	48	50	51	48	48	46	51	50	51
Education of head	Yrs.	10	11	9	9	11	11	10	9	10	9
Money income after taxes	Dol.	5594	5957	4700	4424	6193	6198	6220	4543	5038	4150
Homeowners as percent of total	Pct.	58	54	67	71	54	52	71	64	60	65
Nonwhite as percent of total	Pct.	11	13	6	8	13	14	5	7	6	7
Ave. expenditures for current consumption	Dol.	5038	5381	4296	3594	5581	5585	5657	4086	4592	3806
Percentage of total expenditures allocated to:											
Food	Pct.	24.4	24.3	25.2	24.1	24.2	24.3	23.8	24.9	24.2	25.9
Housing, total	Pct.	28.9	29.4	27.7	25.5	29.5	29.5	29.3	27.6	29.0	26.7
Shelter	Pct.	13.1	13.9	10.5	8.6	14.1	14.3	12.5	10.6	12.2	9.4
Utilities and operation	Pct.	10.7	10.5	11.6	10.7	10.4	10.2	11.2	11.5	11.5	11.7
Housefurn. and equipment	Pct.	5.2	5.0	5.6	6.1	5.1	5.0	5.5	5.5	5.2	5.6
Clothing and services	Pct.	10.4	10.5	9.5	11.9	10.4	10.5	9.7	10.1	10.2	9.4
Medical care	Pct.	6.8	6.7	6.9	8.6	6.7	6.6	6.8	7.2	7.1	7.0
Recreation	Pct.	4.0	4.1	3.8	3.4	4.0	4.0	4.1	3.8	4.0	3.7
Reading and education	Pct.	2.0	2.0	1.6	1.8	2.0	2.0	1.7	1.7	1.7	1.5
Transportation	Pct.	15.1	14.5	17.1	17.1	14.5	14.4	16.3	16.5	15.3	17.6
All other	Pct.	8.4	8.5	8.2	7.6	8.7	8.7	8.7	8.2	8.5	8.2

[a] Data from Table 10B, *Consumer Expenditures and Income, Total United States, Urban and Rural, 1960–61*, Survey of Consumer Expenditures 1960–61, BLS Report No. 237–93.

[b] Data from Table 1C, *Consumer Expenditures and Income, Urban United States, 1960–61*, BLS Report No. 238–38.

[c] Data from Table 1, *Consumer Expenditures and Income, Rural Nonfarm Areas in the United States, 1961*, BLS Report No. 237–88.

[d] Data from Table 1, *Consumer Expenditures and Income, Rural Farm Population, U.S. 1961*, USDA Consumer Expenditure Survey Report No. 5.

TABLE 3.2 Summary of Family Characteristics, Income, and Expenditures: All Urban Families and Single Consumers, United States 1960–61, and for Groups Selected by Income, Occupation, and Age of Head[a]

Item	Unit	All U.S. Urban	Money Income after Taxes			Occupation of Family Head				Age of Family Head in Years		
						Salaried Profes-sional, Official	Clerical Sales	Wage Earners				
			$2–3000	$5–6000	$10,000–$15,000			Skilled	Unskilled	25–34	45–54	65–74
Percent of families	Pct.	100.0	9.9	13.1	7.7	17.7	13.0	15.8	12.8	19.6	19.6	12.3
Average												
Family size	No.	3.1	2.3	3.4	4.0	3.4	2.9	3.6	3.1	3.7	3.3	1.8
Net change in assets and liabilities	Dol.	177	—197	18	868	499	65	191	—32	109	297	131
Age of head	Yrs.	47	53	42	47	41	43	43	45	30	49	69
Education of head	Yrs.	11	9	11	13	14	12	10	9	12	10	8
Money income after taxes	Dol.	5906	2508	5495	11,724	8614	6013	6542	4308	5898	7172	4034
Homeowners as percent of total	Pct.	53	37	51	77	61	48	61	36	37	64	59
Nonwhite as percent of total	Pct.	12	21	10	4	3	6	6	35	13	12	9
Average expenditures for current consumption	Dol.	390	2675	5240	9744	7441	5661	6032	4192	5644	6374	3541
Percent of total expenditures allocated to:												
Food	Pct.	24.3	28.4	25.0	22.2	22.0	23.8	24.7	26.8	23.2	24.0	25.7
Housing, total	Pct.	29.5	34.1	29.7	27.0	29.7	29.8	27.1	29.0	31.3	27.2	32.6
Shelter	Pct.	13.9	18.5	14.1	11.7	14.0	14.5	12.2	14.0	15.0	12.6	15.9
Utilities and operation	Pct.	10.4	11.7	10.3	9.9	10.4	10.2	9.6	9.8	10.3	9.9	12.7
Housefurn. and equipment	Pct.	5.1	3.9	5.3	5.4	5.3	5.1	5.3	5.2	6.0	4.8	4.0
Clothing and services	Pct.	10.4	8.2	9.9	11.9	10.5	11.4	10.3	10.4	10.0	11.4	7.7
Medical care	Pct.	6.6	8.1	6.5	6.1	6.4	6.4	6.5	6.2	6.0	6.0	9.4
Recreation	Pct.	4.0	2.7	3.6	5.0	4.5	4.0	4.3	3.7	4.5	4.1	2.7
Reading and education	Pct.	2.0	1.4	1.6	3.0	2.8	1.9	1.7	1.5	1.7	2.8	1.5
Transportation	Pct.	14.7	8.6	15.4	16.4	15.9	14.1	16.5	13.5	15.6	15.1	12.5
All other	Pct.	8.5	8.5	8.3	8.4	8.2	8.6	8.9	8.9	7.7	9.4	7.9

[a] Data from Tables 1A, 3A, 4A of *Consumer Expenditures and Income, Urban United States, 1960–61*, BLS Report No. 237–38.

TABLE 3.3 Summary of Family Characteristics, Income, and Expenditures: Urban Families and Single Consumers in Four Regions, Farm Families and Single Consumers in North Central Region and South, with Some Subgroupings by Race, 1960–61

Item	Unit	All Urban		North Central Urban[c]			Southern Urban[d]				Southern Farm[f]		
		N.E.[a]	West[b]	Total	White	Negro	Total	White	Negro	N.C.[e]	Total	White	Negro
Percent of families	Pct.	100.0	100.0	100.0	90.7	8.7	100.0	79.6	20.2	100.0	100.0	84.0	16.0
Average													
Family size	No.	3.0	3.1	3.1	3.1	3.4	3.1	3.1	3.2	3.9	3.7	3.5	5.0
Net change in assets and liabilities	Dol.	91	157	326	359	13	128	154	24	709	243	296	—33
Age of head	Yrs.	49	46	47	47	42	48	47	48	50	53	53	52
Education of head	Yrs.	10	11	11	11	9	10	11	7	7	8	8	5
Money income after taxes	Dol.	6295	6324	5934	6095	4391	5153	5653	3200	4878	3592	3878	2086
Homeowners as percent of total	Pct.	47	53	58	61	31	54	59	37	71	68	74	34
Nonwhite as percent of total	Pct.	10	9	9		100	20		100	1	16		100
Average expenditures for current consumption	Dol.	5832	5791	5269	5377	4216	4761	5186	3110	3811	3157	3379	1995
Percentage of total expenditures allocated to:													
Food	Pct.	25.6	23.7	24.0	24.0	23.2	23.4	22.9	25.9	23.9	24.1	23.5	29.0
Housing, total	Pct.	29.9	28.7	29.6	29.3	32.9	29.4	29.3	30.1	26.4	24.4	24.9	20.7
Shelter	Pct.	14.6	14.0	14.1	13.8	16.8	12.6	12.6	13.0	9.0	7.8	8.0	5.8
Utilities and operation	Pct.	10.4	9.7	10.3	10.4	10.4	11.2	11.2	11.5	11.2	10.3	10.6	7.8
Housefurn. and equipment	Pct.	4.9	5.0	5.2	5.1	5.8	5.6	5.6	5.5	6.2	6.2	6.1	7.1
Clothing and services	Pct.	10.6	9.7	10.2	10.1	12.2	10.6	10.3	12.9	12.0	11.9	11.5	15.0
Medical care	Pct.	6.3	7.1	6.5	6.6	4.6	6.7	6.9	5.2	8.7	8.6	8.8	6.5
Recreation	Pct.	3.8	4.5	4.1	4.1	3.4	3.9	4.0	3.2	3.6	3.0	3.1	2.3
Reading and education	Pct.	2.2	1.8	2.0	2.1	1.3	2.0	2.1	1.5	1.9	1.6	1.7	1.0
Transportation	Pct.	12.8	16.0	15.2	15.4	13.1	15.6	16.2	11.6	16.3	18.2	18.4	16.2
All other	Pct.	8.8	8.5	8.4	8.4	9.3	8.4	8.3	9.6	7.2	8.2	8.1	9.3

[a] Data from Table 1A, *Consumer Expenditures and Income, Urban Places in the Northeastern Region, 1960–61*, BLS Report No. 237–34.
[b] Data from Table 1A, BLS Report No. 237–37, comparable report for Western Region.
[c] From Table 7A, BLS Report No. 237–35, comparable report for North Central Region.
[d] From Table 7A, BLS Report No. 237–36, comparable report for Southern Region.
[e] From Table 7, *Consumer Expenditures and Income, Rural Farm Population, North Central Region, 1961*, USDA Consumer Expenditures Survey Report No. 2.
[f] From Table 7, USDA, CES Report No. 3, comparable report for the Southern Region.

tation; and lower percentages to food, household operation, and medical care. These variations reflect differences in "needs" and "wants" related to income, the stage in the family life cycle, the size of the family, and the activities of the family.

3.1.6 Variations with Region, Urbanization, and Race

Incomes and expenditures for current consumption by urban families and single consumers averaged about the same in the Northeast and West in 1960–1961 (Table 3.3). The averages for the North Central Region ran a little lower. Those for the South were markedly lower. The shares of consumer expenditures allocated to food and shelter were relatively high among Northeastern urban families, being compensated by a lower allocation to transportation. Urban families depend more on public transportation, which is cheaper in the Northeast than in other areas. Mass transport is cheaper per trip than private cars.

Expenditure levels and patterns of white urban families in the North Central Region and the South were similar, but those for Negro families in the two regions were rather different. Southern Negro family incomes were much lower. Food needs required a larger proportion of Southern Negro budgets, being offset by smaller outlays for shelter.

Comparison of data in Table 3.3 for white and Negro urban and farm families' incomes and expenditures in the South reveals significantly lower levels for farm people of both races. Again, larger shares for food and smaller shares for shelter are observed for the lower-income farm groups. Clothing shares are consistently larger for Negro than white families in the North Central Region and the South.

3.2 TRENDS IN CONSUMPTION

In Section 3.1 reference was made to the $431 billion which was spent for consumer goods and services in 1965, as well as additional expenditures for residential construction, civilian government services, and national defense. This section provides a longer perspective through the examination of changes in United States consumer expenditures over the last 50 years. To avoid complications raised by World War I, 1913 and 1963 are used for some of the comparisons. In other cases the comparison is between pre- and post-World War II years.

3.2.1 Comparison of 1963 with 1913

Over the 50-year period Gross National Product (GNP) per capita in constant dollars rose 117 percent. In comparable terms, disposable personal income and consumer expenditures just about doubled. Personal consumption expenditures represented 72 percent of the GNP in 1913 and 64 percent in 1963. About 3 percent of the GNP went into new residential construction 50 years ago compared with 4.5 percent in 1963.[8]

Just before World War I a little less than one-tenth of the GNP was allocated to government functions, whereas the proportion had risen to almost a fourth in 1963 (excluding transfer payments such as Social Security benefits). A substantial part of the increase, of course, was due to much greater outlays for national defense. Government purchases of goods and services in 1963 took about three-

TABLE 3.4 Estimates of Shares of Major Government Functions in Total Expenditures by Federal, State, and Local Governments in 1913 and 1963[a]

Function	Approximate percentage of total	
	1913, percent	1963, percent
National defense	9	33
Education	23	15
Welfare, social insurance, veterans' benefits, health and community facilities, and housing	21	24
Transportation	18	7
Agriculture and national resources	2	5
Postal service	10	1
Interest on public debt	2	5
All other	15	10

[a] Based on Table 263 of Dewhurst and Associates (op. cit.) and on data in Table 3.10 of *The National Income and Product Accounts of the United States, 1929–65*, a supplement to *The Survey of Current Business*, August 1966.

[8] Data for 1913 based on appendices in Dewhurst and Associates. *America's Needs and Resources: A New Survey*. Data for 1963 computed from information in *The National Income and Product Accounts of the United States, 1929–65*.

fourths of the total government outlays. The balance was paid out as interest, subsidies, or transfers and aid to individuals. The Federal Government's transfers under the Social Security and veterans' programs amounted to 4 percent of the GNP. Table 3.4 summarizes the shares of total expenditures allocated to a number of major functions of government in the years 1913 and 1963.

Figure 3.3 shows the major changes in publicly supplied goods and services. It excludes national defense, public welfare and social insurance, and agricultural subsidies. The public expenditures identified in the figure averaged about $81 per capita in 1913 and $246 in 1963 (in 1950 dollars), compared with $780 spent for privately purchased goods and services in the earlier year and $1546 in 1963. The public outlays identified in Figure 3.3 accounted for 9 percent and 14 percent of total outlays in the respective years.

For a broad view of the private sector, refer again to Figure 3.1. The bars show the percentage breakdowns for major categories of consumption expenditures in 1914 and 1964. Note that the share allocated to durable goods almost doubled, primarily due to the much larger expenditures for automobiles in current years. In 1914 they were still the playthings of the rich. The other major changes in expenditure allocations are the decrease in the food share from 27 percent to 20 percent and the substantial decline in the share going to the clothing group of items.

3.2.2 Other Major Trends

The use of standard groupings such as food, clothing, and housing covers up several very

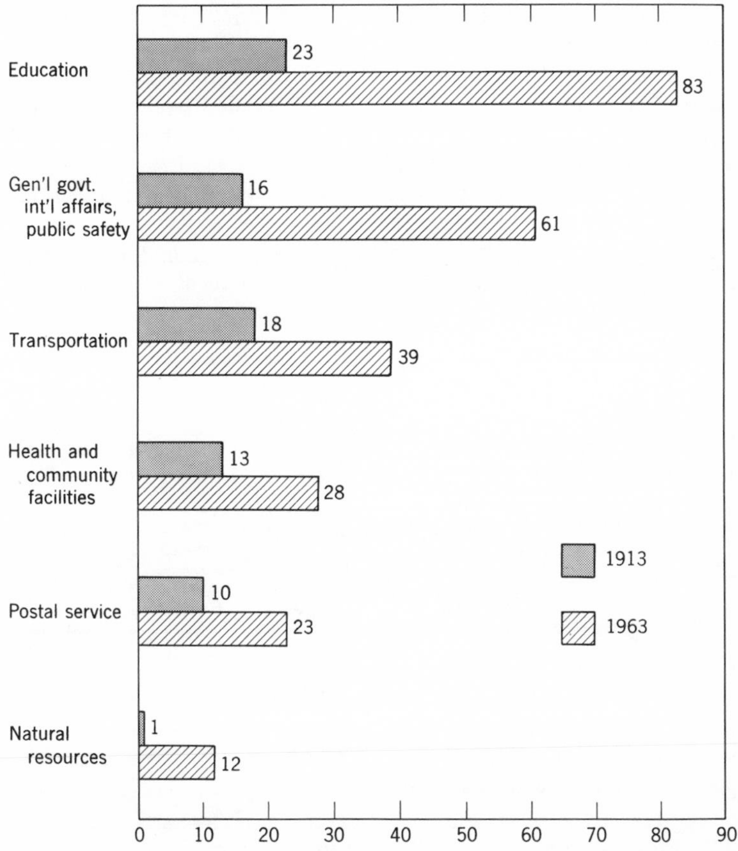

FIGURE 3.3 Public expenditures per capita for selected goods and services, 1913 and 1963 (in 1950 dollars). (Derived from data in Table 263 of Dewhurst and Associates, op. cit., and in *The National Income and Product Accounts of the United States, 1929–65*, a supplement to *The Survey of Current Business.*)

important trends in consumption. The first of these is the great increase in variety of goods from which consumers can choose. Another is the substantial shift from home production of food and clothing to purchases from the market. Whereas families formerly made their food dishes from raw materials bought in bulk and their clothing from raw materials, now they buy factory-made products. In fact, more and more factory processing adds greater convenience.

The last two trends will be studied carefully in later chapters, so here we only need to elaborate on the increased variety. Thousands of food items, for example, are now available in supermarkets in contrast to the small number of staples in bins and barrels that characterized the grocery stores of 50 years ago. Then most fruits and vegetables were available only during the local season. People bought their meats from the butcher who did his own slaughtering. Also, as you know, today we have a tremendous variety of electrical appliances and many kinds of gadgets for housekeeping use that were nonexistent a half century, or less, ago.

The overall figures for food, shelter, and clothing also hide the presence of much more discretionary spending within these categories in recent years. The concept of discretionary spending refers to purchases of luxury-type products, over and above the so-called basic necessities.

3.2.3 Changes since 1940

As incomes in the United States have risen, Americans have shifted emphasis in their expenditures for durable and nondurable goods and for services. Excluding the effects of changes in prices, in the period from 1940 to 1965 expenditures for all goods and services rose about $858 per capita (in 1958 dollars) or by about three-fourths.[9] Outlays for durables more than doubled, accounting for about $215 of the increase. The spectacular rise in housing expenditures and medical care contributed heavily to the $367 increase in real outlays for services. The change in expenditures for nondurable items like food, clothing, shoes, gas, and oil amounted to about $276, an increase of about 40 percent in constant 1958 dollars. (The term *constant dollars* refers to dollars of constant amount of purchasing power, excluding changes in prices.)

Within the food category, changes in the last decade have been relatively minor compared with those over the 25-year period (Figure 3.4). Food consumption measured in both economic and nutritional terms has in-

[9] Based on data in Table 2.6, *National Income and Product Accounts of the United States, 1929–1965.*

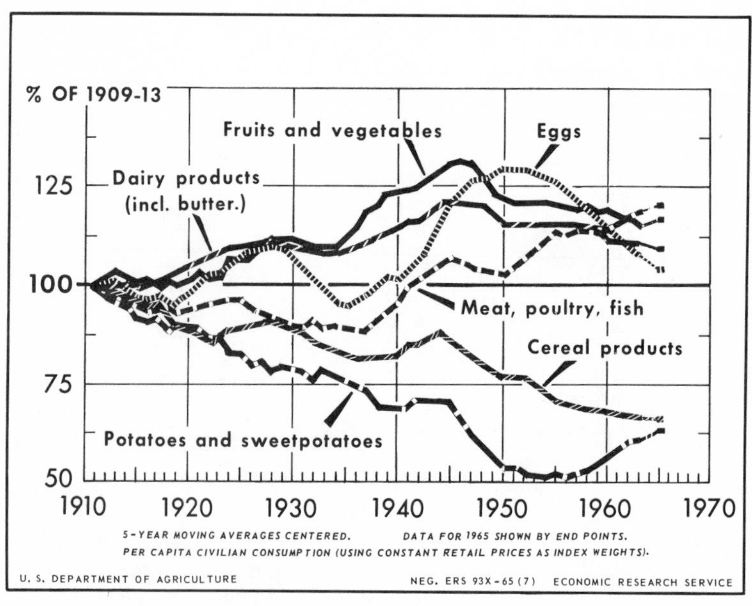

FIGURE 3.4 Trends in United States eating habits.

creased significantly since the years immediately before World War II. Much more of our food now moves through the commercial marketing system instead of being produced in backyards or on farms for home or subsistence use. Part but not all of the decline in subsistence food production (from 16 percent in 1940 to about 5 percent in 1965[10]) has resulted from the farm to city migration. The shift to purchased food has required more labor and more capital investment to handle, process, ship, store, and distribute the food. Bread baking on Saturday morning used to be a necessity in many families. Now it has become an avocation of some housewives and a quality differential for others. (Most Americans take as a matter of course our year-around great variety and plentiful supply of processed and fresh foods.) Only a devastating freeze in Florida or a flood or a major strike can remind us of all the farm and marketing resources that are involved in getting that particular food to our supermarkets or to our favorite restaurant. Per capita use of such marketing services was half again as large in the mid 1960s as in 1965.[11]

Changes in consumption of nonfood commodities and of services have accompanied great changes in the ways Americans live. Particularly striking have been the expansion of automobile ownership and the extensive buying of electrical appliances. By 1960–1961, 9 out of 10 families owned television sets. Only 83 percent owned refrigerators and 70 percent owned washing machines.[12] The latter two items are now commonly supplied in apartment houses.

3.2.4 Changes in Consumption Patterns

Business and labor groups in the United states have been interested for many years in prices paid by clerical and wage earners and in changes in their incomes and expenditures. Data in Table 3.5 have been summarized from six surveys made over a 75-year period. They trace the steady increases in real income per family and in expenditures, measured in dollars of comparable purchasing power. As real incomes have risen, the share allocated to food has declined markedly. In the last 25 years, other major changes have been the increased shares allotted to transportation, medical care, and recreation.

From time to time the home economists and statisticians in the Department of Agriculture have surveyed household food consumption. From studies made in the spring of 1942 and the spring of 1955 we find that urban households spent their food money in these ways:[13]

Item	1942, percent	1955, percent
Meat	22.0	26.3
Dairy products (other than butter)	14.8	15.1
Fats and oils	7.3	4.1
Poultry and eggs	9.6	9.4
Fruits and vegetables	23.3	19.9
Sugar and sweets	2.8	2.7
Cereals and bakery products	11.5	10.4
Other (beverages, fish, nuts, etc.)	8.7	12.1

How income affects food consumption of particular groups of households is revealed by statistics from the 1955 Survey of Household Food Consumption. Consumption of farm foods per person in households with incomes of $10,000 or more was half again as high in the spring of 1955 as in those with incomes under $1000. The variation in average use of livestock products was somewhat greater between households of high and low income than was the variation in use of foods grown as crops.

3.2.5 Future Trends

Most economic forecasters expect that this country will have further increases in real income but probably at a slower rate than in the last 50 years. In the public sector, we are likely to see substantial increases in outlays for education, medical care, recreation facilities, public transportation, and urban development. Changes in legislative apportionment following a 1964 Supreme Court decision will lead to greater emphasis on urban problems. The impact of the post-War War II baby

[10] Estimate for 1940 derived from data in Table 3.4 of Burk, M. C. *Measures and Procedures for Analysis of U.S. Food Consumption*. Estimate for 1965 by author based on related trends.

[11] See Table 12.3.

[12] Page 1132, Tibbets, Thomas R. "Expanding Ownership of Household Equipment," *Monthly Labor Review* 87:10:1131–37, October 1964.

[13] Page 597 of Burk, M. C. "Pounds and Percentages," pp. 591–595 of *Food*, The Yearbook of Agriculture, 1959.

Table 3.5 Average Consumption Expenditures of Families of City Wage and Clerical Workers of Two or More Persons, Selected Periods (in Dollars of 1950 Purchasing Power)

Item	1888–91[a]	1901[a]	1917–19[a]	1934–36[a]	1950[a]	1960[b]
Average family size (persons)	3.9	4.0	4.9	3.6	3.3	3.6
Money income after taxes ($)	1793	1914	2408	2659	4005	5137
Average expenditures for current consumption ($)	1671	1817	2163	2564	4076	4906
Percentage for:			Percentage of Consumption Expenditures			
Food and beverages	47.7	52.4	39.5	40.2	32.8	27.1
Housing (total)	[c]	[c]	25.5	27.8	25.7	28.2
Shelter, utilities, and operation	[c]	[c]	20.5[d]	23.2	18.8	22.5
Housefurnishings and equipment	[c]	[c]	5.0	4.6	6.9	5.3
Clothing and services	[c]	[c]	15.8	12.1	11.6	10.5
Medical care	[c]	[c]	[c]	3.4	5.2	6.1
Recreation	[c]	[c]	[c]	2.6	4.7	4.0
Reading and education	[c]	[c]	[c]	1.5	1.3	1.8
Transportation	[c]	[c]	[c]	8.01	13.2	15.4
All other	[c]	[c]	[c]	4.3	5.5	6.9

[a] From Table 7, p. 49 of U.S. Department of Labor, *How American Buying Habits Change*.

[b] Derived from data reported in Lamale, Helen, H. "Workers' Wealth and Family Living Standards," *Monthly Labor Review* 86:6, 676–686, June 1963. Percentages based on current dollar allocations.

[c] Not available.

[d] Including estimated 3 percent for household operation.

boom and scientific revolution will force heavier expenditures for higher education. The increase in discretionary income and accelerated formation of new households will be reflected in greater demand for housing and housefurnishings and increased emphasis on quality, variety, and convenience.

3.3 USES OF FINDINGS FROM CONSUMPTION STUDIES

Statistics pertaining to production-consumption relationships and to trends and patterns of consumption in the United States, such as those described in earlier sections of this chapter, are gathered, summarized, analyzed, and published for a purpose. Economists and statisticians develop this information to provide operational solutions to questions raised by actual problems.

Data on consumption have been developed by the Federal Government agencies primarily for use in public decision making. Business firms and trade associations often use them to ascertain general trends for their industry and as benchmarks for privately collected sets of data and for analysis to guide business decision making. The remainder of this chapter will review some specific examples of public, business, and consumer problems, policies, and programs for which consumption studies have been or can be used.

3.3.1 Public Uses

Decisions on allocation of our national resources are usually so fragmented that few citizens realize they are making them. When a city has a heated fight over a school bond issue or over teachers' salaries or the Congress passes a great highway program, citizens are deciding on expenditures for publicly supplied services or for public investments to supply such services in the future. Special commissions and groups such as President Truman's Materials Policy Commission (chaired by William S. Paley) and the Outdoor Recreation Resources Review Commission have been directly charged with responsibility for assembly of data and development of economic projections for use in public policy determination. Each of these studies has taken specific note of major trends in the consumption of food or nonfood commodities, capital investment as opposed to current consumption, and needs for investment and conservation of public resources. Their reports are usually weighty economic and statistical tomes unknown to the general public. But their findings are used extensively by administrators and technicians in the government agencies and by staffs of committees of the Congress in the process of formulating policies and legislation, and in making subsequent administrative decisions.

Government agencies and the Congress are major users of data (*a*) contrasting consumption trends and patterns in the United States with those in other countries, and (*b*) relating them to international economic development. Business groups take a very active interest, indeed, in consumption rates when they are arguing for special tariff treatment or supporting trade policies that will affect their expansion in other countries.

Congressmen, farm organization leaders, and U.S. Department of Agriculture officials are generally concerned with matters such as adjustment in farm production to meet changing demands, conservation, food distribution programs, the competition of imports with domestic production, and potential export markets for our surpluses. The USDA is frequently charged with making studies of alternative programs proposed to meet such problems. Congressional committees and congressmen from the predominantly agricultural states want to know how programs related to major commodities in their state, for example, would affect production, consumption, foreign trade, prices, farm income, and costs to the government. An understanding of the forces shaping consumer demand is essential for studies of this kind. We need to know more than we do about how people of different income groups and in different parts of the country would respond to changes in prices and in kinds and qualities of products, especially the newer ones developed to utilize surplus supplies.

Although administrators of government agencies do not determine what the national policy or the program is to be, they do make suggestions to the President and the Congress. Also, they carry out whatever policies and programs are authorized by the Congress. Often they have many difficult decisions to make. One of the key decisions in the U.S. Department of Agriculture under present legislation is that of determining the "normal supply" of an agricultural commodity. In this case the Secretary of Agriculture must determine whether the supply of a commodity is greater or less than normal. Based on his findings, price supports may be raised or lowered significantly. The concept of a normal supply refers to the amount that would normally be consumed both in domestic and foreign markets. Price support programs and other special programs dealing with production of particular commodities can never work well unless the estimates of normal consumption and normal supplies on which they are based are reasonably accurate.

Administrators of research programs also need to know what is happening to the consumption and demand for food and other commodities. Preparing a research budget in the government is no easy undertaking. The research administrators, together with the officials of the Bureau of the Budget, must decide not only how much to request for research, but how this amount should be allocated. For example, how much should go to research on farm production, on the development of new uses for farm products, on agricultural marketing, on the analysis of demand and prices, and for research on many other important subjects? The relative importance of individual problems and subjects changes from time to time. Sometimes we are concerned with the danger of future shortages and high prices. At other times we are concerned with surpluses and low prices.

Here, again, an understanding of trends in the demand for food and other commodities can be of great value in steering our research and the promotion of problem commodities along the most productive lines. In recent years one of the areas of great interest has been that of market development, particularly for the surplus agricultural commodities. A number of agricultural groups have developed "self-help" programs which include compulsory payments to special funds for research and promotion. Also, of course, several large cooperative associations and trade associations have engaged in promoting their products for many years.

Administrators of many nonagricultural programs also have interest in problems of food consumption and in the demand for food as opposed to the demand for other commodities. Among the agencies deserving special mention are the Food and Drug Administration, the Bureau of Labor Statistics, the Department of Commerce, and a number of international agencies including the Food and Agriculture Organization, the World Health Organization, and the International Labour Office.

For example, the Department of Commerce makes extensive use of data on the consumption of individual commodities as a part of its national income accounting. The U.S. Bureau of Labor Statistics collects data like those in Tables 3.1, 3.2, and 3.3, and 3.5 as part of its preparation of the Consumer Price Index. This index is closely watched for indications of inflation and is extensively used in public policy decision making and by business and labor groups in setting wage rates.

The U.N. Food and Agriculture Organization studies trends in food consumption in the United States and throughout the world, comparing supplies and requirements as one of the bases for considering possible courses of action such as technical assistance to improve levels of living.

As American public officials, congressmen, and citizens have become aware of the continued existence of structural unemployment and pockets of poverty, government agencies have collected data on consumption levels by such groups as the low-income families in the Appalachians, in other areas with depleted mines and forests, and in the urban slums. Health and welfare policy and program determination rests heavily on data from cross-section studies and studies of the relationships between actual levels of consumption and estimates of needs. One example is the administration of the Food Stamp Program; another is the conduct of public assistance programs. Agencies responsible for consumer protection frequently refer to consumption data to determine the relative importance of particular commodities in the dietary and expenditure patterns of consumers.

In Chapter 2 the wartime efforts to develop estimates of civilian requirements were discussed. About once a year since World War II, selected representatives of federal agencies have disappeared from their offices to participate in defense exercises, similar to the war games of the Armed Forces, to test plans for national emergencies such as an enemy attack. An important part of such emergency planning is the assembly and use of data on rates of food consumption and food stocks in key metropolitan areas, assumed to be possible enemy targets.

3.3.2 Business Use

Data and analyses of food consumption are further developed than those for most other commodities, with the major exception of automobiles. Private business dealing in nonagricultural commodities has to finance many types of research which are performed by the USDA for agribusiness. One of the functions of consumption researchers in the Federal Government is to supply information to business, as well as to government agencies and the general public, about trends and patterns in consumption. More and more large firms and some of the small firms are devoting time and research money to analysis of consumption trends. Their analyses provide the bases for decisions that are important with regard to investment in plants and facilities, new products, production scheduling, and sales management and promotion.

INVESTMENT PLANNING. The magnitude of investment and rising costs of transportation even in single plants are now so great that considerable expenditure on market research is justified to investigate trends in consumer demand. United States average rates of consumption in a recent year for a broad commodity group are no longer adequate. Therefore researchers use regional data on consumption of individual items from federal surveys as benchmarks for private market research on which investment decisions are based.

NEW PRODUCT DEVELOPMENT. Both large and small firms are exploring possibilities of diversifying their lines to maximize returns on given investments in facilities and distribution systems. In the course of such explorations, they often send representatives to the Federal Government agencies for information on historical trends and cross-section variations in the consumption of their present or prospective products and competing commodities. Many are using federal statistics as a framework within which to set up their own more intensive market surveys and for use in measuring their shares of the market.

PRODUCTION SCHEDULING. More and more firms are turning from production planning based on salesmen's hopes for future sales to use of analyses of trends in consumption and the factors affecting them *plus* the study of their share of the market. The conclusions from such research are very closely guarded in the chief executive offices.

SALES MANAGEMENT AND PROMOTION. Results of research on consumption patterns have long been used by sales managers. More intensive analysis by individual firms of the "whys" of variations in consumption of given products is possible because of the benchmarks from such data as those from the 1955 and 1965 USDA Surveys of Household Food Consumption. When the "whys" are identified, special promotions can be developed to increase consumption in lagging areas or groups of consumers. Of course, no business firm announces the results of its analyses nor its plans. Competing firms, therefore, may not be aware of how outmoded their market research programs may be.

Business firms spend large amounts for consumption data from market research firms such as A. C. Nielsen and Company and the Market Research Corporation of America. Most of the data are never made public. When properly analyzed, they provide vital information for the company supporting the research.

CUSTOMER SERVICE. Some business firms supplying others with materials and services have worked up analyses of trends and variations in consumption of products manufactured by those businesses to whom they sell their own products. For example, several have reported great interest among customers in the data on food consumption which they have carefully organized, summarized, and presented with much skill. They found that market research for their customers was "good business."[14]

Life Magazine's Study of Consumer Expenditures, conducted in 1955–56, was designed to provide updated information for their advertisers.[15] It apparently served some useful purposes, but problems involved in making the survey and in analyzing the data were far greater than expected by the initial planners.

[14] From pp. 398 and 399 of Burk, Marguerite C. "The Significance of Current Developments in Food Statistics," pp. 384–400, Dolva, Wenzil K. (Editor), *Marketing Keys to Profits in the 1960's.*

[15] Ostheimer, Richard H. "Who Buys What? *Life's* Study of Consumer Expenditures," *J. Marketing* **XXII**:3:260–272, January 1958.

3.3.3 Use by Citizen-Consumers

Every American has a stake in the development of consumption economics because everyone is a consumer. His actions are recorded in the statistics which are studied in this book. More important, these statistics and actions based on them have a direct bearing on policies and programs which affect every citizen. It is important that any intelligent citizen be able to find accurate information on a subject which so vitally concerns him. After all, citizen-voters determine what our policies toward food and other consumption goods and services should be and what kinds of programs should implement those policies.

Gradually consumption economists are developing greater knowledge regarding trends and patterns in consumption and the significance of major factors related to them. As such knowledge is passed on to consumers through education programs, Americans will be able to make wiser decisions, not only for themselves and their own families, but also as members of the American economy and polity.

4

CONSUMPTION IN LESS-DEVELOPED COUNTRIES

Levels and patterns of consumption of food and other goods and services vary greatly in different parts of the world. Some years ago writers classified countries as "haves" and "have nots" on the basis of their prosperity and poverty. In postwar years, as economic development has become the great hope of the "have nots" and the ever-present concern of the "haves," we refer to the poor countries as "less-developed countries" or euphemistically and hopefully, as the "developing countries."

Usually classified with the United States as "highly developed" are Canada, Australia, and New Zealand (Oceania), most countries of Western Europe, and Japan in recent years. The kinds of consumption problems encountered in these countries are similar in many respects to those faced in the recent past or currently by the United States so they do not receive separate attention in this textbook.

4.1 INTRODUCTION

The consumption problems of the less-developed countries in Latin America, Africa, and Asia are both more varied and more critical to future economic and social changes than those of the industrialized countries. Consumption patterns within these developing countries are much less homogeneous. Levels of consumption for food and for nonfood goods and services are often very low among large groups of people. Averages for the whole countries are much less meaningful because of the wide disparity in consumption rates and attitudes between people in the so-called "westernized" or industrialized urban centers (described by Chiang as "contact-points"[1]) and in the isolated parts of the hinterland where the indigenous cultures are still predominant.

This chapter is designed to give the student (1) an overall view of variations in consumption, especially consumption of food, between the developed countries and the less-developed countries and within these countries, and (2) some awareness of the significance of consumption problems and of changes in consumption during the process of economic development.

4.1.1 Concern for Consumption Problems of Less-Developed Countries

Governments of the United States and the more developed countries, their peoples, and business firms interested in international trade and overseas operations are all concerned with the consumption problems of the less-developed countries. Threats of famine and major emergencies in any part of the world arouse humanitarian efforts. Substantial overseas shipments of subsidized food, clothing, and medical supplies, as well as various kinds of capital equipment, evidence international concern. In perspective, the first 75 years of the twentieth century appear to be an era of world food emergencies, population explosion, and political and economic warfare.

If the family planning programs and technical agricultural assistance achieve their potentials in the next decade, national and international concerns in the last quarter of the twentieth century and in the twenty-first century will be quite different. The main focuses of concern are likely to be on human resource development and on environmental problems such as air and water pollution, public resource development, land use controls, housing, and supplies of services like marketing

[1] Page 250 of Chiang, Alpha C. "The 'Demonstration Effect' in a Dual Economy," *Am. J. Econ. and Soc.* 18:2:249–258, April 1958.

and mass transportation. But we will also engage in massive efforts to improve education for work and living in the less-developed countries.

4.1.2 Outline of Chapter

Section 4.2 sketches variations in consumption around the world as indicated by income, food expenditures, other food measures, and several measures of environmental conditions. Sections 4.3 and 4.4 describe some of the general characteristics and trends in consumption in the less-developed countries. Sections 4.5 and 4.6 go more deeply into information on consumption in two well-known, less-developed countries—India and Nigeria. The chapter closes with a brief discussion of the significance of consumption changes in the less-developed countries to the United States.

4.2 VARIATIONS IN CONSUMPTION AROUND THE WORLD

Economists have experimented with a variety of indicators of differences in levels of living from place to place and time to time. Perhaps the most common are the per capita measures of money income, gross domestic product, and total consumption expenditures. These money measures pose problems in comparability because of difficulties in converting from one currency to another. There are also difficulties in combining the wide variety of goods and services preferred by different cultural groups. So some alternative measures are used occasionally to supplement income and expenditure data.

4.2.1 Income—Related Measures

Variations in average per capita income from country to country are general indicators of variations in consumption. Data assembled by the United Nations for the early 1950s indicate that per capita incomes averaged less than $100 in most countries of the Far East and Africa, $100 to $200 in most countries of the Near East, and $100 to $250 in most countries of Latin America. In contrast, per capita incomes ran between $750 to $1000 in the Western European countries, around $1000 in Oceania (Australia and New Zealand), and in the neighborhood of $1500 to $2000 in North America.[2]

However, these dollar figures somewhat overstate the extent of variation because they are straight conversions from national income and local currency at official exchange rates. Official exchange rates are often lower than the actual rates of exchange in the business world. Prices of commodities consumed by large proportions of the people in the less-developed countries are often significantly lower than indicated by the straight conversion into dollars. Real incomes frequently permit a higher real level of living than the dollar conversions indicate. For example, disposable income in Great Britain in 1960 averaged £345 per capita, about $966 in American dollars. Although this dollar income level on a per capita basis is close to the often-quoted United States poverty line of $3000 per *family*, the average British family is not on the verge of poverty. A family with £1000 per year in the United Kingdom can buy more goods and services than a United States family can buy with $3000.

A popular indicator of real levels of living is the proportion of income or total consumption expenditures spent on food.[3] Such data for a number of countries are given in Table 4.1, but careful study leads one to question the statistics underlying some of them. For example, the percentages allocated to food reported for El Salvador, Peru, and Jamaica seem quite low in view of their relatively low levels of income and their general consumption situation. Data on food supplies in those countries do not indicate such plentiful food supplies or such low prices as to yield these percentages. One suspects that some of the subsistence food did not get counted in the expenditure figures or in income.

The housing shares of total personal expenditures are affected by the shares required for food in the less-developed countries as well as by a number of supply factors to be discussed later in the chapter. Among the more developed countries, the housing share is affected by government subsidies to housing programs (which do not show up in personal consumption expenditures) and by the relative

[2] Data from page 25 of the *Third World Survey*, FAO. Comprehensive data for later years are not yet available, but other data regarding national output indicate little relative change in the degree of variation.

[3] The term "expenditures" in most of this chapter is used very loosely to include both money outlays and the value of consumption in kind, such as home-produced food.

TABLE 4.1 Selected Countries: Proportion of Private Consumption Expenditures Allocated to Food and Housing in 1964, Except as Indicated[a]

Developed Countries	Percentage for		Less-Developed Countries	Percentage for	
	Food	Housing		Food	Housing
United States	20	18	Jamaica	33	8
Canada	21	19	Taiwan	48	15
Australia	22	13	Korea	58	9
Sweden	26	14	Ghana	59	9
United Kingdom	26	15	Peru[b]	40	20
France	29	10	El Salvador[b]	42	8
South Africa	27	10	Nigeria[b]	70	3
Israel	29	17			

[a] Except as noted, percentages computed from data in United Nations *Yearbook of National Accounts Statistics*, 1965. Food excludes alcoholic beverages; housing includes rent (actual or computed), water, fuel, and light.
[b] Data for late 1950s from pp. 572–573 of *Compendium of Social Statistics*, 1963, U. N. Series K No. 2. Housing includes rent (actual or imputed), water, taxes, fuel, and light.

importance attached to housing in these countries.

4.2.2 Other Indicators

A number of economists have proposed nonmonetary measures for "real income" or "real consumption" to overcome the problem of valuing disparate combinations of consumer goods and services consumed in different countries. For example, Beckerman and Bacon used multiple correlation analysis of data for eleven different countries at two different time periods to find the nonmonetary measures which were most highly correlated with national income and which could serve as independent indicators of real income or consumption.[4] They selected the following per capita measures: (*a*) annual apparent crude steel consumption, (*b*) annual apparent cement production, (*c*) annual number of domestic letters sent, (*d*) stock of radio receivers, (*e*) stock of telephones, (*f*) stock of road vehicles (commercial and domestic), and (*g*) annual meat consumption.

Using (1) the coefficients of these measures to indicate their relative importance in an overall measure, and (2) the matching series of data for 80 countries, they computed a set of aggregates. Finally, they selected the aggregate for the United Kingdom to be the base (setting it equal to 100) and compared the aggregates for the other 79 countries with that of the United Kingdom. The index numbers for 18 of the countries, selected as examples, are:

Countries	Per-cent	Countries	Per-cent
United States	140	Mainland China	15
Sweden	125	Tunisia	13
France	75	Taiwan	12
Japan	46	Ghana	8
Israel	45	Korean Republic	6
Argentina	39	India	5
USSR	35	Nigeria	4
Chile	27	Burma	2
Mexico	22	Ethiopia	1

In general, this ordering matches rather well an ordering of these countries on the basis of per capita domestic product in the early 1960s.

4.2.3 Variations in Food Consumption

Several measures of average food consumption are used to indicate how average food supplies vary among countries and regions of the world. One measure developed by the Food and Agriculture Organization of the United Nations (FAO) is based on farm values of food supplies for human consumption and

[4] Beckerman, Wilfred, and Bacon, Robert. "International Comparisons of Income Levels: A Suggested New Measure," *Economic Journal* **LXXVI**: 303:519–536, September 1966.

compares the values for supplies in each specified year with the world average for 1948–52 which is set equal to 100 percent. Regional variations in per capita food supplies are indicated by this index in the first data column of Table 4.2 and by the information in Figure 4.1. They should not be viewed as precise and exact measurements but as rough indicators. They should be interpreted as showing Far Eastern and African food supplies to be significantly below the world average, whereas those of Western Europe and North America are substantially higher than the world average.

Other measures of overall level of consumption are the food energy and the protein content. Again, the figures in Table 4.2 are really rough approximations, despite their apparent precision. Without doubt, food energy supplies per capita in the Far East are much below those of North America and Europe. But great gaps in our knowledge of subsistence food production in the Far East and in Africa and Latin America lead to the conclusion that African and Latin American food levels should be described as significantly lower than those of North America but probably higher than those of the Far East. The proportion of food energy supplied by the starchy staples and sugar, given in data column 3, is still another indicator of the general level of food consumption, with the poorer countries relying more on these

TABLE 4.2 Per Capita Food Supplies and Supplies of Food Energy and Protein, Major Regions of the World

Region	FAO Index of per Capita Supplies in 1963–65, World Average in 1948–52 = 100[a]	Food Energy, 1959–61 Average[b]		Protein, 1959–61 Average[b]	
		Calories per Day	Proportion from Cereals, Starchy Roots, and Sugar	Total	Proportion from Animal Sources
	Percent	Number	Percent	Grams	Percent
Far East	52	2120	76	54.7	16
Near East (West Asia)	97	2405	71	71.9	22
Africa	54	2400[c]	78[c]	61[c]	20[c]
Northern		2230	73	69.1	25
Southern		2470	80	58.7	19
Europe					
Western	201	2950[d]	52[d]	85[d]	51[d]
Northern		3060	48	88.4	59
Southern		2720	60	78.6	34
Eastern		2990	63	82.5	35
Western Hemisphere		2870	53	80.4	54
North America	309	3180[e]		95.0[e]	66[e]
United States		3190	40	95.3	67
Latin America	100	2600[f]		67[f]	36[f]
Oceania	235	3210[e]		93.5[e]	67[e]

[a] Farm price-weighted index: world average excludes USSR, Eastern Europe, and Mainland China for lack of data. Unpublished data from FAO.

[b] Except as noted, from Table 11, USDA, ERS *National Food Situation*, February 1966.

[c] Computed using 1:3 population ratio for Northern and Southern Africa.

[d] Computed using 2:1 population ratio for Northern and Southern Europe.

[e] Estimated by author to match USDA data, using data for 1960–62 in FAO *State of Food and Agriculture*, 1966, Tables 8B and 8C.

[f] Computed by author from Western Hemisphere and North American averages.

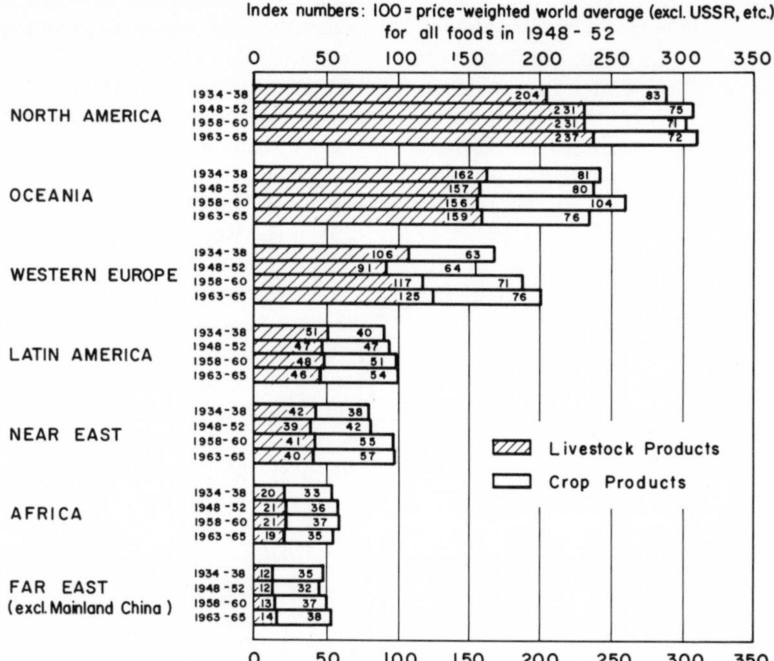

FIGURE 4.1 Index numbers of estimated food supplies per capita by region. (Data from U. N. Food and Agriculture Organization.)

foods and the richer countries turning more to meats, dairy products, and fats.

Variations in protein content of average food supplies are even greater than is the case for food energy. Although cereals, pulses, and roots supply some important types of protein, they are not nearly as rich in several critical types of protein (amino acids) as meats, dairy products, and fish.

At this point, we note that overall measures or average measures of consumption in countries of the Far East, Africa, and Latin America are much less satisfactory indicators of the whole food situation in those countries than such average measures are for the United States. In the United States about 75 percent of the households have an overall level of food consumption per person within the range of 20 percent above or below the national average. Available information on variations in food consumption in less-developed countries indicates far wider differences and a much greater concentration of the population at extreme levels of consumption than in the United States.

The principal staple foods vary from region to region. The United States is a wheat-consuming country, and Mexico relies more heavily on maize (corn). South India is a heavy consumer of rice, whereas North India consumes more of the millets, sorghums, and wheat. Currently, substantial supplies of United States wheat are being consumed in many parts of India to supplement the short supplies of other foods. The northern part of Nigeria is a heavy consumer of millet and sorghums, and the southern diets emphasize starchy roots and plantains. These variations in consumption will be discussed at greater length in the latter part of this chapter. Domestic production is an important key to the kinds of foods consumed in each area. However, relatively rich countries like the United Kingdom are able to import large food supplies to supplement domestic production so their patterns are not necessarily determined by the kinds of foods produced domestically. In the United States 85 to 90 percent of the food consumed is grown domestically.

4.2.4 Variations in Environmental Conditions

The physical environment in which people live is an important aspect of consumption which is receiving increased attention by economists. Housing is only part of the physical environment. Other parts are indicated by public concerns with air and water pollution, environmental health problems, and urban and regional planning regarding land use.

Variations in housing among the developing countries are difficult to appraise easily. Several measures available for a number of countries provide some indications of the variability. One is the average number of persons per room.[5] The average runs 0.7 persons in the United States, Australia, Canada, and the United Kingdom. In Latin America, Argentina has 1.4 persons per room, Brazil 1.3, Chile 1.6, Colombia 1.9, Ecuador 2.5, urban Guatemala 2.1, Mexico 2.9, and Panama 2.4. For countries in the Middle East, data are available only for the urban areas of the United Arab Republic, where the average is estimated at 1.6 persons per room. In Asia the average for urban India is 2.6, for Pakistan 3.1, Ceylon 2.2, and Republic of Korea 2.5, in contrast with 1.2 persons per room in Japan.

Another measure is the availability of piped water. More information is available for Latin American countries than for Asian or African countries. In Argentina and Chile slightly over 50 percent have piped water; in Brazil only 21 percent, Colombia 28 percent, Ecuador 38 percent, Mexico 32 percent, Panama 46 percent, and Jamaica 71 percent. In the Middle East, the percentage for urban Turkey is 56 percent, urban Lebanon 93 percent, for all of Jordan 36 percent, and for the United Arab Republic 40 percent. No estimates are available for India or Pakistan, but in the Republic of Korea 21 percent of the housing units had piped water. In the Philippines 20 percent had piped water inside the house and another 28 percent outside the dwellings.

Sewage disposal presents acute problems all over the world. For example, the city of Lagos, Nigeria, has no central sewage system but depends on individual cesspools which overflow in the torrential rains. Therefore it is little wonder that 85 percent of a sample of school children were infected with parasites and that 54 percent of all deaths in that capital city occurred among children under five years of age.[6] Large sections of many of the cities of developing countries are slums in which the only provision for disposal of human excrement, if any, is by intermittent pail collection. Whereas 90 percent of the dwellings in the United States have flush toilets, 45 percent of those in Chile, 21 percent in Colombia, 38 percent in Panama, 34 percent in Iraq, 8 percent in the Philippines, and less than 1 percent in the Republic of Korea have them.

In countries like the United States and the United Kingdom, economists and health officials are beginning to develop measures of air pollution, especially to guide policy determination with regard to smog, as in Los Angeles and London. No data are yet available for even the Ruhr Valley and certainly not for the developing countries. But this does not mean that air pollution is not a problem there. Visitors to Calcutta, for example, are immediately aware of morning fumes from the use of cow dung as cooking fuel. The odors of human and animal waste in many of the slum areas of the developing world are difficult for inexperienced Americans to imagine. As the population of the world increases in the next decade or two and information on the relationship of environmental conditions to health develops, concern with improving the environment is likely to magnify greatly.

4.3 ECONOMIC AND SOCIAL PROBLEMS RELATED TO CHANGES IN CONSUMPTION

Three sets of socioeconomic phenomena materially affect trends in consumption—those related to production, to allocation for investment versus current consumption, and to population growth. Technical study of these phenomena is part of general economics and demographic sociology, but a few key ideas are needed as background to understanding trends in consumption.

4.3.1 Changes in Production

As taught in elementary economics, changes in national production result from changes in the inputs of capital, labor (including entrepreneurship), and natural resources. New steel, fertilizer, and food processing plants; highways and ports; dams; irrigation systems; and development of improved seeds and breeds of livestock are examples of increased capital inputs. Extension of elementary schooling to a larger proportion of the children, increases in

[5] Data from Table 1307, *Statistical Abstract of the United States, 1966.*

[6] Page 5, Abrams, Charles. *Man's Struggle for Shelter in an Urbanizing World.*

enrollment in institutions for technical and higher education, and on-the-job training in industrial plants and in agriculture are common forms of additions to labor inputs being made in developing countries as they seek to upgrade labor productivity. In effect, they are additions to human capital. Capital investments in roads to open up new lands and in irrigation systems to make better use of the available water supply lead to increases in the inputs of natural resources and increased efficiency in their use.

Data from national income accounts are often used to measure changes in production. One such indicator is the change in per capita product at constant prices, summarized for many countries in the *Statistical Abstract of the United States, 1966*. The percentage increases from 1955 to 1964 for selected countries follow:[7]

Country	Percent Increase	Country	Percent Increase
United States	14	India	18
Argentina	9	Jamaica	46
Burma	21	Mexico	29
Chile	14	Pakistan	20
Taiwan[a]	29	Peru	25
Honduras[a]	11	Puerto Rico	103

[a] 1955 to 1963.

These data on changes in per capita product represent the net effect of changes in production inputs and population.

4.3.2 Investment vs. Current Consumption

Capital inputs into the production of developing countries can be increased through aid from other countries and through increased allocation of current production to investment in capital goods as opposed to use for current consumption. The share of a country's GNP allocated to consumption as opposed to capital investment reflects a multitude of public and private decisions. Examples are government decisions regarding building highways and fertilizer plants and pertinent to direct and indirect taxation; business decisions to accumulate capital to build industrial plants rather than paying out dividends to stockholders; private decisions to save through credit unions and building societies for future homes; and farmers' decisions to increase fertilizer use and build irrigation ditches.

Some data from national income accounts which indicate variations in the allocation of GNP between private and government consumption and fixed capital formation are given in Table 4.3. Note the relatively large shares of the total allocated to private consumption in the developing countries compared with the United States and recall that the total product being divided up is much smaller per capita in those countries. Data on the government shares of consumption include military expenditures as well as public services such as education.

4.3.3 Population Growth

Recent increases in population, described as the population explosion, have offset increases in production in many of the developing countries. They have given rise to near hysteria over future population trends. The population growth rate of Latin America has been 2.8 percent per annum, which can double the population in 25 years. Somewhat lower rates have been calculated for Africa by the United Nations—2.4 percent, and for South Asia—2.2 percent, East Asia (excluding Japan)—1.5 percent. Demographers of the United Nations have made projections of world population for the year 2000, based on varied assumptions regarding the reduction in the fertility rate. The projections range from 5.3 billion to 6.8 billion people compared with the 3.2 billion in the world in 1964. About 85 percent of the increase was projected to occur in the less-developed countries.

Much of the increased rate of population growth experienced in the last two decades has resulted from decreases in the death rate of the developing countries. These were effected by public health measures. Birth rates have remained high in most of the world. However, there have been sharp declines in fertility in some countries of East Asia such as Japan, Taiwan, Singapore, Hong Kong, and the Republic of Korea.

Demographers currently differ considerably in their appraisals of future trends in fertility rates. In contrast with the projections of past trends used by the United Nations demographers, Bogue asserted in November 1966, "Recent developments in the worldwide movement to bring runaway birth rates under control are such that it is now possible to assert with

[7] From Table 1291.

TABLE 4.3 Percentages of Gross National Product Used for Consumption and Fixed Capital Formation in Selected Countries[a]

Country	Year	Consumption		Fixed Capital Formation
		Private	Government[b]	
United States	1964	62	18	17
Bolivia	1964	79	9	15
Brazil	1960	70	14	15
Chile	1964	80	9	14
China (Taiwan)	1964	65	16	14
Ecuador	1964	72	14	17
Ghana	1964	73	12	17
Guatemala	1964	81	7	13
Iran	1963	75	11	13
Korea, Republic of	1964	81	10	11
Mexico	1964	81	6	16
Sudan	1963	81	11	17
Togo	1963	89	7	8
Tunisia	1964	73	17	24
Turkey	1964	73	16	13

[a] Excluding changes in stocks, exports and imports, and net factor income from abroad. Data from Table 1289 of *Statistical Abstract of the United States, 1966.*
[b] Including defense expenditures.

considerable confidence that the prospects for rapid fertility control are excellent. In fact, it is quite reasonable to assume that the world population crisis is a phenomenon of the 20th century, and will be largely if not entirely a matter of history when humanity moves into the 21st century. . . ."[8] Bogue argues that recent trends will not continue because of grass roots approval of family planning, aroused political leadership, accelerated professional and research activity, slackening of progress in death control, a variety of sociological and psychological phenomena promoting rapid adoption of family planning by the masses, and improving technology in contraception.

4.4 EXAMINATION OF FOOD AND HOUSING CONSUMPTION

We turn now to closer examination of food and housing conditions in the developing countries. Our concern here is with some of the critical factors in future changes in consumption levels and patterns.

[8] Page 1, Bogue, Donald J. "The Prospects for World Population Control." Paper presented at the Conference on Alternatives for Balancing Future World Food Production and Needs, Iowa State University, Center for Agricultural Economic Adjustment, Ames, Iowa, November 9, 1966.

4.4.1 Current Food Situation

A very large proportion of available income and total energy of poor families is devoted to obtaining sufficient food. Even so, information outlined earlier in this chapter indicates low levels of food and nutrition in many parts of the less-developed countries. The low levels of food and nutrition result from the compounding of many factors unfavorable to food supplies—greater crowding on the land with much smaller productive area per person to be fed; poorer natural climatic and growing conditions for food production in many cases; primitive methods of cultivation and care of livestock, with little or no use of modern technical knowledge of natural or artificial fertilizer, of improved varieties or hybrid seed with greater productive vigor; and little protection of the crops from natural pests, wet weather, or decay.

On the demand side, the incomes of farm

and city people in the developing countries are generally so low that they cannot afford to import food from abroad to make up domestic shortages in quantity, quality, or variety, except under emergency programs such as the United States' Public Law 480. Illiteracy and ignorance combine with the effects of low incomes to produce poor food habits, that is, poor from the nutritional point of view.

Even for countries with fairly good averages for the whole country over the whole year, there are likely to be either significant seasonal variations in supplies or geographic differences. Substantial numbers of people are poorly fed part of the year or in parts of the country. The marketing systems fail to distribute the supplies from one part of the country to another and to store enough of postharvest supplies to distribute them gradually during the year.

Because of our interest in consumption and demand, let us consider further the factors affecting consumer demand. Cultural inflexibility of food habits and ignorance make people unwilling to try new foods. People must want more food and different foods as well as to be able to produce them. Even if they begin to want the better diets, they often lack the purchasing power necessary to buy them. Therefore underlying every food problem we are likely to find low levels of education and low regard and understanding of public welfare.

Lack of knowledge of the nutritive values of foods and of the requirements for an adequate diet is another factor contributing to the low level of food and nutrition in the less-developed countries. Even in highly industrialized countries, many people are not aware of the nutrient content of the foods they eat nor the vital importance of nutrition to health. Despite the possession of adequate purchasing power, they may not buy and eat the kinds of foods they need in adequate amounts. The developing countries generally have high rates of illiteracy, particularly among low-income families, as well as limited communication facilities. Even existing knowledge of food and nutrition is poorly disseminated. By improper preparation of foods, a large proportion of their nutritive values may be lost. Few people in the developing countries know about the vulnerability of some nutrients to temperature variations, light, or water solubility. Therefore common methods of food preparation may waste substantial but unmeasured supplies of nutrients.

Increases in the total consumption of food and other goods and services are closely related to the size and makeup of the total population. If the population is increasing either because of the reduction in infant mortality or a lower death rate for older people, the number of relatively unproductive people in the population who must be fed out of available food supplies rises. Greater resources may have to be allocated to food production.

Another factor contributing to increases in demand for food and other goods and services is occupational shifts toward jobs that yield higher incomes, usually in urban areas. To some degree, part of the increase in incomes may be an illusion, as more of the population shifts from the subsistence type of economy toward the mixed type (part subsistence, part commercial), or from the mixed to the primarily commercial type of enterprise, with an increasing proportion of productive effort being counted as income. Still another factor related to increases in food consumption is the gradual rise in the level of general education. This tends to make people more aware of the significance of food for health and for higher levels of productivity.

Trends in food consumption under economic development exhibit several common characteristics. Subsistence farmers gradually produce more for their own needs as their expectations and technological knowledge increase. As the basic food needs of their families are met, their wants turn to goods and services they cannot produce and must buy. To buy such goods, they must increase their own output and sell more.

On the other hand, as incomes from commercial agriculture, industry, and trade increase, the demand for purchased food usually goes up faster than the supplies. Prices rise. As a less-developed country increases its demand for food, the demand gradually shifts from the inferior cereals (such as sorghum and millet) first toward wheat and rice, then toward livestock products and fruits. Such shifts raise the demand for foods requiring greater farm resources. The degree to which retail price increases are reflected in prices paid to farmers is very significant. Farm prices measure the degree of encouragement given to farmers to increase their inputs in order to get greater output.

As larger supplies of foods move from farms to other parts of the country, either to rural families or to the urban population, the pressure on the available marketing facilities grows greatly. The marketing system is called upon to handle increased quantities and to supply additional services in the forms of storage, transportation, and processing. Since consumers must pay for these marketing services, their expenditures for food increase. Increased demand for food also usually puts pressure on foreign exchange as people demand more imported food supplies, especially such items as wheat flour and luxury foods, in order to achieve food patterns with greater prestige.

4.4.2 Some Necessary Conditions for Changes in Consumption

Increases in production require increased inputs in the form of fertilizer, better seeds and livestock breeds, more careful husbandry, technological innovations in production, increased supplies of credit at reasonable rates of interest, and greater knowledge on the part of farmers and other producers, such as the processors of farm commodities. Also, increases in production usually mean that producers must break with traditional methods of production and increase their specialization. These changes ordinarily involve more risk for farmers as they change from the old to the new methods. The advantages of the new methods must be clearly understood before the large proportion of farmers will be willing to adopt them.

Inadequate marketing facilities such as transport, storage, and handling greatly increase the losses from spoilage. Processing facilities in the developing countries usually need a great deal of improvement in order to meet minimum standards of sanitation and health. Use of recognized grades and standards is essential for efficient buying and selling of commodities in large quantities. Processing and packaging are important for long-distance transportation and for storage to level out supplies over the crop year. As demand shifts from the staples to the more perishable fruits and vegetables and livestock products, wholesale and retail markets with storage facilities, especially facilities with temperature controls for handling perishable products, must be built.

All of these changes require a willingness on the part of the government, the general public, individual consumers, and producers to break with tradition. Public policy must ordinarily shift *from* the laissez-faire approach with its benefits to wealthy landholders and the business elite *to* concern for the welfare of all parts of the population. The changes usually involve both the raising and the payment of taxes, additional forms of government regulation of business, subsidies for education and small businesses, cooperatives, and farmers.

At this point we should recognize the duality in the economy and society of the less-developed countries. In the cities where there is contact with western culture in the forms of visitors from other countries, businessmen, government agencies, and the like, there is much more acceptability and interest in changing to improve levels of living. In effect, these "contact points" are much more cosmopolitan. In the hinterland, the situation is often very different. Where there is little contact, the traditional ways of living and thinking are predominant. This is described as "localism" in sociological language. A spectrum of variation must be recognized, ranging from very cosmopolitan to very local in outlook and attitude. But there tends to be a considerable concentration at the ends of the spectrum. For many years the wealthy elite of the less-developed countries have been educated and have vacationed in the great urban centers of Europe, so they know cosmopolitan living patterns very well and model their own living after the Parisian or New York ways of life. The elite have been a very small minority in many countries, usually less than 5 percent of the population.

The middle class in most developing countries has been relatively small but is now increasing as more people work for the government, industry, and business. In recent years, urban workers have been assuming more of the cosmopolitan consumption patterns. In the isolated, distant villages and farms we find much more "localism." Most people there are bound almost entirely by traditional ways of living and thinking. The "demonstration effect" appears to work faster in changing consumption in the contact points. In the hinterland there is much greater tenacity of both traditional consumption and production attitudes and methods. But with increasing purchasing power and urbanization and the further development of the communication and transport network, knowledge spreads and the demand for newer types of goods and services increases.

The cases of India and Nigeria described later illustrate a number of these points. Before turning to them, we will look briefly at the housing situation in the developing countries.

4.4.3 Housing Situation and Prospects

As Abrams has written, ". . . Housing is not only shelter but part of the fabric of neighborhood life and of the whole social milieu; it also touches on many facets of industrialization, economic activity, and development."[9] Therefore the finding of the United Nations experts that more than a billion people in the developing countries are homeless or live in housing that is a menace to health and an affront to human dignity is of great importance in considering levels and patterns of consumption in these countries.[10] In fact, housing problems are likely to supersede food problems in the world's attention within the next 15 years. They are likely to be much more difficult to solve than our food problems because of the greater amounts of capital investment needed.

Abrams has summarized information on the serious problem of squatters in the cities of the developing countries.[11] Official estimates, admittedly conservative, indicate that squatters constitute about 1/8 of the Kingston, Jamaica, population; 1/7 of that of Singapore; 1/5 of the population of Istanbul and Manila; 1/4 of Santiago, Chile, and Cali, Colombia; almost 1/2 of Ankara; and 2/3 of Venezuela. Squatter colonies regularly lack water, sewage, and paving, and pose the greatest housing problems next to those presented by homeless street-sleepers.

Rapid increases in urban population, high rates of unemployment, low productivity, speculation in urban land, inadequate public controls and planning for land use, and backward technology in construction industries are some of the major factors in the lag of housing output behind even minimum needs. The gap between shelter cost and income of masses of people is particularly great in most of the developing countries. In most cities of Asia, interest, payments on principal, and overhead costs for a worker's new dwelling unit costing around $1000 would run about $10 per month, according to Abrams.[12] This would require one-fifth of an Asian urban family's income of $600 in comparison with actual incomes averaging between $100 and $200 per year. Only a small part of the urban population of India, for example, has incomes of $600 or more.

Moreover the developing countries cannot afford to subsidize housing to the extent needed to meet annual requirements for new dwellings. A United Nations committee of experts has estimated that these countries would have to build new housing at a rate substantially higher than recent rates per thousand people achieved in the United States and Western Europe if they were to fulfill housing needs.

The United Nations *Report on the World Social Situation* called for a fresh attack on cost-income problems in the form of a minimum cost program to supply the primary need for communal services in the forms of portable water and human waste disposal. In their opinion:

> . . . a developed building-lot on which a family can erect its own temporary structure is the first step towards achieving improved housing conditions. Given the necessary public intervention and funds, this can be provided for every urban family at a rent it can afford. The next steps towards achieving various improved shelter standards must be made through maximum use of non-monetized resources; mobilization of personal savings with a home as a tangible objective; intensive research into economical design; improved use of local materials in place of expensive imported materials; and increased productivity of building labour and management. . . .[13]

Abrams has suggested some complementary steps that need to be taken. One is more careful public land use planning and control so that squatters do not move into newly developed areas, and speculative activity in the urban land market is minimized to keep land costs from spiraling. Another is the use of roof loan schemes to supplement the sanitary core of houses. A third is the training of building technicians at several levels of skill, ranging from rough carpenters and tile layers to plumbers to architects and engineers

[9] Op. cit., page vi.

[10] *Ibid.*, page 7.

[11] *Ibid.* Squatters occupy private or public land without legal rights of tenancy or ownership. See Chapter 2.

[12] *Ibid.*, page 52.

[13] Page 54, 1963 *Report on the World Social Situation.*

and finally to researchers on construction materials and design.

4.5 THE CASE OF INDIA

Consumption problems of India, especially the food situation, have been so much in the news in recent years that India serves as a good example of developing countries. The discussion here centers on food consumption, but some references to nonfood goods and services are made, particularly to housing.

4.5.1 Food Price Problem

Real incomes per capita in India have risen slightly since World War II. There has been some shift of the population to urban areas where they are dependent on commercial food supplies. In recent years domestic production of food grains has failed intermittently, especially in 1965 and 1966, to keep pace with increases in the total population. Also, higher proportions of the food grains are being consumed on farms where produced as incomes of the farm tenants and small owners have risen slightly. The combination of these factors has put heavy pressure on food grain supplies, with the result that free market prices have risen sharply, as much as 30 percent in the single year 1963–1964.[14] Some of the pressure was in the form of the shift in demand from inferior cereals (sorghum, millets, and barley) to maize (corn to Americans), wheat, and rice. The total demand for all grains has risen as people have wanted to eat more. There has been some evidence, too, of increased demand for other higher-priced foods. Price pressures have been magnified by hoarding early in the season by large producers and traders seeking extra profits through manipulating market supplies and prices.

The Indian government has attempted to ease the price situation by establishing a national food trading corporation and by direct action to distribute rice and wheat through "fair price shops" and roller flour mills; regulating markets, credit, and price controls; and special shipments of supplies into deficit areas. To understand the problem, we must look at the production situation, income-food expenditure data, and consumption patterns. The problem is complicated by political relationships between the Federal Government and the states, but they cannot be covered here.

Production of food grains has not kept up with the rise in total demand resulting from the relatively rapid increase in population and the very gradual increases in income. Farmers have not been encouraged and helped sufficiently to expand their output. Indian grain yields per acre are quite low and only about a fourth of India's food grain production moves into marketing channels.[15] The proportions vary from perhaps 1/8 of the small millets to 2/5 of the wheat. The balance is consumed on farms where produced or bartered in the local community and consumed by other families nearby.

Domestically produced supplies have been supplemented by substantial imports of food grains from the United States under Public Law 480 and from other countries. In 1966 the United States shipped 460 million bushels of wheat to India on concessional terms under PL 480. They constituted the largest part of the total Indian imports of food grains.

4.5.2 Income and Food Expenditures

The relatively low levels of income and food consumption in India are indicated by the data given in Table 4.4. These data, based on the national income accounts for the three countries, probably magnify the low level of consumption and income in India, but there is no doubt that consumption levels in India are significantly below those of Japan. (Comparable data for later years are not available, but production data indicate no improvement in the position of India.)

Sinha has analyzed the variations in total value of consumer goods and services and in the value of food consumed in different parts of India using data from the National Sample Surveys.[16] He found differences in the relationships of food value to total value of consumption among regions and for different commodity groups. The ratios of the variations in food value to variations in total consumption (which approximate income elasticities)

[14] Ministry of Food and Agriculture, Government of India, *Review of the Food Situation*, September 1964.

[15] Ford Foundation, Agricultural Production Team, *Report on India's Food Crisis and Steps to Meet It*, April 1959, page 98.

[16] Sinha, R. P. "An Analysis of Food Expenditures in India," *J. Farm Economics* 48:1:113–123, February 1966.

TABLE 4.4 Estimated 1958 Average Per Capita Income and Food Expenditures in India, Japan, and the United States, with Comparisons[a]

Country	Per Capita: Total Income, Dollars	Per Capita: Food Expenditures, Dollars	Proportions of: Income Allocated to Food, Percent	Proportions of: Food Expenditures Allocated to Cereals, Percent
India	63	36	57	61
Japan	258	94	36	56
United States	2069	387	19	10

[a] Data from pp. 7 and 8, Brown, Lester R. *Food Consumption and Expenditures: India, Japan, United States*, USDA, ERS, Regional Analysis Division, ERS Foreign–42, November 1962. Food expenditures include the value of subsistence food supplies insofar as they are included in the national income accounts. Indian and Japanese currency converted at the official exchange rate.

were higher in the rural than in urban areas for all foods other than meat, fish, and eggs.

The food-total consumption elasticities for all of India for major food groups ran about as follows: food grains 0.4; milk and milk products 1.2 to 1.5; edible oils 1.0; meats, fish, and eggs 1.0; sugar 1.2; salt 0.3; other foods 0.8; and total foods 0.7. These figures mean that as the value of all goods and services consumed varied 1.0 percent among families grouped by income, the value of food grains consumed varied 0.4 percent, etc.

A significant measure of variations in level of living in a country is provided by data on the distribution of household members by degree of urbanization and by size of income. According to the National Council of Applied Economic Research of India, about 4/5 of the households are in rural areas. Data in Table 4.5, converted to dollars at the official exchange rate and put on an annual basis, indicate that only 22 percent of the urban population and 8 percent of the rural had incomes over \$95 per year per capita or \$475 for the average family of five. Even if we raised this to \$1000 to allow for differences in buying power and in usual consumption patterns, we still find almost 90 percent of the Indian people having real income less than one-third of the \$3000 which we currently describe as the poverty line in the United States. (The official exchange rate was devalued in 1966 from 4.75 rupees to the dollar to 7.50 to the dollar.)

Cantril, an American social psychologist, directed a survey of Indian personal aspirations and worries in 1962–1963.[17] He found that 40 percent of the people were concerned about their level of living; 25 percent had aspirations to own land, or a farm, and 20 percent to own their own home. Despite the serious problems of illness, disease, and malnutrition in India, only a small proportion of the people mentioned concerns with them,

TABLE 4.5 India: Distribution of Household Members (Normally Residing There) by Level of Income, Urban and Rural, 1960[a]

Monthly per Capita Income in Rupees[b]	Urban	Rural
	Percent	Percent
Under 10	6.7	19.7
11–15	17.9	24.9
16–25	32.7	34.2
26–35	20.5	13.4
36 or more	22.2	7.8

[a] From Tables A33 and 34 of National Council of Applied Economic Research, *Long Term Projections of Demand for and Supply of Selected Agricultural Commodities*, New Delhi, India, April 1962.

[b] One rupee equalled (before devaluation) about 22 cents (U.S.), therefore 36 rupees per month equalled \$95 per capita per year.

[17] Pages 83–97 of Cantril, Hadley. *The Pattern of Human Concerns.*

apparently because of overwhelming concern with economic problems related to levels of living. Cantril concluded:

> . . . by and large, the people of India are still both unaware of their problems and even to a greater extent unaware of or lacking confidence in the capacity of the government to assist them in resolving these problems. . . . (Page 86.)

4.5.3 Consumption Patterns and Problems

During the past 15 years a series of sample surveys of household expenditures have been made in India; each survey is described as a "round" of the National Sample Survey. These have varied in coverage and sample size. One of the more comprehensive was the fourth round taken in April–September 1952. Information on a month's expenditures by a sample of urban and rural households is summarized in Table 4.6. The 40 percent of rural expenditures and 22 percent of urban expenditures allocated to food gains in this period apparently changed little in subsequent years. The shares of total expenditures allocated to food by this sample of households match fairly well with the average of 57 percent that we have noted in the data from the national income accounts given in Table 4.4.

TABLE 4.6 National Sample Survey of India: Average Expenditures per Person per Month (including Value of Home-Produced Food) for All Food. Food Grains, Nonfood Goods, and Services in April–September 1952[a]

Item	Rural Households: Rupees, Number	Rural Households: Percentage of Total	Urban Households: Rupees, Number	Urban Households: Percentage of Total
All food	13.55	62.8%	14.73	51.2%
Food grains	8.74	40.5	6.27	21.8
All nonfood	8.02	37.2	14.06	48.8
Total expenditures reported	21.57	100.0	28.79	100.0

[a] From page 11, Table 4.1, National Sample Survey—Second to Seventh Round—No. 20, *Report on Consumer Expenditure*. Published by Manager of Publications, Civil Lines, Delhi 8, Calcutta: Eka Press, 1959. The fourth round sampled and tabulated data for 2388 rural households and 1074 urban households.

The variations in consumption of particular commodities are summarized in the National Council's conclusions from the sample survey data.[18] They found that per capita consumption of rice in the rural areas is nearly double that in urban areas. The opposite is true for wheat. Consumption of jowar (a type of sorghum) is very low in urban areas compared with rural consumption. Urban consumption of edible oils is about 45 percent higher than it is in rural areas. In general, at a given level of income (both money and nonmoney) rural households consume more food than do urban households. Part of this is because of the availability of subsistence or home-produced foods. Based on a review of a variety of survey data Bansil concluded that urban consumption of cereals in India in 1951 averaged 12 ounces per person per day and rural consumption 17 ounces.[19] These rates yield an average of about a pound per person per day or 365 pounds of food grains per year compared with the average of about 250 pounds per capita for the United States in 1951.

The housing situation in India is even grimmer than the food situation, although housing in a warm country is in some respects less significant to the maintenance of life. For example, Indian census data for Bombay published in 1963 showed that about 1 out of every 66 persons was homeless and thousands of others lived in places not designed for human habitation.[20] A 1948 study found that 6 to 9 people lived in the single room tenements of that city.[21]

India has made considerable effort to construct housing, especially for civil servants,

[18] Op. cit., pp. 72–73.

[19] Page 222 of *India's Food Resources and Population.*

[20] Abrams, op. cit., page 3.

[21] *Ibid.*, page 6.

but the United Nations' report of an ad hoc group of experts concluded that her housing shortage doubled during the decade of the 1950s.[22] Abrams concluded that the gap between shelter cost and income was particularly serious in the case of India where only 1/8 of the urban population could possibly afford to pay the minimum of $10 per month needed to pay for and maintain a worker-type dwelling costing about $1000.[23]

In brief, the current problems with consumption in India include the following: the poor quality of consumer goods and lack of objective standards; poor sanitation in the processing and handling of food; wide price fluctuations during the year and from one area of the country to another; inadequate marketing facilities; low levels of consumption of food and other goods and services by the masses of the population. These low levels are often detrimental to health and full productivity, but they have not been adequately measured. Aside from short supplies, perhaps the most important factor affecting consumption is the traditional ways of living and eating which do not take account of currently available scientific knowledge.

The people of India face some critical public decisions as they allocate their limited resources. Among these is the problem of how far to develop food production and marketing as opposed to channeling investment into industrial development. Another question is the degree to which the government should pressure small producers to change their production methods and how far it should go in instituting additional controls over business.

India, like every other country, faces decisions on the division of available resources between public goods and services and private goods. One of the frequent types of recommendations made by outsiders as they study the Indian food situation is the need to break with tradition. An example here is the problem of taking the cattle off the streets, of sterilizing the bulls, and rendering the carcasses of the animals that have died. Cattle are holy animals to the Hindus so the problem is far greater than outsiders can comprehend.

In the private field, too, there are individual decisions to be made as families break with traditional values that are in conflict with their desires for higher levels of consumption. On the one hand, there is the question of willingness to adopt new production technology, to work harder, and to take more risk to achieve higher levels of income and consumption.[24] On the other hand, families are gradually accepting dairy products, poultry, and even meat in their diets, as well as changes in food preparation.

4.6 THE CASE OF NIGERIA

Nigeria on the west coast of Africa has the largest population of any country in Africa and is also one of the most important agricultural countries of that continent. Its food supply could meet average physiological needs of the population. Large quantities of peanuts and peanut products, cocoa beans, oil palm products, cotton, and rubber are exported. The population appears to be increasing about 2 percent a year, although the population data are subject to considerable question. (Estimates of the total population range from 40 to 56 million.) To meet increased domestic demand of the larger population with rising incomes *plus* greater foreign demand, the areas cultivated have been expanded, the regenerative fallow periods have been shortened, soil fertility has declined, and soil erosion is increasingly evident.[25] Therefore an agricultural development program was started more than a decade ago.

4.6.1 Income and Food Expenditures

Converted at the official exchange rate, Nigerian per capita income in 1960 averaged between $75 and $80.[26] But as Stewart and Ogley have pointed out, the economy of much of Nigeria is still of the subsistence type. A large proportion of the economic activity is performed inside the family and is not counted in the income figure just cited. The urban

[22] Appendix, page 2, United Nations Social Committee, 14th Session, *Report of the Ad Hoc Group of Experts on Housing and Urban Development.*

[23] Op. cit., page 52.

[24] High yielding strains of wheat developed in Mexico are now being introduced, and more fertilizer plants are being built.

[25] Page 159 of Buchanan, K. M., and Pugh, J. C. *Land and People in Nigeria.*

[26] Page 4 of Stewart, Ian G., and Ogley, R. C. *Nigeria: Determinants of Projected Level of Demand, Supply, and Imports of Farm Products in 1965 and 1975,* ERS Foreign–32.

population has been growing faster than that in rural areas because of migration. Data are not available to measure precisely the changes nor to measure changes in urban incomes. However, commercial development, substantial public investments in roads, hospitals, harbors, telephone exchanges, and government offices plus substantial increases in current public expenditures for goods and services during the 1950s have apparently raised both the cash incomes of the urban population and their whole level of living.

From their study of consumer expenditure surveys in urban areas of all three regions, Stewart and Ogley concluded that in low-income households food expenditures took somewhat more than half of total expenditures. In the middle range of income, a little more than 40 percent of total expenditures were allocated to food and at high-income levels no more than 25 percent.[27] Within a given income level Stewart and Ogley found notable variations with tribal background and occupation. A higher proportion of imported foods is used in families of clerks who have greater contact with western culture and a lower proportion by those groups in the urban areas and in the rural areas which are more isolated from the influences of westerners. The proportion of food expenditures allocated to staples by households at successively higher levels of income clearly declines.

4.6.2 Nigerian Diets

The U.S. Department of Agriculture has published estimates of food supplies and distribution in Nigeria for 1958. They include per capita food supplies on a retail weight basis as follows: cereal products—178 pounds; 675 pounds of sweet potatoes, yams, and cocoa yams; 396 pounds of manioc (cassava); 100 pounds or so of bananas and plantains; and about 17 pounds of meat.[28] Cereals supplied about 30 percent of the calories and the root crops about 50 percent of the average supplies of food energy per capita. However, most Nigerians eat a great amount of cereal products *or* the roots and tubers, depending on whether they come from the northern or southern tribes, but not both.

[27] *Ibid.*, page 61.

[28] Based on Table 27 of U.S. Department of Agriculture, Foreign Agricultural Service, *Food Balances in Foreign Countries, Part IV*, FAS–M–108, February 1961.

No later estimates of consumption are available, but more recent production data indicate no significant change in available supplies. Returns to Nigerian farmers have apparently been relatively low and have certainly not encouraged needed investments in agriculture. Recent political crises and civil turmoil undoubtedly are having unfavorable effects on the production and internal trade in food commodities.

After examining some of the urban survey data, Kaneda and Johnston concluded:

> . . . it is virtually certain that the importance of roots and tubers in the cities of Kaduna and Zaria in northern Nigeria is to be attributed to the large numbers of Ibo and other groups from southern Nigeria employed as clerks and in other skilled or semi-skilled jobs in the Northern Region. Kaduna and Zaria lie in a region where millets and sorghum are by far the dominant food crops, but in the survey sample manioc and yams accounted for nearly 20 percent of total food expenditures and the millet and sorghums for only 6 percent of the total.[29]

After extensive study of all available survey information on urban and rural diets in western tropical Africa, Johnston has concluded that consumption of meats, fish, and bread is much higher in the cities, partly because of higher income and higher costs of transporting foods to rural areas as well as greater exposure of urban people to these foodstuffs.[30] Rural diets are largely determined by local production, whereas foods from various parts of the country and from other countries enter into urban diets much more.

Kaneda and Johnston found bread consumption to be much higher in urban than in rural communities: ". . . Recent trends in flour imports in tropical Africa and historical trends in flour consumption in other areas of the world also emphasize that enlarged consumption of bread will be one of the conspicuous changes in diet patterns in tropical Africa. . . ."[31] Urban consumers also tend to

[29] Page 253 of Kaneda, Hiromitsu, and Johnston, Bruce F. "Urban Food Expenditure Patterns in Tropical Africa," *Food Research Institute Studies* **II**:3:229–275, November 1961.

[30] Page 28 of *Summary of Report of Food Research Institute Conference on Economic, Political and Human Aspects of Agricultural Development in Tropical Africa.*

[31] *Ibid.*, page 266.

consume more rice, wheat, or maize (corn) and less of the millets and sorghums.

Urban meat consumption generally runs much higher than rural. However, rural consumption varies greatly with local availability of game or the importance of stock raising in areas outside the zone where livestock raising is practically prohibited by tsetse flies. ". . . Estimates for a number of rural communities in Nigeria reported by Nicol range from less than one kilogram per year in Tangaza to as much as 27 kilograms for male adults and 14 kilograms for women in Tungan Maidubu in northern Nigeria, in a district where livestock are exceptionally important. In most of the survey communities in which Nicol has carried out surveys, per capita meat consumption amounts to no more than 5 or 6 kilograms annually. . . ."[32] (A kilogram is equal to about 2.2 pounds.)

Nicol's intensive studies of diets of northern farmers of three different tribes indicated that 74 to 94 percent of their calories were from cereals and cereal products, mostly guinea corn and millets. In contrast, one tribe of southern farmers obtained three-fourths of its calories from manioc and yams. Another group, the relatively prosperous Warri traders, had 36 percent of their calories from manioc and yams, 18 percent from wheat flour and rice, and about 12 percent from beef and fish. The Soragbemi fishermen obtained about 60 percent of their food energy supply from manioc and yams and 20 percent from fish. Red palm oil is used extensively by southern tribes, supplying 12 to 14 percent of the calories of the three tribal groups studied by Nicol.[33]

A 1962–63 study of food consumption in the rural villages of the Eastern Region of Nigeria concluded that the rural families were consuming too much starch and starchy roots and too little animal protein, fats and oils, fruits, and vegetables.[34] These survey data yielded an average per person supply of only 1700 calories per day. The authors noted the efforts being made to increase food supplies, such as encouragement of rice and fishery production, poultry and pig farming, and market gardens, as well as distribution of free seeds to farmers. They also commented on the need for nutrition education programs to make the rural people more aware of their dietary needs.

[32] *Ibid*., pp. 266–267.

[33] From data taken from Nicol's studies, reported on page 194 of Johnston, Bruce F. *The Staple Food Economies of Western Tropical Africa*.

[34] Page 223 of Mann, W. S., and Nwankwo, J. C. O. "Case Study on Rural Food Consumption in Eastern Nigeria," pp. 221–224 of *Agriculture Situation in India*, July 1965.

4.6.3 Prospects for Changes in Food Consumption

Stewart and Ogley studied all available data relative to the Nigerian food outlook as part of a research program under contract with the U.S. Department of Agriculture (financed by Public Law 480 funds). Their conclusions indicate that Nigerian food production is likely to adjust gradually, although somewhat unevenly, like a ratchet, to incentives of higher prices for food in urban areas as food demand presses on supplies. But the food production potential of Nigeria appears to be able to meet increasing demand without major changes in supplies over the next decade. However, they presupposed continued development of the road system, government programs to encourage adoption of improved technology, and gradual improvements in education and in what economists call the "infra structure" or the institutional structure of the economy.

Despite this quite favorable outlook, the gradual breakdown of traditions surrounding agricultural production and food consumption is necessary but difficult. One example of a serious food problem Nicol found in his surveys was the tradition of not giving 4- to 12-year-old children enough food to meet their energy requirements even when young people over 12 in the same compounds were adequately supplied.[35] Such a practice is completely contrary to current scientific knowledge.

4.6.4 Environmental Situation

No comprehensive information is available on the housing and environmental situation of Nigeria. But Abrams reports some observations based on his participation in a United Nations Mission. He comments on the planless development of the cities such as Lagos, where a two-hour trip to work is common and no central sewage system has been developed.[36]

[35] Page 306 of Nicol, B. M. "The Calorie Requirements of Nigerian Peasant Farmers," *Br. J. of Nutrition* **13**:293–306, 1959.

[36] Op. cit., page 65.

Nigeria has undertaken public housing programs which appear to have been unduly influenced by English and American models and which seem to have been unnecessarily burdensome for the people concerned.[37]

Cantril's study of the personal aspirations and worries of Nigerian people in 1962–1963 reflects both the environmental problems and the impending tribal political chaos.[38] His survey revealed that 69 percent of the people aspired to improved levels of living, 44 percent sought better health, and 37 perecnt wanted better housing. Among their worries, 3/5 of the Nigerian sample mentioned inadequate level of living and ill health for themselves. The aspirations for their country stressed technological advances, education, and public health. Half of the Nigerians expressed concern for political instability, 23 percent for national disunity, 16 percent each regarding dishonest government and lack of law and order. Cantril commented that the survey data indicated a high degree of awareness on the part of the people of political and government troubles of their country and their unusually great concern for political stability. They were quite aware of the importance of resolving regional and tribal conflicts in order to achieve economic development and improved levels of living, including better health facilities. Apparently, their fears have been confirmed by the civil turmoil that began in 1966.

4.7 SIGNIFICANCE TO THE UNITED STATES OF CONSUMPTION CHANGES IN LESS-DEVELOPED COUNTRIES

Changes in consumption of food and other goods and services in the developing countries have economic, political, and welfare implications for us in the United States. As people in Colombia or Nigeria or India earn higher incomes, they are much more likely to buy our products, especially mass-produced items. Such purchases contribute to the incomes of American manufacturers, distributors, and industrial and transportation workers. If the products come from industries with decreasing costs of production, the additional demand may contribute to lower prices to American consumers.

Increased consumer demand in Colombia, for example, for their domestically produced goods is likely to lead to greater specialization of productive effort on output of goods for which Colombia has relatively higher rates of productivity. As production in each country —whether Colombia, the United States, Nigeria, or any other—is concentrated on those goods and services for which it has the greatest comparative advantage, consumers in the producing country and in importing countries (such as the United States) can benefit from better quality and/or relatively lower prices.

In recent years American imports have been increasing and have become significant even in food, despite our surpluses of some foods over domestic demand. For example, slightly over 1/10 of the food consumed in the United States in the mid-1960s was supplied by foreign countries and the U.S. Territories. Nearly half of the total imported was coffee, and much of the balance was tea and cocoa, spices, and other tropical foods. These foods are produced only in Hawaii among the United States. But we also imported much of our sugar and substantial quantities of lower grades of beef. For these foods, several of the less-developed countries rather clearly have a comparative advantage. Import quotas are used to protect American beet sugar producers from the competition of Caribbean cane sugar, for example, and Texas cattle ranchers from South American and Australian beef. Such quotas lead to higher prices for American consumers.

The objective of every developing country is to achieve greater economic independence combined with much higher levels of living than now experienced. Economic independence does not mean self-sufficiency in producing all the goods and services consumed in the country. Instead, it means the stage of economic development in which the country is able to pay for its imports with foreign exchange it has earned, not with grants from the United States or any other country. When this goal is achieved, American taxpayers will be relieved, and American industry and private financial agencies will be busy with commercial financing and private international trade. But achievement of this objective by many countries lies many years ahead.

Consider briefly the political and welfare implications of higher rates of consumption in the less-developed countries and of greater international trade. People experiencing an in-

[37] *Ibid.*, pp. 120–125.
[38] Op. cit., pp. 74–81.

creasing level of real income and living and having hopes for their families' future do not risk war. Instead, they are eager to preserve and enlarge their economic gains, *providing* they have sufficient perspective and are aware of the realities of modern warfare.

Let us now take a long-range perspective. Can we Americans continue to become relatively more affluent in relation to the poverty in which perhaps two-thirds of the world's population lives? According to some data from the United Nations, countries with almost three-fourths percent of the world's population received less than one-fourth of the total income of the world in the mid-1960s. On the basis of altruism, this is not acceptable. On the basis of survival of future generations of Americans, it is clear that this situation must not continue. Such levels of poverty are the basis for extreme efforts to achieve higher levels of living. One symptom of hopelessness for future levels of living and the cruelty of great inequalities is the extensive thievery which surprises United States and European visitors in many of the developing countries. Another symptom is the willingness of many impoverished peoples to try any alternative.

Both United States foreign aid and foreign trade contribute to economic development in this country and in the developing countries. There, our grants for food and financing (much of which is spent for United States goods) and our purchases buy time for their economic changes. One example is our current aid program for India. It is very clear that this is a case of assisting in evolution in order to avoid revolution. But we should not engage in too much self-congratulation because there is solid evidence that our aid often permits the developing countries to avoid needed economic adjustments. Also, our food aid program has helped subsidize certain sectors of United States agriculture which would otherwise have had to adjust to the world price situation. Such policies and programs are considered further in Part III.

PART II

MICROECONOMICS OF CONSUMPTION

Marketing aspects of the microeconomics of consumption are covered in Part II. To illuminate each of the major facets of consumer behavior, we will consider available theoretical contributions and pertinent research. Contributions of the several social sciences, both theoretical and empirical, are integrated in the conceptual frameworks related to the processes of buying and use and to the structure of consumption. Changes in consumer behavior are analyzed in both abstract and pragmatic terms.

Major aspects of consumer behavior are combined in a formal statement at the beginning of Chapter 5. The marketing approach is described and the types of people who cooperate in the study of consumption in business firms are noted. Most of the chapter is devoted to reviews of psychological, sociological, and anthropological concepts and analytical approaches to human behavior in consumption.

Chapter 6 summarizes the content of economic knowledge of consumer response to price and income variations as it existed about 1940. The problems in interpretation and application of this "standard economic theory of consumer behavior" are identified and appraised. Chapter 7 traces postwar developments in economic theory and research which have been concerned with dealing with these problems of standard economic theory, particularly aggregation, response to factors other than income and price, and economic dynamics.

Chapter 8 describes how consumption economists go about solving consumption problems in marketing. One section discusses the formulation and use of conceptual frameworks. Another deals with the types of data needed for empirical analyses suggested by the frameworks. Major surveys of consumer purchases, expenditures, and consumption are reviewed and their methodologies appraised. There is a section on surveys of consumer preferences for product attributes and another on the experimental approach to marketing.

Appendix A supplements this chapter; it contains a more detailed description of procedures for obtaining and using data as well as references to more technical sources of such information.

Processes of choice and use of consumer goods and services are analyzed in Chapter 9. We begin with study of processes of consumer behavior in general. Then several approaches to the process of consumer choice are described, and an interdisciplinary framework is presented.

Several articles reporting empirical research indicate the kinds of problems studied and some findings. Section 9.4 describes how consumer variables in choice making are investigated. The process of use is treated first in terms of conceptual frameworks and then by review of several reports of research.

The several aspects of consumer behavior are integrated in an interdisciplinary approach to the structure of consumption in Chapter 10. This structure has a number of dimensions—behavioral, technical and economic, temporal, and aggregative. They are used in two conceptual frameworks provided for analysis of the structure of consumption. Section 10.5 contains reviews of research on the micro structure of consumption.

Chapter 11 deals with changes in consumer behavior. The major forms and sources of such changes are identified, and the significance of these changes to marketing and economic development is discussed. Three sections describe rather pragmatically the major types of cyclical and secular changes, identify sources of unexpected changes, and discuss the diffusion process for changes in consumer behavior. The final section contains examples of actual research on micro problems of changes in consumption and ties changes in consumption of groups to changes in a whole country. Part III on macroeconomics of consumption deals with changes for large sectors of population and for whole countries.

5

MARKETING AND BEHAVIORAL SCIENCE APPROACHES TO STUDY OF CONSUMER BEHAVIOR

This chapter sets the stage for interdisciplinary analysis of consumer behavior by describing the marketing approach and the contributions of psychologists, sociologists, and anthropologists. In order to understand how the several aspects of consumer behavior and the many parts of our knowledge about the subject fit together, we begin with a rather formal statement about them. Then we identify the marketing approach and discuss how many kinds of people cooperate in the study of consumption. The last three sections of the chapter review the psychological, sociological, and anthropological concepts, analytical approaches, and some empirical work on human behavior pertinent to consumption. Economic knowledge of consumer behavior is reviewed in Chapters 6 and 7.

5.1 ASPECTS OF CONSUMER BEHAVIOR

Major aspects of consumer behavior may be delineated thus:

1. The *psychological, sociological, anthropological,* and *economic phenomena*

related to

2. the *behavior* of individuals, families, and groups as they *take consumer roles*

in

3. individual and group *decision making* or *problem-solving* processes related to *buying* and to *using* products and services

and

4. the economic phenomena of *consumption* and *expenditures* which result

form

5. the *socioeconomic structure of consumption* having these dimensions:
   (*a*) behavioral,
   (*b*) economic and technical (quantity-value-quality),
   (*c*) temporal (situational→dynamic),
   (*d*) aggregative (micro→macro in space and size).

The major behavioral concepts and some of the economic concepts used in alternative approaches to human behavior with regard to consumption are listed in Figure 5.1. They are approximately in the order of their presentation in later sections of this chapter and Chapters 6 and 7. The meanings of these concepts are learned most readily by studying them in the context of the scientific approaches which use them.

In Sections 5.2 and 5.3 we consider how such knowledge of consumer behavior is used by people working on marketing problems.

5.2 MARKETING APPROACH TO CONSUMER BEHAVIOR

Marketing is essentially an applied social science. In relation to consumer behavior, its central concerns are with: (*a*) understanding and predicting variations and changes in such behavior with respect to the purchase and use of consumer goods and services; (*b*) factors bringing about these variations and changes; (*c*) the possibility of influencing them, especially through the communication processes; and (*d*) their impact on market structure and functioning. For example, marketing execu-

Figure 5.1 Psychological, sociological, anthropological, and economic concepts pertinent to consumption (listed in approximate order of introduction).

Psychological

- Motivation
  - Biogenic
  - Sociogenic
- Cognition
  - Perception
  - Attitudes
  - Categorization
  - Structuralization
  - Decision process
- Learning
  - Instrumental
  - Perceptual
  - Affective
  - Social
  - Habit
  - Attitudes

Sociological

- Socialization
- Symbolic interaction
  - Symbol
  - Role
  - Reference group
  - Perspective
  - Tastes and preferences
  - Communication channels
- Structure-function
  - Social system
  - Function
  - Social structure
  - Norms and values
- Developmental approach
  - Family life cycle
  - Careers
- Social differentiation

Anthropological

- Culture
  - Cultural patterns
  - Cultural differences
- Cultural change
  - Processes of change
  - Innovation
  - Invention
  - Diffusion
- Adoption process
- Change agent

Economic

- Demand (in response to price)
  - Utility
  - Alternative goods
  - Market demand
  - Cross-elasticity of demand
  - Inferior goods
  - Price elasticity of demand
  - Diminishing marginal utility
  - Indifference analysis
  - Revealed preferences
- Consumption function (income-consumption relationship)
  - Income elasticity
  - Absolute-income hypothesis
  - Relative-income hypothesis
  - Permanent-income hypothesis
- Statistical analysis of demand
- Distribution system
- Consumption
- Quantity
- Value
- Quality
- Index numbers
- Demonstration effect
- Aggregation
- Attitudes
- Buying intentions
- Economic dynamics
  - *Ex ante*
  - *Ex post*
  - Period analysis
  - Flows
  - Stocks
  - Lag

tives require considerable knowledge of variations in needs and potential wants of different groups of consumers in order to design advertising and promotion programs for a given product so that they will reach consumers with slightly different demands. Such programs seek to influence consumers' perception. Also, many firms use knowledge of the existence of smaller homogeneous markets as segments within the total market for a product as the basis for adjusting their market offerings to expected consumer or user requirements.

Marketing uses many concepts and some propositions developed by theorists in social sciences such as economics, sociology, and psychology. But marketing men insist on testing their usefulness in solving concrete problems related to patterns and changes in consumption. For example, marketing men use the economic concept of the income elasticity of quantity consumed when they compare (*a*) percentage variations in the quantity of their product consumed or in expenditures with (*b*) percentage differences in income. They measure the elasticity, apply it, and evaluate the conditions which affect variations in income elasticity among different groups. Another example is the concept of perception obtained from psychology which marketing people use in exploring the meanings of products for consumers. This leads them into the study of images created by products.

Much of the knowledge of the microeconomics of consumption as well as that of marketing is being evolved by drawing generalizations from empirical research based on observation and experimentation. Marketing researchers often formulate a rough hypothesis, observe phenomena relating to the hypothesis, then revise the hypothesis. Eventually, this sequence permits prediction checked by observation. Then findings can be systematized. This is the inductive method of developing a body of empirically validated generalizations.

5.2.1 Observation and Analysis

One marketing scholar has described marketing as a process of providing *assortments* from which the consumer can choose.[1] Microeconomic analysis contributes particularly to identification of the assortments which groups of consumers have chosen and are likely to select in the future.

As part of marketing research, we study the variety of patterns of actual consumption and use at a given time and in the past. Our objective is to find patterns or evidence of homogeneity. These patterns may be formed by the combination of different kinds of goods and services consumed, by relationships to socioeconomic factors themselves having patterns, and by relationships to changes in microeconomic and social factors.

In marketing we also study consumers' expectations regarding their future needs and the likelihood that certain products will meet their needs. Consumers' expectations are based substantially on their previous experiences and on certain key attributes of products that are expected to meet their needs. But their expectations are also influenced by the expectations and experiences of people with whom they associate or identify themselves—their *reference groups*, in sociological terms.

Appraisal of consumption patterns leads us into consideration of the process of decision making by consumers. Marketing people need to know how consumers decide, first, that they want to buy something, such as meat or some kind of couch, and then, how they decide which items to buy. There are alternative choices in every decision making situation. Otherwise, of course, no decision would be necessary. The strategy of marketing is based on knowledge of these alternative choices and of the factors contributing to the making of particular choices by individual consumers having particular characteristics, such as being rich or poor, urban or rural, old or young.

Analysis of marketing problems is based on conclusions regarding these patterns and the frequency with which they occur. The relationship of one commodity to another which is unique to a single family is of no particular significance to marketing men. But a relationship which is common to a substantial group of potential customers becomes of considerable significance. This can be a market for which the firm can design a product and to which it can be sold.

5.2.2 Prediction and Reappraisal

In marketing, observation and analysis have prediction as their primary objective. We seek

[1] Alderson, Wroe. "The Analytical Framework for Marketing," pp. 15–28 of *Proceedings, Conference of Marketing Teachers from Far Western States*, edited by Delbert J. Duncan. [Reprinted in Bliss, Perry (Editor), *Marketing and Behavioral Sciences*.]

to predict what will be the consumer acceptance of a product of specified characteristics, how that degree of acceptance might be changed by a specific change in the product or a certain change in consumers' knowledge of the product. Expectations or predictions of changes in particular commodities are tied up with predictions of more general changes in consumption patterns which are likely to occur in the future under specified conditions. After marketing men have made their specific predictions and waited to see how they turned out, they face the job of reappraising the consumption situation to determine why their predictions turned out right or wrong. From such evaluations, they learn how to make better predictions.

5.2.3 Experimentation

Large business firms do a considerable amount of test marketing of their products among selected groups of consumers in order to observe reactions to a product before they put it on the general market. This step often follows a kind of laboratory experiment in which they test their product on people within the firm. From controlled market tests, market researchers try to learn as much as possible about (*a*) the kinds of consumers who buy and do not buy a certain product as well as (*b*) the kinds of reaction buyers have to the product being tested. This is the closest that social scientists can come to the laboratory type of experiments made by natural scientists in which "all other conditions" can be held "constant."

Marketing executives have to balance the costs of such market tests against the kinds, amounts, and usefulness of knowledge gained. But there is some evidence that further experimentation and more rigorous controls would often be of advantage, particularly to the larger firms. However, there is always a shortage of time in market research. Each firm seeks a differential advantage which it is likely to lose after a few months. It usually does not take long for other firms to identify the favorable consumer reactions to new products and to develop slightly different products to compete with the recent innovations.

5.2.4 Economic Implications of Patterns of Consumption

This part of marketing research is much closer to general economic analysis. Here marketing men seek to answer the question, "What will be the effect on the market for commodity A if commodity *B*'s sales rise or fall?" As they study the trends and patterns of consumption, they seek to answer questions about whether these trends will continue at the same rate, whether they will accelerate or decline, and when. The decisions of many business firms in recent years to diversify by adding new product lines reflect their awareness that certain commodities are in declining stages of consumer demand. This phase of marketing research involves many of the aspects of macroeconomics of consumption which will be taken up in Part III.

5.2.5 Appraisal of the Marketing Approach

The eclectic approach of many marketing men, i.e., selecting from a variety of ideas, has led to the solution of many problems. But it has provided few generalizations because the problems are often so narrow in focus that generalizations are not possible. Also, much of the research in marketing is ephemeral in character, forming a series of "quickie" studies. Many of them are inadequate in terms of scientific design and statistical rigor. Because of their awareness of the limitations imposed by this type of marketing research, leaders in marketing are turning more and more to the basic disciplines in the social sciences for assistance to gain greater precision in the definition of concepts and in procedures.

5.3 MULTIDISCIPLINARY COOPERATION IN MARKETING

In business firms and organizations concerned with marketing, people of a variety of professional backgrounds must work together on problems related to consumer behavior. A review of the kinds of problems for which each type of professional person takes responsibility will provide further background for appraisal of the contributions of the several social sciences to the study of consumer behavior.

5.3.1 Marketing Specialists

Marketing has been described earlier as the process of bringing together in particular places a large selection of products from the vast array available in the world so that consumers may choose those they want to meet their needs. To accomplish this objective in a profitable manner, marketing specialists must discover the special attributes of individual products which can match consumer needs within the constraints of costs to the firms and prices acceptable to consumers. Individual firms seek to gain a differential advantage over their competitors by putting new versions of old products or new products on the market a little ahead of other firms. If they are too far out in front of a change in consumer demand, they will not sell enough to cover the costs of developing and marketing the new item. If they are very far behind their competitors in putting the product on the market, they may have to spend lavishly on promotion to sell the product to people who are late adopters or to persuade earlier buyers to switch brands.

Even after a firm has put a new product on the market, its market research staff must observe very carefully which distributors or salesmen are selling the product, who is buying it, and who is not. Because initial purchases do not build a sound basis for future marketing, they watch repeat buyers in particular. Repeat purchases usually indicate that the product is fulfilling consumer needs of a continuing nature, not just curiosity.

5.3.2 Economists

People in business firms who are educated in economics are frequently assigned to the job of identifying the consumption patterns and preferences of current and potential buyers of the kinds of products manufactured or distributed by the firm. Then they turn from consumption of the commodity group to the more specific products of their firms. They study consumer reactions to recent product changes and to potential new products. They assist market researchers in many parts of their work, even in developing data for use in promotional materials. Economists are usually given the job of forecasting total consumer demand for the product and of estimating the share of the market their firm might achieve under certain conditions. Most large firms have a group of economists concerned with forecasting the demand and prices for input materials the firm must buy in competition with firms manufacturing products for other sectors of consumer demand. These men must recommend when to buy and when to hold off buying raw materials, partly processed commodities, or final products.

5.3.3 Food Scientists

Food technologists in food firms work with product quality and development, and often study consumer reaction to particular product qualities. They are ordinarily trained primarily in the natural and biological sciences, but they may find that they have to identify psychological, sociological, or economic factors underlying consumer behavior which might possibly be related to the product attributes they are developing. Those who have a broad home economics education with some emphasis in social sciences are qualified to work with economists in identifying interrelationships between the food consumption patterns and preferences of buyers and particular attributes of products as one phase of planning new products. There is strong demand for home economists prepared to work with market researchers in identifying the kinds of product attributes about which consumers have shown concern or for which needs are growing out of socioeconomic changes.

5.3.4 Nutritionists

Nutritionists are employed by food firms and commodity organizations to study both the food habits which lead to ill health and low efficiency and the means of changing food habits. One objective is to learn how the products of the firms or the commodity group can be used to improve health and how consumers can be persuaded to use them. Nutritionists have contributed much to marketing by the identification of food consumption patterns underlying the poor nutrition they observe. Most nutritionists seek to minimize the changes in food habits that homemakers will have to make if they are to be successful in improving the nutritional levels of their families and homemaking practices.

5.3.5 Food Service Managers

Managers of food services must have knowledge of foods, of particular dishes, and of menus acceptable to and popular with their current and potential clientele. This means that they must know something about the economic and social factors affecting the patronage of their firm. Successful managers of food services study the reactions of clientele to prices, menus, and service patterns and to the changes that they make in them one by one on an exploratory basis. Managers of units within large organizations are also concerned with planning locations for new food service establishments and in estimating their potential volume.

5.3.6 Textile, Clothing, and Household Equipment Specialists

Manufacturers and distributors of textiles, clothing, and household equipment are beginning to hire specialists educated in home economics who have some knowledge of the economic and social aspects of these products. The types of problems on which they work are very similar to those encountered by food technologists and home economists in food businesses. Therefore we need not reiterate them.

5.3.7 Specialists in Arts Applied to Home and Business Environment

Manufacturers of housefurnishings and equipment and retailers of these products hire specialists educated in the application of the arts to the environment. These people encounter not only problems of color and design but problems in marketing aesthetics to meet the needs of and to satisfy their customers. This means that they must identify the ways that people actually furnish and decorate their homes and offices and they must learn the reasons for their preferences. They frequently face the series of questions: How would people react to this change or to that change in a product or to this or that new product? Responses to aesthetic aspects of environment are affected not only by psychological but also by social and economic factors. A great deal more research is needed to develop more facts for the use of such specialists.

5.4 PSYCHOLOGICAL APPROACHES

To orient the reader to the contributions of modern psychology, I begin with definitions of a few key concepts and then consider alternative theories in ascending complexity.

5.4.1 Some Key Concepts

First, *motivation* refers to the "drives, urges, wishes or desires which initiate the sequence of events known as behavior."[2] There is no generally accepted definition of motivation in contemporary psychology. It may refer to conscious desire and a whole complex of conscious antecedents to behavior or to unconscious determinants of behavior or to drive as in S-R behavior theory.[3]

Cognition is the term for the area of mental phenomena including perception, memory, judging, and thinking, etc.[4] *Perception* is ". . . the more complex process by which people select, organize, and interpret sensory stimulation into a meaningful and coherent picture of the world . . ."[5]

Learning is evidenced by changes in behavior that result from previous behavior in similar situations or from symbolic experience such as reading or thinking. Reinforcement was long accepted as an important part of learning in S-R theory. Adherents to this theory hold that continued reinforcement affects the cognitive processes by enhancing memory and increasing differentiation among alternatives. Thus reinforcement may decrease the amount of cognitive activity. Some cognitive theorists now de-emphasize the importance of reinforcement.

Neobehavioralists describe the behavior episode as $S \rightarrow \begin{matrix}\text{Black}\\ \text{Box}\end{matrix} \rightarrow R$. Here the S refers to the stimulus, the R to the response, and the Black Box contains the mental processes of motivation and cognition. This formulation bears some resemblance to the economic ideas of input as the S and output as the R. The stimulus contributes to *drive*, identified as need-arousal. Such a paradigm concentrates on the initiation or activation of very simple behavior, particularly that of animals.

Some years ago there was intensive controversy among psychologists as to whether the *push* of the drive was more significant than the *pull* of the goal. Either way, the behavioral approach emphasizes the *how* of behavior, particularly its biogenic aspects. It assumes that the organism is passive and that each episode starts without any history of experience. This approach has been criticized as highly situational and overly simplified, being similar in these respects to the elementary theory of

[2] Page 282, Bayton, James A. "Motivation, Cognition, Learning—Basic Factors in Consumer Behavior," *J. Marketing*, January 1958.

[3] Page 273 of Atkinson, J. W. *An Introduction to Motivation*.

[4] Op. cit.

[5] Page 88, Berelson, Bernard, and Steiner, Gary A. *Human Behavior*.

consumer choice we will consider in Chapter 6. It provides no knowledge of the content of the Black Box. Much of the psychological research in recent years has been on the behavior going on in the Black Box.

5.4.2 Motivation

Motivation involves both motives and the action arising out of the disequilibrium in tension systems which trigger behavior. The sources of drive are commonly identified as primary or biogenic, such as hunger, and secondary or *sociogenic*. In the latter category are learned attitudes, hopes, fears, opinions, and expectancies. Among the motives researched in recent years are the competency motivation which decreases the role of reinforcement in shaping behavior; the strivings for stimulation, information, knowledge, and understanding; the affiliation motive; and the status or dominance motive. These motives are best viewed within the frameworks of the basic theories currently used to explain the motivational aspects of consumer behavior.

There appear to be two major schools of thought or sets of theories. One is identified as the Drive X Habit theory. Its two major formulations have been:[6]

(*a*) Hull's 1943 equation for motivation (*ibid.*, pp. 161–173)

$$_SE_R = f(D) \times f(_SH_R)$$

where E is expectancy or reaction potential
S is stimulus
R is response
D is drive
H is habit

(*b*) Spence's 1956 restatement (*ibid.*, page 191)

$$E = (D + K) \times H$$

where E is excitatory potential
D is drive
K is incentive of object
H is habit

The first of these formulations indicates that reaction potential ($_SE_R$) is determined by drive combined with habit. Both factors operate in the Black Box. In order to take into account expectation aroused by the anticipated goal, Spence developed the second formulation of S-R theory. The K refers to incentive resulting from the frequency and amount of earlier rewards, from expected rewards, and possibly from the delay in reward. This formulation includes in D + K the concept of a nonspecific exciter of habit.

The second line of theoretical development has been the Expectancy X Value approach of cognitive theorists in psychology. *Expectancy* refers to the strength of expectancy of certain consequences following from a given act. *Value* refers to the value of those consequences to the individual. This formulation does not explicitly take account of earlier events, and it overemphasizes the immediate stimulating situation. Atkinson has provided this paradigm (or formal statement) of the relationships (*ibid.*, page 279):

$$T_{r,g} = {_sH_r} \times E_{r,g} \times I_g \times M_G$$

where $T_{r,g}$ is the tendency to a particular goal
$_sH_r$ is habit
$E_{r,g}$ is expectancy
I_g is incentive
M_G is motive
r is activity
g is the goal

Neurophysiological knowledge developed in recent years indicates that the brain is always active. Therefore we need to conceptualize behavior as a continuous stream from one kind of activity to another. This gives us an opportunity to take into account the effects of cognitive controls in assessing motives. Accordingly, motives function as selectors or initiators, and the cognitive processes function as directors.

Atkinson takes into account both the persisting general tendency to action and the tendency to a particular goal in this formulation (*ibid.*, page 311):

$$T_{r,g_f} = (M_G \times E_{r,g} \times I_g) + T_{G_i}$$

where T_{r,g_f} is the tendency to a particular goal at a particular time
I_g is incentive related to goal achievement
T_{G_i} is an inertial tendency or persistent general tendency to achieve success which cumulates balances from earlier unsatisfied tendencies

Thus he attempts to provide for the study of change in activity (*dynamics*) which he views

[6] Atkinson, op. cit., Chapter 10.

as the fundamental problem in modern psychology. He argues that ". . . the immediate stimulus situation (conceived as an influence that is external to the relatively autonomous process of the brain) does not cause a tendency to act . . . but operates on already active tendencies to produce a change in their strength." (*ibid.*, page 310).

Atkinson's book on motivation concludes with the idea that psychologists must ". . . bring together into a single coherent conceptual scheme the impact on behavior of the immediate environment, . . . the effect of stable individual differences in personality, . . . and the constant influence on behavior of the persistent undercurrent of active tendencies to bring about particular effects which can be attributed to previous inhibition or inadequate expression of certain impulses in the past" (*ibid.*, page 314). Such an explanation of behavior permits incorporation of some of the ideas from sociology and is fundamental to analysis of economic behavior through the course of time.

5.4.3 Cognition

Other psychological approaches to consumer behavior have emphasized cognitive processes. Gestalt and Lewinian field theory have contributed much to modern cognitive psychology, but they are now outside the mainstreams of theory. However, two food studies must be mentioned that utilized Lewinian theory. One was Bilkey's study applying vector psychology to family expenditures.[7] The other was Lewin's wartime food study reported in a famous National Research Council bulletin, *The Problem of Changing Food Habits*.[8]

Modern cognitive psychology is concerned with the psychological principles of organization and functioning which govern the different states of consciousness and cognitive processes. *Cognition* encompasses direction and control over reactions, problem solving, and creative thinking. Several lines of research have developed in cognitive psychology. Among them has been the work on cognitive *attitudes*, which are ways of organizing the information received by an individual. In effect, cognitive attitudes may also be defined as intervening variables which establish the rules for shaping forms of experience, such as perception and memory. (The term "intervening variables" is applied here to processes occurring between the stimulus and the response.) Bruner's identification of the motive for categorization and his study of the process are very important for development of knowledge of consumer behavior.[9] Consumers use attributes of products as they perceive them to formulate and discriminate among categories of products and between products.

Bayton has reformulated the S-R paradigm as S→P→R. Thus he gives *perception* the key role in consumer behavior, apparently because of the importance of perception in judging.[10] Many cognitive psychologists do not go that far. They stress other aspects of cognition, particularly those concerned with adaptive behavior. One form of such behavior is the tendency to structuralize in order to deal with the environment.

In connection with a large-scale review of theories of perception, Allport considered a number of psychologists' attempts at *structuralization*. The phenomenon of "set" is a condition of perception as well as other behavioral acts. Sets are learned in a variety of ways, and they affect learning. They are an element in the development of frames of reference by individuals and by groups. Every act as well as every set-stage of an act of behavior, according to Allport, requires "two features in its descriptive model: (1) a 'format' or 'kinematic' aspect (geometry) of motion, connectedness, and events and (2) a 'dynamic,' or energetic, aspect. The energy concerned, in other words, never occurs merely as a quantity or a purely scalar entity; it is always *structured*. . . ."[11] Psychologists concerned with perception substantially agree, Allport says, "in depicting the perceptual act or process as having the characteristics of in-

[7] Bilkey, Warren J. "A Psychological Approach to Consumer Behavior Analysis," *J. Marketing* **18**: 1:18–25, July 1953.

[8] Lewin, Kurt. "Forces Behind Food Habits and Methods of Change," pp. 35–65 of NRC Bulletin No. 108.

[9] Bruner, Jerome S., Goodnow, Jacqueline J., Austin, George A. *A Study of Thinking*.

[10] Bayton, James A. "Contributions of Psychology to the Microeconomic Analysis of Consumer Demand for Food," *J. Farm Economics* **45**:5:1430–1435, December 1963.

[11] Page 408, Allport, Floyd H. *Theories of Perception and the Concept of Structure*.

ternal relatedness, self-closedness or circularity, space and time building, flexibility, constancy of relationships, energic cycle or maintenance, energic or dimensional weighting and pooling, and interaggregate facilitation or opposition. . . . (*Ibid.*, page 605.)

To provide a more general theoretical framework for perception and for other behavioral acts, Allport outlined a "theory of event-structure." The elements of his dynamic structure are (1) ongoing processes such as receptor activities and neural impulses, and (2) events that link ongoing processes (under probability laws) and serve as time points. These form cycles; cycles of cycles form event-systems; and event-systems aggregate into event-regions which have spatial dimensions. By adding a time dimension, Allport ends up with the conceptualization of structural kinematics and dynamics. He used his theory to define the elusive concept of meaning as simply "an energically diminished and kinematically abridged behavioral act (act-structure) . . . ." (page 655.) Then he pointed out that "meanings persist structurally through time, whereas the full energies of the structure of an overt act are present in the structure only for a short time." (*Ibid.*, page 656.)

Because of their interest in the study of thinking, a number of social psychologists have been engaged in research on the *decision process*. Brim, Glass, Lavin, and Goodman used these six sequential phases to study the process: "(1) identification of the problem; (2) obtaining necessary information; (3) production of possible solutions; (4) evaluation of such solutions; (5) selection of a strategy for performance; and (6) actual performance of an action or actions, and subsequent learning and revision. . . ."[12] The last of these phases seems to take the process beyond decision making into problem solving. (The first chapter of the book by these authors provides a good review of literature on the decision process.)

The theory of cognitive dissonance has dealt intensively with cognitive elements in changes in attitude and opinion, although Festinger apparently formulated it in connection with motivation. In brief, the theory pertains to the process of dealing with a disequilibrium between two pieces of knowledge. The amount of dissonance varies with changes in the positive and negative attributes of both the selected and the rejected alternatives and with the degrees of commitment and volition involved in the choice. Recent experiments indicate that this theory has considerable importance for formation and stabilization of tastes and preferences as well as for opinions and attitudes.[13]

5.4.4 Learning

Although hunger is one of the basic biogenic needs, learned psychogenic and sociogenic aspects of the need for food as well as other products and services are very significant in human consumption behavior. One of the two main lines of learning theory is the *association* or *behavioral* or S-R point of view. Hull's behavior theory stressed the importance of reinforcement (based on reward) to develop the habit structure and to reduce the need-state or drive. Currently, research by educational psychologists appears to indicate that reinforcement is not necessary for many types of learning and perhaps not for any. But many psychologists still accept Hull's theory.

Bayton argues that "it is on consumption or use that need-satisfaction will occur—that reinforcement takes place. With reinforcement there is an increase in the probability that when these same needs become active, the same choice will be made. . . . As this continuing reinforcement occurs there are correlated cognitive changes. . . . The discrimination function sharpens . . . and there is a decrease in the amount or degree of cognitive activity involved. . . ."[14] The foundation for habitual purchases is laid.

Spence's paradigm for behavior, cited earlier, indicates that the H (*habit*) is dependent on the number of times the S→R has occurred and does not need reinforcement. He views reward as affecting the incentive motive and not the H. Thus the H appears to depend entirely on experience without refer-

[12] Page 9 of Brim, Orville G., Jr.; Glass, David C.; Lavin, David E.; and Goodman, Norman. *Personality and Decision Process.*

[13] Brehm, Jack W., and Cohen, Arthur R. *Explorations in Cognitive Dissonance.*

[14] Bayton, James. "Conscious vs. Habit Purchases: Implications for Advertising." Paper presented at the Association of National Advertisers, Inc., Workshop on Advertising Research, New York City, April 1, 1959.

ence to reinforcement. This view permits the acceptance of latent learning.[15]

The second line of thought in learning is *field theory* or S→S. This is Tolman's sign-gestalt expectancy, a theory which owes much to Gestalt and Lewinian field theory. It stresses the importance of cognitive structuring or ordering behavior. In fact, ordered behavior may be rewarding in itself and lead to learning.[16]

A "mediation hypothesis" has been proposed, so-called not because it is intermediate between the Hullian behavior theory and the cognitive approach to learning, but because it refers to the capacity of signs or symbols to elicit in an animal or person part of the same behavior which the objects themselves elicit. This hypothesis distinguishes between old learning (in which the process of reacting to signs was reduced from a full sequence of behavior) and new learning in a test situation. Osgood concludes:

> . . . In a very real sense—since it can be shown that most "new" learning comes down to the association of new mediation processes with old stimulus patterns or new instrumental sequences with old mediation processes—this hypothesis places the problem of *meaning* directly at the core of learning theory. . . .[17]

Current knowledge of the learning process has some major limitations. Much learning research has been pertinent to learning *instrumental acts* bearing on the use of products. But there has been little research on the *cognitive* or *perceptual type of learning* through which familiarity is developed or on *affective* learning which leads to liking products. The field of formation of tastes and preferences needs a great deal of basic research. An article by Krugman and Hartley reports several small scale experiments with the learning of tastes, but it is apparently unique.[18]

Social learning has received increased attention in recent years and has considerable significance to the development of consumption habits. The concept encompasses the acquisition and modification of human behavior in dyadic and group situations.[19] Identification with others and imitation of their behavior are key forces in social learning. Social learning "may occur through observation of the behavior of others even when the observer does not reproduce the model's responses during acquisition and therefore receives no reinforcement. . . . Since the eliciting and maintaining of imitative behavior are highly dependent on the response consequences to the model, an adequate social learning theory must also take account of the role of *vicarious reinforcement*, through which the behavior of an observer is modified on account of the reinforcement administered to a model." (*Ibid.*, page 4.)

5.4.5 Special Concerns of Social Psychologists

Social psychologists emphasize factors which affect what goes on in the Black Box between the stimulus and the response. Some argue, for example, that the psychological structure of an individual is determined by external and internal factors and that behavior is a consequence of his central structure or patterning. This provides opportunity for the *socialization* process to have an effect and indicates how sociogenic motives can be formed. Stryker defines socialization as "the process by which the human organism acquires the characteristic ways of behaving, the values, norms, and attitudes of the social unit of which he is a part."[20]

Social psychologists talk in terms of reference groups, symbols, and attitudes. *Reference groups* contribute to the formation of attitudes

[15] Hill, Winfred F. "Contemporary Developments within Stimulus-Response Learning Theory," Chapter II of Hilgard, Ernest R. (Editor), *Theories of Learning and Instruction.*

Latent learning involves developing a cognitive structure made up of relationships among environmental phenomena in contrast, for example, with learning sequences of movements. The term "latent" is used because there is no direct performance. Osgood suggests that "latent performance" is a better term. (Page 416 of Osgood, Charles E. *Method and Theory in Experimental Psychology.*)

[16] Hilgard, Ernest R. "The Place of Gestalt Psychology and Field Theories in Contemporary Learning Theory," Chapter III, Hilgard (Editor), op. cit.

[17] Osgood, op. cit., page 412.

[18] Krugman, Herbert E., and Hartley, Eugene L. "The Learning of Tastes," *The Public Opinion Quarterly* **24**:4:621–631, Winter 1960.

[19] Page 1, Bandura, Albert, and Walters, Richard H. *Social Learning and Personality Development.*

[20] Page 133, Stryker, Sheldon. "The Interactional and Situational Approaches" in Christensen, Harold T. (Editor), *Handbook of Marriage and the Family.*

(which are learned) and are the groups to which an individual relates himself psychologically. Both reference groups and symbols will be discussed in connection with the symbolic interactionist approach in the sociological section which follows.

Attitudes are functional parts of the system through which the individual relates himself to his surroundings and forms a conception of himself. Attitude research focuses on the interaction between individuals and their worlds. In connection with consumer behavior, interaction occurs between individual needs and drives and the products which the consumer wishes to buy or has bought. This relationship is influenced by a variety of psychological, cultural, sociological, and economic influences. Crespi has identified the four dimensions of the underlying structure of an individual's attitudes as follows: "(1) *Cognition*—awareness and knowledge; (2) *Frame of reference*—values and norms that establish the context of reaction; (3) *Evaluation*—positive or negative direction of reaction; and (4) *Affect*—intensity of feeling and involvement."[21] Symbolism enters into the frame of reference and the affect dimensions. Research by the Michigan Survey Research Center under Katona's direction has demonstrated the significance of consumer attitudes and expectations to consumer behavior, especially by large groups of consumers.[22]

From the foregoing review, we conclude that both consumer and product variables enter into consumer behavior. The *consumer variables* include the cognitive and habit dimensions as well as the response to affective appeals and the symbolism of products. Both of these reflect the results of acculturation or socialization.

Product variables refer to characteristics attributed by consumers to the product as well as to certain intrinsic characteristics of the product which are perceived by consumers. Consumers may perceive particular products as symbols of their objectives or as satisfying particular hedonic or aesthetic interests, or they may perceive the functional aspects of products. But here again we find that perception is very important in determining which products will meet the needs felt by consumers. Perception operates by means of cues or clues to categories.

If you look back over the ideas from psychology and social psychology, you will find reference only in Katona's research to a relationship between the micro view of the individual and any macro view of the aggregate consumer behavior of large groups of people, as in a whole country, for example. But the development of psychological theory clearly indicates the shift from the greatly simplified S-R theory toward the complexity of real human consumer behavior. In real human behavior it is frequently impossible to relate a particular stimulus or a particular response to a particular stimulus. This follows from the ideas pointed out by Atkinson regarding the continuous stream of human behavior.

Rose expressed it this way:

> The newer assumptions underlying social-psychological research consider that behavior is a response to selected and interpreted experiences. An individual has an expectation as to how others will act under given circumstances, he has a conception of how others expect him to act, and he has a conception of himself as a conformist or deviant of one of a large number of types. From these conscious or unconscious expectations, conceptions, and "definitions of the situation," the individual guides his behavior. . . .[23]

In addition to their theoretical contributions, psychologists have been particularly helpful in supplying several types of techniques for use in the study of consumer behavior. These include the projective techniques, scaling devices, and factor analysis.

5.5 SOCIOLOGICAL CONTRIBUTIONS

Sociology provides no generally recognized theory of consumer behavior, but many parts of sociological theories pertinent to individual human and group behavior can be translated into terms of consumer behavior.[24] Sociologists view individuals as dominated in many respects by their social environment. Therefore they insist that human behavior cannot be traced solely or mainly to individual psychological processes.

[21] Page 5, Crespi, Irving. *Attitude Research.*

[22] Katona, George. *The Powerful Consumer,* Chapters 3–6.

[23] Page 199, Rose, Arnold, M. *Theory and Method in the Social Sciences.*

[24] For comprehensive coverage, see Faris, Robert E. L. (Editor), *Handbook of Modern Sociology,* and Christensen, Harold T. (Editor), *Handbook of Marriage and the Family.*

Some sociologists view economic processes as one category of sociological processes. Historically, in contrast, sociology was an offshoot of economics, being delegated the investigation of irrational or illogical behavior. This no longer bothers sociologists who simply redefine rationality as a function of the condition of the society as well as the condition of a person. Thus rational behavior can be identified as behavior predictable by others.

The major theoretical approaches of sociologists to the explanation of human behavior and specifically to family behavior are considered next.

5.5.1 Symbolic Interaction

Symbolic interaction assumes that man's capacity for development and use of symbols (of which language is the outstanding example) and his capacity to store a great number of such symbols in memory over long periods of time distinguish him from animals. Rose has defined a *symbol* as "a stimulus that has a learned meaning and value for people" and *value* in this connection, as "the learned attraction or repulsion that they feel toward the meaning."[25] Symbols are used to evoke meanings and values and are the major means of human communication. In the process of human development, man learns to respond to his environment viewed in symbolic terms. An important key to symbolic interaction is man's development and use of categories which have meaning, serve as clues for behavior, and provide bases for organizing behavior. The development of the categorizing skill is an essential part of the socialization process.

Symbolic interactionists assume that symbols—and the meanings and values to which they refer—tend to occur in clusters. Rose uses the term *role* "to refer to a cluster of related meanings and values that guide and direct an individual's behavior in a given social setting. . . ." (*Ibid.*, page 10.) Further, an individual develops self-identification as a role player in a number of relationships such as his family, profession, or firm. *Reference groups* are the groups or relationships in which each individual plays his more highly valued roles. The socialization process molds the behavior of individuals within or aspiring to a particular reference group so that they conform to the group's cultural expectations which change through the course of time.

The way an individual consistently defines a series of situations depends upon his *perspective*. Perspective has been defined as "an organized view of one's world, what is taken for granted about attributes of objects, of events, and of human nature. . . ."[26] People in a particular group who share a common perspective have a common culture in the forms of conventional understandings reflected in acts and artifacts. The perspectives of his reference groups are used by an individual as his frames of reference when he organizes his behavior within his environment. An individual's *tastes and preferences* are formed in this way, but sociologists do not use this economic terminology very often, probably because of its vagueness.

Apparently, people in different social classes or subcultures develop dissimilar modes of life or life styles because similarity of occupation and income level "dispose them to certain restricted communication channels. . . ." (*Ibid.*, page 134.) Common *communication channels* produce shared perspectives and form boundaries for social worlds.

Within the norms of conduct and sets of values of his social world, each individual can carve out his *careers*—as family member, as student, as a member of a profession, and so on. An individual is likely to belong to a number of social worlds and be involved in a variety of communication networks. In seeking to conform in social action and symbolically (as by dress, food habits, and ownership of possessions) to the perspectives of several social worlds or reference groups at the same time, people construct new modes of living because they must reconcile sometimes conflicting norms and values.

By our acts in our several social worlds, each of us gives meanings to the objects within our environment. We continuously judge the suitability of such objects to our actions and make decisions based on our judgment. Blumer says this process illustrates the meaning of interpretation or acting on the basis of symbols.[27] Therefore he argues that an individual's

[25] Page 5, Rose, Arnold M. (Editor), *Human Behavior and Social Processes.*

[26] Page 130, Shibutani, Tamotsu. "Reference Groups and Social Control," Rose (Editor), *ibid.*

[27] Page 182, Blumer, Herbert. "Society as Symbolic Interaction," Rose (Editor), *ibid.*

behavior is not really the result of "such things as environmental pressures, stimuli, motives, attitudes, and ideas but arises instead from how he interprets and handles these things in the action which he is constructing. . . . Each individual aligns his action to the action of others by ascertaining what they are doing or what they intend to do—that is, by getting the meaning of their acts. . . ." (*Ibid.*, pp. 183 and 184.)

5.5.2 Structure-Function

The *structural-functional approach* to analysis of human behavior differs substantially from the interaction approach by conceptualizing *social systems* and by frequent use of statistical analysis in identifying functional relationships. However, functionalists prefer to reserve the term *function* to describe how a part of a whole system contributes to the maintenance of the system or to the interrelationship of the parts within the system.

Social systems are made up of roles. In this approach *role* is defined to encompass "a sector of the individual actor's total system of action. It is the point of contact between the system of action of the individual actor and the social system. . . . The primary ingredient of the role is the role-expectation. Role-expectations are patterns of evaluation. . . ."[28]

Sociologists using this approach are able to deal with internal operations within families and external transactions between families and larger social systems. According to Pitts, Parsons has been seeking to create "a theory of social systems which might permit a classification of concrete social systems and an identification of the functional prerequisites for each classification. He starts with an abstract (analytical) model of the total society and differentiates it into four basic subsystems which specialize in coping with the four functional problems of the total society: *adaptive* (economic), *goal attainment* (political), *integrative* (institutional), and *pattern maintenance* (motivational). . . ."[29] Parsons describes the functional relationships in terms of inputs and outputs between subsystems.

By identifying the household as the pattern-maintenance subsystem of the economy, Parsons and Smelser defined consumer roles of the members of a society as being *outside* the economy.[30] They describe the flow of output of consumer goods and services from the economy as input to the household and the output of labor services by the household as input for the economy. In the course of their examination of the household as a social system, Parsons and Smelser found that the American family system and values imply a certain minimum of possessions and level of consumption of food and other goods and services described as "a standard package." They also pointed out that "a level of spending is required by the consumption unit primarily for the purposes of tension management within the family. In this respect certain aspects of entertainment, leisure, and vacations are important. The primary function of such spending is, for the consumption unit, *latent pattern-maintenance and tension management.*" (*Ibid.*, page 222.)

Another focus for family spending which Parsons and Smelser identified was the urge to symbolize class and prestige. Spending with this objective serves to integrate family units in groups within society. The demands of personality fulfillment and maintenance of community status also contribute to the fixed costs of households and stabilize spending patterns.

Parsons and Smelser contributed significantly to the understanding of consumption patterns by pointing out that (1) the "standard package" expenditure for each group is relatively stable, and (2) the modes of tension management and differential class symbolism vary from class to class of consumers. (*Ibid.*, page 224.) Especially important for projections of aggregate consumption is their conceptualization of a consumption model incorporating "a *structure* of the expectations which govern expenditures at different levels of society. . . . (In using this sociologically derived model) it is necessary to trace income changes to particular segments of society and to note the structured expectation systems of the consuming units in question, since different role expectation patterns govern the spending and saving habits of the various segments. . . ." (*Ibid.*, page 226.)

Parsons and Smelser added that they viewed

[28] Page 190 of Parsons, Talcott, and Shils, Edward A. (Editors), *Toward a General Theory of Action.*

[29] Page 54, Pitts, Jesse R. "The Structural-Functional Approach," Chapter 3 of Christensen, op. cit.

[30] Parsons, Talcott, and Smelser, Neil J. *Economy and Society.*

the job of economists in the consumption area to be formulation of the economic effects of known sociological and psychological facts.

In a 1963 book, Smelser shifted terminology from social systems to *social structure* to characterize recurrent and regularized interaction among two or more persons acting in selected roles.[31] Social controls which regulate interaction in the social structure are values, norms, and sanctions.

This brings up another contribution of structure-function sociologists to the understanding of consumer behavior, namely, the clarification of the roles of *norms and values* in society. Blake and Davis defined a norm as "any standard or rule that states what human beings should or should not think, say, or do under given circumstances."[32] Differences in norms among human groups permit differences in behavior. Although many sociologists try to differentiate values from norms or specific rules of conduct, Blake and Davis argue that norms provide the best evidence of values. "It is the norms, not the values, that have the pressure of reality upon them. It is the norms that are enforced by sanctions, that are subject to the necessity of action and the agony of decision. It is therefore the norms that represent the cutting edge of social control. . . ." (*Ibid.*, page 461.)

Therefore these two sociologists recommend the abandonment of values as factors causing particular behavior. They recommend that values be considered as constructs to serve as links in the total social environment. They also object to the frequent reliance of sociologists and anthropologists on norms and values as determinants of social phenomena because such reliance leads to failure to investigate the norms and to the use of unknowns underlying such norms as explanations of the known or observed behavior. They hold that "far from being fully determinate, the norms themselves tend to be a product of the constant interaction involving the interplay of interests, changing conditions, power, dominance, force, fraud, ignorance, and knowledge." (*Ibid.*, page 464.)

Many norms are highly internalized by some sectors of society so that individuals are emotionally committed to them, but other norms are not. According to Blake and Davis, much of people's orderly conduct results from decisions reached after weighing the consequences of nonconformity. In fact, they view the criss-crossing of commitment and objectivity toward norms as sources of change and stability in society.

5.5.3 Developmental Approach

The third major approach of sociologists to the study of human behavior which is particularly pertinent to consumer behavior is the *developmental approach*. As Hill and Hansen pointed out, it is highly eclectic. Hill and others have formed this approach by borrowing parts of earlier theoretical efforts—stages in the *family life cycle* from rural sociology; the concept of family as a convergence of *intercontingent careers* from the sociology of occupations; concepts of age and sex roles, functional prerequisites, and interaction systems within the family from the structure-function and interactional approaches.[33] The family-development approach focuses on the longitudinal career of the family system. At this stage in its formulation, the developmental approach "attempts both to be micro-analytic and to account for changes in the pattern of interaction over the family's life span."[34]

Hill and Hansen listed the basic assumptions of their approach as follows:

1. Human conduct is best seen as a function of the preceding as well as the current social milieu and individual conditions.
2. Human conduct cannot be adequately understood apart from human development.
3. The human is an actor as well as a reactor.
4. Individual and group development is best seen as dependent upon stimulation by a social milieu as well as on inherent (developed) capacities.
5. The individual in a social setting is the basic autonomous unit. . . .[35]

This framework was used by Hill and Foote in formulating the three-generation study of

[31] Page 27, Smelser, Neil J. *The Sociology of Economic Life.*

[32] Page 456, Blake, Judith, and Davis, Kingsley. "Norms, Values and Sanctions" in Faris (Editor), op. cit.

[33] Page 307, Hill, Reuben, and Hansen, Donald A. "The Identification of Conceptual Frameworks Utilized in Family Study," *Marriage and Family Living* 22:4:299–311, November 1960.

[34] Page 172, Hill, Reuben, and Rodgers, Roy H. "The Developmental Approach," Chapter 5 of Christensen, op. cit.

[35] Op. cit., page 309.

asset accumulation, described in Hill's paper at the Conference of Consumer Behavior Inc., in 1958. Hill and Foote set out to study the content of family culture. The nature of their research is best understood from Hill's statements: "Coping with the demands of the community and of family members, families may develop policies that not only help in making choices in the present but give direction and structure to the future. As the family develops in stature and competence from wedding day on, it builds a history of problem solutions, a pattern of decision making, and a set of rudimentary family policies by which choices can be made involving children and the family's future and by which actions can be judged. These policies, moreover, include the family's time schedule for reaching important goals and objectives—owning a home, completing the family, launching children into jobs and marriage, and retirement. These are the contents of the family culture which, if we knew them, would make family behavior more or less predictable."[36] The reader is referred to Hill's paper for his excellent statement about the theoretical model used.[37]

5.5.4 Other Contributions

Another part of sociological theory and research pertinent to consumer behavior is the study of *social differentiation*. In the process of social interaction, differences evolve between behaviors of individuals and of social groups. Such social differentiation contributes to rank differentiation, particularly social stratification. One research concluded, "Ample documentation shows that social rank differentiation tends to be accompanied by differences in styles of life—attitudes and behaviors. . . ."[38]

A classic article relating social stratification to consumer behavior is Martineau's "Social Classes and Spending Behavior."[39] The article sets forth the hypotheses and assumptions used in a study by the *Chicago Tribune* and some of the conclusions. One was that social class differences have a greater effect on buying behavior than does income.

Sociologists working on social stratification and on a variety of demographic and social problems have exhibited considerable proficiency in the use of survey methods and in developing new methods. Riley provides a useful overview of the social research process and methods used in her chapter in Faris.[40] Straus' chapter in Christensen and books by Lazarsfeld and Rosenberg, by Hyman, and by Selltiz et al. provide helpful information for researchers on consumer behavior who want to use sociological variables, measures, and methods.[41]

5.6 ANTHROPOLOGICAL CONTRIBUTIONS

The concept of *culture* is highly significant in consumer behavior research. Culture refers to the more or less consistent pattern of thought and action which binds people together. Boas defines it thus:

> Culture embraces all the manifestations of social habits of a community, the reactions of the individual as affected by the habits of the group in which he lives, and the products of human activities as determined by these habits. . . .[42]

5.6.1 Cultural Patterns

Social or cultural anthropologists study all the behaviors of man that are learned, seeking to identify *patterns* within each culture. These patterns reflect homogeneity in consumer wants and attitudes of people within cultures and subcultures. Products are a part of culture and often serve as symbols, communicating collections of meanings to members of the culture and to outsiders.

Mead wrote in 1943: ". . . Food habits are

[36] Pages 63 and 64 of Hill, Reuben. "Patterns of Decision-Making and the Accumulation of Family Assets," pp. 57–80 of Foote, Nelson N. (Editor), *Household Decision-Making*.

[37] At this point the author wishes to acknowledge the considerable influence that Hill's writings and seminars have had on her formulation of conceptual frameworks.

[38] Page 555, Svalastoga, Kaare. "Social Differentiation," Chapter 15 of Faris, op. cit.

[39] *J. Marketing* **23**:2:121–130, October 1958.

[40] Riley, Matilda White. "Sources and Types of Sociological Data," Chapter 26 of Faris, op. cit.

[41] (*a*) Straus, Murray A. "Measuring Families," Chapter 10 of Christensen, op. cit.
(*b*) Lazarsfeld, Paul F., and Rosenberg, Morris (Editors), *The Language of Social Research*.
(c) Hyman, Herbert. *Survey Design and Analysis*.
(*d*) Selltiz, Claire; Jahoda, Marie; Deutsch, Morton; and Cook, Stuart W. *Research Methods in Social Relations*.

[42] Page 79, Boas, Franz. "Anthropology," in vol. 2 of *The Encyclopedia of the Social Sciences*.

seen as the culturally standardized set of behaviors in regard to food manifested by individuals who have been reared within a given cultural tradition. These behaviors are seen as systematically interrelated with other standardized behaviors in the same culture. In attempting to estimate the strength of any given item of behavior, e.g., preference for meat, aversion to milk, etc., this item is not treated as isolated, but is referred to the total complex of behaviors which constitute the food habits. . . ."[43] Similarly, items of clothing or kinds of housing or electrical appliances must be considered within the cultural patterns of their use.

Cultural anthropologists are particularly sensitive to *cross-cultural differences* which reflect different ways people within cultures have developed to meet their needs. For example, special studies of the food habits of several subcultures in the United States were made for the wartime Committee on Food Habits.[44] These revealed some differences in food practices and food consumption which had to be taken into account in nutrition education programs and in wartime food controls. But they also showed how rapidly people of different ethnic backgrounds absorb the cultural patterns of people in their new cultural setting.

Writings of anthropologists demonstrate the great variety of ways in which human groups meet their needs for food, clothing, shelter, and leisure time activity. We also learn from them that the parts of consumer behavior must be fitted into total cultures evolving through time. Anthropologists have used quantitative measures only in the measurement of human beings, not in measuring human phenomena. This may explain the tremendous amount of detail included in their writings. But classification systems are now being developed which may permit statistical analysis.

5.6.2 Cultural Change

Many anthropologists have been particularly concerned with the processes by which *changes in cultures* come about. The publication best known to laymen dealing with cultural change may be the UNESCO-sponsored book, *Cultural Patterns and Technical Change.*[45] It is a manual describing studies of several whole cultures and cross-cultural studies of aspects of technical change written to enlighten foreign technicians assigned to help in developing countries.

Barnett's book, *Innovation: the Basis of Cultural Change*, is particularly helpful to people interested in changes in consumer behavior. It provides a systematic coverage of the subject of innovation, assembling many pieces of information gathered by anthropologists. Barnett defines *innovation* "as any thought, behavior, or thing that is new because it is qualitatively different from existing forms. Strictly speaking, every innovation is an idea, or a constellation of ideas; . . ."[46] Popular usage identifies *invention* with a thing, so Barnett uses the term to refer to a technological innovation.

Barnett identifies a number of dimensions in the concept of innovation: first, motivation for innovation; second, factors favoring early adoption of innovation; third, factors favoring wider acceptance of innovation; and fourth, the identification and characterization of the innovators. The sources of motivation for innovation appear to be frustration, prestige, fashion, boredom, and special attributes of new products. The adoption of innovation by individuals is favored by such factors as purchasing power, knowledge, education, and the current experience of innovating firms in mass-production economies that they must keep changing to new products if they want to keep ahead of others.

The basic processes of innovation are fundamental to cultural change, and to changes in consumption patterns and in whole structures of consumption. Barnett argues that innovation represents a linkage or fusion of two or more elements, not previously joined in the same way, so that the result is a qualitatively distinct, new whole concept or product. (*Ibid.*, page 181.) Thus any innovation requires preexisting components and the new combination is the product of mental activity. Development of new products is aided by use of the concept of configuration, rather than the concept of a thing, because configurations have

[43] Page 21, Mead, Margaret. "The Problem of Changing Food Habits," in Mead (Editor), *The Problem of Changing Food Habits*, NRC Bulletin 108.

[44] Summarized by Natalie F. Joffee in "Food Habits of Selected Subcultures in the United States," pp. 97–103 of *The Problem of Changing Food Habits.*

[45] Mead, Margaret (Editor), Manual Prepared by the World Federation for Mental Health, UN Educational, Scientific, and Cultural Organization.

[46] Page 7, Barnett, H. G.

elements or parts organized into wholes. Reorganization or change in the parts comprising a configuration may lead to innovation.

As pointed out earlier, human beings constantly categorize and treat slightly different things as the same. We may ignore the differences for certain purposes. For example, beef and chicken are different, but they are classified as *meat* and used for main dishes by Americans, whereas snake meat is not so used. The cohesion of the parts of a mental configuration, such as the kind of meat suitable for a main dish, is largely determined by culture. Combinations of products are also solidified by custom. The processes of innovation include identification and analysis of configurations, experimentation with incorporating new parts—substitution, and accidental discovery of new configurations, which requires discrimination.

The *diffusion* of innovations refers to rates of acceptance by individuals and groups. To be accepted as an innovation, a novelty must (*a*) have meaning for the potential acceptor, in the sense of being understandable and related favorably to previous experience; (*b*) satisfy a want better than some existing means; (*c*) be congruent or compatible with valued cultural patterns with which it is to be linked; (*d*) be sufficiently divisible so that tentative trials may be made; and (*e*) be communicable from one person to another.[47]

[47] Chapter V of Rogers, Everett M. *Diffusion of Innovations.*

Barnett did not conceptualize the *adoption process* as clearly as sociologists have done in recent years. Rural sociologists' research on the adoption of new farming processes by farm people led to the identification of these stages in the process—awareness, interest or seeking information, mental application or evaluation of the new practice trial, and finally adoption. People are frequently classified in terms of the time of their adoption of an innovation, described as adopter categories. Various bases are used, but a popular one is standard deviations of the normal distribution: innovators—the earliest 2.5 percent; the early adopters—the next 13.5 percent; the early majority—34 percent; the late majority—34 percent; and the laggards—16 percent. (*Ibid.*, Chapter VI.)

The concept of *change agent* has evolved in both anthropology and sociology. Rogers defines a change agent as "a professional person who attempts to influence adoption decisions in a direction that he feels is desirable." (*Ibid.*, page 254.) Change agents are highly significant in achieving planned social changes in developing countries, but marketing people played the role long before foreign technical assistance programs were developed. Specialists in advertising and promotion consciously seek to change consumption patterns of potential cutsomers for the benefit of particular firms. Marketing people can learn much about the processes of change from research summarized by Rogers, for example.

6

ELEMENTARY ECONOMIC THEORY RELATIVE TO CONSUMER BEHAVIOR

6.1 INTRODUCTION

This chapter reviews some of the elementary economic concepts and relationships used by economists in their basic approach to consumer behavior. The brief presentation of a number of topics is based on the assumptions that the reader of this book has been introduced to many of these ideas in his elementary courses in general economics, but that he needs to review and coordinate these ideas as they pertain to his marketing interest in consumer behavior. The standard theories of demand, consumer choice, and consumption-income relationships presented in this chapter approximate the level of economic knowledge generally taught to elementary intermediate students of economics in the 1930s. These theories involve some rather rigid assumptions which received much attention in the succeeding 25 years.

Chapter 7 will review postwar developments in economic analysis. Some of them clarify ideas in basic theory. Still others attempt to make such basic theories more generally applicable and more relevant to observed economic behavior of consumers.

Standard economic theories of consumer behavior have dealt primarily with consumers' purchases in response to variations in price and income. The relation between price and the quantity of a good taken from the market is described by the theory of demand. The decreasing quantities which are demanded at higher prices were first explained by a theory of consumer choice based on the concept of marginal utility, later by preference explanations.

The effect of income on consumption received much less emphasis in standard economic theory before the 1930s, although this relationship was investigated by a series of surveys of levels of living. In the mid-1930s, Keynes proposed a theory of the consumption function, describing the relationship between income and consumption for an entire country. His theory was based on introspection, on general observations of the relationship for individual consumers, and on a simple summation of individuals' expenditures and incomes. This theory is now referred to as the *absolute-income hypothesis*. Extensive empirical work on family living studies during the depression years led to the suggestion of a *relative-income hypothesis* which takes into account the income position of particular families in relation to the income distribution of all families in the area.

The assumptions of the standard theory appeared rather rigid and overly simplified in the light of findings of empirical studies of changes in consumption. Some alternative approaches were formulated even before World War II in attempts to deal with observed complexities of consumer behavior. Examples of alternative approaches will be noted. In the last section we will clarify some of the basic concepts needed for empirical research.

6.2 STANDARD ECONOMIC THEORY OF DEMAND AND THE UTILITY EXPLANATION OF CONSUMER CHOICE

The theories of demand and of consumer behavior as synthesized by Marshall (Sec. 1.3.1) were generally accepted by economists in the 1930s and are still used as the starting point for microeconomic theory in many elementary textbooks. The theory of demand relating to consumer behavior describes the actions of consumers in their role as buyers as they interact with sellers in determining prices at the consumer market level. Here we will follow the usual sequence of considering first the demand of a single consumer and second, the theory describing demand in an entire market. The third step will require backtracking to examine the classical theory of an individual consumer's choice, often referred to as the utility explanation of the downward-sloping demand curve.

6.2.1 Response of a Consumer to Price

The economic concept of consumer demand refers to the quantity of a good or service that the consumer is willing and able to buy at a specified price. More generally, it refers to the variations in quantities the consumer is expected to take at different prices, *assuming* that his income, prices of substitute goods or services, tastes and preferences, and all other pertinent factors do not change. Economists conceptualize the demands (*D*) of two persons, call them Mr. A and Mr. *B*, for a particular commodity, say G_1, in a given period by means of charts such as Figure 6.1. By convention (or usual practice), the price is assigned to the vertical dimension and the quantity is measured on the horizon. Each of these demand curves represents a locus of points, and each point represents an expected or predicted act by a consumer. Such a continuous series of behavioral acts, in economics, defines a behavioral relationship between price and quantity. Data used in drawing such a demand curve are assumed to be supplied by a hypothetical demand schedule showing the behavioral acts in the form of quantities that would be purchased at each price.

Note that Mr. A would take 5 pounds of commodity G_1 if it were priced at $1 but only 1½ pounds at $3. But Mr. *B* would take 5 pounds at $3 and 1½ pounds at $4.50. Which has the greater demand for the commodity? Can you guess why?

The fundamental law of demand is that as the price falls, a consumer is expected to take increasing quantities, and vice versa. These relationships, when graphed, result in the downward-sloping demand curve illustrated in Figure 6.1. This inverse relationship between decreasing price and increasing quantity was first based on general observation of consumer responses in the forms of greater use

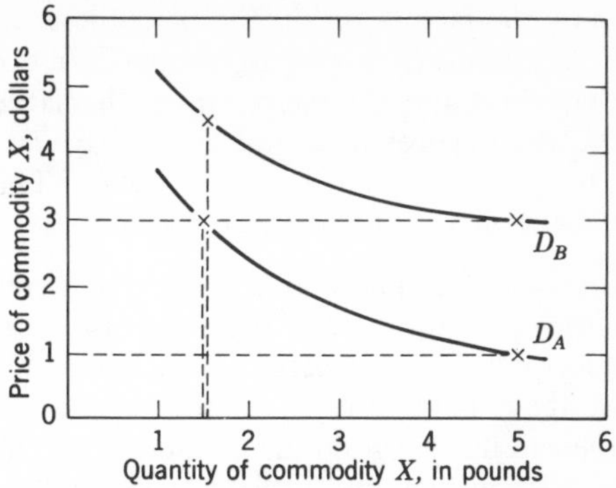

FIGURE 6.1 Demand and price relationships.

of cheaper goods and substitution of lower-priced goods for more expensive items.

This fundamental law of demand provides a simplified, abstract view of consumer response to price. To understand the implications of the law of demand, one must be aware of a large number of qualifying assumptions on which it is based. Unfortunately, some elementary and even intermediate texts on economics do not provide a comprehensive list of the major assumptions. The definition of demand used at the beginning of this section indicates some of them. Others are more subtle. We will identify them step by step, using both words and mathematical notations.

The demand curves in Figure 6.1 reflect the statement that the quantities of a specified commodity G_1 that will be taken by a consumer vary inversely with the price of that commodity G_1, assuming that the prices of *alternative goods*, income, tastes and preferences, all other factors, and the time period are held constant. In mathematical notation, this statement becomes

$$Q_{G_1} = f\,P_{G_1},\ (Y, P_r, X, Z, T)$$

where

Q_{G_1} = quantity of item G_1 demanded
f = function of or related to
P_{G_1} = price of item G_1
Y = income of the consumer
P_r = prices of related items, either substitutes or complements
X = tastes and preferences
Z = all other factors
T = time period

(Y, P_r, X, Z, T) means that these factors are not permitted to vary

Because the factors within the parentheses are held constant, they can be dropped out of the equation and the figure. In mathematical formulations, constant factors do not have rates of change so they are treated as zeros. Thus the figure depicts $Q_{G_1} = f(P_{G_1})$.

In discussing consumer demand for a commodity, your instructor in elementary economics probably presented additional assumptions about holding constant the expectations of the consumer concerning future income and price relationships, the availability and costs of consumer credit, his financial situation with respect to liquid assets, and his inventories of product G_1 and related products. Since all of these might affect the consumer's response to price variations, they too must be held constant in order to appraise separately the consumption-price relationship. We must add to our list of factors the following:

E_y = expectations regarding future incomes
E_p = expectations regarding future price relationships
P_c = cost of credit
A = liquid assets
I = consumer's inventory

Our equation now becomes

$$Q_{G_1} = f\,[P_{G_1}\,(Y, P_r, X, Z, T, E_y, E_p, P_c, A, I)]$$

This equation has expanded too much to keep all the parts in mind so we need to follow the usual scientific procedure of setting up categories. Figure 6.2 lists some additional factors and assumptions that have been hidden from view by the economists' implicit use of *ceteris paribus*, meaning all other conditions remain the same. This assumption is very important in economic analysis of consumer behavior.

6.2.2 Market Demand

For many years economists have viewed market demand as the simple summing or aggregating of individual demands on the buyer side of the market. If Mr. A would take 1½ units of commodity G_1 at \$3 and Mr. B would take 5 units, the total demand of these men would be 6½ units at the \$3 level of an aggregate demand chart.

But if there is actually a third consumer, Mr. C, in the market area, we must add his demand, say 3½ units. We obtain a total market demand of 10 units at the \$3 price. This provides one point on a curve like those in Figure 6.1 except for the extension of the scale for the horizontal axis. Comparable additions of quantities expected to be taken by the three consumers at other prices would, hypothetically, provide the data for locating the entire market demand curve. The same result would be obtained if we drew a new curve for Mr. C in Figure 6.1 and added the distances from the vertical axis to each curve horizontally. We could then study our market demand curve and compare the 10 units that would be taken at \$3 with a total of perhaps 6 units at \$4.

Suppose that there is another commodity G_2 which these three consumers also buy. Assume that its price suddenly declines sharply. The effect of the change in the price of G_2 on the demand schedules of our three consumers for commodity G_1 will depend on the degree to which they are willing and able to *substitute* G_2 for G_1, i.e., as economists say, on their basic tastes and preferences. If the change in the price of commodity G_2 does affect the demand for G_1 by our consumers, we will have to establish a new set of demand schedules and draw new demand curves for each consumer and for the total market. This situation represents a change in demand. The quantities of commodity G_1 expected to be taken from the market at alternative prices are now different from those in Figure 6.1.

Economists use the term *cross-elasticity of demand* to describe the responsiveness of the consumer's purchase of good G_1 to changes in the price of good G_2. If the value of the ratio

$$\frac{\text{percentage change in quantity of } G_1}{\text{percentage change in price of } G_2}$$

is positive, i.e., the degree of change in the quantity of G_1 taken is greater than the proportional change in the price of G_2, G_2 is called a *substitute* for G_1. If the value of the ratio is negative, G_2 is considered to be a *complementary* product for G_1.

If commodity G_2 is very important in the budgets of our three consumers, a decrease in its price may reduce the dollar outlays for it significantly, even if additional G_2 is used to substitute for G_1. If total outlays for G_2 and G_1 are reduced, the consumers will have more purchasing power available for purchase of other items. In such a case, part of the

Figure 6.2 Summary of factors entering into static demand analysis for a commodity G_1 at the micro level.

Factors Identified	*Hidden Factors and Assumptions*
I. Related to the individual consumers	
Y = current income, after income taxes E_y = income expectations in terms of purchasing power E_p = expectations regarding price (and quality) relationships among products I = inventory of consumer goods X = tastes and preferences, undefined A = liquid assets	X = tastes and preferences affected by: age, education, occupation, family size and composition, degree of urbanization, regionality, ethnic background, knowledge of goods and services, tastes and preferences of reference groups, expectations about alternative uses of products
II. Related to specific product	
P_{G_1} = its price	Divisibility Supplies of different qualities
III. Related to other products	
P_r = price of related products, including substitutes and complements	Supplies of related products in terms of their qualities
IV. Related to time	
T = constant length of time periods	Included in X are past experiences with particular products
V. About the economy	
P_c = price (and availability) of credit	Z = competitive forces in the market

decrease in price of G_2 acts like an increase in income. Economists refer to this part as the *income effect*.

Market demand is also affected by changes in the incomes of consumers. If Mr. *B*'s income had doubled, in our example, we would expect his tastes and preferences to change before long. Then we would have to get a new demand schedule from him and derive a new market demand curve. According to standard economic theory, Mr. *B* would be expected to buy more of some items and some new commodities. With double the income, he might also reduce his purchases of work clothes and hamburger and potatoes and shift to more expensive items. Commodities which suffer decreases in demand when incomes go up are referred to as "inferior goods." Those that increase in demand are "superior goods," although often no objective is used to describe them. To be more precise, when the ratio

$$\frac{\text{percentage increase in quantity of } G_1}{\text{percentage increase in income}}$$

is positive, we identify G_1 as a superior good. If the ratio is negative, G_2 is an inferior good.

Another possible type of change in demand is for a new consumer to come into the market, say Mr. *D*. Now that the price of G_1 has gone down so much, he can afford to buy some G_1 if it is priced at \$1 to \$4 per unit. Or there may be new people who move into the area and who want to buy our favorite commodity G_1. Note that these changes involve relaxing some of the initial assumptions.

Economists and marketing people are particularly interested in the degree to which total market demand may rise or fall with variations in price. The concept of price elasticity of demand refers to the responsiveness of the quantity demanded to changes in price. If the demand schedules of every consumer in the market were known and if these schedules were relatively fixed, the answers would be readily available. In the real world, demand schedules are *not* known. But useful information about the price elasticity of demand is provided by a study of historical changes in the prices of a commodity and of quantities sold at the various prices.[1] Also, inferences may be drawn from a study of variations in sales among areas with different prevailing prices concurrently with a study of related phenomena such as incomes and sales of substitute commodities.

Items that are very important in the average consumer's budget and have reasonably good substitutes usually exhibit considerable price elasticity of demand. A rise in price will significantly reduce the quantity taken from the market or a fall in price will induce past buyers to buy more and/or bring more buyers into the market. But the total market demand for a staple, relatively unique item requiring relatively little outlay tends to be quite inelastic. Examples are salt and light bulbs.

The theory of demand just discussed is often called a "partial equilibrium theory" because it takes into account only one commodity or only a few at a time and does not treat all goods and services concurrently.

So far we have not really analyzed why consumers buy what they buy at particular prices. We especially ought to know the reasons for the increased quantities taken at decreasing prices. The standard explanation for many years was built on the concept of *utility* and was described as the theory of consumer choice.

6.2.3 Classical Theory of Consumer Choice or the Utility Explanation

Economists generally start their explanation of consumer choice with the statement that a consumer's utility or satisfaction is a function of the quantities of a good or a bundle of goods being consumed. In recent years some economists have referred to utility as the power to satisfy wants rather than as satisfaction itself. By function, they refer here to the relationship between the variations in the amount of utility and the variations in quantities consumed. (Recall that we used the term *function* earlier when we were relating the quantity taken to its price.) After this general statement, the explanation is focused on the utility expected by a consumer from consumption of a commodity G_1. In effect, economists view the quantity of commodity G_1 as the input into the consumption activity of a household and the utility derived from its consumption as the output. This formulation parallels the production function in which the inputs are identified as land, labor, and capital, and the outputs are the physical products. The physical products yield returns to the factors of production in the forms of rent, wages, and interest.

Let us note the abstractions and assumptions that are involved in such a formulation of the consumption process. We appear to be considering a representative or standard consumer, maybe the average man. We are ignoring his income, how many children he may have, how old he is, what else he is buying, and a host of other phenomena. We are talking about a commodity G_1, ignoring variations between one firm's product and those of other producers.

The concept, *utility,* refers to a general sense of satisfaction. Economists have always been quite vague about its meaning. In teaching the concept, economics professors are inclined to refer persistent questionners among their students to psychology. (I have not been able to find the word in any index to a modern book on psychology.) Economists do not identify *which* wants may be filled to achieve this satisfaction or utility. Also, be aware that economists consider the purchase or consumption of commodity G_1 in a selected period of time without relating a particular event of consumer behavior to other events taking place in the same time period in the life of a representative consumer.

Now that you are alerted to the underlying assumptions of the classical theory, we are ready to take up the explanation of the downward-sloping demand curve in terms of diminishing marginal utility.

Almost everyone has less money to spend than the total cost of all his *desired* goods and

[1] The price elasticity of demand is customarily defined as the negative of the ratio of the percentage change in the quantity of good G_1 demanded to the percentage change in its price. One way of computing it involves measurement of changes in quantity (Q) and price (P) from one point on the demand curve to another. This approach is called arc elasticity. To be more precise, it relates the ratio of the change in price ($\triangle P$, where $\triangle$ means difference) and the change in quantity ($\triangle Q$) to the average of the pairs of prices and quantities and thus standardizes the measure. The formula is

$$\frac{-\triangle Q}{\triangle P} \cdot P/Q = \frac{-(Q_1 - Q_0)}{(P_1 - P_0)} \cdot \frac{(P_1 + P_0)/2}{(Q_1 + Q_0)/2}$$

Where Q_0 and P_0 refer to quantity taken and price paid in the base or initial period, and Q_1 and P_1 refer to the quantity and price in the next period.

services. Therefore economists point out that the consumers must make choices among alternative goods. Being rational, consumers are supposed to do so in such a way as to maximize the utility or satisfaction they can get from their expenditures. In other words, they seek to get the most for their money.

To illustrate the explanation of the classical *cardinal utility theory,* let us analyze a student's expenditure of 70 cents for lunch. He could buy seven apples at 10 cents and obtain a given amount of total utility, 47 utiles according to the hypothetical data in Table 6.1. Or he might buy only two apples and spend the other 50 cents for candy bars or a sandwich. Observe in Table 6.1 and Figure 6.3 that total utility (column 2 of the table) decline after the seventh apple in our hypothetical example. Average utility (column 3) is measured by total utility divided by the number of apples consumed. *Marginal utility* (column 4) is defined as the addition to total satisfaction contributed by the last unit of a commodity consumed. If the student buys and eats only two apples, it is the utility or satisfaction from the second apple, here 10 utiles. *Utile* is the term often used by economists to refer to a unit of utility. The problem of how to define such a unit or how to measure it has never been solved.

Note that all three utility schedules (the last three series of data in the table) rise and then fall. This is based on the intuitive idea that an individual becomes satiated as he consumes more and more of a good. Because goods are imperfect substitutes, additional apples cannot be substituted satisfactorily for coffee or for shoes. Note that marginal and average utility start to decline at the same point, after the first apple in our example. Marginal utility reaches the zero line when total utility is at its peak, here for the seventh apple.

Let us suppose that our student is very wealthy and his expenditures on some other commodity *N* take only a fraction of his current cash and do not affect the amounts of others goods and services he buys. In such a situation, economists argue that we can put an assumed price on each unit of utility, perhaps 2 cents, and multiply each point on the utility scale on the vertical axis by 2 cents. Thus the utility scale becomes a price scale. Now we find that the marginal utility curve is very much like the downward-sloping demand curve. Economists of mathematical persuasion demonstrate that it has the same slope. We will take their word for it.

Actually, consumers are usually buying not

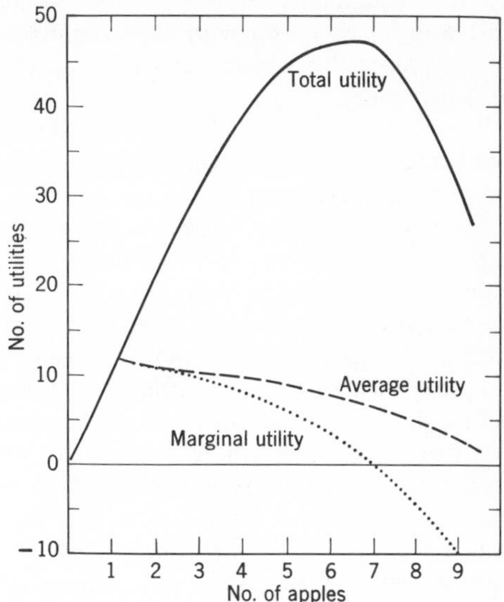

FIGURE 6.3 Hypothetical total, average, and marginal utility functions.

TABLE 6.1 Hypothetical Schedules of Total, Average, and Marginal Utility of a Student Received from Consumption of Apples

No. of Apples Consumed (1)	In Utiles: Hypothesized Total Utility (2)	Average Utility[a] (3)	Marginal Utility[b] (4)
0	0	0	0
1	12	12	12
2	22	11	10
3	31	10	9
4	40	10	9
5	45	9	5
6	47	8	2
7	47	7	0
8	40	5	—7
9	30	3	—10

[a] Total in column 2 divided by number of apples in column 1.
[b] Utility added to total by last unit.

just one commodity at a time but several. Therefore let us go on with the examination of the process by which our student spends his lunch money.

If our student buys only two apples, he could spend the other 50 cents for (*a*) a ham and cheese sandwich or (*b*) a big hamburger and a cup of coffee. In choosing between these two alternatives, he has to compare the potential satisfaction (or utility) from choice (*a*) with that from choice (*b*). He is balancing price and expected satisfaction. Economists can prove with a little algebra that the student will maximize his total satisfaction from apples plus ham and cheese sandwich or apples plus hamburger and coffee at the point where the last penny he spends on each provides equal amounts of utility. If the equation does not balance, our student should seek a more preferred combination of foods for his lunch.

Put in algebraic terms, the following equation represents the student's comparisons as he attempts to equalize his benefits from each item:

$$\frac{MU_{\text{apple \#2}}}{\text{Price}_{\text{apple \#2}}} = \frac{MU_{\text{sandwich}}}{\text{Price}_{\text{sandwich}}}$$

or

$$\frac{MU_{\text{hamburger + coffee}}}{\text{Price}_{\text{hamburger + coffee}}}$$

where MU refers to *marginal utility*. Economists say he is applying the "equimarginal principle" as he seeks the point of equilibrium. You should recognize that we are taking an idealized, short-run view of a consumer's attempts to achieve an equilibrium situation. It is probably quite common for consumers to accept a temporary disequilibrium as they strive for a longer-run balance. In the real world, major expenditures such as buying a new car probably unbalance many consumers' expenditure patterns.

Let us note the assumptions which are involved in the economic theory we are studying: (1) Each consumer can measure the utility derived from each commodity he consumes, referred to as *cardinal utility*. (2) He is aware of all possible alternatives. (3) He is rational so he will select the combination of goods and services which provides the greatest total utility. (4) He is not overly supplied with any of the commodities. (5) No changes are occurring in his income or his tastes and preferences. (6) Nothing is happening which might change the quality of goods and services he is likely to buy.

The assumption that utility is directly measurable in some way has resulted in extensive discussions among economists and in the search for alternative ways of explaining the downward-sloping demand curve. The leading alternative until recent years was the use of indifference curves. They substitute for cardinal utility the assumption of *ordinal utility*. This assumption requires only that each consumer be able to order or rank his preferences for alternative combinations of goods and services.

6.3 THE INDIFFERENCE EXPLANATION OF CONSUMER RESPONSE TO PRICE

Indifference analysis is based on the concept of *ordinal utility,* which involves the ordering of the degree of utility derived from different combinations of goods. It does not require measuring absolute amounts of utility. But it does make use of the utility concept. Indifference analysis rests on a number of assumptions or postulates which will be pointed out after the approach has been described.

Suppose our student likes only candy bars and apples for lunch. First, let us identify the combinations of bars and apples which yield the same total satisfaction or level of utility. Since they are defined as the combinations which satisfy the student equally well, he will be *indifferent* as to which choice to make, whether A, B, C, or D in the following example:

	Hypothetical combinations	
Choice	Apples	Candy bars
A	6	1
B	4	2
C	2	4
D	1	6

Figure 6.4 shows how the points may be joined together to form an indifference curve. Many more could be drawn to represent other sets of combinations, such as I_1, I_2, I_3, I_4 of Figure 6.4. Curves representing different amounts of satisfaction form an indifference map. If you think of the third dimension, total satisfaction or utility, as the altitude, you can visualize the indifference curves as being similar to altitude contours on a topographical map.

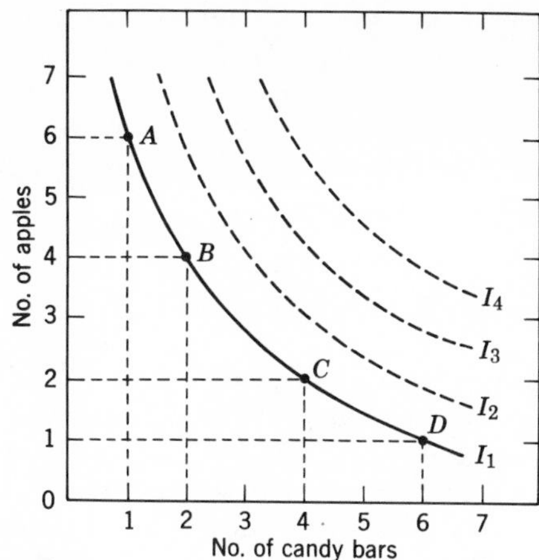

FIGURE 6.4 A student's indifference curves (hypothetical data).

Suppose, again, our student has 70 cents for lunch, and candy bars and apples sell for 10 cents each. He could spend his whole lunch budget for apples or all for candy bars. We assume he acts as a rational consumer and seeks the choice that will put him as high up the hill of total satisfaction as possible. To identify that choice in our hypothetical example, we will use a little mathematics.

First, we must locate our 70 cents budget line (also called an outlay line or consumption-possibility line) in Figure 6.5. If all 70 cents were spent on apples, 7 could be bought. So one end of the line B_1 is the combination of 7 apples and 0 candy bars. Conversely, if all 70 cents were spent on candy bars, 7 candy bars could be bought and 0 apples. The 70 cents budget line B_1 connects these two points. The point at which this budget line barely touches and does not cross (in mathematical language, is tangent to) an indifference curve is the point of highest satisfaction (C_1) and that indifference curve (I_1) is the highest that can be obtained with this budget.

Let us see what happens to our student's choice according to economic theory if we change our example a little by raising the price of apples to 14 cents, keeping the candy price at 10 cents. With the lunch budget of 70 cents our student could buy at the most 5 apples and 0 candy bars or 7 candy bars and no apples. Using these as end-points, we can draw a new budget line B_2. This line touches or is tangent to indifference curve I_2 at point C_2. Curve I_2 is lower down the hill of satisfaction than curve I_1. The rise in the price of apples reduced the total satisfaction obtainable on a 70-cent lunch budget and the likely consumption of apples from 3½ at point C_1 to 2 at point C_2. Theoretically, a series of such price changes and related C's would yield a demand curve for apples by our student, which might look like Figure 6.6.

Similarly, we might hypothesize that the price increase occurred for candy bars and not for apples. In this case our budget line would be B_3 and the point of tangency C_3. Both lines of argument we have just pursued illus-

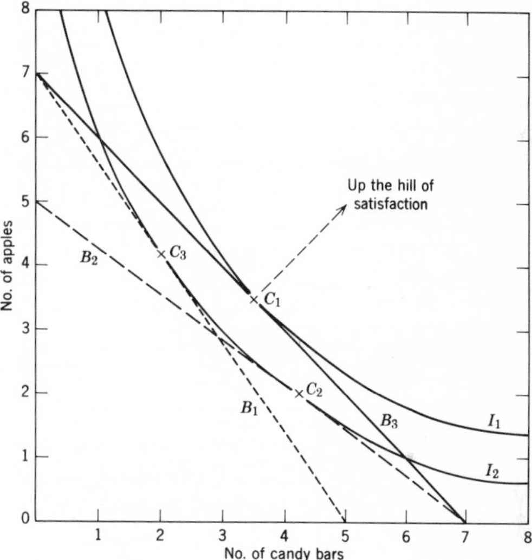

FIGURE 6.5 Effect of change in price.

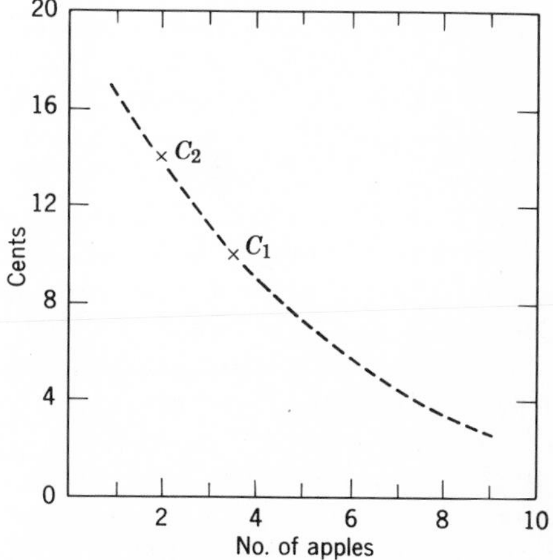

FIGURE 6.6 A student's hypothetical demand curve for apples.

trate the hypothetical effect of an increase in price on the quantity purchased and on total satisfaction.

At each of these consumption points, the C's on the figure, the ratio of the marginal utility of apples to the price of apples will equal the ratio of the marginal utility of candy bars to the price of candy bars. Note in Figure 6.5 that the distances on the budget line (which may be called a *price line* when it is shifting because of price changes) from C_3 to the candy axis, X, and from C_3 to the apple axis, Y, are proportional to their prices.

In the symbolic language we used for the discussion of the cardinal utility approach to demand in Section 6.2.1, the price of apples might be identified as P_{G_1} (the price of the first commodity) and the price of candy bars as P_r (the price of the related good, here a substitute). The lunch budget is comparable with the income concept (Y) in that it places a constraint or limitation on expenditures. Note that it is held constant during this analysis of the effects of price changes just as was done in the earlier exposition of utility theory. Later in this chapter we will hold prices constant and change the budget.[2]

The slope at particular points on the indifference curves in Figure 6.5 indicates the rate of exchange at each point between the two commodities, apples and candy bars. If the student shifted from C_3 to C_2, he would make an even exchange of two candy bars for two more apples. The mathematical value of the slope of the indifference curve at that point measures the *marginal rate of substitution*. Economists have ascertained that it is also the ratio of the marginal utilities of the two commodities.

Consider next the assumptions on which this theory is based. Here, too, we assume no changes in tastes and preferences are occurring and no variation in the qualities of goods and services. The supply of each good is supposed to be homogeneous. Our standard consumer must be able to identify his preferences, be willing to make choices, be rational in seeking to obtain the maximum amount of satisfaction, and not have reached the point of satiety or overabundance for any item. In addition, the consumer must be consistent in his choices. If he prefers A over B, and B over commodity C, he must prefer A over C. Finally, we assume, in the general case, that the marginal rate of substitution is diminishing. This means that when the commodity is scarce, its rate of exchange with other goods is high, and vice versa.

[2] The effects of a change in income (Y) are discussed in Section 6.5.2.

6.4 REVEALED PREFERENCES

Samuelson of Harvard University in 1938 proposed an approach to demand theory which would completely avoid both the use of the utility concept and any reliance on introspection. If a consumer's tastes and preferences do not change and certain other conditions or postulates are met, it should be possible to construct indifference maps from information about preferences revealed by the price and the purchase behavior of consumers. When a consumer spends an observed amount of money for Basket A of goods instead of Basket B, and we know that A costs more than B, that consumer's preference for A is revealed. We must assume that he will be consistent in preferring A to B and never B to A. Under certain conditions, according to economic theorists, it is possible to derive the standard results of the theory of consumer behavior in response to price from the revealed preferences. Among these conditions are the assumptions that the consumer can be induced to buy any collection of goods if its total price is reduced far enough and that he will buy more of a particular good at lower prices unless by so doing he has to cut back on purchases of other goods and services.

Supposedly, consumers can be presented with the alternative combinations of commodities and prices under experimental conditions and their responses can be observed in order to get information needed to construct indifference maps. But the real world of the market place is not this simple. Confirmation of the basic postulates and testing for adherence to them seem to present insuperable problems.

Economic theorists can now demonstrate many of the key ideas of more advanced theory of consumer behavior using revealed preference theory.[3] We will consider the theory further in Chapter 7.

[3] As in pp. 197–205 of Baumol, William J. *Economic Theory and Operations Analysis*.

6.5 RELATIONSHIP OF INCOME TO CONSUMER BEHAVIOR

Up until the last few years, economic theorists were much more interested in the *relationships to prices* of quantities taken from the market than in income-quantity or income-expenditure relationships. In fact, much of the early work on incomes and expenditures was conducted by sociologists or people particularly concerned about social welfare. The surveys of family living mentioned in Section 1.3.3 provided the basis for so-called laws of consumption.

6.5.1 Engel's Law

The best known of the early students of consumption-income relationships was Ernst Engel, a Saxon government statistician. In 1857 he used such data as the basis for his famous law of food consumption (one of the few theories of consumption): ". . . the poorer a family is, the greater the proportion of the total expenditures which it must use to procure food . . ." That law is a simple, empirical and qualitative generalization of the relationship between expenditures and food consumption. It is still widely accepted, but there are some real limitations to its usefulness in analysis of an increasingly complex food economy like that of the United States today.

In effect, Engel used total expenditures as a measure of total purchasing power, rather than income. This has been the usual practice in European studies of cross sections of households, apparently because of difficulties in obtaining income data. In contrast, most American cross-section studies trace the relationships of savings as well as expenditures for different commodities to income. The ratio for food to total expenditures

$$\frac{\text{percentage variation in food expenditures}}{\text{percentage variation in total expenditures}}$$

is somewhat lower than the ratio of food expenditures to income,

$$\frac{\text{percentage variation in food expenditures}}{\text{percentage variation in income}}$$

because part of the variation in income is taken up by the variation in savings. However, Engel's law is stated in such general terms that the term "income" can be substituted for "total expenditures" without changing the interpretation. The latter ratio is called an *income elasticity*, in this instance the income elasticity of food expenditures.

Present-day difficulties in the use of Engel's law do not arise from its failure in application to situations comparable to those from which it is developed. In applications to cross-section survey data, it has failed only when there was a striking lack of homogeneity among the families or when the surveys included only the very poor or the very rich. Furthermore, national averages of income and food expenditures generally seem to conform to the law.

Difficulties are encountered, however, when we seek to quantify the relationship between income and food for analytical use. First, we find that we must specify very carefully the meanings of food and income (or expenditures). Second, as the analysis shifts from static situations described by cross-section data to the dynamic problems of economic development, other variables become relevant. These may be considered either (*a*) as factors to be held constant (*ceteris paribus*) so that the simple form of the law may apply, or (*b*) as additional independent variables in a multivariate relationship. Either way an analyst faces serious operational problems because of a lack of proper measures of the variety of social, economic, and cultural elements entering into economic development.[4]

More directly useful than his law are *Engel curves* (Figure 6.7). These are the curves formed by joining the points for individual observations or group averages for food (either quantities or money values) plotted against comparable data.[5] The slopes of these curves when drawn with double logarithmic scales reflect the relationship between (*a*) the degree of variation in food quantities taken or food expenditures and (*b*) the variation in income among groups of families or households. These slopes measure the *income-elasticity of food consumption* or of food expenditures.

[4] For further discussion, see Burk, Marguerite C. "Ramifications of the Relationship Between Income and Food," *J. Farm Economics* **XLIV**:1:115–125, February 1962.

[5] Some writers apply the term "Engel curve" to curves describing the relationship between the percentage allocated to an item and the level of income.

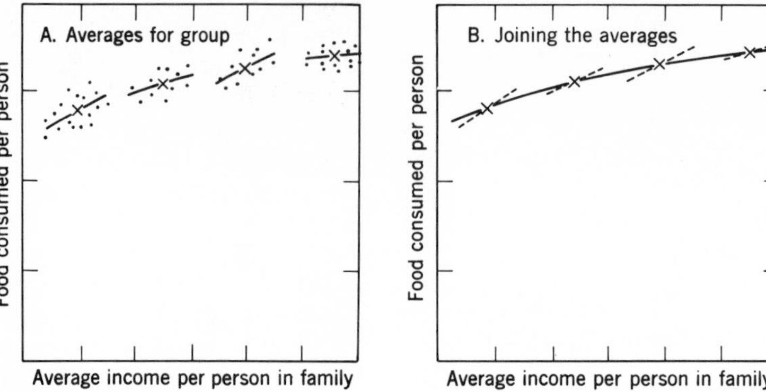

FIGURE 6.7 Hypothetical construction of an Engel curve from survey data for individual households.

6.5.2 Indifference Analysis of Income-Consumption Relationships

Indifference analysis can provide many insights into the potential effects of changes in income on consumer behavior. Let us return again to the student's problem in allocating his lunch budget. Figure 6.8 portrays the same indifference map for apples and candy bars that we used earlier for study of the effect of a change in price. The lunch budget problem illustrates the basic ideas of consumer behavior involved in such choices as between (*a*) cars costing $1000 and $2000 on the one hand and (*b*) the composite of all other goods and services bought by a family plus its allocation of some current income for savings. Exposition of the lunch budget problem is just easier to write and to follow.

Recall our operating assumptions that the student's budget for lunch amounts to 70 cents and that apples and candy bars are priced at 10 cents each. The greatest satisfaction the student could obtain with this lunch budget and his pattern of preferences for apples and candy bars is indicated by the C_1, the point of tangency between curve I_1 and budget line B_1 in Figure 6.8.

Suppose our student loses two dimes down a street grating. His lunch budget is now reduced to 50 cents. The price situation is unchanged. We locate the new budget line as before and identify it as B_3. It is tangent to indifference curve I_3 at point C_3. Therefore with 50 cents to spend our student will get maximum satisfaction if he can buy 2½ apples and 2½ candy bars. We must assume that he can persuade a friend to pool lunch money with him because retail stores do not sell halves of apples and candy bars. Note that the 20-cent decrease in lunch budget resulted in an equal reduction in apple and candy purchases. This follows from the way our hypothetical combinations were set up for the indifference map.

If our student had more than 70 cents to spend for lunch *and* the same combination of preferences *and* faced the same price situation, he would move up the hill of satisfaction along the path identified as the budget-consumption curve in Figure 6.8. This path is in the third dimension crossing the contour lines of the hill. If our problem had involved the choice among cars compared with all other

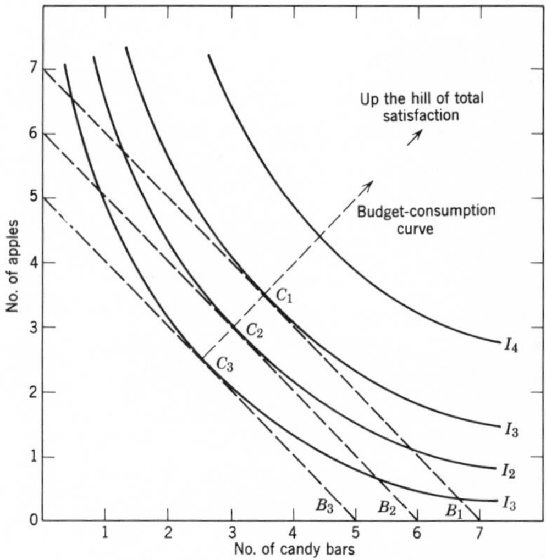

FIGURE 6.8 Effect of change in income.

expenditures plus savings, this path would be called the *income-consumption curve*.

In intermediate books on economic theory, indifference curves are used to analyze a variety of problems. Few of them are concerned with marketing. The possible applications of indifference analysis merit further investigation but not in this introductory text. Next, we must consider other economic ideas about the relationship of consumption to income.

6.5.3 Keynes' Consumption Function

Although Keynes probably knew about Engel's law and was familiar with some of the evidence on income-consumption relationships from statistical surveys, he propounded his consumption function (i.e., consumption as a function of income) on the basis of "fundamental psychological law," which really means introspection. In his words, "The fundamental psychological law, upon which we are entitled to depend with great confidence both *a priori* from our knowledge of human nature and from the detailed facts of experience, is that men are disposed, as a rule and on the average, to increase their consumption as their income increases, but not by as much as the increase in their income. . . ."[6] This phenomenon he called "the marginal propensity to consume." (It is closely related to the concept of *income-elasticity of consumption*. However, it ordinarily is interpreted as referring to the comparison of absolute changes in consumption of all goods and services and income. As you recall, income-elasticity of consumption involves comparison of relative rates of change, usually for one commodity group.) Keynes referred to the proportion of total income allocated to consumption expenditures as the "average propensity to consume."

The statement just cited is the basis for Keynes' two key hypotheses. First, the marginal propensity to consume is positive but less than one. Second, real expenditures for consumption have a stable relationship to real income. His proposition is now described as the *absolute-income hypothesis* because it relates variations in consumption to variations in current income measured in absolute terms.

The underlying assumptions are the familiar ones of rationality on the part of the consumer and of tastes and preferences which do not change during an unspecified time period. The concepts of "*real* income" and "*real* expenditures" are used in referring to changes in income and expenditures *exclusive* of the effects of changes in the price level, e.g., of the effects of inflation or deflation. Thus Keynes followed the conventional procedure of assuming no changes in prices as he focused on the effects of changes in income.

Keynes formulated his microeconomic hypothesis about the income-consumption relationship merely as a step toward his macroeconomic theory that national consumption is a stable function of income. This theory will be considered further in Part III.

In the last 30 years a number of alternative hypotheses regarding income-consumption relationships have been proposed and discussed at length by economists. Among them are several *relative-income* hypotheses. These suggest that consumption is affected by the relationships of one consumer's income to the incomes and consumption of others in his group or to his own past levels of income or consumption. These theories as well as two described as *permanent-income hypotheses* will be discussed among postwar developments in economics in Chapter 7.

[6] Page 96 of Keynes, John Maynard. *The General Theory of Employment, Interest, and Money.*

6.6 SOME PROBLEMS AND LIMITATIONS OF STANDARD THEORY

In order to place later developments of economic theory in proper perspective, we must review the indications of difficulties with standard theory of consumer behavior at its pre-World War II stage of development, note some alternatives proposed concurrently, and summarize some key ideas about important concepts.

Most of the difficulties in empirical applications of the simplified, standard economic theory of consumer behavior can be traced to the assumptions on which each is based. The very abstractness or simplicity of the theory, which is often admired, is the biggest hurdle confronted by marketing people in their attempt to use it in solving the consumption problems encountered in real life. In this section we will consider briefly five types of limitations.

6.6.1 The Concept of a Good

In order to simplify the analysis, standard economic theory of consumer choice assumes a super-standard kind of good without variations in quality, with no separable attributes, and without problems of divisibility. The possibility of different types of goods and services giving rise to different kinds of utility is not considered in the standard theory. However, expositions of the standard theory in textbooks and in economics courses often make use of such differences. The only types of differentiation among goods are the identification of inferior and superior goods, based on income-elasticities, and the discussion of substitutes and complementary commodities.

Thus the economic concept of a good is quite different from the marketing concept. Marketing people are particularly interested in product attributes which need to be identified and matched with present or potential consumer wants. Similarly, marketing theory makes use of several kinds of utility—form, place, time, and possession or exchange. Before World War II, economic theorists paid little attention to the differences between durable and nondurable goods or between goods and services. However, some empirical workers did take these differences into account.

6.6.2 Temporal Dimension

Statements of standard economic theory of consumer choice frequently do not specify the time period in which it operates. This is part of its abstractedness. Marshall's differentiation among market situations, short-run periods, and long-run periods has not been incorporated in the conventional treatment of consumer response to price. Without identification of time periods, standard theory does not provide for analysis of the process of changes in consumer demand and in income-consumption relationships.

With the passage of time, consumer tastes and preferences usually change. Standard theory depicts such changes as raising or lowering the total utility curve and changing the level and location of the marginal utility curve, but it does not provide for analysis of the changes.

Postwar studies of durable goods have clarified the need for a dynamic theory of consumer behavior. Although general economists have continued to abstain from analysis of changes in tastes and preferences, marketing economists analyze such changes along with the study of changes in the supplies of goods and services offered to consumers.

6.6.3 Assumptions regarding the Process of Choice

Economists' emphasis on the process of choice is readily understood when one recalls their basic concern with maximizing returns from the allocation of scarce resources. But the development of consumption economics has suffered from overemphasis on the study of initial or single choices. Most marketing researchers are aware of the significance of consumers' experience in the use of a product for repeat purchases. In contrast, the standard theory of consumer choice considers tastes and preferences to be given or predetermined for each process of choice and makes no provision for interrelationships among choices.

Furthermore, in the opinion of most psychologists and marketing researchers working on consumer behavior, the assumption that consumers have preferences with respect to a good only as a whole and that the whole good yields utility represents a great oversimplification. Even in initial choices, there appears to be a range of consumer expectations regarding the benefits or services or utilities to be derived from a product like an automobile. This matter will be investigated in Chapter 9.

6.6.4 The Robinson Crusoe Characteristics Attributed to the Consumer

Since standard economic theory of consumer behavior with respect both to price and income assumes as given an unchanging set of tastes and preferences for the static situation, there is no provision for examining the effects of wants of the several family members on even initial choices by the household's buying agent. Similarly, this basic assumption has forced many economists to ignore most of modern knowledge being accumulated by other social sciences which is pertinent to interaction among consumers.

Moreover a wide range of problems arising from consumers' lack of knowledge regarding possible alternatives and the characteristics of particular products were considered only by family and consumer economists. But standard theory provided no guidance for their analysis of such problems.

6.6.5 The Standard Consumer

Whereas conventional theory of consumer behavior shifted readily from consideration of the reactions of a representative or standard consumer to the analysis of the total market for a good, economists using the theory to guide empirical studies discovered a variety of inconsistencies. The problems of adding up consumers' characteristics, even such a relatively simple one as income, taxed the analytical ability and the mathematics of a number of economists before the sources of the aggregation problems were understood. (These developments will be reviewed briefly in Chapter 7.) It is now generally recognized that consumers are not all alike and that their differences affect their responses significantly when incomes and prices vary.

The use of a standardized consumer avoided the problem of comparing the utility received by one consumer with that accruing to another consumer from consumption of the same quantity of the same good. Economists have puzzled over this problem for years, although generally viewing it as noneconomic. It still presents difficulties for welfare economics, but that subject matter lies outside the bounds of this book. However, interaction and interpersonal relations have been subjected to some economic study, to be reported in Chapter 7.

6.7 SOME EARLY ALTERNATIVES TO STANDARD THEORY

Despite the general adherence of economists to the standard theory of consumer behavior, either in terms of cardinal or ordinal utility, a number of economists suggested alternatives. As early as 1918, Cassel, a Swedish economist, proposed that the economic theory be based directly on demand functions. But his line of argument led back to preferences.[7] Allen and Bowley, two prominent English economic statisticians, used the marginal rate of substitution between commodities as the basis for consumption theory.[8]

Profiting from the discussions of monopolistic and imperfect competition during the 1930s, Ruby Turner Norris paid particular attention to differences among commodities. She differentiated clearly between commodities requiring careful consumer decision making and petty goods. Consumer demand schedules for the two extreme categories seem to be very different. She argued for a short-run theory of demand which would ". . . treat the main categories of habitually consumed goods in terms of the problem of stocking up and buyer forecast, and should take account of the importance of periodic paydays. . . . The analysis should, further, acknowledge the existence of substantial outlays about which no short-run decisions are made—commitments; it should treat the sometimes large category of purchases made it with complete lack of deliberation—petty goods; and should differentiate sporadic experimental purchases."[9]

Norris's line of argument clarifies the alternative processes consumers use in making expenditures, but it does not help in analysis of the choices made by consumers among alternatives within the categories. Her book contains a number of other ideas which have been explored extensively by economists in recent years.

Statistical analyses of demand became popular in the 1930s and 1940s. They were primarily concerned with macroeconomic relationships. Reference was often made to the theory of demand as the basis for such studies. But analysts like E. Working and Stigler questioned these relationships, and pointed out problems in identifying demand relationships as opposed to supply relationships. Essentially, the statisticians were working with aggregate data and trying to do much the same thing as Samuelson proposed to do on an individual basis with revealed preferences.

6.8 CLARIFICATION OF THE ECONOMIC CONCEPTS OF CONSUMPTION AND EXPENDITURES

The writer has often been surprised by the vagueness with which many economists treat certain key concepts in economics, particularly the concepts of quantity, quality, and value. These three concepts provide alternative meanings of consumption with important differences for economic analysis. The significance of each term appears superficially clear and simple, but actually each is quite complicated. This section will point out some of the complications that must be taken into account as you study consumption aspects of marketing problems. Some of the complications are re-

[7] Page 706, Houthakker, H. S. "The Present State of Consumption Theory," *Econometrica* 29:4:704–740, October 1961.
[8] *Ibid.*

[9] Pages 107–108, Norris, Ruby Turner. *The Theory of Consumer's Demand.*

lated to levels of distribution or stages in the marketing system so we will begin with that concept. The distribution system for food is used as the example because it is more highly developed and better known to most students.

6.8.1 Distribution System

The distribution or marketing system of a country is made up of the firms and agencies engaged in handling, storing, grading, processing, and selling the commodities who operate between the primary *supplier* and the ultimate *consumer*, i.e., the housewife carrying the food out of the grocery store or the patron of a restaurant. Stages in the food distribution system are supplier, wholesale and retail levels, and eating places. Food commodities for United States consumption are supplied by farmers, fishermen, and importers. In some analyses, food processors are treated as suppliers, but they are an intermediate stage. For semidurable goods and durable goods we usually refer to the manufacturer as the primary supplier.

The structure of wholesaling differs so much among commodities that the best way to describe it is to say it is the stage of large-quantity selling and handling for commodities bought in large quantities before the retail level. The term "retail level" usually refers to retail stores, although sometimes eating places are described as retail establishments too. Because eating places add substantial services to the food products they buy, it is helpful to describe them as a separate stage in the distribution system.

The channels of distribution from the producer to the ultimate consumer include some noncivilian channels and the channels to the United States civilian consumer. Supplies flow to non-United States civilian consumers via purchases by the United States armed forces, through commercial channels for export, or through government purchases for export. Civilian consumers obtain their food supplies either from their own subsistence (or home) production or as foods purchased either from the farmers at wayside stands or from distributors, wholesalers, or retailers. Prepared meals and snacks may be purchased in eating places or they may be furnished. For example, many eating places furnish meals to employees as part of their pay. Institutions furnish meals to inmates or patients, as in penal establishments and hospitals. Travelers often receive meals along with other services from air and water transportation agencies.

6.8.2 The Meaning of Consumption

For most economic analyses, food *consumption* means the quantities of food purchased by consumers in retail stores or from other distributors by families or bought as meals or snacks. When economists and marketing people talk about rates of consumption, they usually mean the quantity of a given commodity purchased per person or per family during a specified period, such as a week, month, or year. Because of the relatively great perishability of most foodstuffs, measures of the movements of food through trade channels into domestic consumption are considered to be relatively good estimates of actual consumption in the economic sense of using up resources, although the adequacy of such measures varies widely. Ordinarily, home-produced supplies of food are included in "consumption" or "food use" along with those obtained through marketing channels.

The definition of *consumption of durable goods*, such as automobiles and housing, is much more complex. By definition, durable goods are not entirely consumed in the year in which they are bought. Instead, they have some of the characteristics of capital investments. Therefore analysis of the consumption of durable goods involves the study of changes in inventories, depreciation schedules (describing gradual consumption over a number of years), and variations in the rate of use for durable goods held in inventory.

Let us examine housing consumption to illustrate these differences. Consumption of housing may be defined as the flow of services from the stock of housing structures and sites during a specified period of time. Obviously, the stock of housing cannot be adequately measured by a count of dwelling units occupied. The quantity and quality of services received from a three-room slum apartment occupied by a family of eight differ from services received from an elaborate suburban ranchhouse of eight rooms occupied by a family of three. Therefore it is customary to measure the stock in value terms. The flow of services from owner-occupied and tenant-occupied dwellings has a common denominator of rental value.

To study trends and patterns of housing consumption, we need to identify the principal components of the total stock of residential housing. The categories often used are farm housing and nonfarm housing, and owner-occupied single units, rented single units, and multiple dwellings of different sizes.

Rental value of housing differs from housing expenditures. An elderly couple living in their old home, free from mortage, will have very different current housing expenditures from those of a young couple charged with heavy interest plus payments on a mortgage. Still another reason for the difference becomes clear when you think of a third couple renting a furnished apartment under a contract in which the rent includes heat, all utilities, and rent for the furniture.

Housing has several characteristics which complicate appraisal of its consumption. Consumers face difficult problems in altering their rates of consumption because of the high capital outlays associated with private home ownership, the costs of transfer of ownership, and moving costs. Also, housing has social aspects which are more important than for other consumption goods. A low level of consumption by one group of families, as in a developing slum, materially affects the value of housing consumed by their neighbors and becomes the concern of the whole community.

Consumption of services is even more difficult to define. One definition is the receipt of benefits from performance of certain acts, usually measured by expenditures for them. To be more clear, we also need to review the nature of services. The term "services" refers to such attention as medical care, beauty shops' services, laundry services, and the like. Services have several characteristics which need to be noted as a first step in studying their consumption. They are rather intangible, but they meet some useful purpose or function that consumers want. They have no element of savings so there is no retrievable portion. Often a consumer has the alternative between purchasing a product to supply his services, such as the services of a stove or a clothes washer, or buying the services in the form of factory-prepared foods or laundry services.

Ferber suggests four basic objectives of service expenditures:[10] (1) Consumers buy services for the care and maintenance of their home. These include rent, household utilities, household operation, and domestic service. (2) Another category of service is transportation which may be bought in the form of public transportation, or consumers may derive the services of transportation from operating their own automobiles. (3) Consumers buy the set of services which includes the care and maintenance of other possessions, such as clothing and jewelry services, business services, and furniture and appliance repair. (4) The final category identified by Ferber is the maintenance and improvement of self. Here we find personal care, medical care, recreation, education, gifts, and contributions. Another type of service is the marketing services consumers buy with commodities, such as factory preparation of mixed dishes and meals. But these services are included as a part of the purchase price paid by consumers for meals or for canned chili con carne.

A measurement problem exists for all of these services. We have to rely on costs or expenditures because we have no direct measure of quantity other than times served. Particularly difficult is the element of quality of services because specifications have not been developed. How do you know whether you are getting good dental services or medical services or business services until, in effect, you find that they have not been good?

6.8.3 Quantity

When we use the term *quantity* for a commodity, we are usually measuring quantity in terms of weight or volume or units. But for some services and even for some commodities we have to use value or expenditure as a measure. When a lay person refers to the quantity of food consumed, he usually means poundage. The poundage of a single food is an economically significant measure. But consideration of the total poundage of all foods combined is complicated by the need to distinguish the different poundages as they leave the farm gate, the processor, the wholesale producer dealer, or the retail store. Furthermore, much of the difference in poundage among foods is the difference in water content, and water has not been of such great economic significance in this country that we have to keep track of its content in food.

Quantity problems may arise even for a

[10] Pages 438–439 of Ferber, Robert. "Service Expenditures at Mid-Century," pp. 436–460, Friend and Jones (Editors), *Consumption and Savings*, Vol. I.

single commodity. The obvious example of frozen concentrated orange juice and fresh oranges comes to mind. Should the poundage of the processed product or the weight of the reconstituted juice be added to the retail weight of the fresh oranges if we want to measure in orange consumption? A total which includes the weight of cans of frozen orange juice and the retail weights of fresh oranges obviously has little meaning. Should farm weight equivalents of processed products be added to farm weights of oranges sold to consumers in the fresh form? To handle such problems, a common denominator is needed. There are at least four common denominators for food: (1) pounds at any one of several levels in the fresh or unprocessed equivalents; (2) content of a common ingredient such as fat or calcium in dairy products; (3) food energy value measured in calories; and (4) price-weighted indexes of quantity. An analyst's choice among the alternatives must be based on a clear understanding of what is being measured and why. The common denominator chosen must fit the attributes of the food being studied in a given problem.

Some aspects of the quality of a commodity consumed may vary substantially over time as the technique of production and/or distribution changes. But measurement of changes in quality is so difficult that we usually settle for measuring changes in the quantity, as in the pounds of beef consumed or in the number of cars in use per thousand people. Often we must add qualitative statements about observed changes in the attributes of the units. Combinations of commodities are even more difficult to measure satisfactorily. For many purposes we have to rely on changes in value, using fixed prices, preferably those near the end of the period. This choice of prices for combining the quantities of several commodities becomes particularly significant when we are working on a problem of predicting future changes in the consumption of a group of products.

6.8.4 Price

Prices of commodities are related to the size of the units and to the level of distribution at which the unit is purchased. The level of distribution gives us some understanding, too, of the combination of resources which have gone into bringing the product to that stage of distribution. For example, the on-tree price of oranges represents a very different combination of resources (here purely the farm resources or farm inputs) from the retail price of a can of frozen orange juice. The frozen orange juice incorporates inputs by the farmer in producing the fresh oranges and many types of marketing services. The marketing services include the processing of the orange juice and all of the handling costs for the perishable product. It should be no surprise to anyone to know that prices increase as the commodity moves from the farmer to the consumer.

In this book we frequently use the concepts of current prices and constant or fixed prices. The choice depends upon whether we want to take into account price and quantity changes at the same time or whether we want to hold prices fixed in order to consider changes in quantity only.

6.8.5 Value

The money value of a commodity is determined by multiplying the price per unit by the quantity measured in number of units. *Supplier values* include the values of farm commodities measured at the farm level, the values of fish as caught and sold by fishermen, and the dock or port side values of imported commodities. Dock side prices are used for the imported farm commodities that are not produced in the United States. These are the price and the value which enter into competition with United States-produced commodities. *Wholesale value* data are used extensively for study of some nonfood commodities, but they are not particularly important for study of (overall) food consumption because of the variety of wholesale levels at which they are obtained. *Retail value* data are ordinarily computed using retail store prices. Such value may be based on retail sales. If so, they may involve some problems of coverage because not all commodities sold are included in some of the retail sales data reported by the Federal Government. Often retail value is used as a kind of constructed value series. Such data may or may not include the home-produced or subsistence supplies and the supplies bought in eating places.

Final market value data for food are a combination of (*a*) the farm value of the home-produced or subsistence supplies, (*b*) the retail value of foods sold at retail, (*c*) the wholesale value of any foods sold by wholesalers directly to consumers, and (*d*) the eating place value of meals and snacks. For nonfood commodities the final market value is oftentimes very close to the retail value even though some commodities are bought directly from manufacturers by people having special privileges.

The term *expenditures* is more precisely used to describe money outlays for goods and services by consumers, exclusive of the value of home-produced or subsistence supplies. However, the Department of Commerce series used in Chapter 3 includes the value of most home-produced food and excludes food bought by business firms as meals for their clients.

6.8.6 Index Numbers

In elementary economics you were introduced to the subject of index numbers, particularly with reference to price indexes such as the Consumer Price Index. Such index numbers are based on special kinds of value data. A retail price index involves comparison of the value of the same "market basket" of goods and services at different times or in different places, assuming no change in quality or quantity. A quantity index like the index of per capita food consumption is developed by comparing values of food computed with the same list of prices but with *changing quantities* of individual foods, i.e., changes in the contents of the market basket. Because of lack of detailed data, such quantity indexes may reflect minor changes in quality as well as quantity.

Index numbers are used much more in macroeconomics of consumption than in consideration of microeconomic aspects of consumer behavior so further discussion is deferred to Part III.

6.8.7 The Problem of Quality

Up to this point we have generally ignored the question of the quality of commodities consumed. Quality is usually reflected in the price of a commodity but not always. Just what is quality? A comprehensive definition of quality was developed some years ago by a group of food technologists, economists, statisticians, and home economists: "Quality is the combination of attributes of a product that have significance in determining the degree of acceptability of the product to a user."[11]

It is difficult to evaluate quality, for it may mean a type of food with less waste than another; food that is more mature, more tasty, more tender, or more costly to produce or to market or to buy than some other food; or food that contains more nutrients that are particularly needed. Does a shift from canned to frozen vegetables or from potatoes to leafy, green and yellow vegetables represent an increase in food consumption? Most people would agree that a shift in consumption to a line that is higher priced and that requires more production and marketing services represents an improvement in the quality of food consumed and, for certain analyses, an increase in food consumption.

This leads us back to one of the most difficult problems in economic analysis of consumption—the combinations at the consumer level of marketing services with the raw materials as produced by farmers or fishermen. For example, the addition of some marketing services to food (as in precooking, washing, grading, and so on) may provide attributes desired by consumers; thus its quality is increased. These two elements are distinct to producers and marketing agencies but not to consumers. In this book the distinction between farm and marketing inputs is maintained, with attention directed to the separate contribution of each.

Quality differences in nonfood commodities are even more difficult to measure than for food because of style and fashion elements, lack of industry and government standards for many products, and wide product to product variations in the attributes consumers want. Even casual sampling of the product reports in *Consumers Reports* or *Consumer Bulletin*[12] provides evidence of the difficulties experts have in judging quality differences. Therefore research by business firms on the product characteristics consumers want *and* their ability to identify and use them requires detailed cooperation of their technical staff and market research specialists.

[11] Page 117, *Market Demand and Product Quality*, a report of the Marketing Research Workshop, July 13–21, 1951 at Michigan State College. Report issued by U.S. Agricultural Research Administration.

[12] Published by Consumers Union, Inc., and Consumers Research, Inc., respectively.

7

POSTWAR DEVELOPMENTS IN THE ECONOMICS OF CONSUMER BEHAVIOR

During World War II many economists worked in government agencies on problems related to consumer behavior, such as price controls, rationing, forecasting consumer demand to guide allocations of supplies between military and consumer needs, and development of programs to restrict civilian consumption of critical commodities. These experiences and the improvement in professional preparation of the postwar generation of economists, particularly in mathematics and statistics, have contributed notably to the directions and content of postwar developments in microeconomic theory of consumer behavior and in econometrics.

During the last 20 years there have been serious attempts to deal with each of the limitations in the standard economic theory noted in Section 6.6. Many theoretical articles in professional journals and books on economic theory have been concerned with the assumptions or axioms of the several approaches to consumer choice, especially those of the utility function. Some economists have been trying to reinterpret and broaden the standard theory of consumer choice to differentiate among products and people and to provide a basis for interpreting the structure of consumer preferences. Economic dynamics have been studied in a variety of ways, both for short and extended periods of time. Some knowledge of modern psychology has entered into analysis of short-run shifts in consumer demand. Econometricians have developed mathematical and statistical approaches, variously called models, frameworks, or sets of equations, to take account of interactions among consumers and of changes in consumer behavior, and in factors related to such behavior through the course of time.

This chapter reviews a number of postwar developments. Some of these developments have been based on deductive reasoning using logic and mathematics. Others are really contributions to protheory, i.e., precursors of formal theory, developed by econometricians and other empirical researchers. The selection of topics was based on the criterion of their relevance to the study of consumer behavior from the marketing point of view. Therefore the extensive literature on consumer finances and savings receives only minimal treatment. The presentation of the topics is given in as nontechnical a fashion as possible. For fuller and more precise consideration, students with strong mathematical background should refer to the publications cited. The exposition there is frequently in the precise but abstract language of mathematics.

7.1 DEVELOPMENTS RELATED TO THE UTILITY FUNCTION

Despite the fact that utility analysis has endeavored to relate consumer behavior to prices, there has been little work on such relationships at the micro level in the postwar period. But there has been considerable effort expended on clarification of the axioms or assumptions of the several approaches to consumer behavior, on some extensions, and at least one attempt to redefine the utility function. They are reviewed briefly in this section. More elaborate exposition would require use of mathematics and can be found in the references cited.

7.1.1 Work on Axioms

A number of economic theorists have engaged in painstaking study of the implications and usefulness of each of the sets of axioms underlying the revealed preference explanation of the demand function and the preference or indifference approach based on ordinal utility. If the revealed preference approach can be used to develop all the major ideas of consumer behavior theory, then use of the frequently questioned utility concept could be dropped. In the opinion of some economic theorists, a mathematical economist, Uzawa, has largely succeeded in such a reconciliation, using higher mathematics and symbolic logic.[1] Even if this conclusion becomes generally accepted, certain shortcomings of the successful theoretical basis for demand remain. Revealed preference theory has as yet contributed little to solving the problems of aggregation and interpersonal comparisons.

7.1.2 Extensions of the Utility Function

Some economists had tried to deal with the matters of the existence of commodity groups and their differences within standard theory during the 1930s. But they did not succeed in developing utility theory to distinguish commodity groupings such as food items and clothing items. In the latter part of the 1950s, Strotz and Gorman worked on the concept of the utility tree with branches for major groups of commodities based on assumptions regarding budgeting practices of consumers. If people budget for food separately from clothing, then economic theorists can assume that the two utility functions are separable. In other words, consumer choices within food categories do not affect choices within the clothing category.[2] A number of economists are carrying on further research on this and related problems. Extension of utility theory in this general area is needed to provide a firmer basis for more elaborate demand analyses.

[1] Pages 712–714 of Houthakker, H. S. "The Present State of Consumption Theory," *Econometrica* **29**: 4:704–740, October 1961.

[2] Strotz, Robert H. "The Empirical Implications of a Utility Tree," *Econometrica* **25**:2:269–280, April 1957; Gorman, W. M. "Separable Utility and Aggregation," *Econometrica* **27**:3:469–481, July 1959; Strotz, Robert H. "The Utility Tree—A Correction and Further Appraisal," *Econometrica* **27**:3:482–488, July 1959; Gorman, W. M. "The Empirical Implications of a Utility Tree: A Further Comment," *Econometrica* **27**:3:489, July 1959.

7.1.3 The Utility Function Redefined

A major simplification of utility theory, as noted in Chapter 6, is in the basic view of utility as a function of the good consumed. This view of standard economic theory is very different from the view of commodities held by marketing people who have devoted much attention to attributes of particular products. In two 1966 articles[3] Lancaster suggested a new approach to the utility function, starting from two assumptions: (1) goods are the inputs into consumption activities, and the outputs are characteristics; (2) utility is a function of bundles of characteristics of goods. Lancaster's concept of characteristic seems to be synonomous with the marketing concept of attributes.

The proposed approach is apparently based on the analogies of

(*a*) Consumption activity with production activity

(*b*) Goods with factors of production as inputs

(*c*) Characteristics with commodity output

This approach permits a good to have more than one characteristic so the consumption activity can produce joint outputs. Many characteristics are shared by more than one good. But Lancaster restricts consumer preferences by assuming that they can apply only to the attributes or characteristics and not to the potential of a good to produce the attributes. For the latter, he assumes fixed, technological relationships, *e.g.*, every consumer will view the style of a dress in exactly the same way. This assumption is quite contradictory with the social psychological knowledge of perception. Lancaster considers his assumption of objectivity (the fixed relationships) essential to differentiation between technological adjustments to changes in price (meaning substitution of a less-expensive commodity for a higher-cost item) and private reactions in the form of reordering preference systems (changing basic tastes and preferences).

Lancaster's approach assumes that a con-

[3] Lancaster, Kelvin J. "A New Approach to Consumer Theory," *J. Pol. Econ.* **LXXIV**:2:132–157, April 1966.

———. "Change and Innovation in the Technology of Consumption," *Am. Econ. Rev.* **LVI**: 2:14–23, May 1966.

sumer makes his choices of goods within his total budget according to his choices among bundles of attributes. Such choices are made so as to maximize the utility which can be derived from the consumer's total budget. Lancaster's articles go further in theoretical development and in suggestions regarding possible applications of his theory. A number of difficulties apparently will have to be overcome before general acceptance and empirical usefulness are achieved. The most obvious is the matter of perception previously noted. Another is the inadequate treatment of complex relationships between consumer activity or use and the process of choice. Others are the more usual problems of aggregation and handling of the time factor.

But this innovative economist has opened the door again for possible recognition by economists in general that the processes of choice and use are not identical and that, in modern economies at least, consumers choose products on the basis of their attributes.

7.2 INTERPERSONAL RELATIONSHIPS AND AGGREGATION

One of the important areas of economic theory in which interpersonal relationships now have significance is income-consumption relationships. The adequacy of the absolute-income hypothesis has become doubtful because of inconsistencies between cross-section and time-series data on ratios of consumption and savings to income. Aggregate savings have maintained a relatively stable ratio to income since the 1870s. Experiences with empirical data have led to the proposal of two relative-income hypotheses.

7.2.1 Relative-Income Hypotheses

Based on analysis of data from the 1935–1936 Consumer Purchases Study and the 1941–1942 Study of Spending and Saving in Wartime as well as earlier BLS studies, D. Brady and R. Friedman formed and tested a relative-income hypothesis. They found ". . . a tendency toward a stable relation between the percentage of income saved and the relative income position among families of the same size. . . ."[4] Their evidence indicated that communities with higher general levels of incomes maintained approximately the same proportions for expenditures and savings out of income as communities with comparable distributions of families among different income levels *but* with generally lower levels of average income. They concluded that increases in the demand for goods as real incomes rise are likely to be greater than the income-expenditure relationships across income levels would indicate.

Essential to an understanding of Duesenberry's hypothesis regarding relative income is his argument that the economist's assumption that tastes and preferences are given ". . . implies that the preferences of each individual are independent of the actual purchases of others. . . ."[5] This economist could find no empirical justification for such an assumption. He went on to state, "A real understanding of the problem of consumer behavior must begin with a full recognition of the social character of consumption patterns. From the viewpoint of preference theory or marginal utility theory, human desires are desires for specific goods, but nothing is said about how these desires arise or how they are changed. That, however, is the essence of the consumption problem when preferences are interdependent."[6]

Duesenberry argues that the frequency of contact with superior goods increases primarily as the consumption expenditure of one's neighbors rises. With increased contact, impulses to increase expenditures become most frequent, and the strength of resistance to them lessens. The result is increased expenditures at the expense of saving or through use of credit. He called this phenomenon the "demonstration effect." It parallels sociological reference group theory, but sociologists insist that patterns of role expectations in the reference groups need to be specified before the "demonstration effect" can be ascertained.

7.2.2 Interaction in Household Decision Making

A group of economists participated with other social scientists in a 1958 conference on household decision making. The published papers and discussions indicate general awareness on the part of economists present of the interaction among family members that occurs in the process of consumer choice making by

[4] Page 248, Brady, Dorothy S., and Friedman, Rose D. "Savings and Income Distribution" (Conference on Research in Income and Wealth), *Studies of Income and Wealth,* Vol. 10, pp. 247–265.

[5] Page 13, Duesenberry, James S. *Income, Saving and the Theory of Consumer Behavior.*

[6] *Ibid.*, page 19.

households.[7] Morgan incorporated many of the ideas about the behavior of individuals we reviewed in Chapter 5 in his discussion of the formation of individual preferences. This is the first stage in family decision making.

At the second stage he suggested that ". . . each individual has a strength of preference for a particular alternative depending on his own needs, including his desire to exert power and his desire to give and receive affection by doing what others desire, and that this is weighted by some index of his 'power' in the family. The alternative with the most 'weighted preference' would then win."[8] But he added that power is only potential influence. For a full description of Morgan's model, the reader is referred to the published paper cited.

Sociologists present criticized Morgan's model or framework because it did not encompass group influences. Utilizing small-group theory from social psychology, Thomas reminded the conferees that "an individual's preference, attitude, or opinion may be greatly modified by the group in which he finds himself . . . [and] that the contributions of the individual members often do not combine in any simple manner to produce a group product or decision. . . ."[9] Family variables are probably more indicative of decisions by the family group than individual preferences because of the vigorous exertion of group pressures on individuals to cooordinate their preferences.

The basic idea of economists that a household tends to maximize its collective satisfaction within the limits of its material and nonmaterial resources needs extensive amplification and interpretation before it can be used as a framework for study of decision making by households. As yet, there does not appear to have been any general agreement among economists on the specifications for such a framework.

7.2.3 Problems of Aggregation

As economists worked on data from the 1935–1936 Consumer Purchases Study and on wartime consumption problems, awareness of the magnitudes and implications of variations in consumer reaction grew. Empirical findings indicated wide differences in expenditudes and quantities consumed among families at the same current income level but with different size and age composition, residence, type of employment, race, etc. Analyses of consumer reactions to rationing revealed the great significance of habits and inventories.

Klein, Wold, and Theil, in particular, pointed out that these differences in consumer reactions as well as changes in the distribution of the population by income size raised serious problems. In a comprehensive summary of the problems, Theil identifies the major complication as arising from the fact that in general a macroparameter depends on *all* microparameters, noncorresponding as well as corresponding.[10] For example, when expenditures of individual families are considered to be a function of income and family size, the macroparameter for income depends on both the micro income and size parameters. Over time, the relative importance of the microparameters may change and affect the macroparameters, whereas the microparameters remain relatively unchanged. The assumption of linearity simplifies the aggregation process, but it seems likely that the relationships of a variety of socioeconomic factors to consumption are not linear.

Such problems of aggregation presented part of the challenge to economists participating in the analysis of data from the Bureau of Labor Statistics' 1950 Survey of Consumer Expenditures, Income and Savings, under the auspices of the Wharton School of Finance and Commerce. Their studies employed a variety of formulations to describe relationships of consumer expenditures and savings to a wide range of variables. The studies reported in two volumes edited by Friend and Jones illustrate the fact that advanced methods of econometrics are needed for analysis of the complex problems raised in the process of aggregating behavior of individual families.[11]

[7] Foote, Nelson N. (Editor), *Household Decision Making.*

[8] Page 91 of Morgan, James N. "Household Decision Making," pp. 81–102 of Foote, *ibid.*

[9] Pages 107 and 108 of "Discussion" by Edwin J. Thomas in Foote, *ibid.*

[10] Page 134, Theil, H. *Linear Aggregation of Economic Relations.*

[11] Friend, Irwin, and Jones, Robert (Editors), *Consumption and Saving*, Proceedings of the Conference on: Study of Consumer Expenditures, Incomes, and Savings, Vols. I and II.

7.3 INCORPORATION OF VARIABLES OTHER THAN INCOME AND PRICE

The conventional treatment of other socioeconomic factors (i.e., other than income and prices) has been to combine them in a general factor described as variations in tastes and preferences. This group of factors has often been covered under the economists' assumption of *ceteris paribus* (other factors remain unchanged), or, statistically, they have been included in a residual factor. In the postwar period, economists have used a wealth of new data to explore the relative importance to consumer behavior of three sets of these "other" factors: (1) socioeconomic characteristics of households, (2) financial characteristics, and (3) attitudes and expectations.

7.3.1 Socioeconomic Characteristics

The makeup of families is usually identified in terms of their age, sex, and other family characteristics. Standard economic theory provides no identification of the "consumer." Actually, the consumer unit may be one person or a family living together in a household. A number of empirical considerations, such as the problem of assigning parts of family income and expenditures to individuals within the family, lead most economic analysts to use households as the basic consumer unit. Here, the household is defined as people living together and supported by the common pool of income. Most households are family units. The inclusion of the family in the consumer unit forces recognition of the problems of family decision making, to which reference was made earlier.

David and other economists have concluded that problems in the aggregate preference orderings of individuals within households preclude the relationships of such preference orderings to individual choices. If so, the standard theory of consumer behavior does not appear to be applicable to the internal decision making of families.[12] Therefore David assumed that the preference orderings apply to the entire family. He related family composition characteristics to observations regarding family preferences. He noted the close relationships between (*a*) composition in terms of number, age, family relationship, and sex, and (*b*) the culturally defined needs of the family, the knowledge of the family regarding goods and services, and the expectations and time horizons of families. However, David did not investigate expectations and time horizons.

In order to meet as many of the culturally defined needs as possible, large families take advantage of quantity discounts, do more home production of services wanted by the family, such as gardening and home laundry, and substitute lower-quality goods. Substitution of lower-quality goods is difficult to identify because of lack of data on quality characteristics. But many empirical researchers question the generality of economists' assumption that lower price means lower quality.

For empirical work on the relationship of food composition to consumption, David concentrated on the family-size factor as an independent variable and on consumption of selected durable goods as dependent variables—the value of housing, the value of autos, the expenditures for and frequency of purchases of durable household goods. His statistical analysis revealed significant relationships between family size and the frequency of purchasing durables, the kinds of durables purchased, and the substitution of durables for commercial services. (He excluded the effects of income.) David found larger families to occupy poorer housing, as measured in price per room and number of rooms. The age of the head of the family also influenced the quantity of housing consumed. The consumption of autos was found to be related to marital status, age, and family size in complex patterns.

David concluded that his analysis of the consumption of durables was incomplete because of lack of information on inventories and on the process of changes in family knowledge and cultural adjustments. He also criticized the measures of housing that were available.

Morgan and others at the Michigan Survey Research Center have made a number of studies of the relationships of consumer finances and expenditures patterns to the family life cycle. They have defined a family life cycle as ". . . an idealized construct representing the important stages in the life of an ordinary family. . . ."[13] After considerable experimenta-

[12] Page 6, David, Martin Heidenhain. *Family Composition and Consumption.*

[13] Page 36, Lansing, John B., and Morgan, James N. "Consumer Finances Over the Life Cycle," pp. 36–51 of Clark, Lincoln H. (Editor), *Consumer Behavior*, Vol. II, *The Life Cycle and Consumer Behavior.*

tion, they adopted the following categories: young (head under 45 years), single; young, married, childless; young, married, youngest child under six; young, married, youngest child over six; older (head 45 years and over), married, with children under eighteen; older, married, without children under eighteen; older, single; others.[14]

Because of lack of information on the longitudinal economic history of individual families over their entire life cycle, they were forced to use information on behavior of cross sections of families, classified by these stages in the family life cycle. An analysis of 1953 data indicated that families bought automobiles, TV sets, and homes, in that sequence. Among household items, refrigerators and stoves were particularly important in the early stages of the family life cycle, followed by furniture and washing machines, especially when the children began to arrive. They also found some evidence of a replacement cycle in middle-class families after the children left home.

Among other socioeconomic factors related to consumer behavior which have been studied by economists in the postwar period have been occupation and education. These phenomena apparently influence preferences differently for different types of goods. They have less effect on food and more on clothing, recreation, and outlays for further education. The relationship of formal education to expectations regarding future income and to time horizons for family budgeting has challenged economists in recent years. Morgan studied intensively the impact of education on the consumption of housing and found it to be quite an important factor. However, he concluded:

> . . . the explanation of the effect is probably not because of differential long run or lifetime incomes, past or expected, but because of more immediate direct effects of education, such as short run income security and stability, the capacity to plan ahead, and the resulting willingness to make contractual commitments. . . .[15]

Watts used occupation and education along with several other socioeconomic variables ingeniously in an investigation of the relationship between long-run income expectations and savings. He hypothesized that household expectations of future income over a relatively long horizon are systematically related to current income, occupation, education, race, and location. His investigation of long-run income expectations is related to work on permanent income reported under economic dynamics, Section 7.5. From an analysis of data from the Survey of Consumer Finances, Watts concluded that the demographic variables of age, occupation, race, education, and location are empirically correlated with savings behavior. More precisely, he found that they interact with the more usual economic variables, income and liquid assets. Because the investigation by Watts dealt primarily with consumer savings, we shall not consider further reports on his findings. However, the interested reader is referred to the citation given below.[16]

7.3.2 Family Characteristics

The relevance of recent income changes and of wealth, particularly in the form of liquid assets, has been recognized by economists for many years. Measurement of consumers' wealth has encountered many difficulties, however. Two types of income hypotheses which take variations in income into account have been proposed since World War II. One was Duesenberry's hypothesis relating consumption to past income and two types of permanent-income hypotheses. These will be discussed in Section 7.5.

The postwar availability of data on liquid assets from Surveys of Consumer Finances by the Federal Reserve Board and the Michigan Survey Research Center has expedited economic analysis of the relationships of liquid assets to expenditures on durable goods and to other aspects of consumer behavior. An example of other aspects is discretionary or noncontractual savings. Consumer stocks of liquid assets were built up during World War II and significantly affected expenditure patterns in the early postwar period. Their effect decreased in subsequent years, according to research reported by Klein.[17]

[14] *Ibid.*, page 39.

[15] Page 306, Morgan, James N. "Housing and Ability to Pay," *Econometrica* **33**:2:289–306, April 1965.

[16] Watts, Harold W. "Long-run Income Expectations and Consumer Savings," pp. 101–144 of Dernburg, Thomas S., Rosette, Richard N., and Watts, Harold W. *Studies in Household Economic Behavior.*

[17] Pages 234–238, Klein, Lawrence R. (Editor), *Contributions of Survey Methods to Economics.*

A macroeconomic analysis of postwar expenditure-income relationships by the author of this text used data on changes in liquid assets from Surveys of Consumer Finances and the U.S. Department of Agriculture and U.S. Department of Commerce information on income and food expenditures. The findings supported the hypothesis that extraordinarily high food expenditures in 1947 and early 1948 were due in large part to a temporary lag in the adjustments of consumer expenditure and saving patterns to a changing situation.[18] Short supplies of autos and other durable goods prevented many consumers from using their liquid assets to purchase durable goods as fast as they wished.

Based on analysis of reinterview data from the 1957 and 1958 Surveys of Consumer Finances, Fisher found that the previous use of credit was a significant factor related to subsequent behavior in purchasing durable goods. It was even more significant in the choice between the use of cash or credit to finance such purchases. The effect of liquid asset holdings on subsequent purchase behavior seems to be related to the types of liquid assets available and to previous and current use of credit.[19]

Morgan examined empirical data on the relationships of liquid assets to expenditures and savings for a number of years and formulated the following general statement, which he viewed as the starting point for further research:

> In general, then, assets can be looked at in several ways: as allowing added consumption when pressures exist; as resulting from conscious planning to take care of pressures (e.g., one expects a fluctuating income); as indicating intentions to make large expenditures (e.g., for a house) for which the assets were accumulated; or as indicating a high aspiration level for the accumulation of savings and hence a high average and marginal propensity to save. . . .[20]

[18] Page 292, Burk, Marguerite C. "Changes in the Demand for Food from 1941 to 1950," *J. Farm Economics* **XXXIII**:3:281–298, August 1951.

[19] Fisher, Janet A. "Consumer Durable Goods Expenditures, with Major Emphasis on the Role of Assets, Credit, and Intentions," *JASA* **58**:303:648–657, September 1963.

[20] Pages 185–186, Morgan, James N. "Analysis of Residuals from 'Normal' Regressions," Chapter IV in Klein (Editor), op. cit.

7.3.3 Attitudes and Buying Intentions

Development of knowledge of the role of expectations in consumer behavior has been a major contribution of George Katona, who is both a psychologist and an economist. He has stressed for many years the importance of *willingness* to buy as well as *ability* to buy. Under his leadership, the annual series of Surveys of Consumer Finances was started, first by the U.S. Department of Agriculture and then at the Michigan Survey Research Center. The research on attitudes and buying intentions is largely macro in magnitude and concerned with short-run economic changes, but it is discussed here because of his contribution to knowledge of microeconomic behavior of individual consumers.

This discussion is based almost entirely on Maynes's appraisal of the theoretical and empirical studies of consumer attitudes and buying intentions.[21] The primary focus of the SRC measurement of these phenomena has been to forecast short-run changes in consumer durables, the most important and volatile or changeable part of consumer expenditures. According to proponents of the consumer attitudes and buying intentions approaches, consumers vary for several reasons in responses to stimuli from their objective economic environment. First, their tastes are changing. Second, information they hold about the environment may vary from the more precise knowledge held by specialists, and their understanding of the meaning of the information may vary. Third, a particular change in the environment may be associated with different expectations for the future and result in different spending behavior on the part of different groups of consumers.

These approaches allow changes in responses to stimuli. Maynes puts it this way, ". . . attitudes directly record the decision-maker's perception of economic realities just prior to the period of forecast. Analogously, buying intentions directly record the probable purchase action of the decision-maker again just prior to the period of forecast. . . ." (Page 15.) In effect, the decision maker reports his evaluation of the purchase situation.

[21] Maynes, E. Scott. "Consumer Attitudes and Buying Intentions: Retrospect and Prospect," Manuscript, Instituto Torcuato di Tella, Centro de Investigaciones Economicas, Buenos Aires, Argentina.

Katona and Mueller, the principal proponents of the attitudes approach, argue that the timing of purchases and hence the short-run variations in durable spending are crucially dependent upon the willingness of consumers to buy. Their willingness in turn depends upon their short-run economic expectations or attitudes. Katona and Mueller do not interpret expectations and buying intentions literally but as viewpoints for psychological sets which may affect future behavior. They use only combinations of responses to a number of questions.

In recent years other economists have begun to use a probabilistic approach to buying intentions. This means that they are interpreting buying intentions as probability statements about future actions the respondents intend or expect to take. If this approach is used, then one must recognize that the anchor point of the response scale can differ among respondents and from time to time.

Two tests have been applied to appraise the predictive value of attitudes and buying intentions. One uses the data from cross-section surveys, especially resurveys, relating subsequent actions to preceding attitudes and buying intentions. The second approach compares the time series of changes in consumer attitudes or buying intentions with subsequent changes in aggregate expenditures for consumer durable goods.

Cross-section tests by a number of investigators have indicated that buying intentions have predictive value but that consumer attitudes do not. Also, buying intentions have greater predictive value than disposable income or other objective economic variables.

Time-series tests—incorporating attitudes, disposable income, and buying intentions—indicate that attitudes and disposable income combined have predictive power, whereas the buying intentions variables are not statistically significant. Maynes found that this combination of attitudes and disposable income predicted equally well such dependent variables as the number of cars sold, expenditures on cars, and installment credit extended, and expenditures on nonautomotive durable goods. The general acceptance of attitude measures by economists is indicated by their use in the Brookings Quarterly Econometric Model of the United States. They are the best predictor of expenditures for new cars, which are the most volatile component of consumption.

Maynes points out that attitudes are more important as indicators in a period of relative instability in the economic environment (such as in 1952–1960) than in a stable period (such as 1961–1965). In the more stable economic period, changes in disposable income prove to be a satisfactory predictor of variations in expenditures.

Adams applied factor analysis to individual variables based on responses to eight different questions about attitudes. The three items related to measurement of short-term business outlook explained 52 percent of the variance in the attitudes index; three price expectation questions explained 16 percent; the three buying plans questions explained 23 percent; and personal financial expectations 6 percent.[22]

Other research combined with Adams' work indicates that behavior in buying stocks and behavior in purchasing consumer durables are responsive to common expectational elements.

Maynes has carefully analyzed the two parts of the paradox: (1) cross-section tests indicate that buying intentions are successful predictors, and (2) time-series tests indicate that attitudes are better predictors. He concluded, first, that attitudes are inappropriate for forecasting some types of individual behavior such as that which is based on habit, or on the sequential actions of the period immediately after the purchase of one durable good, a refrigerator, for example. Second, the problem of measuring attitudes is probably much greater than that for buying intentions. In part, this results from the fact that attitudes are more difficult to code. The Survey Research Center's scale for attitudes permits only three responses to each of six questions. Different people are likely to have in mind different anchor points or bases for the scales and different ideas about the intervals between the scale points. Maynes cited Adams' empirical study as evidence for his explanation. Third, he concludes that the problem with buying plans in the time-series tests appears to rise from inadequate sampling. The frequency of plans to buy a particular good in a particular time period is low.

The Bureau of the Census is now carrying on extensive research, seeking to improve the

[22] Adams, F. Gerard. "Consumer Attitudes, Buying Plans, and Purchases of Durable Goods; A Principal Components, Time Series Approach," *Review of Economics and Statistics* **XLVI**:4:347–355, November 1964.

attitude and buying intention approaches to predicting short-run consumer behavior.

7.4 PROCESS OF DECISION MAKING

Economists frequently view the household as a decision-making organism with activities that are counterparts of those of a business firm. After World War II there was great interest in studying decision processes of households. The decision process is described in terms of some objectives or values to be fulfilled, some facts about alternatives, and some inferences drawn from the values and facts.

Von Neumann and Morgenstern proposed a theory of games which explores ways of extending the concept of rational behavior to the decision situations which involve uncertainty in the forms of struggle, outguessing a rival's counterstrategy, and bargaining. Unfortunately, the theory is largely applicable to two-person situations (the two-person, zero or constant-sum type) and is based on very strict assumptions regarding rationality and utility maximization as well as the highly unrealistic assumption of no communication among players. It has not yet proved very useful in empirical study of consumer decision making.

7.4.1 Decision Rules

However, extension of the theoretical approach to games against nature has provided some frames of reference for examining alternative strategies or courses of action. Baumol argues that the appropriate decision rule must vary from person to person and from one situation to another.[23] One decision rule is the maximum criterion according to which a decision maker determines the worst that could happen under several alternative choices (max) and chooses the one whose "worst" would be the least (min).

Another decision rule is called the Bayes criterion. If one has no information about the relative probability of some unknown possibilities, one should assign them equal probabilities. Because of the problem of identifying such unknown possibilities, a variant of the Bayes procedure is for the decision maker to assign subjective probabilities to the sets of outcomes he considers to be possible results of his alternative lines of actions or strategies. Then he can evaluate each strategy as follows:

Valuation of Strategy

$$A = (\text{Outcome}_{1A} \times \text{Probability}_1) + (\text{Outcome}_{2A} \times \text{Probability}_2), \text{etc.}$$

$$B = (\text{Outcome}_{1B} \times \text{Probability}_1) + (\text{Outcome}_{2B} \times \text{Probability}_2), \text{etc.}$$

A third decision rule, called the "minimax regret criterion," has been proposed by Savage. He hypothesizes that people may be more interested in minimizing their regret over unfavorable outcomes of decisions than in maximizing utility. As used here, "regret" refers to the difference between a reward of satisfaction actually derived from the choice and the maximum possible satisfaction which might be viewed later in retrospect. Savage's minimax criterion calls for the strategy of choosing the course of action which minimizes the potential differences between the actual and the maximum possible satisfaction.[24]

The extent to which people utilize alternative decision rules has been researched under experimental conditions by psychologists. But little is known about the actual strategies used by consumers in their decision making. The theoretical development provides opportunity for interesting, creative research which has potential significance for determination of marketing policies.

7.4.2 Real Decision Processes

Decision rules for coping with uncertainties appear quite complex compared with the classical theory of consumer behavior with its assumptions of fixed and known alternatives and known consequences. Modern psychological theories described in Chapter 5 point to the intervention of perception and cognition between the consumer decision maker and his objective environment. Such intervention makes real decisions of consumers far more complex than modern decision theory or economic theory can handle. It is obvious that we need a theory for the process which takes account of the fact that alternative choices for real consumers must be sought—frequently involving expenses, time, and effort—and the likely consequences are generally difficult to ascertain.

[23] Page 552, Baumol, William J. *Economic Theory and Operations Analysis.*

[24] *Ibid.*, pp. 555–556.

The social psychological concept of role is directly applicable to consumer decision making. Simon, an economic expert in the theories of decision making, defines a role as:

> . . . a social prescription of some, but not all, of the premises that enter into an individual's choices of behavior. Any particular concrete behavior is a result of a large number of premises, only some of which are prescribed by the role. In addition to role premises, there will be premises about the state of the environment based directly on perception, premises representing beliefs and knowledge, and idiosyncratic premises that characterize the personality. . . . [25]

The analysis of decision making in terms of decision premises provided a conceptual framework for computer programming of human decision processes. Management scientists have used several programming devices to maximize certain outcomes within specified limitations, using specified relationships of inputs and outputs. An example of programming consumer decision alternatives is Smith's work on alternative diets within certain constraints as to cost, selected consumption patterns, minimum supplies of a number of nutrients, and specified nutrient contents of major foods. The diets that have emerged from such computations have been called "curios" by Peryam, a psychologist formerly affiliated with the U.S. Quartermaster Corps. But Peryam was challenged by the possibility of maximizing probable acceptance or preference by the armed services under a set of restrictions including food preferences as well as nutrition and costs.[26]

Particularly important for future development of the theory of consumer behavior is Simon's hypothesis "that economic man is a *satisficing* animal whose problem solving is based on search activity to meet certain aspiration levels rather than a *maximizing* animal whose problem solving involves finding the best alternatives in terms of specified criteria. . . ."[27]

Empirical research on the process of consumer choice making will be reported in Chapter 9.

In recent years Simon has worked with psychologists in developing a more general theory of human problem solving. It appears to be applicable to both the process of choice and the process of use. As set forth by Newell, Shaw, and Simon, the theory of human problem solving requires a control system consisting of memories, a number of "primitive" information processes ("primitive" meaning fundamental), and a carefully defined set of rules for combining these processes into processing programs. They state that ". . . an explanation of observed behavior of the organism [consumer] is provided by a program of primitive information processes that generates this behavior."[28] They hypothesize that a different program would be needed for each category of situations, but programs should generally be similar for human subjects with similar characteristics and faced with comparable tasks. Their published article defines an information-processing program for discovering proofs for theorems in logic and compares the program qualitatively with the behavior of human problem solvers described in psychological literature.

Finally, we turn to some ideas about consumer behavior reported independently by Strotz and Clarkson. They hypothesize that each consumer decides first for a given period of time what proportion of income to spend on each category of commodities.[29] Clarkson suggests that the next decision is whether to use cash or to make monthly payments to secure the commodity or service. Both economists agree that the consumer then proceeds to decide how to maximize utilities from expenditures within these categories. Clarkson follows Simon in suggesting that the requirement of maximization from all alternatives be replaced by the more operational use of specified criteria to decide when the search for alternatives has been completed. A fourth set of decision

[25] Page 274, Simon, Herbert A. "Theories of Decision-Making in Economics and Behavioral Science," *Am. Econ. Rev.* **XLIX**:3:253–283, June 1959.

[26] See Smith, Victor E. "Linear Programming Models for the Determination of Palatable Human Diets," *J. Farm Economics* **XLI**:2:272–283, May 1959, and the discussions by David R. Peryam and Charles J. Zwick which follow, pp. 302–308.

[27] Page 277, Simon, op. cit.

[28] Page 151, Newell, Allen; Shaw, J. C.; and Simon, Herbert A. "Elements of a Theory of Human Problem Solving," *Psychological Review* **65**:3:151–166, May 1958.

[29] Strotz, Robert H. "The Empirical Implications of a Utility Tree," op. cit., and Chapter 8 of Clarkson, Geoffrey P. E. *The Theory of Consumer Demand: A Critical Appraisal.*

processes would handle expectations regarding future behavior of prices and other important variables utilizing pattern recognition. (The theory of optimization over time, which will be discussed in Section 7.5.1, is pertinent here.) Finally, a set of decision processes would be provided to resolve conflicting situations and govern the use of substitutes and complements over a number of time period. Clarkson's suggestions reflect many of the postwar developments in economic theory and emphasize the need for establishing empirical validity of consumption theory.

7.5 ECONOMIC DYNAMICS

Economists have used a variety of approaches to economic dynamics. In this section we will examine several pertinent theoretical developments and some econometric efforts.

7.5.1 Optimization of Utility Over Time

Modern economic theory of optimization of utility over time is based on the use of credit markets to adjust purchasing power to wants over a number of time periods, such as years. Following some earlier ideas of Irving Fisher, Henderson and Quandt provide a comprehensive exposition in terms of a consumer's borrowing and lending in a bond market as he programs his consumption expenditures on n goods over a horizon or expected duration of time (perhaps a lifetime) containing T periods.[30] At the time of initial planning, each consumer plans as if he knew how his tastes and preferences will change. He can change plans if his tastes and preferences vary from earlier expectations.

Henderson and Quandt also postulate that a consumer has certain expectations regarding earned income each year throughout his life. Changes in bond holdings provide for accumulation and depreciation of assets and permit matching expenditures to wants in particular years. Income expectations plus initial wealth place the budget constraints on purchases of goods and services. The reference cited uses differential calculus to demonstrate the hypothesis that utility maximization requires equating rates of substitution between each pair of commodities in every pair of periods to the ratio of their discounted prices. Selection of an optimal time pattern requires the selection of optimal values for total consumer expenditures on the various marketing dates (dates for shifting assets) and the selection of optimal commodity combinations corresponding to the expenditures planned for each marketing period. The chapter also includes a discussion of the substitution and income effects of a change in the rate of interest, to which students with a substantial background in economics are referred.

In the 1930s Hicks stressed the *ex ante* or expected nature of income in the current income-consumption relationship. After the war, several economists developed hypotheses about the relationship of income to consumption, as mentioned earlier. Duesenberry's version of the *relative-income hypothesis* related the current level of expenditure by a consumer unit to its peak income or expenditures in the past, as well as to current income.[31]

7.5.2 Permanent Income Hypothesis

More elaborate hypotheses have been propounded and tested by M. Friedman and Modigliani, Brumberg, and Ando (identified as M-B-A). Friedman's *permanent-income hypothesis* is based on three sets of assumptions. First, both the current income and current consumption of a consumer unit in an identified period, such as a year, have *transitory* and *permanent* components. *Permanent income* for the period is conceptualized as the product of wealth expected over the consumer unit's lifetime (with the appropriate discounts to derive present values) and the rates at which the expected receipts are discounted. (It should be noted that Friedman uses a moving average of past incomes as a measure of permanent income with effects distributed over a several-year period.)

The second assumption basic to the permanent-income hypothesis is that permanent consumption has a fixed ratio k to *permanent income*. This very complex ratio depends partly on the interest rate, partly on the ratio of material to total wealth, including human resources of the unit, and on age, tastes and preferences, and minor characteristics of the consumer unit. But the k is independent of the level of permanent income. Consumption is defined in terms of quantities of goods and services used up in the period.

A third assumption is that *transitory* and

[30] Chapter 8 of Henderson, James M., and Quandt, Richard E. *Microeconomic Theory*.

[31] Duesenberry, op. cit., Chapter V.

permanent income are not related in a systematic fashion. Similarly, transitory and permanent consumption are uncorrelated. This assumption in particular has been subjected to a variety of empirical tests with controversial results.

In some respects, the M-B-A hypothesis is more of a *permanent-wealth* hypothesis than a *permanent-income* hypothesis. It is sometimes described as a *relative-income hypothesis*. The authors have identified its four basic propositions as: (1) A household's "scale of living" (Friedman's permanent level of consumption) is determined by the members' perception of their present and expected resources. (2) The actual expenditures by the household in any selected period may vary in a random fashion around their "scale of living." (3) The household's income is also related to the overall level of resources to which its standard or scale of living is anchored. Accordingly, income and scale of living are likely to be systematically related. (4) The ratio of the scale of living to the level of resources is expected to be the same at all levels of resources.

The level of resources refers to the total value of resources expected by the household (family) to be available for consumption over its entire life cycle. It is defined as "the sum of the household's net worth at the beginning of the period . . . plus the present value of its non-property income minus the present value of planned bequests, . . ."[32]

The M-B-A hypothesis differs from the Friedman hypothesis primarily because its precise formulation in mathematical form provides for changes in (*a*) the ratio of the scale of living to the value of lifetime resources, and (*b*) the value of such resources. These changes will depend upon changes in family characteristics, such as age and family size. M-B-A did not assume that transitory income and transitory consumption must be unrelated. An example of transitory income was the unexpected dividends paid to veterans in 1950 by the National Service Life Insurance program.

The two hypotheses have challenged extensive theoretical work and empirical research. In a 1962 article Ferber summarized many of the arguments and research endeavors pro and con.[33]

These developments led to general recognition that variabilities in income may have varying effects on consumption patterns. The hypotheses provided a conceptual basis for studying these effects and for contributions to development of a theory of consumer behavior closer to reality.

7.5.3 Period or Process Analysis

Analysis of the process of economic change or economic dynamics has been variously identified as "process" or "sequence" analysis or "period" analysis. The relationship of the three terms may be clearer if we restate the preceding sentence thus: Economists study sequences of events in the process of economic change by analyzing and relating events in one period to events in preceding and subsequent periods. Most of the expositions of the subject are in mathematical terms. Baumol's presentation in Part III of his *Economic Dynamics* is the basis for the following discussion.[34]

The quantities and prices with which economics is concerned may be (1) *flows* through time, such as the quantities consumed day by day, or (2) *stocks* at a moment in time, such as wheat stocks as of January 1, 1966, or a consumer's inventory of durable goods at the time of an increase in his pay. The prices may be the prices of bread bought month by month or the value of a family home. Because many of the prices and quantities are changing continuously, precise economic treatment would require use of time rates of flow at each and every moment of time to study the process comprehensively. To avoid the complexities of such a treatment and to make economic analysis more manageable, economists divide the flows into amounts during specified periods and trace economic changes step-by-step through time for use in *period analysis*. Period analysis seeks to explain the events of one period by considering events of previous periods and changes in outside factors, referred to as exogenous variables. A microeconomic example is the study of purchases of clothing by a family in one year by reference to its rate of purchases in preceding years, its

[32] Page 78, Modigliani, France, and Ando, Albert. "The 'Permanent Income' and the 'Life Cycle' Hypothesis of Saving Behavior: Comparison and Tests," pp. 49–174, Vol. II in Friend and Jones (Editors), op. cit.

[33] Ferber, Robert. "Research on Household Behavior," *Am. Econ. Rev.* **LII**:1:19–63, March 1962.

[34] Baumol, William J. *Economic Dynamics*.

inventory at the beginning of the year, and the exogenous factor of changes in the prices of clothing, the latter being outside the control of the family.

Period analysis makes extensive use of the concepts of the *ex ante* and *ex post*. *Ex ante* refers to expected or planned events; e.g., the *ex ante* concept of the income of the family refers to the income it expects as of, say, January 1st to have in the year 1965. The *ex post* concept describes actual events, such as the family's awareness of its actual income in 1965 when the head of the household added up his income for the Federal income tax forms on January 10, 1966, finding that it totaled $1000 more than he had expected on January 1, 1965, because of wage increases. Thus we can understand more closely that the family did its buying and saving during 1965 based on adjustments of the original or *ex ante* estimate of income in that year.

Theoretical analysis of period to period changes is based on the assumption that plans and expectations are formed at the beginning of each period and that the length of the period provides time for execution of the plans but not for changes in them. The latter is required for the analysis of relationships between *ex ante* and *ex post* magnitudes. Economists analyze inconsistencies or incongruities as examples of variations from the expected equilibrium and seek to determine their effects in the forms of changes in other economic phenomena.

Baumol's presentation includes, *first*, discussion of some simple dynamic models in the form of difference equations which permit measurement of future effects of initial conditions (e.g., initial inventory of durable goods) and specified relationships between independent and dependent variables (e.g., income and clothing expenditures). *Second*, it describes differential equation systems for study of economic changes on the assumption of constant rates of change, using differential calculus. Baumol points out difficulties involved in application of linear models (using first degree or straight line relationships) to a number of macroeconomic problems, most of which are outside the field of consumption economics.

Econometricians have used *distributed lags* to take account of the decreasing effects of past events in subsequent periods. A *lag* is defined as a lapse of time between a causal event and its effect on other events. The lag might have a specified time period, say three months. For most economic phenomena, the effects are distributed over many months. Examples are the time required for consumers to change their buying habits in response to changes in price relationships and the time required for producers to make technological changes, substitution less expensive inputs (e.g., plastics for higher-priced metals). Several analytical approaches have been suggested by econometricians.[35] But these approaches are too technical for presentation here. Instead, we will review two examples of the use of macroeconomic models with lagged variables.

7.5.4 Persistence of Habit

Brown studied the relationship between total Canadian disposable income and total consumption expenditures (both in 1935–1939 dollars) for the periods 1926–1941 and 1946–1949. He used a model or mathematical equation in which consumption expenditures were estimated with a linear function of total disposable income. From comparisons of the estimates with actual expenditures in 1926–1941, he concluded:

> When income is rising, consumer expenditure lags behind the simple relationship . . . and we have a residual; when income is falling, once again consumer expenditures lag behind and we have positive residuals. . . .[36]

Comparable calculations for 1946–1949 led to quite different results. Either the prewar relationship had changed or new phenomena had entered in. The wartime accumulations of liquid assets and deferred wants were likely causes.

Brown explored several hypotheses to explain the lag in consumer expenditures after changes in income, deciding that his analysis supported best the hypothesis that "the lag effect was produced by the consumption *habits* which people formed as a result of past consumption. . . ."[37] He used a time lag of one year and subdivided disposable income into

[35] Pages 111–116, Foote, Richard J. *Analytical Tools for Studying Demand and Price Structures*, U.S. Department of Agriculture, Agriculture Handbook No. 146.

[36] Page 357, Brown, T. M. "Habit Persistence and Lags in Consumer Behavior," *Econometrica* **20**: 3:355–371, July 1952.

[37] *Ibid.*, page 359.

wage and nonwage components on the basis of earlier research. Such research has indicated differences in the income elasticities for salary and wage earners as opposed to the income elasticities for the self-employed group and households receiving interest and rent payments.

Brown explored the implications of the hypothesis that consumers are slow to adjust because of memories of past peaks of real income (Duesenberry's hypothesis, among others) and the hypothesis that "past real consumption patterns and levels form consumption habits which persist long enough to slow down the effects of current income changes on current consumption."[38] The latter hypothesis led Brown to conclude that any level of actual consumption represented the accumulation of all past experiences, therefore a single lag of one time period might be satisfactory. This conclusion raises questions regarding the length of time period to be used in such analyses.

7.5.5 Microanalytic Models of Socioeconomic Systems

Orcutt and his colleagues at the Social Systems Research Institute of the University of Wisconsin have been developing microanalytic, dynamic models for major sectors of the United States economy.[39] To cope with unsolved problems in aggregating microrelations, their models are being built up from microcomponents which are decision units such as individuals, households, and firms. Activities of these units are identified in terms of inputs, status, and output variables which may refer to either stocks or flows. The awesome complexity of the models is indicated by the fact that each component's variables must be identified for each date and has its own behavioral relationships (called "operating characteristics") to generate updated values of status variables and values for output variables.

The second major type of components for their models is the markets through which flow the outputs of decision units which are distributed as inputs to other decision units. To make the models operational it is necessary to obtain data for a large sample of the same components in successive time periods using a scientifically designed and executed sample survey. Computers now being built are almost large enough to handle the data, but Orcutt has estimated the cost of setting up the full-scale model at about 10 million dollars per year for ten years.[40] In a discussion of Orcutt's paper, Summers pointed out that this would represent as much as a tenth of the total economic research resources of the country.[41]

The researchers have been developing approximations of the operating characteristics or behavioral relationships by running regressions on data from the series of Surveys of Consumer Finances of the Michigan Survey Research Center. The Goldberger-Lee paper already cited reported some of their research along these lines, but a number of statistical problems were encountered, and the findings were not particularly satisfactory.[42]

7.5.6 The Houthakker-Taylor Study of U.S. Consumption Expenditures

The econometric demand study by Houthakker and Taylor utilized U.S. Department of Commerce data on personal consumption expenditures in the United States in 1929–1961 and developed projections for 1970.[43] They formulated a dynamic model incorporating the idea that current expenditures depend on current income and prices and on pre-existing inventory of the commodity being studied. They hypothesized that through current expenditures, consumers attempt to bring inventories in line with some equilibrium level and that changes in such factors as income have short-term and long-term effects. They extended their ideas from durable goods to nondurables on the assumption that habit

[38] *Ibid.*, page 370.

[39] Their research has been described in (*a*) Orcutt, Guy H.; Greenberger, Martin; Karbel, John; and Rivlin, Alice M. *Microanalysis of Socioeconomic Systems: A Simulation Study*; (*b*) Orcutt, Guy H. "Microanalytic Models of the United States Economy: Need and Development," *Am. Econ. Rev.* **LII**:2:229–240, May 1962; (*c*) Goldberger, Arthur S., and Lee, Maw Lin. "Toward a Microanalytic Model of the Household Sector," *Am. Econ. Rev.* **LII**:2:241–251, May 1962.

[40] Orcutt, op. cit., page 240.

[41] Summers, Robert. "Discussion," *Am. Econ. Rev.* **LII**:2:252–253, May 1962.

[42] See the discussions by Summers, Suits, and Dingle, reported in the *Am. Econ. Rev.* **LII**:2:252–258, May 1962.

[43] Houthakker, H. S., and Taylor, Lester D. *Consumer Demand in the United States, 1929–1970: Analyses and Projections.*

formation is the exact counterpart of stock adjustment. They hypothesized also that ". . . For habit-forming commodities, the long-term effect is larger than the short-term effect, and their consumption is less dependent on income change than are purchases of durables . . ."[44]

These economists stated their assumptions as follows:

> . . . The effect of past behavior is assumed to be represented entirely by the current values of certain "state variables," of which inventories are a concrete (but not the only) example. These state variables themselves are in turn changed by current decisions, and the net result is that of a "distributed lag": current behavior depends on all past values of the predetermined variables, though more on recent values than on very remote ones.[45]

For their analysis of changes in consumption expenditures, Houthakker and Taylor developed an operational dynamic model incorporating a stock-habit coefficient (β), the coefficient of total expenditures (γ) to represent purchasing power, and a depreciation rate for stocks (δ). These variables were used: (1) per capita expenditures for the commodity in the preceding year, (2) change from the preceding year in total per capita consumption expenditures, and (3) total per capita expenditures in the preceding year.

Houthakker and Taylor followed Nerlove's method of using lags to adjust consumption to an "expected value" and thus ingeniously avoided the problem of estimating stocks directly. They manipulated the β and the δ in developing their structural equation for the flow of commodity expenditures. But the use of the negative β as a stock coefficient and the positive β to represent habit, in effect as alternatives, rests on untested hypotheses that the larger the stock the smaller the current purchases will be and that the more consumers have spent on nondurables in the past, the more they will spend currently.

The coefficients of the variables just indicated and the intercept were derived using the least squares method for most computations. They were then used to estimate the four parameters of their basic model, in the form of a differential equation. These were the intercept as α; the coefficient for changes in stock, β; the coefficient meaning the depreciation in stock, δ, which was assumed to be constant; and the short-term coefficient of total expenditures, γ. The long-term effect of total expenditures is given by the equation:

$$\frac{\hat{\gamma}\,\hat{\delta}}{\hat{\delta} - \hat{\beta}} = \frac{A_3}{1 - A_1}$$

where A_1 is the coefficient of per capita expenditures for the commodity group in the preceding year, and A_3 is the coefficient of total per capita consumption in the preceding year.

Pages 56–149 of their book present the demand equations and projections for 84 categories of personal consumption expenditures. Readers with considerable proficiency in statistics will have no difficulty in reviewing the detailed findings. Chapter 5 contains their evaluation of the demand equations, including comparison of estimates based on equations incorporating early estimates of personal consumption expenditures for 1962 and 1963. Unfortunately, the book was completed before the revision of the estimates by the U.S. Department of Commerce in 1965.

7.5.7 Short-Run Changes in Consumption

Postwar economic research on short-run changes in consumption in the United States has been particularly concerned with the analysis of changes in consumer buying of durable goods and in total personal consumption expenditures. Thus research has relied heavily on data from the Surveys of Consumer Finances and has dealt primarily with implications of attitudes and buying intentions. This subject matter has already been reviewed in section 7.3.3, therefore no further discussion is needed here.

7.5.8 The Process of Consumer Choice in Terms of Dynamic Concepts

The complex relationships involved in the process of consumption activity or use and in the process of choice will become clearer if we restate the processes in terms of expected and actual relationships and also refer to the *ex ante* and *ex post* terminology of process analysis.

(1) From a new product, a consumer expects to obtain satisfaction by matching its attributes (characteristics) to his needs for services arising from his activities. He also

[44] *Ibid.*, page 2.
[45] *Ibid.*, page 8.

expects that the product will have the desired attributes (these are *ex ante*). From use of the new product, he learns relationships between the product and its attributes and between the attributes and his needs for their services (*ex post relationships*). But each consumer's learning is conditioned by his perception of both inputs and outcomes.

(2) For a product with which he has had experience, a consumer has learned and established the relationships. They are subject to revision as changes in perception result from changes in needs and from feedback of other experiences.

7.6 STRUCTURE OF CONSUMPTION

Economic theory of consumer behavior related to the structure of consumption has been primarily concerned with the rise in demand. Lancaster's approach provides an indication of the choice and use aspects of the structure by viewing the choice of goods and services as derived from the choice of attributes. However, he has not described the interrelationship between the processes of choice and use in economic terms which match Bayton's analysis in psychological terms. (See Section 5.4.4.) The preceding section represents a preliminary attempt at identification of the interrelationships. This dimension of microeconomic behavior is not revealed by usual cross-section survey data on expenditures and/or quantities of selected commodities or on all goods and services purchased by families in the preceding period and their socioeconomic characteristics.

Cross-section samples are used to estimate economic relationships which describe behavior of individual units. These relationships are not the simple relationships among income expenditures and prices hypothesized by standard economic theory. Instead, they are multivariate in nature. Empirical economic researchers and many general economists now recognize the existence of complex effects of the psychological and sociological phenomena identified in Chapter 5. Techniques such as covariance analysis and factor analysis are being applied to evaluate the effects of such factors as soon as standard measures for them become available. In later chapters of this book, empirical research along these lines, where pertinent, is reported.

As additional factors are taken into account, economic interpretations of the structure of consumption may eventually encompass study of the consumer market based on categories of users and uses of the commodity and selected economic factors related to uses. The studies of the demand and price structure for agricultural commodities issued by the U.S. Economic Research Service after World War II spelled out the dimensions of the structures being analyzed more explicitly than in most economic studies. These studies made extensive use of simultaneous equations. They were macroeconomic analyses based on time series of aggregates. They did not go very far into the analysis of consumer market sectors, partly because of lack of data. Ultimately, economic analyses of consumer behavior are likely to overlap and even coincide with marketing studies of market segments. Later chapters of this book will consider this topic in greater detail.

8

TOWARD SOLVING CONSUMPTION PROBLEMS IN MARKETING

To study consumption aspects of marketing problems, we need both the wide variety of social science knowledge reviewed in Chapters 6 and 7 *and* knowledge of procedures for application of such knowledge. Some marketing problems arise because of variations in consumer behavior in buying goods or services. Others are related to consumer use of products or services. Still others stem from the present structure of relationships between socioeconomic phenomena and variations in consumption or expenditures. These relationships result from the processes of buying and use. Frequently, study of marketing problems reveals the need to analyze two or three of these aspects as well as past and potential changes in consumer behavior and in the structure of consumption. The same general scientific methods of solving problems are applicable to every type of marketing problem, no matter which aspect of consumption is involved.

This chapter begins with introductions to problem-solving methods and conceptual frameworks. Work on actual problems requires use of data, often from surveys of consumers. Therefore Section 8.3 considers the types of data needed. A supplementary guide to procedures in making surveys is provided in Appendix A. Several major types of consumer surveys are reviewed in Sections 8.4 and 8.5, and some of their findings are included as illustrations.

8.1 INTRODUCTION TO SOLVING MICROECONOMIC PROBLEMS RELATED TO CONSUMPTION

Although masses of data describing consumer behavior in the United States and some theoretical knowledge are available, we do not know many important facts about why consumers make the choices they do in purchasing and use of goods and services. Also, since consumer behavior does change, many descriptive facts about variations in consumption become outdated. Therefore the problem-solving approach is an essential part of the knowledge needed by students who will be working on matters related to consumption for business firms or private and public agencies. This approach provides guidance for incorporating new knowledge as it is developed by others and for original work on marketing problems.

8.1.1 Dewey and Salter on Scientific Method

The problem-solving approach to the development of knowledge is sometimes put in juxtaposition with the theoretical approach, which involves an extensive process of deduction. The ideas of John Dewey and Leonard A. Salter, Jr., about the use of scientific method in the social sciences are pertinent here.[1]

They were critical of the social scientists' frequent practice of assembling masses of data and then trying to organize them to form generalizations about their relationships. Salter and Dewey insisted that we should be concerned with the sources and solutions of problems that arise as people do certain things to achieve certain ends. We must always recognize that our first appraisals of (*a*) problems, (*b*) possible causes, and (*c*) interrelationships between possible causes and

[1] Chapter III of Salter, Leonard A., Jr. A *Critical Review of Research in Land Economics.*

observed effects must be tentative and subject to change as we go along.

Salter provided the following outline for social inquiry:

The substance of this outline of social inquiry is (1) that social science deals with situations in living experience in which there is confusion and conflict with respect to knowing what to do to get specified results (problematic situation); (2) that by the interaction of reasoning and direct and indirect observation of experience a tentative selection is made of those aspects of behavior which appear strategic to the process of acting and getting results (problem formulation); (3) that by further interaction of reasoning and observation of experience a tentative proposal is made that if certain lines of action are instituted, then specified ends-in-view are attained (hypothesis); (4) that this initial hypothesis directs a search for evidence to indicate how it should be modified to be consonant with experience (processing of evidence); (5) that in this processing certain quantitative associations may be found between data bearing on actions and on consequences of action—associations that may be more or less suggestive of modifications in the hypothesis (evidence of relationships); (6) that it is necessary to exhibit the actual sequence between actions taken and results obtained within the experience of individual human beings in order actually to test the hypothesis and to warrant it as a conclusion (evidence of relations in experiment); (7) that the final test in social science is the unity between purposes sought and consequences experienced when the recommended action is taken.[2]

8.1.2 Some Underlying Assumptions

Three assumptions are basic to all modern scientific inquiry: (1) Nature is orderly. (2) Observed phenomena are interrelated in varying degrees. (3) The process of change is continuous but at varying rates. Much of economic research is devoted to the search for patterns of relationships. This search is common to all scientific endeavor.

. . . the great underlying, and essentially unprovable, assumption on which all of science is based is that nature is orderly. A second great dictum of scientific faith is that the order of nature is discoverable by man. . . .[3]

On these assumptions rests our approach to the analysis of consumption problems. Starting from study of the consumption patterns of one family or an individual, we expect to find orderly relationships among the consumption rates and socioeconomic characteristics of a number of families at one time and through time. From these relationships we can form generalizations about the effects of income and other socioeconomic factors on consumption. These generalizations are fundamental to analysis of consumption problems and to prediction of future trends in consumption.

8.1.3 Requirements for Solving Consumption Problems

Study of scientific methods used in the social sciences, review of many research studies bearing on consumer problems, and some years of research in consumption economics have led the author to identify six requirements for solving consumption aspects of marketing problems. As examples, suppose one seeks to understand why more family flour is sold in the South than in other areas of the country or more casual wear in California than in Minnesota or to discover what kinds of transportation consumers will demand in 1985. *First,* one must understand what kind of analysis the consumption problem requires and what steps must be taken to make the analysis. *Second,* every potential problem solver must humbly recognize that he probably is not the first person to tackle a problem of the type with which he is struggling, and that there is probably some knowledge pertinent to the problem available in published form. Accordingly, he must review carefully (*a*) earlier research on comparable problems as well as (*b*) the present store of knowledge about the assumptions and concepts of the several social sciences pertinent to the consumption problems of the type on which he is working, and (*c*) the current ideas of how to use and interpret them.

Third, using information from earlier studies of problems related as closely as possible to the one he is studying and background knowledge about alternative conceptual frameworks, the problem solver must develop an organized way of bringing available knowledge to bear on his problem. This may be in the form of a diagram relating possible causal factors to specified, observable events (a conceptual framework) or in the form of mathematical equations such as those used by econometricians. Identification, in a preliminary fashion, of cause and effect relationships will

[2] *Ibid.*, pp. 246–247.

[3] Weaver, Warren. "A Scientist Ponders Faith," page 8 of *Saturday Review*, January 3, 1959.

expedite selection of the *independent* variables (causal factors) and identify the consumption phenomena to be explained, which should take the form of *dependent variables*. (Section 8.2 discusses the formulation and use of conceptual frameworks.)

Fourth, each of us must develop skill and background knowledge for determining the kinds of data needed to serve as variables and then how and where they can be obtained at least cost in money and energy. *Fifth,* many statistical procedures have been developed and are taught in formal courses in statistics, but such knowledge needs to be supplemented by a knowledge of the inherent limitations of particular types of data and of problems in applying available procedures to such data in order to get important and valid answers.

Finally, every problem solver has a professional responsibility for writing a report on his research to share his findings and his failures with other researchers. Report writing is not easy, even for experienced writers and researchers. The summing up of research on one problem is not really complete until the knowledge gained therein is applied to other problem situations. We must continually seek to move from specific bits of knowledge to more general understanding of consumer behavior.

8.1.4 Preliminary Appraisal of the Problem Situation

The layman and the professional show their colors very quickly in the initial appraisal of problems faced. The layman's approach is usually to describe the situation in general terms, often incompletely. For example, a layman might note that Firms A and *B* sell outerwear. Firm A sells a greater volume, has higher net profits, and advertises more than Firm *B*. The layman might conclude that Firm *B* just needs to expand its advertising and sales promotion programs in order to increase its sales.

A scientific approach to the problem requires identification of the facts and conditions contributing to the confusion and conflict about what to do to get the desired results, which *also* need to be specified. Certainly, we need to know precise details about the location and types of store facilities, the price and quality lines of outerwear sold by both firms, as well as a general description of the consumers patronizing each firm, including their socioeconomic characteristics, such as approximate income, age, family type, occupation, and education.

An economist might quickly identify this problem as an example of imperfect competition. In order to determine the point of maximum profits for each firm, he needs to have information about the demand situation for each firm's line of products, as well as about their cost curves. (The latter lie outside our area of interest.) The information about the demand schedules for the differentiated products of the two firms is not to be found in any book or research report. Therefore it is desirable to apply Dewey's and Salter's scientific problem-solving approach. We need to formulate some alternative but tentative hypotheses based on direct and indirect observations of the firms and on reasoning from preliminary information. One hypothesis might be that Firm A sells more outerwear because it has ten stores and sells more popular-priced lines than does the exclusive store run by Firm *B*. Or perhaps Firm A sells higher-quality lines at about the same prices as inferior lines sold by Firm *B*. Another hypothesis might be that Firm A has located its stores in middle-income suburbs, whereas Firm *B* has stayed downtown in a decaying area.

Soon the problem solver would become aware of the different kinds of facts or data needed to describe the demand situations more precisely and to test hypotheses regarding factors related to differences between the demand for one firm's line of products and the other's. Obtaining such data is a separate stage in the problem-solving approach. Before considering it, a synopsis of the whole process is needed.

8.1.5 Steps in Analysis of Consumption Problems

You will find that researchers divide up the analytical process in different ways. But experienced researchers tend to work in the same general way. The steps this author has identified in research by others and followed in her own are given here in outline form for ready reference:

1. Sizing up the problem
   - (*a*) Realization that there is a problem.
   - (*b*) Understanding for whom it is a problem and why—in general terms.

(*c*) Establishment of objectives for solution.

(*d*) Decision on aspects of consumption involved, including: commodities covered; meaning of consumption—quantity, quality, or value; place in the economic system at which the problem arises—retail, wholesale, manufacturing, farm; kinds and amounts of marketing services involved in the product in the problem situation; whether a problem at one time or place only, or if it is a matter of place to place or time to time variations; differentiation of consumption from consumer acceptances, preferences, consumption habits.

2. Development of tentative hypotheses
   (*a*) Regarding factors entering into the problem.
   (*b*) Regarding how knowledge of elements in the problem can provide leads to its solution.

(Note that these hypotheses should be revised as your work on the problem proceeds. Adhering to one's original hypothesis often reflects one's pride rather than one's analytical ability.)

3. Description of pertinent consumption patterns or relationships
   (*a*) Seek to describe variations and make comparisons—e.g., high and low consumption rates in terms of quantities or expenditures.
   (*b*) Use quantitative measures suitable to the problem being studied. Example—two families may have bought one couch each, one priced at $200, the other at $400. Are the consumption rates the same?
4. Description and measurement of relationships of major socioeconomic factors to observations of consumer behavior

   Major factors in the patterns of consumption by individuals, individual families, and small groups often are the availability of supplies, regionality, degree of urbanization, income, size and type of family, age, education, and occupation. Possible importance of other factors such as facilities or supplies owned by the families should be explored.
5. Measurement of the relative effect of each major factor on total variation in consumption or change in consumption and evaluation of the possible impacts of apparently minor factors
6. Evaluation of possible alternative solutions to the problem, based on findings concerning relative importance of major factors and on information about how influence of major factors can be altered
7. Final step is the attempt to develop generalizations regarding the importance of the major factor and about possible solutions to problems of the type being studied. Although this step is often omitted, it is particularly important to the development of knowledge.

8.1.6 Some Concepts Used in Analysis of Variations in Consumption

In this text we must use a variety of concepts to explore the complexity of variations in consumer behavior. Some have already been introduced. Others are needed in this chapter before they can be introduced in an orderly development of the subject matter of consumption economics. Therefore the following additional concepts are listed and identified:

1. *Private goods*—those owned by individuals; privately supplied services—those bought from business firms by individual consumers.

2. *Public goods and services*—government-supplied goods and services such as public parks, education, and sanitation inspection.

3. *Net worth*—the total value of all of a family's assets minus the total amount owed in such forms as mortgages, installments due, and back taxes.

4. *Credit*—the financial service in the form of the use of another person's or agency's money. Examples—installment credit and mortgage credit.

5. *Supply*—the quantity of goods available in the market at a given time and place or the quantity of goods a consumer may have on hand at a given time.

6. *Regionality*—refers to the state or quality of belonging to or being connected with a region. It reflects the essential and distinguishing characteristics and institutions related to a region.

7. *Urbanization*—reflects a combination of economic and social factors tied in with population density, occupation, and institutions. For consumption analysis, households are often classified according to three degrees of urbanization—urban, rural nonfarm, and farm.

8.2 FORMULATION AND USE OF CONCEPTUAL FRAMEWORKS

In recent decades social scientists have made increasing use of diagrams to identify socioeconomic factors entering into behavioral processes, to trace the sequence of phases in processes, and to describe structural relationships of socioeconomic phenomena. Sociologists have referred to such diagrams as conceptual frameworks, but the degree to which they have been defined has varied. In this text we will interpret conceptual frameworks as diagrammatic presentations of clusters of interrelated but not necessarily interdefined concepts relating to a particular set of behavioral phenomena.

8.2.1 Concepts

Concepts refer to characteristics or attributes of individual things or to relationships among them. You have already become familiar with many concepts related to consumer behavior. Philosophers of science insist that all scientific concepts must be defined in terms of observable characteristics and must have identifiable referents. We defined the meaning of poverty in this way in Section 1.4.1. Concepts are formulated on the basis of common characteristics, by combining old concepts, or through the process of construct development. Constructs are inferred from observations, e.g., family life cycle stage from age and composition of the family.[4]

8.2.2 Guides for Development of Conceptual Frameworks

As a first step toward empirical research, we need to integrate available, pertinent knowledge about consumer behavior. Construction of conceptual frameworks or adaptation of an existing framework is a very helpful procedure. In building or adapting frameworks, a problem solver should build on earlier research by using established concepts. The arrangement of the concepts should be as compact and meaningful as possible and should be designed to indicate the more significant interrelationships.

Conceptual frameworks are particularly important in suggesting systematic cross-tabulations of possibly significant concepts. They encourage the problem solver to go beyond description of relationships to search for the whys of consumer behavior. They can alert the analyst to empirical and analytical problems not apparent from verbal descriptions.

When studying processes, the problem solver should trace the sequence of phases and the interrelationships between phenomena occurring in one phase and those at subsequent stages. When events terminating several processes are to be analyzed, all dimensions or major categories of related phenomena must be taken into account even if a series of frameworks is necessary. In later chapters of this book, a number of conceptual frameworks will be presented which the reader may adapt to his particular needs.

As the problem solver moves on toward development of survey questionnaires, he should keep other guidelines in mind. For example, he should provide for replication of measurements of key constructs and significant relationships by using existing measures where possible or by formulating objective measures which other researchers can replicate. His analysis will be expedited if he uses more than one measure for constructs to test key concepts or clusters still in the developmental stage. He should consult with analytical statisticians about plans for analysis of his data *before* completing work on his questionnaires.

8.2.3 Formulation of Additional Constructs

Many concepts (such as poverty) are so meaningful that it is difficult to differentiate among the possible meanings. Constructs are used to define concepts, and measures are developed to define the constructs. The concept of age is defined in terms of calendar years or ranges of calendar years, such as middle age. Education is measured in terms of years of specified types of schooling or in terms of acquisition of diplomas or degrees. But many concepts needed for intensive study of consumer behavior in market situations are not yet defined to the satisfaction of careful researchers.

To develop new or improved constructs for concepts in conceptual frameworks, it is necessary first to specify the components or dimensions of the concepts. The next steps are to select indicators for them (like years of schooling) and to combine them into index

[4] For rigorous, philosophical discussion of these ideas, see pp. 45–61 of Brodbeck, May. "Logic and Scientific Method in Research on Teaching," Chapter 2 of Gage, N. L. (Editor), *Handbook of Research on Teaching.*

numbers. Before using new measures on costly surveys, they should be tested in pilot studies and put through standardization and validation processes. Suppose your conceptual framework indicates relationships between financial status and expenditures for durable goods. You are aware of the relative and permanent income hypotheses and of research on consumer finances so you want to reflect past income levels, current income level, expectations regarding income changes over the next five years, current level of liquid assets, and current inventory of major consumer durables. These factors in the financial situation are usually handled separately, but there are technical advantages to be gained from development of a combined index for them. The process of developing such a measure is too complex for consideration here, but the challenges to constructors of new measures for consumption research are obvious.[5]

In Section 8.3 we will pay particular attention to data needed to make a conceptual framework operational.

8.3 TYPES OF DATA NEEDED

Dozens of books have been written on statistics and hundreds of tables with statistical data related to consumption have been published. But every problem solver has to decide afresh what data he needs to work on his particular problem and how to use them. Often he must collect new information.

8.3.1 Deciding on Data Needs

There are some guidelines, however, which serve as the voice of experience to guide him in the process of determining the type of data or information needed. An almost limitless mass of data could be collected, but limitations of time, cost, and analytical talent always act as constraints. One begins, of course, with *definition of the problem*. By this we mean the process of determining the question(s) whose solution will be sought through the collection and analysis of information. Consider for the problem situation these aspects: (*a*) the objectives of the solution, (*b*) two or more alternative ways of reaching the objectives, (*c*) the degree of uncertainty as to the best among alternatives for reaching the objectives.

In the process of considering the problem situation in these terms, the wisest procedure is to start with a bibliographical search to discover earlier studies of comparable problems. If the problem has to do with an agricultural commodity, the *Agricultural Index* will usually provide the necessary bibliographical leads. If the problem has to do with public issues or problems, you should consult the *Social Science and Humanities Index* (formerly the *International Index of Periodicals*) and the *Public Affairs Index*. No serious researcher should confine his search to the *Readers Guide* because it indexes few technical or professional journals. Of course, you should search the card index of your library for books related to the problem. A useful habit in research is to check for additional leads the footnotes and bibliographies of every article and book somewhat related to one's problem.

Another step in the process of determining the data or information needed is to clarify further the objectives of the analysis. This often occurs as one considers or discusses the problem with co-workers, with operating people in the firm or agency concerned with the problem, or through reading the background materials just described. Objectives will involve either the overcoming of the difficulties (such as low profits from the product) or the exploitation of opportunities. It is essential to try to state the objectives very explicitly. Each term must be defined precisely. Then the problem must be broken into as many potentially significant parts as possible in order that they may be researched separately. Alternative methods of reaching the objectives often are perceived as one struggles with redefining objectives. Many ideas may be obtained from the bibliographical search, experiences of friends or family members with the commodity or the problem, and conversations with people having a general knowledge of the problem, such as retailers, processors, or other researchers. The researcher must keep an open mind as to possible alternatives throughout his study.

At this point, he is probably ready for the initial *formulation of hypotheses* to match the alternatives. He must decide on the criteria for measurement of results to know whether a hypothesis is supported or disproved by the data obtained. He must determine the type of

[5] For further information, refer to Straus, Murray A. "Measuring Families," Chapter 10 of Christensen, Harold T. (Editor), *Handbook of Marriage and the Family*.

measurement which would lead to acceptance of each alternative and state it in the form of a hypothesis. Hypotheses must be adjusted as he goes along so that they will cover all possible outcomes of the research. But they should be mutually exclusive.

8.3.2 Categories of Data Often Used

When his hypotheses have been tentatively formed, a researcher must decide what kinds of data he needs to test his hypotheses. From our review of the approaches of social scientists to consumer behavior, which have been set forth in Chapters 5, 6, and 7, we can readily identify some possible kinds of data needed within the broad categories of economic, sociological, and psychological information.

Economic data include information on prices paid by consumers for the special products and the quantity and value of those purchased in the preceding week or month or year. Some surveys obtain information regarding the quality of products purchased and what the housewife or another family member thinks of the product. Food and textile surveys include questions to determine whether food and clothing are consumed or purchased or produced at home. Another important type of data is information on where the family shopping is usually done and who shops for what. Of course, many distributors want to know how often certain products are bought or served or used and how they are used. Because of the significance of a family's income to its consumption patterns, questions regarding current income and sometimes income in a preceding year are asked. Occasionally, the questions regarding financial status are put in terms of home ownership or rent paid, either to supplement or to substitute for income as a measure of economic status. Although business firms frequently seek information only for their own products and a competing item or two, most experts on consumption surveys recommend a wider range of commodity coverage to reduce the tendency of the person interviewed, called the "respondent," to exaggerate his purchases of the item or to forget others.

From such data the market researcher or economist can compute the percentages of all people surveyed who used and did not use the given product. He can work out relationships between quantities and expenditures to the total income or total expenditures for all goods and services or the total for the group of items.

Many marketing studies obtain only limited *sociological* information, partly because of costs, but even more because the marketing specialists planning the studies may not think such data are pertinent. But they will usually ask something about social class, using questions about education and occupation of the husband and, perhaps, of the wife as well. Questions about family composition are standard items—number, ages, who lives at home, marital status. Marketing studies sometimes include data on years since marriage and whether the homemaker works outside the home. Ethnic background affects consumption of certain types of commodities so questions concerning nationality of parents and grandparents are sometimes used.

The kinds of *psychological* data used in marketing studies of consumer behavior are much less standardized. But if a psychologist is cooperating in planning the study, you can expect to find measures of attitudes and preferences. These may be in terms of questions about attributes of the product the consumer likes or does not like. They probably utilize a five- or a seven-point scale, varying from "dislike very much" to "like very much." Thus consumers can indicate the degree of their satisfaction or dissatisfaction with the product. Psychologists have several other ways of obtaining data on what people think about products and information bearing on those aspects of personality which appear to be related to buying certain products. We will consider them in Chapters 9 and 10.

8.3.3 Finding Existing Data[6]

Often a market researcher starts his study of consumption of a product by tabulating his firm's (or client's) sales data and by reviewing inquiries or comments from buyers of the firm's products. As he reads up on his subject to clarify the problem, he frequently spots some data collected by the U.S. Bureau of the Census or the U.S. Department of Agriculture (USDA) which indicate quantities of his broad product category sold or consumed in the whole country. Or he will make note of consumption expenditure figures from the

[6] See Gunther, Edgar, and Goldstein, Frederick A. *Current Sources of Marketing Information, A Bibliography of Primary Marketing Data.*

U.S. Department of Commerce comparable to those used in Chapter 3. Often he searches for more detailed data for particular states or cities and comes across data from special sample surveys made by the U.S. Bureau of Labor Statistics or the USDA. Major sets of existing consumer survey data are summarized in Sections 8.4 and 8.5.

To help the reader use survey data correctly and to best advantage, we consider next how information on consumer behavior is affected by the ways it is obtained.

8.3.4 On the Nature of Survey Data

Many students preparing for work in marketing take special courses in market research, but those who major in home economics, agricultural economics, food technology, etc., rarely do. Therefore a brief introduction to survey procedures is provided in Appendix A, with which the student should familiarize himself before studying the remaining sections of this chapter.

Consumer surveys are organized contacts with consumers to get information. Consumers may be surveyed before they buy a product, either in their homes or in the store, while they are shopping or buying, or later at home —before, during, or after using the product. Obviously, the conditions under which questions are asked and the timing of responses in relation to the experience in question affect the consumer's willingness and ability to recall reactions and details of the process of making choices or using a product.[7]

Surveys of consumers' opinions and attitudes can supply information about consumers' perceptions, frames of reference, and even expectations but not *facts* about what they will do. Many factors unforeseen or poorly evaluated by the respondent can intervene before the actual decision to buy or not buy occurs.

Psychological and sociological research has made it clear that people often cannot explain the "whys" of their decisions. They are rarely aware of the full impact of past experiences and social pressures. Or they may conceal some reasons and voice socially acceptable explanations. But the same people may be quite willing to supply information about their socioeconomic characteristics which the consumption student can relate quite well to their choices or pattern of consumption.

Under carefully planned test conditions, consumers can describe their preference ratings for one product compared with another. But the effect of lapse of time may be quite significant in taste or color tests, for example. Similarly, consumers can evaluate the degree of acceptability of particular products, particularly after experience in using them.

One way in which survey methods limit the nature of data obtained is the use of one-time surveys about reaction to a product. Consumer reactions can change rapidly. Only reinterview surveys or continuous panels can catch individual consumers' changes in behavior. However, orderly changes in behavior are predictable, as we will point out in later chapters.

When surveys report the percentage of consumers who prefer a particular product, this finding is not synonomous with the degree to which consumers prefer the product. If a person buys product A, the intensity of his preference beyond the point of choice does not affect that purchase. But it may, of course, affect repeat buying.

Data from consumer surveys can describe the behavior or opinions of only the cooperating consumers. Under some circumstances careful analysis of the characteristics of cooperators compared with information on the total population of an area can provide inferences about noncooperators. Such inferences are very difficult to check.

Finally, data from sample surveys of consumers can describe only the populations actually sampled. For example, surveys of household food consumption tell us nothing at all about the consumption patterns of people living in institutions. Nor can such survey data reveal much about the kinds and amounts of food people eat in restaurants.

8.4 SURVEYS OF CONSUMER PURCHASES, EXPENDITURES, AND CONSUMPTION

Family expenditure data have been collected for centuries. The earliest records extant date from the twelfth century in Western Europe. Until the early twentieth century most of the surveys of family living stemmed

[7] Calvin, Lyle D. "What Do Consumer Surveys Tell Us," pp. 73–77 of Proceedings of the Conference on Consumer Studies and Meat Quality, University of Missouri, Columbia, Missouri, September 9 and 10, 1957.

from concern about the "poor," particularly the working classes. Many of the investigators were social reformers. In the twentieth century, interest in family living has arisen from work on nutrition education, comparisons of standards and costs of living, development of price indices, demand analysis, and market research.[8]

8.4.1 Federal and Nationwide Surveys

In the last 35 years most of the nationwide, large-scale surveys of consumer purchases, expenditures, and consumption have been made by the Federal Government. A number of Federal agencies collaborated with the Works Projects Administration in the 1935–1936 Consumer Purchases Study, the first nationwide survey of both urban and rural families. The next major study, by the U.S. Departments of Labor and Agriculture, was Family Spending and Saving in Wartime, 1941–1942. Since then, the Bureau of Labor Statistics has made two large surveys of urban incomes, expenditures, and savings (1950–1951, 1960–1962) to obtain information on expenditure patterns for use in revision of its price indexes. The U.S. Department of Agriculture surveyed urban families' food consumption in 1948, food consumption by all United States housekeeping households in 1955, farm living expenditures in 1955, rural levels of living in 1961, and food consumption in 1965. The USDA has needed such information to fulfill its responsibilities in connection with the food and nutrition situation of the country, with the demand for farm commodities, and with the incomes and levels of living of farm families. In connection with its marketing research, the USDA has made or financed many studies of selected commodities and population groups.

Since the end of World War II, the Federal Reserve Board has financed surveys of consumer finances, including some information on purchases of durable goods. Until 1960, the surveys were made for the Federal Reserve Board by the Michigan Survey Research Center and published in the *Federal Reserve Bulletin*. Since 1960 their content has been somewhat altered, and the Bureau of the Census has conducted the surveys. The Michigan Survey Research Center has continued to make surveys of consumer finances with foundation and business financing. The findings are published in annual reports entitled *The Survey of Consumer Finances*.

Universities, foundations, farm organizations, market research agencies, advertising firms, and many other businesses have made hundreds of surveys. These include the extensive nationwide survey of consumer income and expenditures by *Life Magazine* in 1956, consumer panel surveys such as those of the Market Research Corporation of America and advertising agencies, a great variety of commodity studies, and many intensive studies for a single area by state agricultural experiment stations and market research firms.

8.4.2 Major Sources of Information regarding Past and Future Surveys

Studies of urban income and expenditures are made by the U.S. Bureau of Labor Statistics (BLS). They are reported in the *Monthly Labor Review* and in special publication series. The U.S. Department of Agriculture has conducted many studies of rural income and family living and of food and clothing consumption and expenditures over the years. These were published by the organization known, first, as the Bureau of Home Economics, then as the Institute of Home Economics, and currently bearing the name, "Consumer and Food Economics Research Division," Agricultural Research Service, U.S. Department of Agriculture. Some of the highlights of such studies are reported in the *Family Economics Review* and listed in other publications of the Department of Agriculture such as the *National Food Situation*. These periodicals also carry references to the much more extensive reports on the surveys that are issued after sufficient time has elapsed for their preparation. Economic and marketing research divisions of the U.S. Department of Agriculture (USDA) were formerly in the Bureau of Agricultural Economics, then in the Agricultural Marketing Service, now in the Economic Research Service. Their studies of supplies, distribution, and consumption of

[8] (*a*) Zimmerman, Carle C. *Consumption and Standards of Living;* (*b*) Williams, Faith M., and Zimmerman, Carle C. *Studies of Family Living in the U.S. and Other Countries:* An Analysis of Material and Method. Washington, D. C., U.S. Department of Agriculture Misc. Pub. 223; (*c*) Stigler, George J. "The Early History of Empirical Studies of Consumer Behavior," *J. Pol. Econ.* **LXII**: 2:95–113, April 1954.

nonfood and food agricultural commodities are reported in the *Marketing and Transportation Situation*, in the *National Food Situation*, and in the commodity situation reports.

State agencies such as the agricultural experiment stations at the Land Grant colleges and universities make studies of food, clothing, textiles, and rural family living. They are indexed in the *Bibliography of Agriculture* and in the *Agricultural Index*. Business research bureaus of some of the state and private universities, such as the University of Illinois, have made some very significant contributions to knowledge of consumer behavior. Such studies are indexed in the *Public Affairs Index*.

Market research firms, advertising firms, and market research groups in the large business firms and trade associations make many studies of consumer behavior. As stated earlier, much of this material is never reported publicly. However, published materials are often indexed in the *Public Affairs Index* and in bibliographies published by the American Marketing Association.

8.4.3 Notes on Methods Used in One-Time Federal Surveys

Two basic approaches to obtaining data from consumers are (*a*) by recall of quantities purchased or used or expenditures in a specified preceding period, and (*b*) by having them keep records. Each approach has some advantages and disadvantages. One study designed to appraise these two approaches is that reported by Murray, et al.[9] Some sections from this report which provide further understanding of survey data follow:

> Methods of obtaining food consumption data from families can differ in at least three respects: The extent to which the memory factor is involved through the lapse of time between the report and the event (purchase, consumption, etc.); the frequency and amount of supervision given the respondent in making the reports; and the detail in which the data are reported. The recall-list depends on the respondent's memory, with the nearly complete listing of foods on the schedule and the aid of the interviewer to assist in recalling items consumed that might otherwise be forgotten. The record method calls for daily recording of food brought into the kitchen for family use, although, even when the record is kept daily, it should be realized that there may be some element of "recall" because of the period elapsing between the time the food is brought into the home and the time the record is made. Amounts are recorded in detail, sometimes with menus, but in diary style, rather than with a list to prod the memory. Frequent visits from the enumerator, at least every day except Sunday, provide a large amount of supervision. (Page 10.)
>
> This investigation has demonstrated that for the groups of families covered, both methods of obtaining food consumption data—the list method and the record method, provided, in general, the same results. Differences of statistical significance appeared for only a few items or food groups; and such differences were scattered among the different types of food data obtained—quantities, money values, and nutritive values. In some instances in which the differences were significant, the list figures were larger than the record figures, and in others the record figures were the larger. Certainly no clear-cut evidence that the two schedule forms provide different results emerged. . . . For most of the food groups or food items tested, and the nutrients in the diet, the differences found between the averages obtained by the two methods were probably due to random variation. . . . (Page 29.)
>
> It is suggested, for example, that consumption of food items of high "prestige" value in the minds of the respondents may tend to be overestimated. The list families in Mississippi reported significantly larger consumption of oranges, a fruit with high prestige value, than did the record families. No other explanation was found, and although the point can certainly not be said to be proved, it has not seemed unreasonable to suggest that this was a case in which families overstated their consumption, reporting as fact that what they wished or knew to be desirable. The prestige factor may, of course, operate when the record method is used . . . through a change in the family's food practices during the week in which records are kept; but this situation would be difficult to detect—and no such instance was detected in this investigation.
>
> The list method is subject to errors of recall, which may result in over- or understatements of amounts consumed. The record method is more subject to understatements through possible omissions (disregarding the problem arising from the possible change in food practices from what they would have been without the recording process, which might lead either to increased or to decreased amounts). An example of a food group that appeared to be understated by the record method because of failure to report an item was found in

[9] Murray, Janet; Blake, Ennis C.; Dickins, Dorothy; and Moser, Ada M. *Collection Methods in Dietary Surveys:* A Comparison of the Food List and Record in Two Farming Areas of the South, Southern Cooperative Series Bulletin 23.

the South Carolina group of families whose reports of sugars were lower than list families, perhaps because of low-recorded amounts of candy.

The list method particularly is subject to certain types of errors which, though avoidable, may occur unless there is very careful training of the enumerators and an awareness on the part of the supervisors of the kinds of problems that might arise under special local conditions. . . . (Page 30.)

Sources for detailed descriptions of the methodologies for major national studies are listed.[10] In general, these surveys follow the methods described in Appendix A.

One-time studies have certain limitations when used for the analysis of how consumption patterns are related to underlying socioeconomic factors. During a limited period of observation, the market availability and demand for goods and services are practically fixed. There may be irregularities in consumption patterns, market structure, and prices peculiar to the particular period, especially those due to seasonal fluctuations. Usually detailed data are available only for products consumed at home by the housekeeping population. Institutional consumption by housekeeping families is included only as expenditures for meals eaten out and consumption of people living in situation must be surveyed separately. Sampling and reporting errors are present to varying degrees. The big USDA and BLS surveys have obtained information on only fairly standard economic and social characteristics. Only in special surveys of the USDA, the U.S. Bureau of the Census, and in the Michigan Survey Research Center surveys has there been much attempt to get at social psychological factors. Identification of commodity attributes has been limited because of the extensive scope of the questionnaires, thus limiting intensive analysis of consumer response to specific qualities.

8.4.4 Panel Surveys

Continuing surveys in which families or individuals report week after week on their purchases and use of specified products and on changes in their socioeconomic characteristics are called *panel surveys*. Quackenbush and Shaffer have carefully appraised the usefulness of this type of survey for obtaining information on consumer behavior. They described the advantages of collecting data from a continuing sample of households in these terms:

> The advantages of collecting data from a continuing sample of households appeared rather obvious. Here was a method of collecting data on purchases from all sources, a problem which plagued researchers obtaining data from store sales, milk routes, etc. It could measure substitution and complementarity of purchases at a point in time and over a period of time within individual purchasing units. It could measure short-time responses to prices and incomes, and if in operation long enough could measure long-time responses or lags in responses. It could be used to determine seasonal patterns. These, among many others, appeared to be valid reasons for using the panel method.[11]

Panel surveys face a number of methodological problems. These include the problem of initial recruitment because many families refuse to commit themselves to continued participation in such a study. Also, there is a gradual bias that develops in the sample because of dropouts and because of some conditioning of those who stay in. The dropouts cause one to question the representativeness of the studies because the higher educated and those more interested in and active in home food preparation, for example, tend to continue in the food studies.

Quackenbush and Shaffer compared expenditures (*a*) recorded by the panel, (*b*) recalled by a special sample of families, and (*c*) re-

[10] (*a*) BLS—Lamale, Helen Humes. *Methodology of the Survey of Consumer Expenditures in 1950*, a monograph of the *Study of Consumer Expenditures, Incomes and Savings*.
(*b*) USDA, Home Economics (1) Clark, Faith, Murray, Janet, et al. *Food Consumption of Urban Families in the United States*, USDA Agr. Inf. Bul. 132, pp. 174–200; (2) Brew, Margaret L.; O'Leary, Roxanne R.; and Dean, Lucille C. *Family Clothing Inventories and Purchases*, USDA Agr. Inf. Bul. 148.
(*c*) *Life Magazine*, "Study of Consumer Expenditures," see pp. 301–319 of Alevizos, John P. *Marketing Research*.
(*d*) Michigan Survey Research Center, *Survey of Consumer Finances*, pp. 357–376 of Alevizos, *ibid*.

[11] From page 5 of Quackenbush, G. G., and Shaffer, J. D. *Collecting Food Purchase Data by Consumer Panel*—A Methodological Report on the MSU Consumer Panel, 1951–58, Technical Bulletin 279, East Lansing, Michigan: Michigan State University Agricultural Experiment Station.

corded by a subsample of the special sample, using the regular panel's questionnaire. An example of the problem of sample losses is the fact that out of 300 families asked to keep a copy of the diary for one week and to *mail* it in to the University, only 195 actually returned diaries. These researchers found: ". . . There is evidence that the recall procedure resulted in the reporting of nearly 20 percent greater expenditures than the panel. . . ." (*Ibid.*, page 37.) When they compared the reports of the 195 families who were both interviewed to obtain recalls and who kept diaries, they found that the products which varied the most were the cooking aids and the vitamins, beverages, meat, poultry, and fish. Those which varied the least were bakery and cereal products, fruits and vegetables. (Page 37.)

From further study of the differences between the recall interview and the panel method, Quackenbush and Shaffer suggested that at least a partial explanation of the difference in expenditures is the higher percentage of families recalling the purchase of the products. Based on analysis of the particular products recalled as bought by a higher proportion of families, these researchers concluded that there may very well have been a problem of "telescoping." This term refers to unconscious extending of the time period backward or forward. From their research Quackenbush and Shaffer concluded:

> The analysis indicates that the two methods of collecting purchase data gave widely different results for some products, some groups of products, and all food at home. The analysis does not prove which gives the most accurate results. Panel members probably underreported and they may have been conditioned in their buying. . . . (Page 39.)

These researchers also explored differences between the panel approach and the telephone interview in collecting data. They found that the difference for three products ran as high as 100 percent. They suspected that the panel members, because of the practice of reporting purchases of all foods weekly, had a much greater awareness of actual purchases. In response to telephone queries, their responses were probably more accurate than was the case for people not experienced in keeping records. These researchers thought the panel members would probably have the same tendency to try to impress the interviewer or to telescope purchases. Quackenbush and Shaffer pointed out that emphasis on three products probably creates a bias that would not be as great if the whole range of food items had been the subject of inquiry. (Pages 40 and 41.)

8.4.5 Alternative Uses of the Data

Information from surveys of consumer purchases, expenditures, and consumption is used to describe the structure of the market for particular commodities in terms of the proportion of total consumption or sales accounted for by a given area or by a specified group of families or people.

These data measure variations in expenditures or purchases or consumption rates among groups of households or families. Groupings may be based on social or economic characteristics like income, urbanization, family size or type, education, or occupation. The relationships between variations in consumption (or purchases or expenditure) and variations in income or urbanization or one of the other characteristics of families are measured statistically. These statistical measures reflect covariance, not cause and effect directly.

Business firms use information on market structure and variations in consumption to plan sales promotion and buying schedules; to lay out their plans for internal administration such as setting sales quotas and evaluating performance of distributors; for new product development; for public relations efforts; and to project demand for their products in order to plan their investments in plant and distribution facilities. Examples of data pertinent to marketing objectives are cited.[12]

Data from such surveys also have many nonmarketing uses. These include development of guides by welfare agencies for use in planning family budgets and in advising families. The information on the ways families actually behave in allocating their financial resources is basic to consumer education. Also, these data are frequently used in public information programs to help the public understand why certain types of public programs are needed to

[12] (*a*) Dickins, Dorothy. *Food Purchases and Use Practices of Families of Gainfully Employed Homemakers*, Mississippi State, Agr. Experiment Station Bulletin 620.

(*b*) Alevizos, op. cit., pp. 343–357, 377–385.

cope with particular types of problems. Two such studies are noted.[13]

Procedures for using such data are outlined in Appendix A. References to more technical descriptions of procedures are given.[14]

8.4.6 Examples of Some Findings

Klein and Lansing used reinterviews of a sample of the Survey Research Center to study factors contributing to carrying out or not carrying out buying intentions.[15] They found a relatively close relationship between purchase plans and actions, between marital status and purchases of durable goods; that buying increases with age up to around 50 years, then declines; and that purchases are related to a feeling of economic well-being.

After working with the data from the 1955 Survey of Household Food Consumption for about a year and a half, Burk and Lanahan formulated a guide for agricultural economists in using such data.[16] The data from the survey showed ". . . that people in the northeastern urban households ranked highest in the market value of food consumed per person, owing to heavier away-from-home expenditures. Also, the average market value of food per person in southern households in each urbanization category fell below the corresponding average for the other regions. Average prices for many foods were lower there, and the proportion of low-income households (incomes under $2,000) was more than twice as high in the South as in the North and West." (Page 94.)

Cues to macroeconomic consumption and marketing problems are also revealed by the comparison of regional production and consumption problems. Consideration of these topics is deferred to Part III.

8.5 SURVEYS OF CONSUMER PREFERENCES: PRODUCT DIMENSIONS

As supplies of goods and services have become plentiful since World War II, producers, processors, distributors, government agencies, universities, and private research groups have conducted thousands of consumer preference and acceptance studies to evaluate consumer response to particular products or groups of products. Psychologists such as Bayton and Woods have helped to identify the complex problems involved in studying consumer preferences. Woods urges that product variables be separated from consumer variables, insofar as possible. He believes that the demands of products on the consumer fall into three classes: (1) those which involve the ego of the consumer in the external symbols conveyed by the product; (2) those which involve the senses of the consumer in terms of pleasure or displeasure, and (3) those which perform functions for the consumer and do not hold much cultural or social meaning for him.[17]

Kiehl and Rhodes of the University of Missouri supply two important definitions: "(1) *Preference* refers to choice or the ordering of choices among two or more alternative products in a given environment by a consumer or group of consumers. (2) *Acceptance* refers to the degree of salability of the product in a given market situation."[18] Their research supported the hypothesis commonly used by economists that group preferences are relatively stable and predictable, although individual

[13] (*a*) Cofer, Eloise; Grossman, Evelyn; and Clark, Faith. *Family Food Plans and Food Costs*, USDA —Agr. Res. Service, Home Economics Research Report No. 21.

(*b*) U.S. Department of Agriculture, Agr. Research Service, *Food Consumption and Dietary Levels of Households in the United States*, ARS 62–6.

[14] (*a*) Burk, Marguerite C. *Measures and Procedures for Analysis of U.S. Food Consumption*, Chapter 4, U.S. Department of Agriculture, Econ. Research Service, Agr. Handbook 206; (*b*) Burk, Marguerite C., and Lanahan, Thomas J., Jr. "Use of 1955 Food Survey Data for Research in Agricultural Economics," *Agricultural Economics Research* **X**:3:79–98, July 1958; (*c*) Clark, Murray, et al. *Food Consumption of Urban Families in the U.S.* (op. cit.), USDA Agr. Inf. Bul. 132, Part II; (*d*) Morgan, James N., and Sonquist, John A. "Problems in the Analysis of Survey Data, and a Proposal," *J. Am. Stat. Assn.* **LVIII**:302:415–434, June 1963.

[15] Klein, J. R., and Lansing, J. B. "Decisions to Purchase Consumer Durable Goods," *J. Marketing* **XX**:2:108–132, October 1955.

[16] Op. cit., (*b*) in note 14.

[17] Page 17 of Woods, Walter A. "Psychological Dimensions of Consumer Decision," *J. Marketing* **24**:3:15–19, January 1960.

[18] Page 1336 in Kiehl, Elmer R., and Rhodes, V. James. "New Techniques in Consumer Preference Research," *J. Farm Economics* **XXXVIII**:5:1335–1345, December 1956.

preferences may vary considerably. They proposed the following areas for further research: (*a*) search for quality factors meaningful to consumers, (*b*) search for measures that will predict homogeneous areas for products, (*c*) formation and development of quality standards, (*d*) study of requirements for maintenance of quality in marketing channels, and (*e*) study of interdependence of preferences, quality standards, production and distribution techniques and costs.

8.5.1 Methods for Study of Product Attributes from the Consumer Point of View

Researchers use several different methods to study product attributes. They include use of informed opinion, ratings by consumers of particular attributes of products, ratings of attributes for their relative importance in the products for specified uses, and ratings of individual products on a scale of some kind.

The use of informed opinion as a form of qualitative market research involves preliminary investigation of facts about the product by unbiased researchers from a series of interviews, then wider exploration with other informed people (perhaps 50), and finally, organization of the information for management decision.[19]

Ratings by consumers of particular attributes of products may be made on the basis of unaided recall (memory of the product characteristic and of reaction to it) or by actual confrontation or handling or tasting the product, as by a taste panel. When consumers are asked only their choice between two alternatives, the results show a majority vote without revealing the gradations around the sample average for consumer preference or the frequency of consumer reactions to each gradation. Manufacturers can obtain such information by providing consumer respondents the opportunity to vote for preferences on a scale between "dislike very much" and "like very much." But a process of establishing gradations which many consumers can identify must have preceded the survey designed to obtain the proportions favoring each degree of difference in the attribute. The technique is particularly valuable in testing new products and planning a line of products such as sweetened and unsweetened canned grapefruit juice.[20]

Although there are some technical reasons for varying and testing only one attribute or factor at a time, there may be compelling reasons for combining several, as, for example, in foods of different varieties.

Business firms often use consumer panels to taste-test new products after they have been developed and taste-tested by trained panels made up of people in the firm, operating under controlled experimental conditions. Preferences for the basic tastes of sweet, sour, salt, and bitter apparently do not vary with income, occupation, and education. But they do vary with age, health, fatigue, and with mouth and sinus infection.

Two USDA marketing research reports on consumer preferences for fibers and fabrics contain examples of ratings of attributes of products for particular uses. Levine found that of the women who preferred cotton for living room draperies:

> 80 percent liked some aspects of its care and laundering characteristics, 38 percent liked its appearance, 35 percent mentioned its durability and wearing qualities, [and] 15 percent considered it economical.[21]

Nolan and Levine studied consumers' concepts of fabric and reported that for winter street dresses, women gave first ranking to ability to hold shape, second to cost, third to color fastness, and lowest ranking (14th) to degree of sheerness.[22]

Researchers at the Quartermaster Food and Container Institute for the Armed Forces have done outstanding research on food preferences. They obtained data on the general like or dislike for individual foods on a recall basis, e.g., on "affective attitudes," using unsigned mail questionnaires. A review of their experiments and findings is provided in *Food Pref-*

[19] For further information, see Wilson, Allan R. "A Qualitative Approach," pp. 248–268 of Ferber, Robert, and Wales, Hugh G. (Editors), *Motivation and Market Behavior.*

[20] Kuehn, Alfred A., and Day, Ralph L. "Strategy of Product Quality," *Harv. Bus. Rev.* 40:6:100–110, November–December 1962.

[21] Page 7 of Levine, Daniel B. *Homemakers Appraise Cotton, Wool, and Other Fibers in Household Furnishings*, U.S. Agr. Marketing Service, Marketing Research Report 279.

[22] From Table 2, page 9 of Nolan, Francena L., and Levine, Daniel B. *Consumers' Concepts of Fabric*, U.S. Agr. Marketing Service, Marketing Research Report 338.

erences of Men in the U.S. Armed Forces.[23] Their findings for particular foods present few surprises, with milk, grilled steak, hot rolls and biscuits, and strawberry shortcake at the top and mashed turnips, broccoli, and cauliflower at the bottom. The men rated some foods as high, medium, and low preference within most of the food classes, of which desserts are an example. These researchers concluded that food preferences form distinct patterns.

8.5.2 Supplementary Notes on Taste Panels

Taste panels are used in attempts to measure characteristics which are highly subjective or subject to psychological factors, such as measurement of sensory differences in food quality. They may be very important to development of products. Conduct of taste panels requires careful attention to factors affecting sensory perception including fatigue, time of day, alertness, distractions, characteristics of tasters, light, color, residual tastes, and order of presentation. Methods differ in ways of presenting products and rating products.

The taste panel approach may be used in determining consumer preferences for nonfood products, where either sensory perception or opinions are involved. But social factors apparently influence variations in senses other than taste more than they affect taste. Reliability of taste panel findings is built upon replication of tests. Researchers find that experience with taste panels can sharpen discriminability of some people's senses but not of others. Even under controlled test conditions, decisions regarding taste can be affected by psychological set or bias based on nonsensory derived knowledge or knowledge based on other senses. Taste panel evaluations are affected by intensity of flavor and odor of food, and by color and texture. The taste panel approach is used by large retailers in deciding on their purchases, and by processors, material suppliers, producers, and agencies working on standardization.

8.5.3 Uses and Limitations of Such Data

Preference is a good predictor of consumption, especially for groups of people. Therefore preference studies are essential to product development on a large scale. They have apparently been used much more in the food field than by producers and marketers of other kinds of consumer goods. Carefully planned and analyzed preference studies contribute significantly to designing new products and changing old ones. However, to react intelligently, consumers must either have some familiarity with the characteristic being tested or be able to relate it to other knowledge or experience.

[23] Peryam, David R.; Polemis, Bernice W.; Kamen, Joseph M.; Eindhoven, Jan; and Pilgrim, Francis S. Report issued by the Department of the Army, Quartermaster Research and Engineering Command.

8.6 THE EXPERIMENTAL APPROACH TO ANALYSIS OF CONSUMER BEHAVIOR

Marketing journals and texts have for many years carried reports of experimental studies of consumers' responses to variations in marketing activity and information. Although some have been statistically sound, few were solidly based on economic or behavioral theory. In recent years, marketing researchers have begun much more scientific research in laboratory situations to test applications of social psychological theories, in particular, to marketing problems. One locus of such research is the University of Minnesota's Center for Experimental Studies in Business. A number of laboratory experiments have been conducted by faculty and graduate students in marketing, using undergraduates and occasionally homemakers as subjects.

Two Minnesota experiments dealt with the problem of the number of alternative items entering into a purchase decision. Both revealed the impact of such numbers on consumer choice.

The Taylor experimental results suggest that as the number of items in a purchase decision increases, the consumer becomes less sensitive to changes in any of the items involved in that decision. The consumer's information per item appears to decline as the number of items increases. Although the experiment does not indicate why this is so, it could be conjectured that as the number of choices increases the purchase decision becomes more difficult. That is, the added advantage of new sources of information for a purchase decision is outweighed by the disadvantages of added time and effort involved in the decision.

The Anderson experiment found that the actual decision process was influenced as the number of choices increased. That is, the greater the number of choices, the greater the postdecision dissonance. This finding would suggest that as the consumer makes purchase decisions in situations where there is a large number of choices, he experiences a considerable degree of anxiety, discomfort, *etc.*, and tends to alleviate these feelings by distorting his purchase decision results. The desirability or undesirability of this phenomenon is yet to be determined.[24]

Professor Holloway, a leader at the Minnesota Center, has been particularly interested in possible applications of Festinger's theory of cognitive dissonance to marketing problems. In 1967 he reported a laboratory experiment in which several dissonance-producing factors were manipulated at two levels of strength, namely (1) inducement to buy, (2) anticipated dissonance, (3) information, and (4) cognitive overlap. From results of the experiment with 80 subjects randomly assigned to 16 alternative experimental conditions, he drew the following implications for marketing:

> Although the results of the experiment were not as positive as anticipated, they did provide a number of *tentative findings* about dissonance and buying behavior:
>
> 1. Consumers who buy when they have *strong inducement* should experience *less dissonance* than those who buy without inducement.
> 2. Consumers who obtain *adequate information* probably will have *less dissonance* than those who buy without sufficient information.
> 3. Product alternatives with very *similar attributes* may cause *greater consumer dissonance* than dissimilar alternatives.
> 4. *Interaction effects* occur when *various dissonance-arousing factors* are combined in one buying situation.[25]

[24] Page 67, Anderson, Lee K.; Taylor, James R.; and Holloway, Robert J. "The Consumer and His Alternatives: An Experimental Approach," *J. Marketing Research* **III**:1:62–67, February 1966.

[25] Page 43, Holloway, Robert J. "An Experiment on Consumer Dissonance," *J. Marketing* **31**:1:39–43, January 1967.

9

PROCESSES OF CHOICE AND USE OF CONSUMER GOODS AND SERVICES

In this chapter we are concerned with the procedural aspects of consumer behavior in choice and use of goods and services. Several aspects of the meaning of process will be clarified as we trace phases in the processes, identify factors related to behavior in these phases, and consider the events terminating each process. We will also note how learning during each process may affect subsequent behavior.

Conceptual frameworks are presented for study of those processes which incorporate concepts and relationships identified in earlier chapters. In addition, in order to relate the concepts to the empirical world of actual behavior, examples of pertinent research are reviewed.

9.1 ON PROCESSES OF CONSUMER BEHAVIOR

A *process* may be defined as a sequence of interrelated actions directed toward some goal, purpose, or end. Implicit in this definition are ideas of a time sequence, subprocesses, and overlaps in processes in the sense that one process often contains components of others. Actions may be symbolic, such as thinking, or physical. This sequence of phases in a process and the subprocesses may be compared to a river with its tributaries.

The shorter or longer length of the time period in which a process takes place may provide little or considerable opportunity for concurrent changes in a consumer's knowledge and in other factors related to his behavior. Therefore particular note will be made of the time dimension.

In the formal statement of the various aspects of consumer behavior given at the beginning of Chapter 5, the terms "decision making" and "problem-solving" processes were used as alternatives. They are not yet well differentiated in the scientific literature, but problem solving appears to be a more general concept and to encompass additional phases. The process of using a commodity to meet consumer wants could be described as a type of problem solving. However, the process of use often requires a series of decisions.

9.1.1 Decision Making

Brim et al. identified six sequential phases in the decision making process in problem-solving terms.[1] These phases included identification of the problem, obtaining necessary information, development of alternative possible solutions, evaluation of the alternatives, selection of a strategy for performance or course of action, and actual performance. Concurrent with the terminating action for one process they identified subsequent learning and revision of strategy. Thus they linked one process with another.

In the case of making a decision about which of two products to buy, identification of the problem would refer to awareness of wants for particular attributes which the goods in question might supply. To obtain information necessary for making the decision or solving the problem, consumers discuss needs with their families and seek information from advertisements, shopping expeditions, their

[1] Page 9, Brim, Orville G., Jr.; Glass, David C.; Lavin, David E.; and Goodman, Norman. *Personality and Decision Processes.*

friends, consumer buying guides, and technical specialists such as home economists. As consumers hunt information, they develop ideas regarding alternative possibilities and other ideas about the criteria which are pertinent to making final choices among alternatives. When a consumer has decided what to buy, he often has to decide where and when to buy it, within what price range, to make the selection, and whether to pay cash or use credit. The actual purchase is the event which terminates the process. However, the process might also be terminated by a decision not to buy at that time any product having the attributes which were being sought.

9.1.2 The Theory of Human Problem Solving

For comparison, recall the Newell, Shaw, Simon theory of problem solving mentioned in Section 7.4.2. At the start of work on a particular problem, the problem-solving consumer already is equipped with a wide range of knowledge. Such knowledge is hypothesized to include alternative strategies for solving different kinds of problems. Newell, Shaw, and Simon suggest that each set contains (1) a number of memories with symbolized information which operate as controls for the procedures to be used, (2) sets of primitive or basic information processes which make use of the information stored in the memories in the search for and selection among alternatives, and (3) rules for combining information processes into programs for processing.[2]

In terms of the theory, we can say that a consumer approaches most problems of choice making with knowledge and habitual procedures for making particular types of choices. Most homemakers already know how and where to shop for food after they have lived in a community for some months. They are also very much aware of the fact that food has usually to be paid for within some kind of budget constraint, and that their family members have certain preferences or likes and dislikes for specific foods. Consumers' memories also contain information about usual price and quality characteristics or attributes of major items and about maximum prices and minimum qualities that would ordinarily be acceptable. These are only part of a wide range of information about needs, preferences, and product attributes that we as consumers store away for future reference.

Among the primitive information processes might be the procedure of checking current inventory and current preferences of family members before starting out on a shopping trip. Another type of process would be procedures for comparing prices and other attributes of products being considered with earlier experiences with comparable products and with current constraints such as cash in one's purse, time to shop further, time available for food preparation, etc. Most consumers probably have well-developed procedures which govern shifts to substitutes for a commodity too high in price or unsatisfactory in quality. These primitive procedures are compared by Newell, Shaw, and Simon with subroutines or subprograms used for digital computers.

The rules for combining the primitive information processes into programs for solving particular problems would prevent excessive time allocation to shopping for pins and needles. An example might be counting all pins in the house before going to the department store to shop for a fur coat and pins. The rules would, in effect, lead to combinations of the subroutines into programs appropriate for different types of purchases and for different occasions.

Thus it becomes clear that the theory of human problem solving now being developed and tested has much broader applications than the process of choice and the process of use. But it provides useful insights into how both probably operate. If the memories include the results of experiences in earlier group processes and if the set of information processes and rules for combining them allow for interpersonal relations and expectations, the theory appears applicable to problem solving by a group such as a family.

9.1.3 Relationship of Processes to Structure

Processes are one aspect of behavior, but we must consider their relationship to structure in order to get a more comprehensive view. One definition of structure given in the Oxford Dictionary is "an organized body or combination of mutually connected and dependent parts or elements." Recall that Allport's ideas about structure related the events

[2] Newell, A., Shaw, J. C., and Simon, H. A. "Elements of a Theory of Human Problem-Solving," *Psych. Review* 65:3:151–166, May 1958.

terminating processes in an event-structure.[3] Using these ideas, we can conceptualize the socioeconomic structure of consumption as being formed by the *processes* of consumers' buying and using products and services and the *events* of consumption or expenditures.

The dimensions of such structures will be discussed in Chapter 10. At this point we must note that they include behavioral aspects (the psychological, sociological, and anthropological phenomena related to consumer behavior); technical and economic aspects of quality, quantity, and value of one or more products; a temporal dimension; and aggregative dimensions in terms of space, number, and sizes (one family, region, an entire country). The processes of buying and using consumer goods and services are interrelated with all of them.

We are all familiar with the idea that changes are continually occurring in our society and economy. But the *process* of change in consumer behavior is difficult to define precisely and to predict, probably because it takes so many forms. Chapter 11 is concerned with changes in consumer behavior and consumption.

9.2 THE PROCESS OF CONSUMER CHOICE

Most strategies proposed for solving the consumer problem of choice or buying goods and services contain stages or phases. Researchers categorize them differently, reflecting the approaches of different social sciences. This section begins with a description of ideas from a sociologist, three economists, and a psychologist.

9.2.1 Alternative Approaches

Roseborough has used a sociological approach. He reasons that the individual accepts the standard of living of his own society, then he consciously or unconsciously decides whether to accept the consumption standards of the majority of the people as a basis for judging quality and performance of its goods and services, i.e., their value system. (An example in the United States is the recent stress on functional design for furniture, clothing, and housing.) Next, the individual must choose the plane of living or life style and a level of living within that plane. Finally, we reach the choice of a particular good or service.[4]

Gartner, Kolmer, and Jones, three economists, identified four interrelated phases in the process of making consumer choices. The *first* was the search for total available alternatives. This search is likely to rest on earlier decisions regarding budgeting, subscription to publications with consumer testing information, and shopping habits, for example. The search builds up knowledge of the alternatives possible for the consumer. Some of the search is incidental to everyday living, but other types of search require careful attention. The *second* phase was to determine which alternatives are relevant to meet one's wants. Here the consumer must consider his limited resources of time, physical goods, income, and energy. The consumer checks with his preference or value system, often quite unconsciously, and decides on a combination of his preferences and his resources. The *third* phase is careful appraisal of relevant alternatives. This requires taking into account the economic, social, and psychological aspects of the product and of his needs, particularly the budget constraint. *Finally,* the consumer makes his actual choice or choices.[5]

Bayton, a psychologist with extensive experience in market research, described the process of consumer choice as starting with need-push, followed by development of awareness of alternative products which can gratify the need. Consumers attach different expectations to these products, depending on past experiences. Such experiences have formed sets of cues to differentiate between products and between brands or types of a given product. Consumers also have learned preferences from their experiences with products and with reactions of other people to products. Such preferences involve ranking or ordering among different products of some kind often identified by trade name. Consumers perform instrumental acts to obtain the object of their wants and to use it. These may have positive or nega-

[3] Allport, Floyd H. *Theories of Perception and the Concept of Structure.*

[4] Page 454, Roseborough, Howard. "Some Sociological Dimensions of Consumer Spending," *Can. J. Econ. and Pol. Econ.* **26**:3:452–464, August 1960.

[5] Gartner, Joseph; Kolmer, Lee; and Jones, Ethel B. *Consumer Decision Making,* Consumer Marketing Bulletin I, Iowa State University and Cooperative Extension Service.

tive values to the individual. If one product is easier to find on the market or can be delivered or saves time in use, it will have positive values.[6]

These analyses of the process of consumer choice tend to be limited by the approach of single social science disciplines. To provide for more comprehensive analysis, the author developed the framework presented next.

9.2.2 An Integrative, Multidisciplinary Framework

A conceptual framework for study of the process of choice is presented in Figure 9.1 which incorporates many of the social science concepts discussed in Chapters 5, 6, and 7. A consumer begins each process of choosing goods to supply the attributes he wants with an accumulation of knowledge learned from past experiences (Box 1 of Figure 9.1), attitudes (Box C_3), style of living (C_1), technical knowledge and a set of other constraints (D). About the same time, the cognitive process of perception may combine his view of the product or a picture or other symbol of it (Box 2) and sales promotion (A) to convert his awareness of needs into awareness of wants and desires for particular attributes. The layman's conception of a consumer's shopping wants is interpreted scientifically in terms of his perception of alternative goods and their attributes (Box 4) and how they are affected by his past experiences, his attitudes, his biogenic and sociogenic needs, and the constraints noted in the figure.

Based on his perception, the consumer goes through cognitive processes of comparing, judging, and thinking. Apparently, he uses a vicarious trial and error method to match attributes of alternative products to his wants within the constraints (the upper and lower limits) set by his budget, his supply of substitutes and complementary goods, his technical knowledge, and his time and energy (Box 5). Then he decides to buy a good with certain specifications (Box 6). It may or may not be one of those actually in view (Box 8). *Or* he may decide to drop the whole buying project (Box 7), at least for that time. The terminating event of actual purchase is generally synchronized with the first phase of the process of use, the arrival of the product at the home of the consumer. This process will be discussed later in the chapter.

Figure 9.1 identifies four sets of factors

[6] Description based on Bayton's article, "Motivation, Cognition, Learning—Basic Factors in Consumer Behavior."

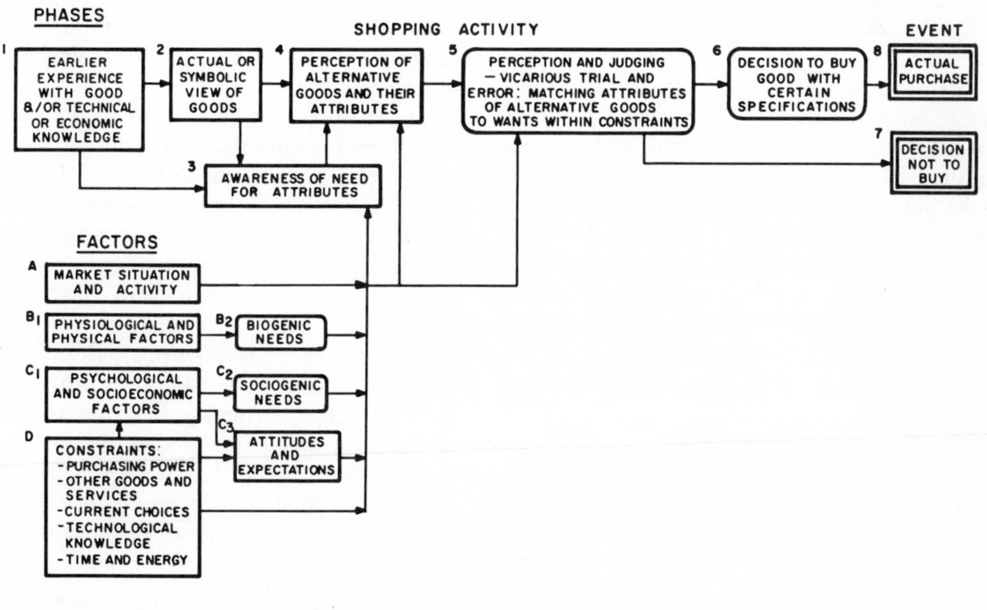

FIGURE 9.1 The process of choice.

entering into the process of choice. These operate through the psychological processes of the individual consumer by affecting motivation and perception (part of cognition). Market situation and activity (Box A) include the supplies, prices, and attributes of products offered on the market, both of the particular product apparently being sought and the potential substitutes and complements. The term "market activity" refers to advertising, sales promotion, and marketing services offered with the product. But consumers' actions are influenced by their knowledge and perception of the market situation and activity, not by possibly different realities as viewed by sellers or by observers. As Alderson, a leading marketing executive, pointed out:

> . . . Marketing creates wants by making consumers aware of needs and by identifying specific products as means of meeting these needs. . . . Marketing assuredly deals with the creation of wants but it starts with the principle that wants spring from needs and are not something alien to be set off in opposition to needs. The transformation of needs into wants is a difficult process and a challenge to marketing skill. The process varies according to the underlying need and nature of the product recommended for meeting it. . . .[7]

Physiological or biogenic needs (Box B_2) include hunger, thirst, and sex. They are affected by one's age, size, health, and so on (Box B_1). Sociogenic needs (Box C_2) may be interpreted to include psychological or psychogenic needs such as those for affection, bolstering one's ego, or protecting it, as well as needs that reflect interaction with others, as in a family. Needs often combine to produce human behavior. Identical behavior may result from different motivational backgrounds. The sociological factors (Box C_1) include the structure and organization of the family, the number of children and their ages, and the number and ages of the adults in the family. Obviously, they affect decisions about what to buy.

Family purchases vary with the number of years since marriage and with the stage in the family life cycle. Several ways have been proposed and used to categorize changes in the family from formation at marriage through birth and school careers of the children to retirement of the husband and dissolution of the family through death. Duvall[8] uses a set of stages based primarily on the age and school placement of the oldest child:

I. Beginning families—married couples without children

II. Child-bearing families with the oldest child from birth to 30 months

III. Families with preschool children in which the oldest child is 2½ to 6 years

IV. Families with school children in which the oldest child is 6 to 13 years

V. Families with teenagers in which the oldest child is in the range of 13 to 20 years

VI. Families as launching centers in which the first child has left the home but before the last child has left

VII. Families in middle years, described as the "empty nest," before retirement

VIII. Aging families, including the period from retirement to death of one or both spouses

Lansing and Kish have related variations in the family life cycle to variations in home ownership and purchases of new cars and television sets.[9] They used nine categories: (1) young single; (2) young married, no children; (3) young married, youngest child under six; (4) young married, youngest child six or older; (5) older married, children; (6) older married, no children; (7) older single; (8) others; (9) not ascertained.

As yet we do not understand all the psychological and sociological phenomena reflected in the relationships among stage in the family life cycle, the behavioral processes, and consumption. But allocation of consumer roles and family interaction regarding consumption probably vary significantly with stage in the life cycle.

Another set of components (Box C_1) includes the elements entering into current social placement. Among them are education of husband and wife; present occupation of head of family and of wife if she is working; location of current residence—urban, suburban, rural nonfarm, or farm; and an index of social

[7] Page 104, Alderson, Wroe. "Conversion of Needs to Wants," pp. 104–105 of Britt, Steuart Henderson (Editor), *Consumer Behavior and the Behavioral Sciences.*

[8] Page 9 of Duvall, Evelyn Millis. *Family Development,* second edition.

[9] Lansing, John B., and Kish, Leslie. "Family Life Cycle as an Independent Variable," *Am. Soc. Review* **22**:5:512–519, October 1957.

position. The amount of formal schooling of the wife affects, for example, her knowledge of nutrition and her willingness to buy inexpensive but highly nutritive cuts in order to save money for the children's college education. The occupation of the husband obviously affects the kinds of clothing he needs and wants. People living in the heart of New York City have quite different ways of spending their money than do people in the Southern Appalachians.

The sociological concept of reference group is important here. Recall that the reference group concept means any group to which a person relates his attitudes. Attitudes are shaped through the setting and enforcing of standards or "group norms" to which members must conform in order to gain acceptance or favor. "Peer group" influence on teenagers' clothes-buying behavior is an example. Reference groups also influence the expectations and aspirations of individuals and families for expenditures and income at each stage of the family life cycle and in each phase of the occupational career.[10]

An index of social position measures social class. The concept of social class refers to status and is indicated by broad patterns of social values, attitudes, and behavior within a culture. The concept has proved to be very useful in differentiating consumers.[11] Social classes are one form of social stratification. This concept implies the existence of social groups which can be ranked within a society.[12]

Economic factors appear to enter into the process of choice in two ways, partly as they contribute to sociogenic needs and partly as constraints. Past and present occupations, experience with levels of expenditures, and patterns of expenditures affect a family's sociogenic needs and wants. The concept of socioeconomic mobility enters here. For example, the family of an owner of an automobile agency who started out as a skilled mechanic (with a vocational school background) is likely to have different preferences for home furnishings than the family of an agency owner who grew up in the upper-middle-class home of a doctor. This would be particularly true if the latter owner had gone to college to study business administration and had entered the automobile business because he was fascinated by automobiles and liked selling.

Similarly, we expect to find different consumption patterns for families who are on their way up financially from those who have skidded down. Social mobility refers to changes along a social scale as exemplified by the efforts of individuals and families to move upward in society. Tensions are aroused in the family as the aspiration levels or desired changes in status evolve. These lead to changes in consumption patterns of families in the course of their life cycles and in the occupational careers of the heads of the families. The employment career of the wife provides still another dimension to the relationship between occupational changes and income and expenditure patterns. These influences operate through successive reference groups which subtly shape consumer preferences through time.

Economic constraints to be included in Box D include purchasing power, supplies of other goods and services, and current competition among different ones. A family's capacity to buy goods and services can come from current income, from liquidation of assets such as bank accounts or corporate stocks or real property, or from borrowing in the form of installment credit or mortgaging one's home. An established family with a home, two cars, and a good supply of household equipment and furniture is in a very different financial situation from a beginning family that might have the same cash income but no supply of consumer durables. Houses and cars are necessarily bought in large units, but they are used up only after a number of years, in contrast with purchases of fluid milk, for example. This characteristic of durable goods introduces the problems related to depreciation, new house demand versus the demand for old houses, remodeling, and so on.

Home economists are much more aware of the constraints of technical knowledge held

[10] For additional understanding, refer to Bourne, Francis S. "The Concept of Reference Group Influence," pp. 1–16 in *Group Influence in Marketing and Public Relations*, a report of a 1956 seminar conducted for and published by the foundation for Research on Human Behavior, Ann Arbor, Michigan. [Reprinted in Holloway and Hancock (Editors), *The Environment of Marketing Behavior*.]

[11] As in Martineau, Pierre. "Social Classes and Spending Behavior," *J. Marketing*, **23**:2:121–130, October 1958.

[12] For empirical use of this concept, see Jacobi, John E., and Walters, S. George. "Dress Buying Behavior of Consumers," in *J. Marketing* **23**:2:168–172, October 1958.

by consumers and of the limitations on time and energy of homemakers than are most social scientists. Substantial parts of home economics research and curricula have been concerned with the development and teaching of knowledge regarding technical attributes of products and how to match them to particular consumer uses. Also, home management research has been concerned with allocation of homemakers' time and energy as well as purchasing power. Home economists have pioneered in measurement of alternative costs and time requirements to prepare foods bought with different amounts of factor preparation.

To avoid further complicating the conceptual framework, the author has included only one type of secondary socioeconomic factors or intervening variables—attitudes and expectations (Box C_3). Attitudes have been described as complex habits.[13] They are developed as we cope with our social and economic environments. Attitudes can facilitate adjustments to subsequent recurring events by regularizing our reactions. Social psychologists have invented rather successful ways of measuring a number of important types of attitudes that are not directly observable. In Section 7.3 reference was made to the work of Katona and others at the Michigan Survey Research Center on measuring attitudes and relating them to purchases of durable goods. According to some social psychologists, we learn two of the components of attitudes—our feelings and reaction tendencies—through association and need-satisfaction. Our thoughts and beliefs are generally acquired by transfer from important people who influence us.

Economic attitudes and expectations of families are those concerned with family evaluations of their own financial situation and outlook and the general economic and market outlook. Here attitudes are defined as a predisposition of an individual to behave in a certain way toward an object or event. Katona and others at the Michigan Survey Research Center have worked extensively with economic attitudes and expectations as intervening variables. Katona argues that all attitudes have situational determinants—such as economic and political conditions—as well as a personality basis. But one or the other set may predominate. The Survey Research Center has been concerned with attitudes which are variable because they are influenced by economic developments, either personal or national in scope. In turn, these attitudes influence our reactions to economic developments.

Katona says that expectations are attitudes which, like other attitudes, may shape behavior, but they are forward-looking attitudes.

> . . . expectations originate in a variety of economic, political, social, and personal developments. The manner in which they are formed is a very complicated process. A study of the multitude of environmental single "facts" would not suffice to show in advance how these facts are perceived and what expectations they will produce. Therefore we have no recourse but to measure directly the prevailing expectations which help to shape business and consumer action.[14]

Expectations are only partly a projection of recent trends. They are influenced also by current perceptions and by information recently received. Attitudes and expectations influence demand for goods and services at the times they are held. Therefore it is not surprising that the Survey Research Center has found that information on changes in attitudes and expectations helps to explain changes in demand, particularly for major items and overall changes in discretionary demand. *Discretionary demand* is demand for goods and services not necessary for maintenance of the basic level of living of a particular social group. The Survey Research Center's Index of Consumer Attitudes measures attitudes and expectations with a fixed set of questions to determine the willingness to buy which combines with ability to buy to produce *discretionary demand.*

Other secondary factors or intervening variables which have been hypothesized as affecting consumer behavior in choice making are family value orientation and family life style. *Family value orientation* refers to the basic behavior patterns formed from past experiences and reflecting the long-range attitudes of the family. Two highly significant sets of values are achievement orientation and security orientation.[15]

The *life style of a family* has to do with its ways and content of living. The life style of

[13] Page 138, Lambert, William W., and Lambert, Wallace E. "Attitudes," in Britt (Editor), op. cit.

[14] Page 65, Katona, George. *The Powerful Consumer.*

[15] Boulding, Elise. "Orientation Toward Achievement or Security in Relation to Consumer Behavior," *Human Relations* 13:4:365–383, November 1960.

a family is both the result of specific consumer choices in the past and the basis on which current alternatives are weighed. One's life style is the means of identifying who one is and what one seeks to become. Thus consumption is instrumental in achieving a life style and is restrained by the conscious and unconscious shaping of one's style.

Note that Figure 9.1 has provided a temporal dimension in the form of a horizontal scale for identification of time periods. The length of these periods will differ among commodities, probably among consumers, and under different circumstances. Scientific knowledge is limited on this point. Generally, economists rather arbitrarily adopt periods like a week, month, or year for their studies of economic events. Some phases of the process of choice take only minutes. This problem of matching phases to a time dimension and serious difficulties in making objective measurements of consumer behavior in the several phases are major factors contributing to the scarcity of research on the sequential process of choice. Most research has concentrated on study of the relationships between selected socioeconomic factors and the event of actual purchase. In the cases of durable goods such as cars and major home improvements, economists have studied such planning periods, which they call "planning horizons."

The Michigan Survey Research Center has established that the degree of deliberation varies with the size of the expenditure required for the item, its meaning and importance for the buyer, his earlier experience of satisfaction or dissatisfaction with such a product, the urgency of his wants, the presence of strong market stimuli, and with his education.[16]

The framework presented in Figure 9.1 provides for all of the ideas underlying the usual economic analysis of choice. It includes the price of the good in question and prices of related goods and services in Box A. Current purchases and inventories of related goods are among the constraints in Box D, along with purchasing power in the form of income. As described previously, past experiences with incomes fit into Box C_1. Tastes and preferences enter both in phase (1) and through sociogenic needs, attitudes, and expectations in the cognitive phases (4) and (5). Changes in tastes and preferences are taken into account by relating the process of choice to the subsequent process of use and then, through learning, to later choice situations as experiences accumulate.

Some economists view the process of consumer choice as stages in the specifications of choices. These begin with allocation of a family's financial resources among broad categories of goods, such as food, clothing, and housing. The next stage is sometimes identified as selection of the kinds of goods within a commodity group, like food, to be bought in a particular period, then the amounts of each. Marketing economists point out how consumers must choose among stores, depending upon the amounts and kinds of marketing services they sell with the products and the price and quality lines they emphasize. The next stage in the case of food involves appraisal by the buyer of relative costs for the same food in different forms and degrees of prepreparation—fresh, canned, frozen, single-food, or mixed food. Next comes the stage of such importance to marketing firms. The consumer decides which brand of the product to buy. In this phase, psychologists argue that "brand image" is significant so market research departments have studied this subject in depth. Finally, the event of purchase occurs.

Some very interesting theoretical developments and empirical studies pertain to the psychological reactions of consumers *after* their purchases. These are not necessarily related to the process of use. They are based on Festinger's theory of cognitive dissonance. The theory has to do with anxiety of consumers over whether they made the best choice when they made their purchase. (See Section 8.6.) Further information can be found in the references cited.[17] Here we must turn to the question of who makes choices and to examination of the implications of learning for the process of choice.

9.2.3 Who Makes the Choices?

The framework does not make explicit the important concept of *role*, from modern so-

[16] Page 34, Mueller, Eva. "A Look at the American Consumer," pp. 23–37 of Newman, Joseph W. (Editor), *On Knowing the Consumer.*

[17] (*a*) Pages 114–121 of Britt (Editor), op. cit.; (*b*) Festinger, Leon. *Conflict, Decision, and Dissonance*; (*c*) Brehm, Jack W., and Cohen, Arthur R. *Explorations in Cognitive Dissonance.*

ciology, which is so significant in the process of choice. It bears on the questions of who is making the choice and for whom. If the homemaker is shopping for new furniture for the household, she is performing the consumer role as an agent for the family. Therefore the family's sociogenic needs enter into her perception.

Sociologists have done some research to answer the question of who makes choices because of their interest in role playing. Roseborough classified the components of roles as those related to executive direction and control, coordinative, supervisory, and technical. For the household, he wrote:

> . . . these role components are compressed into three kinds of role categories: husband, wife, and child. While households vary with respect to the way the executive, co-ordinative, and supervisory components are divided between husband and wife, the child role is ordinarily composed of technical components and a few co-ordinative components—the child is expected to have "confidence" in his parents. . . .[18]

The Michigan Survey Research Center has carried on some research on purchasing decisions. Part of their research was reported by Wolgast in 1958.[19] Wolgast found that the decision-making role varies from problem to problem and among types of families. She concluded that both husbands and wives participate in most economic decisions in American families, particularly in financial management. However, older couples tend to develop certain spheres of major responsibility such as the husband's responsibility for planning for car buying and the wife's planning for home appliance purchases.

9.2.4 Learning

The key ideas on learning pertaining to the process of choice have been discussed in Section 5.4.4 in connection with psychologists' contributions to understanding consumer behavior. But we should go a bit further with the application of Bayton's ideas here. Using his sequence of ideas,[20] we start with the individual's using the goal object, perhaps a particular brand that he has chosen. If actual consumption gratifies the initiating needs, Bayton says there is reinforcement and continued reinforcement leads to learning and habit formation. As noted in Chapter 5, some other psychologists argue that experience itself contributes to habit formation. At any rate, psychologists agree that continued experience with a product affects the cognitive process of memory and particular expectancies are formed. Brand A may rise much above Brand *B* in preference. With continued experience the amount of cognitive activity decreases. A *habit* is formed. A habit is a repeated response pattern accompanied by a minimum of cognitive activity. The strength of the habit is not measured by the frequency of the response but by the extent to which the individual will continue the response after it has ceased to gratify the need.

Students particularly interested in the effects of advertising on choice are referred to some suggestions by Britt on how advertising can use psychology's rules of learning.[21] Howard has also reviewed psychological theory and empirical research pertinent to learning in search of substantive implications for marketing. His review indicates the inconclusive stage of the research as well as the considerable potential relevance of modern information theory.[22] Howard's presentation of demand analysis for marketing management incorporates a substantial amount of both learning psychology and information theory as well as a number of concepts used by economic analysts. However, the emphasis is much more on conceptualization than on development of an operational framework for demand analysis.[23]

9.2.5 Some Limitations and Complications

The foregoing description of consumer choice making covers only the initial buying decisions. It excludes noncommercial decisions regarding the supply of consumer goods to meet needs which may come from home production, gifts, and payments in kind. It also

[18] Page 458, Roseborough, Howard. "Some Sociological Dimensions of Consumer Spending," *Can. J. Econ. and Pol. Econ.* **26**:3:452–464, August 1960.

[19] Wolgast, Elizabeth. "Do Husbands or Wives Make the Purchasing Decisions?" *J. Marketing* **23**:2:151–158, October 1958.

[20] Op. cit., *J. Marketing,* pp. 288–289, January 1958.

[21] Pages 130–132 of Britt (Editor), op. cit.

[22] Pages 100–127 of Howard, John A. *Marketing Theory.*

[23] Chapters 3 and 4 of Howard, John A. *Marketing Management: Analysis and Planning,* revised edition.

neglects subsequent decisions which bear on consumption patterns. These include frequency, time and method of use, repairs, inventory management, and decisions related to complementary goods and services.

Consumer choice making is complicated by a variety of promotional devices, particularly by premium merchandising. Two types of premiums are used, the single premium received at the time of purchase (or nearly so) and a multiple choice among premiums obtained with trading stamps. The use of premiums makes consumers weigh not only the store services and the products they seek but the advantages and disadvantages of buying the product with premium interest, as in the case of trading stamps.

9.2.6 An Alternative Formulation of Consumer Decision Processes

Another marketing scholar, Nicosia, has developed a very elaborate, comprehensive scheme to integrate behavioral knowledge pertinent to the effects of marketing activity like advertising on consumer decision processes.[24] His framework provides for interaction among individuals and is designed with the objective of testing by computer simulation. To the author, Nicosia's description of *a* consumer decision process as *a* structure is very confusing because his framework encompasses a series of decisions and actions by *a* firm and *a* consumer. However, he explicitly describes this statement of his integration of behavioral and marketing knowledge as still preliminary, so the relationships of processes and structure may be altered as Nicosia's study continues.

Nicosia's current presentation of a comprehensive scheme and related models is quite complex, but it holds great promise for further development of experimental research and marketing theory. Although this marketing theorist explicitly refers to the need for analysis of aggregates of consumer actions, his framework at this stage of development is micro-oriented and makes minimal use of economic concepts.

9.3 SELECTED RESEARCH PERTINENT TO THE PROCESS OF CHOICE

In this section we turn to a number of research studies to obtain a deeper understanding of the concepts used in the analysis of consumer choice making. The full citation for each research study will be followed by a summary of pertinent arguments and conclusions.

[24] Nicosia, Francesco M. *Consumer Decision Processes.*

9.3.1 Motivation and Cognition

1. Koppe, William A. "The Psychological Meanings of Housing and Furnishings," *Marriage and Family Living* **XVII**:2:129–132, May 1955.

The human habitat is complex, mainly because the places and objects within the habitat have a variety of meanings which may change from hour to hour and over the family life cycle and only partly because of its variety of physical objects and characteristics. A dining room table may be the place for eating, studying, recreation, and aesthetic display. Koppe surveyed 60 Twin Cities families to obtain reasons for wishing to change housing or furnishings. Only one gave an economic reason for wanting to change his housing. Almost all reasons were related directly to behavior: more bedrooms to achieve quieter sleeping space for children; more play space for children; more special activity rooms; and improved appearance of rooms for the benefit of guests.

Koppe's conclusion was: "Furnishings and housing must be brought in line with patterns of family behavior. In turn, family behavior depends on our value systems. . . ." (Page 132.)

2. Lewin, Kurt. "Forces Behind Food Habits and Methods of Change," pp. 35–65 in *The Problem of Changing Food Habits,* National Research Council, Report of the Committee on Food Habits, 1941–1943, Bulletin No. 108.

Lewin, an imaginative psychologist, viewed the housewife as a gatekeeper controlling the flow of food to her family. In a pilot study he surveyed 107 housewives to ascertain their values behind their food selection and the cognitive structure of their eating situations, as well as other aspects.

Lewin identified four frames of reference used by the women in evaluating foods—expense, health, taste, and status. Money cost was much more significant than the others for all but high-income women, for whom health was most important, followed by taste. He asked questions about which foods would be served if the major consideration was money, if health, if taste, if for guests, to "fill up" people. The women gave for the meat group these answers: short on money—glandular and chopped meat; fill up—meat in general; health—meat in general; taste—steaks and chops; guests—fowl.

In identifying the cognitive structure underlying food choices, Lewin asked: (*a*) What foods the women cooked when their husbands were at home that they did not cook when he was away, and (*b*) what they cooked specially for their children. The most frequent answer for husband's food was meat, for children—vegetables. An important aspect of cognitive structure of food is the variation in attitudes toward foods proper for each meal. Fruits were mentioned for breakfast much more often by high- than low-income women. Similarly lunch foods for the high-income group included fruits and milk, for low income—soups, for Czech housewives—leftovers. Foods for dinner included meat, vegetables, potatoes, and dessert for all groups, plus salads by high-income group. Low-income women frequently referred to bread and butter as important for dinner.

3. Trier, Howard; Smith, Henry Clay; and Schaffer, James. "Differences in Food Buying Attitudes of Housewives," *J. Marketing* **25**:1:66–69, July 1960.

These researchers asked 242 Lansing, Michigan, housewives a number of questions designed to determine the relationships between their decision making and their socioeconomic and psychological characteristics. They found that the cost-of-food factor accounted for about a fifth of the variation in decision-making attitudes. Cost-consciousness was identified with how they viewed their shopping and cooking role for the family. It was not related to any of the socioeconomic characteristics or personality traits studied.

The importance of friends in decision making also accounted for a fifth of the variation. It was higher for better-educated and more dominating types of women. Next in significance as an explanation of decision making was the factor of parents, most important for younger and better-educated housewives. The significance of husbands in decision making was higher for families with higher social status. The factor of importance-of-food-value was not related to sociological characteristics of the families but to the degree of interest in planning and bargain hunting.

4. Bourne, Francis S. "The Concept of Reference Group Influence" in *Group Influence in Marketing and Public Relations*, report of a seminar conducted and reported by *Foundation for Research on Human Behavior*, Ann Arbor, Michigan. (Reproduced in part in Holloway, Robert J., and Hancock, Robert S. *The Environment of Marketing Behavior*, pp. 45–49.)

From his research findings, Bourne concluded that consumer choices of both the product and the brand of cars, cigarettes, beer, and drugs are significantly influenced by what others do. Market researchers believe that product choices, but not brand choices, for air conditioners, instant coffee, and TV sets are influenced by reference groups. In contrast, product choices for clothing, furniture, magazines, and toilet soap are *not* influenced by others, but choices of brands and types are influenced by other people. For common items such as laundry soap, radios, and canned peaches, personal influence on choices turns out to be quite weak.

9.3.2 Learning

Demsetz, Harold. "The Effect of Consumer Experience on Brand Loyalty and the Structure of Market Demand," *Econometrica* **30**:1:22–33, January 1962.

Using data from the *Chicago Tribune* Consumer Panel, Demsetz tested the hypothesis that through the learning process buyers come to rely more on personal experience in purchase and use of products and less on sellers' advertising efforts. He classified brands of concentrated orange juice into a nationally advertised high-priced group and a nonadvertised, low-priced group. After careful statistical treatment of the data, Demsetz found that (*a*) prices paid for frozen orange concentrate declined over the 1950–1957 period, (*b*) the market share of the advertised brands declined, and (*c*) the relation between the market share and price ratio shifted adversely to the advertised brands. He viewed these findings as evidence that "consumers are not mere puppets, but that they learn from experience" (page 33) and that studies of market behavior should incorporate provision for the learning process.

9.3.3 Family Characteristics Related to Purchases

Lippitt, Vernon G. "Determinants of Consumer Demand for House Furnishings and Equipment," pp. 225–246 of Friend, Irwin, and Jones, Robert (Editors), *Proceedings of the Conference on Consumption and Saving,* Vol. I, a part of Study of Consumer Expenditures, Incomes and Savings, University of Pennsylvania.

Lippitt analyzed data for these products from BLS 1950 Survey of Consumer Expenditures with these results: The proportion of total expenditures allocated to these products varied little among family income groups from $1000 to $6000 but declined at higher levels. Expenditures for furnishings and equipment by families buying new homes were much higher than by others. The expenditure percentage declined steadily with age of head and increasing age of children. Car buyers cut back on expenditures for furniture and equipment. The proportion of total expenditure allocated to these items was not clearly related to installment debt or education of head of household.

9.3.4 The Steps in Decision Making

1. Norris, Ruby T. "Processes and Objectives of House Purchasing in the New London Area," pp. 25–29 of Clark, Lincoln H. (Editor), *Consumer Behavior: The Dynamics of Consumer Reaction.*

Professor Norris studied 101 house purchasers in the New London, Connecticut, area in 1952–1953. The stated reasons for buying a house were inability to find a house to rent (especially at a reasonable price), desire to own their own home, and need for a house of a different size. Alternatives explored were renting an apartment or house, buying an old or new house, and building a new house. Buyers of houses in the middle price range made a more intensive search than buyers of houses for higher or lower prices. Most purchasers visited only the house they bought two or more times. House buyers rarely consulted anyone viewed as an expert. Interviewers were struck by how frequently the respondents' views of their homes' characteristics differed from the interviewer's appraisal.

2. Mueller, Eva. "A Study of Purchase Decisions; Part 2 The Sample Survey," pp. 36–87 in Clark, Lincoln H. (Editor), *Consumer Behavior: The Dynamics of Consumer Reaction.*

Miss Mueller reports on a study, by the Michigan Survey Research Center in the fall of 1953, of the kind and extent of deliberation which accompanies the process of purchasing selected durable goods and sport shirts. A United States random sample was used. Five dimensions of deliberation were measured: extent of planning and consideration, extent of information-seeking activity, degree of emphasis on price, degree of brand consciousness, and number of features considered. About 80 percent of the buyers of durables planned at least a few weeks, whereas only about 40 percent of the buyers of sport shirts did any planning to speak of. Only a fourth of durable goods purchasers reported much family discussion, and less than a fifth discussed the subject extensively with friends or relations. Half of the buyers of durables shopped only in the store where they bought the product. About a fifth said they obtained information from advertisements or circulars. Study of "choosing with respect to price" revealed that many buyers paid little conscious attention to price. A third of the durables buyers knew from the beginning what brand they wanted. Buyers of durables were concerned mostly with mechanical properties, new technological features, and performance. But buyers of sport shirts were primarily concerned with the appearance of specific fabrics.

Miss Mueller found that ". . . both individual characteristics of buyers and the conditions under which the purchase takes place had a bearing on the decision-making process. . . ." (Page 80.) A higher degree of deliberation was related to college education, upper-middle-income level, age under 35 years, white collar occupation, and liking for shopping.

9.4 STUDY OF CONSUMER VARIABLES IN CHOICE MAKING

The author hopes that the contents of Figure 9.1, as elaborated in Section 9.2.2, will contribute to your understanding of consumer variables in choice making. It should suggest hypotheses concerning the possible relationships between such variables and the measure of the event or action taken at the end of the process of choice. Before introduction of the complex subject of testing hypotheses, we will review what a psychologist has had to say about consumer variables.

9.4.1 Consumer Variables Related to the Process of Choice Making

Woods defines the consumer dimensions of consumer decisions as those which refer ". . . to differences among consumers in their habits, cognitive structure, and motives which cause them to behave differently in purchase situations."[25] His discussion of consumer variables leads to the suggestion:

> . . . that particular people tend consistently to behave in particular ways. Although it is unlikely that a given consumer always reacts in one way rather than another, people do react predominantly in one way rather than in other ways. The market for consumer products probably is composed of:
>
> 1. A *habit-determined group* of brand loyal consumers, who tend to be satisfied with the last purchased product or brand.
> 2. A *cognitive group* of consumers, sensitive to rational claims and only conditionally brand loyal.
> 3. A *price-cognitive group* of consumers, who principally decide on the basis of price or economy comparisons.
> 4. *An impulse group* of consumers, who buy on the basis of physical appeal and are relatively insensitive to brand name.
> 5. A *group of "emotional reactors,"* who tend to be responsive to what products symbolize and who are heavily swayed by images.
> 6. A *group of new consumers,* not yet stabilized with respect to the psychological dimensions of consumer behavior.[26]

9.4.2 Further Consideration of Hypotheses

Frequently, market researchers start work on identification of elements in a problem situation (e.g., lower sales for an established product than those of a competitor) by dredging up memories of similar or related situations in a brainstorming session. More careful workers search for earlier research plans and findings. Often, the hypotheses simply spell out in greater detail a few of the general ideas outlined in Figure 9.1.

Psychological techniques may be used to investigate new possibilities, especially for those hypotheses related to motivation. They include: (*a*) depth interviewing (a psychoanalytical approach), (*b*) focused group interviewing to obtain group stimulation of ideas, and (*c*) projective techniques. The basic idea of projective techniques is to present ambiguous situations. By disguising the objectives of the survey, the researchers hope to get the individual to reveal his private world of attitudes, feelings, and values—his unconscious motivation.

Projective techniques generally used include: free word association, successive word association, sentence completion, and responses to a variety of pictures which may be only ink blots. The free word association technique begins by presenting a word to the respondent. Then, he is invited to say quickly any words that come to his mind as being related to the stimulus or as being an opposite to the stimulus word. Examples would be *sun* to which respondent might say *rain* or *cigarette* with the response *cancer*.

In a sentence completion test the respondent is asked to complete a sentence which may start thus: "A women who uses instant coffee———." Such a test has the advantages of providing more data than does free word association and of being easier for the researcher to interpret as well as for the respondent to understand.

The picture test may involve showing a cartoon with an empty balloon for the comment of one of the individuals. The respondent is asked to supply the comment. The use of such cartoons has developed from psychological research on the Thematic Apperception Test.

Some researchers are also using the sociological concept of role by having respondents act out their reaction to a given situation or a product. Projective and related psychological techniques are described at length in the book edited by Ferber and Wales.[27]

9.4.3 Empirical Research on Consumer Variables

Study of consumer variables and their relationships to choice uses the procedures outlined in Chapter 8 and described in further detail in Appendix A. Here we will review, first, two examples of research on the consumer

[25] Page 16 of Woods, Walter A. "Psychological Dimensions of Consumer Decision," *J. Marketing* 24:3:15–19, January 1960.

[26] *Ibid.*, page 17.

[27] Ferber, Robert, and Wales, Hugh G. (Editors), *Motivation and Market Behavior.*

buying process and then a number of studies of consumer variables less commonly used than income, age, or family type.

Researchers are frequently asked how much of consumer buying is on impulse, how much is planned, and what effects impulses and planning have on actual choices. Here are two studies which demonstrate the complexity of the problem. Refer again to the study by Eva Mueller summarized in Section 9.3.4.

1. Shaffer, James Duncan. "The Influence of 'Impulse Buying' on In-the-Store Decisions on Consumers' Food Purchases," *J. Farm Economics* **XLII**:2:317–324, May 1960.

Less than half of the purchases actually made were anticipated so a large number of food purchase decisions were made in the store. Comparison between anticipated and actual food purchases of two sample groups showed little difference between anticipated and actual purchases for the population as a group. Shaffer concluded that total food expenditures and their allocation among foods and food groups are not substantially altered by consumers' making purchase decisions in the store.

2. Ferber, Robert. *Factors Influencing Durable Goods Purchases*, Bur. Econ. Bus. Res., University of Illinois Bulletin Series No. 79.

Ferber's interviewers questioned a continuous monthly panel of 150 families in Decatur, Illinois, in 1951 about their purchases of durable goods in the preceding 6 to 9 months, their expected purchases over the next 6 months to a year, and their expectations for income. He repeated the questioning each month for 8 months and compared the results. Among other results he found that about two-thirds of the purchases of durable goods had been planned in advance, and that considerable variation existed in the extent of planning among types of durable goods. (Page 26.) Planning was most frequent for furniture, less so for appliances, and least for clothing. Planning of purchases was most common among lower-income groups. "Families with favorable personal financial expectations reported significantly more major purchases than other families." (Page 27.)[28]

[28] Much more detail on findings is available in the report cited, which was also printed as pp. 75–112 of Clark, Lincoln H. (Editor), *Consumer Behavior* Vol. II: *The Life Cycle and Consumer Behavior.*

The kinds of variables measured in several research reports reviewed next include consumer knowledge of nutrition bearing on biogenic needs for nutrients and food sources of nutrients, psychogenic needs for security or achievement, influences of family members as a type of sociogenic need, and values that enter into both motivation and cognition.

1. Stubbs, Alice C., and Blackstone, J. H. *Nutritional Knowledge and Consumer Use of Dairy Products in Urban Areas of the South*, Southern Cooperative Series Bulletin No. 87.

Homemakers selected one of four possible answers to each of a series of five questions to measure the extent of their nutritional knowledge related to dairy products. Their answers were related to socioeconomic characteristics and to their rates of use of dairy products. Although families using more than the minimum amounts of dairy products tended to have a higher proportion of nutritionally knowledgeable homemakers, a number of other factors also contributed to the higher use of dairy products. Analysis of the data led the authors to conclude that nutritional knowledge did not appear to be a causative factor in increased adequacy in the use of dairy products. They remarked that "recognition of a nutritional fact does not assure application of that fact in planning and buying the family food supply." (Page 19.)

2. Boulding, Elise. "Orientation Toward Achievement or Security in Relation to Consumer Behavior," *Human Relations* **13**:4:365–383, November 1960.

Mrs. Boulding begins the article with comments on the complex interrelationships between attitudes acquired through one's life and situational constraints which summarize one's past and present experiences with income, residence, social class, etc. Her concept of "orientation toward achievement" is closely related to the "achievement motive" of McClelland and his fellow psychologists. Her "security orientation" is rather comparable to their "avoidance motive." Mrs. Boulding's analysis utilizes data from a panel of families reinterviewed several times in 1954–1957 by the Michigan Survey Research Center.

To determine family orientations, the respondents were asked to indicate preference rankings for jobs with steady income, high income, specific security features, chances for advancement, and for their satisfaction with present incomes and levels of living. Answers to the last two questions were used to subdivide those with achievement orientation into consumption-minded and performance-oriented subgroups. The achievers made more cash purchases of durable goods over a two-year span. Within the achiever group, the consumption-oriented bought more durables on the installment plan than the performance-oriented, showing how their aspirations outran their incomes.

3. Dickins, Dorothy, and Johnston, Alvirda. *Children's Influence on Family Food Purchase Decisions*, Miss. Agr. Exper. Station Bulletin No. 671.

For this study 220 boys and girls of 9 and 10 years of age were included, divided between urban and rural residence. They were shown a picture of a boy (John) or a girl (Jane) and asked what foods the child of their own sex should eat each day and for a birthday dinner; whether they ever requested specific foods, and if such requests were granted; whether they asked mothers to prepare school lunch dishes for them at home, etc. Their requests at the grocery for specific foods were usually granted, but roughly a third of the school lunch dishes requested were not prepared at home. Most of the foods they requested, about which they had heard radio advertising, were purchased.

4. John, M. E. "Classification of Values that Serve as Motivators to Consumer Purchases," *J. Farm Economics* **XXXVIII**: 4:956–963, November 1956.

John developed his classification system for social values and in economic decision making from findings of several research studies conducted at Pennsylvania State University. A study of the relative value placed on various items of household equipment and furnishings used these questions to obtain values to serve as criteria in evaluating the utility of the specific items: (pages 956–957.)

(1) "What item of household equipment or furniture were you particularly proud to show your friends when it was new?"
(2) "What was there about this item that made you proud of it?"
(3) "What item of household equipment or furnishings were you glad you purchased in spite of the fact that you were not particularly proud to show it to your friends?"
(4) "What was there about this item that made you glad you had it?"

His classification includes functional values, status-giving values, values giving self-esteem, sentimental values, aesthetic values, and economic values.

5. Beyer, Glenn H. *Housing and Personal Values*, Cornell University Agr. Exper. Station Memoir 364.

Beyer used these nine values for study of their relation to housing: family centrism, equality, physical health, economy, freedom, aesthetics, prestige, mental health, and leisure. Respondents indicated their degree of agreement with each of several statements illustrating each value; then they assigned first, second, and third choices to the values as they related to houses. Next, they were asked to react to a series of statements which guide architects in planning houses to meet most people's wants, such as "having to walk in the rain from the car to the house," and "kitchen noises being heard in the living room." Comparisons of reactions led to findings such as these: People who emphasize family centrism and equality generally favor providing accommodation for collective living. Such values conflict with privacy. People who favored economy actually wanted costly features such as room divisions, protection from rain while walking from the car to the house, and separate baths. Those placing high value on aesthetics were willing at times ". . . to disregard comfort, convenience, and even necessity and physical health for the sake of the 'aesthetic effect.' A typical example of this type of single-mindedness may be found in the case of lighting, where utility and comfort are sacrificed for the sake of effect. . . ." (Page 29.)

9.5 ANALYSIS OF THE PROCESS OF USING PRODUCTS TO MEET CONSUMER WANTS

The concept of *use* refers here to the process of utilizing a product in the home to meet a consumer's need. We will consider factors related to the practices and behavior of consumers as they *use* products, not the quantity of products consumed.

This section begins with discussion of

several economic concepts pertinent to the process of use. They are particularly important in the case of durable goods. Then two conceptual frameworks will be described which have been designed for analysis of the use of nondurables and durable goods. The difference in time periods arises from the definitional distinction between the two categories, i.e., durable goods are used over a longer length of time. During the longer time period, many changes in related socioeconomic phenomena can occur; learning takes place and affects attitudes, knowledge, and wants; and the stock or inventory of products has decreasing value.

9.5.1 Some Additional Economic Concepts

Consumer durable goods like autos and houses have many of the same characteristics as producers' *capital goods* such as trucks, factories, and office buildings. Many consumers invest their savings in their own homes, viewing them as investments, and are shocked to discover that they can depreciate as well as appreciate in value. Development of new features and new fashions in autos and housing can influence consumers' judgment regarding future useability of their current stocks (cars and houses owned). Such judgments are also influenced by changes in the availability of purchasing power (e.g., a legacy from a rich uncle).

Just as manufacturers may buy new types of labor-saving machinery when union wage scales go up, so consumers often buy labor-saving household equipment when alternative demands for the homemakers' time (e.g., chauffering the children) appear to outweigh the initial outlays and upkeep required. A manufacturer can estimate dollar costs of alternative combinations of labor and capital, whereas a consuming household has difficulty in attaching a price tag on the homemaker's time (unless one alternative is a paid job) and on the satisfaction derived from the use of the automatic washer-dryer, for example.

Capital goods play such an important part in the economics of production that economics has a number of significant concepts to contribute. One of these has to do with *depreciation schedules*. These provide for a systematic lowering of the value of an item as its "life expectancy" or future usefulness diminishes. As implied previously, such depreciation may result from physical changes in the item or from diminution in its capacity to fulfill the consumer owner's wants. For example, your car may be only one day older the day after you inherit $100,000, but it might no longer suit your new level of demand for transportation. Comparable in this respect, but very different in others, is the rapid decline in usefulness of a child's playpen after he learns to climb over the side.

A considerable amount of consumer behavior has to do with *saving*. Saving requires foregoing current consumption or using up of a product in order to have it available in the future. This subject is discussed in elementary courses in principles of economics so only passing reference is needed here. Also, it has limited direct pertinence to marketing.

Another concept, the concept of *production scheduling*, does have considerable pertinence, but it has been little developed in this connection. We refer here to the scheduling of the combination of inputs to maximize the return from the outputs. One example would be preparation of food items for a special dish to be served on a special occasion. Another is housing. Think of the need for expanding the home as several of the children enter their teens and have extensive requirements for more space in which to carry on their activities in the home. When the children leave home for college or marriage or jobs, the house has too much space. This leads to a social problem in the sense that many older couples who do not need the space are occupying housing space which is needed by families with children.

TECHNOLOGICAL COEFFICIENTS. In production economics, considerable use is made of the concept of production functions. They are measured by production coefficients which relate the rates of input of labor, for example, to physical output of a product, such as corn. An analogous concept for consumption economics has been suggested by Lancaster, as noted in Section 7.1.3. It would relate the input of goods into the consumption activity to the output of attributes or characteristics. Lancaster assumes that the relationships are fixed and the same for all consumers. The latter assumption appears to contradict observed intervention of differences in perception among different consumers of (*a*) attributes possessed by particular products, and (*b*) the adequacy with which specified attributes meet varying wants and needs of consumers. But it is conceivable that these variations in perception follow laws of probability and can be treated as independent variables. Certainly, much of home economics education is concerned with teaching consumers a standardized body of knowledge regarding product attributes and their usefulness in meeting particular types of needs.

MAINTENANCE. The management concept of *maintenance* encompasses the idea of a program for repairing and servicing durable goods, such as machinery in factories or household equipment in homes. The costs of such a program are related to company, here the family's, policies regarding depreciation and replacement.

WASTE. The economic concept of waste is rather ambiguous. Some waste in homes is really the discard of portions of food regarded as inedible. Other wastage results from spoilage of food and damage of nonfood items. Physical scientists consider wastes and losses to represent reductions in quantity or quality of physical products arising from natural factors inherent in or external to the product or from mechanical causes such as crushing, bruising, marring, or breakage. Economists view wastes and losses of goods in the marketing system or in homes in terms of costs incurred through reductions in value or costs of replacement as opposed to alternative costs of efforts to reduce such wastes. Consumers can reduce physical waste by buying processed foods, but the costs of such processing are included in the retail prices. Careful preprocessing and management of products in the home can reduce spoilage. However, time, effort, and use of equipment, such as refrigerators and freezers, are needed for such preventive actions. The close relationship between waste and maintenance becomes clear.

9.5.2 Multidisciplinary Conceptual Framework for Nondurables

As in the framework for study of the process of choice, the conceptual frameworks for the process of use, presented in Figures 9.2 and 9.3, incorporate concepts and relationships drawn from the several social sciences and discussed in Chapters 5, 6, and 7. The framework for the use of food could apply to either one consumer or to a family or nonfamily household. In the latter cases, the socioeconomic factors and constraints would encompass additional people and interaction among them.

Food provides the best example for nondurables, but some extension of the time dimension would make the framework applicable to the less durable types of clothing and to household supplies. Because most food is consumed within a few days, weeks, or months after purchase, gradual using up of inventories does not complicate the analysis of food use to the extent that the services of consumer durable goods on hand confuse the measurement of consumption or "using up" such goods. In brief, we find that a number of concepts and analyses from the economics of the firm are applicable to consideration of food use by a consumer. The economic functions being performed in the family kitchen are production scheduling, manufacturing, inventory management, and distribution. But some of the socioeconomic factors which complicate analysis of a business firm's operations are magnified in a household's operation.

Referring now to Figure 9.2, note that the arrival of the food product at the home of the consumer (the starting phase of the use process) is considered to occur immediately after the event of purchase. The latter terminated the process of choice in time period T. Upon its arrival, the homemaker must decide whether to assign the product to inventory or to process it for consumption quite soon. These steps are identified as production scheduling and processing. In processing, one food is usually combined with others. Such processing, often referred to as meal preparation, requires use of labor, utilities, kitchen supplies, and equipment. Food items are distributed to the family members either by placing them on the table in the customary form and sequence or by serving them individually. This application of the distribution concept differs from the usual economic interpretation of distribution, which refers to the sharing of returns from the output of production process among the factors of production in the forms of wages, rents, profits, and interest. However, it coincides with the concept of distribution used in marketing.

After menu items are prepared, they are combined with other dishes on dinner plates or put into serving dishes to be distributed to the family. This marketing process may be simple or complex, depending upon the time, energy, equipment, and wants of the family. Consider the variety of service many families demand. Some meals are eaten hastily in the kitchen, others by candlelight with glistening silver in the formal dining room, still others with flying objects on the patio or out by the fireplace. Few food manufacturing firms would cater to the whims of even their best customers the way many housewives do as a matter of course. Their supply of services is exhausted only when their energy or patience runs out.

The process of use for a consumer good generally terminates in the actual consumption or using up of the commodity. Here the eating of the food is a part of the meal, but it may be a between-meal snack. However, provision is made in the framework for the discarding of inedible portions or for the discard of unwanted or spoiled items as waste.

An important part of this conceptual framework is provision for the concurrent operation of the *learning process*. During use, consumers learn more about particular attributes of products they buy, particularly how well those attributes match or fulfill specific wants. Learning may take place at each stage of the process of use. It affects both the subsequent stages in the use of a particular product at hand and subsequent choices of similar products or related goods and services. Learning shapes attitudes and wants, and it changes technological knowledge and expectations. The learning process is also affected by the components of the four boxes of factors, especially by the technological knowledge and expectations held at the start of the process of use. In Figure 9.2, dotted lines connect the learning and use processes to reflect the fact that learning is a separate but related process.

The components of the four boxes of factors, A, B, C, and D, are mostly the same as those described by the process of choice in Section 9.2.2. However, their relationships to the process of use probably differ in degree from the factor-choice relationships. For example, price is probably much more important a factor in the purchase of a meat item than in its use. Even so, expensive beef cuts like prime ribs are rarely if ever used for stews.

Some of the elements of technological knowledge pertinent to processing of a commodity may be rather different from those needed for selection. Knowledge and expectations regarding the usefulness of particular attributes such as the tenderness of meat affect both the selection and use. In contrast, the consumer knowledge of where to get the best

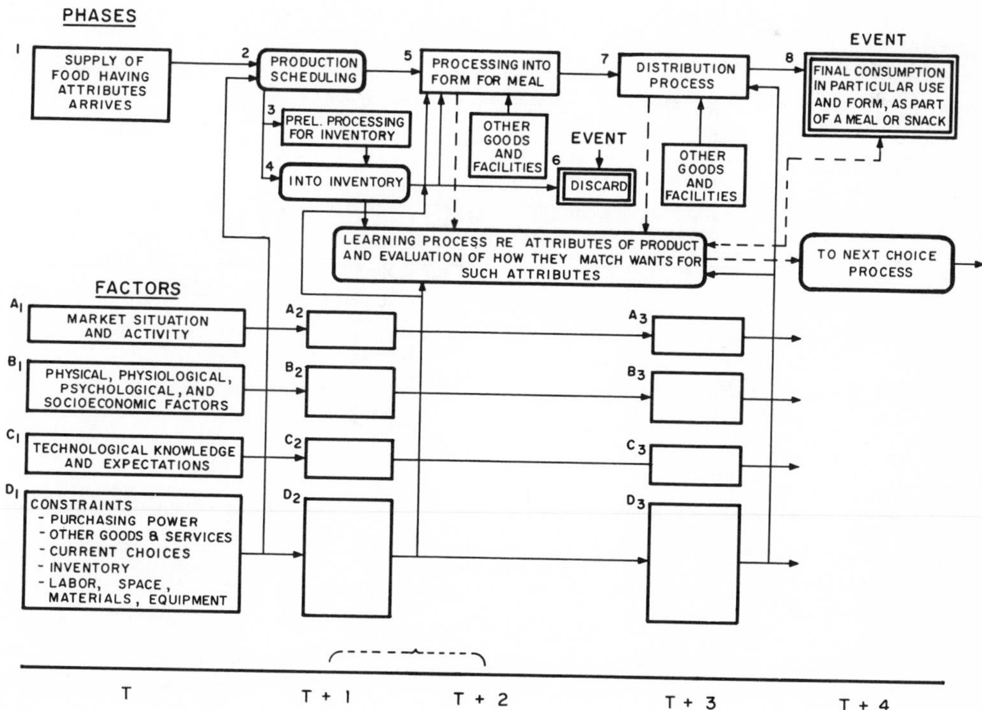

FIGURE 9.2 The process of use of nondurables—food example.

buys on meat is rarely pertinent to preparation of meat cuts for meals.

Finally, the reader should consider the provision of a time dimension for the process of use, as indicated by the horizontal line in Figure 9.2. Here the time periods begin at T, the time of purchase and arrival of the food. Factors related to the process of use may be changing between the time the food arrived and the time(s) of actual use. Household members may come or go. New knowledge regarding food preparation may be acquired. An increase in market prices may cause the consumer to save or hoard the prime ribs for "company" dinner rather than for a usual family meal. Also, the oven might burn out and force the homemaker to prepare the food in a different way than contemplated earlier.

9.5.3 Conceptual Framework for Durables

As consumers use semidurables and durables like clothing, house furnishings, equipment, housing, and automobiles, they make a series of decisions on: the frequency, timing, and method of use; care and repairs of the commodities; how large an inventory they wish to maintain; and what criteria should be used to determine the stage at which a product should be discarded as no longer suitable (as obsolescent) or as worn out.

Such decisions bear materially on the timing and character of their demand for new products. Interrelationships between business and consumer decisions regarding obsolescence are dramatized in Vance Packard's *The Waste-Makers*. Empirical knowledge of consumer practices and factors relating to consumer decisions on use of products is relatively meager. The significance of such knowledge to understanding shifts in consumer demand and business fluctuations is increasingly clear. When consumers are worried about the economic outlook, they can and do make their clothes and cars and furniture last for an extra season or year or even longer. Thus they contribute to slowing down the economy.

The conceptual framework presented in Figure 9.3 for study of the process of use of semidurables and durables condenses the phases identified for nondurables by the use of the concept of an *operating schedule*. To understand the meaning of this concept, think of the use of a washing machine in a family household. A load or two of laundry may be run through the machine every day, or twice a week several loads may be processed. The

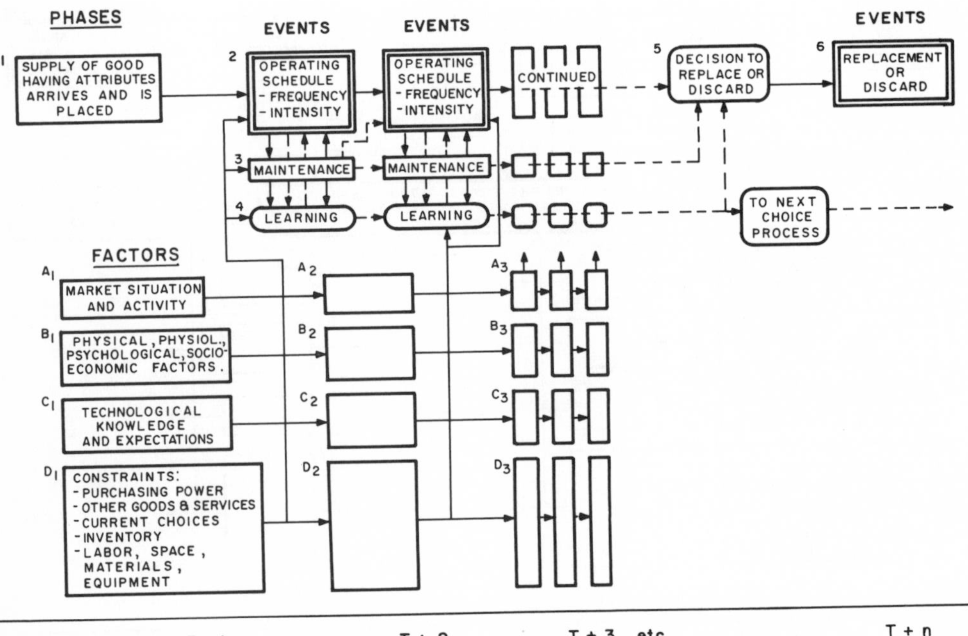

FIGURE 9.3 The process of use of durables.

operating schedule followed will affect the rate at which the machine is worn out, but the maintenance of the machine is also significant. Also, by definition, there is time for learning to change the consumer's stock of technical knowledge and her expectations regarding the use of the item and thus the operating schedule for subsequent periods. Factors influencing use in one period are also likely to have a carryover or lagged effect on use in later periods. An example might be the gradually diminishing effect on a family's buying pattern of the destruction of part of a house by fire.

The events of use are summarized for each time period, e.g., use of the washing machine 9 times per month for 11 months in the year, and compared with concurrent flows or status of the factors related to the process of use. An example of the concept of a flow is the summary of monthly salary payments into total annual income for the current year. A status example is the use of an average for the number of people living in the household during the year, say 3.25 persons for a family in which the son is away at school for 9 months and does not send his laundry home. The use of such summaries for time periods is described by the concept of *period analysis*.

For study of the effects of some factors which have gradually reducing impact, economists use the device of *distributed lags*. However, the way in which they distribute the impact of, say, a sudden $5000 increase in income on the discard and replacement of furniture over the following years has to be rather arbitrary because of lack of information. An analyst might assume that half of the impact of a sharp change in income on furniture use would come in the first year, a third in the second year, and the balance in the third year. By the fourth year, he might argue that other parts of the family expenditure pattern would be altered so that the higher level of the income would be largely absorbed in current living expenses.

As in the conceptual framework for analysis of the use of nondurables, the components of boxes A, B, C, and D are the same categories of factors as described for the process of choice in Section 9.2.2. However, their relationships to the use of durables are probably rather different. A drastic change in the market price of washing machines is not likely to affect the operating schedule for doing the family laundry. But it may materially affect decisions about repairs and regarding the timing of replacement of the washing machine by a new machine.

The opportunity for changes in factors related to the use of durable goods is obviously greater than for nondurables because of the lengthening of the time of use. The longer time period for use is implicit in the definition of durable goods. The potential for consumers' discretion in decisions regarding the lifetime of a durable good has substantial economic significance, as noted at the beginning of this section. This is one aspect of discretionary buying and is particularly important in the year-to-year shifts in purchases of automobiles.

9.5.4 Efficiency

In analysis of production processes, economists are concerned about the *efficiency* with which inputs are used in the production process. They study factors related to improving efficiency. Some of the constraints on efficiency in household operations are similar to those in business. Lack of knowledge of relative costs, materials, technical coefficients, and poor demand forecasting, absenteeism, malingering, inflexible foremen, nepotism, and featherbedding are socioeconomic factors which interfere with production efficiency in manufacturing plants. Long telephone calls, crying babies, late husbands, and chauffering responsibilities upset the operations of food processing in family kitchens. Also, food waste-making ties in with ego-bolstering needs. The ways of family interaction, family values, and cultural patterns cause some families to be extravagant in use of food, equipment, energy, and time.

Efficiency experts can use more measuring devices in a slaughtering plant than home management specialists can apply to measure efficiency in the kitchen. Efficiency in the homemaker's labor during food preparation is hard to measure when she has to feed the baby as she cooks the meal. Also, the selling price for the dishes served in a family meal is really the family's satisfaction. A profit and loss statement for a packer is far more tangible than a family's levels of nutrition and general satisfaction.

Economists measure efficiency by the ratio of valuable output to valuable input. Unfortunately, it is much harder for consumers to appraise the extra satisfaction they get from using a new car as opposed to an old car, particularly when we know that many people are very good at justifying their decisions in retrospect. However, new scaling techniques developed by psychologists should permit some interesting research on consumer evaluation of uses of alternative products.

9.6 SIGNIFICANCE TO BUSINESS FIRMS OF KNOWLEDGE OF CONSUMER USE

The use of a product has a great deal of impact on a consumer's learning concerning the possibilities of the product's meeting his wants in the future. A consumer is likely to be a repeat buyer *if*, in the process of its use, the attributes of a product fulfill her expectations, meet her needs, and give indications of meeting future needs better than alternative products. In other words, the satisfaction derived from use reinforces the choice for purchase.

Both the frequency of need and the degree of satisfaction in processes of purchase and use will affect the rate of use and repeat buying. Dissatisfaction is a negative reinforcer and results in alternative choices or disuse. A business firm that concentrates on initial sales to the detriment of repeat business can only prosper in a seller's market or if new buyers are continually coming in.

Firms frequently survey both users and nonusers of their products. Different kinds of promotion are usually needed for the two groups. Users can supply much more information about product attributes and their reactions to them than can nonusers. Two manufacturers (*A* and *B*) may each estimate average Twin Cities' consumption of their cake mixes at 0.2 pound per household in a week. Suppose 10 percent of the population actually use the "*A*" line and 50 percent use the "*B*" line. If so, the rate of use of "*A*" line by using households is 2 pounds (0.2 ÷ 0.10), whereas the users of "*B*" line consume only 0.4 pound per using household. What kinds of additional information would you advise firm "*A*" and firm "*B*" to seek?

Manufacturers need to do considerable research to match product characteristics to various aspects of consumer use. We are all aware of the products that are designed for special occasions. Examples are party dresses, tuxedos, Christening clothes, and Christmas china. These may be fairly costly and specially designed. They usually carry social connotations. Although some consumers are willing to make substantial outlays for these products for special occasions, other consumers seek to buy them at minimum cost because they are used so infrequently.

Some of the "image" research which market researchers have carried on has revealed that certain foods with convenience characteristics, those partially prepared like instant coffee, are considered acceptable for general use but are not served on special occasions. However, careful research is necessary because many of the attitudes toward suitability of products are peer-group- or class-based.

Products prepared for everyday usage need to have certain characteristics of durability and convenience. Items like stainless steel flatwear and synthetic tablecloths are sold on the basis of cost, durability, ease in laundering, and with the understanding that they lack exclusiveness.

Some commodities with long life expectancies may be so costly as to achieve status. The Rolls Royce and Mercedes Benz automobiles are examples.

9.7 REVIEW OF SELECTED RESEARCH ON CONSUMER USAGE

Most consumption surveys are reported in terms of average rates of use by an entire population including users and nonusers. In many of them, however, the percentages of households using the products are also given, as, for example, in the 1955 Household Food Consumption Survey Reports issued by the U.S. Department of Agriculture. With these percentages the rates of use by users only can be computed. However, it is not possible to separate the characteristics of users and nonusers reported in such publications.

9.7.1 Special Surveys of Consumer Practices in Use of Foods

An outstanding study of consumer use was made by LeBovit and Clark in *Household Practices in the Use of Foods.*[29] They examined practices in the use of eggs, milk, butter, margarine, sugar, baked goods, flour, pur-

[29] LeBovit, Corinne, and Clark, Faith. *Household Practices in the Use of Foods,* Three Cities, 1953, USDA Agr. Inf. Bulletin 146.

chased mixes, shortening, fats for frying, and several vegetables.

Another study by the home economists in the Department of Agriculture reported on consumer practices in the handling and storing of commercially frozen foods.[30] This study developed from concern over consumer handling and storing of frozen foods between the time of checkout at the store and actual cooking at home. Redstrom, Davenport, and Murray concluded from their survey that the data did not support the hypothesis that "considerable quality deterioration of frozen foods occurs in the home, since frozen foods are not often held for long periods in the home refrigerating unit. . . ." (Page 1.)

9.7.2 Product Factors Related to Use

A survey of York, Pennsylvania, homemakers indicated that the criteria related to a particular dress purchase may differ from attributes rated most important regardless of occasion or season, that is: (1) "Ability of the fabric to hold shape; (2) degree to which the fabric will or will not wrinkle; and (3) color fastness. . . ." (page iii) plus cost. The authors added that ". . . experience may play an important role in that selected characteristics are assigned certain values on the basis of habit, which limits their influence at the time of purchase."[31]

A national survey was made by the U.S. Department of Agriculture to determine homemakers' views of the virtues and faults of fibers used in draperies, rugs and carpets, bed sheets, bed coverings, and table coverings.[32] The product attributes most sought by homemakers in soft floor coverings were durability, ease of care, and appearance.

Alevizos has reported on a product research survey of gas and electric cooking ranges that made use of the Good Housekeeping consumer panel.[33] Questionnaires were returned by 78 percent of the 2500 mailing. Respondents described the arrangements of top-stove burners they had and their preference for the next range they would buy. They answered a question on need for an automatic burner control. To a series of questions about features of ranges, they indicated whether they had wanted each or considered it unimportant. They also answered questions about whether they preferred their next range to be gas or electric and why.

9.7.3 Consumer Factors Related to Use of Products

A comparison of homemaking practices among two groups of Georgia homemakers (one employed outside the home, the other not) revealed much smaller differences than expected.[34] The major differences were in the amount of paid help for child care, laundry work, general housework, and sewing. Surprisingly, at each level of income fewer employed than nonemployed homemakers used frozen foods at home during the week studied. A smaller proportion of the employed wives sewed at home (other than mending), but, except in two-person households, they made more garments.

Based on a survey of preferences for a number of major items of household equipment, Nolan concluded, "In general there existed a positive preference between experience with an item and a preference for it. . . ." This was especially true for washers, ranges, and freezers.[35]

In the spring of 1957 a sample of 666 families in Johnstown, Pennsylvania, was surveyed to determine the effects of differences in national background and several other socioeconomic variables on use of dairy products,

[30] Redstrom, Ruth A.; Davenport, Elizabeth; and Murray, Janet. *Consumer Practices in the Handling and Storing of Commercially Frozen Foods, Two Cities, Two Seasons,* USDA Home Ec. Research Report No. 23.

[31] Nolan, Francena L., and Levine, Daniel B. *Consumers' Concepts of Fabric,* USDA Marketing Research Report No. 338.

[32] Levine, Daniel B. *Homemakers Appraise Cotton, Wool and Other Fibers in Household Furnishings,* USDA Marketing Research Report No. 279.

[33] "Good Housekeeping, The Consumer Panel in Product Research," pp. 523–535 of Alevizos, John P. *Marketing Research.*

[34] Holmes, Emma G. *Job-Related Expenditures and Management Practices of Gainfully Employed Wives in Four Georgia Cities,* USDA Home Ec. Research Report No. 15.

[35] Page 34 of Nolan, Francena L. *Factors Associated with Preferences for Household Equipment and Furniture By 351 Rural Families,* Pennsylvania Agr. Exper. Station Bulletin No. 591.

meats, and selected fruits and vegetables.[36] The presence of young children influenced the use of milk, luncheon meats, and meat soups. Educational background appeared to be a significant factor in use of dairy products and fruits. ". . . What appeared at first glance to be major differences in food habits among national groups were in many cases qualified or even eliminated when stage in family life cycle, education, and occupation were introduced as control variables." (Page i.) However, a few differences survived careful analysis. Ice cream and fruits were consistently more popular with families with extended American backgrounds. Veal was clearly more of a favorite for German and Italian families than for others. Italian families served leafy green and yellow vegetables more frequently than was the case for other nationality groups.

[36] Fliegel, Frederick C. *Food Habits and National Backgrounds*, Pennsylvania Agr. Exper. Station Bulletin No. 684.

9.7.4 Inventory Practices

Brew, O'Leary, and Dean made an intensive study of family clothing.[37] They pointed out the significance of the relationship between inventories and acquisitions. It can provide an indication of the lifetime of garments in a wardrobe if one assumes the addition of comparable amounts in each of several years preceding the study. The authors concluded that the Twin Cities men surveyed must have kept their suits slightly over five years, on the average, whereas the women were keeping their dresses two to three years.

Comparison of clothing practices of carefully matched Twin Cities and Minnesota farm families revealed larger inventories held by the urban families and larger outlays for clothing upkeep.

[37] Brew, Margaret L.; O'Leary, Roxanne R.; and Dean, Lucille C. *Family Clothing Inventories and Purchases*, USDA Agr. Inf. Bulletin No. 148.

10

STRUCTURE OF CONSUMPTION

This chapter is concerned with the integration of the major aspects of consumption, described in Chapters 5 to 9, for an interdisciplinary appraisal of the structure of consumption. The several different ways of looking at consumption appear to be concerned with different dimensions. The elements of each dimension are interrelated, as are many of the elements in the different dimensions.

Concurrent handling of the processes of choice and use, for even one product category like food or household laundry equipment, becomes so complex that we must abstract from the details. One way to do this is to omit both all nonobservable phases and those that are difficult to measure. Thus we can concentrate on the events observed and on measurable factors related to them. The processes for different goods occur in different lengths of time. Therefore events have to be summarized in convenient periods such as a week, a month, or a year.

An analysis of the structure of consumption requires at least two conceptual frameworks. One is needed to describe the structure at the micro level. Another must provide for aggregation of purchase events during each time period over the several uses of one good, over all goods, over many households in one market area, and over all markets in an entire country. The second diagram covers only the events of purchase. It should be supplemented by summaries of the statuses and flows of socioeconomic factors related to purchases. These become quite complicated, as indicated by the extensive work of econometricians on problems of aggregating only the effects of changes in income and family composition during recent years. (Section 7.2.3.)

Generally speaking, economists have concentrated their attention on changes in demand measured at the point at which consumers take goods from the marketing channels. Economists and statisticians have worked very little on the analysis of the process of use; therefore there is little knowledge of specific problems in the aggregation of consumer use.

10.1 STRUCTURE AND ITS DIMENSIONS

Although we have used the concepts of structure and dimension in earlier chapters, more precise definitions and some elaboration of their meanings at this point will help in comprehension of the complexity of consumption structures.

10.1.1 Definitions

The concept of *structure* encompasses the ideas of an organized whole and of interconnected and dependent elements. In Section 9.1 we used Allport's event-structure to conceptualize the interrelationships between the processes of consumers' buying and use of products and services and the events of consumption (or expenditure). We are preparing now to examine the dimensions of this structure.

The familiar definition of the term *dimension* is that it refers to a measurable extent of any kind, e.g., length, depth, or breadth. This concept has been expanded beyond the three spatial dimensions to other elements whose functions may be measured analogously to those of space. An obvious example is the quantitative dimension of milk consumption, measured in cups or pounds. Another is time. measured in days or weeks or years. Such dimensions may also be viewed as types of elements in a structure.

10.1.2 Behavioral Dimensions

The psychological, sociological, anthropological, and economic phenomena listed in

Figure 5.1 and discussed in Chapters 5, 6, and 7 may be considered as behavioral elements in the structure of consumption. The processes of consumer buying and use are also elements in the structure. They have subprocesses and subelements, as noted earlier.

Because of the difficulties in tracing processes and subprocesses of consumer behavior, researchers often relate measures of the underlying socioeconomic phenomena directly to measures of the results of the consumption events. For instance, we study the relationship between purchasing power of a family, measured approximately by dollar income in a year, to the dollars spent for food or for rent of their home. Rental value is a rough economic measure of the consumption of shelter. Think how we simplify a great and complex series of processes and many events when we note, for example, that the Jones family spent 20 percent of its disposable income for food in 1965.

10.1.3 Technical and Economic Dimensions

Events of consumption are measured in the dimensions of quantity, quality, and value of the product or service consumed. (See Section 6.8.) Each of these dimensions has both technical and economic characteristics. For example, economists use dollars or other monetary measures for food, whereas a nutritionist immediately thinks of nutrient values such as vitamin A content. Marketing people are concerned with both technical and economic aspects of quality as they match consumers' wants to their firm's potential output of products with desired quality attributes of flavor, style, color, speed, etc.

Many different products and services are consumed in proportions which vary from family to family. Thus a product-service dimension must be envisioned in order to provide for different combinations of such items and different amounts of those included. An example of this dimension would be the fact that the Jones family spends $1500 for food in a year, which accounts for 25 percent of all their expenditures. The tables in Chapter 3 with BLS survey data provide some comparable aggregated information.

10.1.4 Time Dimension

Social scientists frequently simplify their problems by concentrating on individual situations and by the assumption that no changes are occurring. Thus they attempt to avoid complications introduced during the passage of time. But processes and events occur in time. A basic assumption in all scientific research is that the process of change is continuous but at varying rates.

Suppose you are making a survey which requires knowledge of all aspects of consumption by the Jones family in a week. That week might include one event of buying a coat for Junior (perhaps on impulse or perhaps the end result of several weeks of shopping and family discussion), five trips to food stores to shop for groceries (including perhaps 30 purchase events), use of food in 18 meals, going out to eat three times, running six loads of clothing and linens through the washer and dryer, continuous use of housing by the family and their visitors, plus purchase and use of many other items.

In effect, at the beginning of a survey week the researcher cuts into a variety of ongoing processes and leaves unfinished ones at the end of the week when he asks the homemaker to recall or to record the family's consumption or expenditures for a week. If the time period for recall is a year, many more processes and more variation and change in the processes will be included. The total quantities and values of goods and services will be much larger and more socioeconomic phenomena will be taking place. The family might have a new baby; a child might start to school; the head of the family might lose one job or get another; and so on.

Chapter 11 is focused on such changes so this chapter is limited to a rather situational approach.

10.1.5 Aggregative Dimension

Most Americans consider a family income of $5000 in a year to be small and a million dollar income as large, but they can't identify the dividing line between small and large in other than subjective or relative terms. Similarly economists cannot identify the boundary between micro and macro aspects of the problems they study. Variations from micro to macro operate in the dimensions of numbers and variety of consumers and marketing firms, geographic space, and quantities and value of products. As the consumption of one group, say the people in one suburb, is added to that of others in a metropolitan area, or to those in comparable suburbs of other cities, totals or aggregates are formed and the macro zone is reached. As the expenditures of poor families are added to those of middle-income groups and those of upper-income families, the results are macro aggregates consisting of total expenditures by different kinds of groupings of consumers. These will be placed in perspective in Section 10.3.

10.2 CONCEPTUAL FRAMEWORK FOR ANALYSIS OF THE MICRO STRUCTURE OF CONSUMPTION

The structure of consumption at the micro level as outlined in Figure 10.1 involves (1) aggregation of the events of purchase and use for entire bundles of goods and services by an individual family in one or several periods of time, and (2) the summarization of information on factors related to such events.

10.2.1 Summarizing Events

Let us first consider the problem of summarizing all purchases by a family in one period, t_i, which might be April to June, 1965. There are essentially two ways of doing this. One is to add units to derive a total, such as pounds of food. But a total poundage figure for food involving different kinds of foods such as flour and milk is not very meaningful. Nor is total poundage for food, clothing, and shelter at all meaningful. Therefore dollar values are used as a common denominator for all items, although the number of units is also needed for the analysis. To make comparisons of purchases in one period with those in another, it is necessary to hold prices constant. By pricing all items purchased in several periods with prices of one period, we can derive total values in dollars with constant purchasing power. Comparisons of these total values with the total value for one period, called the base period, yields percentages of that period's value which serve as index numbers.

Moreover the total value of food purchased by the families in a period such as April to June 1965 can be compared with the total value of clothing or of all goods and services. Such comparisons indicate to some extent the relative importance placed by the family on a particular category. They also reflect the relative costs of the category in the economy.

Figure 10.1 also provides for summarizing actual total use in each period. This is not overly difficult for items like food, utilities, household supplies, and rented homes. But calculation of the amount of family-owned housing and amounts of household furnishings and equipment used up in a quarter or in a year requires estimation of their economic lives and rates of depreciation. Such estimates are made for rental property for income tax purposes. Another approach to valuation of housing is to ask families to estimate the rental value of owned homes. Estimates of use are generally less precise than purchases during a specified period. But they are likely to provide more meaningful measures of levels of living.

To study usage of some items, it is desirable to identify subcategories of use, such as use of fluid milk as a beverage, with cereal, and in preparing desserts. Consumer goods like clothing and furniture are manufactured from such a variety of raw materials that consumers may or may not know their content, unless labeled. An analysis of uses of specific materials and finished products is particularly important for planning sales promotion and for development of new products by manufacturing firms.

For some purposes, values in current dollars are more useful than values in constant dollars. Therefore Figure 10.1 provides for both. Current dollar values avoid the complication of calculations with constant prices, but they always infer the possibility of changes in prices.

Summaries of events in a number of periods, as indicated by Figure 10.1, are used in *period analysis*. The "mix" or combination of events or even individual events in one period are compared with those of another or a series of periods. Similarly, relationships of events to underlying factors in one period are compared with relationships observed for other periods. This is one type of dynamic economic analysis. A more complex type relates the events in one period to factors in preceding periods, or to previous and subsequent events.

10.2.2 Buying Intentions

For major items like autos and homes, many consumers plan for future purchases during a period of many months. The Michigan Survey Research Center has collected data on buying intentions for such items and found that they are useful predictors of short-run changes in buying behavior, i.e., purchases in periods subsequent to the date of the initial survey. In effect, questions regarding buying intentions ask the respondent to take stock of

FIGURE 10.1 Structure of consumption at the micro level.

Section (*a*)	(*b*)			(*c*)	(*d*)	(*e*)			(*f*)			(*g*)		
Factors Related to Consumption, Measured in Terms of Status and Flows in Specified Periods	Time Period			Consumption Event	Unit	Buying Intentions			Purchases			Actual Use		
	t_1	. . .	t_n			t_1	. . .	t_n	t_1	. . .	t_n	t_1	. . .	t_n
A. Market situation and activities 1. Prices for particular items and for major categories of goods and services 2. Measures of promotion activities 3. Measures of supply and quality . . . *n*. Other B. Social psychological factors 1. Attitudes 2. Expectations . . . *n*. Other C. Socioeconomic factors 1 . . . *n* (Income, assets, occupation, family characteristics, value orientation, life style, education, nonwork time and activities, etc.) D. Technological knowledge and expectations				A. In terms of quantity 1. Nondurables *a*. Food A *b*. Food B . . other foods . *s*. Household supply A . . . *z*. Aggregate for all nondurables, index using constant dollars 2. Durables *a*. Automobiles *b*. Major household item A . . . *s*. House . . . *z*. Aggregate, index 3. Services . . . 4. All goods and services B. In terms of current value (same subheads and items as under A)										

his cognitive process of choice making and to forecast the probable outcome and timing of such an outcome. Of course, many factors can cause individual families to buy sooner than expected, to make unplanned purchases, or not to fulfill their buying plans. But the actions of groups of families appear to be influenced by tempests in the general social and economic climate, such as fears of inflation and concern over near future employment and income situations. When families' willingness to buy is significantly affected by these outside or exogenous factors, the combined impact on the nation's economy can be quite strong.

10.2.3 Factors Related to Consumption

Figure 10.1 provides for measurement of economic, social, social-psychological, and technical phenomena considered to be causally related or perhaps only associated with the events of consumption, in terms of purchases and use. These are the same phenomena discussed at some length in Section 9.2.2 where they were related to the process of choice. Section (*a*) of Figure 10.1 lists most of the major categories used in empirical economic analyses of variations in consumer purchases. Additional factors may be selected from the comprehensive listing in Section 9.2.2.

Some of the factors are measured in terms of status, others in flows in specified periods. For example, we should relate total quantities, i.e., total number of units, of particular food items purchased in a period such as April–June 1965 to the actual prices paid for them. To obtain the average price for a period, a *status measure*, the actual prices should be weighted by the number of units bought at each price. The weighted price can be derived by dividing total expenditures by the number of units purchased. (The process of weighting involves multiplying each price by the number of units bought at that price, summing the products, and dividing by the total number of units.) If none of the particular item was bought in a particular period, a community retail price would have to be used. Because of problems in identifying the qualities of commodities purchased by consumers at alternative prices, economic analysts frequently use the retail prices collected by the Bureau of Labor Statistics for items with carefully identified specifications. These prices form the basis for the Consumer Price Index and for price subindexes such as retail prices for all foods for home use.

Income is a good example of an economic factor measured in terms of flow, such as total wages received in April–June 1965 after deduction of federal and state income taxes, and perhaps social security payments. Figure 10.1 indicates that such a factor as income should be measured over a number of periods. Thus one could relate current level of use of housing by each family to its past peak income, income five years earlier, current income, and income expectations.

The relationships of events of purchase and use to behavioral, economic, and technical factors can be studied in a variety of ways. Sometimes it is sufficient only to describe the characteristics of families and their consumption patterns, in terms of categories indicated in Figure 10.1. Usually, we work with survey data for a sample of families and use graphic and statistical methods.

A preliminary step is to plot two-dimensional charts, such as the Engel curves with quantities on the vertical axis and income level measured on the horizontal axis. (Guidance to such procedures is provided in Appendix B.) The slope of the Engel curves in such charts, if drawn on a double logarithmic basis, provides an indication of the income elasticity of the quantities consumed.[1] Among the statistical measures used to study the relationships are correlation and regression analyses, analysis of variance, and factor analysis. These techniques go beyond the scope of this text so the student is referred to textbooks on statistics.

Students preparing for professional work on analysis of consumer behavior should take several courses in statistics, particularly with emphasis on methods used in psychometrics and sociometrics. Even so, frequent consultation with statisticians and econometricians is desirable. Survey data on consumer behavior often violate some of the assumptions of standard statistical techniques, such as the continuity of variation and mutual independence among independent variables.

Figure 10.1 outlines the comprehensive coverage of a general theoretical model. Op-

[1] If the Engel curve is based on group averages, the income elasticities for the several groups should be weighted by their proportional significance in the total sample.

erationally, economic analysts test hypotheses suggested by such a framework and discard the relationships of minor importance for explanation of the total structure and prediction of major changes.

10.3 THE AGGREGATIVE DIMENSION OF THE STRUCTURE OF CONSUMPTION

Figure 10.2 begins with the aggregation of one household's purchases of one commodity for a number of uses, e.g., value of milk purchased for all uses in all forms. This level of aggregation, and the next, which summarizes the purchases of all goods by the household, replicate the coverage of Figure 10.1 but for one period only. The next level of aggregation covers all households in one relatively homogeneous market, such as all urban, high-income households in the Northeast. Note how the aggregation for one household (h_1) fits into one box of the market level of aggregation. Economists use the symbols $\Sigma(h_1, h_2, h_3 \ldots h_n)$ or $\Sigma(g_1, g_2, g_3 \ldots g_n)$ to indicate summarization across all items, here individual households and individual goods, in the total, here a market, following the example of mathematical practice.

The next level of aggregation summarizes the subtotal for market$_1$, market$_2$, . . . market$_n$ and we reach the total value of purchases in an entire country in *one* time period. The entire aggregation process is in terms of value. If aggregate value in period t_1 is to be compared with aggregate values in t_2 and t_3, it is desirable to know how much of the difference in value is due to changes in price and how much to changes in the quantities or in the mix of the goods consumed. To develop this knowledge, it is desirable to construct comparable value aggregates in constant dollars and to identify aggregates for major categories such as food, clothing, and housing.

If all data were available for every household in the country or if the random sample were properly representative of all characteristics of all types of households, no major aggregation problem would be encountered. Ordinarily, such detailed data are not available, and the analyst must be concerned with the representativeness of his sample and with the distribution of household according to major socioeconomic characteristics which may be affecting the variations in events of consumption or expenditure. Difficulties encountered in connection with such concerns are magnified when events and matching socioeconomic phenomena are aggregated over a number of time periods. To cope with these complex problems, analysts of consumer behavior and related marketing problems need the assistance of the most highly qualified econometricians they can hire. Even these experts lack much of the knowledge they need. However, substantial progress has been made in recent years toward development of the needed knowledge. The aggregation process has led us into the field of macroeconomics of consumption so we will go no further with the analytical problems here.

Before considering applications of these two structural frameworks, the characteristics of supplementary frameworks must be outlined. As indicated in the preceding discussion, the aggregative dimension of events of purchase (Figure 10.2) requires an aggregative structure of factors related to such events or characteristics of families making the choices and using the commodities. The nature of such a structure can be discerned by aggregating the factors listed in Section (*a*) of Figure 10.1 over all households in a market and then over all markets in an entire country. Another two-part structure would relate the events of use to the same aggregative structure of underlying factors as just described to go with the structure of purchase events in Figure 10.2. However, the relationships of these underlying factors to aggregates of consumer use are not likely to be precisely the same as the relationships of such factors to choice in particular time periods.

Finally, the reader should be aware that total use exceeds total purchases even in a country like the United States. Home production of food and do-it-yourself services make up most of the difference. Such subsistence or home-produced supplies of goods (and services) are far more significant in developing countries than in the United States in the 1960s, but 50 years or even 30 years ago they supplied a substantial part of the food and fuel consumed by rural people in the United States. Subsistence food accounted for as much as 20 percent of total United States consumption just before World War II. In contrast, it appears possible that home-production of services such as maintenance of equip-

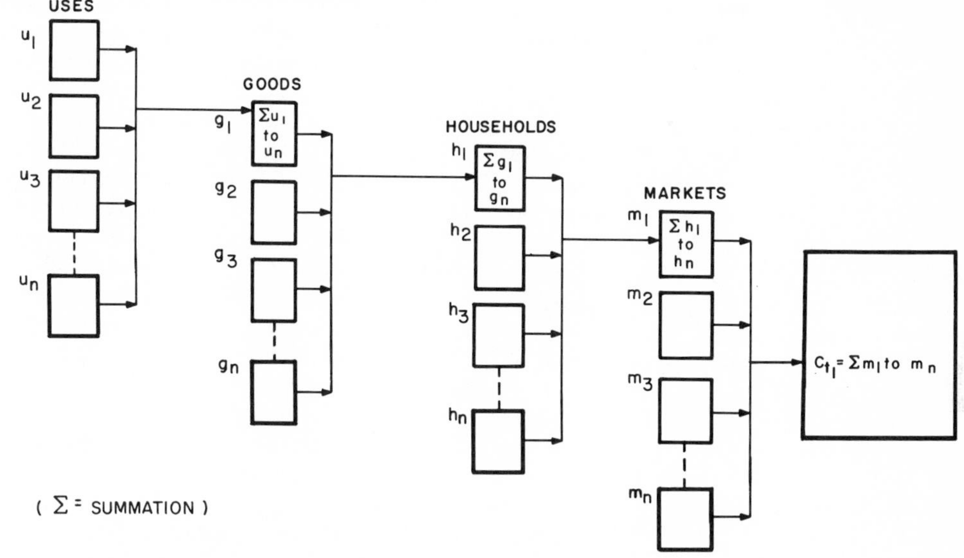

FIGURE 10.2 The structure of consumption—aggregative dimension (micro → macro).

ment and homes and health care may be increasing in this country.

10.4 APPLICATIONS OF THE CONCEPTUAL FRAMEWORK

Economists and marketing people have used the ideas underlying these conceptual frameworks for the structure of consumption for many years. They have generally worked with only two or three factors and a few commodities. Recall that standard economic theory of consumer behavior relates variations in consumer choice of one good to variations in its price, prices of related goods, and income under the assumption that all other factors remain constant (*ceteris paribus*) or have insignificant effects.

10.4.1 By Marketing People

Two characteristics of an affluent society are (1) the large amount of discretionary expenditures, which are made possible by the high level of income, and (2) the variety in supplies of consumer goods and services available in the market. Such excesses of purchasing power and goods over minimum or basic needs challenge marketing men to tailor products with special attributes in order to attract consumer demand.

To identify potential wants, business firms must analyze in detail the components of the total structure of consumer choices and consumer uses. The conceptual frameworks are designed to provide hypotheses concerning possible sectors of consumer markets and to guide appraisal of their relative significance in different periods of time. But analyses based on these frameworks must be supplemented by intensive study of historical trends, recent variations, and future prospects for key factors related to consumption. For example, simple extrapolations of past changes in the population to the years 1985 or 2000 are likely to be grossly in error because of extensive family planning programs and recent changes in technology and attitudes toward birth control.

Similarly, even for small groups of families, it is no longer safe to assume that past relationships between income and food expenditures or between income and housing provide adequate indications of future behavior. Generally, they cannot forecast the turning points or timing of future changes. In a period of major social and economic change, the wisest course of action for a consumption analyst is to hypothesize that a wide range of factors enter into consumption variations or changes through time. Then he must test the significance of each individually and appraise possible interactions. It is becoming increasingly evident from empirical research that socioeconomic and social psychological factors have differing relationships to consumption of specific commodities by major sectors of the population and that these relationships are not constant. Extensive integrated research is needed to provide the understanding and the measurements of the patterns of such relationships and to demonstrate how they may be used to predict consumer response for small and large population groups.

10.4.2 In Consumer Education

A significant part of consumer education is designed to widen the horizon of consumers so that they will examine and choose from a greater range of alternative goods and services. Individual middle-class families frequently want to know how other families in their income, family type, or occupational category spend their money, what goods they select, what their future incomes are likely to be, and how they should plan ahead. The conceptual framework at the micro level, outlined in Figure 10.1, can be used to guide record-keeping and to teach families to study their own data. Data from cross-section surveys such as the BLS-USDA survey of consumer expenditures for 1960–1961 can be fitted into the framework of Figure 10.2 and the matching summary of characteristics comparable with those in Section (*a*) of Figure 10.1. They can provide answers to questions about how other consumers spend their money.

Figure 10.1 might also be used to guide the collection of data and analysis of consumption patterns and problems of low-income families. The consumer expenditure data for low-income families from such surveys as those for 1960–1961 are regularly used as guidelines for development of welfare budgets. They might also be helpful in countering the frequent reaction of welfare families that they cannot live on the amounts budgeted by demonstrating actual consumer expenditure patterns of families with comparable characteristics of income and family size.

10.4.3 To Guide Public Policy Making

Economists have been extensively concerned with appraisals of the effects of alternative public policies. But our appraisals have often been rather divorced from reality because we have failed to take into account some important complicating factors. As knowledge of the structure of consumption grows, the possibilities of taking account of additional socioeconomic and social psychological factors increase. Such knowledge gives us the opportunity to judge the potential effects of public policies relating to prices of farm commodities, family planning programs, or income distribution through changes in social security laws. For such judgments we need detailed analyses of actual relationships of these factors to actual consumer purchases and use of major commodities by subgroups of families. Thus we can expect to shift from heavy reliance on normatively based, deductive analyses (theoretically based "shoulds") to empirically based explanations and predictions. It has become increasingly possible for government analysts to work up estimates of the effects of alternative programs based on alternative sets of assumptions and sets of observed relationships between consumption rates and key socioeconomic phenomena.

10.5 RESEARCH ON THE STRUCTURE OF CONSUMPTION

A number of the research studies reported in Chapter 9 provide findings regarding the nature of the structure of consumption because the events terminating the processes of choice and use form one part of the overall structure. However, findings from four additional research studies are summarized here as an indication of the broad scope of research pertinent to the structure of consumption.

1. Coons, Alvin E., and Glaze, Bert T. *Housing Market Analysis and Growth of Nonfarm Home Ownership*, Ohio State University, Bureau of Business Research Monograph No. 115.

The authors utilized a variety of macroeconomic data on housing along with a sample survey of 100 households in a suburb of Columbus, Ohio. They investigated a wide range of socioeconomic factors possibly related to the home tenure decisions of families in their sample. As hypothesized from knowledge of the relationship of the family life cycle to home purchases, the authors found that the typical homeowner purchased his first house when he was between 25 and 40 years of age. About 10 percent of their sample households were single persons living with others or alone, not normal biological families of two or more persons. Homeowners were found in practically all occupational categories, but the largest group in their suburban sample was comprised of owners in professional and semiprofessional occupations followed by the group of skilled and semiskilled workers. Major reasons for home ownership turned out to be security of residence and expectation of savings to be gained from home ownership. Most families viewed their homes as a consumer durable good rather than as an investment.

2. Caplovitz, David. *The Poor Pay More.*

Caplovitz directed a study of the consumer practices of 464 families living in low-income housing projects in the neighborhoods of three New York City settlement houses. He found considerable evidence to support the hypothesis that cultural pressures to buy major durables reach low-income families as well as those with higher incomes. In fact, he argues that these families engage in compensatory consumption to offset their lack of upward social and occupational mobility (pages 12–13). Caplovitz cites a number of examples of lack of consumer technological knowledge which leads to buying overpriced goods and disastrous use of easy credit. In Chapter 3, this sociologist traced the sequence of buying events related to movement of families into the housing projects. Almost three-fourths of the families bought some furniture at the time of their moves and others did their buying subsequently. The extent of ownership of television sets and automatic washing machines by these low-income families differed little from that for all families in New York City.

Other chapters of the Caplovitz book describe shopping patterns, sources and uses of credit, and the characteristics of the marketing system catering to these low-income, high credit-risk families.

3. Alexis, Marcus; Simon, Leonard, and Smith, Kenneth. *Some Determinants of Food Buying Behavior*, Manuscript, College of Business Administration, University of Rochester, 1966.

This manuscript is a preliminary report on a study of relationships among kinds of stores shopped, socioeconomic variables, and food commodities purchased by a sample of 300 families in the Rochester, New York, Metropolitan Area, stratified in three income groups —low, middle, and high. The authors selected food expenditures as the consumer goods category to measure the influence of socioeconomic class and demographic variables upon consumption patterns. They found that consumers in the lowest economic group tended to buy their food supplies more generally in independent neighborhood stores than do consumers with higher incomes. The major factor related to this pattern was the lack of mobility because of lower rate of automobile ownership. Apparently, less education and the availability of credit, delivery, and telephone service also contributed. The shopping patterns of families with less than $3000 income closely resembled those of families in the next higher income category, $3000 to $5000. But the lower-income groups purchased a somewhat different "mix" of foods.

From their analysis of income-food quantity relationships for individual foods, the authors found that purchases of the following foods increased at successively higher levels of income: frozen orange juice and frozen vegetables, fresh tomatoes and fresh fruit, cartoned orange juice, regular coffee, and butter. The list of items decreasing at higher levels of income included bread, pork chops, canned vegetables and soup, potatoes, instant coffee, rice, sugar, spam, chicken, and powdered milk.

4. Kosobud, Richard. "Fulfillments of Consumer Buying Plans," Chapter 4 of Kosobud, Richard F., and Morgan, James N. (Editors), *Consumer Behavior of Individual Families over Two and Three Years*, Monograph No. 36, Survey Research Center.

Kosobud used data from repeated interviews with the same families from the 1961 and 1962 Surveys of Consumer Finances, to study the relationship between (*a*) plans for purchases of cars, additions and repairs to housing units, and other major durables, and (*b*) actual expenditures for such purposes. Evidence from the surveys supported the hypothesis that buying plans are influenced by consumer income, attitudinal variables, and age and quality of the existing stock of the durable item. Kosobud found that buying plans consistently overestimated actual expenditures in 1961. He traced the lack of fulfillment to unfavorable income events which had not been foreseen and to unexpected price increases and business developments.

11

CHANGES IN CONSUMER BEHAVIOR

Changes in consumer behavior unique to one family or even to a small group of families and changes which follow established cyclical patterns are of no particular concern to the executive in charge of marketing in the typical business concern. However, unexpected innovations in the structure of tastes and preferences of a small group of consumers which spread to larger groups usually attract considerable interest of marketing practitioners. Both sudden changes in consumption of many families, even though in predictable ways, and general trends in their consumption present problems and opportunities for marketing.

Section 11.1 catalogs the major forms and sources of changes in consumer behavior, at the micro level. Then the significance of such changes to marketing and economic development is discussed. The next three sections consider successively the major types of cyclical changes, sources of unexpected changes, and the spread of changes in consumer behavior from one group to another. The last two sections of the chapter provide examples of empirical research and an introduction to changes at the macro level, as in an entire country.

11.1 FORMS AND SOURCES OF CHANGES IN CONSUMER BEHAVIOR

11.1.1 The Conventional Approach

Standard economic theory categorizes changes in consumer behavior in three principal forms: (1) a shift from one point on a particular indifference curve to another, as in the case of a change in price demonstrated in Figure 6.5; (2) a shift from one indifference curve to another, as with a change in consumer income (Figure 6.8) or a change in real income; and (3) a major shift in tastes and preferences requiring identification and measurement of an entirely new map of indifference curves to reflect changed relationships, especially with respect to variations in income and price.

From this listing of the forms of changes in behavior you can identify most economists' primary interest in those changes which result from changes in price and income. By assuming tastes and preferences as "given," conventional economic theorists avoid the questions of how and why they change.

Because of price or income changes (or for other reasons), consumers may acquire wants for new products or lose interest in familiar items. Such changes can be handled reasonably well by manipulating indifference maps. But changes in behavior related to ways of solving consumer problems, sometimes described as changes in problem-solving strategies, are more complex and difficult to explain with indifference analysis.

11.1.2 Suggested Categories

To clarify and amplify the economists' rather abstract views of changes in behavior, let us examine how the situational formulations of processes of consumer purchase and use of goods and services and the micro structure of consumption in Chapters 8, 9, and 10 relate to changes in behavior. Many changes in consumer behavior might be categorized as changes (1) in the processes of purchase, (2) in consumption or expenditure events measured in terms of rates per period of time and forming part of the structure of consumption, and (3) in the processes of using goods and services.

Factors bringing about changes in consumer behavior fall into three categories. *First,* socioeconomic phenomena related to the processes of choice or buying and use and to the structure of consumption of a family, for instance, constantly change. Let us exclude the factors related to supply from this category. (Such phenomena are described in Section 9.2.2.) *Second,* the relationships between socioeconomic phenomena and the structure of consumption probably change continuously but at varying rates. The *third* category could be subsumed under the first, but changes in technological and supply factors are so frequent and important to marketing that they merit separate attention.

11.1.3 Process of Buying or Choice

The multidisciplinary framework for study of the process of choice in Figure 9.1 provides clues to the ways in which changes in the process of buying take place. Biogenic needs of individuals change gradually, but sociological phenomena such as changes in reference groups or in family interaction may change awareness of sociogenic needs rather suddenly or gradually. A series of bad experiences, favorable new experiences, newly acquired knowledge, or changes in perception may change the awareness of specific needs. At the final judging stage, still more forces of change can crowd in. They may result from changes in the market situation (among which are price changes) or from changes in the constraints or limitations placed by purchasing power (income change), by choices of substitute or complementary products, by knowledge of use of the product, and the limitations of time and energy related both to shopping and to potential use.

To illustrate, let us consider the hypothetical case of Family *F* which has been on relief. Suppose Mr. *F* enters a special training program under the Economic Opportunity Act and, upon finishing it, gets a job paying $400 per month. The family income level rises substantially, reducing the constraint on purchases. The family can move up the hill of satisfaction on their indifference map. Everyone in the family wants new clothes, a new TV, and steaks or pork chops every night. But suppose they move to a low-cost housing project in a better part of town. There the children acquire new friends and new wants. Thus sociological factors begin to affect their perception of needs and wants, a part of the process of choice. Perhaps the pressures of accelerated demands and the availability of a nursery school will lead to Mrs. *F*'s taking a homemaker course in order to get a job to supplement the family income.

The foregoing illustration started with changes in the socioeconomic phenomena of education, income, and occupation. These changes triggered other changes in socioeconomic characteristics and in the psychological phenomena of needs, perception, and other cognition processes. Through interaction we would expect some changes in the relationships of these phenomena to the process of consumer buying. But we lack empirical evidence for positive, precise statements about changes in these relationships. Such knowledge would be very helpful in formation of public policies and programs for breaking the poverty cycles of individual families.

11.1.4 Changes in Micro Structure

In Section 10.1 the behavioral, technical and economic, temporal, and aggregative dimensions of the structure of consumption were explained. Here we are concerned with the changes in the behavioral and the technical and economic dimensions through time. In marketing terms, we must consider how and why changes occur in rates of consumer purchases of individual products and services and combinations of products bought by individual consumers or families.

The rate of purchase and consumption of one product by one family can change simply by repeating the process of purchase more often in a given period. Also, changes in the process described previously, such as purchase of a larger quantity at a time, may affect the rate of purchase. If the rate of purchase for one item changes significantly, we expect to find either offsetting changes in purchases of other items, in savings, or in income. For a group of families, the average rate of purchase can be affected by changes in the proportion of the group buying the product.

Empirical economists and marketing specialists are particularly attentive to the direction of changes in the "mix" or combinations of products and to the degree of change in purchases in relation to the degree of change in income or price. As noted in Section 6.2, the relationship between the proportional change in price of an item and the proportional change in purchases which results is called "price elasticity" or "elasticity of demand." The comparable relationship between the ratio of change in income and that for purchases is called "income elasticity of demand." Both assume all other conditions remain unchanged. Because of difficulties in obtaining data on incomes and purchases from families free from interaction with other socioeconomic changes, economists frequently calculate approximate income elasticities from data on differences in purchases among families with differences in income at a given time, e.g., the year 1965. Thus they treat the cross-section elasticities as estimates of how purchases would change if people's incomes were to change, assuming *ceteris paribus*. Price elasticities are ordinarily calculated from aggregative data for a series of months or years because we lack observations of the reactions of small groups of families to identified changes in prices.

Changes in purchases accompanying changes in prices or income may represent the effects of alternative relationships, e.g., movement along the same indifference curve or from one curve to another on a given indifference map. But changes in purchases may also result from changes in price-consumption or income-consumption relationships (i.e., in the behavioral dimension) or from interactions with other socioeconomic phenomena. For theoretical analysis, an economist often assumes "all other conditions remain the same" (*ceteris paribus*). When other conditions do change, economists say that tastes and preferences have changed. In empirical work we try to find out whether and how much changes in other factors have altered structural relationships, and whether the changes are likely to recur or to continue. Thus we try to sort out fixed and changing relationships to factors other than income and price.

So far we have been concentrating on changes on the supply side (price to consumer) and in the consumer's economic situation. Section 9.2.2 described many other socioeconomic factors that are susceptible to changes and are likely to have repercussions on consumption rates. These repercussions may be predictable from earlier experiences, or they may change in intensity and direction, indicating changed relationships. If they occur for many families, they are of concern to marketing people.

11.1.5 Changes in Process of Use

Although changes in use often affect later purchases and the structure of consumption (or expenditures), the sequence of purchase and use caused the author to defer consideration of changes in use until this point. The schedules of the process of use or of maintenance may be changed and affect consumption rates—providing the constraints of economic resources permit. Either type of change is important to marketing because of the significance of repeat buyers to total sales and to holding a market position.

Economists have devoted little attention to this subject. Although marketing researchers have apparently done some fact gathering, as in the two nationwide surveys of menus made by the Market Research Corporation of America, few analytical results have been published. Home management specialists and foods specialists have carried on small scale studies, but few generalizations have been formulated for marketing use.

Having reviewed the more abstract or general approaches to changes in consumer behavior, we are now ready to consider some rather pragmatic material.

11.2 THE PROBLEM OF CHANGING TASTES AND PREFERENCES

Business firms carry on empirical research in consumer behavior to explain past and present actions of consumers, and, probably more significantly, to predict future consumer behavior. Changes in the consumer behavior of individuals are partly preceded by changes in tastes and preferences and partly reflected in these changes. Many empirical economic researchers have been indistinguishable from marketing specialists in their concern for and preoccupation with the study of changing tastes and preferences.

In an affluent society, as well as in developing economies, marketing is engaged in meeting current consumer wants and in contributing to the fulfillment of new kinds of wants. Just as firms which fail to engage in a vigorous search for new products and new markets wither away, so societies that do not change have a strong tendency toward apathy and stagnation.

The American economy has the productive potential to supply both (*a*) current average rates of consumption for most of the kinds of goods and services to those families now below the poverty line, and (*b*) increased demand from the whole population. More and more families have incomes well above anyone's definition of a "subsistence level." Subsistence level refers to the minimum levels of consumption necessary to maintain life and health. Income above the variously defined "minimum" to buy necessities is called "discretionary income." The use of discretionary income appears to be little influenced by usual factors related to urbanization and regionality. Instead, sociological and psychological factors seem to be more important.

Viewing the problem from a different perspective, we see that the predictive value of changes in income and urbanization for most foods and some other commodities currently considered to be necessities in the United States is diminishing. A very large proportion of the United States population is reaching the flatter part of the Engel curves for food (with lower income elasticity) and other necessities. Also, most of the population is now either urban or behaves that way. However, future changes in income will continue to be very significant for prediction of changes in consumption of housing, new products, and luxuries.

To support the need for studying changes in tastes and preferences, here is a summary of expectations concerning future changes in consumption.

> . . . Only a small increase in per capita food consumption is expected in the coming decade, with most of the change likely to be in improved quality, greater variety, and changes in form. For clothing we expect still more changes in use of fibers and synthetic products. In the next decade the demand for house furnishings and equipment probably will be highly related to the changes in the distribution of the population by age and stage of the family life cycle. For other semidurable and durable goods there is likely to be greater emphasis on quality and variety and further technological change. Changes in quantities and types of commodities will tie in with changes in our ways of living. These changes are also likely to lead to further increases in demand for services. Changes in the ways we live will be affected by a wide range of technological and social changes. The potential significance of these changes to future demand for food and nonfood goods and services indicates both the urgent need for a new approach to demand forecasting and the starting point for our search for that approach.[1]

[1] Page 620 of Burk, Marguerite C. "Development of a New Approach to Forecasting Demand," *J. Farm Economics* **46**:3:618–632, August 1964.

Just as economists identify movements of a consumer along his income-consumption curve up the hill of satisfaction (Figure 6.8) as his income changes, so we can think of consumers moving rather predictably along other statistical curves, such as the aging cycle of individuals and the family life cycle. But sometimes consumers develop new sets of tastes and preferences which result in discontinuities in their behavior. Often they are brought about by changes in the goods and supplies offered on the market, such as technological changes in products. Or unemployment may force a cut-back in expenditures and realignment of preferences. We consider these expected and unexpected changes in behavior in more detail in Sections 11.3 and 11.4.

11.3 CYCLICAL AND SECULAR SOURCES OF CHANGES IN CONSUMER BEHAVIOR

Among the types of changes in behavior of individuals and families expected or predictable from cyclical changes in natural and socioeconomic phenomena affecting our lives is the obvious adjustment to seasonality. Most Americans eat much more turkey during the November–December holiday season than in summer, although the seasonal variations are much less now than 20 or 30 years ago. Fuel oil consumption in private households goes up in winter, down in summer. However, changes in technology are altering many seasonal patterns. Other sources of change, such as secular increases in urbanization, have continued for many years, with predictable effects.

11.3.1 Supply-Induced Changes

For individual consumers, changes in supplies appear mostly in the forms of changes in price or in the quality of goods on the market. Consumers react to such changes in ways already described briefly in connection with demand in Section 6.2.1. In price analysis, economists work out much more elaborate analyses of reactions to price and changes in supplies of substitute and complementary goods. Therefore the author introduces only a few ideas here.

Some of the seasonality in consumption reflects historical variations in supply, such as the traditional reduction in livestock slaughter in the summer. The great reduction in output of durable goods for civilians during World

War II and the postwar flow of supplies had generally predictable effects on consumer behavior. However, the magnitude of consumer demand at the end of the war was much greater than expected by many firms and by government economists.

The effects of supply on consumption lead us into macroeconomics, therefore further consideration is deferred to Part III.

11.3.2 Physiological and Psychological Aspects of Aging

Many changes in consumer behavior are related to the physiology of aging and to societally established norms for behavior at each age. For example, infants and young children in the United States are heavy milk consumers. Most families follow the recommendations of nutritionists regarding the calcium needs of growing children. But numerous studies have indicated that many teenage girls reduce their milk consumption to very low rates because they are hypersensitive about their weight and usually not well informed about nutrition. (The nonavailability of skim milk in the schools and many in-plant feeding establishments apparently reduces total milk consumption by people avoiding use of milk fat.) Elderly people buy few clothes and probably few steaks and boats in comparison with people in the middle-age groups.

11.3.3 Family Life Cycle

Data from cross-section surveys reviewed in earlier chapters clearly indicate rather close relationships between the stage in the family life cycle and consumer behavior. Few longitudinal studies of families have been conducted, and those that have been are largely confined to analysis of financial records of account-keeping farm families. The Hill-Foote study of three generations of a hundred families, when published, will yield some data contrasting the consumption patterns of the three generations.[2]

A variety of changes are expected as the family increases in size and changes in age composition. These changes respond to the needs of young children, then of teenagers, and then of the parents in the so-called "empty nest." The larger households have to spend more for food, for example, compared with smaller households at the same level of income. Many families change their housing expenditures and move from the central city to the suburbs when the children need play space and their parents want particular types of educational facilities for their children.[3] Based on cross-section studies by the Michigan Survey Research Center, Fisher has described the kinds of changes in consumer behavior that are expected to take place over the family life cycle.[4] Further research by the Survey Research Center on relationships between household purchases and family life cycle has been reported by Lansing and Kish.[5]

But considerable care must be taken in inferring longitudinal changes from cross-section data. Allowances must be made for changes in group influence on individual families, for changes in macro type factors, such as supplies and prices, and for major sociological changes.[6]

11.3.4 Occupational Career Patterns

Comparisons of consumption patterns of different occupational groups and their related social classes, referred to in Chapter 9, indicate that consumption patterns of families may be considerably influenced by the occupational career patterns of the individual earners in the family. For example, workers doing heavy manual work require more high energy foods than do sedentary workers, and different types of clothing than office workers. But some of the differences in expenditure patterns are less obvious. Several studies have indicated that relatively high-income wage-earners spend more for durable goods than do families of businessmen with comparable incomes. Some

[2] Hill, Reuben. "Patterns of Decision-Making and the Accumulation of Family Assets," in Foote, Nelson N. (Editor), *Household Decision-Making.*

[3] Pages 34–51 of Foote, Nelson N., Abu-Lughod, Janet, et al. *Housing Choices and Housing Constraints.*

[4] Fisher, Janet A. "Family Life Cycle Analysis in Research on Consumer Behavior," pp. 28–51 of Clark, Lincoln H. (Editor), *Consumer Behavior: Volume II, The Life Cycle and Consumer Behavior.*

[5] Lansing, John B., and Kish, Leslie. "Family Life Cycle as an Independent Variable," *Am. Soc. Review* **22**:5:512–519, October 1957.

[6] Major differences between longitudinal data and cross-section data related to family development are described on page 204 of Hill, Reuben, and Rodgers, Roy H. "The Developmental Approach," Chapter 5 in Christensen, Harold T. (Editor), *Handbook of Marriage and the Family.*

sociologists have suggested that this may be a compensation for frustrations experienced in the occupational sphere.[7]

Sociologists have found some general patterns in occupational changes during the careers of workers who started at different levels.[8] Related to such changes are changes in income and social status, which are major determinants of consumer behavior. Therefore we may hypothesize that there is an expected life-income cycle matching the expected work cycle for each major occupational group and an expenditure cycle related to the family life cycle. Both expected and unexpected family economic behavior might be appraised by measuring such expectations and comparing actual experiences of particular categories of families with their expectations. Such comparisons might yield useful marketing information. For example, it is generally recognized that families adjust their buying patterns to those identified with the reference groups to which they aspire or to which they belong. Suppose that increasing automation forces many skilled workers to take retraining courses and to move up to semiprofessional levels, out of the manual worker category. What changes in their demand for individual commodities and services would be expected to result?

11.3.5 Residential Shifts

Problems of food consumption of urban families differ from those of farm families at the same level of real income because of less production for home use, less need for high energy foods, differences in the availability of perishable, commercially produced and distributed supplies, and the effects of accumulated habit patterns and social influences. Such differences and the knowledge of the significant influence of reference groups on consumption lead to the inference that families moving from rural areas to urban areas gradually change their consumption patterns toward those of families in urban areas. Of course, part of the change comes about as a result of significant shifts in real income. But no major study has ever traced such families to discover the rates and degrees of change in consumer behavior.

Let us follow through a hypothetical example. Suppose the "*F*" Family has moved into town from the farm where the garden was bountiful and they were eating beef and chicken they had produced for their own use. In town, Mr. *F*'s new job as manager of the petroleum cooperative pays very well. Let us consider the process of change in the *F* Family's outlay for food. They start spending more for food than when they had home-produced supplies. Obviously, the change is in response to a problem—the need for food. It is a rational change to adjust to a discrepancy between what exists in the new environment and what is desired. Soon (but just how soon we do not know) new patterns of consumer behavior are formed and become habitual. We hypothesize that they will be quite similar to the food expenditure patterns of established urban families with similar socioeconomic characteristics.

Similarly, as families move from the South to the North or from the East to the West, we expect their consumer behavior to adjust to their new setting. But we do not have detailed information with which to test this hypothesis.

11.4 UNEXPECTED CHANGES IN CONSUMER BEHAVIOR

Economic theory has relatively little content pertinent to explanation of changes in behavior which are *not* in response to changes in prices or incomes or in degree of urbanization. Such changes are herded together under the tent of changes in tastes and preferences. Economists often refer to the shifts in demand curves resulting from changes in tastes and preferences, but they have done relatively little work on reasons for such changes.

Although many socioeconomic phenomena change in predictable ways and have predictable effects, others do not. Sometimes emergencies such as wars, natural catastrophes, sharp economic changes, and political upheavals are accompanied by rapid shifts in institutions, policies, and programs which lead to unexpected shifts in consumer behavior. The processes of choice and use and the structure of consumption may be affected individually or together. Sudden shifts in behavior may also result from major technological

[7] Chinoy, Ely. "The Tradition of Opportunity and the Aspirations of Automobile Workers," *Am. J. Soc.* **LVII**:5:453–459, March 1952.

[8] Form, William H., and Miller, Delbert C. "Occupational Career Pattern as a Sociological Instrument," *Am. J. Soc.* **LIV**:4:317–329, January 1949.

changes in products available or the impact of such changes on the supply situation.

Perhaps the most unpredictable shifts occur when one set of relationships is disturbed by changes in another set. To understand more about such changes, let us review two psychological approaches.

11.4.1 Psychological Approaches

Psychologists such as Bayton remind us that perception of a product by an individual may change because the product changes (structural factors) or because the individual's power of perception changes (functional factors). Perhaps the housewife has learned by experimenting with a new product that it meets the *wants* of her family quite satisfactorily.[9]

A number of psychologists have delved deeply into attitude and preference changes. Recently, the concepts of balance, congruity, and dissonance have assumed considerable prominence.[10] The key to these concepts is man's striving for consistency. Festinger's theory of cognitive dissonance has attracted particular attention. (See Section 5.4.3) Dissonance results when two elements of knowledge, whether fact or value, are held by an individual and have characteristics such that the converse of one element would follow from the other. They are completely inconsistent, in other words. The hypothesis of Festinger is that dissonance makes people psychologically uncomfortable and will cause a person to make efforts to reduce the dissonance in order to achieve consonance. An individual will actively avoid situations and information which are perceived as likely to increase dissonance.[11]

11.4.2 Anthropological Interest in Innovations

In Section 5.6 we noted the major interest of anthropologists in cultural change. We are concerned in this chapter with the micro dimension of behavioral changes and recognize that cultural changes begin with individuals and small groups. Read again the discussion of Barnett's study of innovation in Section 5.6.2. Anthropologists' contributions to the understanding of the processes of innovation and cultural change will be considered further in Section 11.5.

11.4.3 Marketing Approach to Unexpected Changes

Research on the process of change in tastes and preferences in the past is essential to the development of a new approach. Marketing researchers search for factors that have brought about such changes in the past and for knowledge of the kinds of people who changed first. There is fairly general agreement that the major constraints on changes probably are a conservative point of view and the limitations of finances and other resources. From past research there is evidence that the conditions conducive to changes in tastes and preferences are higher levels of education, the status incentive, the achievement incentive, higher communication receptivity, extensive association with other people, and the incidence of these changes related to the family life cycle which are characterized by mobility and excess of income over urgent needs.

Motivation researchers for business firms have been concerned with want creation. There appear to be about four different broad sources of wants or ways in which wants are created: (1) the search for new ways of satisfying old needs, (2) socially created new needs such as those based on changes in customs and institutions, (3) psychological creation of new wants based apparently on curiosity and the urge for variety in human experience, and (4) technological innovation. We will consider innovation in more detail after a brief look at the relationship between economic growth and changes in tastes and preferences.

11.4.4 Impact of Such Changes on Economic Growth

Analysis of unexpected changes in consumption is particularly significant to development of greater understanding of the stimulation, acceleration, and continuation or decline in economic growth. Although research in this area has been meager, some challenging ideas and hypotheses have been presented in recent years. One set of ideas comes from McClelland, a psychologist, who argues that achievement

[9] Bayton, James A. "Contributions of Psychology to the Microeconomic Analysis of Consumer Demand for Food," *J. Farm Economics* 45:5:1430–1435, December 1963.

[10] Zajonc, Robert. "The Concepts of Balance, Congruity, and Dissonance," *Public Opinion Quarterly* 24:3:280–296, Winter 1960.

[11] For further study, see Festinger, Leon. *Conflict, Decision, and Dissonance.*

motivation is in part responsible for economic growth.[12]

A significant component of economic change is change in consumer behavior. Hagen, an economist, has used some of McClelland's ideas and has studied empirical data on factors related to economic growth. He wrote: "The interrelationships between personality and social structure are such as to make it clear that social change will not occur without change in personalities. . . ."[13] Then he investigated the hypothesis that changes in personality among homogeneous groups of people develop from changes in the environment of children which encourage the seeking of new solutions to problems, often newly perceived.

Moore has criticized the theories of McClelland and Hagen because both deal exclusively with personality formation in early socialization. He writes:

> . . . In view of the overwhelming evidence for adolescent and adult socialization—the internalization of values and norms appropriate to contexts of social action that could not possibly be learned in infancy—exclusive attention to infant socialization represents a radical distortion of the interaction between the individual personality and the social order. Yet it would be improper to deny the importance of "marginal" and even "disaffected" groups as initiators of social change. . . . If, however, social circumstances provide a measure of both opportunity and immediate rewards for novelty, then the structure and personality may interact in ways that produce useful novelty.[14]

11.5 SPREAD OF CHANGE IN CONSUMER BEHAVIOR FROM ONE GROUP TO ANOTHER

There have been relatively few research studies on processes of innovation, especially with respect to consumer goods, despite the significance of the subject. Barnett has indicated that the concept of innovation has a number of dimensions: (1) motivation for innovation, (2) factors favoring early adoption of innovation, (3) factors favoring wider acceptance of innovation, and (4) the identification and characterization of the innovators.[15] People apparently adopt new products in order to offset frustration, achieve prestige, keep up with fashion, because they are bored, or because of special attributes of new products. The prestige factor or desire to be different has been noted for years by many observers and has been discussed earlier in this book. Adoption of an innovation by individuals is favored by such factors as purchasing power, knowledge, education, and the fact that innovations are quickly mass-produced. Therefore recent innovators must keep changing to new products to keep ahead of others.

The process of acceptance of innovation is described as the *diffusion process.* Rogers examined six major traditions of research on this process—in anthropology, early sociology, rural sociology, education, industrial and medical sociology.[16] He related the adoption process, through which diffusion operates, to learning theory and decision making. Although researchers have used various means of identifying stages in the process, they have agreed that adoption is a process with a number of stages. Rogers followed the lead of such rural sociologists as Beal and Bohlen in using the following stages in the adoption process—awareness, interest or information seeking, mental application or evaluation of the new process, trial, and finally adoption.

Earlier research has revealed some evidence that high-income families are in the forefront of changes in tastes and preferences, especially for new products. Despite much research on how the process operates, we still know little about the "whys" of the process. Without knowledge of the whys, we cannot evaluate how far this approach could be used to forecast demand. One step toward learning about the process of change is intensive study of the whys of variations in preference patterns at a given time for one group of families such as those with moderately high incomes.

The significant *unknowns* include: (1) reliable knowledge of variation in consumption patterns of moderately high income families and of the relationship of such variations through socioeconomic factors; (2) precise knowledge of the relationships of value orientations to consumer decision making

[12] McClelland, David C. *The Achieving Society.*

[13] Page 86, Hagen, Everett, E. *On the Theory of Social Change.*

[14] Moore, Wilbert E. "Social Aspects of Economic Development," page 897 of Faris, Robert E. L. (Editor), *Handbook of Modern Sociology.*

[15] Barnett, H. G. *Innovation: The Basis of Cultural Change.*

[16] Page 23 of Rogers, Everett M. *Diffusion of Innovations,* op. cit.

on specific types of food and nonfood commodities and of the interrelationships among such sets of values; (3) documentation of the characteristics of families which are related to the process of innovation and consumption patterns for old and new products.[17]

11.5.1 The Tastemaker Study

A significant pilot study of America's tastemakers was made in Ridgewood, New Jersey, by Opinion Research Corporation to test a new strategy for predicting change in consumer behavior, i.e., by study of "high mobiles." Their research with a sample of 105 households with incomes over $5,000 yielded generally higher Early Product Adoption scores for higher income families, but there was a considerable variation within this group as well as within lower income groups. . . . These researchers found the lowest scores on Early Product Adoption by the highest income families in their sample to be roughly equal to the highest scores by the lowest income families. Variations in adoption timing appeared to be closely related to travel, breadth of social contacts, reading habits which the researchers described as aspects of geographic, social, and intellectual mobility.[18]

11.5.2 A Study of Upper-Income Families

A new approach has been suggested to the problem of forecasting demand or consumer behavior based on the hypothesis that upper-income families act as forerunners of changes in demand and consumption. The author and her research assistants have undertaken research to explore the validity of this hypothesis. This conceptual framework given in Figure 11.1 provided the general plan.[19] We identified the purchasers and users of recently developed products in a group with substantial discretionary income. Currently, we are relating socioeconomic characteristics and con-

[17] Page 628 of Burk, Marguerite C. "Development of a New Approach to Forecasting Demand," *J. Farm Economics* **46**:3:618–632, August 1964.

[18] *Ibid.*, pp. 621–622. The author is grateful to Walter G. Barlow, President of Opinion Research Corporation, for access to the confidential reports on this study.

[19] Most of the ideas underlying the conceptual framework have been developed further for Chapters 9 to 11 of this text.

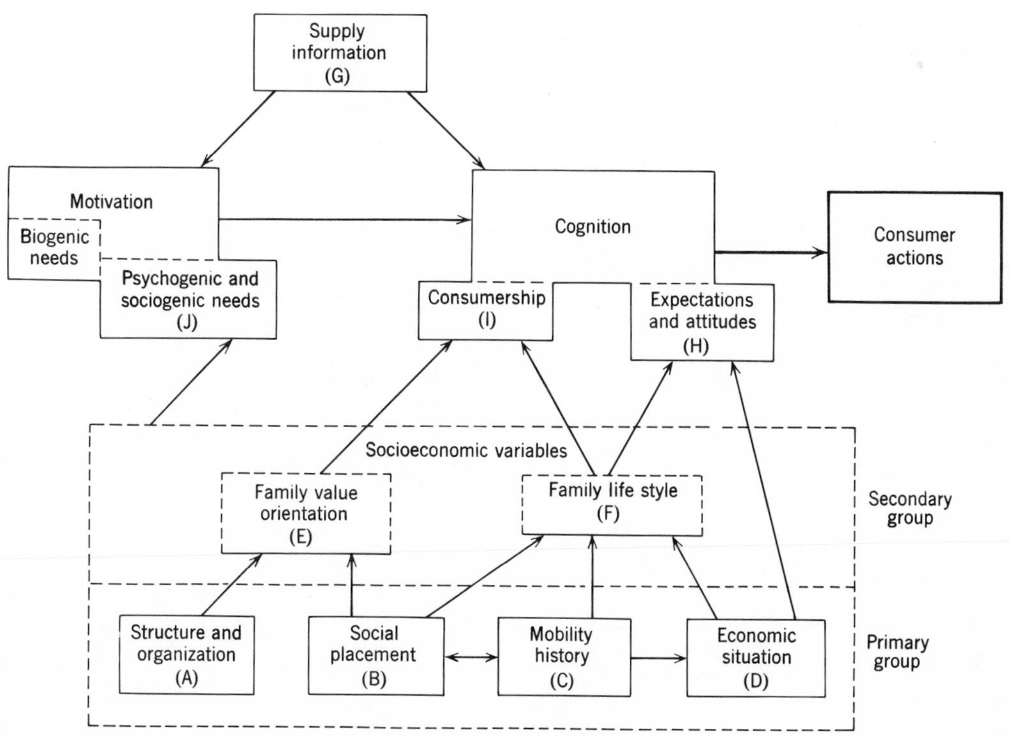

FIGURE 11.1 Conceptual framework developed for analysis of consumption patterns of upper-income families.

sumer orientation to these innovation characteristics. From extensive measuring of the interrelationships, we hope to identify more of the key characteristics of people who have recently adopted innovations and to measure their relative importance.

11.6 EMPIRICAL RESEARCH ON CHANGES IN CONSUMPTION BY THE SAME GROUP OF FAMILIES

Two approaches have been used to study changes in consumption by the same group of families. One has involved reinterviewing families who had been contacted in surveys at an earlier date. Data obtained relating to consumer behavior and consumption patterns at the later dates are compared with those at the earlier date. The second approach involves comparison of data obtained at two different times from families reporting continuously under a consumer panel operation.

Simmons traced the respondents who had cooperated in the study of consumer meat purchases in Syracuse, New York, in 1942. He found ". . . a definite association between rate of change in per capita income between 1942 and 1948 and the changes in per capita purchases, price paid, and expenditure for meat. . . ."[20]

Quackenbush and Shaffer reported findings of the panel study of consumers in Lansing, Michigan. Weekly average per capita expenditures of these families for major food groups by four-week periods varied significantly from season to season, but their general level was remarkably stable over the period.[21]

Other panels which have supplied data useful for further technical research are the nationwide panel of the Market Research Corporation of America and the panel of families in Atlanta run for a few years under auspices of the Georgia Agricultural Experiment Station.

Neither the reinterview approach nor the panels have yet supplied much-needed information about rates of change in consumption by particular families or factors affecting lags in adjustment to changes to socioeconomic factors. Furthermore they have as yet told us practically nothing about the dynamic changes in sociological factors underlying observed changes in consumption.

11.7 CHANGES IN CONSUMPTION OF THE ENTIRE COUNTRY

Analysis of changes in consumption of large sectors of the population of a country and of nationwide changes is the area of macroeconomics of consumption considered in the next part of this text. In brief, the total change in United States consumption of a commodity, say, chicken, from one year such as 1941 to another year, say 1955, is composed of changes in: (1) the number of people in each group of the population and (2) consumption rates of people grouped by specified characteristics such as income and urbanization.

Although we can identify some of the factors contributing to changes in consumption rates, such as income, urbanization, education, technological innovations, and price relationships, there are often unexplained factors underlying people's changes in behavior. As research accumulates, we can expect the "unexplained" portion to diminish, but some changes probably never will be understood. People are not machines.

[20] Page 4, Simmons, Will M. *Consumer Meat Purchases in Syracuse, New York, 1948 and Comparison with 1942*, Cornell University Agricultural Experiment Station Bulletin 869.

[21] Pages 21 and 22, Quackenbush, G. G., and Shaffer, J. D. *Collecting Food Purchase Data by Consumer Panel*—A Methodological Report on the M.S.U. Consumer Panel, 1951–1958.

PART III

MACROECONOMICS OF CONSUMPTION

Individual actions of individual consumers aggregate into totals for small groups of consumers, then to the aggregates for market segments within the total consumption structure of the whole country. These aggregates, subaggregates, and averages computed from them, and their relationships to the socioeconomic phenomena at one point in time and through time, are the next subjects. Part III is designed to help the student integrate knowledge of trends and patterns in consumption processes and structures at macro levels with knowledge of the marketing system and total economy on the one hand and behavior of individual consumers, developed in Part II, on the other.

Analysis of variations in consumption of major groups of commodities and selected items requires study of their relationships to the marketing system and to other economic and social phenomena. Such cross-sectional studies are basic to analysis of historical changes and to forecasting future changes. Knowledge developed from such studies contributes to the depth and breadth of understanding needed to analyze major types of macroeconomic problems with consumption aspects.

In the following chapters, attention frequently focuses on food consumption problems encountered in agriculture, business, and government. We know more about these problems and more pertinent data are available for study. Wherever possible, data on nonfood consumption are incorporated. The kinds of knowledge needed for analysis of macroeconomic problems of consumption are identified and summarized, including underlying ideas, methods, procedures, and data, as well as some applications of such knowledge.

Consumption may be measured at several different points in the marketing flow of a commodity from the producer to the consumer. Therefore Part III begins by tracing several commodities from primary producers through the marketing system to the ultimate consumers. Problems in measuring consumption of groups of commodities are introduced in Chapter 12, as are contrasts between food and durable goods and between farm food commodities and food marketing services.

Consumption rates of different groups of people vary in every country. Sample surveys are used to measure variations in consumption. Only a brief review of survey methods is included in Chapter 13 because a fuller treatment has already been given in connection with empirical research on consumer choice and use described in Part II. Variations in consumption rates usually form patterns of relationships with measures of the characteristics of the population groups to which they refer. These patterns provide important insights for analysis of changes in market segments and in the total consumer market for goods and services.

Chapter 14 begins with a summary of the kinds of generalized knowledge needed for analysis of various types of consumption patterns, followed by a review of pertinent macro concepts. Then the macro relationships postulated by conventional theories of demand and of the consumption function are examined. Subsequent consideration of alternative approaches includes an integrated conceptual framework for use in macro analysis. Such a framework appears necessary for study of relationships between the structure of consumption and the whole range of socioeconomic phenomena, not just price and income.

Using concepts and measures developed in the preceding chapters, Chapter 15 provides a closer view of historical changes in consumption and of a number of major problems and policies bearing on consumption in the United States. Three sections deal intensively with trends in the United States food market. The last section of the chapter is an introduction to difficult problems in the analysis of changes of consumption in the developing countries.

Chapters 16, 17, and 18 review research on macro aspects of consumption for business firms, on problems of agriculture, and on other national and international problems. They provide some summaries and some comprehensive examples of consumption studies on a wide variety of problems.

Appendix B is a guide to some of the procedures used in macroeconomic analysis of consumption. It is designed to serve as both a working tool for the student and for later reference use.

12

ECONOMIC FLOW OF GOODS INTO CONSUMPTION

This chapter relates production and marketing to consumption by using economic measures to trace the flow of goods into consumption. It begins with clarification of concepts and brief descriptions of the structures of production and marketing. In Section 12.2 some ideas about marketing processes pertinent to consumption are reviewed. Economic dimensions of marketing-consumption relationships at macro levels are demonstrated by considering the flow of, first, single commodities through the marketing system to ultimate consumers, then groups of commodities. Agricultural examples are used extensively because pertinent data are more readily available than is the case for nonagricultural commodities. However, the processes and structures of the two categories differ primarily because of perishability and inventory operations.

12.1 BRIEF DESCRIPTION OF THE STRUCTURES OF PRODUCTION AND MARKETING

12.1.1 On the Meaning of Structure

The concept of structure includes ideas about an organized whole and interrelated, interdependent parts. Structures have dimensions. Laymen think first of the dimensions of height, width, and length. But scientists have expanded the concept of dimension to include measures of other variables like time, value, form, and behavior. As noted in Chapter 5, behavioral scientists like Parsons and Allport describe social structures in terms of systems and subsystems. Although production and marketing involve physical quantities, they are operated by people. Therefore we must relate the behavioral aspects of the structures of production and marketing to consumption, as well as their economic aspects.

Alderson has identified a number of *elements* in these structures, which other people might describe as characteristics of their operations or processes. He gives the term *seriality* to the sequence of steps and stages observed in the processes. *Parallelism* is common in marketing in the sense of separate but parallel flows from suppliers to buyers. These are partly geographic but partly socioeconomic in origin. Alderson says that *circularity* is a special case of seriality in the sense of the circular flows of the complete economic system, often the starting point for elementary textbooks on economics. *Centrality* is the fourth element, referring to the frequent arrangement in which channels flow together at a common point and processes flow in or out. This is common in the process of assembly for mass transport, for example.[1]

Figure 12.1 portrays the seriality, parallelism, and centrality characteristics of economic flows from producers to consumers. To simplify, it omits contributions of other industries to food production and marketing and does not trace details of the flow of agricultural food commodities into nonfood uses. These contributions are part of the circularity to which Alderson refers.

12.1.2 Structure of Production

Economists and marketing people do not generally agree on how to differentiate between production and marketing. They do agree that production of raw materials in

[1] Pages 75–79 of Alderson, Wroe. *Marketing Behavior and Executive Action.*

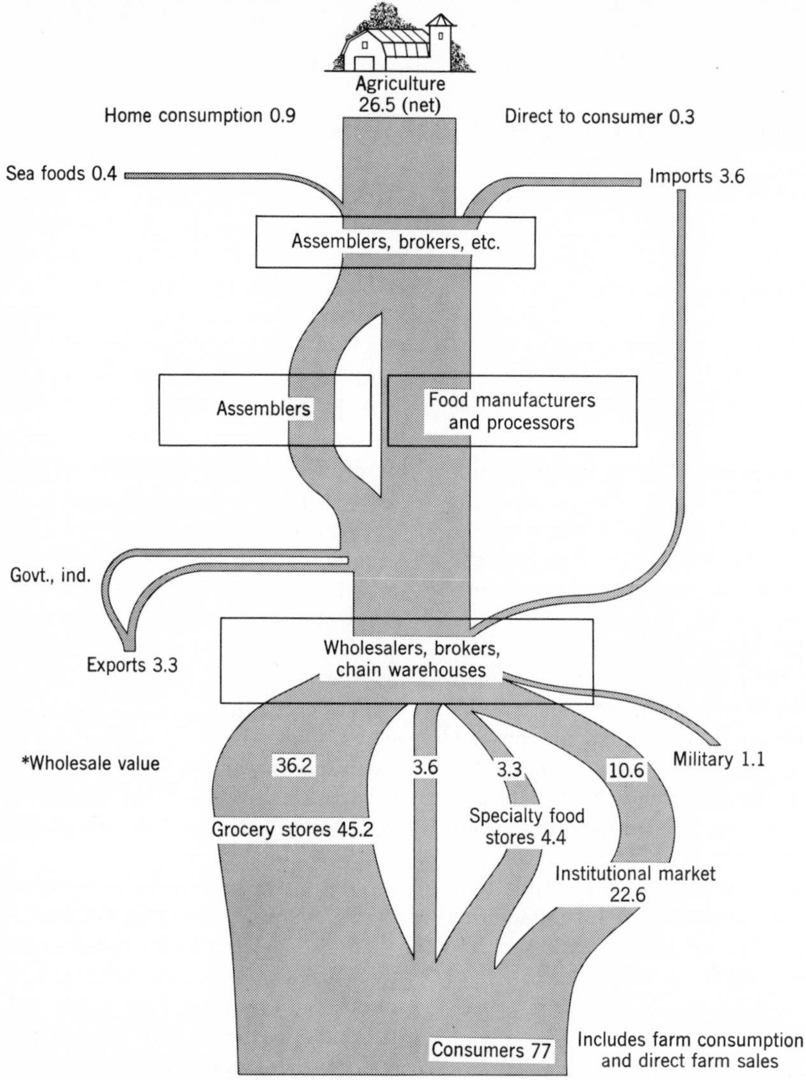

FIGURE 12.1 Flow of food from sources to destinations, 1963 (figures in billion dollars). (Source: Figure 1 of Report of the National Commission on Food Marketing, *Food from Farmer to Consumer*, June 1966.)

mines, from fisheries, and on farms is production. But they differ on whether manufacturing such as food processing is production or marketing. Most agricultural economists argue for the latter, but other people engaged in marketing teaching and operations view manufacturing as production. This follows from their describing *production* as the process of creating "form utility" of products and *marketing* as the activities involved in creation of place, time, and possession utilities.[2] Much depends on what industry is being studied.

Some economists compromise by referring to *primary* production (in mines, farms, forests, and fisheries) and *secondary* production (manufacturing). The two categories of structure have similar dimensions. They include

[2] For example, pp. 1 and 2 of Converse, Paul D., Huegy, Harvey W., and Mitchell, Robert V. *The Elements of Marketing*.

geographic (space); kinds and values of resources involved—labor, land, and capital; number and size of firms; and the time dimension for completion of processes. Output of services (such as medical care and dry cleaning) may be categorized as a third form of production with comparable dimensions for measurement but very different amounts of each.

Alderson maintains that ". . . the basic economic process is the gradual differentiation of goods up to the point at which they pass into the hands of consumers. . . . Under this concept there is no basic difference in the kind of utility created by production and that created by distribution. Every step along the way consists of shaping a set of materials more and more completely to fit the needs of specific consumers. . . ."[3] You can understand this process if you think of the steps from the mining of iron ore, the manufacture of steel plates, the formation of automobile bodies, the assembly of the hundreds of parts of an automobile, to the distribution of finished cars to dealers and on to consumer-buyers.

12.1.3 Structure of Marketing

Where we draw the line between production and marketing does not really matter as long as we alert others to its location and recognize the somewhat arbitrary basis for the delineation. For now, let us classify the manufacturing process as production and concern ourselves with the structure of the detailed processes by which goods are moved from producer to consumer. McInnes has described the market as the gap or separation between producer and consumer within dimensions of space, time, perception, valuation, and ownership.[4] His dimensions of perception and valuation need to be broadened to mesh with the dimensions of the structure of consumption used in Chapter 19, i.e., behavioral, economic, and technical. Also, we need to make explicit the micro-macro or aggregative dimension inferred by McInnes' discussion.

As in the case of consumption, we can identify marketing processes within processes and systems and subsystems, all in motion, to move goods and supply services at the place, time, value, and perception level desired by consumers. In fact, McInnes defines marketing as actualization, meaning the force which actualizes or activates the potentialities of the market relation between producer and consumer.[5] Alderson defines marketing as a phenomenon of group behavior and makes extensive use of Parsons' sociology of systems in describing the operations of individual firms, including firms engaging in transportation, wholesaling, and other processes within marketing.[6] He wrote: "Behavior systems may be described as operating systems when they are characterized by processes involving inputs and outputs. The functions of an operating system should determine its structure if the system is to operate efficiently. . . ."[7] Both of these interpretations of marketing omit the distinctive economic characteristic of the process, namely, the determination of value and price. Suppliers and buyers adjust prices to balance available supplies and demand at successive stages in the marketing process.

Alderson helps us grasp the idea of economic flow of goods from production into consumption with these sentences: ". . . Inputs and outputs may be viewed as the terminal points of some process. In a continuous process involving whole sequences of steps, the beginning and ending points of the process can be selected arbitrarily according to the convenience of the analyst, and inputs and outputs defined correspondingly in relation to these terminal points. . . ."[8] Figure 12.1 traces the sequence of marketing processes that occur in the economic flow of food commodities from farmers to consumers.

12.2 MARKETING PROCESSES RELATED TO CONSUMPTION

The relationship of marketing to consumption can be clarified by reference to three key concepts in marketing—marketing channels, marketing processes, and value added. The treatment of these concepts must be brief here, but they are covered in most courses in marketing. The student can find additional

[3] Op. cit., pp. 69–70.

[4] Page 60 of McInnes, William. "A Conceptual Approach to Marketing," Chapter 3 of Cox, Reavis; Alderson, Wroe; and Shapiro, Stanley J. (Editors), *Theory in Marketing.*

[5] *Ibid.*, page 61.

[6] *Op. cit.*, page 13.

[7] *Ibid.*, page 65.

[8] *Ibid.*, page 65.

detail in marketing texts and in references cited.

12.2.1 Marketing Channels

One writer has defined marketing channels as ". . . institutional configurations for directing and supporting the flows, from production to use, of things of value. . . ."[9] and as social systems which have technological, economic, sociological, and psychological features. To match the terminology of this text, we must become more precise and describe marketing channels as having final terminals at the point of final consumer purchase, not at the point and time of actual use by consumers in their homes.

Matthews, Buzzell, Levitt, and Frank have provided a useful chart of alternative channels in the marketing system of the United States.[10] (Figure 12.2.) Current changes in marketing and in the structure of consumption necessitate greater flexibility in use of marketing channels by producers. There is a definite trend from exclusive distribution policies toward use of a number of different channels by major firms.

12.2.2 Processes in Marketing

Marketing texts usually go into the marketing processes in depth, covering packaging, selling, advertising, physical distribution, servicing, and so on. Here we can only note the highly pertinent sorting aspects of exchange identified by Alderson:[11]

[9] Page 176 of Balderston, F. E. "Design of Marketing Channels," Chapter 12 of Cox, Alderson, Shapiro, op. cit.

[10] Matthews, John B., Jr.; Buzzell, Robert D.; Levitt, Theodore; and Frank, Ronald E. *Marketing: An Introductory Analysis.*

[11] Op. cit., pp. 200–201.

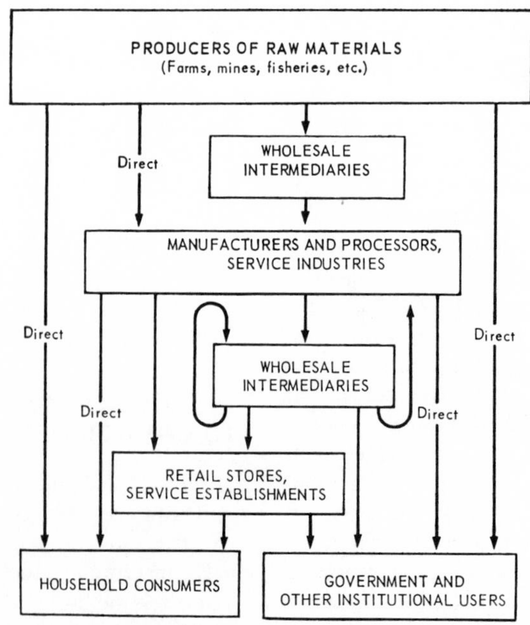

FIGURE 12.2 Channels of distribution in the marketing system of the United States. (From *Marketing: An Introductory Analysis* by Matthews, Buzzell, Levitt, and Frank. Copyright McGraw-Hill Book Company, 1964. Used by permission of the McGraw-Hill Book Company.)

(1) *Sorting-out* —breaking a conglomeration or collection of *different items* into various types of goods
(2) *Accumulation*—of a larger supply of *homogeneous* products
(3) *Allocation* —of breaking down a *homogenous* supply
(4) *Assorting* —using additional supplies to build up assortments of *different* kinds of goods

Alderson argues that the whole economic process starts with conglomerations and ends with assortments as it proceeds from frequently heterogeneous output to meet consumers' demand for heterogeneous supply of goods. Again, however, we must note explicitly the pricing process that goes on concurrently. In addition, the storage operations required by the sorting process should be recognized.

12.2.3 Value Added

Agricultural economists' preference for categorizing manufacturing as part of marketing is related to their intensive study of values added (in connection with price-spreads) as commodities flow from producers to consumers. The existence of a series of markets linking buyers and sellers in modern capitalistic economies provides stages in the productive process at which "services are performed and value is added. The succession of market transactions that occur as goods move from basic resources toward the consumer theoretically presents us with a succession of appraisals of values added as the stream of goods progresses from stage to stage. These cumulative appraisals give us a constant linkage between the uses to which we put our resources and the ultimate values which the market system expects the final consumer transaction to validate." [by consumer's purchase][12]

12.3 FLOW OF FOOD COMMODITIES FROM PRODUCERS TO CONSUMERS

To illustrate the marketing process, we consider first the case of wheat and then the case of milk.[13] The terminology of agricultural economics is used, describing the whole flow from farm gate to consumer as marketing. Thus the manufacture of food products is included as a step in marketing and the term "producer" is applied primarily to farm producers of farm commodities and only secondarily to manufacturers as producers of food products.

12.3.1 Wheat Marketing

Farmers sell the grain they have threshed to country elevators or they may ship directly to terminals if they are large operators. Country elevators then send the wheat by rail or truck to terminal markets or directly to mills. Terminals add the services of weighing, inspection, cleaning, drying, storage, trading, insurance, and financing. From the terminals wheat moves to the mills. After milling, the mill feeds go back to farms through feed dealers, but the flour goes to bakeries, wholesalers, retail stores, and restaurants (referred to as "eating places"). The wheat cereal products produced by the mills go through wholesalers to retail stores and eating places.

Figure 12.3 shows changes in the broad categories of postwar wheat supplies and utilization. The flow of wheat through major United States marketing channels for wheat in the 1963–1964 marketing year is summarized in Figure 12.4.

Information about the quantity of wheat flowing through the several channels comes from many sources.[14] Usually, every five years farmers report how much they have produced in the preceding year for the Census of Agriculture. Such data serve as benchmarks. Annual data on *farm production* are based on estimates of the change from the most recent census or base year developed through a voluntary crop reporting system which uses information from key farmers, elevators, terminal markets, and other informed people. *Stock* data are reported for specific dates by key farmers plus formal reporting by elevators and

[12] Page 214 of Arthur, Henry B. "Market Structures and Functions in Agricultural Control Programs," Chapter 14 of Cox, Alderson, Shapiro, op. cit.

[13] An atlas of marketing is given in the last part of the 1954 Yearbook of Agriculture, *Marketing*, issued by the U.S. Department of Agriculture.

[14] The kinds of data and their sources are described in various reports of the U.S. Department of Agriculture. The most complete single source now available is Chapter 6 of *U.S. Food Consumption* Statis. Bulletin No. 364.

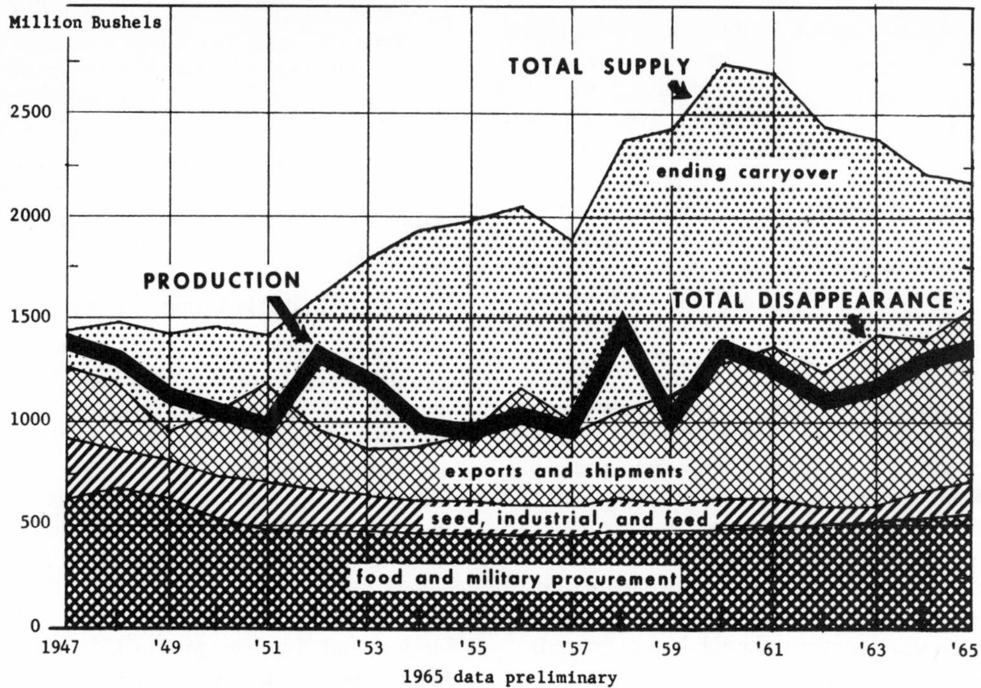

SOURCE: U. S. Department of Agriculture

FIGURE 12.3 Wheat utilization, production, and carryover.

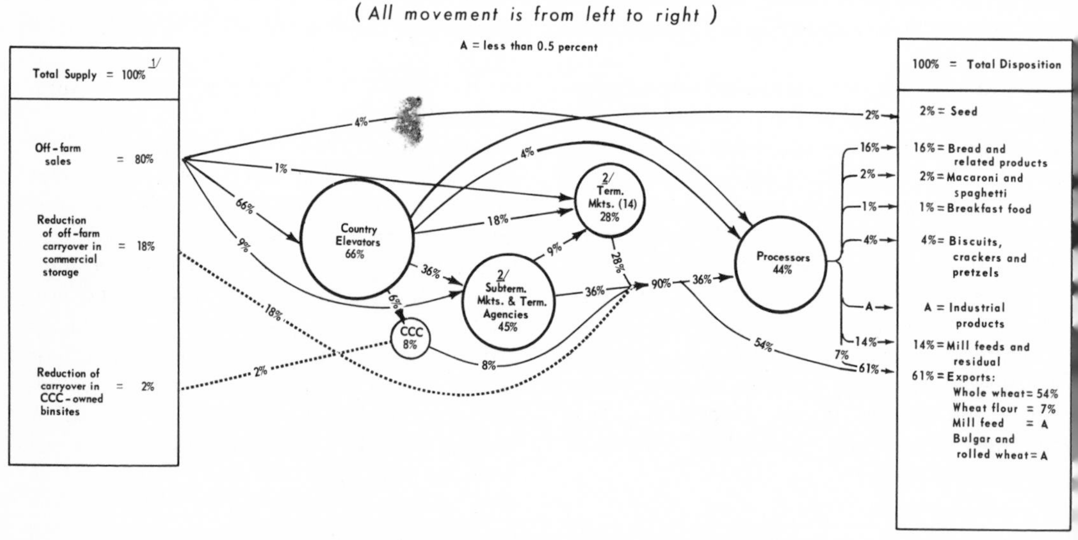

1/ TOTAL SUPPLY DURING THE 1963-64 MARKETING YEAR WAS 1,378 MILLION BUSHELS. OFF-FARM SALES (97 PERCENT OF TOTAL PRODUCTION) TOTALED 1,103 MILLION BUSHELS, OR 80 PERCENT OF THE TOTAL SUPPLY. REDUCTION OF OFF-FARM CARRYOVER IN COMMERCIAL STORAGE TOTALED 249 MILLION BUSHELS, OR 18 PERCENT OF THE TOTAL SUPPLY, AND ENTERED THE MARKETING CHANNELS FROM THE TERMINAL AND SUBTERMINAL ELEVATORS. REDUCTION OF CARRYOVER IN CCC-OWNED BINSITES TOTALED 26 MILLION BUSHELS, OR 2 PERCENT OF THE TOTAL SUPPLY, AND ENTERED THE MARKETING CHANNELS FROM CCC STORAGE SITES.

2/ TERMINAL RECEIPTS ARE BASED ON THE VOLUME OF INSPECTED RECEIPTS. FOURTEEN TERMINAL MARKETS INCLUDE CHICAGO, DULUTH, HUTCHINSON, INDIANAPOLIS, KANSAS CITY, MILWAUKEE, MINNEAPOLIS, OMAHA, PEORIA, SIOUX CITY, ST. JOSEPH, ST. LOUIS, TOLEDO AND WICHITA.

U.S. DEPARTMENT OF AGRICULTURE NEG. ERS 3535-65 (2) ECONOMIC RESEARCH SERVICE

FIGURE 12.4 Major United States marketing channels for wheat, 1963–1964.

warehouses, terminals, and mills. All large mills must report their *output of flour* each month to the Bureau of the Census. Information on *imports* and *exports* comes from reports filed at the time of loading or unloading by the shippers and sent to the Bureau of the Census for tabulation. Information on *military takings* is based on estimates of the U.S. Department of Defense. The estimate of wheat going for *nonfood* purposes is based on information from processors, from farmers (obtained in census reports), and estimates made by the crop reporting system. A full reporting is provided in the Census of Manufactures and in the Census of Agriculture. In the Census of Manufactures, millers report the wheat and other commodities they use. Also, bakeries report the flour they use as well as other food products that are components of the bakery goods.

Marketing specialists use data similar to those in Table 12.1 to answer a number of important questions about the flow of wheat from producers to consumers, or, more broadly, from sources to destinations. Some of their questions and identifications of pertinent data in Table 12.1 follow:

(1) What are the sources of wheat used in the United States and how much comes from each?
  (*a*) Measure in terms of bushels of wheat grain—lines 1–7.
  (*b*) Measure in terms of constant dollars, i.e., 1957–1959 farm prices—lines 11–14.

(2) How do United States civilians share in total wheat use?
  (*a*) Measure in terms of bushels of wheat grain—lines 17–21.

  The per capita figure for line 22 is calculated by multiplying the total in million bushels by 60 pounds per bushel and dividing the total poundage by the total civilian population, comparable with the data in line 40.

  (*b*) Measure in terms of value in constant dollars—compare line 31 and lines 15 and 16.

  Utilization includes exports and nonfood use, such as feed, seed, and industrial purposes. The farm value of civilian food use of wheat must exclude the value of the bran part of the grain. These values at the farm level have to be estimated using the shares of food and nonfood components of total wholesale value.

Flour is measured in hundred pound bags (cwt.) and valued in 1957–1959 wholesale values in line 23, priced at 6.422 cents per pound. Some wheat is processed into wheat cereals for breakfast, having an average 1957–1959 price of 25.5 cents a pound. The byproducts of the milling process are the mill feeds or bran. The farm value of all wheat products represented about 54 percent of the total wholesale value of these products in 1965. Applying this ratio for each year to the wholesale value of civilian flour plus the wheat cereals, we get the estimate of the farm value of these products going into civilian use.

(3) In what forms do consumers buy wheat flour? Measure in pounds of flour—lines 35–39.

  Note the great shift from purchases of flour in the form of pounds of "family flour" for home processing to flour purchased in the forms of processed foods like bread, other baked goods, and mixes.

(4) How does the consumption of wheat compare with consumption of other cereals and how have the consumption rates per capita changed?
  (*a*) Consumption rates per capita, flour equivalents—lines 45–53.

  Detailed data on consumption of cereal products in final form are available only for years in which the Census of Manufactures is taken. But data from millers on the amounts of the flour milled and sold to domestic distributors provide good measures of changes in terms of milled products. Current production is adjusted for foreign trade in developing the total and per capita consumption data.

  (*b*) Measurement of change in consumption of all major cereals combined—value aggregates in constant (1957–1959) dollars in line 54 and the index numbers in line 55.

The computation of the retail value of cereal products consumed in each year is complicated by that shift from family flour to

TABLE 12.1 Wheat Flow from Production into Consumption, Calendar Years

Line	Item	Unit	1940	1955	1965
	Part A—Farm and wholesale quantities and values				
	Supplies				
1	Stocks in all positions (excl. flour), Jan. 1[1]	Mil. bu.	606	1,481	1,449
2	United States production[1]	Mil. bu.	815	937	1,327
3	Sold by farmers (crop of year)[2]	Mil. bu.	643	845	1,236
4	Imports[1]	Mil. bu.	Negl.	6	2
5	Ending stocks on Dec. 31, including USDA[1]	Mil. bu.	724	1,567	1,339
6	Total utilization including feed and seed[1]	Mil. bu.	697	857	1,439
7	Total processed[3]	Mil. bu.	495	523	576
	Farm price and value				
8	Average price received by farmers (season average for new crop)[2]	Per bu.	$0.68	$1.98	$1.33
9	Farm value of new crop—current dollars[2]	Mil. $	556	1,859	1,770
10	Average farm price in 1957–1959 dollars[2]	Per bu.	$1.85	$1.85	$1.85
11	Farm values in 1957–1959 dollars[4]				
12	Production	Mil. $	1,508	1,734	2,455
13	Imports	Mil. $	1	14	4
14	Stock change[5]	Mil. $	−218	−159	+204
15	Total utilization	Mil. $	1,289	1,589	2,663
16	Total processed	Mil. $	916	968	1,066
	Distribution of wheat in all forms				
17	Com'l exports and shipments[1]	Mil. bu.	37	117	162
18	Net purchases by U.S. Dept. of Agr. including change in stocks[1]	Mil. bu.	—	300	747
19	Military purchases[1]	Mil. bu.	—	9	5
20	Nonfood use—feed, seed, alcohol[1]	Mil. bu.	176	99	190
21	Total used for civilian food[1]	Mil. bu.	484	472	512
22	Per capita	Lb.	220	174	160
	Wheat products				
	Utilization, *wholesale* level, measured in 1957–1959 values				
23	Wheat flour[6]	Mil. $	1,396	1,455	1,638

Line	Item	Unit			
24	Wheat cereals[7]	Mil. $	113	121	130
25	Wheat mill feeds[8]	Mil. $	191	186	194
26	Total products	Mil. $	1,700	1,762	1,962
27	Total civilian flour[6]	Mil. $	1,313	1,280	1,423
28	Total civilian cereals[7]	Mil. $	111	120	142
29	Total civilian flour and cereals	Mil. $	1,424	1,400	1,565
Farm level					
30	Ratio of farm value of wheat processed to wholesale value of products used[9]	Percent	53.9	54.9	54.3
31	Total civilian flour and cereals, measured in 1957–1959 farm value[10]	Mil. $	768	769	850
	Part B—Wholesale and retail quantities of civilian supplies				
32	Total civilian flour[11]	Mil. lb.	20,698	19,970	22,165
33	Per capita[11]	Lb.	158	126	116
34	Processed for farmers[12]	Mil. lb.	531	94	Negl.
35	Sold to consumers (line 32–line 34)	Mil. lb.	20,167	19,876	22,165
36	As family flour	Mil. lb.	10,667[12]	6,376[12]	3,100[12]
37	In bread and rolls	Mil. lb.	6,900[12]	8,600[12]	12,800[13]
38	In other baked goods, biscuits, pretzels, crackers	Mil. lb.	1,800[12]	3,300[12]	3,800[13]
39	In other cereal products and mixes	Mil. lb.	800[12]	1,600[12]	2,465[13]
40	Total civilian population—July 1[14]	Mil.	130.9	159.1	191.9

Part C—Index of per capita retail consumption of major cereal products[15]

Line	Item	1957–1959, Retail Price (cents)	1940	1955	1957–1959	1965
			Weighted average retail price (cents)			
41	White and whole wheat flour (combined price)	18.4	16.0	[16]	18.4	[16]
			Percent of total used			
42	Retailed in processed products	22.0	45	64	64	(77)
43	Retailed in mixes	14.1		8	(8)	(9)
44	Other (family flour)	11.0	55	28	28	(14)
			Per capita quantity (lb.)			
45	White and whole wheat flour, combined	(See above)	150.0	122.0	115.0	110.0

TABLE 12.1 (Continued) Wheat Flow from Production into Consumption, Calendar Years

Line	Item	1957–1959, Retail Price (cents)	1940	1955	1957–1959	1965
46	Semolina and durum flour (from durum wheat)	23.0	4.7	1.4	5.1	6.0
47	Wheat cereal	33.7	3.3	2.9	2.8	2.9
48	Rye flour	27.6	2.4	1.4	1.2	1.1
49	Rice	20.4	5.9	5.5	5.4	7.6
50	Corn meal and flour	12.9	21.8	8.7	7.4	5.7
51	Corn cereal	32.9	1.9	1.7	1.8	2.1
52	Hominy	12.0	1.7	2.7	3.5	4.7
53	Oat food products	19.6	4.0	3.3	3.5	3.7
54	Total value aggregate		$32.48	[16]	$27.36	[16]
55	Index (1957–1959 = 100)		118.7[17]	[16]	100.0	[16]

Part D—Analysis of bread price (approximate)[18]

Line	Item	Unit	1940	1955	1965
56	Retail price per pound of bread	Cents	8.0	17.5	20.9
57	Amount of flour in a pound of bread	Lb.	0.65	0.65	0.65
58	Wholesale value of flour in a pound of bread	Cents	1.5	3.9	4.2
59	Farm value of wheat in a pound of bread	Cents	0.9	2.7	2.7
60	Farm value of all ingredients in a pound of bread	Cents	1.1	3.2	3.3

[1] From Table 76, USDA Statis. Bulletin No. 364, *U.S. Food Consumption* and its Supplement for 1965.

[2] From annual *Agricultural Statistics*.

[3] Grindings of wheat as reported in U.S. Dept. Commerce *Business Statistics* and currently in *Survey of Current Business* under Food and Kindred Products.

[4] Calculated from data in preceding section and 1957–1959 farm prices.

[5] Negative indicates increase in stocks; positive indicates decrease.

[6] Values calculated using quantity data from Table 77 of Statis. Bulletin No. 364 and Supplement for 1965 and average 1957–1959 wholesale price of $6.422 per hundredweight.

[7] Values calculated using 1957–1959 wholesale price of 25.5 cents per pound and data on total processed supplied by Economic Research Service (ERS) and civilian aggregate calculated from per capita data in Table 26, Statis. Bulletin No. 364 and its Supplement.

[8] Values calculated using quantity data and 1957–1959 wholesale price of $40.80 per ton; data from ERS.

[9] Line 16 divided by line 26.

[10] Calculated using data in lines 29 and 30.

[11] From Table 77 of Statis. Bulletin No. 364 and its Supplement.

[12] Unpublished data from ERS, derived from Census of Manufactures.

[13] Estimated by author from data in Technical Study No. 5, *Organization and Competition in the Milling and Baking Industries,* National Commission on Food Marketing, June 1966.

[14] From Table 100 of Statis. Bulletin No. 364 and its Supplement; 50 states covered in 1965 total.

[15] Revised quantity data for 1955, 1957–1959, and 1965 from Table 26 of Supplement for 1965 to Statis. Bulletin No. 364; 1940 quantity data and price weights from original bulletin Tables 2 and 26, and text table page 13. Distribution of flour by type of product for 1965 estimated by author from data in Technical Study No. 5, op. cit.

[16] Data to be computed by student.

[17] Differs slightly from index number published by ERS which is based on linkage at 1955 of 1947–1949 price weighted index with series based on 1957–1959.

[18] 1940 data from *Marketing Margins for White Bread,* USDA, AMS Misc. Pub. 712; 1955 and 1965 data (except wholesale value) from retail price spread data published in *Marketing and Transportation Situation*; wholesale value data from ERS.

bakery products indicated in Part *B* of Table 12.1. Because the data matching Part *B* are not available for all years, an approximation of the average prices for flour and bakery products sold each year has to be developed for use in deriving the total retail values of the per capita quantities in line 45.[15] The object of computing such retail values is to arrive at an economic measurement of the change from 1940 to later years in the quantity of all cereal products consumed. This procedure takes into account the shifts from lower-priced to higher-priced cereal products. These value data can also be combined with comparable data for other products, as we will note.

(5) How important are the costs of wheat and other farm commodities in the retail price of the finished product such as bread?

Measure in cents per pound developed in lines 56–60.

12.3.2 Milk Distribution and Consumption

Milk production has varied between 120 billion and 125 billion pounds per year since the early 1950s, although the number of milk cows has been decreasing. In 1965 about 125 billion pounds of milk were produced in the United States. What happens to milk produced by farmers is traced in Figure 12.5.

Farmers do one or more of five different things with the milk they produce: (1) They feed it to calves as whole milk. (2) They may use some of the milk for their own family in the form of whole milk or products. (3) They may separate it into skim milk and cream and sell the cream. (4) They may sell whole milk to assemblers or processors. (5) They may retail the milk directly to consumers.

In 1965 only 5 percent of the 125 billion pound output of milk was fed to calves or used on farms by the farm families as milk or butter. Sales of farm-separated cream formerly required as much milk as sales of whole milk. Now most of the milk is collected as whole milk by milk tankers and taken to milk processing plants. Few farmers now sell milk and cream directly to consumers.

In 1965 about half of the whole milk sold was processed and used as fluid milk and cream (57 billion pounds). About 62 billion pounds of milk were factory processed into these products: butter (29 billion pounds),

[15] *Ibid.*, page 13.

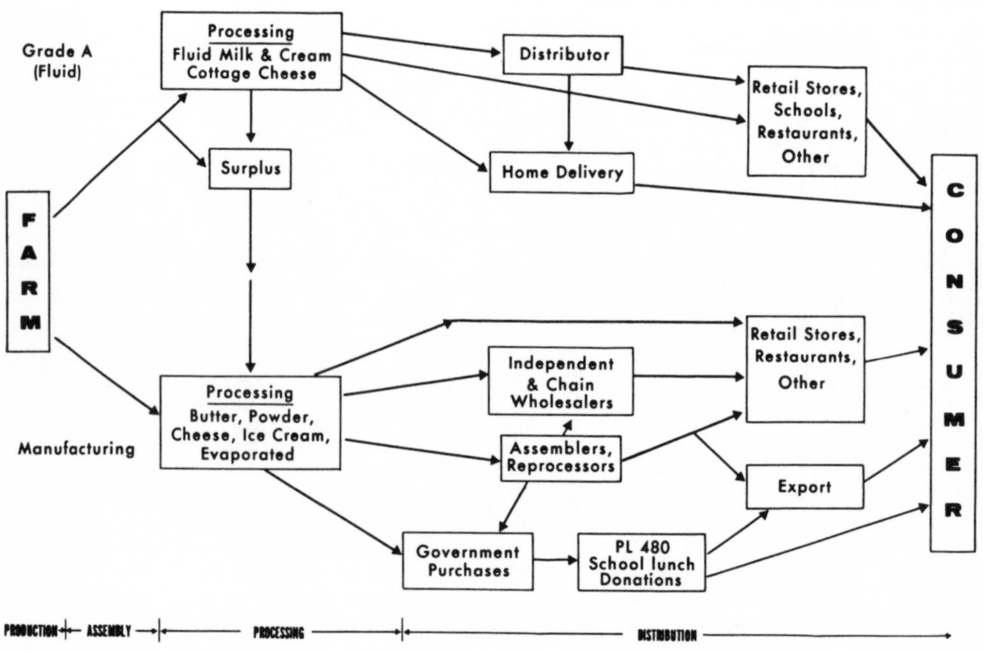

FIGURE 12.5 Marketing channels for milk and dairy products. (Source: Figure 7 of *Organization and Competition in the Dairy Industry*, Technical Study No. 3, National Commission on Food Marketing, June 1966.)

cheese (16 billion), canned milk (5 billion), frozen dairy products (11 billion), and miscellaneous products.

As you can see from the price and value data in Table 12.2, farmers receive very different prices for milk depending on quality and the form in which it is sold. Compare the $10.42 average price for a hundred pounds of milk and cream sold directly to consumers in 1965 with the $2.18 price for a hundred pounds of milk equivalent to cream sold to creameries and the $4.24 for the hundred pounds of whole milk sold to dairies, lines 6, 9, and 12 of Table 12.2.

This table provides a variety of data measuring the flow of milk from production into distribution. Those in Part A include the total quantities of milk produced on farms and the diminishing quantities consumed on farms where produced. You will also find the breakdown of milk marketings by farmers among retail milk and cream, farm separated cream, and whole milk. Total cash receipts from farm marketings of milk and cream plus the farm value of milk consumed on farms where produced add to the gross farm income from dairy products, line 15.[16]

Part *B* of Table 12.2 traces the supply and distribution of all dairy products in terms of billion pounds of whole milk equivalents, down through line 25. Lines 26 and 27 show the shifts in the consumption of fat and nonfat components of total milk. Whole milk includes about 87 percent water, 4 percent fat solids, and 9 percent nonfat solids, by weight. All dairy products can be expressed in *whole milk equivalents.* For example, a hundred pounds of fluid milk yields the following quantities of the products indicated, in rounded numbers:

5 pounds of butter
4 pounds of butterfat
11 pounds of cheese
96 pounds of skim milk
12 pounds of dry whole milk
9 pounds of 40 percent cream

Another way of expressing milk equivalents is the following: To get 1 pound of butter, you need 21.7 pounds of whole milk; for 1 pound of natural cheddar cheese you need 8.7 pounds of whole milk; and 1 pound of evaporated milk requires 2.14 pounds of whole milk.

These expressions are in whole milk equivalents. Are there other equivalents that we can use? The answer is yes. All dairy products can be expressed in terms of fat solids or nonfat solids. Thus we can use the 0.035 pounds of fat solids consumed as an equivalent of 1 pound of fluid milk or 0.086 pounds of nonfat solids. Dairy marketing specialists and consumption economists are much more careful now to keep track of fat and nonfat solid contents of milk because the demand for the two types of components is changing.

Let us look at the farm value figures in Table 12.2. Note that the farm values are quoted in terms of 1957–1959 farm prices in lines 31–36. These match the poundage data for the same items in the preceding section of the table.

Part *D* shows the same kind of calculations of total retail value in fixed prices of changing quantities of individual dairy products as we developed in Part C of Table 12.1 for cereal products. The value aggregates for 1955 and 1965 are not given in the table in order for the student to have the opportunity to compute them and thus to gain experience in calculation of index numbers.

12.3.3 Consumption of Bread and Milk

Suppose we want to find out how much of the combination of wheat (or bread) and milk is consumed per capita and how the total has changed from prewar to postwar years. Should we add the 220 pounds of wheat for 1940 from line 22 of Table 12.1 to the 818 pounds of milk from line 28 of Table 12.2? No, because we do not eat the bran part of the wheat and we feed to animals some of the skim milk, a by-product of the processing of butter and cheese. Should we add the pounds for processed wheat products, given in lines 45–47 of Table 12.1, and the pounds for the dairy products (in lines 37–48 of Table 12.2)? If we added in the other ingredients used in bread, that total will give us an idea of the quantities of wheat and dairy products we carry into our kitchens per capita per year.

But are economists really interested in the weights of our bags of groceries? Isn't value the significant key? Compute some total values for wheat and milk at the farm, wholesale,

[16] Data like those in Table 12.2 are reported each year in the USDA publications *The Dairy Situation* and *Agricultural Statistics.*

TABLE 12.2 Milk Flow from Production into Consumption, Calendar Years

Line	Item	Unit	1940	1955	1965
	Part A—From farmers into distribution[1]				
1	Milk production on farms	Bil. lb.	109.4	122.9	125.1
2	Fed to calves	Bil. lb.	3.0	3.3	2.1
3	Consumed on farms as fluid milk, cream, butter	Bil. lb.	20.2	11.4	3.8
4	Value in current dollars	Mil. $	359	495	171
Milk marketed by farmers					
5	Retailed by farmers as milk and cream	Bil. lb	6.1	2.7	1.8
6	Price per 100 lb. (2.15 lb. per qt.)	$	4.79	9.67	10.42
7	Value of sales	Mil. $	294	258	182
8	Milk equivalent of farm-separated cream	Bil. lb.	33.0	14.7	3.8
9	Price per 100 lb. of milk equivalent derived from value of sales	$	1.06	2.14	2.18
10	Value of sales	Mil. $	350	315	83
11	Sold as whole milk	Bil. lb.	47.2	91.0	113.6
12	Price received per 100 lb.	$	1.82	4.01	4.24
13	Value of sales	Mil. $	858	3,644	4,819
14	Total receipts from farm marketings	Mil. $	1,521	4,217	5,084
15	Gross farm income from dairy products	Mil. $	1,880	4,712	5,255
	Part B—Supply and distribution of all dairy products, whole milk equivalents[2]				
16	Milk production—total including nonfarm	Bil. lb.	111.5	123.0	125.1
17	Beginning commercial stocks (milk eq. of prods.)	Bil. lb.	2.7	3.2	4.3
18	Imports	Bil. lb.	0.3	0.5	0.9
19	Total supply for year	Bil. lb.	114.5	126.7	130.3
20	Ending commercial stocks	Bil. lb.	2.7	3.6	3.9
21	Commercial exports and shipments	Bil. lb.	0.7	1.2	1.7
22	Fed to calves	Bil. lb.	3.0	3.3	2.1
23	Net purchases by U.S. Dept. of Agr. for export	Bil. lb.	–	0.8	0.2
24	Military takings	Bil. lb.	–	3.2	3.2
25	Total civilian consumption—total milk	Bil. lb.	108.1	114.7	119.0

26	Total civilian consumption—milk fat	Bil. lb.	4.29	4.41	4.40
27	Total civilian consumption—milk solids not fat	Bil. lb.	5.03	7.24	7.89
28	Per capita civilian consumption—total milk	Lb.	818	706	620
29	Per capita civilian consumption—milk fat	Lb.	32.5	27.2	22.9
30	Per capita civilian consumption—milk solids not fat	Lb.	38.1	44.6	41.1
	Part C—1957–1959 farm value data[3]				
31	Milk production	Mil. $	4,650	5,133	5,076
32	Imports	Mil. $	10	15	29
33	Stock change	Mil. $	−30	−151	28
34	Total utilization	Mil. $	4,630	5,299	5,133
35	Civilian food use—total value	Mil. $	4,150	4,393	4,486
36	Civilian food use—per capita	$	31.42	27.07	23.38

(continued)

TABLE 12.2 (Continued) Milk Flow from Production into Consumption, Calendar Years

Part D—Index of per capita consumption of major dairy products (retail)[4]

Line	Item	1957–1959 Retail Price (cents)	Per Capita Quantity in Retail Weight (Lb.) 1940	1955	1957–1959	1965
37	Fluid whole milk	11.4	265	306	298	270
38	Fluid low-fat milks	10.0	47.3	28.5	26.7	34.7
39	Fluid cream	50.3	10.6	9.9	9.6	7.7
40	Cheese, whole or part whole	72.4	6.0	7.9	7.9	9.4
41	Condensed milk	21.3	0.7	0.8	1.1	0.8
42	Evaporated milk	16.6	17.5	14.2	12.4	8.4
43	Ice cream	49.3	11.4	18.0	18.2	18.4
44	Other frozen desserts (excl. mellorine)	45.6	0.9	4.5	5.4	8.5
45	Nonfat dry milk	46.9	2.2	5.5	4.5	5.9
46	Dry whole milk	47.6	0.1	0.2	0.3	0.3
47	Cottage cheese	31.4	1.9	3.9	4.6	4.7
48	Butter	74.6	17.0	9.0	7.8	6.5
	Total value aggregate		Dol.	Dol.	Dol.	Dol.
49	Including butter		68.06	[5]	70.33	[5]
50	Excluding butter		55.38	[5]	64.52	[5]
	Index: 1957–1959 value = 100		96.8[6]	[5]	100.0	[5]
51	Including butter		85.8[6]	[5]	100.0	[5]
52	Excluding butter		Mil.	Mil.	Mil.	Mil.
53	Total civilian population[7]		132.1	162.3	171.5	191.9

[1] Series published in *Agricultural Statistics*.

[2] From Tables 44, 45, and 46 of USDA Statis. Bulletin No. 364, *U.S. Food Consumption*, and its Supplement for 1965, plus ending 1965 stock data from ERS.

[3] Data for 1955 and 1965 from ERS; data for 1940 estimated by author from supply and utilization data on whole milk equivalents for 1940 and prices derived from 1955 value data in 1957–1959 farm prices and poundages.

[4] Most of the quantity data are from Table 10 of Statis. Bulletin No. 364 and its Supplement for 1965, op. cit.; data for condensed and evaporated milk excluding use in other dairy products supplied by ERS; price data from Table 2 of Statis. Bulletin No. 364.

[5] For student to calculate.

[6] Differs slightly from index published by ERS because the ERS index was derived by linking at 1955 the series based on 1947–1949 prices with the new series based on 1957–1959 prices.

[7] From Table 100 of Statis. Bulletin No. 364 and its Supplement for 1965, op. cit.

and retail levels by adding the appropriate sets of data from Tables 12.1 and 12.2. What is the purpose of such measures? What do they mean? Compare the values you obtain when you use current dollars and those derived using constant 1957–1959 prices. When constant prices are used, the relationships you obtain reflect changes in the quantity of the commodities consumed. But when you use the values in current dollars, you are including changes in quantities and prices. Your choice between these measures will depend upon the uses to which you want to put them.

12.4 VALUES MEASURED AT SEVERAL STAGES IN THE MARKETING PROCESS

From the preceding work with data for wheat and milk, we know that consumption can be measured at the farm and retail levels. But some food is bought in eating places as meals and snacks. Its prices are higher than retail prices because of the services of restaurants, dairy bars, and so on in preparing the food and in serving it, as well as providing the attractive rooms for eating. Because of lack of information on sales of individual food commodities by eating places, we cannot compute the final market value of individual commodities and have to stop at the retail store level.[17] For all foods combined it has been possible to estimate the value of foods bought at retail and bought as meals and snacks. We will examine those figures in Section 12.4.3.

12.4.1 Supplier Level Measures for Food[18]

Farmers are the primary *suppliers* of food for the American market. Therefore we must measure such supplies in terms of values and quantities. No tonnage figure for all foods is computed regularly because a tonnage total for wheat, milk, sugar, cattle, hogs, etc., has little meaning except as a very gross indicator of transportation requirements. Certainly it does not have economic significance. Therefore we turn to value measures to evaluate changes in the total quantities of all foods consumed.

Lines 3–6 of Table 12.3 provide the data measuring the contributions of four sources of food supplies for United States consumption in a year. First, we have the supplies from subsistence or home-produced food. These refer to the amount of milk consumed on farms where produced, or home garden production, or meat slaughtered by farmers for their own use. Next, we have the values of quantities of the commodities sold by farmers for civilian use or for export. The third category is the import or dockside value of imports. And the fourth category is the wharf values of fishery products caught by United States fishermen. These data are in terms of current dollars.

In *constant* dollars, we can measure the same flows of food by adding data computed for all farm commodities comparable to the wheat data in lines 12–15 of Table 12.1 and the milk data in lines 31–35 of Table 12.2. The total of such constant dollar figures is given in line 7 of Table 2.3. Because the farm price for each commodity has been held at the 1957–1959 level[19] for all calculations of totals for all the farm foods over a period of years, the total values reflect the changes in overall *quantities of farm resources* supplied and used. The average values per capita for all farm food are derived from these total values of food moving or disappearing into civilian distribution channels in a given calendar year by dividing the totals by the size of the civilian population at the middle of the year. Such civilian per capita data are given in the last three columns of Table 12.3.

[17] Commodity breakdowns of the total marketing bill and consumer expenditures for farm foods published in Table 28 of Gale, Hazen F. *The Farm Food Marketing Bill and Its Components*, USDA, Agr. Econ. Report No. 105, rest on very inadequate information regarding the proportion of such items sold by eating places. One of the sources is a pilot study of 20 eating places in Minneapolis and 13 in Fairmont, Minnesota, in selected weeks of 1950, in which this author cooperated. Much improved bases for such estimates will come from the 1967 phase of the survey of eating places sponsored by the Marketing Economics Division, ERS, USDA, and from the incorporation of commodity line detail from the 1963 Census of Business.

[18] A more technical description is given in Sections 3.1.2.2 and 3.2 of Burk, M. *Measures and Procedures for Analysis of U.S. Food Consumption*, U.S. Department of Agriculture, Agriculture Handbook No. 206.

[19] For further information see *ibid.*, Sections 3.1.2.1, 3.1.2.3, and 3.3.

Table 12.3 Selected Data Measuring All Food Consumed by United States Civilians in 1940, 1955, and 1965

Line	Item	Total United States Civilian Consumption			Civilian Consumption per Capita		
		48 States		50 States			
		1940	1955	1965	1940	1955	1965
		Mil.	Mil.	Mil.			
1	United States civilian population[1]	132.1	162.3	191.9			
		Bil. $	Bil. $	Bil. $	Dol.	Dol.	Dol.
2	SUPPLIER VALUE data, current dollar total	7.7	24.6	30.8	58	151	161
3	Farm value of subsistence or home produced[2]	1.4	2.3	1.0	10	14	5
4	Farm value of domestic farm food sold to civilians[3]	5.6	18.7	25.5	42	115	133
5	Import value of imported food[2]	0.6	3.3	3.8	5	20	20
6	Wharf value of domestic fish catch for civilian use[2]	0.1	0.3	0.5	1	2	3
7	Equivalent farm value *in 1957–1959 prices* for United States civilian farm food[4]	17.7	23.0	27.0	134	142	141
8	RETAIL VALUE data, current dollar total	19.5	59.4	80.0	148	366	417
9	Subsistence or home-produced food valued at retail prices[5]	3.2	4.8	3.0	24	30	16
10	Retail value of all domestic farm food sold to civilians[6]	14.1	47.0	66.0	107	289	344
11	Retail value of imported and nonfarm food[5]	2.2	7.6	11.0	17	47	57
	QUANTITY of all food per capita						
12	Valued at 1957–1959 prices[7]				351	375	377
					Index Numbers		
13	Index numbers: 1957–1959 = 100				95	101	102
					Pounds		
14	Total pounds in retail equivalents[8]				1548	1479	1417
					Index Numbers		
15	Index numbers: 1957–1959 = 100				107	102	98
		Bil. $	Bil. $	Bil. $	Dol.	Dol.	Dol.
16	MARKET VALUE data, current dollar total including taxes and tips	18.4	61.8	87.9	139	381	458
17	Farm value of subsistence food	1.4	2.3	1.0	10	14	5
18	Expenditures for all foods including taxes and tips[9]	17.0	59.5	86.9	129	367	453

	TOTAL MARKETING BILL for all foods, excluding taxes and tips						
19	In current dollars[10]	10.4	36.0	55.0	79	222	287
20	In 1957–1959 dollars[11]	23.6	39.6	50.9	179	244	265
						Index Numbers	
	Index numbers: 1957–1959 = 100				72	98	106
21	Index of marketing margin[12]	44	91	(108)	–	–	–

[1] Table 1, USDA, Economic Research Service, Statis. Bulletin No. 364, *U.S. Food Consumption* and 1965 Supplement.

[2] 1940 and 1955 data from Table 3.3, Burk, M. C. *Measures and Procedures for Analysis of U.S. Food Consumption*, USDA Agr. Handbook 206; 1965 figure estimated by same author.

[3] 1940 figure from Table 3.3, Agr. Handbook 206; revised 1955 and 1965 data from Table 5, *Marketing and Transportation Situation* (*MTS*), August 1966.

[4] USDA data unavailable for public use. 1957–1959 average estimated by author from farm value of domestic farm foods sold plus 3 billion dollar estimate for imported farm foods. Index numbers published in May 1965 and February 1967 issues of *National Food Situation* applied to base period average to derive estimates for this table.

[5] 1940 and 1955 from Table 3.4 of Agr. Handbook 206; 1965 figure estimated by same author.

[6] 1940 figure from Table 3.4, *ibid.*; 1955 and 1965 estimated from farm value data used previously and farm-retail price spreads for farm food market basket, Table #1, *MTS*, May 1966.

[7] Estimated from value aggregate in Table 2 of Statis. Bulletin No. 364 and index numbers published in Table 2, *National Food Situation*, February 1967.

[8] Table 5, Supplement for 1965 to Statis. Bulletin No. 364.

[9] 1940 figure from Table 3.7, Agr. Handbook 206; 1955 figure slightly revised because of change in farm value estimate. Conceptually matching estimate for 1965 derived from estimate of total food expenditures, Department of Commerce, Office of Business Economics, by adding approximate values of business purchases, food supplied with services, government distribution, and excluding home-produced food.

[10] Derived by subtracting supplier value of all food sold and estimated taxes and tips from total food expenditures in line 18.

[11] Computed by dividing current dollar estimates by index of marketing margin.

[12] Based on series published in Table 1, *MTS*, May 1966 and earlier issues. Preliminary estimate for 1965 adjusted upward slightly by author, based on indications from corporate profits and volume of sales.

12.4.2 Retail Level—Food[20]

The quantity of all food consumed is sometimes measured by totaling the approximate retail weights for all foods, usually on a per capita basis. Line 14 of Table 12.3 gives such data. A measure with much more economic meaning is calculated by valuing the retail weights for individual commodities in each of several years using fixed prices (e.g., the average prices for 1957–1959), then comparing the total values for all commodities for each year with the average for the base period to derive index numbers. Such data are in lines 12 and 13. This method is based on the Laspeyres formula for index numbers:

$$\frac{\Sigma P_0 Q_i}{\Sigma P_0 Q_0}$$

where P_0 = average price in base period

Q_0 = average quantity consumed in base period

Q_i = average quantity consumed in given year

Retail value data have been computed to combine the variety of foods and the several channels through which foods flow to United States civilian consumers. Compare the coverages of lines 9, 10, and 18 in Table 12.3. Remember that retail value *equivalents* can be estimated for subsistence or home-produced food which never leaves the farm or the suburban home. This is done simply by multiplying the quantities consumed or estimated to have been consumed from subsistence supplies in farm homes and suburban homes by the average retail prices charged by the food stores. Similarly, foods sold at higher than retail store prices in the form of restaurant meals may be valued at retail prices for purposes of comparison.[21] The Census of Business data on sales by retail food stores differ from the total retail value of food sold at retail because retail stores other than food stores sell food (for example, department stores and discount houses) and retail food stores sell nonfood commodities.

12.4.3 Final Market Level—Food[22]

The concept of the final market level differs from the retail level concept (*a*) by taking into account the costs of extra marketing services added by restaurants and other eating places when meals are eaten away from home, (*b*) by pricing subsistence or home-produced food at the farm level, and (*c*) by taking into account that some people pay wholesale prices for food or even farm prices if they work for food distributors or buy from friends or relatives.

Several alternative measures of the value of food consumed at the final market level exist. One pertains to domestic farm foods only, that is, only the foods produced on American farms. Such a measure of the value of food consumed is of particular importance when we are dealing with matters of farm policy. Another measure refers to all food consumed. It includes domestic farm foods, all imported foods, and the domestic fish catch for civilian food consumption. The value of food sold at retail (or wholesale) plus the market value of food consumed in eating places equals *expenditures* or *dollar outlays*. In making use of expenditure data, the student would do well to read the fine print because expenditure figures often include the value of home-produced food, which is technically not a part of expenditure figures.[23]

12.4.4 Marketing Services[24]

Marketing services include assembly, transportation, warehousing, wholesaling, retailing,

[20] Another year or group of years could be used as a base, but economists try to use relatively recent "normal" years.

[21] See Appendix B, of Burk, M., *Measures and Procedures.*

[22] Estimates in Table 12.3 are consistent with those in Tables 3.3 to 3.6 and 3.8 of Burk, M. *Measures and Procedures*, as described in Sections 3.2 to 3.5. When necessary adjustments are made for differences in coverage, they are also consistent with the U.S. Department of Commerce series on personal consumption expenditures for food. However, expenditure data are somewhat lower than the new series recently issued by the Marketing Economics Division (MED) of ERS, USDA, when necessary adjustments for coverage are made. (Gale, Hazen F. *The Farm Food Marketing Bill and Its Components*, Agr. Econ. Report No. 105.) The new MED series of estimates of consumer expenditures for domestic farm foods is based on the commodity-flow method, also used by the Department of Commerce. It appears likely that further research using the 1963 Census of Business data on merchandise line sales and data from the 1966 and 1967 phases of the survey of eating places will lead to closer reconciliation of the MED estimates with the Commerce data and with USDA data on quantities of food consumed and BLS price data.

[23] See the Department of Commerce series, described in Burk, M. *Measures and Procedures*, Section 3.6.2.

[24] *Ibid.*, Section 3.5.

TABLE 12.4 Industry Components of Personal Consumption Expenditures at Producer and Distributor Levels, for Selected Commodity Groups, 1958[a]

Commodity	Value at Producer Prices, Mil. Dol.	Allocation to Transportation and Insurance, Mil. Dol.	Allocation to Distributors ("Trade"), Mil. Dol.	Value at Producers' Prices, Mil. Dol.
Shoes and footwear	2,337	61	1,676	4,075
Women's and children's clothing	7,912	217	5,227	13,356
Furniture	2,441	87	1,818	4,346
New cars and purchases of used cars	9,568	237	3,453	13,258

[a] Data from page 8, Simon, Nancy W. "Personal Consumption Expenditures in the 1958 Input-Output Study," *Survey of Current Business*, October 1965.

and processing, as agricultural economists define the term. Some economists describe the manufacture of food products as "production," but most agricultural economists reserve the term "production" for the stage of primary output of the farm commodity, that is, the wheat or the milk. In fact, food preparation and serving of meals by eating places are included among marketing services. Marketing services are so varied in nature—by supplying the utilities of time, place, and form—that they are very hard to measure. They include the inputs of labor, capital, and management beyond the farm level, e.g., between the farm gate and the final purchase by the ultimate consumer.

The only measure of the combination of marketing services yet devised is cost or value. *The value of all marketing services for all foods* (line 19 of Table 12.3) was computed by subtracting the total supplier value of all foods *sold* from their total market value. The total market value for food sold is better termed *food expenditures* (line 18 of Table 12.3).

Marketing services bought with food per se represent *marketing resources* as opposed to *supplier* or *farm resources* used to produce the farm commodities. We often want to know how the two sectors of the food supply and distribution system have changed. As yet, there is no direct measure of changes in the quantity of marketing services bought through time comparable to the quantity measure for farm food use, which is constructed by combining changing quantities and fixed prices. But economists often shift from current value series to constant value series by the process of deflation, e.g., dividing a value series by a price index. The only available price index is the food marketing cost part of the farm market basket series of the U.S. Department of Agriculture, Economic Research Service.[25] The total marketing bill for all foods divided by the index of the marketing margin yields the data presented in line 20 of Table 12.3. These values in 1957–1959 dollars for a series of years were compared with the average for the three years 1957–1959 to derive the index numbers in the next line. This index serves as an approximate measure of changes in the overall quantity of marketing services.[26]

12.4.5 Values of Nonfood Products at Producers' and Retail Levels

Information on the flow of nonfood commodities into consumption has been much less developed than for farm food commodities. Fortunately, a relatively new type of data are now being prepared by the U.S. Department of Commerce, called *input-output data.* The study for 1958 provides the data in Table 12.4. The distributors' shares of retail values for shoes and footwear, women's and children's clothing, and furniture ran around 50 percent. In contrast, the distributors of new and used cars received only 26 percent of the

[25] See Misc. Pub. 741, op. cit., or page 24 of Burk, M. *Measures and Procedures*. . . .

[26] A slightly different procedure used by Waldorf produced a generally comparable measure of changes. See Waldorf, William A. "The Demand for and Supply of Food Marketing Services: An Aggregate View," *JFE* 48:1:42–60, February 1966.

consumer purchasers' value, the smallest share for any industry group identified in the study.

Figure 12.6 summarizes the 1958 ratios of producers' value to purchasers' value for 27 commodity categories.

12.5 SIGNIFICANT QUESTIONS FOR ANALYSIS

In order to be sure that you understand the concepts and data introduced in this chapter, a series of questions follows:

(1) How do you go about answering the questions:
How have United States food supplies changed?
What kinds of measures, sources of data, and kinds of computations would you use?

(2) Has United States food consumption increased?
For what commodities have the consumption rates gone up, down?
How much have they changed?

(3) How far does the increase in the total retail value of food from 1940 to 1965 reflect an increase in the population?
In quantity?
In price?
In services?

(4) How far has domestic food consumption fallen behind available supplies?
How do you find out?

(5) Has the use of marketing services risen as much as the consumption of supplier food (food per se) in the last 20 years?
How do you know?

12.6 SUPPLEMENTARY NOTES ON CONCEPTS, RELATIONSHIPS, AND MEASURES INTRODUCED IN THIS CHAPTER

The concepts, relationships, and measures which have been used in this chapter will be used many times in the rest of the book. Therefore you will gain much from careful study of their use in the context of this chapter. To supplement your understanding, here are some definitions and elaborative notes.

12.6.1 Index Numbers

Index numbers measure changes in quantity or price or value, usually for combinations of commodities. (See Section 6.8.) Values in constant dollars are used to derive indexes of quantity if the prices are held constant, as in the Laspeyres index. However, a quantity index for homogeneous commodities may be derived very simply by comparing the total poundages for two different periods, for all fresh fruits, for example. The best known price indexes in the United States are the Consumer Price Index and the Wholesale Price Index of the U.S. Bureau of Labor Statistics, and the wide variety of price indexes developed in connection with the parity price computations of the Department of Agriculture. Indexes of value may use either constant prices or constant quantities, but in general both the quantities and the prices will vary.

12.6.2 Other Concepts

Data such as those on wheat and milk are often referred to as *disappearance* data. In this concept we are referring to the fact that we have a calculated total supply which disappears into distribution except for the stocks identified as being held at the end of the period. In this case total disappearance is equal to total utilization.

Consumption is measured in a variety of ways. The choice of measure depends on the objective of the measurement and the availability of information. We are concerned in this text with measuring economic quantities, for example, the farm or the marketing inputs or the farm plus the marketing inputs rather than being concerned with the straight poundage of a food consumed or the number of pieces of furniture sold in a year.

Civilian use of a commodity may refer to either or both food and nonfood use. Nonfood use includes use for feed or clothing or for all items not consumed directly by human beings, for instance, industrial alcohol. Noncivilian use refers to takings by the United States military and to the quantities exported or shipped to United States Territories.

Joint products are illustrated by the flour and the mill feeds produced in the process of milling grain.

In this text we make extensive use of *averages* or arithmetic means. The use of such averages relies on the significance of the measure of general tendency or central tendency. Averages are most useful if the population has relatively homogeneous rates of consumption. Therefore averages are not as satisfactory for

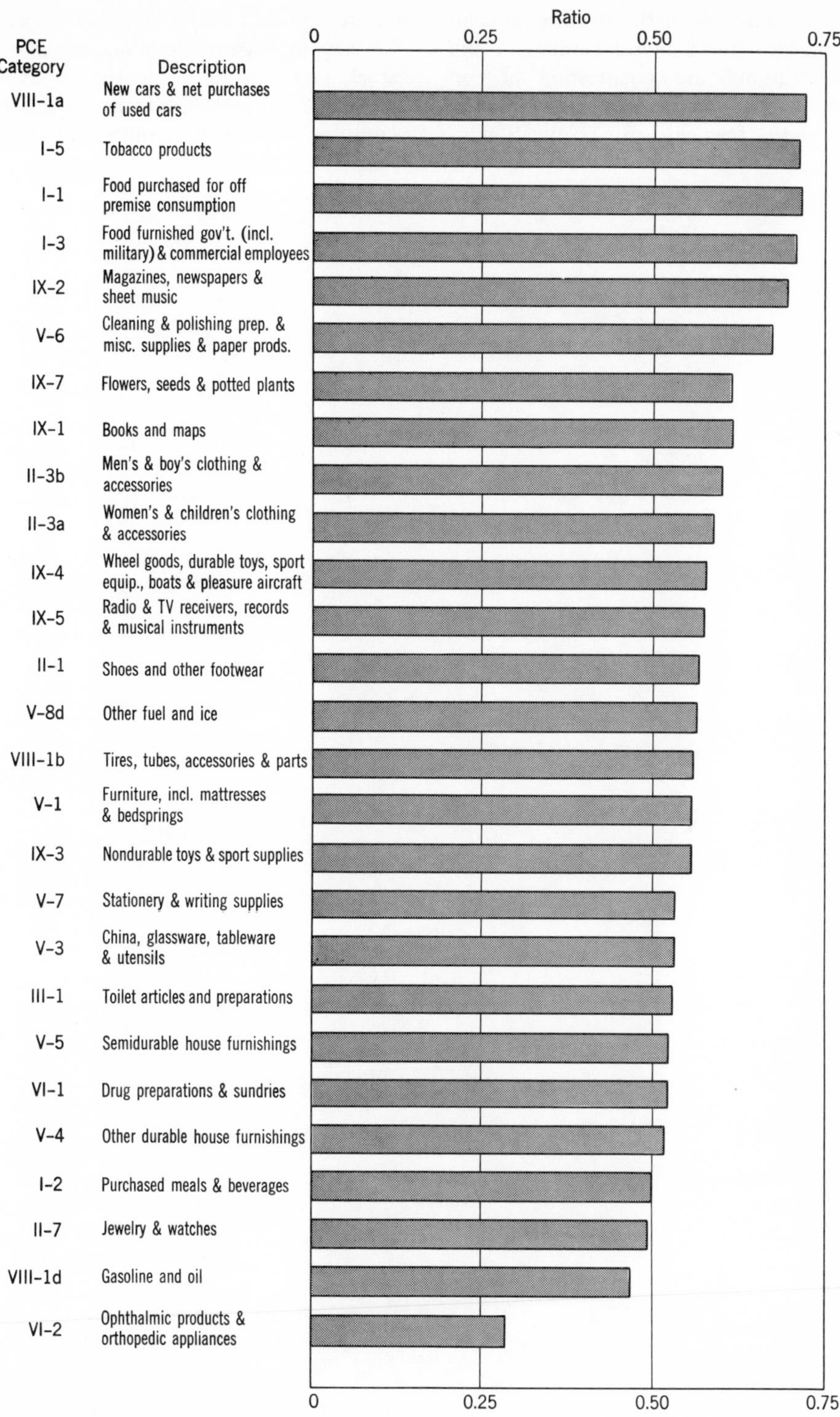

FIGURE 12.6 Categories of personal consumption expenditures for commodities[1] arrayed by ratio of producers' value to purchasers' value, 1958. (Source: *The Survey of Current Business*, October 1965, Chart 5, page 12.)

study of consumption in the developing countries as in the United States because of substantial variations and polarization of consumption rates there for the masses of poor people and the few elite. By polarization we mean here that a small number of people may be very high consumers, for example, of livestock products and expensive foods, whereas the large proportion of the population may consume very small quantities of these foods.

13

MARKET SEGMENTS WITHIN MACRO STRUCTURES OF CONSUMPTION

Knowledge of the structures of the market for the products being sold and for their substitutes and complements is fundamental to every consumer marketing program and to economic analysis of trends in consumption. Business firms operate with varying amounts of knowledge about different facets of the processes and structure of consumption, often because the knowledge has not yet been developed. But some business managers are not aware of knowledge available from public sources or they are unwilling to pay the costs of data collected by private market research firms.

Public data on expenditures and consumption rates for broad categories of products sold in the entire country and on purchase by subgroups of the United States population are used in most studies of the macro structure of consumption. A valuable set of benchmark data is now available in the form of the breakdown of retail sales by merchandise line for regions, states, and metropolitan areas for 1963.[1] They are somewhat comparable in coverage with data from the censuses for 1939 and 1948. Public data on the market for food commodities are far more comprehensive than for most nonfood commodities and for services.

A number of market research firms maintain a continuous reporting system under which a stratified sample of households or distributors report detailed information on the quantities of particular brands of foods and nonfood commodities purchased by people in selected areas. The household data reveal patterns of consumer choices in relation to family characteristics, whereas the distributor data tell more about the market channels through which the commodities are moving. Market research firms design and make special surveys to obtain data on consumer preferences and attitudes regarding specific product attributes with which their clients are concerned. Private market research data related to market segments occasionally become public information through professional articles published after their private usefulness is exhausted.

This chapter begins with general consideration of economic and marketing approaches to analysis of the macro structure of consumption. Then there is a review of some patterns of average expenditures for current consumption in the years covered by major government surveys. Sections 13.3 and 13.4 describe in some detail variations in consumption for selected foods and all foods to serve as examples of the types of knowledge needed in early stages of the analysis of market sectors. Section 13.5 illustrates an economic analysis of a macro structure of consumption. Section 13.6 provides several examples of the use of nondemographic criteria for segmentation of the market for nonfood products. Sections 13.7 and 13.8 utilize food data to demonstrate the development and use of cross-section or cross-segment measures of consumption as well as analytical uses of patterns of consumption.

13.1 ECONOMIC AND MARKETING APPROACHES

Economists and marketing people approach the study of sectors or segments within the macro structures of consumption somewhat

[1] U.S. Bureau of the Census. *1963 Census of Business, Retail, Trade, Merchandise Line Sales*. Merchandise line refers to commodity groups such as food or clothing.

differently. Most economists analyze the demand for a product by seeking to identify groups in the population having different demand schedules and related demand curves. Because information needed for theoretical demand schedules is not obtainable, in practice economists rely primarily on consumption and expenditure data for population groups formed on the bases of current income, region, and urbanization category. Thus they subdivide the macro structure into segments based on socioeconomic characteristics of consumers who have bought or consumed the product in the past.

Marketing specialists have used three different sets of criteria for identification of homogeneous markets. (1) They have supplemented the usual socioeconomic characteristics of consumers with social-psychological information on attitudes, social class, etc. (2) They have made detailed studies of consumer response to product attributes, especially to brand symbols, to guide product development and promotion. With such information somewhat different products and promotion appeals can be tailored for separate segments of the total market. (3) Some firms have carefully investigated consumer responses to alternative types of promotional activities and used different market promotion programs for individual segments of their market.

Consumption economists use ideas from both general economics and marketing. We begin by identifying in as much detail as possible the subcategories of the consumer market, based on the usual socioeconomic characteristics and additional knowledge as the behavioral dimension, such as family life cycle and family value orientation. We examine economic and technological differences in products purchased, such as prices, value, and quality attributes. Although routinely studying seasonal variations in expenditures and consumption, economists have not gone as far as some market researchers in identifying consumer characteristics of seasonal markets. Consumption economists have paid more attention than most marketing specialists to problems of aggregating components of the total market, e.g., population groups, products, and brands, and to forecasting changes in the total market.

Analysis of the segments of the total consumer market for a product often requires a dual approach. On the one hand, a business firm needs micro knowledge of the individual submarkets for its products, in terms of the several dimensions used by consumption economists. Conceptual frameworks for integrating such knowledge are described in Chapters 8 and 9. As more micro knowledge of consumption has accumulated, it has become increasingly evident that no one dimension or set of criteria can provide sufficient information for developing and maintaining successful marketing programs. Researchers are always limited in their efforts to develop pertinent information by constraints on research time and costs. But they must be aware of the potential limitations of their knowledge imposed by incomplete study of all dimensions of the micro structure of consumption.

The other approach to analysis of the macro structures of consumption uses disaggregative procedures, often called market segmentation by marketing specialists. The first step in macroeconomic analysis obviously entails definition of the market with which the research and marketing program are concerned. For example, analysis of the market for furniture produced by one manufacturer must begin by disaggregating total furniture sales into office furniture and home categories in which the firm is interested. Next, the objectives of the analysis, whether for product development or sales promotion or both, must guide the selection of criteria for the process of dissecting the market and development of pertinent data along the lines indicated previously. Ordinarily, an analyst investigates the availability and potential costs of obtaining additional data needed to map the market in terms of product and consumer variables. Examples of these variables are (*a*) price lines, style categories, and distribution channels; and (*b*) socioeconomic characteristics of consumers with high and low rates of purchase or using the product in different ways.

Although they lie outside the scope of consumption economics, we should note here two additional steps involved in the development of market segments. One is the analysis of economic costs and potential returns from investment in market development of particular segments, such as the export market for a particular line of office furniture. A second is the formulation of time schedules and strategies for development of major segments, within the constraints of the firm's resources and expectations regarding marketing programs of competing firms. Formulation of strategies for developing market segments should take into account special requirements for product development and production scheduling, possible needs for additions to the firm's distribution system, as well as planning for special promotion programs.

13.2 CONSUMER EXPENDITURE PATTERNS IN THE UNITED STATES

As indicated in Part II, the effects of socioeconomic forces on consumer behavior are revealed by the generally consistent patterns formed by relationships between variations in consumption rates and variations in socioeconomic characteristics. In this section we examine some of these patterns.

13.2.1 Variations with Income

Expenditures for categories of consumption in actual dollars and as percentages of total income vary widely among groups in the population. Income was considered to be the major determinant of consumption long before Keynes wrote about the consumption function. Variations in expenditures for major categories of foods and services by urban families and single individuals at the several levels of income and averages for the other two urbanization categories (when available) are shown in Table 13.1, using 1941, 1950, and 1960–1961 data from the surveys of the Bureau of Labor Statistics and the U.S. Department of Agriculture.

Although average dollar outlays for every consumption category are greater at successively higher levels of income, their shares in income vary considerably. The proportions allocated to food and the combination of housing and household operation decline substantially. Some of the others take larger shares in the middle-income range than at higher or lower incomes, except for the rather freakish lowest-income group. The lowest-income group often includes many individuals drawing on accumulated assets for current expenditures or using credit.[2]

[2] Variations in food consumption indicated by annual value data are described in Section 4.2 of Burk, Marguerite C. *Trends and Patterns in U.S. Food Consumption*, Agriculture Handbook 214. Section 4.4 of the same reference describes variations in expenditures for food.

13.2.2 Variations with Other Socioeconomic Characteristics

Many analyses of survey data have revealed several family characteristics whose variations are accompanied by significant variations in consumer expenditures and consumption. Among these are region of the country, degree of urbanization, family size and type, and occupation. To demonstrate variations in expenditures with other economic and social characteristics of families, here are some data extracted from the 1950 Survey of Consumer Expenditures conducted by the U.S. Bureau of Labor Statistics. These data for housing expenditures include fuel, light, and refrigeration as well as shelter itself. They pertain to urban families with disposable incomes of $5000 to $6000.[3] (Disposable incomes refer to incomes after payment of income taxes.)

(*a*) By region of country: suburban families in North, $813; in South, $789; and in West, $683
(*b*) By city size in North: large cities, $733; suburbs, $813; small cities, $753
(*c*) By family size, United States: 2, $719; 3, $763; 4, $732; 5, $679
(*d*) By occupation, United States: salaried and professionals, $795; clerical and sales, $805; skilled workers, $696; unskilled workers, $607.

Similar data on housing expenditures by the $5000 to $6000 income families of different sizes are available from the 1960–1961 urban survey reports. They indicate that the housing and utility expenditures in 1960–1961 varied with family size in this way: families of two spent $927; families of three persons, $993; four persons, $1066; and families of five, $1042.[4] Other detailed data for this income group from the survey are available from reports issued by the Bureau of Labor Statistics and by the U.S. Department of Agriculture.

13.2.3 Degree of Variation Affected by Measured Used

One factor in the degree of variation in consumption among regions and urbanization categories is the measure of consumption

[3] Data from Volume IV, pp. 10–11, and Volume XVIII, pp. 15 and 39 of the *Study of Consumer Expenditures, Incomes and Savings*.

[4] From Supplement 3, Part A to BLS Report 237–38.

TABLE 13.1 Income and Expenditure Data for United States Urban Families and Single Individuals, Calendar Years 1941, 1950, and 1960–1961 with Some Comparisons (in Current Dollars, Averages per Unit in Group)

Annual Money Income Class	Pct. of Total	Average Disposable Money Income, Dollars	Average Money Expenditures for Current Consumption	Food and Beverages: Amount, Dollars	Food and Beverages: Pct. of Disp. Income	Housing, Utilities, Household Operations: Amount, Dollars	Housing, Utilities, Household Operations: Pct. of Disp. Income	Furniture and Equipment: Amount, Dollars	Furniture and Equipment: Pct. of Disp. Income	Clothing and Related Services: Amount, Dollars	Clothing and Related Services: Pct. of Disp. Income	Auto and Other Transportation: Amount, Dollars	Auto and Other Transportation: Pct. of Disp. Income	Personal, Medical Care, Recreation, Reading, and Education: Amount, Dollars	Personal, Medical Care, Recreation, Reading, and Education: Pct. of Disp. Income
				Average Money Expended for Major Categories of Consumption											
				A—1941 urban survey data[1]											
Urban															
Under $500	7.7	310	425	170	55	124	40	8	3	30	10	24	8	61	20
500– 1,000	14.7	734	744	295	40	209	28	22	3	71	10	47	6	78	11
1000– 1,500	14.2	1,244	1,243	437	35	325	26	59	5	138	11	108	8	136	11
1500– 2,000	16.8	1,749	1,639	561	32	417	24	74	4	186	11	149	9	200	11
2000– 2,500	15.1	2,227	2,099	656	29	497	22	110	5	227	10	270	12	269	12
2500– 3,000	12.0	2,732	2,555	829	30	560	20	159	6	306	11	332	12	292	11
3000– 5,000	14.0	3,707	3,223	949	26	688	19	208	6	428	12	412	11	446	12
5000–10,000	3.9	6,120	4,717	1,330	22	958	16	202	3	663	11	633	10	787	13
10,000 and over	1.6	13,357	8,510	1,895	14	2,283	17	314	2	1,112	8	1,336	10	1,412	11
Urban average	62.3	2,372	2,060	637	27	494	21	104	4	247	10	247	10	272	11
Average for rural nonfarm	21.5	1,300	1,147	361	28	229	18	79	6	137	11	154	12	145	11
Farm	16.2	1,130	823	250	22	108	10	66	6	135	12	109	10	121	11
All United States	100.0	1,948	1,666	516	26	375	19	93	5	205	11	205	11	220	11
				B—1950 urban survey data[2]											
Under $1,000	6.3	614	1,278	442	72	398	65	55	9	80	13	92	15	159	26
1000– 2,000	12.3	1,532	1,768	642	42	466	30	87	6	163	11	140	9	204	13
2000– 3,000	18.7	2,534	2,718	943	37	592	23	174	7	280	11	296	12	337	13
3000– 4,000	24.0	3,487	3,570	1,171	34	711	20	237	7	385	11	476	14	482	14
4000– 5,000	16.9	4,462	4,450	1,382	31	848	19	329	7	509	11	639	14	606	14

5000– 6,000	9.5	5,449	5,257	1,588	29	969	18	379	7	645	12	814	15	699	13
6000– 7,500	6.4	6,618	6,043	1,756	27	1,109	17	433	6	774	12	944	14	846	13
7500–10,000	3.5	8,434	7,108	2,055	24	1,331	16	454	5	963	11	1,098	13	1,009	12
10,000 and over	2.4	15,914	10,773	2,641	17	2,419	15	907	6	1,519	10	1,378	9	1,488	9
Average	100.0	3,910	3,808	1,195	31	774	20	261	7	437	11	510	13	508	13
C—1960–1961 urban survey data[3]															
Under $1,000	2.4	654	1,307	373	57	493	75	40	6	62	9	62	9	218	33
1000– 2,000	8.7	1,513	1,770	548	36	627	41	64	4	108	7	95	6	254	17
2000– 3,000	9.9	2,508	2,675	792	32	809	32	103	4	219	9	230	9	416	17
3000– 4,000	11.4	3,516	3,716	1,019	29	989	28	175	5	336	10	486	14	567	16
4000– 5,000	13.2	4,506	4,501	1,214	27	1,118	25	220	5	437	10	693	15	646	14
5000– 6,000	13.1	5,495	5,240	1,394	25	1,277	23	277	5	517	9	809	15	775	14
6000– 7,500	16.3	6,710	6,229	1,615	24	1,472	22	344	5	642	10	953	14	958	14
7500–10,000	14.9	8,573	7,534	1,942	23	1,679	20	404	5	840	10	1,207	14	1,182	14
10000–15,000	7.7	11,724	9,744	2,349	20	2,105	18	525	4	1,157	10	1,596	14	1,634	14
15000 and over	2.4	21,889	14,745	3,095	14	3,590	16	783	4	1,813	8	2,101	10	2,483	11
Urban average	72.6	5,906	5,390	1,401	24	1,311	22	277	5	558	9	793	13	836	14
D—Averages for other urbanizations and all United States, 1960–1961															
Rural nonfarm, 1961[4]	21.1	4,700	4,296	1,133	24	949	20	240	5	408	9	737	16	653	14
Farm, 1961[5]	6.3	4,424	3,594	893	20	697	16	220	5	427	10	613	14	603	14
All United States, 1960–1961[6]	100.0	5,557	5,047	1,313	24	1,195	22	266	5	518	9	770	14	783	14

[1] From U.S. Bureau of Labor Statistics *Family Spending and Saving in Wartime*, BLS Bulletin 822.

[2] From U.S. Bureau of Labor Statistics Survey, published by Wharton School of Finance and Commerce, U. of Pennsylvania in *Study of Consumer Expenditures, Income and Savings*, Vol. XVIII.

[3] U.S. Bureau of Labor Statistics *Consumer Expenditures and Income: Urban United States, 1960–61*, Survey of Consumer Expenditures and Income, BLS Report No. 237–38.

[4] Page 2, U.S. Bureau of Labor Statistics *Consumer Expenditures and Income: Rural Nonfarm Areas in the United States, 1961*, Survey of Consumer Expenditures 1960–1961, BLS Report No. 237–88 (USDA Report CES–10).

[5] Page 14, U.S. Dept. Agr., Agr. Research Service *Consumer Expenditures and Income: Rural Farm Population, United States, 1961*, USDA Cons. Exp. Survey Report No. 5.

[6] Page 11, U.S. Bureau of Labor Statistics *Consumer Expenditures and Income. Total United States, Urban and Rural, 1960–61*, Survey of Consumer Exp. 1960–1961, BLS Report No. 237–93.

Measure	North Central		South	
	Urban	Farm	Urban	Farm
1. Market value of all food at home and away	$9.67	$7.80	$8.34	$8.12
2. Expenditures for food at home	8.00	4.60	6.79	4.09
3. Expenditures for food and beverages away from home	1.43	0.73	1.21	1.45

being used. Such variations are illustrated by the following data for families with $5000 to $6000 disposable money incomes. The food value data are in terms of averages per person in a week of spring, 1955.[5]

The market value of all food consumed in a week of spring 1955 by farm families in this relatively high-income group averaged practically the same per person in the North Central Region and the South. In contrast, expenditures for food at home were much higher among the North Central farm families than in the Southern group. But this difference was offset by lower expenditures for food away from home.

The average outlays per urban family in this income group were practically the same in the North Central Region and South. Larger family sizes in the South made the significant differences in per person averages shown previously. Urban households spent considerably more for food at home in both regions than did rural households, both on a family and on a per person basis. The value of home-produced food enters into the total market value food measure. Urban and farm households in the South at the same $5000 to $6000 level of income had practically the same market value of food, on both bases. Although this income group of farm households in the North Central Region had a market value of $38.54 per family compared with $33.74 per urban family, their family size averaged much higher, 4.9 persons compared with 3.5 for urban families. Therefore the per person average for urban families was significantly higher than that average for the farm families of this income group in the North Central Region.

13.3 VARIATIONS IN CONSUMPTION OF SELECTED FOODS

For most market research, the average consumption rates per person computed from household survey data are satisfactory. But market analysts using such data for small groups of families must be aware of the possible influences of differences in family types. Such differences can be checked by reference to age composition of families in the various income groups, for example. Intensive analysis of consumption patterns often raises questions regarding the general types of variations in consumption to be expected within families. In the past we have not been able to handle such questions satisfactorily. But a subsample of the 1965 Survey of Household Food Consumption will yield data on food consumption of individuals.

13.3.1 Variations in Flour and Milk

Let us look more closely now at the data from household food consumption surveys. Surveys such as that for spring 1955, conducted by the U.S. Department of Agriculture, provide a great deal of valuable information about food consumption at home by American families, both for all families and for groupings of families based on region, urbanization, income, and other characteristics. In Table 13.2 you will note the marked differences in average consumption per household of flour and milk by $5000 to $6000 income families between the urban and farm urbanization categories, both in the North Central Region and in the South and between the urban families of the North Central and the South and farm families in the North Central Region and the South. Farm families are much higher consumers of cereal products and dairy products than urban families with the same money income, even after one makes allowances for differences in the size of family. Southern farm families use more purchased flour and less purchased bread than comparable families in the North Central Region.

13.3.2 Comparison of Cross-Section Data and Time-Series Data

A number of problems develop when one compares cross-section survey data, such as

[5] Data from Table 2 of Survey Reports 3 and 4 of the 1955 Survey of Household Food Consumption.

TABLE 13.2 Average Quantity and Value of Selected Foods Consumed per Household in a Week of Spring 1955 in Urban and Farm Households of the North Central Region and South and in All United States Households Having $5000 to $6000 Disposable Incomes in 1954[a]

Item	Unit	North Central		South		United States, All Urbanizations
		Urban	Farm	Urban	Farm	
Flour other than mixes	Lb.	1.57	4.64	2.80	6.57	2.03
bought as such	Dol.	0.16	0.45	0.28	0.61	0.21
Prepared flour mixes	Lb.	0.80	0.96	0.53	0.46	0.78
	Dol.	0.22	0.26	0.12	0.13	0.21
Breakfast cereals (excluding	Lb.	0.90	2.03	0.71	0.70	1.01
baby cereals)	Dol.	0.27	0.58	0.22	0.20	0.30
Bread	Lb.	5.56	7.72	5.15	4.02	5.91
	Dol.	1.04	1.39	0.91	0.73	1.11
Baked goods other than	Lb.	2.35	2.14	2.65	2.03	2.53
bread	Dol.	0.96	0.78	0.91	0.66	0.97
Total for grain products —flour equivalent	Lb.	8.13	14.28	10.18	16.55	9.56
Money value	Dol.	2.95	3.76	2.80	2.90	3.14
Grain products—retail cross-section index[b]	Index	94	107	95	116	100
Fresh fluid milk—whole	Qt.	12.01	20.52	9.04	11.92	12.18
	Dol.	2.39	3.93	2.13	2.83	2.59
Fresh buttermilk, skim	Qt.	1.05	1.48	1.60	5.80	1.10
and chocolate milk	Dol.	0.21	0.25	0.33	1.02	0.22
Cheese, all types	Lb.	1.19	1.85	1.08	0.81	1.26
	Dol.	0.52	0.75	0.57	0.44	0.60
Milk fat in dairy products, excl. butter	Lb.	1.53	2.94	1.48	1.61	1.66
Milk solids not fat in dairy products	Lb.	3.13	5.23	2.99	4.12	3.31
Fluid milk equivalent of all dairy products on calcium basis	Qt.	16.11	27.19	15.96	21.66	17.35
Dairy products, excl. butter—money value	Dol.	4.04	6.65	4.14	5.27	4.42
Dairy products, excl. butter—retail cross-section index[b]	Index	109	140	96	109	100
Average household size[c]	No.	3.42	4.89	3.75	3.92	3.69

[a] Data from 1955 Household Food Consumption Survey Reports 3, 4, and 1 except for total grain products in flour equivalent, which are from Table 15 of Reports 8, 9, and 6.
[b] Cross-section indices from Tables B. 2 and 3 of Agr. Handb. 214 *Trends and Patterns in U.S. Food Consumption*. All-United States average = 100.
[c] From Table 3 of Household Food Consumption Survey Reports 1, 3, and 4.

those in Table 13.2, with supposedly matching time-series data. All-United States averages must be used, of course, but the commodity data from the surveys cover only the food eaten in private households in a week of spring. So the seasonal problem is immediately raised. For some foods, such as those eaten particularly by children, consumption rates at home may run higher than rates away from home, as in restaurants. The averages given in the reports are on a household basis. Conversion to a per person basis is best accomplished by using average household sizes computed as the number of people who ate 21 meals at home in a week. The per person rate for a spring week can be converted to an annual basis by multiplying by 52 *only* if one assumes that the spring rate approximates the weekly average for the year. Some research indicates that this holds true for all foods combined, but not for some of the more seasonal individual foods. In making comparisons of commodity data, one must watch for differences in coverage. An example is that the bakery product category of cross-section data includes the fats and oils, milk, and sugar which are counted in the individual commodity groups in the time-series data.[6]

13.4 PATTERNS OF CONSUMPTION FOR ALL FOODS COMBINED

In this section we will examine the patterns of relationships between several measures of consumption of all foods combined and differences in regional location, degree of urbanization, and income. These three are, in effect, key factors into which merge a wide range of economic and social characteristics or factors. They are frequently used as a basis for subdividing the population into groups in order to study patterns of consumption.[7]

13.4.1 Regionality

Regionality refers to the state or quality of belonging to or being connected with a region. It reflects the essential and distinguishing characteristics and institutions related to a region.

The Censuses of Retail Trade provide more adequate data on regional differences in the consumption of food than is the case for most other commodities. This is because retail food stores and eating places are separately identified in these censuses and food constitutes a large proportion of the sales by these firms. Regional differences in overall food consumption rates indicated by such census data for 1954 and by the Survey of Household Food Consumption in spring 1955 were found to be quite similar. However, the levels of the two sets of data are not comparable because of differences in coverage.

Alternative measures for overall food consumption provide somewhat different indications of regional variations. There is much more regional variation in expenditures for food than in the market value of all food (including home-produced supplies). This reflects regional variations in the degree of urbanization and income. As the North Central Region and South become more urban and as incomes rise in the South, we may expect greater increases in food *sales* per capita in those areas than in the Northeast and West.

Three cross-section indexes for the quantity of food consumed, based on the 1955 household survey data, yield indications of differences in overall use of farm food commodities from all sources, purchased farm foods only, and food consumption measured in retail terms. They show that average use per person of farm food commodities varied from 7 percent above the United States average in the North Central Region and West to 9 percent below in the South. Average purchases of farm foods varied from 85 percent of the United States average in the South to 112 percent of the United States average in the West. Regional variations in the retail measure for all foods were quite similar to those for farm food commodities from all sources.

In the South per person food use of farm commodities averaged lower on farms than in urban households, whereas farm households in the Northeast and North Central Region used more farm foods per person than did urban households. The farm and urban rates of use in the West averaged about the same. In each region except the West, farm households used half as much purchased farm foods per person as urban households. These facts underlie our great expectations for increases in the market for commercially produced and marketed farm foods in the South and in other regions where the off-farm movement will be substantial.

Regional differences in the use and purchases of major groups of foods in terms of

[6] See Appendix A of Burk, Marguerite C. *Measures and Procedures for Analysis of U.S. Food Consumption* for further detail.

[7] See the procedures outlined in Appendix B of this text. Much more detailed discussions of the relationships among these factors and variations in consumption are provided in Chapters 3 and 4 of Burk, M. *Influences of Economic and Social Factors on U.S. Food Consumption.* The procedures used in such analyses are described at greater length in Sections 4.2 and 4.3 of Burk, M. *Measures and Procedures for the Analysis of U.S. Food Consumption,* cited hereafter as *Measures and Procedures. . . .*

their farm values can be studied by means of the detailed data published in the July 1959 issue of the *National Food Situation*.[8] The ramifications of such analyses are too extensive for description here.

13.4.2 Urbanization

The term *urbanization* is a shortened form of the phrase "degree of urbanization." Urbanization reflects a combination of economic and social factors related to population density, occupation, and institutions surrounding urban and farm living. For many analyses households are now classified according to three degrees of urbanization—urban, rural nonfarm, and farm.

Subdivision of households according to this criterion leads to a greater degree of standardization or homogeneity of consumption patterns of the subgroups. Accordingly, urbanization seems to reflect some of the more important economic and social factors related to consumption in the past, but perhaps it will be less significant in the future. Among the elements reflected are probably the amount of home production; the accessibility to particular types of food stores; economic factors related to occupation, nonmoney income, and prices of the nonfood goods and services in the area; social and cultural factors such as schools and other institutions, the mass media, the employment of homemakers, education, and other elements underlying differences in the ways of living among subgroups in the population.

Within each urbanization category there has appeared to be some cultural standardization. The great expense involved in surveys precludes the possibility of samples large enough to study each of the social and economic factors separately. Therefore it is useful to have a key factor like urbanization to represent a package of subsidiary factors. Furthermore because of the long-range interest in studying the patterns of consumption in order to predict future trends in consumption, it is important to note that there are adequate measures through time of changes in only a few of the factors such as urbanization, income, and population size.

Among urbanization categories, households differ much more in the way they spend their money for food than in the value of food consumed, which includes supplies that are received without direct expense, either from home production or gifts of payments in kind. The most significant of these is the extent of home production. In spring 1955 farm households spent only half as much as did urban households for their food, on the average. The variations were, of course, traceable to differences in home production and in eating away from home. At the level of average income, farm households spent almost 40 percent less for all food than did urban households, on a per person basis. Rural nonfarm households spent about a tenth less than the urban rate.

When the quantities of foods consumed per person were converted to farm equivalents and combined with farm prices, it was revealed that farm households used about 14 percent more farm food commodities than did urban households at the level of money income equal to the United States average. Rural nonfarm households also exceeded slightly the average rate of use by urban households at this level of income. The higher rate of farm than urban consumption indicates, on the one hand, the extra supplies available from home production, and on the other, the fact that money income excludes the nonmoney components of purchasing power of farm households.

These differences are illustrated by data in Part *B* of Table 13.3, which are some indexes derived from the 1955 food survey data for the South. Since some rural nonfarm households have substantial amounts of nonmoney income in the form of home-produced food and fuel, there were probably households in the \$3000 to \$4000 money income group that had total income (including nonmoney income) approximating that of urban households in the \$4000 to \$5000 range. Since nonmoney income has much greater significance for farm families, data for the \$2000 to \$3000 money income group are also considered. These data clearly indicate that rural nonfarm and farm households with \$4000 to \$5000 money income per family, after taxes, ate better than did urban households of comparable money income. But when one takes into account the possibility of nonmoney income and looks at the next lower money income group, this higher level appears questionable. However, urbanization clearly affects the use of purchased foods.

Farm households vary less in the market

[8] A quarterly publication of the U.S. Economic Research Service.

TABLE 13.3 Relationship of Region, Urbanization, and Income to Cross-Section Indices of Food Consumption per Person during a Week of Spring 1955 (United States All Household Average for Each Index = 100)[a]

Part A—Regional differences, illustrated by data for urban households with money incomes after income taxes of $4000–$5000

Index	United States	Northeast	North Central Region	South	West
Food use of farm commodities (farm level):					
All sources	100	99	102	99	100
Purchased	111	112	113	109	110
Consumption of all foods (retail level)	101	100	103	97	104

Part B—Urbanization differences, illustrated by data for Southern households roughly comparable in money plus nonmoney income

Index	Urban	Rural Nonfarm		Farm		
	$4–5000	$4–5000	$3–4000	$4–5000	$3–4000	$2–3000
Food use of farm commodities (farm level):						
All sources	99	102	92	103	97	95
Purchased	109	101	92	59	57	56
Consumption of all foods (retail level)	97	99	90	101	95	92

Part C—Income differences, North Central urban households in selected groups based on money income after income taxes

Index	All[b]	Under $2000	$3–4000	$5–6000	$6–8000	$8–$10,000	$10,000 and Over
Food use of farm commodities (farm level):							
All sources	107	104	102	111	109	110	117
Purchased	119	116	113	124	122	124	131
Consumption of all foods (retail level)	108	100	103	110	112	113	122

[a] Developed from data obtained in the 1955 Survey of Household Food Consumption as described in Appendix D of Burk, M. *Measures and Procedures. . . .* Regional data given in Appendix B of Burk, M. *Trends and Patterns. . . .*
[b] In those households of two or more persons reporting income.

value of all foods at home and away from home than do nonfarm households. There is less variation above the average level of income than below. Expenditures for food at home and away vary much more with income for each of the three urbanization categories and for all three combined than do the food value measures which include home-produced food. The level of *expenditures* by urban households is substantially above that for rural nonfarm households which in turn is above the farm level. Expenditures for food away from home are much more income-elastic than other measures for food. Here, too, the general level of urban expenditures exceeds that for the rural nonfarm which is again above the farm level.[9]

13.4.3 Income

The more one studies income and relationships between income and consumption the more complex seems to be the variety of problems that are involved. There are many ways to define income and consumption. Also, there are a number of relationships which exist between income and food from which the analyst may choose. Ideally, one seeks to get as pure a relationship between the factor "income" and consumption as possible, but available data are often complicated by differences in family size and composition, occupation, regionality, urbanization, supply influences, and even some temporary additions or subtractions from income which affect purchasing power. Since World War II there has been a great deal of attention paid to the definition of income and to these relationships. The three alternative hypotheses concerning income-consumption relationships have been noted earlier in Sections 7.2 and 7.5. They will be considered further in Chapter 14.

In spring 1955, United States households with incomes per person about 50 percent above the average level of income used only 8 percent more farm-produced food than did those at the average level of income. But among households with incomes three times as large as the average per person for the United States, food use was up only 16 percent from the average of the households at the mean level of income. Food use varied much more with money income among nonfarm households than among farm households.

Regression techniques are used extensively in study of the relationships between food consumption and income. Pertinent data and descriptions are given in the publication on trends and patterns in food consumption of the United States.[10] Statistical tests indicate that the variation in the use of farm foods from all sources with variation in income was significantly higher for rural nonfarm households than for the urban. For the farm households it was significantly lower.

A summary of findings from some extensive analyses of the cross-section relationships between income and food, utilizing the spring surveys for 1942 and 1955, follows: Average consumption of food from all sources varies more with income among nonfarm households than among farm households. There is greater variation with income below the mean level of income than above. Use of purchased farm foods varies much more with income than does the use of food from all sources. For the quantity of food consumed income elasticities are lower than for the corresponding measures of value, reflecting differences in prices paid.

13.5 ANALYSIS OF SERVICE EXPENDITURES BY AN ECONOMIST

Ferber's study of the 1950 BLS consumer expenditure data on expenditures for services provides a useful example of an economist's approach to the structure of consumption. He began by differentiating between goods and services, noting the intangible, nonsaving characteristics of services and the fact that many services can be home-supplied by purchased durable goods such as washing machines. Next, he categorized services as follows:

Care and maintenance of a home—rent, household utilities, household operation, domestic service

Adequate transportation—purchased transportation, auto operation

Care and maintenance of other possessions—clothing and jewelry services, business services, furniture and appliance repair

Maintenance and improvement of self—personal care, medical care, recreation, education, gifts, and contributions[11]

Using these categories, Ferber calculated (1) the percentages of total current family expenditures allocated for particular services, by level of income, and (2) income elasticities

[9] Extensive information on income elasticities of food consumption is given in Table 4.4 of Burk, M. *Trends and Patterns in U.S. Food Consumption.* Income elasticities are defined as the ratio of the percentage variation in expenditures (or consumption) to the percentage variation in income. They are frequently calculated using the least squares method for linear regressions. If the linear regression is calculated in logarithms, the coefficient of the income variable measures the elasticity.

[10] See Chapter 4 of Burk, M. *Trends and Patterns in U.S. Food Consumption.*

[11] Page 439, Ferber, Robert. "Service Expenditures at Mid-Century," pp. 436–460 of Friend, Irwin, and Jones, Robert (Editors), *Consumption and Saving,* Vol. I.

TABLE 13.4 Percent of Current Family Expenditures Spent for Different Types of Services, by Selected Characteristics

Characteristic	Category	Average Income after Taxes	Object of Expenditure: Home	Transportation	Other Possessions	Self	All Services
Family size	1	$1895	22.6%	5.7%	4.0%	14.6%	46.8%
	2	3601	18.5	7.0	3.5	12.6	41.6
	3	4221	16.9	6.8	3.4	11.4	38.5
	4	4793	16.0	6.5	3.5	10.8	36.8
	5	4981	15.6	6.0	3.5	11.1	36.2
	6 or more	4948	14.3	5.7	2.9	10.0	32.9
Age of head	Under 25	3050	16.3	7.7	3.1	9.9	37.0
	25–35	3876	17.0	7.0	3.5	9.9	37.4
	35–45	4464	16.8	6.2	3.6	10.7	37.3
	45–55	4500	15.6	6.7	3.5	12.6	38.4
	55–65	3850	17.5	6.8	3.4	13.0	40.7
	65–75	2687	20.6	5.9	3.4	14.2	44.1
	75 and over	2161	24.5	4.6	4.3	16.1	49.5
Occupation of head	Self employed	5432	17.3	5.7	4.2	13.4	40.6
	Salaried, prof., official	5406	17.8	6.8	4.0	12.7	41.4
	Clerical—sales	4077	17.9	6.4	3.8	11.7	39.8
	Skilled wage earners	4219	15.7	7.5	3.0	10.6	36.8
	Semiskilled	3673	15.7	6.6	2.8	10.6	35.7
	Unskilled	2839	17.2	6.0	3.1	10.4	36.7
	Not employed	2232	21.7	5.2	3.5	13.0	43.4
Number of full-time wage earners	None	2248	20.3	6.2	3.4	11.9	41.8
	1	4229	17.1	6.5	3.5	11.6	38.7
	2	5638	14.9	7.0	3.6	12.9	38.4
	3 or more	7226	10.9	7.1	3.1	11.3	32.5
Education of head	8 yrs. or less	3191	16.7	6.1	3.0	11.3	37.1
	9–12	3976	17.3	6.9	3.4	11.4	39.0
	13–16	5197	17.9	6.6	4.2	12.9	41.6
	Over 16 yrs.	6268	19.1	6.3	5.0	13.0	43.4
All families		3910	17.3	6.5	3.5	11.7	39.0

Source: Derived from *Study of Consumer Expenditures, Incomes and Savings,* Vol. 18, Table 1, as presented in Table 3 of Ferber, *ibid.*, page 447 of Vol. I, Friend and Jones, op. cit.

for particular services bought by each income group. A third set of calculations is indicated by data in Table 13.4.

These explorations led to a number of hypotheses. One was that expenditure patterns differ widely among items within the service categories as well as between categories. Another hypothesis related service expenditure to ownership of particular material or human resources, either as complements or substitutes. A third hypothesis was that the principal determinants of service expenditure patterns vary substantially by category. He tested the last hypothesis, with the following conclusions:

	expenditure share on home and other goods	expenditure share on transportation	expenditure share on self
As income increases . . .	falls, then rises	rises, then falls	rises
As age of head increases . . .	falls, then rises	falls, then rises	rises
As family size increases . . .	falls	rises, then falls	falls[12]

Finally he studied interactions among independent variables, arriving at the following findings:[13]

	expenditure share on home and other goods	expenditure share on transportation	expenditure share on self
Income by age	rises with age much more at low incomes than at high incomes	is lowest at low incomes for older people . . .	rises much more with rising incomes among older people than among younger people
Income by family size	declines with rising family size much more at low incomes than at high incomes	not significantly related	falls much more at low incomes than at high incomes as family size rises
Age by family size	rises with age for very small families, but falls with age for larger families	has a much sharper peak at 45–65 ages among middle family size, but little or no peak for same family size at other ages	falls uniformly at younger ages as family size rises, but exhibits an inverted U pattern among older people as family size rises

13.6 OTHER CRITERIA FOR MARKET SEGMENTATION—NONFOOD EXAMPLES

Although the total market or aggregate consumption may be subdivided most readily using demographic characteristics of age, family size, location, or income, new criteria are actively sought by market researchers. For many years, the automobile industry has marketed varied lines of cars, from the stripped-down economy models to the super-luxury models. In part, this segmentation has been based on value or price line, but aesthetic concepts and susceptibility to change may also enter in.

Yankelovich has reported a variety of other criteria being used.[14] Researchers for U.S. Time found watch buyers to be subdivided by differences in values attached to watches. One category includes the people who pay the lowest possible price for a watch that runs reasonably well. In the second and largest group are people who want long-lived, really good watches. The third category seeks good watches plus qualities giving emotional value, e.g., diamond cases and very well-known brands.

Cleanser companies have used segmentation based on preventive cleaning vs. therapeutic cleaning after the fact. Yankelovich reports also that the bathing soap market is divided into people who just want soap to clean and people who seek a sensuous experience along with the cleaning process.

He states that the market for retail soft goods has four parts based on the different conceptions of value held by women: (1) willingness to pay a little more for quality, (2) value identified with merchandise on sale, (3) value based on lowest possible price, and (4) good value for the money only if bought as seconds or discounted for some reason.

Business firms buying computers can also be subdivided into categories, based on degree of confidence their executives have in their own ability to evaluate computers. Yankelovich says that this element of confidence has differentiated the IBM users from the users of other makes of computers.

[12] *Ibid.*, page 451.

[13] *Ibid.*, page 452.

[14] Yankelovich, Daniel. "New Criteria for Market Segmentation," *Harv. Bus. Rev.* **42**:2:83–90, March–April 1964.

He concludes that:

> . . . Market should be scrutinized for important differences in buyer attitudes, motivations, values, usage patterns, aesthetic preferences, or degree of susceptibility. These may have no demographic correlates. . . .[15]

Brandt, a marketing consultant, has proposed that the "segmentation syndrome" be dissected on the basis of variations in potential consumer response to market promotion activities. He recommends research on identification of consumer groups homogeneous in expected reactions to a producer's marketing efforts.[16] Brandt cited the example given in Figure 13.1 of two categories of consumers interested in car waxes.

> 1. *Demographic data or statistical facts about consumers:* age, income level, family size, sex, education, occupation.
> 2. *Behavior traits of consumers:* social-class membership, life-cycle status, ethnic origin, life-style habits.
> 3. *Performance facts about consumers:* heavy versus light buyers, early versus late adopters, etc.
> 4. *Psychological characteristics of consumers:* personality profiles, attitude measurements, etc.[17]

13.7 CROSS-SECTION MEASURES OF CONSUMPTION

The concept of patterns of consumption has been used frequently in this book. Patterns are formed in at least three ways: (1) by

Private Car-owners Interested in Waxing	*Product expectations*	*Objective of waxer*	*Other characteristics of the use system*
Residential interest	Separate wax and cleaner Highest quality Systematic application required	Proper maintenance Pride in doing	Tools Gardening Home repairs
Social interest	Combination wax and cleaner Easy and fast to apply Long-lasting	Appearance of car to others	Travel Social activities Personal appearance

FIGURE 13.1 Two consumption systems for car wax. (Source: Brandt, *ibid.*, Figure 4.)

Because of difficulties inherent in scaling all consumers according to their reactions to different kinds of promotions for different products, Brandt was forced to come back to familiar criteria. The criteria he used are closely related to the behavioral, economic-technological, and process dimensions we have used in this book in considering the structure of consumption. They were:

variations in consumption of a single commodity or expenditure within a group of families or between groups based on socioeconomic characteristics such as region, urbanization, income, or family types; (2) by combinations of consumption rates for two or more commodities by a single family or group of families—although micro in character when they pertain to single families but moving toward macro for the groups of families; (3) by relationships between variations in consumption rates and variations in income, urbanization,

[15] *Ibid.*, page 89.

[16] Page 25, Brandt, Steven C. "Dissecting the Segmentation Syndrome," *Journal of Marketing* 30: 4:22–27, October 1966.

[17] *Ibid.*, page 26.

or age, both for groups of families and averages through time.

Variations in consumption are measured by a number of types of data. In Section 13.2 we have considered expenditures for major commodities reported by samples of families and single consumers subdivided by urbanization and income. Table 13.2 contains data which are averages per household for individual commodities in terms of total pounds, total dollars, equivalents based on common ingredients, and special quantity indices derived from retail value data.

After a brief review of information on survey data described in Chapter 8, we will examine in detail the construction of the indices used for groups of commodities. Such data have significant uses as well as several limitations. The limitations are noted in Section 13.7.5. The uses are described in Section 13.8.

13.7.1 Review of Survey Procedures

The most obvious method of obtaining information about what people consume is to ask them. Because of the time and money required, as well as for technical reasons, samples of population groups are used. Even if perfect sampling were possible, difficult problems would arise in obtaining adequate information for particular purposes. Questions must be phrased very carefully to elicit answers corresponding to the concept being measured. Take this simple question—how much meat do you consume? What kinds do you want your respondent to include? For what period do you want the data? Is the "you" singular or plural? At home, in restaurants? How well do you think your respondent can recall what she or her family consumed?

A great deal of knowledge about procedures for obtaining such information has been accumulated. Some is summarized in Section 6.2.2 and Appendix A. Sources for additional information are listed in that appendix. The reader should look back over these procedures in order to understand how they determine the kinds of data available for study of patterns in consumption. Then review the description of the surveys of consumer purchases, expenditures, and consumption given in Section 8.4. By the way, cross-section data are sometimes called "family budget data," especially by Europeans, even though they represent actual expenditures, purchases, or use and *not* "budgeted" or planned expenditures.

Next, let us consider more carefully the household food consumption surveys by the U.S. Department of Agriculture. Over a 40-year period home economists and statisticians in the Department have evolved procedures and questions which produce reliable statistics on household food consumption. They have been particularly concerned with the appraisal of family diets. Therefore they have concentrated on obtaining the best possible estimates of quantities of food consumed, as well as data on economic status and a few social characteristics of families.

The 1955 survey utilized personal interviews to obtain, by recall, information on food consumed by the household in the preceding seven days, prices paid, and some information about the family. Table 13.5 summarizes the major types of food quantity and value data obtained and computed from the survey, especially as published in survey reports 1–5. Twelve other reports were published by the U.S. Department of Agriculture, supplying dietary evaluations, information on home food production and processing and on relationships of consumption and dietary levels to age and employment of homemakers and size of family.[18]

Information on purchases of food outside private households is much more limited than is the case for the family households. Some data have been estimated from expenditures for hospital services from purchases by state and local institutions that report their financial operations and from sales of those types of eating places that report separately in the Censuses of Distribution.[19] A number of special surveys have been made to obtain data on food purchases of selected types of nonhousehold establishments such as restaurants, penal and special-care institutions, inplant feeding facilities, school lunch and school milk programs. They have utilized some of the survey procedures outlined in Appendix A. The first nationwide sample survey of consumption in restaurants and institutions was made in 1967. A group representing many large business firms selling to these institutions cooperated with

[18] A special series of articles using the commodity and regional data from this survey to measure consumption patterns of significance to food marketing firms was published in the *National Food Situation* from October 1956 to July 1959.

[19] Described in Section 5.5 of *Trends and Patterns. . . .*

TABLE 13.5 Types of Food Data from First Five Reports on 1955 Survey of Household Food Consumption

Data given in survey reports 1 to 5

(1) Average money value per family of:
- (*a*) All foods and beverages used in a week at home and away from home, including purchased and without direct expense
- (*b*) Purchased food for home use and meals, snacks and beverages consumed away from home
- (*c*) Food used at home received without direct expense from home production or as gifts or payment in kind.[a]

(2) For each of some 230 food items separately and for groups of foods, from all sources and purchased only:
- (*a*) Percentage of households in group using item in week
- (*b*) Average quantity used at home per household in week
- (*c*) Average money value of the quantity used per household.

(3) Use of major home-produced foods by rural nonfarm and farm households:
- (*a*) Percentage of households in group using item in week
- (*b*) Average quantity used at home per household in week
- (*c*) Average money value of the quantity used per household.

Averages reported for households grouped by:

Area	Urbanization category	1954 money income of family after income taxes[b]	
United States	All combined	Under $1000	$5–6000
Northeast	Nonfarm	$1–2000	$6–8000
North Central Region	Urban	$2–3000	$8–10,000
South	Rural nonfarm	$3–4000	$10,000 and over
West	Farm	$4–5000	

Data computable from reported statistics for each group

(1) Per person averages for each type of data for individual foods and for groups of foods.
(2) Per household averages for those households using item during week.
(3) Estimates of regional, urbanization, and income shares of (*a*) the commercial market for all food and for individual foods, (*b*) home-produced foods, (*c*) all food consumed at home.
(4) Breakdown of the money spent for food at home among commodities.
(5) Average prices paid by selected groups of households for individual foods and groups of foods.
(6) Cross-section indexes of food consumption per person (retail level), of total food use per person (farm level), and of use of purchased foods per person (farm level).

[a] Valued at prices paid for purchased item by households in the same urbanization category and region.
[b] Some income classes were combined in some urbanizations of some regions because of small number of cases in sample.

the U.S. Department of Agriculture in planning for and raising funds to finance this survey. Reports on the survey have not been issued as yet.

13.7.2 Value Measures

Reports on U.S. Department of Agriculture and Bureau of Labor Statistics surveys of food consumption and consumer expenditures contain data on the money value of food and beverages used at home in a week, both purchased and obtained without direct expense, and on expenditures for food and beverages away from home. Money value data are equivalent to market values. Values of purchased foods and beverages are actually expenditure figures. Since World War II home production and gift foods have been valued in most such surveys at the average prices paid for purchased foods by families in the same category (grouped by area, urbanization, and income).

No commodity breakdown is available for meals, snacks, and beverages consumed away from home, but considerable commodity detail is available for the items consumed at home.[20]

13.7.3 Measures of Quantity

The U.S. Department of Agriculture surveys of consumption regularly obtain and report much information relating to the quantities of individual foods consumed and commodity group totals. A few commodity groups are summarized in terms of ingredient equivalents such as flour, milk fat, milk solids, nonfat and whole milk equivalents based on the calcium content. But most totals are just aggregates of retail weights reported by families.

To measure the structure of overall food consumption in quantitative terms, three new indexes were developed from the 1955 food survey and reported in *Measures and Procedures for Analysis of U.S. Food Consumption*, Section 3.7.5.5. Two of these match the definitions of the time-series indexes of per capita food use of farm commodities, one covering consumption from all sources, the other only purchased foods. For them, the consumption data from the 1955 survey were converted to their farm commodity equivalents and valued at 1947–1949 farm prices. The third index measures the variations in consumption from all sources in terms of average retail value at 1947–1949 average prices. This index matches the time-series retail index of per capita food consumption when it is computed on a 1947–1949 base.

The overall indexes for United States households grouped by urbanization and income are given in *Measures and Procedures*, Table 3.13. Details of the methodology and subseries for the commodity groups are reported in Appendix D of that publication. The overall food data are quite reliable and generally representative of food consumption at home in all of the year 1955. The subindexes for commodity groups are subject to the same limitations as the weekly data from which they are computed—seasonality and sampling, in particular. The regional indexes matching the all-United States indexes are given in Appendix B of *Trends and Patterns*. These indexes use the all-United States average as their base, that is, this average is set equal to 100.

13.7.4 Measures of Marketing Services

The 1967 survey of away-from-home eating will supply a direct measure of the total amounts of different kinds of food eaten away from home, but we will still lack a direct measure of other marketing services used by different groups of families. However, surveys conducted by the U.S. Department of Agriculture and Bureau of Labor Statistics obtained households' estimates of their expenditures for meals, snacks, and beverages away from home. The U.S. Department of Agriculture surveys give us information on the quantities of purchased foods, both fresh and processed to several degrees. Using these 1955 U.S. Department of Agriculture data on expenditures for purchased foods and calculations of equivalent farm values of such foods, the author derived approximations of the marketing costs paid by different groups of households.[21] These data indicate a very wide range in such marketing costs. For example, the estimate of average marketing costs paid for food at home by United States households with disposable money incomes over $10,000 in 1954 was three times as high per person as the estimate for households with less than $1000 in family income. The range for all food both at home and away from home was even greater.

Regression analyses were used to compare variations in the food marketing costs per person, calculated as just described, with variations in income. They indicated that the income elasticity of these costs is two to three times as high as the income elasticity of food alone. The cross-section income elasticities of marketing costs for all United States households are close to those based on postwar time-series data.[22]

[20] Further information on the data is in Section 3.7 of *Measures and Procedures*. The United States data are in *Measures and Procedures* Tables 3.14, 3.15, and 3.16. Comparable regional data are in Tables B.13, 14, 15, and 16 of *Trends and Patterns*. . . .

[21] *Trends and Patterns* Section 5.6.2 and Table 5.2.

[22] See pp. 71 and 83 of *Trends and Patterns*.

13.7.5 Limitations

Some limitations of available cross-section measures of food consumption have been mentioned earlier or have been inferred, and we summarize them here. Changes in commodity classifications and household coverage create problems in comparing sets of data. These require so much detailed attention that we must omit them here and simply refer to more detailed coverage.[23] Nonhousekeeping households do not report their food consumption in detail, and the first details on food commodities eaten away from home by the United States population will come from the 1967 survey.

Analysis of findings from surveys of a week's food consumption must take into account these facts: During a limited period the market availability of goods and services is practically fixed. Demand is relatively fixed or static because outside influences and intrafamily relationships have no time to change during the single week reported on by each respondent, although the interviewing may be spaced over a several-month period. The data may reveal irregularities in consumption patterns, market structure, and prices which are peculiar to the particular period. Problems for some individual foods arise because of seasonality. Only housekeeping families are included. An adjustment for meals eaten at home and away from home is made on a pro rata basis in obtaining per person averages for food at home, 21 meals at home being set equal to one person. Although such adjustment is necessary, it may introduce some bias, particularly if there is a notable difference in the kinds of foods eaten out. Sampling and reporting errors have varied, reflecting improvements in sampling and collection methods on the one hand and difficulties such as obtaining cooperation of employed respondents and recall of data on more items, on the other.

One-time cross-section surveys cannot reflect changes in a particular family's consumption in response to changes in prices, family income, and other socioeconomic factors. Such changes are reflected in data from panels of families, but significant sampling problems develop in this approach.

Field work and processing costs for large-scale cross-section surveys are so great that the samples do not represent as detailed subdivisions of area, types of families, and commodities as many business firms wish for their market research.

[23] *Measures and Procedures* Sections 3.7.7.1 and 3.7.7.2.

13.8 ANALYTICAL USES OF PATTERNS OF CONSUMPTION

The expectation of patterns of consumption is basic to all analyses of consumption and market demand. Economists and marketing specialists, like all scientists, operate on the basis of three fundamental assumptions: (1) Nature is orderly. (2) Observed phenomena are interrelated to varying degrees. (3) The process of change is continuous but at varying rates.[24]

We hypothesize that socioeconomic forces affect consumer behavior in consistent ways, and then we seek to identify their effects by categorizing people according to the characteristics reflecting those forces. Next, we relate the measure of the rates of consumption of such groups to variations in these characteristics. The major problem is with the implicit assumption that "all other factors remain the same" or *ceteris paribus*.

13.8.1 Examples of Patterns of Consumption

Food consumption has averaged significantly lower in the South than in other regions of the country. Lower rates in the South are related to lower incomes, relatively smaller supplies of livestock products, and some institutional factors.[25]

Household food surveys indicate that food use varies much more with money income among nonfarm households than among farm

[24] These undergird several sets of hypotheses that are implicit in the macroeconomic analysis used in this book. Further information is given in Section 1.7 of Burk, M. *Influences of Economic and Social Factors on U.S. Food Consumption*, op. cit. These three assumptions were used in Part II of this text in connection with microeconomic analysis.

[25] Further analysis of patterns of consumption is reported in Burk, Marguerite C. "The Study of Regional Food Consumption," *J. Farm Economics* **XLI**:5:1040–1049, December 1959; in four regional articles in the *National Food Situation*, 1957; and in the article entitled "Introduction of New Regional Indexes for Food Consumption Analysis" by Robert J. Lavell in the *National Food Situation*, July 1959.

households. But the degree of variation is much less among high-income than among middle-income households.[26]

Engel's law is a good example of a generalization based on the observed pattern of relationship between expenditures and income. A translation of his law is: ". . . the poorer a family is, the greater the proportion of the total expenditures which it must use to procure food."[27] Dozens of studies over the last hundred years have indicated the general applicability of Engel's law. The exceptions have been instances of striking lack of homogeneity among families surveyed or surveys including only the very rich or the very poor. Similarly, national averages or trends in national averages of income and food expenditures generally seem to conform to the law, although the law was stated in terms of cross-section rather than time-series data.

There are complications in using the law today when we seek to quantify the relationship between income and food for analytical use.

> First, we find that we must specify the meanings of food and income (or expenditures). Second, as the analysis shifts from static situations described by cross-section data to the dynamic problems of economic development, other variables become relevant. These may be considered either (*a*) as factors to be held constant (ceteris paribus) so that the simple form of the law may apply or (*b*) as additional independent variables in a multi-variate relationship. Either way an analyst faces serious operational problems because of lack of proper measures of the variety of social, economic, and cultural elements entering into economic development.[28]

There are a number of alternative meanings of food which can be used. These are described in the article and are familiar to the reader of this textbook. Similarly, several different comparisons with income can be made, as mentioned earlier.

One of the major complications in the use of Engel's law as originally set forth is that it gives no basis for projecting the total expenditure–food relationships through time. However, reinterpretations in the last 50 years or so have compensated for this deficiency. The time element has very significant economic importance.[29] By their very nature, cross-section studies of income–food relationships exclude the effects of changes in other economic and social factors on them. Therefore we certainly cannot expect operational measures of income elasticity derived from household survey data to match those derived from regressions of time series. Through time, income–food relationships are influenced on the supply side by changes in the food-nonfood price relationships brought about by changes in the general economic situation, in industrial and agricultural production, and in exports or imports as well as by changes in the availability of food in the retail stores and in home food production. On the demand side we note changes in the degree of urbanization, in the activity and age composition of the population, in food tastes, and in relative emphasis given to food. We also must watch for variations in purchasing power during the short run which may result from changes in assets.

I have proposed ten ramifications of Engel's law to adapt it to the needs of macroeconomic analyses of present-day problems related to food consumption. These ramifications represent the attempt to be more precise in dealing with the meaning of food, temporal specification, the handling of economic and social factors other than income, and the degree of change in income elasticity.

The first five proposals are concerned with income–food relationships at a given point in time. The following generalizations pertain directly to economic and social conditions and the food supply situation of the United States in the midtwentieth century:

> (1) The quantity of all food per se, excluding marketing services, consumed per person varies with the level of income within each urbanization category, but has a quite low income elasticity.

[26] Detailed descriptions of such variations are given in Section 4.5 of *Trends and Patterns*. Charts in Chapter 4 of *Trends and Patterns* illustrate variations in food consumption measured in a number of ways. Figure 3.1 in *Influences . . .*, op. cit., indicates differences among several indexes. Tables 4.6 to 4.10 of *Trends and Patterns* provide data on the variability of food quantity and value measures among population groups.

[27] The following section is based on the article, "Ramifications of the Relationship Between Income and Food," *J. Farm Economics* **XLIV**:1:115–125, February 1962.

[28] *Ibid.*, page 118.

[29] Pages 84–88 of Burk, M. *Influences of Economic and Social Factors on U.S. Food Consumption.*

(2) The quantity of purchased foods consumed per person varies much more with level of income among rural families than does the quantity of *all* foods, which includes home-produced supplies.

(3) The value of food marketing services per person bought with food per se, both in retail stores and in eating places, varies with level of income 2 to 3 times as much as the quantity of food per se consumed among families within each urbanization category.

(4) Expenditures for food at home and away from home per person in rural nonfarm families vary with income about a third more than does the value of all food, including home-produced supplies. For farm families, the variation of average food expenditures with income is almost twice as great as for money or market value of all food.

(5) Income elasticity of food expenditures is less among families with higher real incomes than for lower income groups. . . .[30]

13.8.2 Uses of United States Data on Variations in Food Consumption

Data on variations in consumption have been used to describe and analyze the structure of the retail market, to study similarities and dissimilarities of demand by different groups in the population, to compare regional production and consumption patterns, to derive estimates of consumption in subregional areas, and for demand analysis.

The structure of the food market can be reasonably well appraised with data on the total market value of all foods and beverages consumed at home and away from home from such surveys as the 1955 survey. They provide a reasonable basis for regional breakdowns and for indications of variations in such expenditures by income level. However, one must be very careful in interpreting the away-from-home data because of limitations on coverage and problems with reporting.[31]

Data on the average market value of all food consumed per person in this country for segments of the population grouped according to region, urbanization, and income, computed from the household averages, are the only available statistics for analysis of so-called food expenditures by groups of consumers (including nonhousehold members). Some marked differences in the dollar value of food consumption from region to region are revealed by similar data for each level within the same urbanization category, as well as the expected variations by income and between farm and urban households. These variations are one indicator of the possible range of expansion or contraction in per capita food use and food sales in the future.

These at-home patterns of food expenditures can be used as rough approximations of the commodity breakdown of total food expenditures during the mid-1950s, including those away from home. Data for broad commodity groups were developed and described in a series of articles on regional and commodity food patterns published in the *National Food Situation*. These articles provide further detail and some discussion of the factors back of consumers' allocations of their food dollars to particular foods.

Estimates of shares of the United States food market by region, urbanization, and income show, for example, that farm households accounted for only 7 percent of the sales of food, meals, and snacks, in the spring of 1955, compared with the 69-percent share taken by urban households. Why this picture emerges is easy to explain in general terms: There are five times as many urban as farm households, urban families have more purchasing power, and they produce little of their own food.

Survey data on the proportion of households in each group using each commodity in the preceding week supply clues to the vital *marketing* question: Is the average consumption rate coming from very high rates of relatively few households or from relatively general usage?[32]

For example, consumption of butter and margarine in all urban households of two or more persons in the North Central Region averaged 0.82 and 0.64 pounds *per household*, respectively, in a week of spring 1955. But consumption of margarine in all households

[30] From pp. 122–123 of "Ramifications of the Relationship Between Income and Food," op. cit.

[31] Cross-section data from the survey differ from the food and beverage expenditure series of the Department of Commerce, partly because the Commerce data cover the whole population and the survey data apply only to housekeeping households. Also, survey data on money value of all foods include home-produced foods used by nonfarm households and all payments in food, some of which are excluded from the Commerce series on food expenditures.

[32] The percentage of users generally increases with the lengthening of the time period covered, so these data for the seven-day period of this survey are not directly comparable with those for longer periods.

that used this commodity averaged precisely the same as consumption of butter by those who used butter.[33] Accordingly, the higher average for butter among households in the North Central Region resulted because relatively more households used butter than used margarine.

Estimates of the regional distribution of the United States market for farm food commodities *only,* as well as for all foods, can also be derived from survey data. Food expenditures by the nonhousekeeping population are excluded, but they make up no more than 6 percent of the total population eating from civilian food supplies.

Estimates of the regional pattern differ slightly according to the precise definition of "food market." In spring 1955 the total market value of farm-produced foods consumed by housekeeping families both at home and away from home was divided among the regions thus, in percentages: Northeast 30, North Central 32, South 26, and West 12.

In economic terms, this measures the regional allocation of the demand for farm inputs in the form of primary food production plus the demand for inputs of marketing resources in the form of all services performed from the farm gate to the ultimate buyers in retail stores and eating places.

At the consumption end of the flow of food from production to consumption as compared with farm output, the four regions share differently. Whereas in 1954 the North Central Region produced half of the food in the country, a few months later households in that region accounted for only a third of the United States domestic market. In contrast, the Northeast consumed three times as large a share as it produced.

Based on the relationships of food consumption to the key factors of regionality, urbanization, and income, the author and her former colleague, Robert J. Lavell, have experimented with making state estimates for food consumption. (The process is described in detail in *Measures and Procedures* . . ., Section 4.3.4, to which the reader is referred.) It is necessary to estimate these data because of the high cost of sample surveys of household food consumption or of retail store sales for individual states and the impossibility of collecting data on all commodities moving across state lines. Such data would be needed to adjust production data to derive estimated "disappearance" within a state.

[33] These averages are derived by dividing the average for all households in the cell or income group by the percentage of households using each commodity.

14

CONCEPTUAL FRAMEWORK FOR MACROECONOMIC ANALYSIS OF CONSUMPTION

Several kinds of knowledge are needed for macroeconomic analysis of consumption. First, one must have in mind the broad outline of the marketing processes which prepare and distribute commodities and services to ultimate consumers, as described in Chapter 12. Second, one must know quite a lot about the sectors of the consumer market, so as to produce and distribute goods and services with the attributes consumers want (Chapter 13). Third, analysis of a new consumption problem is easier and of better quality if the analyst is familiar with the general characteristics, objectives, and findings of earlier empirical research. Fourth, an analyst must know and be able to use available scientific knowledge pertinent to the study of his consumption problem. Such knowledge includes concepts of and relationships among macro socioeconomic phenomena, some understanding of microeconomics of consumption, and understanding of the alternative analytical approaches which can be used. This chapter is concerned with the last two kinds of knowledge.

14.1 ON THE NATURE OF MACROECONOMIC ANALYSIS OF CONSUMPTION

Macroeconomic analyses of consumption problems have supplied explanations and predictions of consumption trends and patterns for use by government agencies, business firms, private research and trade organizations, and citizen-consumers. Just as families make wiser choices if they investigate alternative uses of resources, so public decision making concerning the desirability of developing public resources and providing publicly supplied services requires information regarding consumers' needs and requirements for privately and publicly supplied goods and services.

Examples of public alternatives which require analysis are allocations to develop land for recreation or urban redevelopment, and subsidies for food consumption by low-income families in the United States or developing countries. Other studies back up decisions regarding controls on private use of resources, as in farm price supports accompanied by acreage controls. Examples of such studies are provided in Chapter 17.

Marketing people working for firms producing and marketing consumer goods and services study general market trends, shifts in consumer demand among commodities, and changes in demand for marketing services such as processing, storage, and retail services. Examples of their empirical research on consumption aspects of marketing problems are given in Chapter 16.

Both government agencies and business firms carry on programs to inform individual consumers about trends and patterns in consumer purchases and use of goods and services. Government agencies do this in order that citizens will understand current actions of the government and be prepared to act through their legislative and executive representatives in deciding public policies. Also, many of the agencies assemble data and make analyses for use by business. Business firms and trade associations communicate consumption data to consumers as part of public relations and sales promotion programs.

Macroeconomic studies of consumption which supply explanations and predictions regarding variations in consumption at particular points in time and changes through time have some general characteristics. They usually investigate some of the same kinds of questions. We will review these similar characteristics and questions next.

14.1.1 General Characteristics of These Consumption Problems

By definition, macroeconomic problems of consumption pertain to consumption by large numbers of people, usually living in different parts of the country, in different types of communities, and often having varying socioeconomic characteristics. Some relate to consumer actions during varying periods of time. Many have implications for the value, quantity, and price of goods and services bought and consumed. Thus they have the dimensions of behavior, technical and economic aspects, time, and aggregation. As one studies these problems, one frequently finds interrelationships among several commodities if not among a considerable number of commodities. Therefore one may say that the essential characteristic of macro problems of consumption is their *aggregative* nature.

Income continues to be a key economic factor underlying differences between sectors of the consumer market. But a number of other socioeconomic factors that are frequently considered, particularly in an affluent economy, were noted in Section 13.1. In addition to the obvious importance of the number of people in the market, the age, urbanization, and regional distributions of the population are related to consumer demand. Some socioeconomic factors apparently interact with income, age distribution, and degree of urbanization, and have independent effects on consumption patterns. Among such factors are employment, occupation, education, accumulated assets, and family value orientation.

Other elements common to many problems are the reaction of consumers to price changes, technological changes, and to the availability and costs of consumer credit. In effect, the availability of consumer credit permits consumers to shift the time schedule of their consumption, e.g., buy now and repay the principal in installments plus interest in later periods. The use of borrowed money is a service consumers can buy. Economic theory relative to optimization of utility over time is summarized in Section 7.5.

The time element is present in every problem. Therefore the ways an analyst handles the time element and the data related to the time period inevitably affect the conclusions reached in the analysis. At one point in time, little or no opportunity is provided for changes in supply and demand toward equilibrium. We must recognize that a week may be "a point in time" when one is considering demand. The supply of a commodity like food or seasonal clothing in the market during a given week can change considerably. Similarly, supplies of some items change markedly over a two-year period which may be described as a "short-run period." The purchasing power of consumers and supplies and prices of alternative goods and services also may change considerably. Ordinarily, consumption patterns of particular groups of people change relatively little over a period as short as two years. Marshall's statement that supply leads over demand in the short run apparently holds here. For the longer run, Marshall argued that demand leads supply. It is in the longer run that patterns of consumer wants become more significant because they have time to change.[1]

Several economic theories related to the dynamic aspects of macroeconomics of consumption are considered in Section 14.2.

14.1.2 Some Questions Common to Many Problems

Three sets of questions are often inherent in problems requiring analysis of the consumption aspects. The *first* set has to do with trends and patterns in consumption. It includes such questions as these: What have been the major trends in the past? Who consumes how much of the commodity or commodities? How are these consumption rates related to social and economic characteristics of consumers? How do quality and prices paid vary with the consumption rates? How important is that commodity in the overall consumption pattern?

A *second* set has to do with the whys of consumption: Why do consumers take a particular quantity and quality at a particular price? What factors entered in from the supply side, whether from production, trade, or costs? Where and from whom was the commodity obtained by consumers? The "whys" often include income, urbanization, regionality, demographic factors, availability of alter-

[1] Further discussion of this point will be found in Section 1.4 of Burk, M. *Influences of Economic and Social Factors on U.S. Food Consumption.*

native goods and services, and other economic and social factors.

The *third* set has to do with the future prospects. Regarding them, an analyst commonly asks questions such as these: Will past trends be continued? What economic and social changes should be specified and taken into account in developing projections? What major technological changes appear to be in the offing and what effects will they have on the demand and the supply for the particular commodity in question? Is it possible for the marketing firm to influence future demand or the future total supply significantly? Does the commodity seem to be changing in relative significance within the total consumption picture? Are the rates of change significant and can they be altered?

An introduction to general problem-solving methods has been provided in Section 8.1 in connection with microeconomic analysis. These general methods are applicable with minor adjustments to macro problems, therefore the student should review them at this point.

14.1.3 On the Components of Theory

Workers in a scientific field use its theory as a language for communicating ideas. The components of formal theory are identified in different ways by different philosophers of science, but the following categories are generally included: (1) concepts, (2) assumptions or postulates, (3) generalizations or laws relating phenomena, and (4) rules of interpretation regarding the relationship of theory to observed phenomena or facts. These rules are often called operational definitions. In a deductive science one also needs rules of inference, which are usually from logic, in order to derive theorems or postulates from the primitive postulates.

Concepts are names or labels which have both meaning and significance. The meaning of a concept is its observable referent; e.g., the *quantity* of an item consumed is defined in terms of size, weight, or another unit. The significance of a concept is based on its relationship with other things, often set forth in generalizations about relationships among phenomena. For example, the concept of retail value refers to monetary value of some good or service measured at the retail level and has significance when compared with value at some other level in the distribution system or with retail value at another time.

Concepts usually have complex meanings and are defined by *constructs*. Constructs are postulated attributes, e.g., economy-mindedness of a consumer. Measures are developed to reflect the constructs. For example, the concept of retail value of food consumed requires use of the concepts of monetary value, retail level of distribution, and all food. Several measures of retail value of food consumed in the United States have been developed in the past, using different sets of basic data and somewhat different procedures. One retail measure in current dollars for all types of food consumed has been used in Chapter 12. Measures of this type can be useful in evaluating variations in food consumption among population groups and through time.

Straus has spelled out two approaches to the conceptualization and measurement of constructs.[2] In brief, the *rational* approach has these steps: conceptual definition, specification of components, selection of indicators, index construction, standardization, and validation. The *empirical* approach uses a collection of items and pragmatically sorts out those which differentiate between criterion groups. Supposedly, the conceptual basis for such a construct is developed *ex post facto*.

An example of assumptions or postulates is provided by the set of postulates needed for indifference analysis described in Section 6.3. Other examples are three assumptions basic to all science and particularly relevant to the macroeconomics of consumption: (1) Nature is orderly. (2) All phenomena are related to varying degrees. (3) The process of change is continuous but at varying rates. Economics makes extensive use of these assumptions in the process of abstracting simple models from the complexity of modern economics *and* the assumption that other conditions remain the same (*ceteris paribus*).

Kemeny stresses the importance of measurement to the development of a science. Measurement requires categorization for ordering or scaling. He states that classification is a fundamental process in all science.[3] It is the first step in the formation of scientific explana-

[2] Pages 339–341 of Straus, Murray A. "Measuring Families," Chapter 10 of Christensen, Harold T. (Editor), *Handbook of Marriage and the Family.*

[3] Page 161, Kemeny, John G. *A Philosopher Looks at Science.*

tions. Kemeny provides in his Chapter 5 a particularly helpful discussion of the cycle of the scientific method. It begins with the inductive process of forming hypotheses, then deduces the consequences in terms of an observable statement, and concludes with verification of the prediction.

Generalizations regarding relationships of concepts state that one instance of a concept is always connected with an instance of another concept, usually in a certain way. *Hypotheses* are generalizations still being tested. *Laws* are well-established generalizations about relationships. An example of a law is Engel's law. A *theory* is a deductively connected set of laws. It is designed to explain and predict as well as to describe and unify phenomena.[4] Examples are the theory of demand and the formal theory of consumer behavior.

Operational definitions provide information about the observable conditions under which a sentence containing a concept is true. Here is an example of such a sentence: The *quantity of food used* per capita in the United States in 1965 was significantly higher than in 1935. An example of a definition is: The *quantity of food used* refers to the farm resources contained in the food and is measured by value at the farm level.

Economic theory is concerned with the principles through which scarce resources are allocated among alternative wants so as to maximize satisfaction. It is also concerned with the effects of such allocations on the economy. Analysis of consumption requires consideration of a wide range of factors entering into wants. These factors include technological changes and the behavioral phenomena described in Chapter 5. The adaptability of micro theory to macro problems will be considered in the following section.

14.2 CURRENT MACROECONOMIC THEORY RELEVANT TO CONSUMPTION ASPECTS OF MARKETING PROBLEMS

Much of the microeconomic theory related to consumer behavior as set forth in Chapters 6 and 7 was developed in order to study macroeconomic problems. Before World War I, most economists were largely concerned with national economic problems. Not having many data to match their macro concepts, they speculated about the responses of all consumers in a market or an entire country to possible changes in prices and income on the basis of assumptions and hypotheses concerning the behavior of a representative or individual consumer.

In the period between World Wars I and II, microeconomic theory relative to consumption developed to the stage described in Chapter 6. Concurrently, some initial steps were made toward development of macroeconomic theory of consumption, but most macro theory has developed since World War II. In the following discussion of current macroeconomic theory, references to its history will be made only incidentally. The student is referred to fuller treatment in Chapter 7 and to references cited there. Here we will consider, in order, economic concepts for macroeconomic analysis, then relationships generally used by economists, and period or process analysis.

14.2.1 Macro Concepts

Both micro- and macroeconomics of consumption utilize the concepts of demand, price, income, value, economic attitudes and expectations, supply factors, consumption, quantity, quality, alternative goods, stocks, consumer choice, consumer use, and decision making, among others. The meanings of these concepts have already been discussed in connection with microeconomic theory. Their macroeconomic meanings will be clarified as we consider the relationships of price, income, and other phenomena to variations in consumption. In general the changes needed to adapt the micro concepts to macro analysis are primarily related to the process of aggregating (*a*) from individuals and families to (*b*) groups of people with homogeneous characteristics who form subcultures and to (*c*) aggregates for entire national populations.

To describe the economic flow of goods from producers to consumers in Chapter 12, we used a number of macro concepts. They included the concepts of market structure, economic flow of goods through marketing channels, marketing processes, stages in the marketing processes, changes in supplies, and market trends. Also, index numbers were introduced and used to permit the aggregation of nonhomogeneous commodities.

[4] Brodbeck, May. "Logic and Scientific Method in Research on Teaching," pp. 44–93 of Gage, N. L. (Editor), *Handbook of Reseach on Teaching.*

Consideration of the sectors within the consumption structure in Chapter 13 required use of the concepts of urbanization, regionality, and the demographic characteristics used to form groups, such as age groups of the population. These serve as key factors in the simpler forms of macroeconomic analysis.

To provide understanding of the structure of consumption, in Chapter 10 we made use of the idea of aggregation, as in Figures 10.1 and 10.2. This concept and that of disaggregation will be used in the section describing analytical approaches so we need not elaborate them further here.

14.2.2 Market Demand

The concept of market demand usually refers, in economics, to the aggregate of individual consumer demand in a market with geographic boundaries or other specified limits. Standard economic theory of consumer demand says, in effect, that the demand of an individual for a given product at each price is determined by his income, a given set of tastes and preferences (reflected in his indifference curves), and prices of related commodities. At first glance, one would think that the only additional factor needed to get market demand would be the number of people. Conceptually, this is true. Operationally, the estimation of market demand relationships, i.e., price–consumption relationships, is complicated by concurrent changes in supplies, incomes, tastes and preferences, disparate changes in prices of other goods, and random disturbances. The usual assumption that the demand of each individual is independent of demands of all others is contradicted by sociological findings regarding the impact on consumption of reference groups and the socialization process within subcultures. In Section 6.2.2 we discussed price elasticity of demand, including cross-elasticities.

Recall that formal economic theory pertinent to market demand assumes consumers' tastes and preferences to be given or already set. In contrast, marketing is concerned with how such tastes and preferences are formed and how they change. Marketing people are also concerned with how groups of people derive satisfaction as they use the product to meet their needs. Thus the very knowledge that is assumed by most economists is sought by marketing people.

Statistical demand analysis by agricultural economists has been largely concerned with the effects on prices for specific agricultural commodities of (*a*) changes in supplies of the particular product, (*b*) prices of related goods (usually substitutes but sometimes complements), (*c*) incomes of consumers, and (*d*) sometimes other specified socioeconomic factors. Often a catch-all factor is added, labeled *t*, to represent changes in tastes and preferences through time and/or technological changes. Most of the demand and price analyses have been developed to explain and predict short-run price changes.

In contrast, economists studying demand for nonagricultural commodities have more often tended to define variations in consumption or expenditures as the dependent variable. Frequently, they have been concerned with predicting short-run changes in aggregate expenditures or long-run shifts in levels of consumption. Price is an important factor in short-run predictions, but difficulties in long-range forecasting of price relationships are so great that economists usually operate with sets of assumptions regarding price relationships in longer-range analyses of consumption.

The subject of market price analysis is now considered intensively in special courses in agricultural economics and in courses in econometrics. Therefore we go no further with it in this text.

14.2.3 Income–Consumption Relationships

The relationship between aggregate consumption in an economy and aggregate income has been a subject for intensive study by economists in the last 40 years. Some theoretical and empirical work has suggested a relatively stable relationship of proportionality. Other findings indicate gradually declining proportions of income allocated to consumption as income levels rise, as was hypothesized by John Maynard Keynes.

Three types of hypotheses have been proposed regarding income–consumption relationships. Each originated in *a priori* reasoning regarding microeconomic relationships of individual consumer expenditures to consumer income. Each has been applied to the study of aggregative income and consumption relationships. Keynes' theory of the consumption function, now known as the *absolute income hypothesis*, has been discussed as part of micro theory in Section 6.5.3. Relative and permanent income hypotheses support the idea of a proportionality relationship between income and consumption. Relative income hypotheses proposed by Brady and R. Friedman and by Duesenberry have been introduced in Section 7.2.1. The assumptions of M. Friedman's permanent income hypothesis and of the Modigliani-Brumberg-Ando "permanent wealth" or family life cycle hypothesis were discussed in Section 7.5.2. Here we will consider some of the macro aspects of the hypotheses.

Keynes developed his *theory of the consumption function* as an integral part of his general theory of employment, interest, and money. This theory has served as a cornerstone of modern macroeconomic theory. Keynes was concerned only with total consumption, defined as real consumption expenditures for all goods and services. He clearly stated the hypotheses that (*a*) real consumption expenditures are a stable function of real income, and (*b*) the marginal propensity to consume is positive but less than one. These hypotheses were based largely upon introspection, finding a "fundamental psychological law." Keynes used the terms "marginal propensity to consume" and "average propensity to consume." Marginal propensity to consume is the ratio of an absolute change in consumption to an absolute change in income. By dealing with absolute changes, it differs from the income elasticity of total consumption which is based on proportional changes. Average propensity to consume is the proportion of total income spent for consumption.

Keynes proposed two other hypotheses: The marginal propensity to consume is less than the average propensity, which declines at higher levels of income. The marginal propensity to consume probably declines as income increases. With a decline in the marginal propensity to consume, there is necessarily a decline in the average propensity.

As in the cases of the utility and indifference approaches, Keynes assumed that tastes and preferences are given and that consumers do not learn or develop new tastes; they are unresponsive to what goes on in the world about them. He found the principal "objective factors" influencing the propensity to consume to be real income, windfall changes in capital, changes in the rate of time-discounting, fiscal policy, income, and income expectations. His second category of factors included the following "subjective" motives for consumption: enjoyment, shortsightedness, generosity, miscalculation, ostentation, and extravagance.[5]

Despite the fact that Keynes explicitly noted the possible effects of these factors on total consumption expenditures, he considered them to be much less important, even in total, than real income insofar as short-run changes in consumption were concerned. But we should recall that Keynes' interest was in the study of factors related to unemployment and in appraisal of alternative economic policies during the Depression when real incomes were very low.

During the Depression, there was very little evidence that the desire for consumption goods might have a causal effect on income or that individual families might be able to vary their incomes at will. Keynes treated income as a constraint on consumption and operated with a stable, linear, nonproportional relationship which was reminiscent of a linear function fitted to the Engel curves of income–food relationships.

Following the publication of Keynes' *General Theory . . .*, economists and statisticians were very excited about calculating consumption functions from time-series and cross-section data. However, they encountered a variety of statistical problems and became aware of serious conceptual limitations of the theory. The theory applied primarily in the short run and failed to take significant socioeconomic factors other than income into account.

Data on national income and national consumption expenditures developed by Simon Kuznets for the period 1869–1938 indicated a stable proportional relationship until the 1930s.[6] Among the hypotheses proposed to support the proportionality principle were Duesenberry's relative income hypothesis and M. Friedman's permanent income hypothesis. (See Sections 7.2.1 and 7.5.2.)

Duesenberry suggested that the failure of consumption to maintain its proportion relative to income in some short-run periods could be explained by lags in adjustment to changes in fluctuating income. He argued that consumers experiencing decreases in income cut back on savings in order to maintain their level of living as close to the past peak as possible,

[5] Page 108, Keynes, John Maynard. *The General Theory of Employment, Interest and Money.*

[6] See the discussion in Ackley, Gardner. *Macroeconomic Theory*, pp. 236–246.

although over a longer period they will make the necessary adjustment in consumption. If and when incomes recover, consumers gradually increase consumption but they are likely to rebuild savings first. If new high levels of income occur, then consumption will increase expenditures. A graph of such relationships for successive periods will look like a ratchet, therefore these varying impacts of income on consumption are referred to as the "ratchet effect."[7]

M. Friedman's *permanent-income hypothesis* is to the effect that *permanent* consumption is proportional to *permanent* income. He argues that observed, current income consists of a *transitory* component and a *permanent* component and that observed consumption has comparable parts. Permanent income during a given period cannot be observed but is hypothesized to be the discounted value of wealth expected over a consumer unit's lifetime. Consumer expenditures in a given period will differ from the expected value because of lumpy expenditures for durables, special expenditures for emergencies and unusual vacations or their counterparts in extra savings before or after sporadic, heavy outlays. Friedman insists that there is no correlation between transitory components of income and expenditures, i.e., between variations in income and expenditures from their expected values.

In formal terms, Friedman's permanent income hypothesis is

$$y = y_p + y_t$$
$$c = c_p + c_t$$
$$c_p = k(i, w, u)\, y_p$$

where c = actual consumption in some time period

c_p = expected value of consumption or *permanent consumption*

c_t = *transitory* consumption

y = actual income in the same time period

y_p = expected value of income or *permanent income*

y_t = *transitory* income

k = fixed ratio of c_p to y_p

i = rate of interest available to spending unit

w = ratio of nonhuman wealth to *permanent* income

u = collective effect of factors including family life cycle, tastes and preferences, and a variety of other socioeconomic phenomena[8]

The Modigliani-Brumberg-Ando (M-B-A) hypothesis is comparable in a number of respects to M. Friedman's hypothesis. M-B-A argue that a household's scale of living depends partly on current income and partly on resources expected over the family life cycle. Actual expenditures or level of consumption may vary from the general scale of living. The level of income is also related to the family's expectation concerning its long-run resources. (Note that this proposition assumes that the family has some control over its income.) Finally, M-B-A assumed that the scale of living bears a stable relationship to the level of resources at all levels of resources, but the relationship can be changed by other socioeconomic factors. The M-B-A formulation makes no reference to the relationship between transitory income and consumption, as defined by Friedman.

The Duesenberry, Friedman, and M-B-A hypotheses have been tested extensively with a variety of time series and survey data. A number of appraisals of these tests have been made by competent economists. Ackley concluded that the evidence is clear that variations in current disposable income alone do not adequately explain variations in consumption expenditures in either the short or medium run, e.g., by quarters or by years. But he found the several formulations of longer-run income–consumption relationships to be overly simplified, although fundamentally correct. Certainly the consumption function is far more complex in an economy like that of the United States than followers of Keynes have envisioned.[9]

Suits notes that studies by Ferber and others have revealed (*a*) significant differences between income–consumption relationships in postwar and prewar periods, and (*b*) the importance of introducing dynamic factors into analyses rather than reliance on Keynes' largely static theory. Suits' examination of the quarterly behavior of income and consump-

[7] Chapters V and VII of Duesenberry, James S. *Income, Saving and the Theory of Consumer Behavior.*

[8] Pages 17 and 26, Friedman, Milton. A *Theory of the Consumption Function.*

[9] Ackley, op. cit., page 266.

tion expenditures in the postwar period revealed no useful Keynesian-type consumption. In the very short run, income turned out to be more stable than consumption expenditures. Consumption expenditures were affected by lags in income and in other factors not specified in his analysis. A significant negative correlation between consumption and income appeared.[10] These findings fit in well with the research results of Katona and Mueller on the influence of consumer attitudes and buying intentions, which will be discussed in Section 14.2.4.

Such highly aggregative relationships are not directly useful for marketing purposes. But they do indicate the importance of a longer view of income expectations than the current year in making analyses of factors related to consumption of individual products. These hypotheses also provide theoretical bases for alternative ideas about handling income–consumption relationships in empirical research.

There is empirical evidence that the transitory component of income (such as windfall inheritances or other receipts) often is spent on vacations, durable goods, or education. For such items, current expenditures may be related to current income. This is especially true in prosperous times when the wives go to work to get the extra income for college educations of their children or to help pay for more elaborate home furnishings or a higher-priced house than one earner's income could finance.

14.2.4 Attitudes and Expectations

Katona and his colleagues at the Michigan Survey Research Center have constructed measures of consumers' attitudes and expectations regarding their economic situation for use in predicting changes in consumer buying at the macro level. Katona argues that such attitudes and expectations vary with economic developments and in turn influence reactions to such developments.[11]

Theoretical and empirical studies of consumer attitudes and buying intentions have been carefully appraised by Maynes. His findings are discussed in Section 7.3.3, to which you should refer.

14.2.5 Other Macro Theories

Empirical studies of consumption conducted in the postwar period have indicated the importance of other socioeconomic factors and variations in consumption. Some of the evidence has already been discussed in Chapter 13. Additional findings derived from survey data are described in Section 7.3.1. These demonstrate the relationships between (*a*) the consumption of particular categories of goods and services and some specific items and (*b*) such factors as family composition, stage in family life cycle, occupation, education, liquid assets, and stocks of durable goods. Although these relationships have not been integrated in formal economic theory, their significance is generally recognized and taken into account by economists.

One theory from production economics deserves special mention, the principle of economies of scale. In production economics it is generally found that firms producing larger volumes have lower costs than firms with smaller volumes. Similarly, it has been found that larger households often have lower costs per consumer by purchasing large quantities of supplies and being more efficient in household use of such supplies. Home economists in the U.S. Department of Agriculture have estimated that a four-person family has a 5-percent cost advantage over a three-person family in buying food and a 10-percent advantage over a two-person family. They also found that economies of scale permit the five- and six-person family to buy food to feed their families as well as the four-person family at 5 and 10 percent less cost per person, respectively.[12] Economies of scale are obvious in the cases of the use of durable goods such as washing machines, automobiles, and certain types of furniture.

14.2.6 Period or Process Analysis

Modern macroeconomics of consumption is largely concerned with economic dynamics. Even an analysis of the consumption structure of a cross section of the population incorporates concepts which reflect the history of the consumers, such as years of education, parents'

[10] Pages 26–39 of Suits, Daniel B. "The Determinants of Consumer Expenditure: A Review of Present Knowledge," Research Study One, Committee for Economic Development, Commission on Money and Credit, *Impacts of Monetary Policy*.

[11] Page 57, Katona, George. *The Powerful Consumer*.

[12] Page 2, *Food Consumption and Dietary Levels of Households of Different Sizes—United States, by Region*, 1955 Household Food Consumption Survey Report No. 17.

socioeconomic status, residential background, income in the preceding year, and stocks of specified durables on hand at the beginning of the year.

As pointed out in Section 7.5.3, *period or process analysis* has been formulated in theoretical and empirical terms since World War II. Recognizing the impossibility of studying continuous flows of all economic processes, economists divide time into periods and study aggregates of the flow of various kinds of economic phenomena for a sequence of periods. The objective is to explain consumption events in one period in terms of data for concurrent economic events *and* for events in preceding periods. The impact of events in earlier periods is reflected in some instances by stocks of durables on hand at the beginning of the current period and for other events by use of *distributed lags*. *Distributed lags* are rather rough statistical devices designed to reflect the hypothesis of the economic investigator that the impact of an event such as a major step-up in income may be spread over one or several succeeding periods, e.g., one-half in the first year, one-third in the second, and the balance in the third year.

The persistence of habit has been suggested by Brown as an explanation of the lag in consumer adjustments to changes in income. Sections 7.5.4 and 7.5.5 describe Brown's findings and the Houthakker-Taylor study of United States consumption expenditures. The latter study is a large-scale econometric demand analysis of most of the subcategories in the U.S. Department of Commerce's data on personal consumption expenditures for 1929–1961.

14.3 PERTINENT MACRO THEORIES FROM OTHER SCIENCES

Macroeconomic analysis of consumption has made increasing use of concepts and relationships developed in other social sciences in recent years.

General understanding of the psychological concepts listed in Figure 5.1 and discussed in Chapter 5 is essential for the study of the behavior of consumers. They underlie a number of the economic concepts and relationships. For example, the concepts of habit, expectations, and social learning are fundamental to the permanent and relative income hypotheses discussed previously. Attitudes and expectations regarding the economic outlook are now used extensively in macro analyses of short-run fluctuations in the economy. Attitudes are also significant in research on consumer preferences for specific items conducted by marketing people. However, satisfactory measures are still to be developed for constructs needed to make a number of the psychological concepts operational.

14.3.1 Sociological and Anthropological Concepts

Macroeconomic analysis now incorporates such sociological concepts as family life cycle, social differentiation or stratification, occupational differences, and subcultures. As soon as measures are developed by sociologists which are suitable for macro analysis, we are likely to make greater direct use of the concepts of reference groups, communication channels, and family value orientation. (These concepts are all discussed in Chapter 5, to which the reader is referred.)

Such demographic factors as age, sex, head count, and degree of urbanization have contributed to macroeconomic studies of consumption for many years. In recent years, the potential implications of several important sociological theories for macro analysis have been considered. These include the sociological theory relative to the functioning of social systems (such as the structural-function theory of Parsons), the ideas regarding the formation of cultural patterns which are supplied by the theory of symbolic interaction, and the complex of concepts related to social stratification. (See Chapter 5.) As yet, few economists are sufficiently sophisticated in modern sociological theory to make extensive use of such theory. Also, many of the measurement problems encountered are still unsolved.

All of the anthropological concepts discussed at the micro level in Chapter 5 have potential use in macro analysis. They are pertinent to study of subcultures within regions and countries as well as for macro analysis at the international level. Many economic analyses of changes in consumption in different countries appear to assume that such changes will follow the trends of consumption in the United States. It is quite possible that conceptual and data limitations introduce major biases in this direction which may be revealed as more anthropological theory is applied in development of much-needed social indicators and in improvements in national income accounting in the developing countries.

The frequent failure of American-type agricultural extension programs to speed up technological change in the agricultural economies of many of the Asian and Latin American countries has been traced by economic analysts to lack of understanding of the processes of change. Sociologists and anthropologists have developed a considerable body of theory about the relationships of innovation and diffusion of innovation to cultural change. Brief introductions to such theory have been given in Chapters 5 and 11. Further discussion will occur in Chapter 17.

14.3.2 Marketing

Several sections of Chapters 12 and 13 have described the kinds of marketing knowledge used in macroeconomic analysis of the structure and trends in consumption. The author refers particularly to the concepts of market sectors, market flows, market channels, stocks, and values at several levels in the distribution system.

14.4 TOWARD DEVELOPMENT OF NEEDED THEORY

Scientific theory develops in various ways. Usually, the prerequisite is an awareness of observable facts which are inconsistent with current concepts and generalizations about relationships between concepts. There appear to be several different bases for development, with varying mixes of the inductive and deductive approaches. These ideas will be elaborated in the following paragraphs.

14.4.1 Needs for Knowledge Regarding Macroeconomic Structures and Trends

The lack of continuous-type variables to measure some of the rather common socioeconomic variables, such as family life cycle stage, and of measurements of other socioeconomic concepts leads to problems with hidden variables. Knowledge to fill such needs will have to come from experimental studies and statistical research and will be incorporated much later in formal theory. Statisticians have already studied the relationships between consumer purchases and net worth, family size, and other socioeconomic characteristics and changes in supplies. But these contributions have been highly descriptive and have not yet been integrated to any extent into formal theory.

We have no organized body of knowledge about the processes whereby tastes and preferences change, only inferences from sociological and anthropological studies. Also, research on the interaction between consumption and income is needed. Morgan and others have pointed out that wives often go to work in order to raise their families' levels of living.[13] Economists have done a considerable amount of theorizing on the subject of uncertainty, but we have had little empirical research to measure the effect of uncertainty on consumption. Probably uncertainty affects middle- and high-income families very differently from the way it affects poor families. Recent writings on poverty have indicated that the hopelessness of very low-income families encourages bursts of splurging with pay checks or any unexpected funds. In contrast, middle-income families are likely to ration expenditures and save for the proverbial "rainy day."

We lack generalizations regarding the relationships between socioeconomic variables measuring many concepts of socioeconomic factors and the level of expenditures or consumption. Nor do we have generalizations regarding rates of change in these variables through time within individual cultures and comparisons for different types of cultures.

14.4.2 Developmental Processes

Based on his studies of the history of economic theories, Stigler has concluded that successful new theories are always more general than the ones they supplant, they often use weaker assumptions to reach comparable conclusions, they often encompass a wider range of phenomena, and usually systematize and explain a portion of the empirical knowledge of the time. He added that progress in economic theory development has been delayed by the lack of a criterion of refutable implications of theories.[14] Samuelson and Stigler are apparently in the minority among economic theorists in insisting that economic theory should be a strategically simplified description of observable and refutable empirical regularities.[15]

[13] Pages 23 and 24 of *Income and Welfare*, op. cit.

[14] Pages 148–155, Stigler, George J. *Essays in the History of Economics*.

[15] Samuelson, Paul A. "Professor Samuelson on Theory and Realism: A Reply," *Am. Econ. Rev.* LV:5:1:1164–1172, December 1965.

As is to be expected, econometricians have moved closer to reality than has the current theory of consumer behavior. Both inductive and deductive procedures are required to develop economic theory, to make use of theory from other social sciences, and to incorporate empirical research findings regarding consumers' behavior. Merton described as "theories of the middle range" those that are "intermediate to the minor working hypotheses evolved in abundance during the day-by-day routines of research, and the all-inclusive speculations comprising a master conceptual scheme from which it is hoped to derive a very large number of empirically observed uniformities of social behavior."[16]

Statisticians and economists have made major contributions to the analysis of aggregative consumption data by using insights from standard economic theory and other social science theory to guide the measurement of relationships between variations in consumption and variations in specified characteristics of large groups of consumers. This has been the approach of operational demand analysis. It produces useful findings, but they are rarely integrated systematically.

The problem-solving approach starts from work on problems requiring macroeconomic analysis. Ideas and hypotheses are gradually developed, tested, and reworked. Eventually this approach might lead to the development of a body of theory, but great efforts would have to be expended to integrate the findings.

Homans suggests the following strategy:

> . . . The strategy starts with the empirical findings themselves and seeks to invent the more general propositions from which these same findings, and, under different conditions, other findings may be derived. This is the strategy by which deductive systems are inductively arrived at.[17]

Another approach is to develop a conceptual framework, starting with scientific principles and insights from economics and other social sciences. This approach must start with a preliminary approximation or a general view of the content of a conceptual framework needed to deal with a group of problems in consumption. Considerable experimentation and analysis of statistical data are necessary. Concepts and hypotheses about relationships must be formulated, tested, and reformulated. The next section outlines such a framework.

Frameworks are needed to integrate social science knowledge pertinent to the four dimensions of consumption—behavioral, quantity-quality-value, temporal, and aggregative. Such frameworks must meet a number of criteria if they are to contribute to empirical research and to development of contingent theories, i.e., corresponding to actual behavior. The framework(s) should

1. Build on earlier research by using known concepts and by providing for replication of measurements or relationships.
2. Expedite operational analysis (*a*) by providing for use of one or more operational measures of constructs to test use of each key concept or cluster of concepts and (*b*) "by stating the observable conditions under which a sentence containing the term is true or false."[18]
3. "Suggest the *systematic* cross-tabulation of presumably significant concepts and . . . sensitize the analyst to types of empirical and theoretic problems which might otherwise be overlooked . . ." and thereby "promote analysis rather than concrete description."[19]
4. Use observable actions as measures of dependent variables.
5. ". . . Provide a compact parsimonious arrangement of the central concepts [from the basic disciplines] and their interrelations as these are utilized for description and analysis. . . ."[20]
6. In the case of analysis of process, not stop with comparative statics, but develop the dynamics by indicating the sequence of phases. If possible, the matter of stability under conditions of change must be considered.
7. Build toward a theory encompassing the several dimensions of the structure of consumption, possessing the characteristics of logical consistency and completeness, and having predictive power.

[16] Pages 5 and 6, Merton, Robert K. *Social Theory and Social Structure.*

[17] Page 975, Homans, George Caspar. "Contemporary Theory in Sociology," Chapter 25 of Faris (Editor), *Handbook of Modern Sociology.*

[18] Page 49, Brodbeck, May. "Logic and Scientific Method in Research on Teaching," Chapter 2 of Gage, N. L. (Editor), *Handbook of Research on Teaching.*

[19] Page 15, Merton, Robert K. *Social Theory and Social Structure.*

[20] Page 14, *ibid.*

14.5 OUTLINE OF A GENERAL CONCEPTUAL FRAMEWORK

A general framework integrating the several dimensions of the structure of consumption at a highly aggregative level is presented in Figure 14.1. It has been built on the foundation of the structure of consumption at the micro level (Figure 10.1) and represents the culmination of the process of aggregation described in Figure 10.2.

The aggregative nature of the macro structure of consumption is so complex that its analysis requires a number of simplifying assumptions. Phases in the processes of purchase and use, and their aggregation, are implied, not stated explicitly. Thus psychological phenomena of motivation, cognition, and learning are subsumed under concepts such as attitudes, expectations, and consumer knowledge, but period analysis permits their effects to change through time.

At the macro level, consumption problems generally require analysis of changes in the structure of consumption through time. The longer the time period, the more opportunity there is for the market situation to change and for market activities to affect consumer demand. But in longer time periods, demand factors such as population size, income distributions, and the cultural interests and attitudes of large segments of the population can also shift significantly. These ideas are elaborated in the following section.

14.5.1 Introductory Comments

The framework is presented in generalized form in Figure 14.1 under the assumption that alternative versions should be developed for use in analysis of specific problems. The framework can be adapted for use in situational analyses of cross sections of consumption or market sectors, in study of market trends or changes in aggregate use of specified services, or in specified leisure-time activities.

For example, if the analyst is working on a problem requiring comparison of regional markets for a particular processed food or household equipment item, he might develop details of structure of each regional market in the country in a recent year (identified as t), variations in purchases in t or between t and t_{-5} might be selected as the events to be explained, i.e., as the dependent variable. The author would expect him to accumulate information related to the independent factors for both time period t and the earlier period t_{-5}. For some factors he might consider changes in the periods t_{-10} to t_{-5} and t_{-5} to t to have important effects on structure of purchases in the two years t and t_{-5}.

Note that the time dimension is indicated for investigation of both independent factors and the dependent phenomena. It is designed to permit investigation of lags in the effects of independent variables on the dependent variables. But observations of independent variables for a sequence of years, e.g., time series of average retail prices of particular foods, can also be used in the framework without lags. The time periods may be measured in hours, days, weeks, or other units dictated by the problem at hand.

The level of aggregation is assumed by definition to be high, such as a region or an entire country. But the degree of aggregation, such as coverage in terms of different commodities and different population groups, will depend on the problem being studied.

14.5.2 Independent Factors Related to Demand

Factors influencing, causing, or associated with consumption are often categorized by economists according to their relationship to consumer wants or demand or to their origin in the production and marketing processes, i.e., stemming from the supply side of the economy. Many social scientists use the concepts of primary and secondary levels. The secondary level of socioeconomic factors includes the complex factors which result from interaction of the primary factors in the socioeconomic, social-psychological setting but appear to make contributions to variations in consumption over and above the influence of primary factors.

The selection of factors to be included here is based on the theoretical and empirical contributions to understanding consumer behavior reviewed in Chapters 5, 6, and 7.

Four groups of *primary socioeconomic factors* are identified in Figure 14.1. A number of concepts are subsumed under each of the brief titles.

Demographic characteristics (A) are useful indicators of biogenic and sociogenic needs, and factors related to needs and wants. Demographers often categorize people by age,

FIGURE 14.1 General conceptual framework for macroeconomic analysis of structures and changes in consumption.

INDEPENDENT FACTORS

$t_{-n} \ldots t_{-3}, t_{-2}, t_{-1}, t, t_{+1}, t_{+2}, t_{+3}, \ldots t_{+n}$

Related to Demand

Primary socioeconomic factors: status at specified points in time and cumulative history

A. Demographic

B. Social stratification

C. Consumer knowledge

D. Economic factors

Secondary factors acting as intervening variables:

E. Attitudes and expectations

F. Family life style

Supply Aspects

Market situation and activity: status and history

G. Price, quantity, and quality of goods and services offered in the market

H. Resource components

I. Marketing channels

J. Information flow

K. Technology

→

DEPENDENT FACTOR

$t_{-n} \ldots t_{-3}, t_{-2}, t_{-1}, t, t_{+1}, t_{+2}, t_{+3}, \ldots t_{+n}$

Alternative Sets of Events

I. Purchases of specified quality of goods or services in specified time periods, measured in quantitative terms
- —by total population group
- —by buyers only

II. Uses of goods and services in specified time period
- —by total population group
- —by users only

III. Expenditures for specified goods and services in specified time period
- —by total population group
- —by buyers only

IV. Value of flow of specified goods in specified period measured
- —at different levels in marketing system
- —including or excluding subsistence supplies

V. Activity and time allocation
- —work and leisure

sex, size and type of families, age of family head, stage in family life cycle, years since marriage, degree of urbanization, number of earners in family, and geographic area. They also use some of the characteristics the author places in separate social and economic groups. These characteristics reflect for the macro structure of consumption some of the phenomena related to structure and organization of individual families. Most of these characteristics are measured with Census of Population statistics for large areas and with data from cross-section surveys for population groups.

Social placement of individual families becomes *social stratification* (B) within large aggregates. Sociologists often use education and occupation of the head of the family in identifying social classes. For analysis of the consumption of many products, the education and occupation of the wife and children are also important so they should be included here too. Education is usually measured by years of formal schooling and completion of high school or college degree requirements. As adult education programs expand, better measures probably will have to be developed. The U.S. Department of Labor has a very elaborate occupational code, but most consumption analysts use eight to ten broader categories or groups such as blue collar, white collar, self-employed nonfarm, and farmer group.

Consumer knowledge (C) refers to knowledge of consumer technology. This includes knowledge of attributes desirable in particular products for particular uses, awareness of the characteristics of particular brands—including going prices, understanding of the workings of the marketing system, and services offered by different types of distributors. It also covers knowledge pertinent to consumer decision making regarding family finances and that pertinent to use of products.

Among the *economic factors* (D) are the usual income (measured in alternative ways), net worth, and liquid assets. The inventory of durables owned by consumers should be specified either as part of net worth or separately. Credit availability enters in too. For example, the limited availability of mortgage credit and high interest rates can materially reduce housing starts, as was the case in 1966. Consumption problems are affected by different types of credit situations, therefore different credit measures are pertinent.

The effects on current consumption patterns (as in time t) of past income levels, occupational experiences, and changes in other socioeconomic phenomena can be worked into the analysis in several ways. One is to use a lagged form of the variable (e.g., income two years earlier) as a separate variable. Another way is to disaggregate large samples into subsamples based on past experiences. A third is to work out moving averages such as average income in 1950–1952, 1951–1953, 1953–1954, etc., which can be used as the measure of the income factor. Some tests of the permanent income hypothesis have used the last method mentioned.

The behavioral sciences make considerable use of secondary factors described as *intervening variables* because they are intermediate between the primary stimuli or variables and the resulting response. Among such factors which seem to have separable influences are *attitudes and expectations* (E) *and family life style* (F). Katona has emphasized general economic attitudes and expectations in his research, but marketing researchers have been much more interested in consumer attitudes toward particular types of products or product attributes and in consumer expectations regarding buying specific goods or concerning the attributes particular brands or particular stores should or do possess. Attitudes and expectations are important components in family value orientation so the latter is not listed separately. Further discussion of such factors is given in terms of the micro situation in Section 9.2.2.

Family life style (F) is a complex concept which has been studied by a number of sociologists in the past 20 years. Direct measures of style of living tend to involve the analyst in circular reasoning because consumption goods provide an easy measuring stick. But if measured that way, style of living cannot be an independent factor causally related to consumption patterns. One direct measure utilized kinds of newspaper and magazines read. This is an example of a potentially useful concept for which researchers are seeking a construct and a measure.

14.5.3 Independent Factors with Supply Aspects

In the short run, events of purchase and expenditures for individual commodities or commodity groups are materially affected by the *prices, quantities, and qualities of products and related goods* (G) offered to consumers in the market. Prices have been used by economists for many years as an independent variable when quantity taken is treated as a dependent variable, and vice versa. Quantities offered in competitive markets largely determine short-run price situations so they cannot be used concurrently. However, for some types of problems, it is important to develop data on quantities of a given commodity offered in different price lines or quality categories.

Some highly macro analyses of the structure of consumption require study of relationships between (*a*) inputs of raw materials and resources used in processing and distribution, and (*b*) goods and services consumed. For example, preparation of long-range projections of economic development involves research on the flows of agriculturally produced materials, energy materials, and construction materials into major industries and then research on the flows of manufactured products into the consumption sector, government, and other industries. Another type of data on flows consists of information on imports and domestic production. As input-output analysis and data develop further, we can expect greater use of *resource components* (H) in study changes in consumption.

Sales through different *marketing channels* (I) are studied by market researchers to develop part of the background for making business policy decisions regarding use and development of distribution systems. Currently, U.S. Department of Agriculture data on civilian food consumption sort out food donations moving through a special distribution system but do not measure sales to users of food stamps by retailers.

Information flow (J) provides for the introduction of trade or private business information on advertising and special consumer information programs. To my knowledge, little use has been made of it in macro analysis, but the developing science of communications is likely to produce some more pertinent public measures of information flow than numbers of newspaper subscribers, numbers of TV sets and stations, and total advertising outlays.

Changes in technology (K) of production and distribution can materially affect consumption of particular goods. To date, no valid constructs have been developed. Economic statisticians have occasionally used a catch-all "trend variable" in a mechanical fashion to accumulate the effects of changing technology and other unidentified socioeconomic factors, but many econometricians question the use of such an expedient. Here, again, is a concept of considerable significance, particularly in developing economies, without a good construct or measure.

14.5.4 Dependent Phenomena

The five sets of events listed in Figure 14.1 are intended to be used alternatively as the dependent variable, according to the requirements of the consumption problem being analyzed. *Purchases* (I) may be measured in units if the product is homogeneous or by a price-weighted index or in value at constant prices, if nonhomogeneous. Different relationships to the independent factors will be found for average purchases in specified periods for the total population and for buyers only. The same comments apply to *uses* (II).

Expenditures (III) differ from *purchases* (I) by including price effects, e.g., price × quantity. This difference is especially significant in historical or trend analyses.

The set of phenomena described as *value of flow of specified goods* in specified periods measured at specified level in the marketing system (IV) is useful in problems requiring study of the farm level value of food consumed or of wholesale value of imports, etc. The note about subsistence supplies is particularly significant in analysis of problems relating to agricultural development or marketing changes in the developing countries. When value data are used, it is necessary, of course, to take account of price changes, either by deflation or by inserting a separate price variable in the supply group of independent variables. Changes in the general price level may differ from changes in the price of the product being studied, so price ratios may be needed.

The last of the five sets of dependent phenomena, *activity and time allocation* for work and leisure (V), is included to provide for analysis of expected changes in consumer demand for leisure time and participation in activities utilizing leisure time.

Probably one or more of the alternative sets of dependent phenomena should be treated as an independent factor affecting another set of

the analysis of some problems. For example, increases in active participation in sports would be expected to affect expenditures for sporting goods or expenditures for tickets to sporting events.

14.6 ANALYTICAL APPROACHES

The objective of macro analyses of consumption events may be to describe the current market structure, to identify key factors in it, and to explain historical future changes. To use such a framework as that outlined in Figure 14.1, an analyst must find or develop measures for each concept and for relationships among the concepts. Such measures may come from one-time cross-section surveys like those used in Chapter 13, from repeated cross-section surveys or consumer panels, or from time series of average observations for large areas, such as an entire country. Although some aspects of trend analysis are discussed incidentally in this section, the subject is so complex that it will receive separate treatment in Chapter 15.

We must now consider several general ideas which underlie empirical research on the structure of consumption. In Section 13.8 and earlier in this chapter we noted three basic assumptions used by scientists about orderliness, relatedness, and continuity of phenomena. On these three assumptions rest other assumptions or hypotheses which lead us to expect, *first*, to find patterns and trends in consumption and, *second*, to find that such patterns and trends are related to economic and social factors.[21]

Analysis requires a variety of concepts related to consumption or, in other words, different ways of looking at consumption. A particular problem may require a unique combination of these concepts. For example, problems differ in commodity coverage, whether they involve nonfood commodities or food commodities or services. The economic meanings of consumption pertinent to the problem also vary. One problem may require closer appraisal of the quantity consumed; another may focus on the quality of the products being consumed. Most problems require some attention to the value of quantities being consumed. But values and quantities may be measured at different levels in the distribution system. The problems may be limited entirely to the farm level or to the retail level. Or the problem may involve analysis at several levels, including the wholesale level.

In sizing up a macro problem, one has to consider the alternative *sources of the commodity and its uses*—whether by civilians, noncivilians for food, or for industrial purposes. Then, too, the channels through which the commodity reaches consumers are very important for some problems. Through study of marketing channels one can learn something about the kinds and amounts of marketing services bought by the consumer with the commodity. These are of vital importance to market analysis.

Many marketing problems require careful attention to variations in consumption among population groups at given points in time. As discussed in Chapter 13, these variations provide clues to the factors affecting consumption. Variations in consumption also occur through time. They may encompass changes in average consumption or changes in the consumption patterns among population groups through time.

The concept of consumption is not identical with consumer acceptances, preferences, and habits. *Consumer acceptance* is fairly close to that idea of consumption which is defined in terms of quantities taken from the market in a given period. But the idea of consumption also includes such meanings as value which are not included in consumer acceptances. *Consumer preferences* may not be entirely apparent from the quantity, quality, and value of food actually bought or consumed. Preferences may not be fulfilled in that products with the desired attributes may not be available on the market. Or consumers may not have the necessary purchasing power to fulfill their preferences. *Consumer habits* refer to both the combinations of commodities bought and used in a particular period and to the ways in which they are shopped for and used in the household. The concept of consumer habits is considerably more complex than is usually assumed.

A significant part of the knowledge of consumption needed for analysis is an understanding of how socioeconomic factors are related

[21] For further detail, see Section 1.7 of Burk, M. *Influences of Economic and Social Factors on U.S. Food Consumption.*

to variations in consumption at one point in time and to changes through time. It is helpful to subdivide them into factors operating primarily from the supply side and from the demand side, as in Figure 14.1.

14.6.1 Using One-Time Cross-Section Surveys

Description of variations in consumption among groups of people with several socioeconomic characteristics identified is based on a straightforward process of running frequency distributions and averages. But measurement of relationships between characteristics representing socioeconomic factors and rates of consumption becomes more complicated. For example, by subdividing cases in the Bureau of Labor Statistics' sample surveys of consumer expenditures and income according to level of income, one can derive average expenditures for food by families at each income level. However, the total amount of variation in average food expenditures cannot be attributed to variation in income because families at different levels of income will have different numbers of members, different age composition, different proportions in the several urbanization categories, and different characteristics for many other variables in the macro conceptual framework outlined in Figure 14.1.

Often available data from survey questionnaires only permit adjustment for size of family and further subdivision of the sample population by region and urbanization. If no other adjustments are possible, income elasticities can be computed by least-square regression methods (preferably using logarithms) for families classified within each urbanization category of each region or the whole United States. But if information is available to measure variations in other socioeconomic factors, an analyst will certainly want to take them into account. The procedure is not complicated if the data are in the form of a continuous variable, e.g., age of head of family reported in years. But discontinuous variables complicate the analysis. For example, occupation of the head of the household or of the wife may be quite significant in clothing purchases, but occupational categories are discrete not continuous. We categorize occupations according to blue collar, white collar, or professional work or service work, etc. At this point most marketing people will need to call for help from statisticians and econometricians.[22]

Econometric methods are necessary for aggregating cross-section data for prediction of changes. Some of these methods assume, for example, that if two groups of families differ in income, occupation, or other characteristics and have different consumption rates as revealed by a survey, their consumption rates would become the same if time were allowed for change in their income and occupation. Another common assumption is that all other characteristics of the families are the same or do not yield differences in consumption.[23] Some economists describe relationships between socioeconomic characteristics and consumption rates, found in cross-section surveys, as "long-run" in character. Others disagree because such an identification fails to take account of many changes in the society and economy which occur through time and cannot be measured by cross-section data at a given point in time.

A simplified approach to prediction using aggregation is to reweight the averages for subgroups found by the survey methods with frequency distributions projected independently from other sets of data. Such a procedure is described briefly in Section 2.3 of Appendix B and at a greater length elsewhere.[24] This procedure assumes that the relationships between (*a*) key factors used as the basis for the frequency distribution and (*b*) consumption rates will remain the same. For example, families at given real income levels will continue to buy the same amount of food or clothing. No allowance is made for changes in unidentified variables.

14.6.2 Use of Repeated Cross-Section Surveys

Repeated cross-section surveys can reveal changes in relationships between key factors

[22] Helpful guidance is provided by (*a*) Morgan, James N., and Sonquist, John A. "Problems in the Analysis of Survey Data, and a Proposal," *J. Am. Stat. Assn.* 58:302:415–434, June 1963; (*b*) Ben-David, Shaul, and Tomek, William G. *Allowing for Scope and Intercept Changes in Regression Analysis*, Cornell University, Department of Agricultural Economics, A.E. Res. 179.

[23] See Klein, Lawrence R. *An Introduction to Econometrics*, Chapter 2.

[24] Section 4.3 of Burk, M. *Measures and Procedures. . . .*

such as income or urbanization and consumption. These changes can then be taken into account using either fairly simple reweighting procedures or preferably more complicated econometric procedures.

Marketing people use repeated surveys to monitor the consumer market for their brands. An article describing such analyses has been written by Mainer and Slater.[25] It is discussed briefly in Section 16.4.1.

Repeated cross-section surveys and information from time series should be compared in order to appraise the major components of changes in average rates of consumption. Averages derived from the time series can be compared with averages for subsectors of the population at different points in time. To use this procedure, the reader must understand more about the general process of disaggregation.

14.6.3 Disaggregation

Macroeconomic analysis often involves the process of successive disaggregation of the great aggregates and overall averages of national consumption into their components, such as quantity and price or several groups of people. Or such analysis may proceed from all goods and services down to all commodities in one group combined, to subgroups, and to individual commodities consumed in a year, then to a season. One may disaggregate from all United States consumers to United States civilians grouped by region, then to urbanization groups within each region, and to income groups within the urbanization categories. Another type of disaggregation is illustrated by subdividing total food consumed into subsistence and retail food, then subdividing all retail or purchased food into sales at retail and sales by eating places. Or the value of a commodity may be disaggregated into its price and quantity components (approximately) or into the supplier and marketing service components.[26]

Suits illustrated the usefulness of disaggregation in his analysis of the consumption function for 1948–1959. He subdivided total consumption expenditures into four components, automobiles and parts, other durables, nondurables, and services.[27] His analysis revealed the importance of automobile purchases in the short-run behavior of total consumption and the dynamic effect of changes in stocks of autos and other durables. Because this analysis is concerned with changes in consumption in relation to national policy, further discussion is deferred to Chapter 18.

[25] Mainer, Robert, and Slater, Charles C. "Markets in Motion," *Harv. Bus. Rev.* 42:2:75–82, March–April 1964.

[26] Cf. pp. 4–8, Burk, M. *Influences of Economic and Social Factors on U.S. Food Consumption*, op. cit.

[27] Pages 32–34 of Suits, op. cit.

15

INTRODUCTION TO STUDY OF TRENDS IN CONSUMPTION

A large part of the macroeconomics of consumption is concerned with analysis of trends. This chapter provides an introduction to the very complex subject of changes in the macrostructure of consumption by examining major trends, especially for food. It begins with an exposition of the kinds of changes which can occur. Section 15.2 describes changes in United States consumption of all goods and services in the last 35 years. The next three sections deal with food consumption trends in this country.

Although the description of trends is a necessary part of the study of consumption economics, a more important undertaking is to clarify the major problems related to such trends. Public policies which have been adopted in this country to deal with these problems also merit scrutiny. Such trends, problems, and policies are, in effect, a framework within which business firms must plan their operations, especially over longer periods. Section 15.6 points out special problems in the analysis of consumption trends in the developing countries.

At several points in this chapter your attention will be directed to key concepts used in the measurement and analysis of changes in consumption. Thus you may acquire gradually the depth of understanding needed for your future analytical work.

15.1 CATEGORIES OF MACRO CHANGES

Basic to study of changes in the structure of consumption is an understanding of the kinds of changes which can occur and have occurred. One immediately thinks of changes in the several categories of *dependent* phenomena listed in Figure 14.1. Different magnitudes of purchase or use may result from changes in the processes of purchase and use by large enough groups of consumers to affect overall rates of purchase or use. But per capita or per family rates of purchase or use in major population groups can remain unchanged, although shifts in the relative significance of such groups within the total population result in changes in aggregate and average purchase or use or expenditure. Similarly, the structure of consumption for all goods and services may be altered by changes in one or a few items within the set of dependent phenomena while the rates for others stay relatively constant. An example is the sharp impact that changes in automobile purchases have had on total consumption expenditures in the United States in several postwar years. The "mix" of goods and services consumed may change with respect to quantity, value, and/or quality.

At least a few of the socioeconomic and market factors, which serve as *independent* variables, are likely to change noticeably even in a short span of time. New products appear on the market frequently and may affect the demand for the particular item under study. Over a period of several years, a number of significant changes can and usually do occur. Real incomes, price relationships, the size of the total population, and market activities of producers and distributors are examples.

Changes in relationships occur within sets of both independent and dependent phenomena and between one or more independent factors and individual dependent events, or sets of events. An illustration of a change in relationships among independent factors is a shift in consumer attitudes of two or more parts of the population grouped on the basis of income or urbanization. The change in relationships might have offsetting effects on consumption rates, or there might be a net change in total and average consumption. A good example of offsetting changes in consumption is the fact that per capita consumption of wheat in the United States has declined at about the same rate during the last 50 years as the total population has increased. Consequently, total consumption now approximates the annual total for the years just before World War I.

The intense interest of economists in possible changes in income–consumption relationships has been noted frequently in earlier chapters. There is substantial evidence that changes do occur for individual goods and services and for groups of items in both short and long spans of time. Short-run fluctuations are frequently observed in the relationships of total consumption expenditures to current income for the entire United States, but findings regarding long-run relationships are precariously based on inadequate data for years before World War II. However, Morgenstern, in particular, has pointed out that wide, but unpublicized, ranges of error in many of the macro data of the national income accounts raise substantial doubt about the reality of apparent short-run changes in some of the aggregates involved in measurement of income–consumption relationships.[1] Data problems will be considered further in Chapter 16.

It is obvious that the span of time under consideration, i.e., the *temporal dimension*, is an important factor in the kinds of changes which may occur in the macro structure of consumption. Economists since Marshall's time have frequently contrasted the possibilities for changes in the supply–demand situation in the very short-run or market situation (meaning a few days, weeks, or months according to the nature of the problem being studied), in short-run time periods (from a few months to a few years), and in long-run periods. Another way we subdivide changes in the course of time is by use of the categories of cyclical and secular changes. During the 1930s in particular, economists and marketing people were greatly concerned with changes in the rates of consumer purchases during business cycles. There was much controversy over whether changes in consumption were among the causes or the effects of ups and down in the economy. Keynes generally treated changes in consumption as a result of changes in employment and income.

Cyclical changes in food consumption are common because of natural cycles in production of some fruits and price-induced production cycles for a number of agricultural commodities such as hogs. The long-term downtrend in per capita consumption of wheat in the United States and the continued rise in automobile purchases are examples of secular trends in consumption.

15.2 CHANGES IN UNITED STATES CONSUMPTION OF GOODS AND SERVICES

Great economic and political events occurring in the United States in the last 35 years have had sharp repercussions on consumer incomes and outlays. Although 1929 was a year of record incomes and expenditures up to that time, it was also the year of the stock market crash. This marked the beginning of a severe economic depression. By 1933 per capita expenditures for goods and services, in real terms, had fallen to the lowest point of the twentieth century. Although recovery began about 1934, the drought years of the mid-1930s reduced the incomes of families dependent on agriculture and held down the level of food consumption for several years.

The outbreak of war in Europe and our defense buildup sparked rapid increases in income and consumption expenditures in 1939–1941. During World War II, shortages of durable goods and price controls reduced expenditures for them. Outlays for food, many other nondurables, and services rose as demand outran supplies and prices increased faster than controls could be devised. Sharp price adjustments occurred soon after the end of the war when controls were removed and supplies could not expand as rapidly as demand. By 1955 most of the severe shortages had disappeared, with the exceptions of housing and publicly supplied goods and services.

Table 15.1 provides data of the type used to trace changes in income and expenditures for consumption, at approximately ten-year intervals, thus skipping the depression years and the World War II period.

[1] Chapter XIV, Morgenstern, Oskar. *On the Accuracy of Economic Observations*, Second Edition.

TABLE 15.1 Department of Commerce Data on Income and Expenditures, 1929, 1940, 1950, 1960, and 1965, with Comparisons[a]

Item	1929	1940	1950	1960	1965
Disposable personal income					
Total in current billion dollars	83.3	75.7	206.9	350.0	469.1
Per capita in current dollars	683	573	1364	1937	2411
Per capita in 1958 dollars	1236	1259	1646	1883	2214
Personal consumption expenditures					
Total in current billion dollars	77.2	70.8	191.0	325.2	431.5
Per capita in current dollars	634	536	1259	1800	2218
Per capita in 1958 dollars	1145	1178	1520	1749	2036
Food expenditures					
Total in current billion dollars	19.5	16.6	46.0	70.1	85.4
Per capita in current dollars	160	125	303	388	439
Per capita in 1958 dollars	300	319	357	390	410

	1929		1940		1950		1960		1965	
	Bil. dol.	Pct. of total	Bil. dol.	Pct. of total	Bil. dol.	Pct. of total	Bil. dol.	Pct. of total	Bil. dol.	Pct. of total
Personal consumption expenditures										
1. Food, alcoholic beverages, tobacco	21.24	27.5	22.03	31.1	58.12	30.4	87.51	26.9	106.79	24.8
2. Clothing, accessories	11.19	14.5	8.85	12.5	23.71	12.4	33.03	10.2	43.43	10.1
3. Personal care	1.12	1.4	1.04	1.5	2.44	1.3	5.32	1.6	7.51	1.7
4. Housing	11.53	14.9	9.45	13.3	21.29	11.2	46.30	14.2	63.16	14.7
5. Household operation	10.74	13.9	10.48	14.8	29.46	15.4	46.91	14.4	61.88	14.3
6. Medical care and expenses	2.94	3.8	3.02	4.3	8.79	4.6	19.12	5.9	28.12	6.5
7. Personal business	4.16	5.4	3.33	4.7	6.86	3.6	14.97	4.6	22.05	5.1
8. Transportation	7.61	9.9	7.14	10.1	24.67	12.9	43.13	13.3	57.82	13.4
9. Recreation	4.33	5.6	3.76	5.3	11.15	5.8	18.30	5.6	26.30	6.1
10. Private education and research	0.66	0.8	0.63	0.9	1.62	0.9	3.72	1.1	5.59	1.3
11. Religious, welfare activities	1.20	1.6	1.01	1.4	2.28	1.2	4.75	1.5	5.61	1.3
12. Foreign travel and other, net	0.51	0.7	0.09	0.1	0.63	0.3	2.18	0.7	3.21	0.7
Durable commodities	9.21	11.9	7.77	11.0	30.48	16.0	45.29	13.9	66.06	15.3
Nondurable commodities	37.69	48.8	37.02	52.3	98.11	51.3	151.30	46.5	190.60	44.2
Services	30.32	39.3	26.04	36.7	62.42	32.7	128.65	39.6	174.81	40.5

[a] From U.S. Department of Commerce, *Supplement to Survey of Current Business,* August 1966, *The National Income and Product Accounts of the United States, 1929–1965.*

Probably the most important change in United States buying patterns in the last 15 years has been increased buying of services. They are now back in the same position relative to expenditures for all goods and services as they held in 1929. Services now take about 41 cents out of each consumer dollar spent for goods and services, compared with the low of 31 cents in 1947. Half of the increase has been due to the recovery of prices of services in relation to prices of goods from the abnormal relationships after the war. Particularly significant in the increased outlay for services in the last decade has been more spending for housing, household utilities, physicians and dentists, private hospitals, interest on personal debts, and the expenditures for education and research.

Housing costs are counted as services in the national accounts because they are given in terms of rental values, even for family-owned homes. Although in the last few years rent increases have been slowing down, the housing share in consumer expenditures has gone up from 11 percent in 1950 to 15 percent in 1965. Apparently, the quality of housing has been improving.

Relative importance of nondurable goods has declined from its very high position after the war as food and clothing prices and supplies have shifted in relationship to prices and supplies of other goods and services. Per capita expenditures for *food* have increased only slightly when the general rise in prices is taken into account. The share of disposable income per capita allocated to food has dropped from 26 percent around 1947 to 18 percent in 1966. There has been a substantial shift in food consumption toward more processed foods and more livestock products, and away from potatoes and cereals. In the last 20 years a significant part of the increase in retail food store sales has been to replace food formerly home-produced. Per capita expenditures for *clothing* have risen markedly in the last few years, perhaps because of the relative increase in the teenage population.

Transportation expenditures are partly classified as nondurables and partly as services. The long period of considerable upgrading in car purchases, which began with the model change in 1949, was reversed for several years by the purchases of small foreign cars and the new domestic compacts but seems to have started again in the mid-1960s. Per capita consumer expenditures for gas and oil have increased in the last 15 years; in terms of dollars of constant purchasing power they rose almost 70 percent, from 1950 to 1965. These figures exclude expenditures by business firms for gas and oil.

The share of *durable goods* in outlays for all goods and services is about the same now as it was 15 years ago but well above the 1929 proportion. The high level is closely related to expenditures for autos. Expenditures for durable goods are particularly subject to fluctuation with changes in income.

Data with which these trends have been measured are taken from the Department of Commerce's annual publication of the national income accounts, published in the *Survey of Current Business*. The national income number is usually a part of or a supplement to the July or August issue. There the reader can find estimates of the goods and services consumed by the American public for individual years for many subcategories.

15.3 HISTORICAL TRENDS IN THE UNITED STATES FOOD MARKET

This section illustrates the process of identifying important trends in consumption of a commodity group and introduces the student to sources of basic data. It is easy to get lost in the masses of statistics available in the United States which relate to consumption problems. Among them are the expenditure data and the new input-output data indicating industrial origins of consumer goods and services (developed and published by the U.S. Department of Commerce), and the food data in the current reports of the Economic Research Service of the U.S. Department of Agriculture. Summaries and descriptions of the food data are provided in several handbooks cited.[2]

[2] The U.S. Department of Agriculture led the government parade in publishing compilations and descriptions of its data when it published Misc. Pub. No. 691, *Consumption of Food in the United States, 1909–48*, in 1949. Later, it published Agriculture Handbook 118 *Major Statistical Series of the U.S. Department of Agriculture*, a series of volumes with data and information on all kinds of series published by the Department. Volume 5, "Consumption and Utilization of Agricultural Products," describes consumption data in nontechnical terms. Misc. Pub. No. 691 was superseded by Agr.

A number of series measuring overall food consumption, i.e., all foods combined, are published and appraised in Agriculture Handbook 206, *Measures and Procedures for Analysis of U.S. Food Consumption*. The trends and patterns in consumption of food are described in much greater detail than herein in Agriculture Handbook 214, *Trends and Patterns in U.S. Food Consumption*, which also includes a small amount of analysis.[3]

Next, let us consider eight of the major changes in United States food supplies and consumption over the last two or three decades, taking them up one by one and identifying supporting data.

Handbook No. 62 (with the same name), which has now been updated and reorganized as USDA. Statistical Bulletin No. 364 *U.S. Food Consumption* (1965). Annual supplements are issued to carry the series forward, but current data for major series are published each quarter in the *National Food Situation* by the Economic Research Service.

[3] Data in these publications have not been updated since their publication. Therefore the author has had to develop approximately matching data for subsequent years, mostly from published reports, for use in tables in Chapter 12, in the figures of this chapter, and in Appendix B.

15.3.1 Per Capita Use of Food, Farm Level

In the last 25 years domestic food production has increased relatively more than the United States population, and incomes have risen. Therefore per capita use of food has increased. Contribution of imports and inshipments showed some increase in the late 1950s as consumers used more tropical foods, but the admission of Hawaii and Alaska lowered totals for inshipments into the 50 states. Stocks of grains in particular accumulated after the war, but subsidized exports have sharply reduced them in the last few years.

United States domestic production of farm food commodities generally has supplied 85 to 90 percent of civilian food use of farm commodities, with the balance being imported. The foods we import are largely the tropical commodities like fruits and coffee not produced in the United States except Hawaii. Some countries have a comparative advantage for some other commodities and would like to ship them to us, but pressure of domestic producers on Congress and the U.S. Department of Agriculture has led to the establishment of quotas on the importation of some

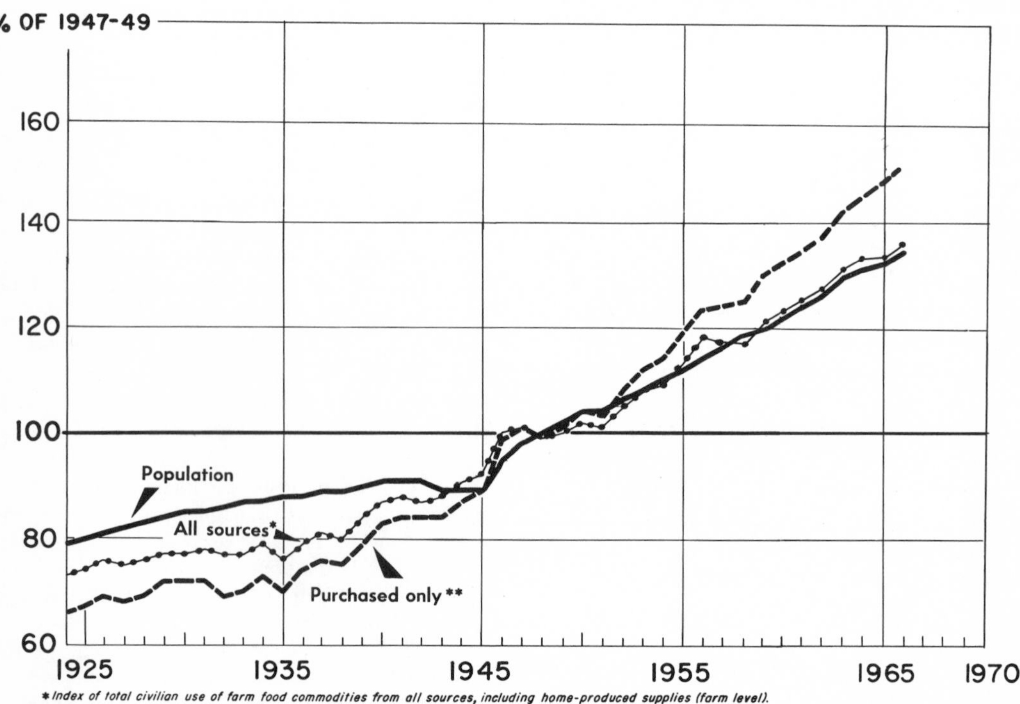

FIGURE 15.1 Total civilian population and food use of farm commodities.

commodities either under law or through government agreements. Examples are sugar, dairy products, and beef.

During recent years, total civilian food use has accounted for about three-fourths of each year's flow of farm commodities into utilization. This proportion is slightly lower than the rate of flow into civilian use in the mid-1930s but higher than during the war period when the Armed Forces and our allies were taking substantial quantities of food.

The increase in per capita use of farm resources converted into food is indicated in Figure 15.1 by the changes in the relationship of the index of civilian population and total civilian food use of farm commodities. The figure also shows how commercially produced farm foods have been increasing in importance in the total civilian use of foods. Within the overall totals, there have been some shifts in commodity makeup, depending partly on current production and partly on changes in consumer preferences. Their net effect over the last 30 years has been a small increase in the relative importance of livestock products. The shift toward livestock products has resulted in a net gain in the use of farm resources. For example, a shift in consumption involving a ten-pound reduction in per capita consumption of wheat flour and an increase of ten pounds in per capita consumption of meat means a $500,000 increase in the use of farm resources (in 1947–1949 dollars), aside from changes in marketing services. This demonstrates the major significance to United States farmers of the makeup of the total poundage of food that the civilian population eats.[4]

The data used in these comparisons are similar to those we used in Chapter 12. They are part of the master index of supply–utilization of farm commodities. This index measures the annual flows of commodities from the broad categories of source into broad categories of use and users. It was designed for analysis of changes in supply and use of all agricultural commodities as a coordinated whole. Thus it permits the analysis of interrelationships among the sources and channels of distribution.

In Chapter 12 we traced the flow of wheat and milk from producers to consumers. Data for all commodities similar to the data given in lines 12 to 15 and 31 of Table 12.1 and

[4] Further detail is given in Section 2.3.4 of *Trends and Patterns. . . .*

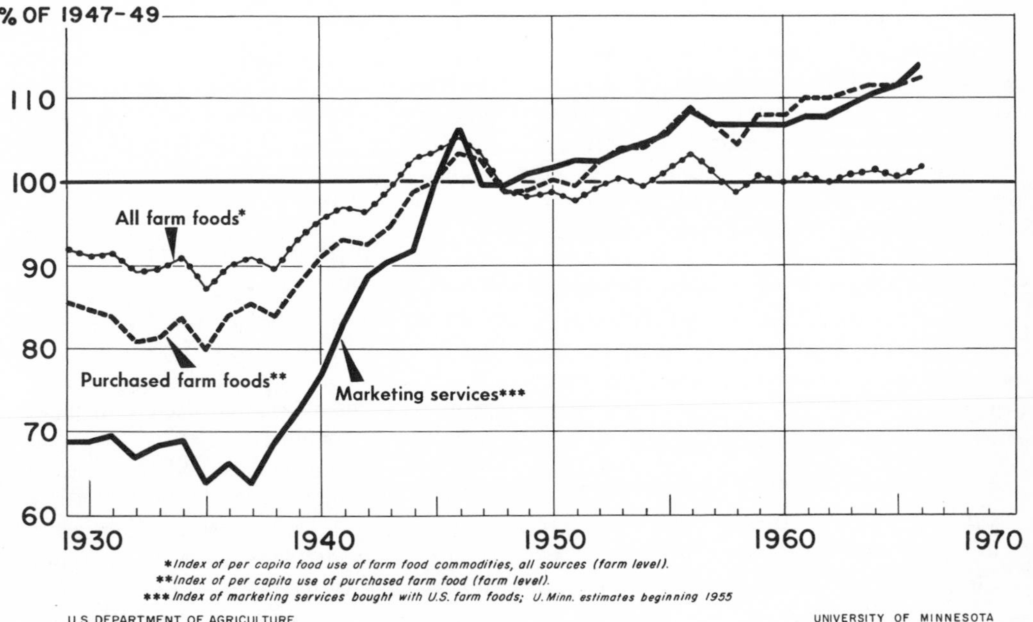

FIGURE 15.2 Per capita use of farm foods and of food marketing services.

in lines 31 to 35 of Table 12.2 are added together to form the value aggregates from which this master index and its subindexes are computed. The subindex *excluding* home production is described as purchased only. The indexes used for the chart were related to the 1947–1949 average. Population data for the table come from the Bureau of the Census. Indexes of the data based on 1947–1949 are derived by dividing the total number for a particular year on July 1st of that year by the average population on July 1st during the three years 1947–1949. The chart was drawn by plotting the index numbers calculated as percentages of the 1947–1949 average, and then connecting the dots.

15.3.2 Home Production

Home production of farm food commodities for household food use has decreased greatly in the United States over the last 35 years. Figure 15.2 shows the much faster rise in the use of purchased farm foods than in the use of farm foods from all sources. Whereas home production supplied about a fifth of civilian food supplies in the mid-1930s, the proportion was down to around 5 percent in the last few years. The output of both livestock products and crops for farm family or rural family use has fallen very significantly. The decreases in the farm population combined with the problems of raising livestock in the increasingly urbanized areas have reduced the proportion of civilian consumption of home-produced livestock products more than is the case for crop items. Changes in the use of marketing services needed to get the food from farmers to consumers have naturally been closely tied to these changes in the use of purchased foods.

Data for measuring changes in subsistence or home production at the farm level are calculated by multiplying the farm quantities for each item times the 1957–1959 average farm prices for the item. The products are value aggregates. Then the ratio of the value aggregate in each year to that in the base period must be derived.[5]

15.3.3 Retail Measures of Consumption

Although poundage is not a satisfactory way to measure overall food consumption from an economic point of view, as discussed in Chapter 12, it is used so often that we need to note the changes in poundage at retail. Just before World War I about 1600 pounds of food were consumed per capita per year in terms of retail weight. In recent years the per capita poundage of food consumed has declined to about 1400 pounds as more processed foods have been used. For example, we consume more of the frozen concentrated juices and less of the bulky foods such as the fresh oranges. But several economic and nutritional measures of consumption indicate significant increases in consumption have occurred in overall level.

Economists are primarily interested in the value, not the water content, of commodities like food, so they use price to compute total values such as those in Part C of Tables 12.1 and 12.2. The changes in such totals in the course of time are studied with care. You will recall from the tables in Chapter 12 that price and quantity may be measured at the farm level or at the retail level of distribution. Figure 15.3 shows how the retail price-weighted index of per capita consumption increased from 1910 to current years. Note that calcium and protein from animal sources moved along close to this index, but that calories per capita declined as people needed less food energy.

Retail poundage data are published in Table 5 of Statistical Bulletin No. 364 *U.S. Food Consumption* and its annual supplements. The index of per capita food consumption measured at retail is carried in Table 1 of that bulletin and in the *National Food Situation*. The index of per capita civilian food use of farm commodities is published in Table 4 of the statistical bulletin.

15.3.4 Changes in Makeup of Food Consumption

Significant changes in the relative importance of individual foods in overall United States food consumption during the last 50 years were the substantial decline in potatoes and cereal products, the substitution of vegetable for animal fats, and the increase in poultry consumption. In the post-World War II period, per capita consumption of most livestock products has averaged substantially higher than in the 1930s.

In Chapter 12 we traced the development of per capita consumption data for flour and milk. You will recall that in Tables 12.1 and

[5] Such data were given in Table 47 of the Supplement for 1959 to Agr. Handbook 91 *Measuring the Supply and Utilization of Farm Commodities.* No later edition has been published.

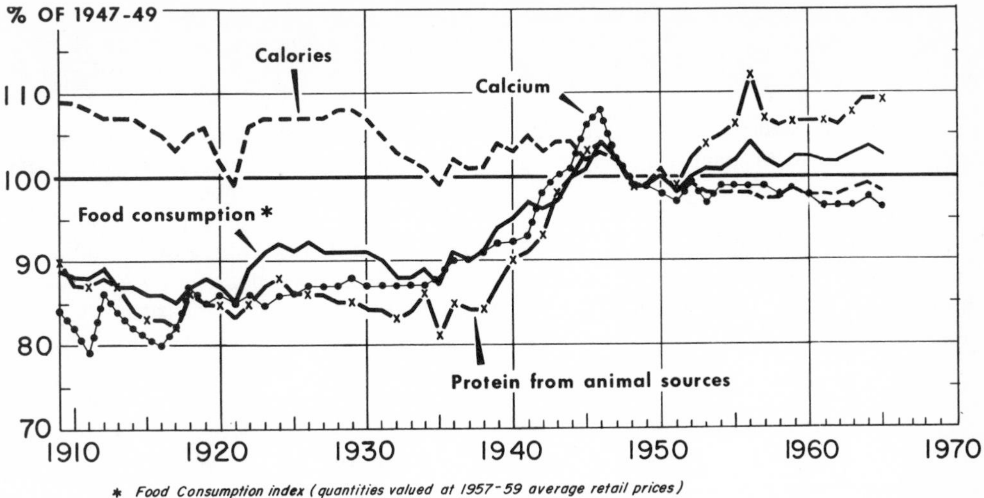

FIGURE 15.3 Food consumption and available supplies of selected nutrients, per capita.

12.2 we worked out the retail value data and the index of per capita retail consumption for cereal products and dairy products. Comparable data for all commodities are described in Statistical Bulletin No. 364 and Volume 5 of Agr. Handbook 118, to which references were cited earlier. These data were used for Figure 3.4 of this text. The value data for individual years in terms of base period prices were combined into five-year moving averages (e.g., 1910–1914, 1911–1915, etc.) and then compared with the average for the 1909–1913 base period for that chart. The annual per capita consumption data for major commodities, which are used in such calculations, are published each quarter in the *National Food Situation*.

15.3.5 Increased Use of Processed Foods

There has been a substantial shift from the use of fresh foods to those commercially processed. Part of this shift can be traced to the decline in home food production. Another part of the change reflects tremendous institutional changes in food marketing in the United States.

Basic to the study of changes in the use of marketing services is the problem of defining such services as processing. One analytical approach has been that of identifying stages or degrees of processing within the overall area. Practically all foods purchased by consumers undergo some form of processing. The amount of processing or degree of processing varies from trimming, grading, and washing to complete pre-preparation of elaborate dishes and meals such as the TV dinners. Also, some foods go through several forms of processing. For one study, four stages of commercial processing were identified, and the flows of food through them were measured. Operations performed by farmers and by households for their own use were excluded because the objective was to measure changes in the volume of foods to which were added services supplied by commercial marketing agencies operating between the farm gate and the kitchen door.

Out of the total civilian supply of farm foods, marketing agencies handled about 80 percent in 1925 but 91 percent in 1954. Over this period the proportion of the total food supply commercially processed beyond the minimum degree necessary for retail sale as fresh or raw, such as that canned, dried, cured, frozen, or baked, went up from 25 percent to 35 percent.[6]

The stages of processing used for this study were these: the first stage was the least possible amount of processing for foods to be sold in retail stores, often described as fresh or raw foods. The second stage covered all additional

[6] Page 1 of Burk, Marguerite C. *Consumption of Processed Farm Foods in the United States*, U.S. Agr. Marketing Service Mktg. Res. Report No. 409.

processing of single commodities whether by canning, quick freezing, drying, curing, manufacturing of butter, etc. The third stage included the preparation of all the older mixed foods such as the canned soups and the older flour mixes, baked goods, and ice cream. The fourth stage was used to identify newer mixed foods, often considered to be "convenience foods." But "convenience foods" also should include such old-fashioned items as fluid milk and sliced bread. The prepared foods classified in the fourth stage were those which have been extensively marketed only since World War II.

"The greatest changes among the forms or types of processing over the 30-year period from 1925 to 1954 were a ninefold increase in frozen foods and a 275-percent increase in the total civilian use of canned foods. In contrast, the consumption of milled grains without further commercial processing into bread, other bakery products or mixes decreased 40 percent in the 30-year period."[7] Unfortunately, a comparable analysis based on the 1958 and 1963 censuses has not been reported by the Economic Research Service, if made.

15.3.6 Increase in Eating Out

The relative importance of eating away from home has increased, and there has been a marked shift from eating in boarding houses to restaurants, hotels, lunch counters, and school and industrial feeding facilities. In 1963 about 19 percent of all food reached consumers through the institutional market, compared with 13 percent in 1929.[8]

The variety of establishments in which Americans can eat meals and snacks greatly complicates measurement of the extent of such eating. It is relatively easy for the Bureau of Census to obtain total sales data from restaurants and cafeterias, but it is much more difficult to get the department stores, variety stores, and filling stations to report separate sales data for food. For the 1954 and 1958 Censuses of Business no commodity details were obtained, but some data on retail sales subdivided by merchandise line are supplied by the 1963 census reports.

The first nationwide survey of all types of food distributed by United States eating places was made in two phases in 1966 and 1967, sponsored by the U.S. Department of Agriculture and the trade association of food firms selling to the institutional market. Data from that survey will provide much needed information about that market.

One measure of changes in the eating place business is the market value of all meals and food handled by eating places. Such data for 1929–1959 were developed for an ERS handbook by this author using information from the Censuses of Distribution, some household survey data, and unpublished data from the Department of Commerce.[9] To relate the volume of operations of eating places to the total food flow, it is necessary to make comparisons with the value of all food sold or consumed at the same level in the distribution system, either retail or wholesale. Apparently eating places currently are handling about 18 or 19 percent of the total United States food supply.[10] But they handle a larger proportion of the food moving through commercial channels, which excludes the home-produced supplies. During the war there was a boom in restaurant eating because so many people were away from home or working overtime or they were avoiding rationing problems. In the immediate postwar period, the relative share of eating places in the total food business declined somewhat. Renewed prosperity in the 1950s and 1960s apparently again increased the extent of eating out by the United States population.

15.3.7 Ratio of Food Expenditures to Income

The proportion of disposable money income allocated to food expenditures has declined

[7] *Ibid.*, page iv.

[8] Estimate for 1963 from page 5 of *Food from Farmer to Consumer*, Report of the National Commission on Food Marketing. Estimate for 1929 based on retail value data on page 92 of Burk, M. *Measures and Procedures. . . .* The NCFM figure for 1963 appears to be about one percentage point too high, on the basis of preliminary data available from the 1966 phase of the USDA nationwide survey of eating places. See Van Dress, Michael G., and Freund, William H. *Survey of the Market for Food Away from Home:* A Preliminary Overview of Basic Tabulations From Phase I of the Survey, ERS–197, May 1967.

[9] Procedures used are described in Appendix B of *Measures and Procedures. . . .*

[10] The estimate based on retail values is fractionally lower than that of the National Commission on Food Marketing. Both are only approximations.

significantly since 1947, and a decreasing proportion of food expenditures by consumers has gone to farmers. Up to this point we have been talking about farm value and retail value. Now we will use expenditures or dollar outlays for food by consumers. Figure 15.4 shows how these three series compare. The retail value series comes so close to the expenditure series for the years before 1948 because significant quantities of food were apparently sold to consumers by farmers and distributors at less than retail store prices, and offset the extra costs of eating out. This practice is apparently much less common now.

Estimates of food expenditures based on data of the national income accounts (developed by the Office of Business Economics, U.S. Department of Commerce) are generally used to estimate the proportion of disposable money income allocated to both domestically produced and imported food. (Table 15.1.) However, they *include* the farm value of farm home-produced food for family use and *exclude* (*a*) business purchases and (*b*) food furnished either as a part of employees' pay or with transportation and institutional services.

Expenditures for domestically produced farm foods have been estimated since 1958 by the Economic Research Service of the U.S. Department of Agriculture. The estimation process used from 1958 to 1966 started from data on civilian consumption derived from supply and distribution data. When the necessary adjustments were made to match the concepts used in the Commerce and Agriculture sets of data (which were designed for different purposes), the two sets matched reasonably well until the USDA series was changed in 1966. The old USDA series involved pricing USDA estimates of foods consumed at retail and adding an eating-place markup for food moving through that channel. The new USDA series was estimated by means of the commodity-flow method, also used by the Department of Commerce. However, the two series are now somewhat inconsistent in level.

Table 12.3 and the charts in this chapter incorporate estimates by the author consistent with the earlier USDA series and with estimates of the Department of Commerce.[11]

A more extensive discussion of trends in food values and their relationships to income for years before 1960 is given in Chapter 6 of

[11] See footnote 22 in Chapter 12.

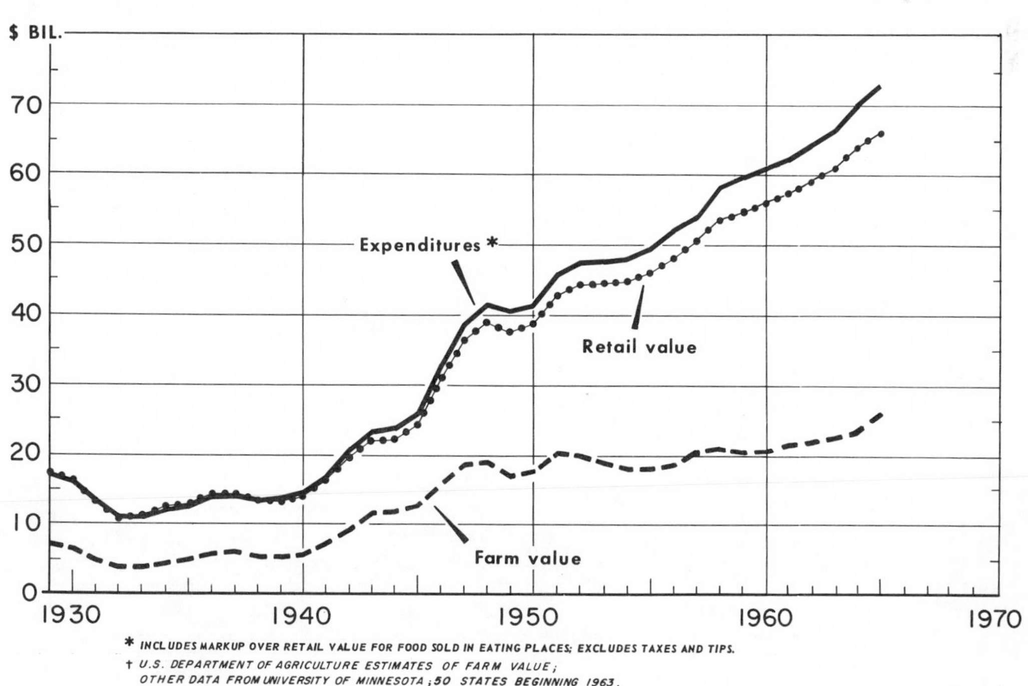

FIGURE 15.4 United States-produced farm foods sold to civilians,† farm value, retail value, expenditures.

Trends and Patterns in U.S. Food Consumption, op cit.

15.3.8 Increases in Food Expenditures

Changes in the composition of civilian food expenditures are indicated in Figure 15.5. The share going to food marketing services increased sharply after wartime controls on prices, labor, and construction were removed. The trend in food expenditures summarizes a number of trends already mentioned, such as increased demands for higher-cost, higher-quality foods with more factory preparation, and for additional marketing services connected with processing, retailing, and restaurant service.

Accompanying these changes have come a number of major changes in the economic and technological structure of the food industry. They include the growth of supermarkets; reduction in numbers and increases in size of establishments engaged in retailing, food processing, wholesaling, and assembly of farm products; and growth and development of new types of establishments distributing food to consumers, e.g., in-plant and school feeding facilities, vending machines, drive-in restaurants, and convenience food stores.[12]

15.4 MAJOR PROBLEMS AND POLICIES RELATED TO FOOD CONSUMPTION TRENDS

In this section, five major food trends are used to identify the kinds of economic problems that are related to changes in consumption. Also, some examples of public policies that have evolved to cope with these problems will be noted. People in marketing positions need such knowledge to guide their production

[12] Further information on these changes is available in a number of government reports, such as:

(*a*) *The Marketing and Transportation Situation*, May 1966;
(*b*) The summary report and technical studies issued in June 1966 by the National Commission on Food Marketing;
(*c*) U.S. Economic Research Service, Marketing Economics Division *Agricultural Markets in Change*, USDA, ERS, Ag. Econ. Report No. 95.

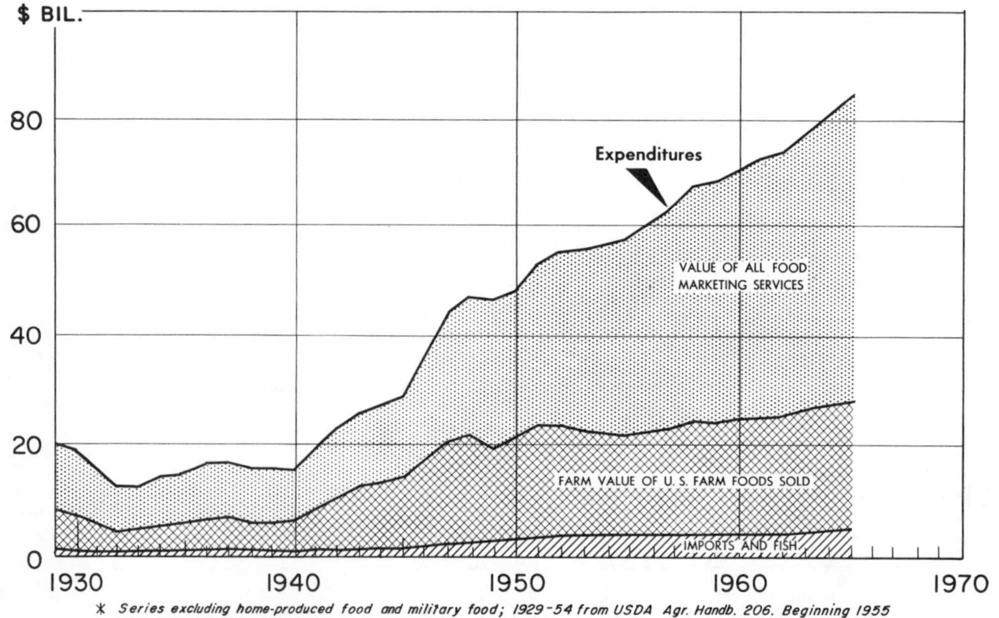

FIGURE 15.5 Civilian food expenditures (excluding taxes and tips).*

and distribution planning and to gain sensitivity to future problems that may develop from changes in trends and patterns of consumption.

15.4.1 Consumption Lags behind Output

Increases in United States food consumption have not kept pace with increases in farm output in the last 20 years. Therefore supplies of many commodities have exceeded demand at prices necessary to maintain farm income at high wartime and immediate postwar levels. Accordingly, pressures put on the Congress for farm price support programs have resulted in a variety of programs, originally designed to provide time for production adjustments. Farm surpluses of grains, cotton, oilseeds, and dairy products accumulated under the price support programs. Most programs operated by controlling one input factor, acreage, without controlling other inputs. These surpluses have incurred substantial storage costs as well as handling and transportation costs on foods moving to United States low-income people under domestic distribution programs and to foreign countries under partial subsidy or gift programs. The adjustment problems turned out to be greater than expected because agricultural productivity has continued to rise, whereas consumer demand for some products of food crops continued to fall.

Under policy directives given in legislation passed by the Congress, the Department of Agriculture has attempted to support farm prices of grains and potatoes by restricting production through use of acreage controls. For other commodities, price and marketing controls have taken the form of marketing quotas, direct payments to producers, and marketing agreements. A related policy has been the attempt to increase consumption by subsidizing distribution of food supplies to special groups of domestic consumers. Programs related to this policy are the direct distribution programs to institutions and families on relief, the school lunch and milk programs, and the more recent Food Stamp program. These programs have contributed significantly to meeting the food needs of low-income families and to supplementing the diets of school children.

A fourth set of policies has been the attempt to dispose of surpluses by gifts to charity programs operating abroad, such as "CARE," to foreign governments for special relief program sales abroad for local currencies under Public Law 480, and sales at world prices with the difference between United States prices and world prices being subsidized by the U.S. Treasury.

15.4.2 Commodity Shifts in Demand

Consumer demand has been gradually shifting from emphasis on crops to greater emphasis on livestock products. The shift is clearly indicated by the kinds of commodities in surplus. The output of grains exceeded demand at farm prices acceptable to farm groups, which were, for example, 90 percent of the very favorable 1910–1914 relationships, especially for certain qualities of wheat. There have been periodic surpluses of potatoes, some other crops, and even of some of the livestock products.

Several types of policies have evolved to cope with these problems. The government loan and purchase programs to hold supplies off the domestic market, subsidies for domestic distribution of surpluses, and the subsidies for exports have just been noted. Another category, less familiar to many people, has been the substantial financial support for research on marketing and utilization. The returns for the investment in research on marketing and utilization are difficult to measure, but it is no doubt true that they have yielded much more knowledge and understanding of marketing and utilization problems than was available before.

15.4.3 Food Marketing Services

As noted at several points in this chapter, the demand for food marketing services has grown substantially in the last 25 years. The spread in prices between those received by farmers and those paid by consumers has increased. From time to time the Congress has authorized special investigations to find the culprit in such price spreads. Farmers have experienced what they called "price squeezes" and have had emotional reactions to their decreasing share of consumers' food dollars. The increased demand for food marketing services has resulted in some disadvantages for commodities which could not become "convenience foods" and for some producing areas which have distribution problems.

To deal with these problems, there have been periodic investigations of marketing costs and marketing agencies, such as that by the National Commission on Food Marketing,

1964–1966. A number of producer groups have joined together to advertise commodities. And there has been a substantial amount of research in search of marketing inefficiencies and to identify marketing and utilization alternatives in the United States and abroad for the commodities in surplus of United States demand, especially the crop items.

15.4.4 The Need for Public Decision Making

The accumulation of surpluses from the excess of United States production over domestic demand has led some people to suggest that we should not make further public investments in reclamation and development of resources for agriculture. Rather, public funds should be diverted to other resources. Farm producers in some parts of the country continually ask for land reclamation and irrigation projects to be federally subsidized. Others demand subsidies for the use of fertilizers and lime. Such federal subsidies have continued to increase the output of agricultural commodities, including some in surplus. Only in recent years under the Soil Bank and successor programs has there been serious investigation of alternatives for the submarginal agricultural land, such as parks, public forests, and conservation areas. These have a political disadvantage in that they reduce the population which supplies business for local communities and votes for legislators.

The policy during the 1950s and 1960s was to continue land reclamation, irrigation, reservoir programs, and subsidies for soil conversation. The Soil Bank was sponsored during the 1950s. Since its terminal dates, much of the land retired under it has come back into production to yield still more supplies. It seems obvious that longer-range land retirement programs are needed. Another type of policy has been that of rural development. This means subsidies for development of recreational resources and rural industries.

15.4.5 Low-Consuming Groups

As noted earlier, not all Americans eat equally well or have equal amounts of consumer goods and services. Some families have inadequate purchasing power to buy the kinds of things they want. Others lack knowledge about commodities, such as knowledge of food and nutrition, food buymanship, and how to prepare food. Some families have poor consuming habits. Low consumption rates for protective foods and for some nonfood goods and services result in poor health and low personal efficiency.

The policies and programs which have been developed over the last several decades to do something about these low consumption rates have included special educational programs and the use of subsidies and special distributions of the commodities in short supply to consumers. Federal, State, and local governments have cooperated in programs of food and nutrition education and in urban redevelopment. Programs instituted during the 1930s and 1940s have provided minimum levels of income such as those under Social Security, under special state relief programs, and allotments for dependent children. Since the days of the depression, we have had direct distribution of surplus foods to people receiving public welfare assistance and to institutions. Before World War II and in the last few years, there has been a Food Stamp Plan, currently being extended to larger proportions of the low-income population. The principal public information program for food was the Consumer Marketing Program under the Agricultural Extension Service. To build up information which could help these population groups, some research in foods and nutrition and a small amount in consumption economics has been financed.

15.4.6 National Emergencies

We are all aware that national emergencies such as natural disasters and national defense emergencies do occur from time to time and that food has an essential role in coping with such emergencies. From time to time the Department of Agriculture has cooperated with other statistical agencies to obtain some current information on the amounts and location of supplies of many products, especially the more staple types of food. But we lack any firm scientific knowledge of consumer needs and consumer behavior under emergency conditions. Although we have had some national exercises to simulate activities required to handle the emergency of a foreign attack, we do not know very much about how to allocate and distribute supplies in emergencies of less serious nature. Because of our experiences during World War II, a standby system for emergency controls over food production, processing, and distribution has apparently been formulated.

The Department of Agriculture has cooperated with the Civil Defense authorities in developing and running practice experiences with emergency food distribution programs. There have been attempts to educate the public and to obtain business cooperation in maintenance of minimum supplies. Despite some fairly elaborate exercises, there does not appear to have been much in the way of research on needs, distribution plans, and alternative sources of supplies for emergencies of varying degrees of seriousness.

15.5 INTRODUCTION TO ANALYSIS OF PROBLEMS GROWING OUT OF CHANGES IN CONSUMPTION

Now that we have identified some of the kinds of problems that result from changes in consumption, we are ready to take the first steps toward analysis of such problems. One way to understand the meaning and process of analysis is to think of it as the process of breaking down a complex to find the simpler components. Another is to recognize it as a process of getting answers to a series of questions such as: What happened? Why? What did it lead to? What also happened at the same time?

The approach of this section is to point out the kinds of data, relationships, and changes to be used in considering different aspects of problems arising from changes in consumption. The material presented here demonstrates analytical work on macro problems. Certain similarities are found among the requirements for analysis of such problems growing out of changes in consumption. These similarities are handled as separate clusters of problems in the following sections.

15.5.1 Comparison of Historical Rates of Change

Many problems involve comparison of historical rates of change in supplies, total consumption, population, and prices. One cue is the rates of change in *supplies*. Supplies may be studied at different stages in the flow from producer to consumer, as at wholesale or retail. In agricultural economics we usually start at the farm level or at another level of basic supply. For a single commodity we work with farm quantities or dockside measures for imports or the "round" or "landed weight" for fish and with the matching price data. But for combinations of commodities, we must shift to supplier value data which are computed by multiplying the supplier prices times the quantities. To measure changes in quantities, we hold *prices* constant. To measure changes in prices, we hold *quantities* constant in forming an index. We often compare percentage changes in supplies from domestic production of imports, and in total consumption with percentage changes in the United States population.

Because prices reflect the degree of balance between supplies and demand, we compare changes in prices for commodity groups and in the all-commodity farm price level. These are usually measured at the farm level by the index of prices received by farmers which is published by the Department of Agriculture. If we are considering food only, we use the farm part of the U.S. Department of Agriculture's "market basket data."[13] For comparisons between farm prices and the general price level, the Consumer Price Index, issued by the U.S. Bureau of Labor Statistics, is used to represent changes in the general price level.

As mentioned in earlier sections of this chapter, two of the important dimensions of supplies are: (1) the breakdown between subsistence or home-produced foods and the supplies moving through commercial channels, and (2) the difference between supplies produced in the United States and imports of competing and complementary commodities. An analyst always looks at these components of the total supply picture to see what is happening and to understand the impact of general economic changes on consumption.

15.5.2 Variations in Rates of Change in Consumption of Different Commodities

Another cluster of problems having to do with food consumption involves study of variations in rates of changes in the consumption of different commodities or commodity groups. Here we are looking for answers to the questions: Why does this commodity increase and that one decline? Why does this one change more than that one? We work with percentage changes in quantity if we are dealing with a

[13] See Section 3.3.2 of *Measures and Procedures. . . .*

single commodity or with a homogeneous group such as canned vegetables. But if we are comparing fluid milk plus butter and cheese, we must use another common denominator. Because the mix within the group is likely to be changing, it is more desirable to work with value data. If our problem involves primarily changes at the supplier level, we measure all commodities at that level in order to exclude possible effects of rates of change in marketing services which are combined with the supplier foods when bought by consumers. On the other hand, if we want to take marketing services into account as well as the supplier services, we measure consumption at the retail level. Remember that these values will exclude the extra services of eating places because we do not yet have an adequate measure of the amounts or values of individual foods consumed away from home.

Almost every analysis will require some use of value measures. We can study price and quantity changes by comparing changes in current value series and in measures described as "constant dollars," as "in 1957–1959 dollars" or "in 1957–1959 prices."

Often we relate changes in average rates of consumption of particular commodities or commodity groups to changes in average income, preferably using disposable personal income per capita. Another significant common denominator for food commodities used in certain types of comparisons is the fat content or the food energy content, measured in calories, or the protein content. But such common denominators should not be confused with values involving price which generally have much more meaning for economic analysis.

15.5.3 Geographic Changes

Marketing people are greatly concerned with geographic changes in areas of production and consumption because these indicate a major type of adjustment which must occur in the marketing system. Although there are farm production data for most commodities available for the major producing states, we do not have annual consumption data of the disappearance type for individual states, only for the United States as a whole. You can understand the reason for this if you stop to think that to get data for individual states we would have to obtain information on all commodities crossing state lines. However, it will eventually be possible to develop working approximations for state data on major commodities because we have regional data from some of the post-war sample surveys of food consumption by households. The first nationwide survey that gave really reliable data was the Household Food Consumption Survey of 1955. Another was taken in 1965.

To compare production and consumption, the use of the supplier level is recommended. This avoids the complexity of adding marketing services on one side and not on the other. Quantity data can measure geographic changes in the production and consumption of an individual commodity. A common denominator such as whole milk equivalents is needed for a commodity group like dairy products. For other types of combinations, one must shift to value data. A first approximation of studying shifts in consumption is often made by relating shifts in production areas to shifts in population among areas.

15.5.4 Comparison of Trends in Supplier Food and in Marketing Services

A great many problems require comparison of trends in supplier food and in marketing services. For them the use of value data pertaining to all foods sold is essential. Changes in supplier values (excluding subsistence food) should be compared with changes in values of marketing services. The United States retail value equivalents formerly issued by ERS for commodity groups matched the farm value data.[14] The marketing bill data could be derived by subtraction. But there is no basis for developing commodity breakdowns of sales of all eating places in the United States or by area. Commodity problems often require tracing changes in costs of marketing services combined with the farm commodity. Examples are those related to increased commercial processing of the food consumers want and buy.

A significant part of the upward trend in marketing services results from the needs of a larger proportion of the population being employed in nonfarm occupations and living in urban areas. Also, many specialized farmers now buy a large proportion of the food that

[14] See Note 17 in Chapter 12 regarding the 1967 estimates of expenditures for commodity groups.

they need for their families. The substantial increase in incomes has contributed significantly. When people have higher incomes, they buy both more food and more marketing services with the food in order to reduce the amounts of time and energy spent by the housewife. Moreover, the increasing proportion of homemakers employed outside their homes has had some effect on the demand for marketing services. This effect is difficult to measure separately from the effect of the increase in family income.

15.5.5 Shifts in Sources and Channels of Distribution for Food Supplies

Another set of problems requires study of shifts in sources of food supplies and in the channels of distribution to consumers. Here, too, we need the kinds of knowledge, described in Section 15.5.1, regarding subsistence as opposed to commercial supplies, and domestic farm and fisheries output as opposed to imports. The information in Section 15.5.3 regarding shifts in production areas is pertinent too. Changes in channels of distribution from producers to consumers involve shifts in marketing services added in those channels, as already noted. You will recall the increases in away-from-home eating, both in restaurants and in school feeding programs, which were mentioned earlier in this chapter. Remember that the data on United States food consumption include supplies received under the direct distribution programs for surplus foods and other public welfare programs, as well as foods purchased under the Food Stamp Plan and food consumed in schools under the school milk and school lunch programs. Such quantities can be studied only with special sets of data based on government shipments or sample surveys.

15.5.6 Variations in Consumption among Groups

Analysis of variations in consumption among population groups is a major part of macroeconomic analysis of consumption. An introduction to such analysis has already been provided in Chapters 13 and 14. But we must note here several changes in rates of consumption by subgroups in the United States population. Average consumption of all food per person in urban, rural nonfarm, and farm households increased substantially from the period early in World War II (spring 1942) to spring 1955. Differences in food consumption and expenditures among the three urbanization categories were materially reduced, partly because of changes in income. The amounts of food consumed by households at the same real income levels within the three urbanization categories also changed to some extent.

In 1955 there was much less variation in market value and expenditures for food at home and away from home in all urbanizations between the *lower*-income households and those of *average* income than was the case in 1942. On the other hand, the differentials between the market value and expenditures for food by *higher*-income households and those at the level of average income in 1954 increased substantially between 1942 and 1955. This indicated the possibility of further changes in the future. Households in each urbanization category and at most income levels increased their use of meat and poultry and commercially processed foods between 1942 and 1955. Also, they shifted significantly from butter and lard toward margarine and shortening.

15.5.7 Changes in Income–Food Relationships

In Chapter 14, income–food relationships derived from cross-section data at one point in time were summarized in the form of five ramifications proposed for Engel's law. Through time, income–food relationships are influenced on the supply side by changes in the food–nonfood price relationships brought about by changes in the general economic situation, industrial and agricultural production, and exports or imports. They are also affected by changes in the availability of food in the retail stores and in home food production. On the demand side, we note changes in the degree of urbanization, the activity and age composition of the population, food tastes, and relative emphasis given to food. We also must watch for variations in purchasing power during the short run which may result from changes in assets.

From analyses of cross-section data for different time periods and of time-series and per capita real income, price relationships, urbanization, food expenditures, and food quantity data, the author has developed five ramifications of Engel's law pertinent to changes in relationships through time. The following ramifications refer to changes in national averages:

(1) When a country has reached as high a level of average food consumption as the United States in the 1960's, further increases in average real income may be expected to raise average consumption of food per se only slightly. Consumption will vary, however, with changes in the distribution of income and in the quantity and quality of food supplies in relation to supplies of all other goods and services.

(2) Increases in the density of the population and in the proportion residing in urban areas combine with increases in average real income to raise average purchases of food per se substantially more than the consumption of food from all sources.

(3) Changes toward a higher degree of urbanization and in ways of living may lead to further increases in the average quantity of marketing services bought with food without increases in average income. If average real income rises concurrently, the use of food marketing services may rise about twice as much as the increase in the average quantity of food consumed.

(4) As farm and rural nonfarm families become accustomed to using more food marketing services, the income elasticity of average food expenditures decreases—both among groups of families and through time. But the increased expenditures for food marketing services cause the proportion of average income spent for food and services to decline more slowly with rising incomes than would be the case for the value of food alone.

(5) At successively higher levels of average real income, the rate of increase in food expenditures may be expected to decline, relative to changes in income. The timing and the degree of this change will depend upon changes in the ways we choose to live and in the structures of both our food and overall economies. . . .[15]

In addition, I concluded that:

. . . Short-run changes, such as the availability of purchasing power from sources other than income, or changes in the supplies of major foods, may temporarily reverse or halt general trends in income–food expenditure relationships, but only the effects of such phenomena as war or other global disasters are likely to last more than two or three years.[16]

[15] From pp. 123–124 of "Ramifications of the Relationship Between Income and Food," *JFE* **XLIV**: 1:115–125, February 1962.

[16] *Ibid.*, page 124.

15.6 ANALYSIS OF TRENDS IN CONSUMPTION IN DEVELOPING COUNTRIES

Analysis of trends in consumption in developing countries is made much more difficult by a variety of special problems with measures and procedures. It seems obvious to Americans that measurement of consumption depends on the availability of physical measures such as bushels, tons, pounds, and quarts, and the use of scales and a system for reporting production and distribution. We have had standardized weights and measures for so many years in the United States that we find it difficult to envision the chaos which exists when there is a wide variety of local measures having varying interpretation in communities only a few miles apart. In such cases one needs conversion factors to know how many of this measure equal how many of that. But the contents are not standardized and the use of the measures is not standardized. Therefore the conversions cannot be standardized.

All empirical analysis in marketing and consumption economics rests on measurement, and somebody must do the measuring. United States economic data have developed fairly rapidly in the last thirty-five to forty years and are now based on benchmarks from periodic censuses of population, agriculture, manufactures, and business which are taken two to ten years apart. New programs of sample surveys are added from time to time to supply public and business needs for special data. In addition, we have more frequent reporting on critical operations of business firms which everyone in the industries wants to know about or which may have considerable significance for the country as a whole. As the demand for information has grown over the last fifty years or so, new reports have been instituted and summarized by federal agencies or by groups of business firms, such as the trade associations.

In contrast, in the developing countries the systems for reporting farm production, processing, and trade are usually in the beginning stages. Even much-needed census benchmarks are often unavailable. But this should not surprise us so much when we realize that even a country like France had not had a census of business until recent years. In the developing countries, subsistence food is relatively very important and usually largely unreported. By relatively important, the author means about 60 to 70 or 80 percent of the nation's food supplies may be produced by the people who consume them. Also, substantial amounts of foods are bartered at the local level and never really have prices attached to them. Commercial production of many foods eaten by people in these countries is still on a small-scale basis. Farmers produce a number of commodities for family use and sell the excess.

Very significant factors inhibiting the development of reporting systems in the developing countries are the distrust of government and the widespread avoidance of taxes. These factors also contribute to the general lack of statistical information on major social and economic factors and thereby to the lack of information on changes in these factors. Markets for nonexport commodities are usually poorly developed. Prices of individual commodities vary greatly from place to place and from time to time. Consumption patterns often differ considerably between areas only a few miles apart.

But the developing countries are fortunate in that they do not have to originate the procedures for obtaining information. Rather, it is a matter of adapting available procedures and methods to their particular institutions and cultures. For example, the system of cross-section surveys on a sampling basis has been formed and tested. These countries can adapt questionnaires to their own needs and use such surveys either on a one-time or a panel type of operation. Such cross-section surveys are particularly important in obtaining information from producers and consuming households. In order to obtain information on marketing, it is probably desirable to set up special survey points at crossroads, local markets, or bridges such as those used in Ghana.[17] Just as the data on agricultural production and distribution and on marketing operations in the United States have been developed through efforts of individual researchers, so it will be necessary in these developing countries to involve students at all levels of education in developing data on production, trade, and consumption. There is no better way to learn how to carry on analysis than to go out to collect the data and then to analyze them one's self.

Analysis of consumption changes depends on information regarding economic and social changes such as shifts in agricultural output, manufactures, trading patterns, income, and so on. American economists transported to developing countries to furnish technical assistance for agriculture, marketing, or other sectors of the economy have a tendency to urge a speedy construction of counterparts of their own statistical system without recognizing the institutional aspects of reporting.

A very different approach has been described by Rivkin who acted as a consultant for the Turkish Department of Regional Planning.[18] Rivkin reported that in the early years of this department the people attempted a number of studies requiring data on national economic and population trends but used secondary sources. All of them were dropped because they became too big, too amorphous, or simply beyond the ability of the personnel to handle. Both the morale of the workers and the leadership of the department were greatly frustrated by these failures. They began to question whether regional planning could be done in any way in Turkey. But the need for such planning was so great that outside consultants were brought in to work with the planning people, especially to identify the problems. They found that the objectives of earlier studies were far too lofty and did not take into account the minimal resources available. Therefore Rivkin led them to see that it was necessary at the outset to undertake projects which were within their range of accomplishment.

One stage was the development of simple sets of specific facts which later could be welded into larger reporting systems. At the early stage they gathered data on industrial activity and location, agricultural activity and land use, population characteristics, and so on. They obtained such information only for a limited sector. Although there were inconsistencies and wide gaps, they began to understand the characteristics of the regions and how they might be recorded.

[17] Pages 164–166, Poleman, Thomas T. "The Food Economies of Urban Middle Africa: The Case of Ghana," *Food Research Institute Studies* **II**:2:121–174, May 1961.

[18] See Rivkin, Malcolm D. "Let's Think Small for Development," pp. 152–163 of Hambidge, Gove (Editor), *Dynamics of Development.*

Even with the elementary sets of information, it was possible for the central planning agencies to become aware of relationships among activities in each area which affected the very nature of these activities. They began to see the population growth and the increase in demand for commodities and services which were directly traceable to economic growth of certain types. As the usefulness of the information became clear, greater resources were put into this kind of basic fact-finding. But still it was a long process. It was absolutely necessary to adopt a pragmatic approach geared to the resources of the staff and budget and directed to clarifying limited issues of great importance to the nation. This approach paid off far better than attempts to do everything all at once. Rivkin describes this as the courage "to think small" and to recognize that it is necessary to take many tiny, but essential, steps between the conception of a new idea and its realization.

This step-by-step approach to build a body of knowledge for use in the study of specific problems recapitulates the United States experience. Although the first Census of Agriculture from which consumption data have been developed was in 1910, the first comprehensive set of food consumption data resting on a relatively firm base was not published until 1941. Many of these data had to be reworked when the deficiencies were revealed during wartime administration of food supplies. It was 40 years from that first Census of Agriculture to publication of the current range of statistics on United States food consumption by the Department of Agriculture in one bulletin, Miscellaneous Publication No. 691, *Consumption of Food in the United States, 1909–48.*

16

RESEARCH ON MACRO ASPECTS OF CONSUMPTION FOR MARKETING DECISION MAKING

The underlying objective of this chapter is to present examples of consumption research at the macro level which are pertinent to several types of decisions made by marketing executives. The chapter treats only the consumption economics aspects of subjects developed extensively in books on market research and marketing management. As emphasis on planning for marketing has grown in recent years, awareness of the significance of macroeconomic research on consumption trends and variations has started to develop among marketing executives.

The chapter begins with a discussion of the relevance of consumption trends to the modern concept of marketing. Then it covers, in succession, examples of the use of consumption studies in product development and deletion, long-range planning, distribution management and promotion, and membership and customer service. Section 16.6 deals briefly with the potential market for consumer services.

16.1 RELEVANCE TO THE MODERN CONCEPT OF MARKETING

In recent years marketing academicians and executives have been evolving a much broader concept of marketing than the old one which focused only on the flow of consumer goods from the manufacturer to the consumer. King defined the modern concept as ". . . a managerial philosophy concerned with the mobilization, utilization, and control of total corporate effort for the purposes of helping consumers solve selected problems in ways compatible with planned enhancement of the profit position of the firm. . . ."[1] He pointed out that most discussions of the marketing concept had focused on consumer orientations and organizational structuring while neglecting such elements as the role of marketing intelligence, formal long-range planning, and the significance of the new product function of marketing staffs. It is to these elements that consumption research is particularly relevant.

16.1.1 Keith's Description of the Marketing Revolution

The classic description of the reorientation that has been occurring in marketing is that of Robert J. Keith, now chief executive officer of the Pillsbury Company: "In today's economy the consumer, the man or woman who buys the product, is at the absolute dead center of the business universe. Companies revolve around the customer, not the other way around."[2] He traced the marketing revolution at Pillsbury in terms of four eras. In the first era, 1869 to the 1930s, Pillsbury was manufacturing- or production-oriented. The basic function of the company was to mill flour; selling it was described as *almost incidental.*

In the second era, the 1930s and 1940s, Pillsbury (and other flour millers) became

[1] Page 85, King, Robert L. "The Marketing Concept," Chapter 5 of Schwartz, George (Editor), *Science in Marketing.*

[2] Page 209 of Holloway, Robert J., and Hancock, Robert S. (Editors), *The Environment of Marketing Behavior*, pp. 209–212, reprinted from Keith, Robert J. "The Marketing Revolution," *J. Marketing* **24:**3:35–38, January 1960.

much more aware of the consumer and established a commercial research department to gather facts about the market. The firm was sales-oriented. In order to dispose of its product at a favorable price, the sales force was backed up by consumer advertising and market intelligence. Great attention was paid to consumer reactions to package shapes, sizes, and colors used for the consumer products.

In the third era, the 1950s, the successes of the baking mixes brought realization that research and production could produce hundreds of different new products from which management had to select those for manufacture and sale. According to Keith, ". . . The company's purpose was no longer to mill flour, nor to manufacture a wide variety of products, but to satisfy the needs and desires, both actual and potential, of our customers."[3]

But underlying this purpose was still the obvious objective of making profits. No matter how much some consumers may like a new product, firms like Pillsbury and General Mills will discontinue it within a few months or even weeks if it does not shown signs of being a volume seller. Keith added:

> In the early days of the company, consumer orientation did not seem so important. The company made flour, and flour was a staple—no one would question the availability of a market. Today we must determine whether the American housewife will buy lemon pudding cake in preference to orange angel food. The variables in the question have multiplied, just as the number of products on the grocers' shelves have multiplied from a hundred or so into many thousands.
>
> When we first began operating under this new marketing concept, we encountered the problems which always accompany any major reorientation. Our people were young and frankly immature in some areas of business, but they were men possessed of an idea and they fought for it. The idea was almost too powerful. The marketing concept proved its worth in sales, but it upset many of the internal balances of the corporation. Marketing-oriented decisions resulted in peaks and valleys in production schedules, labor, and inventories. But the system worked. It worked better and better as maverick marketing men became motivated toward tonnage and profit.[4]

At the beginning of the 1960s, Keith believed that Pillsbury stood at the brink of its fourth major era in the marketing revolution.

[3] *Ibid.*, page 211.

[4] *Ibid.*

> Basically, the philosophy of this fourth era can be summarized this way: "We are moving from a company which has the marketing concept to a marketing company."
>
> Marketing today sets company operating policy short-term. It will come to influence long range policy more and more. Where today consumer research, technical research, procurement, production, advertising, and sales swing into action under the broad canopy established by marketing, tomorrow capital and financial planning, ten-year volume and profit goals will also come under the aegis of marketing. More than any other function, marketing must be tied to top management.
>
> Today our marketing people know more about inventories than anyone in top management. Tomorrow's marketing man must know capital financing and the implications of marketing planning on long-range profit forecasting.
>
> Today technical research receives almost all of its guidance and direction from marketing. Tomorrow marketing will assume a more creative function in the advertising area, both in terms of ideas and media selection.[5]

16.1.2 Impact of Consumption Changes

The great increase in discretionary purchasing power of consumers has posed both a threat and an opportunity for business firms. A growing proportion of American business is concerned with production and marketing of goods and services not essential to the maintenance of physical life and welfare of the United States population. Instead, it is dependent on increases in the material levels of living and on development of consumer demand for nonmaterial services. In many respects, the great marketing infrastructure of the American economy has provided the setting for intense competition in supplying bundles of attributes in forms of goods and services to attract consumer interest and demand. Although there is much argument regarding some aspects of marketing like advertising and rapid product change, American consumers apparently encourage creative marketing efforts and eventually discriminate between those firms that do and do not satisfy their wants.

The preponderance of consumers have moved up the real income scale and can afford to buy the food, clothing, and basic equipment they want. Therefore family income no longer serves satisfactorily as the key explanatory variable for variations and changes in consumption of basic products. This is particularly

[5] *Ibid.*, pp. 211–212.

true for different commodities and types within the commodity groups. Other factors such as education, family life cycle stage, occupational group, and market location are becoming relatively more important for some items. Study of their relationships to variations and changes in consumption is a much more complicated process than development of simple correlations between per capita consumption or expenditure and per capita income. Interrelationships among several of these socioeconomic factors complicate the analysis too.

One group of market researchers has described two methods used in forecasting the effects of such changes on sales of selected consumer durables—ranges or "cookers," refrigerators, vacuum cleaners, and washers—in the United Kingdom.[6] Their data came from a large continuous sample survey. Their first method was built on analysis of brand shares of the initial purchase and replacement sectors of the market. They subdivided the initial purchase market for each durable by type of durable, then by region and social class in order to study rates of penetration or saturation. Their analysis of the replacement market depended on "death rates" or life expectancies and the age distributions for the durable items owned by sectors of the population.

The second approach they developed for sales forecasting rested on analysis of (*a*) the probabilities that households in the several socioeconomic categories would purchase each type of durable good, and (*b*) the related priorities among items observed in different groups of British households. They utilized the relationships among observed ordering in purchases, the overall rate of acquisition of durable goods, basic socioeconomic characteristics, and media exposure in making their forecasts.

A number of different articles have appeared in trade and business magazines in recent years describing the great potentials of expanding the consumer market for different kinds of goods. Notable among them was a series of seven articles in *Sales Management*, reprinted in 1961 under the title, *America's Lush Leisure Markets*. The series set forth in lavish journalistic style a variety of estimates of recent and prospective changes in the consumer market for goods and services related to boating, skiing, hunting, fishing, camping, do-it-yourself activities, family recreation, travel, and community recreation. Incidental references were made to surveys by specialized periodicals, government agencies, and trade associations related to participation in the activities, recorded and potential sales of the main items of equipment and apparel, admissions, and a variety of peripheral marketing activities. Unfortunately, the documentation is too limited to appraise the analyses used or to judge the adequacy of the data. Expectation for expansion in these markets is widely held, but many data pertinent to development of the kinds of demand forecasts needed for decision making by marketing firms are lacking.

[6] Brown, D. A., Buck, S. F., and Pyatt, F. G. "Improving the Sales Forecast for Consumer Durables," *J. Marketing Research* **II**:3:229–234, August 1965.

16.2 PRODUCT DEVELOPMENT AND DELETION

Some marketing academicians argue that the modern concept of marketing begins with appraisal of consumers' needs and desires, which are to be measured *qualitatively* in terms of attributes of products and product mix and *quantitatively* in terms of the market potential for different kinds of products. The concept encompasses a wide range of business activities related to the flow of these products from the manufacturer to the consumer and ends with servicing products in the hands of consumers. Microeconomic analyses of consumption described in Part II are particularly pertinent to detailed planning for product development and product and market testing. But macroeconomic analyses of trends in consumption also contribute to these efforts by (*a*) identifying and measuring the changes in factors in the marketing environment for particular products, (*b*) contributing a longer-range perspective for product planning, pricing, and distribution, and (*c*) providing the broader framework within which market segmentation can be planned.

Record levels of United States production, plant expansion, and affluency among consumers challenge producers to a continuous search for ways to improve old products and for innovations. Diversification of product lines and geographical distribution are both an opportunity and a necessity. Auto manufacturers compete with each other, with boat firms, aircraft producers, and home builders for consumers' dollars. Some new products for the competition may come unexpectedly from laboratories, but more and more they are built to the specifications dictated by consumers through market research.

16.2.1 Key Role of Research on Consumer Wants

As Reynolds wrote in a 1961 paper:

Since product decisions are based in substantial part upon market research and since in a short run research and development manpower and budgets are relatively fixed, marketing managements have an increasing responsibility to be sure that the wants and needs which they are communicating to research and development personnel are more real than imagined. These must be supplemented with a rigorous examination of factors such as competition, trends in the industry, investment requirements, advertising appropriations necessary, channels of distribution, and a host of other critical factors. For despite the wants and needs of the consumer, and they are many and varied, corporate managements are asking for a more realistic assessment of the total risk.

In its final form the identification and interpretations of consumer wants lead ultimately to a prediction problem; and the information which managements are really asking of marketing management is prediction of consumer behavior at some future point in time. Under these conditions, and if research and development effort is not to be misdirected, it would appear that the tools and techniques to be applied in predicting consumer behavior now need the same kind of scrutiny that predictive mechanisms in the physical sciences have undergone for a hundred years. . . .

Even assuming that the ability to predict future consumer behavior becomes more sensitive as we learn to live with the marketing concept, the responsibilities of marketing managements do not end here. The reason for this is that the purpose of predicting and interpreting is to provide intelligent outlines for research and development programs which, if successful, will find acceptance with the consumer. The consumer, however, is not the only governing factor. Research managements must at the same time evaluate their applied projects in view of a total evaluation of the future climate in which the proposed products will find themselves competing. Research and development departments have a real responsibility in technological forecasting just as marketing managements have a responsibility in demand and business forecasting. The rate at which technology is growing has accelerated to the point where decisions must be made today on the possible impact of tomorrow's technology. The rate at which our decisions can be made obsolete is truly staggering.

An enlightened total marketing concept requires three major technical programs. These are a fundamental research program engaged in a search for new knowledge, an exploratory research program which becomes more immediate than the fundamental program, and an applied product development program aimed specifically at introducing new products in time and with particular characteristics which will satisfy consumer wants as interpreted through marketing managements. With these three programs, it is possible to work not only from the consumer back toward development, but also to work from a developing technology toward the consumer.[7]

16.2.2 Matching Product Attributes to Consumer Wants

An alternative marketing strategy to product differentiation is market segmentation. ". . . in its simplest terms, *product differentiation* is concerned with the bending of demand to the will of supply. . . . *Segmentation* is based upon developments on the demand side of the market and represents a rational and more precise adjustment of product and marketing effort to consumer or user requirements. . . ."[8] Companies like General Motors, General Mills, and Procter and Gamble use both product differentiation and market segmentation. These firms produce and market a wide range of products under different brand names in order to match product offerings to varying product preferences of major segments of the total market for their products. Such product preferences are determined by both intensive and extensive consumer surveys.

European car designers pay particular attention to the desires of European motorists to avoid some of the obstacles set up by government regulations.

. . . Englishmen often buy small panel trucks instead of passenger cars because there's no purchase tax on commercial vehicles—but to make that kind of sale motor companies have to build passenger-car comfort into the vans. Frenchmen cavil at buying engines with five-liter crankcases; they want four-liter ones that save them from investing an "extra" 60 cents—40 cents of it tax—on each oil

[7] Pages 174–175 of Reynolds, W. B. "Research and the Marketing Concept," pp. 170–175 in Holloway and Hancock, op. cit.

[8] Pages 304–305 of Smith, Wendell R. "Product Differentiation and Market Segmentation as Alternative Marketing Strategies," pp. 303–307 of Holloway and Hancock, op. cit., reprinted from *J. Marketing* **XXI**:1:3–8, July 1956.

change. In Germany, where the annual registration tax is based on cubic centimeters of engine displacement, designers have to exercise their ingenuity devising ways to get acceptable horsepower with minimum engine size. . . .[9]

The great variety of eating places also illustrates the strategy of matching products to market segments. In 1965 one of the big food service chains, Marriott-Hot Shoppes, Inc., decided to diversify by setting up a subsidiary chain of Hot Shoppes, Jr. to specialize in 15-cent hamburgers. *Business Week* reported these statements by J. Willard Marriott, Jr., president of the company:

> We believe that this market's potential is unlimited. . . . There is an ever-increasing number of young middle-income families, increased automobile travel, increased leisure time and an increasing public demand for low-priced, conveniently served food.[10]

Yankelovitch has pointed out a variety of criteria for market segmentation.[11] The U.S. Time Company has found segmentation by value of the watch to be the best way to analyze the market and plan production. (See Section 13.6.)

16.2.3 Market Testing

Marketing firms rarely publish detailed information about new product development, but comparable procedures are used for new products from agricultural commodities by the U.S. Department of Agriculture. Bird described them in an article in the *Marketing and Transportation Situation*.[12]

> The invention of a new product and process does not complete the evolution of new product development. Before the process or product can achieve its desired place in the market, some market testing is usually necessary. USDA market economists work closely with the laboratory scientists. Economists test products and processes and make recommendations as to their acceptability. In addition, they study the market feasibility for new uses of foods, new crops and new processing methods. These studies bear indirectly on the lab program. Sometimes they suggest areas of needed research for technical workers of the labs. Several examples show the type of research that provides commercial firms with marketing data on new developed products or processes.
>
> The study of white potato flakes is a good example of retail marketing. In 1957, the tri-city area of Binghamton, Endicott, and Johnson City, N. Y., was selected as a test area. First step was to conduct store audits to establish benchmark sales of all closely competing food products prior to the actual market test. Then, all 41 supermarkets and a sample of smaller stores in the area were stocked with potato flakes. Retail prices were set at a level consistent with those of other processed potato products on the market. The Maine Potato Commission financed the promotion campaign. Store audits and a followup consumer survey were used to determine repeat purchase patterns. On the basis of this test and other indicators, several manufacturers went into production and put a commercial product on the market. The successful introduction of flakes validated findings of the market test—that the product did indeed have a favorable sales potential. Other products, when tested, do not always show such favorable results. These may be dropped or returned to the laboratory for improvement.
>
> Successful introduction of a dehydrated potato product and its widespread acceptance in institutional and household markets had a salutary effect on the potato processing industry. It triggered growth of a large number of other forms of dehydrated potatoes and facilitated growth of other processed forms such as frozen potatoes. In 1958, 18 percent of the total U.S. potato crop went into processing; by 1963, the proportion had risen to 29 percent. Ensuing years saw American potato processing develop from 210 million pounds of finished product to the one billion pound industry of today.[13]

Often a new product results from applying a new process to an old product to meet identified consumer wants. An example is the "WURLAN" process developed as part of research in interests of wool producers and tested by the U.S. Department of Agriculture.

> . . . WURLAN is a process whereby all-wool fabrics are treated to give them more of the desired laundering characteristics. This study was conducted among retail buyers of wool clothes. In total, 40 firms, operating 3,300 retail outlets, were shown samples of "WURLANIZED" wool fabrics

[9] Page 101 of Smith, Richard Austin. "The Onrushing Auto Makers," *Fortune*, August 1963.

[10] Page 160, "Hot Shoppes adds to its menu," pp. 160 and 162, February 13, 1965.

[11] Yankelovitch, Daniel. "New Criteria for Market Segmentation," *Harv. Bus. Rev.* **42**:2:83–90, March–April 1964.

[12] Bird, Kermit. "Developing and Testing New Foods and Fibers," *The Marketing and Transportation Situation* **155**:35–41, November 1964.

[13] *Ibid.*, pp. 36–37.

and similar samples of untreated wool fabrics. Information obtained concerned sales of presently available machine-washable wool apparel. These retailers described what laundering improvements in wool fabrics they thought were needed. They estimated future sales of wool fabrics if launderability were improved. Retailers said their present machine-washable wool fabrics lacked several characteristics needed for easy laundering and discussed washable wool apparels that had not satisfied market needs. Results showed WURLAN could improve retailers' ability to merchandise many all-wool apparel items. Now introduced into the market, WURLAN gives wool a lasting new market dimension by adding complete launderability to the present desirable properties of natural wool.[14]

16.2.4 Deletion Problems

Not all new products and new product lines prove successful. *Fortune* has reported on one General Foods' experience thus:

> Anyone who understands the enormous changes that have come over the American diet in the last half century might suppose that the customers are restlessly searching for innovations. Such a supposition can be dangerously misleading. The food market is basically conservative and the introduction of new products or product lines has to be carefully timed. Despite its experience, General Foods seriously misjudged the market for "gourmet foods." The line it introduced in 1957 included such fancy items as a green-turtle soup laced with Madeira wine, and a Rock Cornish game hen stuffed with wheat pilaf and roasted in a spicy sauce. A market was there. But companies that have succeeded with gourmet foods gear themselves to make money with extremely limited distribution. This is not General Foods' game. Most of its customers avoided the exotic foods; as far as the mass market was concerned, the time of green-turtle soup had not come.[15]

Alexander has provided some useful guidelines for decision making regarding deletion of sick products.[16] He calls attention to the need for study of (*a*) trends in sales, prices, and profits, (*b*) the appearance of substitute products, as well as (*c*) product effectiveness in meeting consumer wants, and (*d*) managerial problems. But he does not cite specific examples of analyses used.

[14] *Ibid.*, page 38.

[15] Page 163, "General Foods Is Five Billion Particulars," *Fortune*, March 1964.

[16] Alexander, R. S. "The Death and Burial of 'Sick' Products," *J. Marketing* 28:2:1–7, April 1964.

16.3 PLANNING FOR PRODUCTION AND MARKETING, ESPECIALLY FOR LONGER PERIODS OF TIME

Many firms still make production decisions based on careful studies of production costs and then tell their salesmen to "move the product." Under such circumstances the emphasis is on advertising and other forms of promotion. Each firm attempts to persuade all groups of consumers that they really want not different products but the particular product offered by the producing firm. This strategy is designed to build volume sales for the standardized, mass-produced item with characteristics set by production cost considerations. It makes only superficial use of knowledge of consumption trends and patterns, as in advertising appeals.

More frequently in recent years manufacturers and distributors have based their decisions regarding major investments on data regarding consumption trends and variations in addition to data on production and marketing costs. To be specific, large food and other consumer good manufacturers study long-time trends in consumption of commodities they now produce, they might produce, or that compete with their products before building new plants for production or distribution. Such trends also influence decisions on size and plans for research and product development facilities and programs.

An administrative vice-president of the United States Steel Corporation, Bennett S. Chapple, Jr., has stressed the significance of long-range marketing planning to top management in the following text for a symposium of the National Industrial Conference Board:

> Long-range forecasting and long-range marketing planning are the first steps in working toward better selling and higher profits. Longer-term projections are generally less specific than short-term forecasts. But, at United States Steel, our plans for the five to ten years in the future are in considerable detail as to markets and products. This is necessary since our entire facilities planning program is predicated on these studies.[17]

[17] Page 15, "Long-range Marketing Planning," in the National Industrial Conference Board, *The Development of Marketing Objectives and Plans*, A Symposium, Experiences in Marketing Management No. 3, 1963.

Top management needs a framework for effective use of long-range marketing planning. Mr. Chapple stated further:

> The first step in constructing this framework is to require that every plan, whether short or long range, start with an appropriate forecast. Secondly, it is extremely important that such a forecast be developed in the commercial—*i.e.*, marketing—end of the business.
>
> If a company makes long-range planning decisions without appropriate forecasts covering the time periods involved and the product and area details required, and if such forecasts are not developed in the sales end of the business, management is neglecting one of the most important resources of knowledge of the future.[18]

16.3.1 The Old Order Changeth

The production and marketing operations of the Cudahy Packing Co. of Omaha provide a good example of the old approach to marketing.[19] Early in 1963, a new management group found that the firm had long experience and large capacity for meat processing but no personnel policies, no research, and no real long-range planning. There were apparently only seven college graduates (all lawyers and accountants) among the 6000 employees. The firm had never had a major study of consumer wants or reactions made for it. During a period of marketing changes by other packers, it is not at all surprising that a meat packing firm like Cudahy which continued its production-oriented ways of operating should drop in sales volume and profits. The management that took over in 1963 brought in a marketing staff and many management changes. In 1964 the firm earned a $1.7 million profit after a series of annual losses.

Donald R. Burrus, manager of advanced economic planning for Texas Instruments, Inc., noted early in the 1960s that top management's interest in long-range planning was increasing, but that a Stanford Research Institute study indicated that only 20 percent of the 3600 manufacturing firms in this country with yearly sales over $10 million had full-time formal planning organizations.[20] He added, "I believe that future long-range planning will shift away from the mere projecting of numbers and estimating of over-all corporate goals to the more difficult tasks of establishing specific marketing strategy, of actively thinking through the problems that must be faced in years to come, and of finding solutions that can lead to action programs."[21] Furthermore, "long-range marketing strategy can be effectively conceived and planned only within the long-range economic environment. When marketing researchers are working on plans for three to ten years ahead, they should have a knowledge of the economic system and of the various economic forces that affect their own future markets. . . ."[22] A substantial part of the kind of knowledge Mr. Burrus was discussing is the subject matter of the macroeconomics of consumption.

16.3.2 Examples of Long-Range Planning

Carlos Campbell, formerly Executive Vice President of the National Canners Association, used U.S. Department of Agriculture data on production and consumption trends in his article, "Commercial Canning—What Does the Future Hold?"[23] He pointed out the considerable increases in per capita consumption of canned vegetables since 1939. Meanwhile, fresh vegetable consumption changed little, and frozen was rising within a stable per capita average in fresh equivalents. Canned fruits became more important in the non-citrus fruit total from 1947–1949 to 1957–1959 but declined in the citrus category. The latter reflects the growth of frozen orange juice concentrate. He argued that economies in processing and marketing favored the canned products so that prices were held down. Although he referred to variations in purchases of canned vegetables among different income groups and urbanization categories, his analysis seems rather cursory. He did not trace differences in patterns among regions nor the impact of expected technological developments. However, his conclusion that per capita consumption of canned fruits might hold at the 1961 rate and that consumption of canned vegetables might rise slightly by 1975 seems feasible but not dramatic for the canning industry.

---

[18] *Ibid.*, pp. 17–18.

[19] "Young Blood Puts Life Into an Old Packer," pp. 142 and 144 of *Business Week*, February 13, 1965.

[20] Page 24, "How Marketing Research Can Contribute to Long-range Planning," in The Conference Board, *The Development of Marketing Objectives and Plans*, op. cit.

[21] *Ibid.*, page 28.

[22] *Ibid.*, page 32.

[23] *J. Marketing* **26**:2:44–47, April 1962.

Anderson, Clayton, and Co., the world's largest cotton broker, saw the handwriting on the wall back in the 1930s and gradually moved from oilseed processing into food processing. The firm developed vegetable oil products such as margarine, shortening, and salad oils. Their food line for the Latin American market also includes a variety of mixes plus soft drinks and peanut butter in Brazil, roasted coffee and jams and jellies in Peru, and chocolate in Mexico. According to a 1965 report in *Business Week,* the firm hoped to see food revenue pass cotton within a couple of years.[24]

The U.S. Department of Agriculture's technicians have participated extensively in planning for new terminal wholesale markets in many cities—Boston, New York, Houston, Philadelphia, Detroit, to name a few. An essential ingredient of their planning has been the estimation of the total flow of fresh produce and other foods into the areas. Their estimates have been based in part on per person data from the 1955 Household Food Survey and on local data on unloads of fresh foods. Each time, the economists have sought better data. Despite the inadequacies of available data, they have had to go on to develop very rough estimates of the volume of different items to be handled by the proposed facility.

In 1957, according to *Business Week,* William M. Batten, Vice President of the J. C. Penney Co., proposed a merchandising character study to the board of the company:

> The proposal, soon approved by the board, tackled three areas: (1) an assessment of Penney's immediate position in merchandising, compared to its chief competitors; (2) a forecast of market opportunities, examining changes in population and trends in shopping, work, and leisure; (3) a forward determination to spell out desired changes in goods and services, and voids that had to be filled.
>
> "Until then," says one Penney official, "we had no real market research. Batten started it all."[25]

Based on the study, Batten led the company in setting up a consumer credit program, adding new lines such as appliances, paint and hardware, bedding, mail order distribution, and new outlets in suburban areas showing greatest population growth. The firm is also experimenting with discount operations to develop comparative figures on which to base future decisions.

GEM International, Inc., of St. Louis decided several years ago that the United States was about saturated with its kind of one-stop suburban shopping centers and began to look overseas for future growth opportunities.[26] It was attracted to Britain by the rapid growth in auto ownership, the move to the suburbs, and rising incomes. In the United States, GEM runs a members-only operation at discount prices and licenses its departments to specialty companies. "After deciding to move into Britain, GEM spent a year examining British cities, looking at potential markets, and analyzing habits of British consumers. Then came a year of looking for land, lining up financing (GEM has a 65% stake in the West Bridgford center, the London merchant bank of S. G. Warburg & Co., Ltd., the balance), and looking for operators to handle the store's 50 departments."[27] It succeeded in enlisting a number of the most important British retailers. The first two months of operations appear to indicate that British shoppers are even more price conscious than Americans. GEM immediately began construction of two more centers, pushing quality and private brands at highly competitive prices.

In a stimulating study of the "marketing myopia" of growth industries, Levitt argued that an apparently automatically expanding market for a product is conducive to little market development work.[28] He cited (page 161) the example of the petroleum industry's focus on improving the efficiency of getting and making its product, not really on improving the generic product or its marketing. The industry has done practically nothing to create a demand for its product. In fact, the major improvements in gasoline quality have originated outside the industry, and the marketing innovations have been developed by firms not directly affiliated with production or processing. Even the natural gas industry was developed by outsiders, although the oil companies owned the gas.

[24] "Cotton's King Tills New Fields," pp. 138, 140, 142, *Business Week,* January 23, 1965.

[25] From pp. 69, 72, 74 of "The Memo That Moved a Mountain," *Business Week,* December 12, 1964.

[26] As reported in "Will It Go in Britain?" pp. 86–89, *Business Week,* January 9, 1965.

[27] *Ibid.,* page 88.

[28] Levitt, Theodore. "Marketing Myopia," pp. 158–169 of Holloway, Robert J., and Hancock, Robert S. (Editors), *The Environment of Marketing Behavior.*

Levitt argued further that mass-production industries like the oil and automobile industries emphasize selling, "moving the product" to suit the needs of the sellers. He said that they largely ignore the needs of the buyers, including the whole cluster of things associated with creating, delivering, and finally consuming the product. Thus they emphasize production as an end in itself, not as a means toward consumption. Preoccupation with the product appears to preclude the development of really new products to meet customers' needs except under critical circumstances such as lucrative defense contracts or zooming imports of foreign compact cars.

16.4 CONSUMPTION RESEARCH RELATED TO DISTRIBUTION AND SALES PROMOTION

Consumption analysis is used for at least five different purposes related to sales: (1) evaluation of the current sales situation through use of share of the market studies, (2) planning and realigning distribution organizations either in old or new market areas or for old or new products, (3) planning advertising programs and selecting communications media, (4) development of special promotions, and (5) setting sales quotas.

16.4.1 Sales Evaluation

First, let us consider the kinds of data available for such analyses. The firm's share of the total market is measured by comparing its sales with total sales data from censuses of retail–wholesale business and manufactures and from special market surveys by government agencies, trade associations, and private research firms. Current data on shares in areas or among market segments must be purchased from research firms such as the Market Research Corporation of America, A. C. Nielsen Company, or from newspapers' consumer polls. Income and population data must be related to those on sales. A supplement to the *Survey of Current Business*, called *Personal Income by States*, is issued intermittently to summarize the state income estimates.

Information of particular value for analysis of sales results must come from cross-section surveys. Some of these are continuing consumer panel operations. Consumer panels have been operated for many years by advertising agencies, but two specialized firms have made panels big business in the postwar period. The Market Research Corporation of America operates a very large panel of consumers who record in weekly diaries their purchases of many items, in return for premiums. The data are assembled and analyzed largely for sales purposes. Impressive collections of data and charts are sold to business firms and, on occasion, to trade associations, farm groups, and government agencies. These data on week to week changes in purchases by families of specified demographic characteristics provide current indications of market shifts for different brands and competing items. The ever-present problem with attrition of the random sample has been discussed at length in the literature.

Other indexes of market changes are provided by the A. C. Nielsen Company, based on their periodic audits of purchases and inventories of a panel of retail firms. Their estimates of retail sales by the types of firms that are willing to cooperate provide another set of estimates of changes in brand shares of the market and the effectiveness of special promotions.[29] The Nielsen indexes for food and drugs measure movement of selected commodities (procurement plus change in inventory) through the sample of retail outlets.

Mainer and Slater have proposed a program to study the shifting parts of the market for individual products by means of analysis of series of cross-sectional studies. The first step is to identify major segments of the market, followed by initiation of a program to collect information about consumer behavior in each segment. Then ". . . the marketer can spot changing patterns in consumption and brand preference within specific consumer groups long before over-all sales figures begin to mirror the underlying shifts in consumer behavior."[30] Entry of new consumers may result in sharp changes in apparent preferences, perhaps for only a short period of adjustment but possibly because of the pertinence of some attribute of the product for their particular wants. From a series of consumer surveys, the proportion of the volume of each segment taken by recent brand-switchers can be iden-

[29] See pp. 326–343 of Alevizos, John P. *Marketing Research*.

[30] Page 77, Mainer, Robert, and Slater, Charles C. "Markets in Motion," *Harv. Bus. Rev.* **42**:2:75–82, March–April 1964.

tified and intensive market research can be directed at the switchers to determine factors related to the brand change. The shifts may result from competitors' product changes, new advertising programs, changes in relative prices, or changes in consumer demands. Although such research is expensive, it can serve as a warning system for manufacturers and distributors to avoid obsolescence of their investments in plant, marketing organizations, and promotion.

16.4.2 Distribution Planning

Intensive analysis of the market flows of products into consumption is basic to making decisions about changes in distribution setups. Felton cites two pertinent examples:

> In the case of a firm making a product for interior decoration, an important factor in the market naturally was the number of interior decorators. In a market study, management turned to the Census, which indicated that there were some 1,300 interior decorators. According to this figure there was not a great deal of room for increasing sales of the present line, so the management, being aggressive, decided tentatively to branch into new product lines.
>
> As subsequent events showed, this would have been a sad mistake. But, fortunately, the management did what few managements do: it had a more professional survey made. By just taking the further steps of checking the circulation data of an interior decorators' magazine, talking with an informed credit service, interviewing company salesmen, and making a spot mail survey, it was learned that there were actually 9,700 interior decorators and that they spent some $75 million a year for this product alone. The company's biggest and best market for expansion was the one it was already selling![31]
>
> Some sales executives have become so deeply involved with one method of distribution that they overlook the possibilities of other methods which, though once inappropriate, are now more closely attuned to the company's needs. Often the answer is not a single method but a combination of methods. Thus, one large manufacturing company that recently found it could no longer afford to service a large percentage of its retail accounts has turned away from tradition and carefully selected several distributors to handle a large volume of small repetitive orders at an attractive discount—and at lower cost to the manufacturer.[32]

[31] Page 314 of Felton, Arthur P. "Conditions of Marketing Leadership," Section 31 of Seelye, Alfred L. (Editor), *Marketing in Transition.*
[32] *Ibid.*, page 315.

The rapid increases in consumer incomes and consumer demand for goods and services in Japan and Western Europe is providing new market opportunities for American manufacturers. *Business Week* reported that Lenox' success with its new bone line of china, called Oxford, in the United States (a product line selling for 10 percent more than the Lenox brand) has encouraged it to work out agreements with distributors in Japan, Europe, and New Zealand. Even though import duties will result in higher prices for the Lenox products than for domestically produced china, Lenox hopes to attract sophisticated consumers.

> If the overseas venture works, the company expects a not-so-hidden bonus back home. If Europe, for years the center for prestige china, accepts Lenox, the prestige that Lenox has built so carefully in its home market will gain reflected glory in the U.S. where half of the buyers still turn to imports for their best china.[33]

The Singer Sewing Machine Company is a good example of what can happen to an old, complacent company when new management is brought in to cope with new competition, here from Japanese sewing machines. The Singer firm has diversified its product offerings at home, bought up companies manufacturing new types of products (e.g., Friden calculating machines), and moved into new markets abroad, even in Japan. Consumption research played an important role in such developments, as indicated by this quotation from *Fortune:*

> In 1959, with Singer's U.S. comeback under way, Kircher [the president] turned his attention increasingly to diversification. In a lengthy memorandum he not only spelled out criteria for acquisitions but launched Singer's first big effort to sell other products in its stores. The Stanford Research Institute had just studied the European consumer-goods market for Singer, and Kircher concluded that steeply rising purchasing power and low market saturation made this a most inviting area in which to try to retail other appliances. Accordingly, test-marketing of vacuum cleaners, washing machines, refrigerators and other appliances got under way in Europe in 1960, and results were good. Since then the new business has grown to an expected $33 million this year [1963], or a fifth of Singer's European sales.[34]

[33] Page 70, "Lenox Takes A Fast Boat for China," *Business Week*, January 2, 1965, pp. 69–70.
[34] Page 154, Faltermayer, Edmund K. "It's a Spryer Singer," *Fortune*, December 1963, pp. 145–148, 154.

16.4.3 Competition for Advertising

Competition among media for advertising contracts has contributed to research on consumer behavior and on trends in consumption for many years. In fact, a pioneer in market research was the Curtis Publishing Company which used data and findings to attract advertising to the *Saturday Evening Post*, *Ladies Home Journal*, and the *Country Gentleman*. Several examples of consumer surveys sponsored by national periodicals are given later. But first attention must be called here to the significant amount of consumer research, sometimes of good quality but rarely reported publicly, carried on by many advertising firms as part of their services to their clients. This research ranges from "quickie" market surveys to running nationwide, highly professional consumer panels and to maintenance of extensive libraries of statistical data, special studies, and published reports pertinent to trends in consumption of products of interest to present and potential clients.

Reference was made at several points earlier in this book to the nationwide survey of consumer expenditures in the mid-1950s by the Politz research agency for *Life* magazine. It appears to have been one of the most ambitious and expensive undertakings to obtain information regarding consumer behavior in the whole country as a service to attract advertising.

A number of surveys of car buyers, sponsored by magazines, have been reported publicly. One was the 1961 study of compact car ownership by R. L. Polk and Company for *Redbook* magazine.[35] The survey obtained the following types of data—age group of compact owners by make, marital status, sex of drivers; plans to buy a car in 1961 or 1962, including body style desired, expectations regarding change in makes; degree of shopping for compacts; rating of present make owned in terms of a variety of attributes; and uses of the compacts. It is not surprising that the report concluded that the best market for compacts was among young adults since *Redbook* claims to be *the* magazine for young adults. Unfortunately, no statistical analysis was reported with indications of measurements of socioeconomic factors and marketing practices to actual car ownership. Only frequency data and percentages were published.

Another study of the same general type was *Newsweek's 1963 Census of New Car Buyers*.[36] This study was designed to indicate the usefulness of *Newsweek* as media for advertising communication to the new car market and to develop information regarding new car buyers. Particular attention was given to the attitudes and opinions of the new buyers about their new cars. Questionnaires were mailed to a sample of 15,691 buyers of 1963 model domestic automobiles registered in November 1963 and to 1000 buyers of new imported cars. Out of the total mailing, 50.7 percent of the questionnaires were returned. The survey covered information on type of car bought, number of cars owned, other makes owned, years, models, and how purchased; information regarding disposal of old car; opinions about new car styling, mechanical reliability, roominess and comfort, dealer service, future buying plans, planning period for recent purchase, shopping pattern, magazine readership; comparative cost analysis per 1000 readers or viewers; and several socioeconomic characteristics of new car buyers. Very little analysis of the data was reported.

Look's research people have intermittently interviewed appliance manufacturers regarding marketing problems. They used this information and the help of survey specialists to design surveys to broaden marketing knowledge regarding marketing problems and, of course, to sell advertising space. The 1963 survey of a sample of all United States households obtained information on appliance sales, brand loyalty, market saturation, buying decisions, characteristics of buyers purchasing top-of-the-line models, methods of financing purchases, servicing of appliances, sales by type of outlet, and the replacement market. Again, little analysis was reported.[37]

16.5 MEMBERSHIP AND CUSTOMER SERVICE

Studies of trends and variations in consumption are also made as a service to customers of suppliers of materials and for members of

[35] *Compact Car Owners*, a study made by R. L. Polk and Co. for *Redbook Magazine*.

[36] Third Annual *Newsweek* Report.

[37] *National Appliance Survey*, 1963. Vol. One: Major Appliances, Cowles Magazine and Broadcasting, Inc.

trade associations. Examples are the research reports on trends and patterns of consumption of canned foods developed by researchers on the staffs of can manufacturers and made available to their customers, the canners. A number of trade associations have a long tradition of collecting and summarizing data. National Canners Association has a reporting system to assemble data on production and stocks, and performs some market research for its members. The American Meat Institute, the American Dairy Association, the Frozen Food Manufacturers' Association, the National Association of Margarine Manufacturers, the Wool Bureau, and the Textile Bureau are other trade groups performing research functions.

A 1964 report of the Wool Bureau by Jackendoff analyzes trends in consumer apparel revealed by the expenditure estimates of the Department of Commerce in connection with their work on national accounts. The report stresses interindustry competition for consumers' dollars and the need for active promotion of apparel. The author states, "The outlook for consumer apparel expenditures is especially favored by the inevitable maturing of the war and postwar babies into adult men and women. During the current and next decades, this will expand the most dynamic sectors of the apparel market. If the dominance of separates and casual wear in today's apparel market persists, these fashions should be traded up via better materials and workmanship to enhance the profitability of the textile and apparel trades."[38] The analysis of changes from 1935–1939 to 1963 in apparel expenditures is in terms of comparisons with trends in the population and income. Trends in apparel prices are compared with price changes for other goods and services. Production data are used in lieu of consumption data to identify trends within the overall apparel categories.

Still another way of viewing customer service is in terms of services supplied to consumers. Some are in connection with commodities being sold or previously sold. Others are services such as insurance and personal services. One of the sharpest notes about consumers' needs for services and their relationship to sales has been written by Levitt in the article "Marketing Myopia," as follows:

> As for taking care of other customer needs, there is not enough being done to write about. The areas of the greatest unsatisfied needs are ignored, or at best get stepchild attention. These are at the point of sale and on the matter of automatic repair and maintenance. Detroit views these problem areas as being of secondary importance. This is underscored by the fact that the retailing and servicing ends of this industry are neither owned and operated nor controlled by the manufacturers. Once the car is produced, things are pretty much in the dealer's inadequate hands. Illustrative of Detroit's arm's-length attitude is the fact that, while servicing holds enormous sales-stimulating, profit-building opportunities, only 57 of Chevrolet's 7,000 dealers provide night maintenance service.[39]

16.6 MARKETING OF CONSUMER SERVICES

Now that United States consumers are better supplied with goods than ever before, their demands for services are increasing rapidly. These include education, medical care, personal care, and many others. The Department of Commerce tabulates expenditures for 55 different categories in its National Income Supplement. Since the end of World War II, the proportion of personal consumption expenditures allocated to services has reached the share estimated for 1929. Regan has hypothesized that ". . . the United States is well advanced into a *service revolution* that may in time bring to its beneficiaries wholly new quantitative and qualitative patterns of service consumption."[40] He supports this hypothesis with these five propositions for which he marshalls substantial evidence:

1. Market potentials for business expansion today are greater in the area of human wants that are classified as services by the Department of Commerce.
2. Mass production techniques used in manufacturing commodities are being adapted to develop service technologies.
3. Use of service systems leads to the arbitrary administration of standard services and the impersonalization of services.
4. Substitution of manufactured equipment for

[38] Page 1, Jackendoff, Ruth. *Consumer Apparel Expenditures:* An Analysis of Trends, Average 1935–39—1963, Wool Bureau.

[39] Page 164 of Holloway and Hancock, op. cit.

[40] Page 57 of Regan, William J. "The Service Revolution," *J. Marketing* 27:3:57–62, July 1963.

personalized attention encourages a reduction in the extrinsic quality of service in the short run and a general "massification of taste."

5. A desirable proliferation of services will emerge in the long run that is adaptable to a wide variety of tastes in much the same manner that mass production of goods led to diversity in commodity choice today.[41]

[41] *Ibid.*, page 60.

17

CONSUMPTION ANALYSES PERTINENT TO PROBLEMS OF AGRICULTURE AND OTHER RESOURCE INDUSTRIES

In this chapter we will examine some macroeconomic analyses of consumption aspects of problems relating to resource industries. Many of them deal with agriculture because they are made by public agencies and are generally available. As in Chapter 16, there will be only brief reference to econometric methods because of the introductory character of this book. Another limitation of the chapter is the absence of studies demonstrating cost–benefit analyses, usually carried on by production economists.

Consumption aspects of production problems vary with the time period under consideration. Short time periods provide little opportunity for changes in consumption patterns except temporary adjustments in response to price changes. Therefore price analysis is much more significant than consumption analysis in the short run. However, the underlying consumption situation is an important factor in consumer response to changes in supplies which bring about short-run changes in price. Section 17.1 reviews a number of short-run analyses.

Sections 17.2 and 17.3 are concerned with middle-range and long-range problems. Section 17.4 takes up the problems surrounding current issues regarding agricultural and food aid to the developing countries. Section 17.5 goes further into the complexity of income–food relationships in the process of development. They are of major significance for agriculture, marketing, and national policy determination.

As you read this chapter, you should evaluate the empirical studies reported herein against the key ideas of the scientific approach to problem solving set forth in Chapter 8.

17.1 ANALYSIS OF SHORT-RUN SITUATIONS

The U.S. Department of Agriculture, state agencies, farm groups, and financial groups pay close attention to appraisals of the current situation and outlook. These appraisals form one part of the information entering into marketing decisions by producers and into buying and pricing decisions by marketing agencies. They are used also to inform the public about reasons for supply and price changes.

17.1.1 The Annual Outlook for Food

Examples of such appraisals are regularly reported in the outlook and situation reports of the U.S. Department of Agriculture. One is the annual outlook for food, summarized in the November issue of the *National Food Situation*. The objective is to appraise prospects for changes in food expenditures, overall food consumption, retail food prices, and for consumption rates and prices for major commodities. Consumption economists and commodity statisticians in the Economic and Statistical Analysis Division of the Economic Research Service develop estimates of the supplies of each major commodity, overall civilian demand, indications regarding possible changes in civilian demand for each commodity, and military and export demand. They rely heavily on careful analysis of changes in the preceding decade and on their experience with successes and failures in predicting the likely effects of changes in food supplies, incomes, and marketing costs.

During the summer, economists of the Division develop estimates for many indicators of economic changes in the following year which affect the agricultural sector. They are checked with the staff of the Council of Economic Advisers to the President. With these general economic projections as a framework, each commodity specialist works up supply, price, and consumption data for his commodity group. He compares the outlook for the coming year, season by season, with recent experiences with supply, price, and marketing changes. These data must be coordinated with projections for substitute or competing foods, e.g., meats and poultry, and fitted into overall measures such as farm and retail price indexes, farm output measures, the supply–utilization index, and the retail level consumption index. The projections are checked with trends in each series. Such research culminates in official statements like these from the November 1964 *National Food Situation:*

> Rising consumer incomes and continued population growth are expected to further expand the domestic demand for food in 1965. Although continued economic expansion and rising incomes appear likely, the rise in consumers' after-tax income probably will not equal the large gain this year. Per capita food consumption is expected to about equal this year's high level. A smaller retail price advance than in recent years appears likely; price pressures developing in some parts of the economy do not appear to be affecting food. (Page 4.)
>
> Per capita food consumption in 1965 is expected to about match this year's high level. Consumption of food from animal products is expected to decline for pork, animal fats, and lamb and to increase further for beef, veal, and turkey. The only important change in consumption of crop products in 1965 is an expected substantial increase for fruits, as a result primarily of citrus consumption climbing from depressed levels of 1963 and 1964. (Page 7.)
>
> Retail food prices in 1964 are up about 1 percent from the 1963 average; in 1965, prices are expected to increase slightly from this year's level. . . . The upward pressure on prices of foods from crops, primarily fruits and vegetables, that has persisted for the past 2 years is not likely to continue next year if growing conditions are about average. Production of citrus fruit and potatoes are expected to increase in 1965, so prices likely will decline from this year's high levels. Further demand expansion and moderate production gains for animal products are expected to maintain retail prices for these products near current average levels. But, price increases for pork and lamb may result if prospective declines in production materialize. Prices of such items as cereal and bakery products likely will continue their postwar uptrend. An increase in prices of foods purchased and consumed away from home is expected to tilt upward the average price of all food in the coming year. (Page 10.)

Problems in short-run forecasting are best understood when one examines actual events to see how they matched the forecasts. In the case of the outlook for food in 1965, the information is available in the February 1966 *National Food Situation* and in other USDA reports on production, prices, and consumption. The forecast of only a slight increase in per capita domestic demand for food from 1964 to 1965 rested on the projection of a minor increase in per capita real income, whereas real income went up about 5 percent. The USDA staff expected food consumption and per capita supplies to average about the same as in 1964. Pork supplies declined more than expected, perhaps because of underestimation of the effect of the low corn–hog ratios in 1963 and 1964. Beef supplies did not continue their upward trend. Per capita meat consumption fell about 5 percent so the full force of increased consumer demand hit meat prices, causing them to go up 7 percent. Import quotas held down imports of meat.

Concurrently, military procurement of food in this country apparently exceeded expectations. Poultry and fish prices and those for fats and oils reacted to the short meat situation. Cereal and bakery product prices also rose again. Instead of advancing less than one percent as expected, retail food prices rose 2.4 percent.

17.1.2 The Import Situation for Beef and Veal in 1962–1963

A good example of an analysis of a price–consumption situation is a brief study of the import situation for beef and veal, published in the *Livestock and Meat Situation* of November, 1963 (pp. 35 ff.). The problem developed out of cattlemen's price difficulties in the fed cattle market in 1962–1963 during a period of increasing imports of beef and veal. The researchers in the Economic and Statistical Analysis Division assembled data pertinent to the relationship between imports and prices of fed cattle. They presented data on quantities and types of beef and veal imported and produced, countries of origin for imports, prices of cow beef (Utility) and fed beef (Choice steers and heifers at Chicago), quantities of other meats consumed, and disposable real income.

The import data showed that most of the beef imported came from Australia and New Zealand and was boneless, frozen, lower-grade beef for the meat processing industry. The volume of imports has tended to vary with the United States cattle cycle, being high when United States cow slaughter was low. Prices for Utility cows at the Chicago market had changed little since 1959, and per capita supplies of cow beef in 1962 (domestic plus imports) were lower in 1962 than in 1954–1957.

To determine the possible effects of lower grade beef on fed beef prices, they ran these regression analyses for the 1948–1962 period: the influence of variations in (*a*) per capita supplies of steer and heifer beef, (*b*) per capita supplies of cow beef (domestic production plus imports), (*c*) per capita consumption of other meats, and (*d*) per capita disposable income (in constant dollars) on fed cattle prices. They also studied the influences of the same factors on cow beef prices. The statistical analyses revealed that fed cattle prices were influenced primarily by the supplies of fed beef which were four times as significant as the supplies of cow beef (including domestic and imported quantities). In contrast, cow beef prices were very responsive to supplies of steer and heifer beef and only one-third as responsive to cow beef supplies.

A special analysis of the influence of levels of imports on fed beef prices indicated that when imports are running about 10 percent of total domestic beef production, an increase of 10 percent in imports leads to a 1-percent drop in the price of choice steers. When imports are less significant in the total picture, the effect of a 10-percent increase in imports on fed cattle prices is less than 1 percent, and vice versa.

Despite such evidence of minor effects of imports of lower grade beef on the price of fed beef, cattlemen's pressures on the Secretary of Agriculture contributed to the formation of agreements between the United States and governments of Australia, New Zealand, and Ireland to limit meat exports to the United States. They were signed in February 1964. Imports and inshipments of beef and veal totaled 1677 million pounds in 1963, then dropped to 1085 in 1964 and to 942 million in 1965.

17.1.3 Other Short-Run Examples

The sharp rise in retail coffee prices early in 1964 led to an analysis of the coffee supply and demand situation by U.S. Department of Agriculture economists, reported in the May 1964 issue of the *National Food Situation.* Higher retail prices reflected sharply rising green bean prices, largely the result of world supplies being reduced by the poor crop in Brazil, the world's largest producer, in 1964–1965 and the possibility of adverse weather conditions for the 1965–1966 crop. Short supplies and higher prices of coffee brought per capita consumption down from 15.7 pounds in 1963 to 14.8 in 1965.

A quite different objective of short-run appraisals is held by some land investment companies operating in California. *Business Week* has reported that several apply key economic indicators to evaluate properties to be selected for purchase. ". . . These include employment base, quality of employment, income levels expected in an area in 10 years, availability of water, regional and master planning for future growth, how finance and insurance companies feel about the area, and climate."[1] These firms are reportedly buying land for quick turnover and capital gains, although they do get into some development operations.

17.2 MIDDLE-RANGE PROBLEMS

Economists always have difficulty in agreeing on the interpretation of long- and short-run time periods, but they make frequent use of these concepts and of the in-between middle range. For this section we may consider the middle-range time period to cover 18 months to four or five years. Again, more attention is devoted to study of price adjustments in shorter periods of two or three years, with basic consumption patterns reflected in demand curves or schedules which are assumed to be fixed. Over a longer period (with the length depending on the degree of flexibility in resources), assumptions are made about levels of prices or supplies, and major consideration is given to changes in demand.

[1] "Still More Gold in California Land," January 23, 1965, pp. 112–114.

17.2.1 A Projection for Wheat, Feed, and Livestock

Both production and marketing adjustments can be made during this span of time. We examine first the consumption aspects of a study by U.S. Department of Agriculture economists entitled *Production Prospects for Wheat, Feed, and Livestock, 1960–65*.[2] The researchers started with the familiar problem of excess of United States agricultural output over domestic demand despite production restrictions and special disposal programs. They examined recent trends and projected changes in production for wheat, feed grains, and livestock. They concluded that 1959 levels of exports and domestic per capita consumption of livestock products could be maintained during the following 5-year period on 15 to 18 million fewer wheat and feed-grain acres than were harvested in 1959. But if consumption of red meat increased about 7 pounds per capita from the 1959 level, the excess acreage would run 10 to 12 million. On the other hand, if wheat and feed grains were produced on the excess acreage and fed to additional meat animals, the number of pounds of red meat available for consumption per capita would rise from 158 pounds in 1959 to about 173 pounds in 1960, and 181 pounds in 1965. They predicted that such a rise in supplies would result in price trouble for livestock producers. Therefore they suggested that other methods of dealing with excess wheat and feed grain capacity should be explored.

[2] Raymond P. Christensen, Sherman E. Johnson, and Ross V. Baumann, USDA Agr. Research Service, ARS 43–115.

How have their projections turned out? In 1964 red meat consumption reached 174 pounds per capita with retail meat prices close to the 1959 level. The situation changed sharply in 1965, as discussed previously, when short meat supplies forced consumption back to 167 pounds and prices up 7 percent. Meat consumption did not reach 180 pounds, but prices received by farmers for meat animals were lower in 1960–1964 than in 1958 and 1959. They rose sharply and then declined in 1966.

The production control programs reduced acreages, but yields per harvested acre ran substantially higher than expected as shown by the data given below. However, subsidized exports reduced stocks sharply by the end of 1966.

This comparison provides an example of a frequent experience with postwar projections. Each time they are developed it appears that demand might catch up with supplies several years later. Then yields increase so much more than expected that the hoped-for balance of food production and domestic consumption seems to be the Great Illusion.

17.2.2 The Production–Consumption Balance for Dairy Products

Milk production exceeded domestic demand during the early 1960s. The U.S. Department of Agriculture purchased substantial quantities of dairy products under the price support pro-

Commodity	Unit	Projected for 1964	Actual[b] 1964	Actual[b] 1965
Wheat	Bushels	22.6	25.8[c]	26.5[c]
Corn	Bushels	50.6[a]	62.6[d]	73.1[d]
Oats	Bushels	38.7	43.1	50.2
Barley	Bushels	31.6	37.9	43.5
Sorghum grains	Tons	31.6	41.1	50.0
Four feed grains	Tons	1.13	1.37	1.62
All hay	Tons	1.68	1.72	1.82
Soybeans for beans	Bushels	23.7	22.8[e]	24.5[e]

[a] All corn
[b] *Feed Situation*, November 1966
[c] *Wheat Situation*, March 1967
[d] Corn grain, slightly higher than all corn
[e] *Fats and Oils Situation*, January 1967

gram. Net expenditures for such purposes reached $603 million in 1961–1962. But production fell to 121.5 billion pounds in 1966, and prices received by farmers rose substantially. Declines in per capita consumption of fluid cream, butter, and fluid whole milk accompanied the 7 percent reduction in milk consumption on a whole milk equivalent basis from 1960 to 1966. Meanwhile, sales of fluid skim milk rose from 24 pounds per capita to 38 pounds.

Because of the surplus situation early in the 1960s, the dairy industry engaged in a number of efforts to strengthen the market for its products. Dairy farm groups spent as much as $25 million annually for advertising and other forms of promotional activity.[3]

. . . The bulk of these expenditures has been allocated to direct consumer advertising with a smaller proportion being spent for promotional activities in public eating places. The industry is interested in expanding and strengthening its promotional programs in public eating places because these establishments, with annual sales of $12 billion are significant outlets for food. It is estimated that about 25 percent of the consumer food dollar is spent in public away-from-home eating places.

As an important outlet for food, restaurants can significantly influence market demand for individual products. Consumer choice and ultimately market demand is affected by the manner in which products, including dairy items, are integrated into the overall operation of the restaurant. The price structure for dairy products, the manner and frequency of offering them to consumers, and the attention they are given in the restaurants' promotion activiites all influence consumer demand. (*Ibid.*, page 1.)

Data from a nationwide consumer survey for the American Dairy Association, based on recall of the preceding day's milk consumption, indicated that less than 2 percent had been consumed in commercial establishments.[4] To ascertain merchandising and promotion practices employed for dairy products by public eating places, managers of samples of such establishments in the Hartford, Connecticut, and Indianapolis, Indiana, areas were surveyed. The findings indicated underestimation of the profit margins for milk by the managers, that menus frequently did not list milk, little effort was made to promote milk purchases, and recipe and menu suggestions regarding use of milk products would be welcomed. In Hartford establishments the table spread generally offered to customers was butter, whereas in Indianapolis it was margarine. This was essentially a fact-finding study so the findings are more suggestive of possible local promotional activities than analytical.

[3] Page 1 of Clement, Wendell E. *Use and Promotion of Dairy Products in Public Eating Places*, U.S. Department of Agriculture, Marketing Research Report No. 626.

[4] Page 6, *Dairy Promotion Topics*, American Dairy Association, November–December 1962.

17.3 LONG-RANGE STUDIES

Planning for long-term adjustments among major categories of enterprises within agriculture and other natural resource-developing industries is a very complicated process. Adjustments may involve shifts in investments or location, changes in qualities of products, and major changes in market structure and marketing programs.

Study of resource needs and alternative allocations of resources within agriculture are necessary:

(*a*) To balance uses of land, water, labor, and capital to produce the needed food supply

(*b*) To direct production–consumption adjustments for commodities and related production and price policies and programs

(*c*) To plan for emergency needs

(*d*) To guide production research

17.3.1 Changes in Raw Materials Consumed in the United States

To provide perspective for consideration of long-range problems, data on changes in the United States consumption of broad categories of raw materials are reviewed here.[5] The share of agricultural materials in the total declined from 65 percent in 1909 to around 59 percent in 1961, with the larger part of the decrease in crops. Fish and wildlife products changed relatively little, but the share of forest products dropped from 14 percent to 6 percent. The importance of minerals (including oil) rose from 20 percent to 34 percent over the 50-year period.

In terms of categories of use, there were also some major changes in United States consumption of raw materials. Food use fell in

[5] Based on Tables A4 and A5 of Spencer, Vivian Eberle. *Raw Materials in the United States Economy, 1900–61*, U.S. Department of Commerce, Bureau of the Census, Working Paper No. 6.

relative importance from 58 percent in 1909 to 51 percent in 1961. Use of physical structural materials declined from 26 to 23 percent, with the decline in lumber more than offsetting the increase in the use of minerals. In contrast, the use of raw materials as a source of energy rose from 16 percent of total use to 26 percent.

17.3.2 Long-Range Projections of Demand for Agricultural Commodities

Long-range projections of changes in demand rely heavily on analyses of historical trends in consumption and on their relationships to changes in socioeconomic factors. Analyses of changes in resources are used to study problems at the supplier level, so farm level time series are used for the consumption projections. These series include the per capita use of all farm food, use of purchased farm foods only, and matching farm value and price data. Variations in cross-section data are compared with the trend data.

The most explicit description of analytical steps involved in making long-range projections of demand for any of the basic resources is provided in a 1960 paper by Koffsky.[6] Most of them had been developed for a study, *Land and Water Potentials and Future Requirements for Water,* for a Senate Committee. Koffsky described the major guidelines for the demand projections as follows: (*Ibid.,* pp. 2–5)

1. *Population Growth*

How fast our population grows will largely determine the potential demand for farm products. The domestic market for U.S. farm products accounts for some 90 percent of the total market and food uses account for about 90 percent of the total domestic market. Presently, population increases about 1.6 percent a year. By 1980, according to the projections of Resources for the Future, which provided the basic framework for the Senate Committee Study, population of the U.S. could range from a low of 225 million to a high of 278 million, depending on possible future rates of fertility, net immigration, etc. (This is a somewhat wider range than the Census Bureau projections of from 231 million to 273 million.) The medium projection of 244 million persons is at about the middle of the range. Thus, population could increase by 50 to 100 million persons over the next 20 years or so, or from 30 to 60 percent. In the past 20 years, population has increased some 35 percent. It is worth noting that the possible range in population that might be forthcoming by 1980 is much wider than the excess of farm output over commercial takings of farm products in recent years.

There is a corollary question as to whether the changing age composition of the population will have a significant effect on the per capita takings of food. Much of the increase in population will likely come in the younger age groups, particularly heavy-eating teen-agers, but also in the older age brackets. By and large, these would appear to be offsetting in their effect on average per capita food consumption. . . .

2. *Economic Growth and Per Capita Consumption of Farm Products*

The effect of economic growth and rising consumer incomes on food consumption per person is relatively small and appears to be diminishing. . . . Upgrading in diet is reflected in the Department's index of per capita food use, inasmuch as it is a price-weighted index giving allowance to the trend toward more expensive foods—a factor which has meaning for the farmer since more resources are required to produce a pound of meat than a pound of grain. Thus, over the past 20 years, the index of per capita [use] of food has risen about 10 percent. In the post-war period, there are some indications, as Daly reported a year-and-a-half ago, that the long-term income elasticity of demand for domestically-produced food of about 0.20 may be getting smaller. The same may be the case for price elasticities—and prices appear to be somewhat more sensitive to changes in supplies than before World War II. It is logical that as purchasing power rises (at the rate of 2 percent or more a year) more and more people are eating the kinds of food they want to eat. If we apply this income elasticity of food consumed to the projected 45 percent increase in real income per person, per capita food consumption might rise an additional 9 or 10 percent over the next 20 years.

There is some support for this estimate from the cross-section analysis of the 1955 Survey of Food Consumption (*National Food Situation,* July 1959, pp. 17 ff. USDA). When we compare indexes of per person food consumption for the average income group, \$4,000-\$5,000, with the group some 50 percent higher, the latter shows an increase of 8 percent. These cross-section indexes also show a leveling off at about that income level; suggesting that after 1980, further gains in food consumption per capita might well be quite negligible.

. . . the response to income growth varies among the major food groups. Table [17.1] shows the historical income and price elasticities for major

[6] Koffsky, Nathan. "Potential Demand for Farm Products Over the Next Quarter Century," presented to the Seminar in Dynamics of Land Use at Iowa State University, May 3, 1960.

TABLE 17.1 Income and Price Elasticities for Major Groups of Farm Products

Item	Income Elasticity	Price Elasticity
Livestock products		
Meat animals	0.48	−0.30
Dairy products[1]	0.09	−0.05
Poultry	0.62	−0.50[3]
Eggs	0.04	−0.10
Crops		
Fruits and vegetables	0.16	−0.06
Cereals, potatoes, and beans	−0.23	−0.002
Other crops[2]	0.16	−0.02

[1] Based on price-weighted combined consumption of fat and nonfat milk solids.
[2] Excluding imported crops.
[3] This equation also included a cross elasticity of demand for poultry with respect to relative price of meat animals of 0.05.
[Source: Koffsky, Nathan M. "Potential Demand for Farm Products Over the Next Quarter Century," paper presented at Ames, Iowa, May 3, 1960.]

groups of farm food products. . . . In projecting into the future, there must be some measure of judgment. Trends do change. For example, the decline in the use of cereals appears to be flattening out, and some experts in nutrition suggest we might do well to increase our consumption a little. Nor does it seem likely that the recent sharp increases in broiler consumption can continue as large in the future.

Among the non-food products, the downtrend in cotton consumption per capita has come to a halt and with new technology, particularly the blending with other fibers, might well show some increase in the years ahead. On the other hand, technology in the tobacco industry has slowed the increase in requirements at the farm level.

So, there is a substantial element of judgment in the long-term projection do-it-yourself kit.

3. *Total Domestic Requirements*

We have now reached the point where we can put together population growth and per capita consumption and arrive at some total domestic requirements for farm products (Table [17.2]). According to the rate of population growth assumed, domestic use of all farm products might increase from 50 to 80 percent by 1980, with meat animals showing a larger rise. However, you will note that feed requirements do not rise as much, reflecting the trend toward rising feeding efficiencies per animal. Non-food uses are projected to rise somewhat faster than food uses. This could well occur in view of the expanding research effort in this field.

4. *Foreign Requirements*

Our colleagues in the Foreign Agricultural Service developed estimates of the potential foreign commercial demand for U.S. agricultural products for the purposes of the Senate Committee report. These were based on projections by the United Nations of population growth in the rest of the world, some increase in real per capita income and some improvement in diets in underdeveloped areas. They also assessed the likely trends of production in other surplus-producing areas and their ability to meet world needs. Summarizing very briefly, the major opportunities for increases in commercial channels appear to be for fats and oils, particularly in low-income areas, and for feed grains in Europe, where an increasing volume of imports will be required for an expanding livestock industry.

On this basis, an increase in our exports of some 25 percent is projected from 1958 to 1980 (also Table [17.2]). Quite recently, with economic growth proceeding rapidly in Europe, some additional optimism over commercial export potentials has been generated, particularly for feed grains and poultry which have shown substantial gains in the past year or so. Further, it is difficult to assess how the role of food might develop in the economic cold war between East and West and the needs of newly emerging countries. To keep perspective, we need to remember that we now export about 10 percent of our production, including a substantial amount under Public Law 480. While events may turn out that exports might rise appreciably beyond those projected, the effect on total requirements—the sum of domestic and foreign—would not be large. For example, we could double the recent level of exports by 1980 and total requirements would rise 5 percent or less. Further, the possible alternative levels of exports that might prevail 20 or 25 years ahead will probably depend to a considerable extent on how well domestic demands are met. In other words, if our population increases relatively slowly, a higher level of exports is more likely than if population and domestic requirements increase rapidly.

Total Requirements

Table [17.3] summarizes for major crops the projected requirements, domestic and foreign, for 1980 according to the 3 population projections. You will note that for some commodities, production in 1958 was within or above the range of projected requirements. These include wheat, rye, potatoes, soybeans, flaxseed, grain sorghums, and in 1959, corn. Pasture production would need to increase

TABLE 17.2 Total Requirements for Farm Products, 1954 and 1958, and Projections to 1980 (Index Numbers, 1954 = 100)

Item	1954	1958 Total	Projections 1980, Total Low	Medium	High
Population	100	107	139	150	171
Domestic utilization of all farm products	100	106	157	169	192
Food	100	107	155	167	189
Nonfood	100	101	171	185	211
Livestock products:					
Food	100	107	156	168	190
Meat animals	100	104	162	175	199
Dairy Products	100	107	148	160	182
Poultry	100	129	168	182	206
Eggs	100	99	137	148	168
Nonfood	100	86	105	114	129
Crops:					
Food	100	107	152	165	188
Cereals and potatoes	100	102	129	136	151
Fruits and vegetables	100	113	164	176	201
Nonfood	100	113	138	150	171
Feed and seed	100	117	131	143	162
Other	100	100	164	177	201
Exports total	100	136	172	172	172
Livestock exports	100	126	100	100	100
Crop exports	100	138	188	188	188

Source: *Water Resources Activities in the United States: Land and Water Potentials and Future Requirements for Water*, a report by USDA to the Select Committee on National Water Resources, U.S. Senate; as quoted in Koffsky, op. cit.

by 30–60 percent from 1958 to support the increase in output required in the livestock sector.

In view of our present surplus situation and prospective continuing feeding efficiencies, total farm output would need to increase about 35 percent from the 1958 level to meet requirements for the low population projection, about 45 percent for the medium projection, and 60 percent for the high projection. Keep in mind also that in 1958 some 27 million acres were in the acreage reserve and conservation reserve of the Soil Bank.

We have not made allowance for possible changes in requirements for stocks. Clearly in the case of wheat, there would be no need for a higher "normal" carryover than presently—and very substantially below the existing carryover stocks level. For corn, "normal" stocks 20 years from now might well be 30–50 percent greater than present needs—but again still substantially below what we actually have. For cotton, we might well consider an increase of 50 percent in our "normal" stock level by 1980—perhaps not much different than the level of stocks we have at present.

SUMMARY

What have we learned from our exercise? In essence it is that agriculture faces a wide range of possibilities. If population grows slowly, there is little prospect, in view of current technology and persistently rising costs, for demands to rise fast enough to alter significantly the current situation of surpluses and lagging incomes in agriculture. If, on the other hand, population increases rapidly, we may be hard put to meet requirements, and the low price elasticities for farm products, which are agriculture's weakness today, could become a source of strength in terms of the prices and incomes that farmers might then realize. Crop and livestock inventory requirements could add some further tightness. We might well have to find room not only for 100 million more people, but also for 100 million more livestock.

Considering the range in possibilities, it is very difficult to be dogmatic. To narrow the range appreciably, we need to be able to project population with closer tolerances. Perhaps as a nation we

TABLE 17.3 Production of Major Crops, 1954 and 1958, and Projected Requirements in 1980

Commodity	Unit	Production		Projected Requirements, 1980		
		1954	1958	Low	Medium	High
Corn	Mil. bu.	3,058	3,800	4,310	4,643	5,234
Oats	Mil. bu.	1,410	1,422	1,551	1,683	1,905
Barley	Mil. bu.	379	470	720	769	858
Sorghums	Mil. bu.	235	615	354	381	428
Hay	Mil. tons	108	122	137	149	170
Cotton	Thous. bales	13,890	12,059	21,296	22,247	24,507
Tobacco	Mil. lb.	2,244	1,758	2,697	2,734	3,001
Wheat	Mil. bu.	984	1,462	1,217	1,287	1,411
Rye	Mil. bu.	26	32	28	30	33
Rice (rough)	Mil. cwt.	53	43	64	66	71
Potatoes	Mil. cwt.	220	266	257	278	317
Sweet potatoes	Mil. cwt.	17	17	27	28	32
Sugar (raw)						
Beets	Thous. tons	2,186	2,202	2,654	2,654	2,654
Cane	Thous. tons	610	579	757	757	757
Dry beans	Mil. lb.	1,694	1,898	2,079	2,254	2,567
Soybeans	Mil. bu.	341	574	512	532	568
Flaxseed	Mil. bu.	41	40	37	39	43
Peanuts (Farmers' stock)	Mil. lb.	1,008	1,886	2,283	2,449	2,744
Cottonseed	Thous. tons	5,709	4,798	6,889	7,467	8,502

Source: *Water Resources Activities in the United States: Land and Water Potentials and Future Requirements for Water*, reported in Koffsky, op. cit.

should aim at the mid-point as being the most likely, recognizing that demands could be plus or minus some 10 percent or so. In our programs, we might hope to retain enough flexibility so that if either eventuality occurs, we would not be unduly embarrassed.

The land and water study for the Senate Select Committee on National Water Resources, for which Tables 17.1, 17.2, and 17.3 were prepared, was in response to the Senate's need for information about future needs for water to increase agricultural crop production. The Committee asked for considerable detail about requirements for agricultural products for 1970, 1980, 2000, or 2010, the effects of further irrigation and reclamation, and the costs of achieving increased output—all to be prepared in three months' time. After almost six months' work by many technicians, these conclusions were reached, among others:

It is apparent that most of our increased production to meet future requirements must come from increased yields and increased efficiency in use of resources. Public efforts in conservation and development should recognize this fact.

The loss of productive crop, pasture, and forest land to urban and other special uses can be replaced only at high cost. With high population increases, policy regarding these shifts should be reexamined. Wherever a choice exists, public programs should encourage the use of unproductive land for these special uses.

The estimated irrigation development and improvements in efficiency of water storage, transportation, and application could not be achieved without changes in State water laws and their administration. . . .

While we are currently faced with problems of overproduction and surplus disposal, we should not lose sight of the longrun requirements for land and water resources. This report indicates that we have great productive capacity, yet our land and water resources are relatively fixed. We cannot afford to waste them or to allow irreplaceable depletions. Where there is a choice we should preserve our more productive land.

It is clear that requirements for land and water for agriculture, urban development, industry, highways, and recreation will increase in the future. The rate of increase in requirements will be dependent on the level of population growth. The improvement and application of technology to keep pace with this increase, and the more intensive use of our land and water will require increased research and acceleration of programs for conservation, development, and management of these resources.[7]

17.3.3 Demand for Marketing Services with Food

Because the studies just described did not involve directly the relationships between demand for food per se and for food marketing services, a note on the data and analyses required for them must be added. One must use per capita farm quantity and value data to measure trends and variations in food use and quantity and value data for marketing services between the farm gate and the ultimate consumer. Changes in distribution channels are often involved. To study them, use retail value data for all foods, such as those in Appendix B of Burk, M. *Measures and Procedures for Analysis of U.S. Food Consumption.* For some items, commodity flow data are available in special studies. Use of farm equivalents and values at the several levels of distribution permits evaluation of changes in distribution channels and marketing services.

The projections of food consumption used in the 1960–1965 production study and for 1980, cited previously, were based on analysis of changes in total output and in use of food from all sources. Because of the historical significance of the decline in home production to expansion of commercial production, some years ago this author examined changes in *rural* food consumption (most affected by the change in subsistence output) to measure their potential impact on commercial food output and marketing.[8] Based on Daly's 1957 economic framework,[9] historical changes in consumption of purchased foods by urban, rural nonfarm, and farm populations and estimates of changes in urbanization and extent of home food production by 1975, she concluded that the quantity of commercially produced and marketed farm foods might increase 16 to 18 percent per capita from 1955 to 1975, measured at the farm level. This projection was consistent with Daly's projection of a 10 percent increase in per capita use of farm foods from all sources (home production and commercial output).

Of this 16 to 18 percent increase in purchased foods, about 10 percentage points would come from the expected shift in urbanization plus the changes in income and consumption patterns of the rural population. Although the rural food market accounted for roughly one-third of the food sold for consumption at home in 1955, increased urbanization of the population by 1975 is likely to reduce the importance of the rural sector to about one-fifth of the total for purchased food at home.

Section 17.5 will consider the significance of alternative food measures and changes in marketing for demand forecasting in the developing countries.

17.3.4 Qualitative Changes in Food Consumption

At the request of the editor of *Economie Rurale*, the French journal for agricultural economics, the author studied major qualitative changes in United States food consumption. She appraised their implications for agriculture in the United States and in Western European countries experiencing comparable changes.[10] The major categories of qualitative changes investigated included: (1) changes in economic values of resources used for consumer food products; (2) improvements in the quality of farm commodities; (3) shifts among foods to higher preference items; (4) changes in marketing services related to qual-

[7] Pages 2 and 3 of *Water Resources Activities in the United States: Land and Water Potentials and Future Requirements for Water,* report for Select Committee on National Water Resources, U.S. Senate, 86th Congress, First Session, 1960.

[8] Burk, Marguerite C. "An Economic Appraisal of Changes in Rural Food Consumption," *J. Farm Economics* **XL**:3:572–590, August 1958.

[9] Daly, Rex F. "Prospective Domestic Demands for Food and Fiber." Paper submitted for hearings on Policy for Commercial Agriculture, Joint Economic Committee of the Congress, November 22, 1957.

[10] Burk, Marguerite C. "Les Changements Qualitatifs dans l'Alimentation et leur Répercussions sur l'Agriculture: L'Expérience des États-Unis," *Economie Rurale* **66**:31–38, October–December 1965; also published in the German journal of agricultural economics as "Qualitative Veränderungen im Nahrungsmittelverbrauch und die Landwirtschaft-Erfahrungen in den USA," *Agrarwirtschaft* **15**:5:149–156, May 1966.

ity, especially processing; and (5) changes in nutritive value.

The paper began by pointing out that quality has both product aspects and consumer aspects. The product attributes making up product quality may be either inherent in or may be developed in a commodity. But they are important to quality only insofar as they contribute to acceptance of the product and to satisfaction of present or potential needs of consumers.

Comparison of data on per capita use of purchased farm foods and those from all sources revealed that the former increased twice as much as the latter over the preceding 30 years. Home production supplied about a fifth of United States food in the 1930s but probably less than 5 percent in the mid-1960s. The major part of the decrease has been in subsistence production of livestock products due to the increasing urbanization of the population and to higher incomes. Meanwhile, marketing services bought with food have risen about 60 percent. The shift from home-produced to purchased foods has been a major factor in this rise.

Search for evidence of changes in quality led to the following conclusions. Changes in marketing to self-service require more uniformity and standardization. Considerable research on quality testing and developing of new instruments leads to the inference of improvements in quality of foods sold. In 1947 one-half of the beef produced and consumed was graded good or higher. By 1965 the proportion had reached 56 percent and has continued to rise. Improvements in the quality of milk are indicated by the changes in its keeping quality. Quality fresh foods are available during longer periods of the year.

Shifts in the commodity makeup of the food supply evidence changes in the quality of farm resources demanded. These have already been described in Chapter 15. Contributions of marketing to improved quality are illustrated by the increases in grading, inspection, packaging, and research on quality maintenance while in marketing channels. The proportion of the food supply processed rose from 25 percent in 1925 to 35 percent in 1954 and more since then. In postwar years there has been extensive use of enrichment and fortification of foods with vitamins and minerals.

Two key factors in the increased demand for quality have been higher real incomes and increased urbanization. Consumer tastes and preferences for food commodities and qualities have changed as American ways of living have altered. The relatively affluent sectors of the population place greater importance on quality, variety, convenience, and service. The doubling of the proportion of American married women employed outside the home over the last 25 years has been a contributing factor. With higher levels of education homemakers tend to discriminate more carefully among alternative qualities of food to meet particular uses.

Agricultural research has scored some notable successes in terms of quality. The development of the fast-growing broiler bird, both chicken and turkey, is one. The meat-type hog is likely to be another. Many new varieties and characteristics of crops have been developed to meet the requirements for mechanical harvesting and new types of processing.

Among the achievements of marketing research have been the development of dehydrated potatoes, improved refrigeration in retail stores and homes, the knowledge of specific refrigeration and humidity needs of individual commodities, the development and partial adoption of hog carcass grading, major advances in the measurement of the color, flavor, and texture of foods, and much greater knowledge of packaging requirements for individual foods.

Plentiful food supplies in the United States have forced many farmers and processors producing low-quality commodities out of business. The demand for high-quality farm commodities has apparently favored larger producers with greater capital resources and more technological knowledge. These human and capital resources have proved essential to use of improved methods and equipment and to adoption of new varieties and breeds.

Development of quality standards and grading systems offsets the common inclination of farmers to plant varieties most likely to produce the highest yields per acre and weights per volume unit of measure. When the profit incentive shifts from quantity to quality plus quantity, farm output shifts also.

Intensive competition in the processed food business has led to increased efforts to achieve and maintain high quality. Food industries have urged research agencies, seedsmen, and breeders to develop improved varieties and breeds. Moore and Hussey wrote:

. . . Market orientation requires that food processors assure themselves of a continuous flow of uniform raw materials at all times which are priced at levels that reasonably reflect their end-use values. The demand for farm products must be viewed as a derived demand and the products be priced accordingly.[11]

To summarize, increased consumer demand for quality and convenience in food products has led to increased demand for processed foods and increased use of standards and grades. Part of the increase in demand for processed foods may be traced to the greater increase in the costs of marketing fresh foods of high quality.

The United States has a substantial amount of unfinished business in development of standards and grades more suitable to consumers' matching quality attributes of products to end uses. Such standards and grades should also fit in with quality characteristics used by producers, wholesalers, and retailers. Where sets of quality standards differ, transmission of price impulses from consumers to producers is impeded. In the United States retail prices of some foods appear to be quite unrelated to present quality standards. A group of specialists at the 1955 National Workshop of Agricultural Marketing concluded:

Grades and standards should provide quality and size categories which have utility to producers, processors, distributors and consumers. With few exceptions, existing grades and standards are based on requirements of producers, processors, shippers, and wholesale receivers. Greater consideration should be given to the requirements and preferences of consumers, revising present consumer standards and developing new areas for additional commodities.[12]

Continuing research is needed to develop the desired quality characteristics in farm commodities, to maintain quality of the food commodities in marketing, and to process the food products so that they may have the attributes consumers want. Research must be designed to discover the individual qualities and the composites of quality factors that have meaning to consumers. Such research should recognize the importance of groups in the population with different preferences and different needs for different types of products. Market research can define the characteristics of products desired by important preference groups. Then operational techniques and biological requirements must be established for maintenance of quality to meet the standards desired by consumers.

Delivery of food products changed in quality and increased in uniformity from producers to consumers leads to changes in production and marketing. These changes may work to the disadvantage of established, relatively inflexible producers, distributors, and processors. They may force changes in institutions which have been developed to protect established marketing channels and structures. As food industries accept the concept of "market orientation" or consumer orientation, major innovations in business arrangements between agriculture and firms marketing agricultural commodities are to be expected.

17.3.5 Projections of Regional Changes

Regional groups of commodity producers have long been interested in the development of long-range projections for demand for their commodities in the several major regions of the country. A study of prospective changes in production, processing, and marketing of farm food products in the West was made by the Economic Research Service in the early 1960s.[13] Estimates of production and consumption of major commodities were developed for the 11 western states and published for California, Washington-Oregon, the Mountain States, and the whole region for 1947–1948, 1954–1955, and by 5-year intervals to 1985.

To make the estimates of consumption, per person food consumption and income data were derived from the 1955 Household Food Consumption Survey, and income–consumption relationships were computed for the nonfarm population, using a double logarithmic

[11] Page 424, Moore, Hugh L., and Hussey, Gorham. "Economic Implications of Market Orientation," *J. Farm Economics* 47:2:421–427, May 1965.

[12] Page 259, Report of Work Group IX, "Relation of Fruit and Vegetable Quality Maintenance to Marketing Efficiency," pp. 248–267 of *Marketing Efficiency in a Changing Economy*, a report of the National Workshop on Agricultural Marketing, June 17–24, 1955 held at the University of Kentucky, published by the U.S. Department of Agriculture, Agricultural Marketing Service, AMS–60.

[13] Stallings, Dale G. *Long-Run Projections of Food Processing and Marketing in the West*, Agr. Econ. Report No. 78.

model. These adjustments were calculated from trend data developed for individual foods by Daly.[14] However, the basic factor in the projections was income.

Stallings concluded from the study that the West should expect increases in net surpluses of fresh and processed fruits and vegetables, nuts, and beet sugar for shipment outside the region. But the deficit of production compared with consumption of meat, poultry, dairy products, and flour might be likely to double by 1985.

17.4 AGRICULTURAL AND FOOD AID FOR THE DEVELOPING COUNTRIES

In recent years, the U. S. has supplied the world with about one billion dollars' worth of food per year, at least a third of the food imported by food-deficit countries. We have exported about half the wheat and two thirds of the rice we produce. The subsidized export market is very important to American farmers, and vast quantities of food are needed in many of the less developed countries. (Page 199.)[15]

Consideration of agricultural and food aid for the developing countries in the last third of the twentieth century rests on knowledge regarding four key questions: (1) What are the requirements for food and how do they compare with supplies from domestic production and commercial exports? (2) What are the possibilities of additional supplies from the United States and other surplus producing countries and of moving the supplies to people who need them? (3) What would be the impact of increased food aid on both the exporting and the importing countries? (4) What are the alternatives to food aid, especially the possibilities of all-out efforts to increase domestic production in the developing countries?

In the following sections, we will examine the evidence pertinent to each question.

17.4.1 Estimates of Food Needs

There is considerable discussion on minimum standards for national average levels of food consumption. Scientific knowledge about dietary needs of people in the food-deficit countries is lacking, but there is solid evidence that there *are* areas of the world where people are seriously short of food energy at least part of the year and that many millions suffer from malnutrition. (Page 200.)

Problems encountered in making estimates of food consumption for the developing countries have been noted earlier in Section 4.2.3.

Available data on domestically produced food supplies in most of the less developed countries pertain largely to the commercial crops. Estimates of food produced or gathered for home use by rural people, which provide the largest proportion of their supplies, are mostly "informed guesses." Furthermore, projections of food output tend to be conservative. Recent technological improvements in varieties of food grains indicate potentials for tremendous increases in yields. But agricultural leadership in the developing countries needs reinforced will to accomplish such ends and incentives must be provided to domestic producers. . . .

Officials of the U.S. Department of Agriculture and the Food and Agriculture Organization of the United Nations acknowledge problems in estimating future food supplies and requirements for the world. But they have prepared such estimates in order to dramatize the world food problem. The USDA estimates a deficit in needs for food energy in 1970, for instance, which would require 54 million metric tons of grain in addition to supplies now foreseen. For comparison, U.S. food use of grains in 1959–61 averaged 19 million metric tons per year. USDA values the world food deficit for 1970 at $6.8 billion, including $2.5 billion for the so-called "Free World." The critical fact here is that about sixty-two percent of the deficit would be in Communist Asia, the area for which basic data are most questionable. (Page 200.)

The U.S. Department of Agriculture's estimates were developed as background for consideration of international food policies; they were published in *The World Food Budget: 1970*.[16] The researchers started the estimating process with the "food balance sheets" or supply and distribution tables for the periods 1956–1958 and 1959–1961 assembled by the Foreign Agricultural Service, the U.N. Food and Agriculture Organization, the Organization for Economic Cooperation and Development, plus some supplementary ERS estimates. Their demand projections were based primarily on population growth (United Na-

[14] Daly, R. F. "Agriculture in the Years Ahead," talk presented at the Southern Agricultural Workers Conference, Atlanta, Georgia, February 3, 1964.

[15] This paragraph and a number of others quoted in this section are taken from Burk, Marguerite C. "Can or Should the U.S. Fill the World Food Gap?" *AAUW Journal* 59:4:199–201, 214, May 1966. (By permission.)

[16] USDA, Economic Research Service, Foreign Regional Analysis Division, Foreign Agricultural Economic Report No. 19.

tions projections) and projected income changes where available. Otherwise, trends were extrapolated to 1970. The projections of supplies, both domestic production and imports, relied heavily on historical trends, as did those for nonfood uses. The several elements for the food balance sheets for 1970 were entered:

. . . and balanced by successive approximations. It was at this point that price effects were considered in balancing supply and demand in each country. Also, where commodities did not balance, analysis was made of production, consumption, and trade policies to determine where further adjustment in demand and supply would probably occur. . . .

Adequacy of diet: The food balances for 1959–61 and 1970 for each country were measured against nutritional reference standards that have been developed by the Consumer and Food Research Division of USDA's Agricultural Research Service. Countries whose diets were deficient in calories, total protein, animal protein, pulse protein, or fat were identified and the magnitude of the deficiency was calculated.

For a realistic measure of the deficits, they were expressed in terms of commodities which are of interest to the United States or which are commonly consumed in the countries. [Wheat, rice, other grains, nonfat dry milk, fish protein concentrates, dry beans and peas, soygrits, and vegetable oils.]

Country food balances were summarized into 10 commodity groups and 22 subregions, and an average diet for each subregion was calculated. However, the magnitude of the deficit for a subregion was not determined by the average subregion diet but is a weighted average of the country deficits within the subregion.[17]

Based on this research, the highlights of the report were:

Two-thirds of the world's people live in countries with nutritionally inadequate national average diets. The diet-deficit areas include all of Asia except Japan and Israel, all but the southern tip of Africa, the northern part of South America, and almost all of Central America and the Caribbean.[18]

In view of the tenuous nature of the "rough estimates" of food supplies in Communist Asia, some food researchers outside the U.S. Department of Agriculture are concerned that that area accounts for 62 percent of the 1970 food deficit, valued at $6.8 billion. Latin America's share was estimated at 2.3 percent, Africa's at 3.4 percent, India—13.2 percent, other Asian countries (excluding Japan and Communist Asia)—18.7 percent. These estimates are playing a significant role in discussions regarding the continuation of food export programs to aid the developing countries. All concerned wish they had a more substantial statistical basis, especially since they are also important in decisions regarding United States agricultural adjustment and the national budget.

The USDA estimates that food grain requirements of the less developed countries in 1980 may run about 300 million metric tons, or seventy percent above the requirements annually available in 1958–61. This is about three times the size of the increase in food grain supplies from 1959–61 to 1970 projected by USDA.[19]

The USDA estimates of food deficits rest on the U.N. population projections which may be overestimating the increases, as discussed in Section 4.3.3. Bogue's adjusted estimates referred to there, which assume a linear decline in growth rate to zero by the year 2000, yield an estimate for the world's population in 1980 that is 200 million lower than the U.N. medium estimate of 4.3 billion people. All of the difference is in the developing countries.

17.4.2 Availability of Supplies from United States and Other Developed Countries

A recent summary of the U.S. farm production potential for 1980 indicated that expected increases in farm output on ninety percent of our cropland could supply the total domestic demand plus a seventy-five percent increase from the 1959–61 average in crop exports by 1980.[20] If we also used all of the sixty million acres now diverted from crop production, total output of crops might run sixty percent above the 1959–61 average by 1980. If all of this increase were exported, exports would reach 250 percent of the 1959–61 average. Grain exports could amount to 75 million metric tons in 1980.

Increases in yields have also outrun population growth in Canada and Western Europe. Experts believe sufficient food could be produced in the U.S. and other developed countries to fill the food gap of the next ten to fifteen years, but problems of logistics, economic and political costs, and long-run repercussions on production potentials in the developing countries merit careful consideration.[21]

[17] *Ibid.*, page 90.

[18] *Ibid.*, page iii.

[19] Page 200, Burk, M. *AAUW Journal*, op. cit.

[20] Pages 7–8, Daly, R. F., and Egbert, A. C. "A Look Ahead for Food and Agriculture," *Agr. Econ. Research* **XVIII**:1:1–9, January 1966.

[21] Page 200, Burk, M. *AAUW Journal*, op. cit.

17.4.3 Impact of Expanded Food Aid on United States and Recipients

Pertinent to the U.S. decision on greatly expanded, long-range food aid commitments is the evidence of adverse effects on domestic production in recipient countries in recent years. The Institute of Development Economics in Pakistan found that bulk supply food aid to that country reduced its farm income. Extensive reliance of Colombia on P.L. 480 supplies of wheat in 1955–60 so depressed the domestic wheat price that wheat output failed to change while spectacular increases were achieved for crops with price incentives.[22]

The proposed expansion in domestic production to fill the world food gap would incur costs in terms of consumers' doing without the output of nonagricultural goods and services, magnifying the farm problems in other food-exporting countries, and extensive subsidies for port, storage, transport, and processing facilities in the recipient countries. We would have to make long-range commitments to subsidize distribution in the developing countries. These commitments would probably raise conflicts in those countries with commercial traders who are important in the political power structures. The political problems at home and in diplomacy would be magnified in dealings with Communist Asia. . . . [*Ibid.*]

In a special study for FAO, Dr. Dandekar of the Gokhale (India) Institute of Politics and Economics argued that foreign food aid has reduced economic stimuli for small farmers in the developing countries to use more fertilizer and better seeds and improve their land. He also pointed out that the use of food aid to create employment on public works contributes to inflation in prices of nonfood commodities bought by farm families and thereby reduces their purchases and probably their productive efficiency.[23]

A third pertinent fact comes from an econometric analysis of food aid to India by Dr. J. S. Mann of the University of Minnesota. He found that imports of 2.9 million metric tons of cereals into India in 1962 probably depressed wholesale prices of cereals about four percent. He estimated a net gain over a six year period of one half pound in Indian cereal consumption from each pound of cereals imported per capita. Half of the import appears to be offset by the resultant cut in domestic output.[24]

U.S. prices of some major agricultural commodities for food use are above world average prices and much higher than prices in some of the food exporting but less developed countries. For example, U.S. rice costs about $150 to $170 per metric ton, to which must be added transport, storage, and handling costs involved in shipping rice to India. The U.S. government could save money by buying the rice in Thailand and Burma. However, to step up output there to meet the new demand, large amounts of fertilizer, relatively high-priced in that area, would be needed, as well as improved varieties of rice.

Finally there is the question of whether the developing countries could accelerate their food output and improve their marketing systems sufficiently to cope with their own food problems by 1982. A recent USDA study reports that between 1948 and 1963 twelve developing nations achieved rates of increase in crop output higher than those of the U.S. and many other developed countries.[25] They proved that rapid advances in agriculture are possible providing there is national determination to achieve them. If so, researchers from the developed countries can help by joining forces with those in the developing countries to adapt technology to local conditions. Meanwhile, short run expansion of U.S. food output, such as that recommended by the Administration's draft of a bill to replace Public Law 480 could help the poorly fed countries over the intervening years.

U.S. food aid has also magnified some political and social problems in the developing countries, in our own, and in other food exporting countries. Continuation of government purchases of agricultural surpluses and of export subsidies has stretched out the postwar period for adjustment in U.S. agriculture to twenty years. By stressing the emergency aspects of food aid, we have avoided making long-range commitments to a multilateral food distribution agency which is needed to make expanded assistance by the higher income countries to the less developed nations politically acceptable and economically efficient.

Political and social problems experienced under conditions of emergency food aid would be magni-

[22] *Ibid.*, page 200. Information from (*a*) page 8, FitzGerald, D. A. *Operational and Administrative Problems of Food Aid,* FAO World Food Program Studies No. 4; (*b*) page 30, Dandekar, V. M. *The Demand for Food and Conditions Governing Food Aid During Development,* FAO World Food Program Studies No. 1.

[23] *Ibid.*, page 201, information from op. cit., page 31.

[24] *Ibid.*, information from pp. 161 and 179 of Mann, Jitendar Singh. *The Contribution of United States Public Law 480 to Indian Economic Development,* unpublished Ph.D. Thesis, University of Minnesota.

[25] Page v., U.S. Department of Agriculture, Economic Research Service, Foreign Development and Trade Division. *Changes in Agriculture in 26 Developing Nations, 1948 to 1963,* USDA, ERS, For. Agr. Econ. Report No. 27, November 1965.

fied by any indication of U.S. willingness to supply food aid indefinitely. There would be no incentive whatever for governments of the developing countries to clash with their powerful elite over much needed economic and social changes. So the basic problems could continue to fester.[26]

17.4.4 Public Decision Needed

We must soon choose between two sets of policies regarding use of our resources to help developing countries meet their food problems: Either substantial expansion of inputs in our agricultural sector, including extensive price supports and subsidies as needed and concurrent programs to distribute the food where needed, or development of a massive program of agricultural research and education to expedite the increases in agricultural output in the food-deficit parts of the world and extensive research and education on the problems of population control. (*Ibid.*)

17.5 PERTINENCE OF INCOME–FOOD RELATIONSHIPS TO ECONOMIC DEVELOPMENT

A comprehensive analysis of the potential effects of income changes in the course of economic development on the demand for agricultural and marketing resources has been made by Stevens.[27] He uses the concepts for food at the retail and supplier level and for marketing services introduced in Chapter 12, with slightly different terminology. Based on careful review of time-series and cross-section income elasticities for many countries, he demonstrates how income elasticities vary at different points in the macro structure of consumption.

The starting point of Stevens' analysis is the demand for *total food,* defined as food sold at retail plus the farm value of home-produced food. (This concept matches the market value of all food minus markup over retail of food sold by eating places.) Depending on level of income, the income elasticity of total food varies from 0.4 to 0.9; the usual elasticities are about 0.7.

The relative importance of *home-produced food* has a great impact on the income elasticity of *food at retail* (retail value of all food sold). The share of home-produced food in total food appears to increase with income at very low levels of per capita income and then to decrease, based on cross-section data for the less-developed countries and on United States time series. The ratio of changes in retail food to changes in income runs significantly higher than the income elasticity for *total food* (as much as 0.6) and ranges between 0.8 and 1.2. Stevens utilizes three "retail food paths" to show the varying effects on the demand for food at retail of shifts in the population from rural to urban areas, a major structural change in the economies which accompanies economic development. Lacking the appropriate information on the proportion of food marketed, Stevens used estimates of the ratios of nonfarm to total labor force to approximate the ratio of retail food to total food. His analysis reveals a much more rapid increase in the ratio of food at retail to total food at lower per capita income levels than at higher levels. This is consistent with observed price pressures in the developing countries as incomes begin to rise.

Based on these high income elasticities for food at retail:

> . . . it is evident that the demand for Food at Retail can be expected to remain high in countries undergoing rapid development. For low-income countries increases in per capita income of $25 to $50, increases which would be considered modest amounts for the United States, can mean appreciable increases in the consumption of Food at Retail; because of this, there is likely to be considerable strain on the marketing system during development.[28]

The measure of value of farm and nonfarm food sold, valued at supplier prices at the farm gate and wharf, is called by Stevens *food for wholesale.* The income elasticity of food at this stage in the market structure is greatly influenced by changes in the marketing margin, i.e., the share of payments for total food taken by marketing agencies. (For simplicity, Stevens holds relative prices constant throughout his study, although he explicitly notes their potential effects.) If there is no change in the marketing margin, the income elasticity of food for wholesale is the same as that for food at retail, as is the income elasticity of marketing costs. From his analysis, Stevens concludes that relatively small percentage

[26] AAUW *Journal,* op. cit., page 201.

[27] Stevens, Robert D. *Elasticity of Food Consumption Associated With Changes in Income in Developing Countries,* USDA, ERS, For. Agr. Econ. Report No. 23.

[28] *Ibid.,* page 38.

point changes in the marketing margin can result in substantial differences between income elasticities of food at retail and food for wholesale. Increases in the marketing margin dampen the income elasticity of food at wholesale. But they do not often occur in the early stages of economic development because marketing charges are generally very high in the poor countries, and the governments try to reduce them.

Stevens notes that the significant effect of even small changes in the marketing margin on demand for food at wholesale "has important implications for nations undergoing development. If, for example, a nation succeeds in reducing Marketing Costs and hence the marketing margin appreciably, it should expect greatly increased demand for Food for Wholesale. On the other hand, if development in a nation results in a certain amount of disorganization in traditional marketing channels with increased uncertainty and turmoil in marketing, the increases in the marketing margin which would probably result would depress the demand for Food for Wholesale."[29]

The income elasticity of food at wholesale is highly significant for planning and evaluating food production programs in the developing countries. It is likely to be at least 0.6, according to Stevens' research, and will always be higher than the income elasticity of total food or supplier food (which include home-produced food). The demand for food at wholesale appears to increase at about the same rate as per capita income during the early stages of economic development. Stevens expects the income elasticity of food for wholesale to be at least as great as the income elasticity of food at retail, i.e., ranging from 0.8 to 1.2.

Supplier food refers to supplier level values of all food sold and home produced. The income elasticity of supplier food appears to be 0.4 to 0.6. The elasticity of this measure differs from that for food at wholesale according to changes in the relative importance of home-produced food. It differs from the elasticity of total food, a retail level measure, according to changes in farm–retail marketing margins and in the proportion of food marketed, apparently running about 0.1 or 0.2 less. Thus the demand for agricultural resources does not increase as rapidly as per capita incomes rise as does the value of total food, farm resources plus marketing resources.

Stevens concludes from his analysis:

> Important implications of high income elasticities on the rate of growth in national food requirements emerge from a dramatic rise in the rate of growth of food consumption as development gets underway. For example, the transition of an economy from a stagnant state, where population and income remain constant to an economy with high levels of per capita income, is likely to increase the rate of growth in food requirements at the farm gate by as much as 5 percent per year in the early stages of economic development before it finally decreases to about 3 percent.
>
> Governments planning economic development should be aware that rapid increases in food flows through marketing channels are likely to cause inflationary pressures on food prices unless marketing channels are made capable of handling these increased flows. An alternative policy for reducing the pressure on marketing services would be one to slow the movement of population into urban areas. If this were achieved, less food would need to be transported into urban areas.[30]

[29] *Ibid.*, pp. 40–41.

[30] *Ibid.*, page iv.

18

CONSUMPTION STUDIES RELATED TO OTHER NATIONAL AND INTERNATIONAL PROBLEMS

This chapter gives examples of empirical consumption studies pertinent to the formulation of national and international policies and programs. It concludes the series of chapters that have focused on research for marketing, agriculture, and now on public policy.

There is no attempt to discuss here some of the interesting questions related to the aggregate demand for all goods and services or to the welfare of the American public because these topics are part of the constant of general economics, especially in intermediate and advanced courses. But a number of consumption studies related to public issues are summarized even though their analyses are not as comprehensive as economists wish. For example, consumption aspects of the development of human capital offer great challenge, but the greater availability of data pertinent to investment for future earnings has limited most of the economic analyses to that aspect. A sampling of this kind of research is included here because of the current interest in the economics of education.

We begin with examples of consumption research pertinent to analysis of economic growth and to planning for resource development. Then we consider research bearing on public decision making regarding government controls and subsidies. Next we deal with research on problems of foreign aid to developing countries. (This section supplements Section 17.4.) Finally, we conclude with brief extracts from studies of the consumption aspects of international trade policies.

18.1 ECONOMIC GROWTH

Researchers on problems of economic growth are devoting increased attention to the consumption aspects of their problems. In recent years, additional government and university resources have been allocated to the study of trends in consumption expenditures and to the study of factors related to the demand for housing, education, recreation, health, and medical care.

18.1.1 Relation of Consumption to Monetary Policy

Suits reviewed the details of consumer expenditures in connection with the investigation of the effects of monetary policies on various aspects of the economy, under the auspices of the Commission on Money and Credit of the Committee for Economic Development.[1] (See also Section 14.2.3.) He concluded that the structure of consumption has a relatively long time-dimension. One part of his chapter is a careful review of the Keynesian consumption function and some extensions and modifications by empirical researchers. Another part reports several investigations of the consumption function. Suits notes the great importance of total consumption in total income and how this relationship may give a misleading impression regarding the uniformity of responsiveness of consumption to income. He provides evidence of the difference in consumer behavior between the prewar and postwar periods, particularly of the substantial increase in the importance of liquid assets (Table 18.1).

[1] Suits, Daniel B. "The Determinants of Consumer Expenditures: A Review of Present Knowledge," *Impacts of Monetary Policy*, copyright 1963. Reprinted by permission of Prentice-Hall, Inc., Englewood Cliffs, New Jersey.

TABLE 18.1 Suits' Disaggregated Consumption Equations, Prewar and Postwar[a]

A—Prewar equations

	Equation	R^2
Automobiles	$\Delta A = .0893\ \Delta Y + .0199\ \Delta L_{-1} - .401\ A_{-1} + 1.243$	.93
	(.008) (.0177) (.076)	
Other Durables	$\Delta D = .0967 \Delta Y + .0403\ \Delta L_{-1} - .0928\ D_{-1} + .484$	.93
	(.008) (.0174) (.057)	
Non Durables	$\Delta ND = .247\ \Delta Y - .0251\ \Delta L_{-1} + .164\ \Delta ND_{-1} + .870$	.79
	(.065) (.132) (.193)	
Services	$\Delta S = .130\ \Delta Y - .004\ \Delta L_{-1} + .220\ \Delta S_{-1} - .166$	.87
	(.0265) (.0501) (.475)	
Total (summed)	$\Delta C = .563\ \Delta Y + .0311\ \Delta L_{-1} + \dots + 2.431$	

B—Postwar equations

	Equation	R^2
Automobiles	$\Delta A = .194\ \Delta Y + .220\ \Delta L_{-1} - .551\ A_{-1} + 5.042$	.74
	(.075) (.075) (.136)	
Other Durables	$\Delta D = .178\ \Delta Y + .0709\ \Delta L_{-1} - .0391\ D_{-1} - .363$	.95
	(.067) (.016) (.034)	
Non Durables	$\Delta ND = .207\ \Delta Y + .146\ \Delta L_{-1} + .299\ \Delta ND_{-1} - .085$	.68
	(.056) (.060) (.150)	
Services	$\Delta S = .108\ \Delta Y + .0447\ \Delta L_{-1} + .601\ \Delta S_{-1} + .413$	.76
	(.028) (.028) (.153)	
Total (summed)	$\Delta C = .687\ \Delta Y + .482\ \Delta L_{-1} + \dots + 5.007$	

Where A = total consumption expenditures for automobiles and parts
Y = current disposable income
Y = income in preceding period
L = liquid assets
D = expenditures for durables other than autos
ND = expenditures for nondurables
S = expenditures for services
C = total consumption expenditures

[a] From page 33, Suits, Daniel B. "The Determinants of Consumer Expenditure: A Review of Present Knowledge." Fitted in first differences to annual data, 1930–1941 and 1948–1959; all variables measured in billions of 1954 dollars.

Suits also investigated the quarter-to-quarter variations and found that the correlation between consumption and income vanished:

> [and] . . . that on a true quarterly basis a useful Keynesian-type consumption function does not exist at all! Income is more stable in the very short run than is consumption expenditure. The general level of expenditure in a given quarter is a function of a distributed lag, not only of income, but of other factors as well. The deviations of quarterly expenditure from this general level are the result of such factors as very short-run alteration in consumer attitudes, and accidents in the timing of receipts, requirements, and expenditures. . . .[2]

[2] *Ibid.*, page 39.

In another section, Suits examined available evidence relating four monetary factors explicitly to consumer behavior: the price level, the interest rate, liquid assets, and consumer credit. Direct effects of price inflation have not been empirically studied, but price increases have been found to depress consumer expenditures indirectly. The rate of interest appears to have little direct or indirect influence on consumer expenditures.

The accumulation of conflicting empirical evidence from cross-section studies added to the highly unstable coefficient found for liquid assets in the time series analysis of the preceding section is convincing evidence that the role of liquid assets in the consumption function has not yet been discovered.[3]

The role of consumer credit is likewise confounded with other aspects of behavior. The overall statistical evidence does not indicate any clear cut effect on expenditure. In part this may be due to the rather poor quality of the data available—particularly for credit terms. In part it may be due to the complex interaction of credit with liquid assets and above all with the determination of income itself.[4]

The financial variables play a part in this complex process, but it is difficult to isolate their effects, and in particular to separate the results of behavior from its determinants and constraints. This greatly increases the difficulty of properly assessing the influence of policy controls on behavior, and it is evident that in our present state of knowledge we must rely for policy guidance primarily on the obvious direction of the effect of the policy step.[5]

Policy evaluation calls for the study of changes over time, not differences in status. We need to know what change in expenditure will be accompanied by a change in liquid asset holdings, credit terms, income or other factors. These changes can only be observed over time. But because of the greater resolving power of cross-section data, and because behavior varies from spending unit to spending unit, we need both cross sections and time series over the same units.[6]

18.1.2 Studies of Economic Growth

The effects of income and other household characteristics on household auto ownership were investigated by economists in the Office of Business Economics, U.S. Department of Commerce, for the Interagency Economic Growth Project.[7] Friedman, utilizing data collected from 15,000 households in July 1964 as part of the Bureau of Census's *Quarterly Survey of Intentions*, studied the economic and social factors related to the ownership of automobiles. After adjusting for the age of the household head, employment status, housing tenure, region of residence, and place of residence, the income elasticity of auto ownership, over the $2000 to $15,000 income range, was found to be "approximately constant with a value somewhat above one for ownership of two or more cars. The elasticity is approximately constant and somewhat below one for ownership of cars less than 3 years old. . . . In contrast, the income elasticity for ownership of one or more cars is only about 0.25 among households with incomes of less than $6,000 and is even smaller for high income households. For cars 3 to 8 years old, the income elasticity is about 0.40 for incomes under $4,000; it declines to zero as income approaches $7,500 and becomes negative at higher incomes. For cars 8 years old or older, the income elasticity is negative for all income classes tested."[8]

Friedman concluded from his analysis that there is a clear relationship between auto ownership and the density of population in an area—the larger the population, the lower the ownership rate.[9]

Two housing analyses, made in connection with the interagency study of growth, have been reported by Atkinson. One was concerned with alternative projections of the number of housing units to be constructed around 1970. Atkinson reported as follows:

> The general technique used here to estimate new housing construction in future years begins with projections of households, which are equivalent to occupied housing units. To these is added a projection of vacant units. By definition, occupied plus vacant units equal the total housing stock. Changes in the stock, plus an estimate of removals, yield projections of the number of housing units to be constructed.[10]

> Housing construction, like fixed investment generally, is not only a determinant of the level of economic activity but is also dependent upon it. The housing projections presented here are not based on specific assumed levels of income and other relevant economic variables, principally because it was not possible to develop usable relationships between them and the available housing data. The projections assume high levels of prosperity. In general, the alternatives are consistent with a range of economic conditions varying from a continuation of the historical average rate of growth in total output to a somewhat faster growth. Adequate financing for residential construction, no major changes in the relative price of housing, and sufficient flexibility in the construction industry to

[3] *Ibid.*, page 43.
[4] *Ibid.*, page 49.
[5] *Ibid.*, page 51.
[6] *Ibid.*, page 52.
[7] Friedman, Charles S. "Auto Ownership by Households in Mid-1964; Influences of Economic and Other Socioeconomic Factors," *Survey of Current Business* **46**:10:14–24, October 1966.
[8] *Ibid.*, page 18.
[9] *Ibid.*, page 23.
[10] Page 8 of Atkinson, L. Jay. "Long-Term Influences Affecting the Volume of New Housing Units," *Survey of Current Business* **43**:11:8–19, November 1963.

meet the demand for new housing units are implicit in the projections.[11]

> . . . Under varying assumptions consistent with continued high levels of prosperity, the number of new housing units projected for the end of this decade ranges from a 1.66 million annual rate to an intermediate estimate of 1.85 million and a high of 2.12 million annual rate. The latter figure is consistent with a rate of economic growth faster than the historical average. These projections may be compared with an annual average of 1.4 million total housing starts for the period of 1960 to date.[12]

The second study by Atkinson dealt with factors affecting the purchase value of new houses in an attempt to estimate the average value per unit for later years. It utilized cross-section data from the 1960 Census of Housing and some time-series data. However, available data did not prove adequate for development of projections. Atkinson wrote:

> . . . The regression analysis is the heart of this report. The basic regression took this general form: The value of a newly built house acquired by a family or individual depends upon the current income of the household; the age, sex, race, education, occupation, and marital status or length of time married of the household head; and the location of the housing unit. Some modifications of this regression were also explored.
>
> A feature of this study is its treatment of a large number of nonincome variables, for which data have not ordinarily been available until recently. The use of such data in statistical analysis had been limited not only because they were scarce but also because many of the variables were nonnumerical. The development in the last few years of new statistical techniques involving the use of "dummy" variables and the availability of large computers have overcome these obstacles.[13]

All the independent variables combined explained only about half of the total variation in prices paid for new homes in the cross section. Income explained about 50 percent of the total explained. The income elasticity was between 0.41 and 0.47 when computed holding all other factors constant and omitting the extreme income groups. Contrary to the findings of some other analysts, Atkinson found income elasticity to be constant over much of the range of income.

[11] *Ibid.*, page 8.

[12] *Ibid.*, page 9.

[13] Page 20, Atkinson, L. Jay. "Factors Affecting the Purchase Value of New Houses," *Survey of Current Business* 46:8:20–36, August 1966.

A simple relationship between family income and house value through time was estimated from price, credit, and income data on new homes insured by the Federal Housing Administration. The relation was found to be about 0.8.

> The price elasticity of new homes was estimated to be less than unity, with the usual inverse relationship between price and real value of house purchased. An inverse relationship was also found between house value and a credit variable in the form of monthly mortgage payments, i.e., the lower the monthly payments, the higher the value of house acquired.[14]
>
> A major contribution of the time series analysis is the fact that credit terms appear to have significant and important effects on house value and that relative prices are important in some formulations. The extent to which the various net regression coefficients derived from the 1960 cross-section household data were affected by the particular pattern of prices and credit terms prevailing at that time cannot be determined, as was already indicated.
>
> The net coefficient on income from the FHA time series data (after the introduction of price and credit variables) turned out to be considerably greater than the cross-section estimates based on individual household data. The two sets of data are, of course, not comparable in terms of coverage. . . .[15]

18.1.3 Trends in the Composition of Aggregate Consumption

When input-output data for later years (now being developed by the Office of Business Economics) are available to match the data issued in the *Survey of Current Business* in 1965–1966, it will be possible to study intensively the trends in the industrial origin of resources utilized in consumer goods and services. Input-output data subdivide data for conglomerate firms into specific industries. However, industrial contributions to national income, as measured in the national income accounts on a value-added basis, provide some general indications. Table 18.2 shows that the contribution of agriculture, forestry, and fisheries decreased from 9.8 percent in 1929 to 3.7 percent in 1965. Mining and construction changed relatively little, but manufacturing rose from 25.3 to 30.5 percent, with all of the increase in the durable goods sector. Transportation's share fell from 7.6 to 4.1 percent, but communications rose from 1.3 to 2 percent.

[14] *Ibid.*, page 20.

[15] *Ibid.*, page 34.

Table 18.2 National Income by Industry, Selected Years, 1929 to 1965[a]

	1929		1939		1948		1958		1965	
	Bil. Dol.	Pct. of Total	Bil. Dol.	Pct. of Total	Bil. Dol.	Pct. of Total	Bil. Dol.	Pct. of Total	Bil. Dol.	Pct. of Total
All industries	*86.8*	*100.0*	*72.6*	*100.0*	*224.2*	*100.0*	*367.8*	*100.0*	*559.0*	*100.0*
Agriculture, forestry, fisheries	8.5	9.8	6.0	8.3	21.6	9.6	17.9	4.9	21.0	3.7
Mining and construction	5.9	6.8	4.0	5.5	16.0	7.1	24.7	6.7	34.8	6.2
Manufacturing	*22.0*	*25.3*	*18.1*	*24.9*	*68.7*	*30.7*	*107.7*	*29.3*	*170.4*	*30.5*
Nondurable goods	10.6	12.2	9.1	12.5	32.9	14.7	45.7	12.4	65.6	11.7
Durable goods	11.3	13.0	9.0	12.4	35.8	16.0	62.0	16.9	104.8	18.8
Transportation	6.6	7.6	4.6	6.3	12.8	5.7	16.6	4.5	22.9	4.1
Communications	1.1	1.3	1.1	1.5	2.8	1.3	7.0	1.9	11.2	2.0
Electrical, gas, sanitary services	1.6	1.8	1.8	2.5	3.2	1.4	7.4	2.0	11.6	2.1
Wholesale and retail trade	13.5	15.6	12.6	17.4	39.9	17.8	58.3	15.9	83.6	15.0
Finance, insurance, and real estate	12.8	14.8	8.0	11.0	18.4	8.2	40.9	11.1	61.0	10.9
Services	8.9	10.3	7.6	10.5	20.0	8.9	38.4	10.4	63.0	11.3
Government and government enterprises	5.1	5.8	8.5	11.7	19.8	8.8	46.9	12.8	75.2	13.5
Rest of world	0.8	0.9	0.3	0.4	1.0	0.5	2.0	0.5	4.3	0.8

[a] Dollar data from pp. 18–21, *The National Income and Product Accounts of the United States, 1929–1965*, Supplement to the *Survey of Current Business*, August 1966. Data for years beginning 1948 based on 1957 classification.

Finance, insurance, and real estate dropped from 14.8 to 10.9 percent of the total national income. Governments and government enterprises rose from 5.8 percent in peaceful 1929 to 13.5 percent in 1965, a postwar year with substantial defense outlays.

18.2 PUBLIC INVESTMENT IN RESOURCE DEVELOPMENT

The resources that should be included in this section cover the whole spectrum of natural resources of land, water, forests; human resources, and technology but, for the sake of brevity, we shall use a sampling approach. The usual analytical approaches for decision making have been cost–benefit analysis (relying heavily on cost and expenditure data in alternative situations) and the more theoretical welfare economics approach, often without recourse to empirical data. The lack of market price data and of economic measures of quantity and value of benefits to people affected by the resource change have impeded analysis.

18.2.1 Introduction

A somewhat different and perhaps naive approach is sketched first, based on consumption aspects. It is organized in terms of the steps in analysis that we used in earlier chapters. In sizing up the problem involved in proposal for public investment, we must recognize that the demand for public goods varies among groups in the population and through time, but information for analysis of these variations can be collected with modern survey techniques. For example, the Michigan Survey Research Center conducted a nationwide survey of adult participation in outdoor recreation,[16] and the Bureau of the Census made a nationwide survey of the outdoor recreation habits and preferences of Americans 12 years of age and over.[17] Very long-range projections are needed for consumption trends because of the long life of the resource developments usually being planned. These projections require rather elaborate assumptions. The development of criteria to guide public investment is a difficult problem in itself. We should notice that groups in the population with the greatest demand for public goods and services frequently pay the least taxes; they are the least articulate; and they have the least political power.

In the process of formulating tentative hypotheses, a researcher often finds factors such as public desires to continue past trends or desires of one group to depart from them in a certain way, uncertainties about costs of alternative programs of resource development, and indications of advantages that might accrue to particular pressure groups. The possibility of long-range shifts in public demand in response to social changes is still scarcely recognized. During background surveys of the problem, needs for public goods or services may be revealed that may vary from unfilled minor but aggravating requirements to very fundamental needs growing out of recent social changes. The level of public awareness of needs for public goods is often very low. Problems with water pollution are a case in point.

Description of pertinent consumption patterns can be accomplished by careful identification of the economic and social factors related to consumer actions and of the components of such actions. The outdoor recreation studies indicate how complex the quantification problem can be. What units should be used to measure recreation services? Some researchers have chosen user-days, that is, man-days spent in a national park or at a beach. Others have used dollars spent per recreation episode or trip to a park, on a per capita basis. The recreation surveys noted earlier provide data along these lines. For analysis of some of these data, see ORRRC Study Report 24, *Economic Studies of Outdoor Recreation* and the reports noted previously.

In connection with the water resource study for the Senate Select Committee, referred to in Section 17.3.2, we noted that consumption rates for food and fiber were projected as one factor in estimating future needs for water for irrigation. The study provided some alternative levels. This author has not come across information indicating how much further the Select Committee carried its research. For fully informed policy making, we should be able to consider alternative investment programs

[16] Reported in Study Report 20 of the Outdoor Recreation Resources Review Commission (ORRRC), *Participation in Outdoor Recreation: Factors Affecting Demand Among American Adults* by Eva Mueller and Gerald Gurin.

[17] *National Recreation Survey*, Study Report 19 of the ORRRC.

and their potential impacts on public supplies of goods and services.[18]

Currently, in connection with attempts to reduce unemployment, the Federal Government is subsidizing several kinds of aid programs for unemployed workers who could obtain employment outside their home areas. The amounts of assistance vary from grants to cover all costs of moving the family and its effects and settling at the new location to partial loans at subsidized interest rates. Essentially, these are experiments in public investments in human resources.

18.2.2 Other Studies of Outdoor Recreation

The task of the Outdoor Recreation Resources Review Commission was identified by Hauser as seeking answers to these questions:

> What are the recreation wants and needs of the American people now and what will they be in the years 1976 and 2000? (2) What are the recreation resources of the nation available to fill those needs now and in the years 1976 and 2000? (3) What policies and programs should be recommended to insure that the needs of the present and the future are adequately and efficiently met?[19]

Hauser considered the problem of estimating future outdoor recreation needs to be:

> . . . a complex one involving the evaluation of a dynamic set of forces affecting leisure time activity as a whole and, within that framework, a dynamic set of forces affecting outdoor recreation activity, in general, and specific forms of such activity, in particular.

The general procedures used by the Commission and its collaborators to achieve its task may be described as follows. The present patterns of outdoor recreation activity were ascertained by means of an analysis of available administrative statistics and sample surveys of the outdoor recreational behavior of the general population. Trends in factors affecting demand for outdoor recreation facilities such as national income, hours of work, leisure time, consumer expenditures and the size and composition of the population were projected to the target dates. Differential outdoor recreational participation rates revealed by the outdoor recreation surveys, together with the projections of population and other relevant factors, provided a basis for gauging future demand for outdoor recreation resources.[20]

The demographic and ecological factors affecting the demand for outdoor recreation were examined by Hauser in some detail, separating their relationships to "resource-based areas," such as national parks and forests; intermediate recreation areas, e.g., state parks and reservoir areas; and "user-oriented areas," which are largely city, county, and regional parks.

> . . . The hard fact is that as a result of population growth, the resource-based recreation area can no longer make the full contribution to American leisure activity that was originally planned and hoped for it; and that this situation will inevitably grow worse rather than better. All that can be done is to alleviate the situation as much as possible.[21]
>
> . . . despite their obvious limitations, the intermediate type of recreation land must be regarded as the chief source of expanded outdoor recreation facilities which can be made available to most of the population, other than parks and recreation areas immediately within the urban setting. . . .[22]

Hauser noted that intermediate recreation areas cover about 9 million acres at the present time and provide about 0.05 of an acre per capita. With the increases in population, this provision of space for intermediate recreation purposes would shrink to about 0.03 by the year 2000. Clawson of the Resources for the Future estimates that an additional 1 to 5 million acres would be needed even now to meet the potential demand for recreation in such areas. By the year 2000, his estimate increases sixteenfold.

Perhaps the greatest shortage of recreational area space will be in the category identified as "user-oriented." Even to maintain present standards, it appears that city and county park area would have to be doubled within the next 40 years. But, meanwhile, it appears that the

[18] Further references: (*a*) For a thought-provoking article on a major form of public investment, see Gramm, Warren S. "Water Resource Analysis: Private Investment Criteria and Social Priorities," *J. Farm Economics* **45**:4:705–712, November 1963. (*b*) Pages 5–6 of a Senate Committee report on Water Resources indicate the close relationship between consumption projections and public investment. *Water Resources Activities in the United States: Land and Water Potentials and Future Requirements for Water*, Select Committee on National Water Resources, U.S. Senate, Eighty-sixth Congress; First Session, Committee Print No. 12.

[19] Page 28, Hauser, Philip M. "Demographic and Ecological Changes as Factors in Outdoor Recreation," pp. 27–59, *Trends in American Living and Outdoor Recreation*, ORRRC Study Report 22.

[20] *Ibid.*, page 28.

[21] *Ibid.*, page 42.

[22] *Ibid.*, page 43.

demand for user-oriented, close-in recreational areas may increase fourfold by the year 2000.

In the study cited here, Hauser examined differentials in attitudes and recreational activities of subsectors of the urban population—by region, residential type, race, and age. See ORRRC Report No. 22 for further details of his analysis.

Another study in the same report conceives outdoor recreation in "systems" terms. Perloff and Wingo view the core elements of outdoor recreation in terms of various recreation "populations," the outdoor recreational activities in which they participate, and the facilities which make their activities possible. They wrote:

> The first step, then, is to disaggregate the population into groups which are reasonably homogenous by criteria discussed below. These outdoor recreation groups are the basic units of the system, and are so drawn as to exhaust the population: every member of any population will fall into one of the boxes. Under this condition any change in group behavior identified by the criteria can be described as a shift among outdoor recreation classes and structural changes are defined out of the problem. The prediction of recreation behavior is then achieved by the process of assigning the members of a population to the outdoor recreation groups through estimates (1) of the characteristics of the new population increments and (2) of the probabilities that individuals will shift among the outdoor recreation classes in the interim.[23]
>
> The second set of elements is the broad array of outdoor recreation activities which people will pursue when opportunity permits. . . . In the system we are describing, activities are the fulcrum which fixes the overall relationship of the recreation propensities of outdoor recreation groups to the array of facilities which are in different degrees available to users. They relate in specific ways to the behavior patterns of the outdoor recreation groups and each has certain requirements for the nature of the facilities that support it. To make these relationships clear, outdoor recreation activities can be classified by some specific criteria. . . .[24]

These criteria include the skill requirements, the role of group participation, personal expenditure requirements, seasonal and climatic orientations, and kinds of facilities required for specialized activities.

[23] Page 88 of Perloff, Harvey S., and Wingo, Lowdon, Jr. "Urban Growth and the Planning of Outdoor Recreation," pp. 81–100 of *Trends in American Living and Outdoor Recreation*, ORRRC Study Report No. 22, Outdoor Recreation Resources Review Commission, Washington, D. C., 1962.

[24] *Ibid.*, page 89.

The third category of elements in the systems is the facilities.

> From the policy point of view, facilities for outdoor recreation have several key characteristics which influence the manner in which the system operates. A facility may be highly specialized in use, so that one, or at best, a few activities can be carried on in it. Unspecialized facilities permit several activities to be enjoyed concurrently by different users, where the activities are themselves unspecialized. A facility may be "multiple-purpose" in the sense that it is arranged to permit a number of specialized and unspecialized activities to be carried on simultaneously. The faciilty can be viewed as an intermediate product in the production of outdoor recreation services, which are consumed when the facility is used. Since the technology of this product is an essential feature of the system, it is useful to examine the nature of the inputs.[25]

The inputs include areas of land and water and capital investments in improvements. Location is not an input, but it greatly affects the intensity of use of facilities by influencing the recreational decisions of consumers.

> A systems-analysis approach to a problem requires a focus on the relationships which connect the elements of the system and which are the pathways by which changes are communicated among the elements. Effective public policy must work its purposes through these relationships. If the problem is seen to be one of relating a set of demand conditions to a set of supply conditions, these interactions stand in the place of the market. If the problem is basically construed as a matter of minimum standards of welfare, the interactions are the mechanism by which such an objective must be achieved. Both views might, of course, be applied.
>
> The outstanding feature of a system is the interdependence of its parts, and interdependence is abundantly apparent in the complex array of outdoor recreation demands, activities, and facilities across the Nation. . . .[26]
>
> . . . Thus, given the nature of the demand side of the market for an activity, as well as the number, sizes, and locations of facilities producing the relevant services, there is an equilibrium distribution of users among the facilities such that the quality of the service at any facility is valued by the user at the private costs associated with it. If all users valued the quality of service in the same way, and had common sets of private costs, there would be no economic problem, and where the number of users exceeded the capacity constraints some form of rationing would be required. As is more realistically the case, private costs vary tremendously, and uniformity in the manner in which people

[25] *Ibid.*, page 89.

[26] *Ibid.*, page 90.

appraise and evaluate quality in the recreation experience is an untenable assumption. The aggregate of demand is a summation across a mix of demanders who vary with respect to the private costs of the experience and quality valuation, so that, although the equilibrium condition is pertinent, it is also subject to the nature of the demand "mix."[27]

These then are some of the central economic characteristics of the system of outdoor recreation. It consists of facilities which produce the services of outdoor recreation, services whose quality declines (or whose implicit prices rise) with increasing density, and hence with intensity. These facilities turn out specific products at given locations. Further, the system includes a set of consumers with propensities to engage in certain kinds of recreation, budgets in both money and time, knowledge of alternatives, and an inclination to act rationally to maximize their net satisfactions. The location of all of the facilities and the residential locations of the users determine the distance costs, which relate the behavior of the consumers to the nature of the products of the various parts of the system. The scale of consumer behavior here is dominated by the severe peaking of demand and the extremely low load factors. . . . (Load factor: the ratio of average demand for all periods to peak period demand.)[28]

This double budget calculation exerts an important influence on the consumer decisions about outdoor recreation through its implications for the relative locations of facilities vis-à-vis the consumers. To engage in outdoor recreation generally involves travel to and from a facility, and this costs the consumer time and money, neither of which he can evade. Both the time-costs and the money-costs tend to be proportional to the distances involved, so that distance can be interpreted as a loose measure of the access costs confronting the user of a facility. Access costs can thus be taken as the principal variables within the system influencing user decisions about the consumption of outdoor recreation services.[29]

. . . In short, the function of the time-budget in the private costs of outdoor recreation and the dominance of access costs in the consumer decisions about recreation are salient features of recreation demand which require a dual accounting framework to organize these pertinent areas of information for purposes of analysis and projection.[30]

18.2.3 Economics of Education

Economists' interest in analysis of the relationship of education to economic growth and in study of a number of other economic aspects was reawakened in the 1950s. A number of researchers found that output per manhour had been increasing steadily in the United States over the preceding 50 years. The only reasonable explanation seemed to be that the heavy outlays by this country for education (both public and private) were, in effect, investments in human capital.

Professor Schultz stimulated a variety of research studies after he became interested in the economics of education. In one essay, Schultz discussed ". . . the proposition that people enhance their capabilities as producers and as consumers by investing in themselves and that schooling is the largest investment in human capital. . . ."[31] ". . . When viewed as economic attributes, the returns consist of satisfactions, a consumer component, and of acquired capabilities, a producer component. . . ."[32] Schultz includes estimates of earnings foregone along with direct private and public costs of education. But he does not subtract student earnings from his totals. Comparison of returns in the form of lifetime earnings, when properly discounted, with these costs indicates as high or higher a rate of return on education as on investment generally, according to Professor Schultz.

The satisfaction that people obtain from schooling is the consumption component. It consists of values associated with education that are not as a rule vocational, occupational, or professional. Schooling to acquire abilities to increase future earnings is not consumption. When it is consumption, its value can be moral, or a refinement in taste, or some other source of satisfaction. To the extent that schooling is a consumer "good," it is predominately an enduring component, even more enduring than most consumer durables. It is hard to find plausible examples of schooling that represent primarily present consumption. As an enduring consumption component, it is a source of future satisfactions which enhance future real income. But these satisfactions are not reckoned in *measured* national income.

Treating the expenditures for schooling as economists do other consumer expenditures opens the door for demand analysis to determine, among other things, both the price elasticity and the income elasticity for the demand for schooling. . . .[33]

[27] *Ibid.*, page 91.
[28] *Ibid.*, page 92.
[29] *Ibid.*, page 93.
[30] *Ibid.*, page 94.

[31] Page x, Schultz, Theodore W. *The Economic Value of Education.*
[32] *Ibid.*, page xi.
[33] *Ibid.*, page 8.

Schultz did not attempt to allocate costs of schooling between consumption and investment in earnings. But he does divide conceptually the contributions of schooling to consumption between those that serve consumption in the present and those that contribute to future consumption, thus being similar to investments.

If all the fruits of schooling enter directly into final consumption, additional schooling would not contribute to economic growth. . . . Only if schooling increases future productivity and earnings, do the contributions of schooling become a *source of measured economic growth*. . . .[34]

Denison has identified education as one of the major sources of economic growth.[35] He estimated that the increase in education has contributed about one-fifth of the growth rate from 1929 to 1957. Higher education also contributed substantially to the share of advance in knowledge, another one-fifth of total economic growth, because about half of the country's research is carried on by educational institutions.

Another facet of research on the economics of education with significant consumption aspects is illustrated by the following extract. It deals with the problems of estimating demand for college education and is taken from a paper by Alice Rivlin.

The first question which those who make decisions about education generally want answered is: How many students do we have to plan for? What will enrollment be 5 or 10 years from now? Perhaps because college enrollment has grown rapidly and fairly steadily for a good many years, educators have come to think of it as having an inexorable trend of its own with which they have to cope, rather than as something under their control. They have clamored for enrollment projections on which to base their future plans, and the Office of Education and others have attempted to produce such projections. The usual method has been to estimate enrollment ratios (college enrollment as a percentage of the population in the college age group, sometimes broken down by sex) for the recent past, to fit a trend to these ratios and project it into the future, and then apply the projected ratios to estimates of the college-age population in future years.[36]

Such trend projections can be useful if they are not taken too seriously, but several things about them should be remembered. One is that the tendency of young people to go to college is influenced by their family income, their parents' education, their estimates of job opportunities, and so forth, not just by the march of time. Projecting a time trend in enrollment is therefore a substitute for trying to estimate the effect of changes in these other variables. Furthermore, enrollment projections cannot be very useful to decision makers until they are broken down into different types of enrollment (full time and part time, graduate and undergraduate, etc.). . . .

Finally, and most important, enrollment itself depends on the policies adopted by educational institutions, particularly as to the level of tuition, the availability of scholarships and loans, the distribution of college facilities, and the type of education offered. When educators ask, "What is enrollment going to be?" they are really asking the wrong question. The right questions are, "What would enrollment be if certain policies were adopted?" and "What policies should be chosen in order to obtain the size and quality of college enrollment the Nation needs?"[37]

18.3 PUBLIC CONTROLS AND SUBSIDIES

Public decisions are continually being made regarding public controls and subsidies for production facilities or materials, controls over imports and subsidies for exports, and marketing services for the general public or for specific groups. Here are some specific examples: the national highway system, federally financed meat inspection, river and harbor improvement, public terminal markets, import quotas and tariffs, export subsidies for agricultural commodities and shipping services and air lines, and public market research for agricultural commodities and forest products.

---

[34] *Ibid.*, page 38.

[35] Page 266, Denison, Edward F. *Sources of Economic Growth in the United States and the Alternatives Before Us.*

[36] "For some refinements of this method, *see* Louis Conger, ch. 1 of this publication. Earlier examples include: Fund for the Advancement of Education, *Teachers for Tomorrow* (Fund for the Advancement of Education Bulletin No. 2), November 1955; Educational Policies Commission, *Higher Education in a Decade of Decision*, Washington, the Commission, 1957, p. 31; Ronald B. Thompson, 'Projected College Enrollments, 1950–1975' (by States), *College Blue Book*, ninth edition, 1959, p. 919–934."

[37] Pages 373–374 of Rivlin, Alice M. "Research in the Economics of Higher Education: Progress and Problems," Chapter 21 of Mushkin, Selma J. (Editor), *Economics of Higher Education*.

18.3.1 Assistance to Suppliers

The sequence for analysis of proposals for controls on production, distribution, prices, or for subsidies runs about as follows. In sizing up a problem described as affecting consumption rates of the general public unfavorably, we frequently find that the issue is basically a question of income to a group of suppliers. In some instances incomes may have declined because of failures or unwillingness of suppliers to adjust to changes in demand. In other cases technological or economic changes may have put a group of suppliers at great disadvantage.

Public-policy questions may also arise from the apparent need to protect the productive capacity in order to supply demand that will revive over the longer run or in emergencies, or there may have to be a decision between higher prices for consumers or subsidies from the public treasury or decreases in the supplies of a good or service desirable for welfare reasons (e.g., hospital services). Or the public through the Congress may be forced to consider gradual reduction in a favored position of one supplier or marketing group to bring it into line with other producer groups. The postwar struggles over agricultural price supports provide vivid examples. In assembling the data for such analyses, analysts generally work with consumption measured as close to the supplier level as possible. Production and marketing functions and costs are studied separately.

In formulating and testing hypotheses, trends and patterns in consumption of pertinent categories of goods are compared with variations in potentially important socioeconomic factors. Frequently, proposals are developed (and sometimes tested and adopted) to alter underlying factors or to change the relationship of a specified factor to consumption. Price discrimination in the form of special rates for certain sectors of a market is a favorite device. The variety of postal rates is a good example. Congressional hearings on proposals to change rates yield evidence of supplier interest. When the rates for educational materials are in question, publishers' representatives appear. When the rates for bulk mail are being reviewed, mail order firms, direct advertisers, and printing interests are well represented. Higher rates for such mail services are higher costs to such firms and change the ratio of their costs to expected returns. But a major argument used by such firms deals with the harm that increased mail charges would do to consumers, that is, to the public interest.

The School Milk Program provides another example of a program that combines price discrimination and subsidy and serves both producer interests and a consumer group. As milk production increasingly exceeded consumer demand in the late 1940s and early 1950s, butter, dried milk, and occasionally other dairy products were purchased by the U.S. Department of Agriculture (USDA) and were distributed to the School Lunch Program, some individual consumers, institutions, and to special foreign consumer groups. But fresh fluid whole milk yields a much higher return to producers. Therefore, producer groups, congressmen from the heavy milk-producing states, and the Department of Agriculture designed the School Milk Program, initiated in 1954. Under this program, consumption by school children is encouraged by selling fluid milk with school lunches and at nonmeal times with an average subsidy by the USDA of about three cents per half pint. Federal contributions to the School Milk Program increased from 60 million dollars in 1957 to 97 million dollars in the 1966 fiscal year.

A number of research studies have been financed by special funds from the act setting up the School Milk Program. Halvorson and Cook analyzed pupil response to price reductions for the whole Wisconsin public school system for a two-year span. They reached these conclusions:

(1) School children may be expected to buy about 40 percent more penny milk than they will buy of three-cent milk, and perhaps 10 to 20 percent more pupils will buy milk at the lower than at the higher price, when the decision to buy milk is not coupled with the decision to buy lunch. At price levels in between these extremes the response is roughly proportionate. Price response (both in terms of consumption per participating child and number of participants) was much less in the aggregate than under those experimental conditions where availability was improved and refrigeration was good.

(2) The seasonal pattern of consumption throughout the year tends to emphasize the importance of availability and refrigeration.

(3) Over the two year span, the initial responses to lowered prices were largely maintained as measured both by consumption per participant and by participation rates. Within matched schools as between the two years, the changes in consump-

tion per participating child associated with price reductions was negligible (in fact, response did not become positive until price was reduced as much as three cents). This is further evidence of persistency because the major price reduction had been made in most schools during the first of the two years. However, participation rates increased substantially.

(4) In the matched schools, consumption was greater for each month of the second year (1955–56) than for the same month a year earlier, up to March. This was true at each level of price reduction, but the increase tended to be greater where the reduction was as much as three cents per half pint.[38]

Johnson et al. summarized their intensive analysis of the effect of price on school milk consumption in Connecticut public schools:

The scope of the Program in Connecticut has continually increased since 1954. During the fiscal year 1959–60 it was estimated that $1,000,175 was expended in reimbursing 31.8 million half-pints of milk. During January 1960, low-cost milk was available through the Program in 76 percent of the 976 public grammar and high schools in Connecticut. Thirty-seven percent of the participating schools were enrolled in only the Special Milk Program, and 63 percent were enrolled in both the Special Milk Program and the School Lunch Program.

In this study it was found that the price elasticity demand for milk in grammar schools serving milk only at lunch time was approximately −.55. The demand for milk in the grammar schools offering milk during a morning milk break was relatively more elastic. The elasticity was −.98 in the 71 Connecticut grammar schools included in the sample. This indicates that in these schools a 10 percent reduction in the price would cause a 9.8 percent increase in milk consumption. Elasticity of demand for milk in the high schools offering hot lunches and a-la-carte milk ranged between −1.4 and −.47.

The free milk experiment indicated what the consumption rate would be when there is no charge to the students for milk. During the base period when milk was five cents per half-pint, the average daily per student consumption was .68 half-pint. The average daily consumption during the six-week period when free milk was available was 1.14 half-pints. The increase of 68 percent in consumption stemmed mainly from three sources: more students drank milk, less milk was brought from home, and more milk was consumed per student.

Increased availability of milk such as during a morning milk break appeared to be an effective way of increasing consumption, particularly in schools where a large percentage of the students go home for lunch.[39]

In studying the problems related to public controls and subsidies, we must use cross-section surveys to identify high and low consumers and to relate consumption of the commodity in question to other consumption rates. Key factors related to variations in consumption usually turn out to be income, urbanization, public welfare problems such as unemployment in economically depressed areas or special deficiencies in knowledge or information, family composition, or cultural background. Precise measurement of the relative importance of the major socioeconomic factors to the problem is rarely possible, but approximations by relatively unbiased analysts generally suffice. Analysis of these relationships should take into account historical changes, the current situation, and prospective changes under specified assumptions. These analyses should be carried to evaluation of alternative solutions with appraisals of costs and benefits and of potential effects of alternative programs on domestic consumption.

A good example of such an analysis is the study of alternative policies for expanding the demand for farm food products directed by Willard Cochrane under the auspices of the Interregional Committee on Agricultural Policy of the state agricultural experiment stations.[40] This study traced the history of proposals, policies, and the programs for expanding the demand for food in the United States from about 1930 into the 1950s. It identified the five major themes of proposals for increasing consumption as pertaining to income, price, nutrition, marketing, and the Malthusian population solution. The analysts

[38] Page 698, Halvorson, Harlow W., and Cook, Hugh L. "Pupil Response to Changes in School Milk Prices in Wisconsin," *J. Farm Economics* **XLII**:3:692-698, August 1960.

[39] Pages 27–28 of Johnson, Stewart, Brinegar, George K., Howes, Richard R., Maina, James W., and Lundquist, Lynwood. *Economic Analysis of the U.S. Special Milk Program with Particular Reference to Connecticut* (University of Connecticut), College of Agriculture, Agricultural Experiment Station Bulletin No. 356.

[40] Wetmore, John M., Abel, Martin E., Learn, Elmer W., and Cochrane, Willard W. *Policies for Expanding the Demand for Farm Food Products in the United States, Part I History and Potentials*, University of Minnesota Agricultural Experiment Station Technical Bulletin No. 231.

tested the possible effects of changes in income, and of improving the nutritional content of the diet by statistical manipulations of 1955 Household Food Consumption Survey data for quantities used, purchased, and matching money and nutrient values. These data were supplemented by estimates of price elasticities to test the effects of price changes. The estimated effects on food consumption were translated into farm resource use in order to evaluate their significance for farm policies.

Here are some of the conclusions:

Through the Income Approach

The estimates of food consumption potentials, where the income restriction is eased, yield hope for the complete elimination of surpluses by this route only at the higher levels of achievement considered. If incomes of all families with per capita incomes below $1,000 were raised above the $1,000 level, total consumption would increase 7.3 percent. Stated in terms of farm resources this would mean an increase of 7.1 percent in the resources employed in the production of food for domestic consumption. When viewed against the 8.0 percent diversion of resources required for elimination of surpluses this is almost sufficient to solve the problem. But the likelihood that the body politic of the United States would adopt a policy designed to accomplish such a level of achievement is exceedingly remote. *Such an operation would involve raising income for half the people in the United States.*

At a more realistic level of achievement, such as raising incomes for all families with per capita incomes below $500, the increase in total consumption amounts to only 2.4 percent. The utilization of farm resources would increase 2.2 percent or much less than would be required to fully utilize the surplus resources in agriculture. At this level of achievement about 18 percent of the population would be affected by the proposal.

There is little possibility that the surplus problem in agriculture can be fully alleviated by lifting the income restriction on food consumption for low-income families. However, a partial solution is available by this approach, and furthermore, the adoption of a policy to increase food consumption for low-income families may be justified on welfare considerations alone. The favorable effect on surpluses would lend further support.

Through the Price Approach

The estimates of food consumption potentials where retail prices of food are reduced suggest the possibility, although not necessarily the probability, of relatively large reductions in surpluses through the price reduction approach. The largest increase in farm resource use for the various levels of achievement considered is 5.9 percent. This occurs when the retail prices of all livestock and livestock products are reduced 20 percent. (The price reductions here and throughout this section refer to the 1955 level of retail prices.) The corresponding increase in the index of all food consumption is 3.3 percent. The discrepancy between the change in farm resource use and the food consumption potential exists primarily because livestock and livestock products receive a greater relative weight in the use of all farm resources than in a value-weighted index of consumption at retail. This, in turn, occurs because marketing margins for livestock products are, in general, less than for other foods.

A reduction in the retail price of all foods by 20 percent leads to a 4.6 percent increase in all food consumption and a 5.2 percent increase in the total employment of farm resources. Where the prices of all foods are lowered, as compared with price reductions on livestock and products alone, the substitution among food groups leads to a smaller increase in the consumption of high-resource-using livestock products—a change that is only partially offset by increases in the consumption of other lower-resource-using foods.

Retail price reductions of 10 percent result, of course, in much smaller changes in resource use. If all retail food prices are reduced 10 percent, the employment of farm resources increases only 2.4 percent. The corresponding figure where all livestock product prices are reduced is 2.6 percent. . . .

Through the Nutrition Approach

. . . the nutrition approach to demand expansion could also effect a relatively large reduction in surpluses at the highest level of achievement. Adjusting food consumption for all people to the liberal-cost diet plan would increase all food consumption by 2.3 percent. But the total resources employed in the production of civilian food supplies would increase 7.6 percent. As indicated in chapter VI, this significant difference between the increase in resource use and the increase in the food consumption potential is largely explained by the increased relative importance of livestock products in terms of farm resources and by the exclusion of sugars and sweets from the resource use calculations. Under the liberal-cost plan, consumption of sugars and sweets would decrease 18 percent.

Consumption adjustments to the moderate-cost diet plan would yield less satisfactory results with regard to surplus removal. In this case, all food consumption *decreases* 5.5 percent while farm resource use declines 0.4 percent. This more realistic level of achievement offers no hope for removing this surplus.

In terms of the nutrition approach, the realization of the food consumption potential at the liberal-cost level could eliminate the farm surplus problem in the United States as of 1955. But it seems doubtful that the consumption adjustments at this level of achievement would be acceptable under the banner of good nutrition. It means achieving the goal of nutritional adequacy at a high level of cost; it means programming to achieve nutritional adequacy by substituting a costly diet for cheaper diets.

The interdependence of the various approaches to demand expansion was discussed in Chapter V in connection with the income and nutrition approaches. Any proposal to increase consumption by easing the income restriction, or the price restriction, would undoubtedly improve nutrition levels, thereby lowering further the potential under the nutrition approach per se.[41]

18.3.2 National Policies Regarding Consumption Minima

Although policies and programs proposed and adopted to put a floor under consumption of food and other subsistence items are essentially welfare oriented, their significance for marketing and the pertinence of consumption analysis merit some consideration of them here. The Food Stamp Plan and public housing programs are good examples.

We begin by tracing steps in analysis of a proposal such as the Food Stamp Plan. In sizing up the problem, we must ask: Is the policy proposed on grounds of public welfare or to benefit a group of suppliers such as farmers? Are rates of consumption of some significant groups of families in the population below levels recommended for health, such as the National Research Council's recommended dietary allowances, or below publicly accepted levels for decency?

Hypotheses are formed from such a question as this: Are the low levels of consumption by some families the result of their free choices or do they result from lack of purchasing power or lack of knowledge? Then variations in consumption rates must be studied to answer: Who is high and low in consumption of this commodity as opposed to that one? What proportion of the income of this group of families or that group is allocated to each commodity group? To other goods and services? What scientific knowledge is available that can provide criteria for judging the adequacy of rates of consumption of a given commodity? What are the variations in consumption measured in quantities, in value terms?

[41] *Ibid.*, pp. 98–100.

Next comes the job of relating socioeconomic factors to observed patterns. In addition to income, urbanization, and regionality, we often note possible effects of lack of education, age and size composition of families, health and living conditions, outside employment of homemaker, and occupational history. We must evaluate the relative importance of these key factors in the past, in the current situation, and expected in the future, based on specified assumptions.

When most of the components of the problem have been analyzed, researchers are faced with evaluation of possible alternative solutions in the forms of policies or programs. They must consider the impact of possible minimum levels of consumption on available supplies of the commodity, on government budgets, and the feasibility of administering the alternative programs. One part of the study must be analysis of the possible effects of subsidizing a minimum level of consumption of one commodity group on expenditures for other goods and services. The political feasibility of introducing a program favoring one sector of the population is outside the consumption analyst's technical competence, but it is highly pertinent to the final decision on the solution to the problem he is studying.

The demand expansion research carried on under Cochrane's direction at the Minnesota Agricultural Experiment Station included a study of alternative programs, prepared by Martin Abel.[42] This study reviewed social, political, and administrative considerations related to past and potential demand expansion programs. It outlined provisions for a food allotment program modeled along the lines of the Food Stamp Plan that operated in the late 1930s, a compensatory payments program, an indemnity price program, and several ways of implementing the nutrition approach. Using the 1955 Household Food Consumption Survey data, program costs were estimated and the impact of demand expansion programs on farm resource uses was evaluated. Its general conclusions were:

> Demand expansion programs provide a means for partially eliminating surplus agricultural production.

[42] Abel, Martin E., and Cochrane, Williard W. *Policies for Expanding the Demand for Farm Food Products in the United States, Part II Programs and Results,* University of Minnesota Agricultural Experiment Station Tech. Bulletin No. 238.

Total food consumption is highly price and income inelastic. Large changes in food prices or consumers' incomes are needed to achieve a small increase in total food consumption. At best, reasonable levels of expenditures on the demand expansion approach would reduce the agricultural surplus by about one-fourth to one-third. The former estimate is possibly the most realistic.

The goal of improved nutrition dictates a preference ordering of the programs presented in this analysis. Within the imposed cost restrictions, the programs that most effectively attack the problem of nutritional shortages are most desirable. Consequently, the National School Lunch and Special Milk Program have top priority. These programs directly attack the problem of nutritional shortages. Moreover, they operate for the benefit of the group most sensitive to the ill effects of nutritional shortages (i.e., the Nation's children of elementary and secondary school age).

Next in order of preference is the Food Allotment Program. It, too, is directed at a segment of population exhibiting the highest incidence of nutritional shortages; namely, low-income consumers. It does not attack the nutrition problem as directly as the National School Lunch or Special Milk Programs because income is not the only restraint to good nutrition.

Finally, the Indemnity Price Program is the least preferred of the programs presented. It does not directly come to grips with the problem of nutrition. It operates for the benefit of all consumers rather than for those with the largest incidence of nutritional shortages.

The people of the United States are, in general, well fed. Improving consumer diets will not result in major or even moderate increases in food consumption. The extent to which demand expansion efforts can reduce the agricultural surplus depends in large measure on how seriously the public views the problem of nutritional shortages and the amount it is willing to spend to remedy this problem through increased food consumption.[43]

18.4 FOREIGN AID TO DEVELOPING COUNTRIES

Most United States aid to the developing countries has been in the forms of food and military assistance. Agricultural and food aid are discussed in Section 17.4. The importance to the United States of increasing consumption levels in the developing countries has been noted in Section 4.7. Here we will consider consumption aspects of two other types of foreign assistance programs. One of these is in the form of helping develop economic analyses needed for allocation of national resources among investments in industries producing different kinds of consumer goods. The second is related to housing.

18.4.1 Studies for Resource Allocations

More specifically, problems of resource allocations include determination of the optimum balances between food and nonfood goods and services, between agriculture and other basic resource industries and the manufacturing and distribution industries; among current consumption, national defense, and private and public investment; and among population groups based on area, economic occupation, and economic wealth. A description of the steps in the process of analyzing the allocation of resources between agricultural and industrial development illustrates the analytical process for study of such problems.

The research team begins by assembling information on the current economic structure of the country, using national income accounts and all available data on levels of living of major sectors of the population and on historical trends in patterns of consumption of agricultural and nonagricultural products. It is helpful to compare such information with data for several other countries with generally similar socioeconomic background and at least as far along the road to economic development.

Tentative hypotheses must be developed which indicate potential economic trends relating to consumption and marketing with and without government or organized business intervention. Other hypotheses should set forth the possible impacts on consumption and marketing of alternative allocations of additional resources through such intervention.

The necessary detailed and reliable information on consumption patterns for foods and for nonfood goods and services of major population groups and on their sources of supplies must come from sample surveys covering various parts of the country. Survey techniques must be adapted to institutions of the country, especially if information on subsistence supplies is to be satisfactory. With such survey data the researchers can identify and measure the relationships of key factors such as availability of supplies, regionality, urbanization, and income to current and prospective consumption patterns.

Evaluation of possible alternative decisions usually requires preparation of alternative sets

[43] *Ibid.*, page 76.

of projections regarding economic growth, industrialization, production, development of marketing institutions, demand of population groups, and related consumption rates at specified stages in later development. In research on consumption and marketing, careful attention must be given (1) to contrary trends in subsistence and commercial production and to requirements for developing the infrastructure of marketing facilities, and (2) to administrative and informational programs necessary to redirect and restrain consumer demand as purchasing power is expanded. It is highly desirable to organize supply and consumption projections under each alternative decision in terms of ranges, with indications of factors determining where in the ranges the actual rates might occur.

The present food situation in India, noted in Chapter 4, and the political nature of the decision-making process for the Five-Year Plans[44] indicate the problems involved in allocating resources among sectors in an economy. Although the Five-Year Plans included reference to raising food consumption levels, the investments in agriculture were not sufficient to yield the increases in output needed to feed the increasing population. Foreign experts have repeatedly recommended greater investment in agriculture at the expense of the more prestigious investment in heavy industry. Apparently, even greater consideration should be given to the development of marketing facilities and institutions. Whereas emergency food aid from the United States can substitute for domestically produced grains and milk, there is no substitute for docks, other transportation and storage facilities, processing facilities for domestic fruits and vegetables, and wholesaling and retailing facilities and expertise. India's inadequate marketing system overprices its services, thus discouraging consumption by poorer people. It deters production changes by failing to reward efficient agricultural producers and encourage specialization.

India has some outstanding economists and statisticians, and some major efforts have gone into developing sample data on food production and consumption. But the findings do not appear to have been sufficiently focused as yet on the major investment decisions. Apparently, the 1965–1967 food crisis is forcing a reexamination of the alternatives. Further information on such problems of economic balances and on the Indian food outlook can be found in the references cited.[45] The National Council of Applied Economic Research has reported findings from a study financed with Indian counterpart funds derived from sale of PL 480 commodities. The underlying American objective was to obtain information useful in forecasting future commercial demand in India for American farm commodities.

[44] Letwin, William. "What's Wrong with Planning: The Case of India," *Fortune* **LXVII**:6:118–121, June 1963.

18.4.2 Housing Aid Programs

A limited program directed at improved housing and environmental conditions is one part of the Alliance for Progress program. Most of the other direct United States assistance to housing has been in the form of contributions to U.N. technical advice, which Abrams sums up as "telling officials to do what they are in no position to do."[46] (Abrams has frequently served as a United Nations and United States consultant to the missions to developing countries.) However, United States financial contributions represent 35 to 40 percent of U.N. funds for technical assistance. Abrams has identified the following reasons for the lack of constructive aid to housing and urbanization: overemphasis on defense and prestige projects based on self-interest or self-protection; frustration arising from the magnitude of the problems encountered; vagueness of the ideas on the priorities; unawareness of the problems and of possible alternatives; international competitiveness; unwillingness to assume responsibilities and inexperience in dealing with urbanization problems; and international parsimony.[47]

Available information on housing and environment planning in relation to foreign assistance programs indicates much less analysis of both the supply and demand aspects than

[45] Johnston, Bruce F., and Mellor, John W. "The Nature of Agriculture's Contributions to Economic Development," *Food Research Institute Studies* **I**:3:335–356, November 1960.

National Council of Applied Economic Research (India) *Long Term Projections of Demand for and Supply of Selected Agricultural Commodities, 1960–61 to 1975–76*, New Delhi, April 1962 (in cooperation with U.S. Department of Agriculture).

[46] Page 243 of Abrams, Charles. *Man's Struggle for Shelter in an Urbanizing World.*

[47] *Ibid.*, page 244.

has been made for agricultural and food aid programs. The need for such analyses, if foreign assistance is to be effective and efficient, is obvious. The author has gleaned the following essential steps from international reports and Abrams' book:

1. Study of a developing country's needs and priorities requires solid information on current supplies of housing and environmental services in terms of quantity and quality related to present and potential demand of major sectors of the population. According to Abrams:

> After World War II, every American embassy and consulate throughout the world was required to supply the government with information on housing conditions, laws, and policies in the country in which it was situated. The product, varying greatly in quality, represented at least the first contemporaneous compilation of housing conditions and policies in the world, but it was never publicized or evaluated. To fill this gap, therefore, the U.S. State Department should order new studies. Furthermore, existing studies at the United Nations and elsewhere should be withdrawn from the archives, evaluated, and released.
>
> Foreign business firms and their field executives can be useful to U.N. missions and aid programs. They play an important part in a country's economic development; their executives are trained, remain for long periods, and learn the customs, problems, and language. They are often influential in local business circles and in government. But the services of those who might be willing to help are rarely solicited by the aid agencies or embassies. Most British and American businessmen who would happily donate their services at home to such organizations tend to be indifferent or isolated in the underdeveloped areas. A large British-based international corporation in Ghana thought its obligation for the country's progress was settled when it made a gift of a small playground. It could have contributed much more by helping to organize a thrift association, which it was asked to do and refused.[48]

2. A comprehensive evaluation needs to be made of each country's laws and regulations and enforcement practices as well as its institutions related to land use, financing urbanization improvements, and security of tenure.

3. The current situation and outlook for the supply and marketing of resources required for construction of housing, water, sewage, transportation, and other environmental construction projects must be appraised. Such appraisals require knowledge of the country's public and private capital market, its materials industries, and labor market as well as knowledge of the status of construction technology, particularly in the urban areas.

4. An essential prerequisite to commitment of foreign aid to a developing country for housing and environmental improvements must be the development and adoption of laws, regulations, and institutions which will be supportive of rational, orderly changes. Abrams writes:

> There are many reforms that seem trivial but lie at the root of capital shortage for building. The institution of title registration systems is one. The improvement of foreclosure laws is another. This reform is needed because the failure to give mortgagees reasonable rights upon default may be the main block to mortgage lending. And the home buyer pays the penalty. Revision of rent controls is another imperative. A private entrepreneur will not build an apartment house, nor will a bank finance it, if the allowable rent is inadequate or is likely to become so because of currency inflation. When rent controls are taken off new buildings, initial rents may be high for a time, but the supply of dwellings will be increased and will ultimately help ease the shortage. Rent controls on existing buildings should simultaneously be revised to allow owners adequate returns on investment and reasonable compensation for repairs and improvements. Controls on industrial and commercial properties that impede industrial settlement should be relaxed. Regulations should be clear and independent of the *ad hoc* decisions of administrators. Quick reviews of determinations should be provided, and the myriad loopholes that now permit the practice of chicane by landlord and tenant should be plugged. Here foreign specialists can be of inestimable value in helping to clear the way for international loans. Their recommendations not only can point the way for action but, when publicized, can ease the political pressures that keep officials from recommending what they know is the right policy.[49]
>
> Unless a constructive land policy is adopted by underdeveloped countries, aid money for urban development will be wasted. The solution of the land cost problem can be achieved more practically by national policy than by international monetary aid. Thus international aid for urban development and housing should be conditioned upon urban land reform.
>
> A direct loan to the Philippines for a housing program, for example, would see most of its proceeds going into the hands of land speculators

[48] *Ibid.*, pp. 255–256.

[49] *Ibid.*, pp. 263–264.

Since loans used to fatten their purses would serve no national or international purpose, a major revision of Philippine land policy would have to be a condition of any aid given for home building or utility development. This should not, however, preclude loans for land improvements, the development of the country's materials industries, or for housing in localities where the cost of undeveloped land is, say, 10 to 20 percent of total home cost.

A proper land policy should aim to bring more land into use at reasonable prices and to permit public purchase when essential, particularly for lower-income housing.

Lack of a land policy is due partly to the fact that industrially less developed countries are also politically underdeveloped. Relationships between government and enterprise have not yet matured, and eminent domain, realistic taxation, and even reasonable regulation are still viewed in some quarters as invasions of property rights.

An ad valorem tax on land (such as that levied on all land by cities in the United States) would discourage withholding land and put more on the market. It would not only reduce prices and check a powerful inflationary force but also encourage subdivisions for moderate- and lower-income families, help relieve the squatter problem, and provide important revenue.

Simultaneously, legislation should authorize special assessments for streets, utilities, roads, and other public improvements from which benefits accrue to owners. . . .[50]

5. Frequently, it has been found that special programs are needed if supplies of labor and capital are to meet additional requirements. These may include special training programs for construction workers and small contractors, building credit, and technical assistance as well as investments in materials-producing industries.

6. A number of schemes have been used to subsidize part of the construction of private homes in the less-developed countries. One is the building of cores with water, sewage connections, and electrical facilities. Another is the provision of roofs, doors, and windows. Still another has been to supply water, sewage, and electrical lines to the new housing areas, leaving connections to the central system to be made by the homebuilders.

Abrams argues for making international loans to individual countries for specified uses, such as home construction for low-income families at low rates of interest (as needed in Jamaica), to finance utilities and house cores (as in the case of Pakistan), for self-help housing (such as in Chile), to thrift associations with limitations on interest rates (as needed in Peru); for construction of transportation, utility, and sewage facilities, and for regional centers for design and building research.

Such loans might well be contingent on institution of measures for curbing speculation and accelerating land use, including zoning; charges to new owners for new roads, streets, sewers, and other property improvements; and laws and regulations to force development of areas designated as ripe for development with penalty of the institution of special taxes for failure to put the property to adequate use.[51]

In sum, the potential demand for housing and environmental services at prices with alternative degrees of subsidy must first be estimated. Then, government agents and private businessmen must be encouraged and prodded to improve the supply and market situation so that families with limited incomes can buy, first, minimum housing such as the cores, and then supplement the minimum with their own work or with later additions and improvements. Thus higher levels of housing consumption can be reached through combinations of foreign and local government assistance and commercial and subsistence efforts in the local areas.

18.5 FOREIGN TRADE AND DOMESTIC CONSUMPTION

Foreign trade affects consumption levels in three ways—through purchasing power earned by families, via prices and supplies of goods and services, and through political and welfare developments.

18.5.1 Appraisal of the American Situation

Two ideas are basic to the appraisal of economic effects of foreign trade on incomes earned. The first of these is that incomes are higher as foreign trade increases. The second is that the best customers for our products are the more highly developed and the higher-income countries.

Why are incomes higher as foreign trade increases? Imports add to the total supply of goods and services available for purchase and therefore to real incomes, especially in a full employment economy. Foreign trade helps

[50] *Ibid.*, page 264.

[51] *Ibid.*, page 265.

direct our productive resources toward output of commodities and services for which our land, labor, and capital have the highest rates of productivity. Explanations of the economics of this process are readily available in general economics texts and in books on international trade. The author illustrated the multiplier effect of foreign trade on the American economy for an Oregon audience as follows: Let us take the Libby plant in Portland which cans pears, as an example. Suppose some are for export to England. Libby buys pears, tin cans, sugar, cardboard boxes, and other materials for, say, $50,000 and it sells the canned pears for, let's say, $100,000. The $50,000 differential received by Libby goes for wages and salaries, overhead, and profits. Joe Jones who works at Libby's buys food, clothing, and pays on his house with his weekly pay check. The supermarket where he buys his food pays its employees, and then in turn they buy consumer goods and services. So income is generated by that Libby sale of canned pears to England.

In 1962 the Department of Commerce issued information based on its survey of manufacturers to obtain data on their 1960 export shipments and on some research by the Departments of Labor and Agriculture. In connection with this study the Bureau of Labor Statistics estimated "that the employment required in exporting the more than $20 billion of merchandise exported from this country in 1960 was the equivalent of 3.1 million jobs," on a man-year basis in production, transportation, and marketing of goods for export.[52] About half of these workers were engaged directly in production and handling of products and half in the supporting industries providing supplies and equipment used in production and handling. But the estimate does not include employment in the production of food consumed by workers in the export industries, for example. These 3.1 million jobs represented 5.8 percent of all jobs in the private economy, including 13 percent of farm jobs.[53]

Imports of goods for consumption in 1965 totaled about $21 billion, in comparison with $27 billion exported. According to traditional terminology, this represents a "favorable balance of trade." That concept was based on the idea of exporting to bring back more gold, rather outdated in a high employment economy when an increasing supply of gold means inflation of prices because goods and services are not thereby increased except through the multiplier effect.

The theory of comparative advantage or comparative costs underlies economists' appraisal of the advantages of importing supplementary goods and services which can substitute in varying degrees for American products. These include such items as aluminum, tin, chrome, carpet wools, Swiss watch movements, cane sugar, and corned beef. Few people argue against the importance of complementary goods like coffee, tea, cocoa, oriental rugs, Thai silk, Scotch whiskey, or services like a two-week vacation in Japan. True enough, Scotch whiskey competes with Kentucky Bourbon for some consumers' dollars but not for others.

Ricardo showed that it was *not* the actual costs in labor and other productive resources for food and clothing that determine the advantages but the *ratio* of costs for food and clothing in two or more countries. This is explained in detail in every economic principles text, but the reader will see it most clearly if you think of the allocation of time in your own household. Many homemakers could process most of their own food, but they do not because they believe their time is better spent on professional or voluntary work. Most professional people concentrate on their jobs and buy their canned pears. Thus they specialize.

It is certainly to the advantage of the United States public to have United States producers specialize in what they can produce most efficiently. Consumers want to buy commodities of desired quality as cheaply as possible, e.g., transistors, burlap, and firecrackers. The theory of comparative advantage can also be described as the theory of greatest relative efficiency. Consumers and producers both benefit from specialization in commodities yielding the highest output for the inputs. Consumers buy at cheaper prices and producers make higher wages or profits or rent. This explains why most economists favor free trade. With free trade American consumers can get both more food and more clothing.

Many of our American industries are operating at levels of production where increased volume can lower the cost per unit. This is

[52] From page 5, *Export Origin Study, State of Oregon*, U.S. Department of Commerce, 1962.

[53] Page 9 of *The American Worker's Stake in Foreign Trade*, U.S. Department of Labor, 1962.

particularly true in the industries producing machinery and mass-produced goods, requiring heavy capital investment which can be spread over more units of output. United States consumers benefit when the volume of output in decreasing cost industries is increased by export demand.

Most people like to have somewhat different packages of clothing and household goods than their neighbors. Some prefer oriental rugs, others broadloom carpeting, others colonial hooked rugs, some Numdah rugs. Often American mass producers cannot be bothered with the full range of variations desired, so our gift shops buy imported items. Also, some commodities like tropical foods are simply not produced in this country, except in Hawaii. Consumers clearly benefit from a range of choice to supplement mass-produced commodities, many of which are relatively inexpensive at the middle range of quality.

The effect of the law of comparative advantage on foreign trade is indicated by the following quotation from Wayne Darrow's *Washington Farm Letter* of October 2, 1964. The author quotes from page 4: "The purpose of the Wool Act of 1954 was to expand production of wool and mohair and increase their domestic consumption. . . . All the increase in consumption of apparel wool came from imports of wool and woolen products from 1954 through 1962." Even Federal subsidies amounting to $30 out of every $100 received by wool producers have not been sufficient to offset the impact of comparative advantage on our relatively high-cost wool producers. The American public has paid for these incentive payments through Federal taxes.

Foreign trade contributes to both internal and international peace. Our imports and exports significantly affect incomes in the developing countries. Hopelessness and the great inequality in levels of living of the less-developed countries lead to extensive thievery and internal strife. People with an increasing level of income and with hope for their families' futures do not risk war and are eager to preserve the gains, providing they have sufficient perspective and are aware of the realities of modern warfare.

Let us now take a longer perspective. Can Americans continue to become relatively more affluent in relation to the poverty in which perhaps two-thirds of the world's population lives? According to some data from the United Nations, countries with about 70 percent of the world's population received less than 25 percent of the total income of the world in 1957–1959. The survival of future generations of Americans may depend on our contributions to changing this situation. Such extreme levels of poverty lay the groundwork for extreme efforts to achieve higher levels of living.

One argument against free trade is that the United States needs a minimum base in industries having strategic importance for defense. This is one of the arguments made for the present tariff on watches. Also, it has been an argument for subsidizing the United States merchant fleet. But this argument does not appear pertinent to the present 40 percent tariff on some plastic items such as those made by Dupont. The Dupont firm is not an infant industry, and it is not likely to disappear if tariff protection were withdrawn.

18.5.2 International Comparisons

As individual countries evolve new forms of economic interrelationships with other countries, consumption studies are required to make comparisons in levels of living, to provide factual data to resolve conflicts over trade and tariff policies, to identify economic needs of less-developed countries, and in connection with international defense planning and the economic and political communities among countries.

Consumption analyses for these problems follow the general outline used for comparisons of current levels of consumption and projections for the European Economic Community.[54] The researchers assembled each country's historical series and cross-section data on personal incomes and on expenditures and consumption for major categories of foods and for all goods and services, plus retail price data and information for construction of quantity and price indexes. They analyzed price and income elasticities and the Engel curves for major commodities. They developed tentative hypotheses regarding the most important factors entering into future trends, such as income, population growth, lowering tariff barriers, other supply changes, and overall economic trends.

To describe pertinent consumption patterns,

[54] Communauté Économique Européenne *Le marché commun des produits agricoles: Perspectives "1970,"* Étude Serie Agriculture Nr. 10.

many adjustments of historical national data were needed to achieve comparability. Some special surveys were made with community encouragement. The relationships of key factors to those patterns were examined. Factors in food patterns were historical supply and price relationships reflected in national and regional consumption variations, as well as income and urbanization. The relative importance of each key factor was appraised.

Projections from the three-year period centered on 1958 to the three-year period, 1969–1971, with the average identified as "1970," were developed under given assumptions regarding changes in key factors. The projections for consumption for major commodities for each country and for the six were compared with projections of agricultural production for each commodity group. Adjustments were made in line with the basic assumption that a series of approximations based on statistical and economic analyses would yield the most reliable results. Finally, the implications of the projected production–consumption balances for prices, imports, and the agricultural economy were identified and considered.

APPENDIX A

OUTLINE AND GUIDE TO PROCEDURES FOR OBTAINING AND USING SURVEY DATA

A.1 RELATIONSHIP OF SCIENTIFIC APPROACH TO RESEARCH PROCEDURES

A.1.1 Analytical Procedures for Use with Survey Data Rest on Assumptions of Orderliness, Interrelationships, and Change

Collection of data must be planned on the basis of careful formulation or definition of both the problem being studied and the hypotheses regarding its solution. The soundest procedures will be those which are tailored most carefully to use (*a*) available measures of established constructs concurrently with exploratory work on new measures and accumulated knowledge of interrelationships, (*b*) the phases in consumers' decision making on buying and use of products, and (*c*) observable variations in characteristics of consumers.

A.1.2 Development of Additional Information Should Start from the Current Accumulation of Knowledge

(1) Painstaking library search for published research reports usually yields valuable guidance to data and/or procedures for obtaining data pertinent to the problem at hand.

(2) For most problems, general background data are available in government publications such as the Censuses of Population, Agriculture, Business, and Manufactures, or in reports of large-scale surveys of consumption (by the U.S. Department of Agriculture and the U.S. Bureau of Labor Statistics), or in reports of special market surveys (by the U.S. Bureau of the Census, U.S. Department of Agriculture, or U.S. Department of Commerce). The first place to look for Federal statistics is in the *Statistical Abstract of the United States*, an annual summary issued by the Bureau of the Census. It updates *Historical Statistics of the United States, Colonial Times to 1957*. Annual compilations of agricultural data are issued in *Agricultural Statistics*, and business and national income and expenditure data are in supplements to the *Survey of Current Business*. The quarterly situation and outlook reports of the Economic Research Service, USDA, frequently list new publications of data and research studies pertinent to agricultural commodities.

Guidance to business and trade association sources, as well as government data, is provided by the Bibliography Series of the American Marketing Association. See, for example, Edgar Gunther and Frederick A. Goldstein, *Current Sources of Marketing Information*, American Marketing Association Bibliography Series No. 6.

A.1.3 Significance of Social Science Concepts

(1) The interaction of socioeconomic and psychological elements in consumer behavior requires cooperative efforts of specialists from the several disciplines in most stages of problem solving. Planning for collection of data cannot be left to the sampling or survey statisticians for they are rarely trained in the subtle meanings of economic, sociological, and psychological concepts sufficiently to think through their possible ramifications in application to particular problems. It is very unusual for a person to be familiar with research literature in more than one discipline. For example, a marketing economist must work with the sampling statistician in designing a sample for a survey of food marketing practices. This is particularly true when cost limitations dictate the survey of representative areas rather than random samples of a whole region, for instance.

(2) Cooperation of people with varied backgrounds is particularly valuable in development of questionnaires. For example, nutritionists are not generally aware of the complexity of the problem of obtaining data on why children eat the way they do. They do not know how the complex concept of motivation affects formulation of questions on homemakers' reasons for buying particular

foods in particular forms. Analysis of the "whys" of consumer decisions and consumption patterns requires information on the socioeconomic characteristics of individual families or other social groups involved. Psychologists rarely know more than a few standard questions to use in determining the purchasing power or incomes of consumers. This is an area in which economists have special know-how. Rarely is an economist or a psychologist equipped to devise new approaches to investigate social status. But the sampling statistician usually insists on certain questions about race or occupation or housing facilities in order to check the final sample against the information he has for the universe being sampled.

(3) The whole process of planning for collection of data is greatly affected by the decisions on what aspects of the consumption problem should be studied. These are reflected in the initial hypotheses to be tested. The analysts who will use the data should participate in or be represented in formulation and development of the survey plans. Full participation of the several social sciences in the planning stage of data collection is especially important because it is generally impossible to go back to respondents when an analyst later finds vital data to be missing.

(4) Many concepts from the social sciences, such as those summarized in Chapters 5, 6, and 7, are used in the process of analyzing data bearing on a problem. Such concepts enter into the determination of interrelations of the parts of consumption patterns, e.g., certain foods are used primarily for breakfast (breakfast cereals), others are used extensively by children. Based on earlier research and economic theory, an analyst expects to find significant variations in consumption of high-priced items with variations in income. So he arranges his data to sort out such relationships. Such seeking for patterns is common to analytical procedures used by each type of social scientist. Ordinarily, each scientist relies mostly on the basic concepts and procedures of his own discipline.

A.2 BRIEF DESCRIPTION OF SURVEY PROCEDURES

INTRODUCTORY NOTE. The objective of this section is to provide both an overall view of a very complex subject and references for further study. Practically every marketing specialist, social scientist, and home economist makes use of survey data at least occasionally in his or her professional life. Increasing use of consumer surveys in business and government has resulted in demand for knowledge, at least general knowledge, of the subject in order to work on research teams and to use research data more intelligently. Before undertaking work on a survey, the research team should have defined its problem, developed its working hypotheses, and checked on published research and other projects currently under way. Chapters 5, 6, and 7 of this book are concerned with understanding the social science aspects of consumer behavior pertinent to microeconomic problems of consumption. Section 8.1 provides an introduction to problem solving.

A.2.1 Development of an Overall Research Plan

(1) *Reason.* To force agreement of the research group and those requesting research on the nature of the problem, operational approach, time schedule, resources to be allocated to the job, and expectations regarding results.

(2) *Content.* (a) Objectives of the investigation stated realistically and operationally and their relationships to the problem clarified, (*b*) description of the general approach and of methods to be used to attain each of the objectives, (*c*) general description of the types of data to be obtained and the form in which they will be summarized, (*d*) time schedule for each stage, (*e*) administrative plan including personnel needs and their responsibilities and budget proposals, and (*f*) tentative plans for preparation and presentation of final report.

(3) *Methods.* Such plans may be developed by group action or by a project leader based on conferences with technical personnel experienced in the problem area. Reference to market research cases and texts and to books on survey methodology is an obvious way to develop background knowledge and to avoid at least some of the pitfalls so common in consumer market research.

(4) *References for further information:*

(*a*) Alevizos, John P. *Marketing Research*, pp. 29–47. (A useful casebook in marketing.)

(*b*) American Marketing Association. *The Design of Research Investi-*

gations, Marketing Research Techniques Series No. 1.

(*c*) American Marketing Association. *The Technique of Marketing Research,* Chapter I. (Standard and good.)

(*d*) Parten, Mildred. *Surveys, Polls, and Samples,* Chapter II. (Out of print but very readable, worth a trip to the library.)

(*e*) Ferber, Robert, Blankertz, Donald F., and Hollander, Sidney, Jr. *Marketing Research,* Chapters 7 and 8.

A.2.2 Identification of the Universe To Be Studied

(1) The term *universe* refers to the total population of units to be studied. Is it all people in the United States, or all housekeeping households, or all housekeeping households in one area, or those with young children, or those consumers who might shop in a given store? The answers must come from consideration, first, of the problem, and then of feasibility within limitations of costs and time. Sampling is usually necessary, but the sample must be drawn so as to provide indications of each key characteristic of the whole population of the universe.

(2) In planning the approach for the study, one must consider who can supply the desired information about the universe. Business firms have information about production or total sales of particular items. If a large proportion of their sales is to charge-customers, they can check on the residence and occupation of these purchasers. But their detailed knowledge of other characteristics of purchasers and of the whys of such purchases is limited and often imprecise. To get such information, one must contact households or individuals with the characteristics pertinent to one's problem.

(3) Care must be taken to include the whole population and not to bias the study from the very beginning. For example, a survey of department store buyers can yield no information about people who buy from specialty stores or mail order houses.

(4) Reference: Huff, Darrell. *How to Lie With Statistics,* Chapter I.

A.2.3 Alternative Survey Methods

(1) *Personal interviews* are conducted by trained *interviewers* with selected individuals, called *respondents.* Selection of people to be interviewed may be made by a sampling expert in the survey office or by the interviewer using precise instructions. People may be interviewed at home, at work, in special offices, on the street, etc. Interviewers ordinarily use a specially developed *questionnaire* to read off the questions and record answers. Most people are willing to cooperate in personal interviews. Personal interviews yield the most correct information of any survey method other than controlled experiments. But they are expensive because of higher time and travel costs. Call backs to get supplementary information add substantially to costs.

(2) *Observational methods* are used by market researchers, especially to discover on-the-spot reactions of shoppers to advertisements, displays, new products, and selling techniques. Trained observers may classify and record reactions, or automatic recording devices such as candid cameras may be used, as in surveys for shoplifters.

(3) *Telephone interviews* are widely used to obtain information on a few selected questions. They are particularly popular for radio and TV audience checks and are inexpensive and quick. But some well-to-do people and public figures have unlisted telephone numbers, and many low-income people do not have telephones. Therefore the sample may easily be biased. Because of frequent telephone solicitation under pretense of interviewing, refusals are increasing. Also, people object to detailed interviewing, may give unreliable answers, and do not want to be bothered with sensitive or complex questions.

(4) *Mail questionnaires* are widely used and widely criticized. They may be sent out from the survey office or published in news media, or attached to products. Mailing costs are relatively low, and the questionnaires can reach all kinds of people. But people do not have to fill them out nor mail them back. People who return them are rarely representative of the whole group contacted. However, new systems of follow-ups can raise the response rate well above the usual 10 to 20 percent. Even so, it is difficult to check responses to get incomplete schedules filled out.

(5) *Radio and TV appeals* usually rely on prizes for respondents. They can provide helpful information on listening and viewing habits and audience reaction, *but* they can also be

very misleading because respondents rarely represent the whole audience.

(6) *Panel techniques* are used by many market research firms and producers of consumer goods. A group of homemakers may be asked periodically to report their reactions to particular products or to report on a weekly schedule (diary record) their purchases of a number of products with brand and price data. In return, they receive prizes or stamps toward desired commodities. The continuous record-keeping panels provide the best available information on the behavior of particular consumers over the course of time. Among the well-known panels are those operated by the Market Research Corporation of America (purchases), the *Chicago Tribune* (purchases), and the A. C. Nielsen Company (media measurement). The major difficulty with panel techniques is to maintain a probability sample because of the very high rate of refusals (close to 50 percent) to participate even at the beginning and the gradual increase in dropouts. Consequently, the sample soon becomes a quota sample and is not completely representative of the universe. Also, some researchers argue that panel members develop a special point of view and that their attitudes may become unrepresentative. However, panels provide very useful data on trends in volume, shares of the market, and number of brands in the market.

(7) *References*

(*a*) American Marketing Association. *The Technique of Marketing Research*, Chapters II, VII.

(*b*) Blankenship, Albert B. *Consumer and Opinion Research*, Chapter 4.

(*c*) Ferber, Robert, and Verdoorn, P. J. *Research Methods in Economics and Business*, pp. 207–213.

(*d*) Lamale, Helen Humes. *Methodology of the Survey of Consumer Expenditures in 1950*, part of *Study of Consumer Expenditures, Incomes, and Savings*, Wharton School of Finance and Commerce, University of Pennsylvania.

(*e*) Parten, Mildred. *Surveys, Polls, and Samples*, Chapter III.

(*f*) Ferber, Blankertz, Hollander, op. cit., Chapter 10.

(*g*) United Nations. *Handbook of Household Surveys*, A Practical Guide for Inquiries on Levels of Living, Studies in Methods Series F No. 10.

A.2.4 Sampling

(1) *Sampling* is a very technical field in which some statisticians specialize. But marketing specialists, agricultural economists, home economists, and other people concerned with obtaining survey data must acquire enough general information about sampling problems to be able to work with the sampling experts. We must tell them the characteristics of the universe to be surveyed and give them some ideas about what proportions of the total may have each characteristic. The sampling specialist works on questions about who should be sampled, when, how many should be in the sample, how to handle refusals and substitutions, and interpretation of findings for the total universe. In laying out their samples, some market surveyors use source lists for whole population, e.g., a telephone or city directory. These may introduce serious bias, e.g., the *Literary Digest* poll in 1932 which indicated a landslide for President Hoover.

(2) *Classes and types of sampling.*

(*a*) Probability sample. A sample so drawn that every unit in the population or universe has a known positive chance of being drawn. If equal chance, it is called a random sample. If heterogeneous population, it is safer to divide total into strata based on a characteristic such as income or population density and sample randomly within each. Size of sample for each stratum may be in proportion to its significance in total population, or it may be disproportionate (for example, if more precision is desired for one section of population than for others).

(*b*) Nonprobability samples can be a useful expedient, *if properly used*, to overcome cost and the difficulty in reaching a probability sample. Nonprobability samples include so-called "area-quota samples," quota samples, and purposive, controlled samples. In nonprobability samples the interviewer is usually responsible for making one or more decisions in the selection process.

(*c*) Within the probability category one may use types of samples based on area or special lists. Nonprobability samples include quota or traffic samples.

(3) *Sample size* depends on heterogeneity of population, precision needed, tabulation

plans, collection and response problems. The objective in sampling decisions must be to allocate available resources (time, money) to get maximum amount of reliable and useful information.

(4) *References*

(*a*) American Marketing Association. *Sampling in Marketing Research*, Mktg. Res. Tech. Series No. 3. (Recommended.)

(*b*) Backstrom, Charles H., and Hursh, Gerald B. *Survey Research*, Chapter II. (Paperback, written for nontechnicians in political science but highly recommended for marketing students.)

(*c*) Ferber, Robert. *Statistical Techniques in Market Research*, Part two.

(*d*) Ferber and Verdoorn, op. cit., pp. 237–266. (Technical.)

(e) Parten, op. cit., Chapters 7–9. (Out of print, but very good.)

(*f*) Hansen, Morris H., Hurwitz, William H., and Madow, William B. *Sample Survey Methods and Theory*, Vol. I, Methods and Applications. (Quite technical.)

(*g*) Ferber, Blankertz, Hollander, op. cit., Chapter 9.

A.2.5 Development of Questionnaires

(1) Before writing questions, preliminary decisions must be made on who will make entries on the schedule, the type of survey method to be used (mail or personal interview, for example), probable intellectual level of interviewers and respondents, form of reproduction (e.g., printed or mimeographed), and whether to use a sequence which expedites the interviewing or the tabulating.

(2) Size and form of the questionnaire will depend on financial and time limitations and on expected problems with responses. A structured questionnaire specifies all questions and answers, whereas an unstructured questionnaire provides opportunity for comments in the words of the respondent. The latter type is used in depth interviews and in pretests to develop the final form of the questionnaire.

(3) The first section of a questionnaire should supply identifying information such as schedule number, name and address of interviewer, address of respondent (if not name), area or section of sample, and date of the interview to provide for check on interviewer and to help keep track of the schedule.

(4) Several sets of questions may be used to supply socioeconomic data for checking the sample and classifying replies. They provide factual information such as age, country of birth, marital status, education, religion, political preference, veteran status, home tenure, rental value of home, color or race, family size and composition, occupation, employment of earner or homemaker, family income, car ownership, and socioeconomic status.

(5) Questions dealing with opinions and attitudes may touch on emotional areas and must be carefully written and placed. Where possible, questions tried out in earlier, successful surveys should be used. By so doing, each researcher can contribute to the accretion of knowledge and provide opportunities for comparison and testing of his findings.

(6) Information questions are used to find out people's level of knowledge of a product and where they obtained specific pieces of information.

(7) Respondents may also be asked to evaluate some aspects of their behavior in relation to others, their "self-perception." These responses are used to trace the web of influence and social and political contacts.

(8) Questions to supply information regarding the subject matter of the study should be pertinent, keeping tabulation plans in mind, and they should be comparable insofar as possible with questions used in other surveys to expedite analysis. They should avoid embarrassing respondents (with personal questions, unfamiliar language, questions outside the experience or memory of respondents), avoid leading to misinformation (bias or deliberate), or requiring too much work.

(9) When the questionnaire is in near-final form, a comprehensive review is desirable to be sure that the questions will yield data needed to examine the hypotheses raised by the original problem. Often the questionnaire has to be cut to come within budget limitations. Also, a policy review may be required at this stage either by the U.S. Bureau of the Budget (in the case of Federal surveys) or by top company or association officials (in the case of privately financed research).

(10) *References*

(*a*) American Marketing Association. *The Technique of Marketing Research*, Chapters III, IV, VII.

(*b*) Backstrom and Hursh, op. cit., Chapters III and IV. (Very good.)
(*c*) Blankenship, op. cit., Chapters 5 and 6.
(*d*) Ferber, Blankertz, Hollander, op. cit., Chapter 11.
(*e*) Kahn, Robert L., and Cannell, Charles F. *The Dynamics of Interviewing,* Chapters 5 and 6.
(*f*) Lorie, James H., and Roberts, Harry V. *Basic Methods of Marketing Research,* Chapters 13–17.
(*g*) Parten, op. cit., Chapter V.

(11) Because of the precision needed in reporting of food quantity data for dietary analyses, statisticians have worked intensively on methodology for such surveys. Their methods are described briefly in many of the reports on food consumption surveys. One study was designed to compare the food list and food record methods. (Murray, Janet, Blake, Ennis, et al. *Collection Methods in Dietary Surveys,* Southern Cooperative Series Bulletin 23.) Two bulletins of the U.S. National Research Council provide good background material and instructions for studies of food habits and nutrition:

Bulletin 111, *Manual for the Study of Food Habits*

Bulletin 117, *Nutrition Surveys: Their Techniques and Value*

The U.N. Food and Agriculture Organization has issued a guide for dietary surveys by Emma Reh, *Manual on Household Food Consumption Surveys* (FAO Nutrition Studies No. 18).

A.2.6 Interviewing

(1) *Characteristics of good interviewers.* Extroverts, keen observers, persistent, honest, reliable, good memory, interest in research, pleasant personality, energetic, high school education or more, depending on who is to be interviewed, etc. Mature women make the best interviewers of housewives because they appear "safer," they tend to "empathize," and they are more willing to take part-time assignments. Home economists are particularly valuable for consumer product surveys.

(2) Interviewers must be trained in the objectives of the survey; interpretation of questions; interview procedures regarding sampling, time of day, approach, sequence of questions, probing for answers, and recording responses; handling problem respondents; and closing interviews.

(3) Supervision of interviewers is always necessary to assure conformity and honesty, to handle subsequent questions which may arise, to minimize bias in interviewing, and to keep up morale.

(4) *References*
(*a*) American Marketing Association. *The Technique of Marketing Research,* Chapter VIII.
(*b*) Backstrom and Hursh, op. cit., Chapter V.
(*c*) Ferber and Verdoorn, op. cit., Section 5.4.
(*d*) Hyman, Herbert. *Interviewing in Social Research.* (Authoritative reference.)
(*e*) Kahn and Cannell. *Dynamics of Interviewing,* op. cit.
(*f*) Lorie and Roberts, op. cit., Chapters 20 and 21.
(*g*) Parten, op. cit., pp. 138–145, Chapter X.
(*h*) Reed, Vergil D., Parker, Katherine G., and Vitriol, Herbert A. "Selection, Training, and Supervision of Field Interviewers in Marketing Research," *J. Marketing,* January 1948, pp. 365–378.
(*i*) Richardson, Stephen A., Dohrenwend, Barbara Snell, and Klein, David. *Interviewing: Its Forms and Functions.*

A.2.7 Pilot Tests and Pretests

(1) Pilot tests are often used to explore problems with preliminary questionnaires. A pretest may be a pilot test, but it is usually made at the stage when the questionnaire is about set. It provides a final check on wording or new techniques and a dry run of procedures for interviewing, editing, coding, and tabulating. Either a pilot test or pretest may use alternative phrasings of questions for groups of respondents. Some kind of pretest is a "must."

(2) *References*
(*a*) Blankenship, op. cit., Chapter 7.
(*b*) Ferber and Verdoorn, op. cit., Section 2.4.4.
(*c*) Parten, op. cit., pp. 55–59.

A.2.8 Editing and Coding

(1) *Editing*

(*a*) Objectives of the editing process are detailed review of each schedule to check for internal consistency, uniformity, accuracy; making necessary conversions for coding and tabulation; and development of procedures for handling open-end comments. Open-end comments are responses to unstructured questions such as, "What other characteristics did you like?"

(*b*) Preliminary review by field supervisor while the interviewers are still working in the neighborhood or city is important to ascertain whether a follow-up by interviewers is needed. Actual editing is usually done by a special office crew.

(*c*) In a large-scale survey or in an office handling several surveys at a time, it is essential to establish and follow a procedure to keep track of schedules as work proceeds on editing and further processing.

(*d*) To maintain uniformity, written and detailed instructions for editing should be developed and followed precisely.

(2) *Coding the data*

(*a*) Coding consists of assigning a number or symbol to each answer to indicate its category as a preliminary step to tabulation. Some questions may provide self-coding answers, such as by having respondents check boxes beside them. Or interviewers may do this as the respondent replies. More often, an office staff does the classifying and coding, using a specially developed coding manual.

Extensive use is made of precoded questionnaires or schedules. This involves providing columns for entering codes and identifying the card and column numbers into which the data will be punched. This practice is generally preferred to use of transcription sheets for entry of data from schedules. Transcriptions are used in unstructured questions such as having people write down the food they ate each meal during a day. In laying out a code, always provide for "don't know" and "refused."

(*c*) Coders need to be reminded that data are confidential and that they must keep track of all questionnaires. *Do not destroy any questionnaires.*

(*d*) The form of coding depends on plans for tabulation. If preparatory to use of ordinary punch cards, for example, codes must be arranged for punching on 80 vertical columns with boxes numbered 0 to 9. It is necessary to carry some identifying information on every card pertaining to a given schedule.

(3) *References*
- (*a*) American Marketing Association. *The Technique* . . ., op. cit., pp. 184–213.
- (*b*) Backstrom and Hursh, op. cit., Chapter VI.
- (*c*) Blankenship, op. cit., pp. 152–160.
- (*d*) Parten, op. cit., Chapters XIII and XIV.
- (*e*) Ferber, Blankertz, Hollander, op. cit., Chapter 14.

A.2.9 Tabulation of Data from Questionnaires

(1) Tabulation is the arranging and classifying of data into forms or tables which make the data meaningful. It should be planned as an adjunct of the final report tables either during the process of developing the questionnaire or even sketched out *before* that process. Tabulation is actually one step in analysis of data. (See A.3.)

(2) Tabulation may be done by hand, semimanually, by tabulating machine, or by electronic computers.

(3) For hand tabulation, first decide on key sorts to be used (for example, region, urbanization, income) and set up tables to receive counts. One may either tally directly on a tabulation sheet or use small "take-off" or code cards which carry identification and employ numbers, heavy lines, or colors for easy classification and hand sorting before tallying on tabulation sheets.

(4) Semimechanical methods use cards with holes punched. One sorts and records data by connecting or breaking the holes.

(5) *Machines used for tabulation*

(*a*) Card sorters—machines which sort tabulation cards according to numbers in specified columns.

(*b*) Tabulators—giant adding machines capable of totaling many columns at a time.

(*c*) Machines to multiply and divide—large-scale calculators. (These are now superseded by computers.)

(*d*) Computers—complex electronic machines which do routine procedural work of selecting sets of data to be combined or completed as well as the actual calculations.

(*e*) Printers—very large typewriters which type out the data coming from computers.

(6) *References*
- (*a*) American Marketing Association.

The Technique . . ., op. cit., Chapters XII and XIV.
(*b*) Backstrom and Hursh, op. cit., Chapter VI.
(*c*) Blankenship, op. cit., pp. 160–180.
(*d*) Coleman, John A., Murray, Edward, Judson, C. H., Jr. *Tabulation: Elements of Planning and Techniques,* Am. Mktg. Assoc. Marketing Research Techniques Series No. 5.
(*e*) Parten, op. cit., Chapter XV.
(*f*) Ferber, Blankertz, Hollander, op. cit., Chapter 14.

A.3 INTRODUCTION TO ANALYTICAL PROCEDURES FOR MICROECONOMIC ANALYSIS OF CONSUMPTION PROBLEMS

A.3.1 Relationship between Tabulations and Analysis

(1) All phases of collection of data must be developed in line with plans for use in analysis of the problem at hand. It is especially important that tabulations of data provide the bases for major parts of analytical work. Additional tabulations or re-runs are costly, time-consuming, and delay analytical work and reporting.

(2) Analysis often begins with a preliminary check on adequacy of hypotheses regarding factors affecting consumption rates. Therefore an analyst eagerly studies summaries of data about which families consumed or bought how much of each type of commodity or service.

A.3.2 Major Objectives of Analytical Procedures

(1) Description and measurement of variations in consumption at one time or through time.

(2) Description and measurement of relationships between (*a*) socioeconomic factors *and* consumption rates and patterns, and (*b*) psychological measures *and* consumption.

(3) Evaluation of relative significance to consumer behavior of socioeconomic and psychological factors under varying conditions.

(4) Development and evaluation of alternative solutions to problems being studied.

A.3.3 Preliminary Investigation of Relationships

(1) Begin by *studying totals and averages* (examples follow):

(*a*) Calculate averages such as average consumption of bread by all families in survey.

$$\frac{\text{Total for all families}}{\text{Number of all families}} = \text{average consumed per family}$$

(*b*) Calculate averages for subgroups which are formed by subcategories of respondents or groups of items.

(*c*) Compare averages for subgroups, either subgroups of families or subgroups of commodities.

(i) $$\frac{\text{Av. expenditure for bread}}{\text{Av. expenditure for all cereal products}} = \text{percent spent for bread}$$

(ii) $$\frac{\text{Av. expenditure for bread by highest-income families}}{\text{Av. expenditure for bread by lowest-income families}}$$
= ratio which gives first hint of how income may be related to expenditures

(*d*) What is the range in totals, in averages?

(2) Next, study the *numbers* of families and their *proportions* in total (of all families reporting) which have certain characteristics, buy certain items, do certain things, or have certain opinions.

(*a*) Calculate percentages such as:

$$\frac{\text{Number of families buying chicken}}{\text{Number of families in survey}} = \text{percent buying chicken}$$

(*b*) Compare percentages, such as proportion who bought chicken with the proportion of families who bought turkey.

(3) Develop *frequency distributions* by tallying how many families fell in certain categories, e.g., number in $1000 to $2000 income group, $2000 to $3000, etc., *or* number of girls having one sport coat, two sport coats, etc.

(4) Develop *cross tabulations* as indicated in the following:

(*a*) First, subdivide the total number of cases into groups according to a major socio-

TABLE X Number of Families in Area Buying Given Amounts of Meat in a Week, 19—, by Income[a]

Income Group	Number of Families Buying: Less than 3 lb.	3–5 lb.	6–8 lb.	9–11 lb.	12 lb. or More
Less than $2000	3	4	3	2	1
$2000 to $4000	2	4	5	6	3
$4000 and over	1	2	3	5	6

[a] *Note:* Most books on report writing provide guidance for setting up tables.

economic characteristic such as level of family income.

(*b*) Then subdivide each subgroup by another characteristic (e.g., family size) or by amount of given product bought (e.g., pounds of meat in a week). This procedure will yield data for a table like the above.

(5) Use *graphic analysis* to identify patterns and significant relationships. (See p. 316.)

(6) *Preparation of work tables.* In the early stages of work on a problem, it is usually desirable to label work tables with that name and to number them as they are developed, in order to simplify cross-referencing. Every table should be dated and initialed at the time its heading is written, and all sources of data should be footnoted, in brief form at least. Subsequent entry of revised data should be made by crossing out earlier figures, *never by erasing*, and the date of revision should be noted as well as the reason for change if it is not obvious. Development of report tables is greatly expedited by adequate work tables. In general, work tables should not be destroyed unless proven to be entirely useless or revised.

(7) *Need for selectivity.* It is usually impossible to explore all possible combinations of data from a survey. An analyst must keep his objectives clearly in mind and be *selective* about his experimental investigations. Imagination counts but so does self-discipline. This is the stage at which background information from other studies can provide fertile clues as well as warnings of blind alleys.

A.3.4 Simple Statistical Methods

(1) *Ratios and percentages*

(2) *Frequency distributions.* How many cases in each group, what percentage of total?

(3) *Cross-classifications.* Refer to Section C 4 above (Ref. Ferber and Verdoorn, op. cit., Section 3.2.).

(4) *Relation between two or more variables*

(*a*) Begin with graphic analysis (*b*) Regression equation (*c*) Calculation of coefficient of determination (*d*) Rank correlation (*e*) Multivariate regression	Refs.: Ferber and Verdoorn, op. cit., Chapter 3 or statistics textbooks

(5) *Reweighting procedures*

(6) *Reference:* Appendix B of this book or Burk, M. *Measures and Procedures for Analysis of U.S. Food Consumption,* U.S. Agr. Handbook 206, Section 4.3.

A.3.5 More Advanced Statistical Measures

References

(*a*) For general guidance to analysis in market research analysis, see American Marketing Association. *The Technique . . .,* op. cit., pp. 236–297.

(*b*) Ferber and Verdoorn, op. cit., Section 4.4 and Chapter 6.

(*c*) Statistics textbooks.

A.4 BRIEF GUIDE TO REPORT WRITING

One objective of report writing is to report findings to others, either in the business firm or the government agency sponsoring the research or to other researchers and laymen. A second

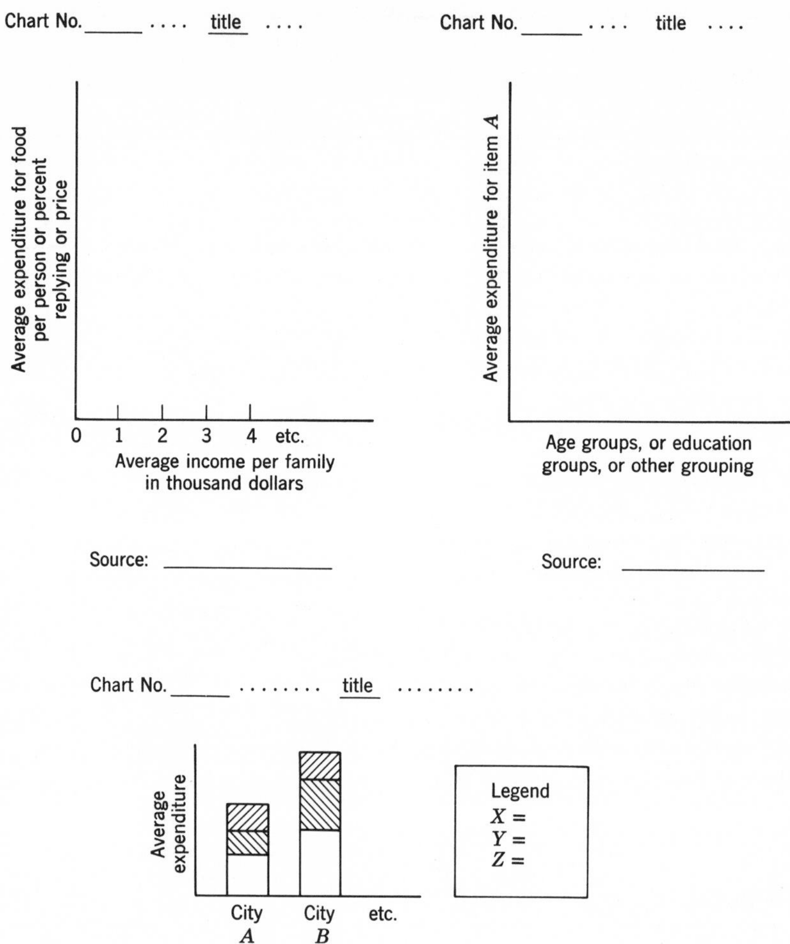

For ideas about charts, see U.S. Department of Agriculture Outlook Chartbooks or a paperback on statistics, some elementary textbooks on statistics, or F. V. Waugh's *Graphic Analysis: Applications in Agricultural Economics,* USDA Agr. Handbook 326.

objective is to add to the store of knowledge. Unfortunately, few commercial market research reports are ever published because of the confidential nature of the research for the use of the private firm financing it. Occasionally, however, professional researchers in business write in professional journals so that others can learn something about the nature of the research they have carried on.

The process of report writing should begin concurrently with initiation of the research. A researcher must always keep in mind what kinds of information he must have for his final report, especially for the full technical report. Certainly, every researcher who is properly trained keeps in mind the fact that the material that he picks up from other sources must carry proper citations to the sources. All quotations and direct paraphrases should carry the full citation. If more than a phrase is quoted verbatim, quotation marks must be used. Not to do so is plagiarism, a civil crime. Several references to guides for report writing are cited.[1]

[1] (*a*) Thurston, Marjorie H. *The Preparation of Term Papers and Reports,* Fourth Edition; (*b*) Hubbell, George Shelton. *Writing Term Papers and Reports;* (*c*) Emberger, Meta Riley, and Hall, Marion Ross. *Scientific Writing.*

Each report should contain these sections: (1) An introduction should give the nature and purpose of the problem and the purpose and scope of the present investigation. (2) A brief summary of findings is optional at the beginning but very helpful. (3) A review of the literature describing earlier research pertinent to the problem should set the stage for the study. (4) A description of the materials used and the methods and the procedures followed is needed to provide evidence for judging the quality of the research. (5) A description of the experiment or nature of the survey supplements item 4. (6) A summary of the analysis and a list of findings with discussion of the high points are desirable. Details may be given in tables and charts. (7) Conclusions should be stated in the form of generalizations. Limitations should be indicated, particularly with reference to unexplored areas. (8) A bibliography or list of literature cited is essential. (9) An appendix may supply additional materials.

For help in preparation of market research reports, refer to textbooks on market research, to the American Marketing Association's *Technique of Marketing Research* (op. cit.), to Blankenship (op. cit.) Chapter 13, or to Parten (op. cit.) Chapter 17.

A.5 OTHER REFERENCES FOR RESEARCH METHODS

(1) Festinger, Leon, and Katz, Daniel (Editors), *Research Methods in the Behavioral Sciences.*

(2) Hyman, Herbert. *Survey Design and Analysis.* (A manual for designing and analyzing surveys in public opinion, marketing, and social research.)

(3) Lazarsfeld, Paul F., and Rosenberg, Morris (Editors), *The Language of Social Research.* (Readings illustrating the nature and applications of the methodology of social research.)

(4) Morgan, James N., and Sonquist, John A. "Problems in the Analysis of Survey Data, and a Proposal," *J. Am. Stat. Assoc.* 58:302: 415–434, June 1963.

(5) Selltiz, Claire, Jahoda, Marie, Deutsch, Morton, and Cook, Stuart W. *Research Methods in Social Relations.* Revised One-Volume Edition.

(6) Ferber, Robert, Blankertz, Donald F., and Hollander, Sidney, Jr. *Marketing Research.*

(7) Luck, David J., Wales, Hugh G., and Taylor, Donald A. *Marketing Research.*

APPENDIX B

GUIDE TO PROCEDURES FOR MACROECONOMIC ANALYSIS OF CONSUMPTION PROBLEMS

This appendix provides only a brief introduction to some of the procedures used in consumption analysis at the macroeconomic level. It supplements rather than substitutes for an elementary text on statistics. For further information on several of the methods described herein, see Chapter 4 of Burk, M. *Measures and Procedures for Analysis of U.S. Food Consumption* (USDA Agr. Handb. 206)[1] and Waugh *Graphic Analysis: Applications in Agricultural Economics* (USDA Agr. Handb. 326). Croxton and Cowden *Applied General Statistics* is a good reference for information on charting. Treatment of logarithms and correlation analysis is quite cursory here because each student will gain more from reviewing correlation methods in his elementary statistics book than from a new, brief presentation.

Every hour spent on careful preparation and organization of data before starting computations in consumption analysis is likely to save at least two hours at later stages, either in puzzling over confusing results or in redoing all computations. Clarification of the objectives of the analysis and careful consideration of which concepts and matching data are most suitable are essential. Chapters 12 to 16 of this book provide considerable information on the types and sources of data used for consumption analysis. Additional information on data pertaining to food is available in Section 4.1 of Burk, M. *Measures and Procedures*. . . . That section also contains data on distributions of the housekeeping population by size of income which may be useful for work on class projects and special studies.

Appendices B and C of USDA Agr. Handb. 187 *Meat Consumption Trends and Patterns* provide some guidance for analysis of consumption of a commodity group. This handbook assembles a great variety of material on all aspects of meat consumption and demonstrates the scope of such information available for business and public decision making.

The following sections of this appendix are designed to help the student to learn how to: (1) describe trends and patterns in consumption, (2) identify and measure relationships among consumption data and pertinent socioeconomic factors, (3) estimate consumption in subareas such as states within regions, and (4) project future trends and patterns.

[1] This handbook has been out of print for several years. However, it may be consulted in most university and large public libraries. Several sets of data used in this appendix are taken from *Meassures and Procedures*. . . .

B.1 HOW TO DESCRIBE TRENDS AND PATTERNS

B.1.1 Arrangement of Data in Tabular Forms

(1) Assembly and organization of data in tables contribute significantly to the understanding of the problem at hand, both by the analyst working on it and by users of the study.

(2) Most books on report writing provide guidance to setting up tables. See also USDA Agr. Handb. 121 *Preparing Statistical Tables for Publication: A Guide to Usage in AMS* by Viola Culbertson and Marguerite Higgins.

(3) For information on preparation of work tables, see Appendix A.3.3 (6) or B. F. Stanton's *Table Talk* (Cornell University, Department of Agricultural Economics, A.E. Res. 98).

B.1.2 Arithmetic Methods

(1) *Use of index numbers*. Economists frequently need special combinations of data that are not readily available. Such needs can often be filled by calculation of simple index num-

bers using the Laspeyres formula. Two examples with hypothetical data follow:

(*a*) Quantity-weighted *price* index:

Formula is

$$\frac{\Sigma p_i q_0}{\Sigma p_0 q_0}$$

where p_i = price in given year
p_0 = price in base period
q_0 = quantity in base period

(*b*) Price-weighted *quantity* index:

Formula is

$$\frac{\Sigma p_0 q_i}{\Sigma p_0 q_0}$$

where q_i = quantity in given year
q_0 = quantity in base period
p_0 = price in base period

Comments: Note that fixed or constant quantities are used as weights for the price index and that fixed prices serve as weights for the quantity index. The value aggregates for the quantity index are thus in *constant dollars.* Most indexes of the Federal Government are based on these formulas.

(2) Measurement of change in price or in quantity using data from 1 (*a*) and (*b*).

(*a*) Change in average price of fluid whole milk from 1929 to 1959 is calculated thus:

$$\frac{p_{59}}{p_{29}} = \frac{0.12}{0.08} = 1.50 \qquad \text{or } 50\% \text{ increase}$$

(Increase = 1.50 − 1.0 = 0.50)

(*b*) Change in average consumption of fluid whole milk from 1929 to 1959. Data are from 1 (*b*).

$$\frac{q_{59}}{q_{29}} = \frac{300}{270} = 1.11 \qquad \text{or } 11\% \text{ increase}$$

(*c*) Change in average price of fluid milk and butter *combined.*

$$\frac{p_{(m+b)59}}{p_{(m+b)29}} = \frac{\Sigma p_{59} q_0}{\Sigma p_{29} q_0} = \frac{\$42.00}{28.00} = 1.50$$

or 50% increase

TABLE B.1 Hypothetical Data on Fluid Whole Milk and Butter for *Price* Index: Quantity, Price, and Value

Item	Average Quantity Consumed in 1947–1949 in Pounds (q_0)	Price (*P*) and Value (*PQ*)					
		1929		1947–1949		1959	
		P	*PQ*	*P*	*PQ*	*P*	*PQ*
Fluid whole milk	300	8¢	$24.00	9¢	$27.00	12¢	$36.00
Butter	10	40¢	4.00	80¢	8.00	20¢	6.00
Total value			28.00		35.00		42.00
Index: 1947–1949 = 100			80		100		120

TABLE B.2 Hypothetical Data on Fluid Whole Milk and Butter for *Quantity* Index: Quantity, Price, and Value

Item	Average Price in 1947–1949 Cents per Pound (p_0)	Quantity (*Q*) and Value (*PQ*)					
		1929		1947–1949		1959	
		Q	*PQ*	*Q*	*PQ*	*Q*	*PQ*
Fluid whole milk	9¢	270	$24.30	300	$27.00	300	$27.00
Butter	80¢	18	14.40	10	8.00	8	6.40
Total value			38.70		35.00		33.40
Index: 1947–1949 = 100			111		100		95

or

$$\frac{\dfrac{\Sigma p_{59}q_0}{\Sigma p_0 q_0}}{\dfrac{\Sigma p_{29}q_0}{\Sigma p_0 q_0}} = \frac{120}{80} = 1.50 \qquad \text{or } 50\% \text{ increase}$$

(*d*) Change in quantity of fluid milk and butter *combined* from 1929 to 1959. Data are from 1 (*b*).

$$\frac{q_{1959}}{q_{1929}} = \frac{\Sigma p_0 q_{59}}{\Sigma p_0 q_{29}} = \frac{\$33.40}{38.40} = 0.87$$

or 13% decrease

or

$$\frac{q_{1959}}{q_{1929}} = \frac{\dfrac{\Sigma p_0 q_{59}}{\Sigma p_0 q_0}}{\dfrac{\Sigma p_0 q_{29}}{\Sigma p_0 q_0}} = \frac{95}{111} = 0.86$$

or 14% decrease

Note the small difference between the two estimates which results from rounding the indexes and percentages.

(3) Measurement of relationships, using data from Tables 3 and 7 of Agr. Handb. 187 *Meat Consumption Trends and Patterns.*

(*a*) Quantity of beef used per person in farm households in North Central Region in a week of spring 1955 compared with average United States farm use at same time. (Table 3.)

$$\frac{q_{NCR}}{q_{US}} = \frac{1.61}{1.17} \text{ lb.} = 1.38$$

or 38% more in NCR than in US

(*b*) Quantity of *purchased* beef used per person in farm households in North Central Region in a week of spring 1955 compared with average United States farm use of purchased beef at same time. (Table 7.)

$$\frac{q_{NCR}}{q_{US}} = \frac{0.48}{0.44} \text{ lb.} = 1.09$$

or 9% more in NCR than US

(*c*) What conclusions can you draw from comparison of data in 3 (*a*) and (*b*)?

B.1.3 Graphic Methods

(1) The use of graphs to highlight trends and patterns should *precede* any more elaborate method such as regression analysis.

(2) Two types of scales are commonly used, natural (or arithmetic) and logarithmic. Absolute changes or variations are best studied using natural or arithmetic graphs. Logarithmic graphs are particularly useful for work on rates of change. Recall that plotting of logarithms of a series of data on arithmetic paper provides exactly the same configuration as plotting the original data on logarithmic paper. Equal distances between points of natural or arithmetic scales indicate equal absolute changes in a variable, such as per capita consumption of meat. In contrast, equal distances between points on logarithmic scales indicate equal proportional changes.

(3) Two types of logarithmic paper are used in the following examples—semilog and double log. Semilog paper has a logarithmic scale on one axis and an arithmetic scale on the other. Double log paper has logarithmic scales for both axes. Note how logarithms magnify small variations and reduce large variations, often to more manageable proportions.

(*a*) Semilog graphs are used for

(i) Comparison of percentage changes in one variable (plotted on arithmetic scale) with actual changes in the other (plotted on log scale). An example is the comparison of the percentage of income allocated to food with level of per capita income.

(ii) Study of rates of change in a variable (log scale) through time (arithmetic scale). An example is Figure 6.2 in Burk *Trends and Patterns . . .* which compares several different value series for all food per capita.

(*b*) Double log graphs are particularly useful for comparison of the rate of change in one variable with the rate of change in another or for comparison of variations in two measures. Figure 4.1 in *Trends and Patterns . . .* utilizes several food value measures for cross sections of United States families.

(*c*) See high school or college textbooks on algebra for the mathematical meaning, properties, and methods of computing with logarithms. But keep these properties in mind as you use log paper for graphing: There are no logs of a negative number. The log of a positive number less than unity or one is negative. The log of one is zero.

(4) To trace historical trends in series—examples:

(*a*) Using arithmetic paper
(*b*) Using semilog paper (2 cycles)

Instructions for Charts 1 and 2

The data for the two charts are the same. On scale (*A*) plot the index of per capita food use of purchased farm foods, given in Table B.3. For scale (*B*) use per capita disposable income data from Table B.3. Write a title, identify the scales by name and unit, indicate sources of data in footnotes, put your name and the date in the upper right-hand corner of the page.

The key idea in laying out a logarithmic scale is to multiply each number within a cycle by the same factor. For example, the *1* at the bottom of the lowest cycle might be

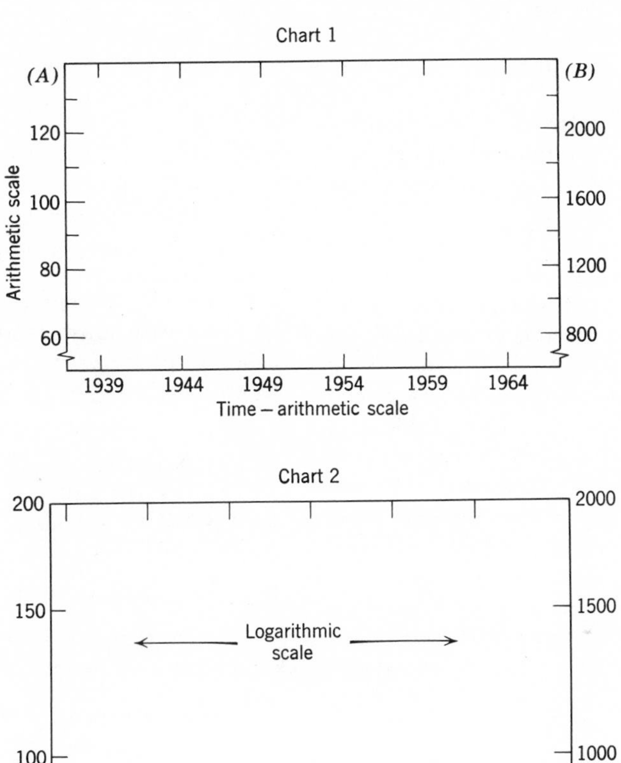

TABLE B.3 Per Capita Food Use of Purchased Farm Foods[a] and Disposable Money Income in 1958 Dollars, 1929 to 1964 at 5-Year Intervals[b]

Item	Unit	1929	1934	1939	1944	1949	1954	1959	1964
Per capita use of purchased farm foods	Index: 1947–1949 = 100	85	84	87	99	99	104	108	112
Per capita disposable money income in	1958 Dollars	1236	952	1190	1673	1547	1714	1881	2116

[a] Data for 1929 to 1959, series PFQ-lb in Table 3.1 of *Measures and Procedures*. . . . Estimates for 1964 by author at the University of Minnesota from published USDA data.

[b] From Table 7.6, U.S. Department of Commerce, *The National Income and Product Accounts of the United States, 1929–1965*, a 1966 Supplement to the *Survey of Current Business*.

multiplied by 100. If so, the 9 at the top of that cycle should also be multiplied by 100. Then it is obvious that the *1* at the bottom of the second cycle should be identified as 1000. It follows that all the figures in the second cycle should be multiplied by 1000. The *1* of the third cycle becomes 10,000, and the figures in that cycle should be multiplied by 10,000. You can begin with any multiplier, such as 2 or 5 or 50. Just keep it constant within each cycle.

(5) To describe patterns of consumption for one variable which varies continuously and another which varies in discrete units, use *arithmetic* paper.

Instructions for Chart 3

On scale (A) lay out average money value of all purchased food (or food expenditure) per family member in urban families having $5000 to $6000 income for families of 2, 3, 4, 5, and 6 members. Take basic data from Table 2 of any of 1955 Household Survey Reports 1–5 (or from comparable reports on the 1965 survey) and do the necessary computing. (For Northeast and West, use $4000 to $6000

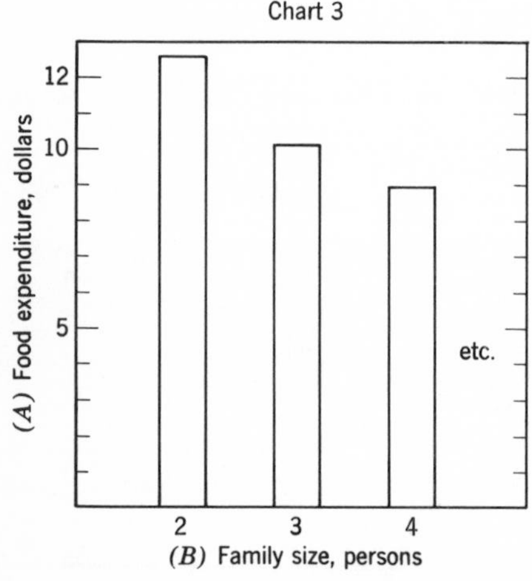

group.) On scale (*B*) lay out the 5 different bars to represent each family size. Plot the data, write title, scale identifications, footnotes, and other information, as needed.

Instructions for Chart 4

On scale (A) lay out the average money value of all purchased food per family member in 3-member families having $5000 to $6000 income for urban, rural nonfarm, and farm families. (From same table as for Chart 3.)

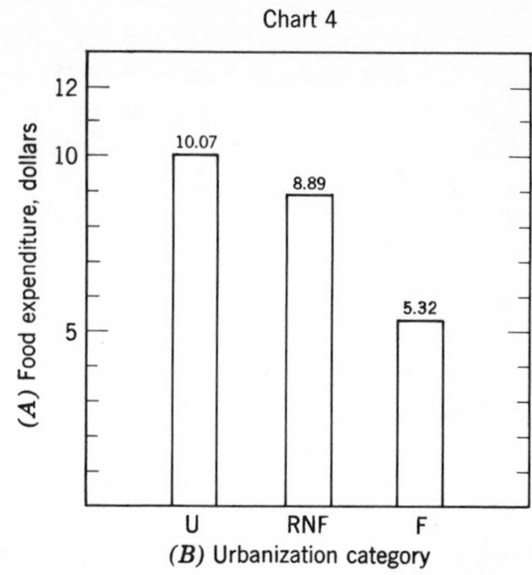

On scale (*B*) lay out the 3 different bars to represent each urbanization category. Plot the data, write headings, footnotes, and other identifications.

B.2 HOW TO FIND AND MEASURE RELATIONSHIPS BETWEEN CONSUMPTION AND ECONOMIC OR SOCIAL FACTORS

B.2.1 Graphic Methods—Examples

(1) To compare historical trends in per capita food consumption and income.

(*a*) To compare absolute changes, use arithmetic paper and plot a chart like Chart 1 or a scatter diagram like Chart 5.

(*b*) To compare rates of change, use semilog paper as in Chart 2 or develop a scatter diagram on semilog or double log paper. Chart 6 illustrates the last type.

Instructions for Chart 5

Set up scale (A) for the index of per capita food use of purchased farm foods for the series given in Table B.3, as in Chart 1. The income measure from the same table should be laid out on scale (*B*). To plot the points, first identify the location on the vertical scale of the figure for the food use index for the first year you are plotting. Then move to the right on the horizontal scale until you find the location for the matching income figure for that year. Identify the point which suits both measures with a little x and place the number for the year beside it very lightly, e.g., '29. Continue the same procedure until you have identified all the points. If necessary, erase and

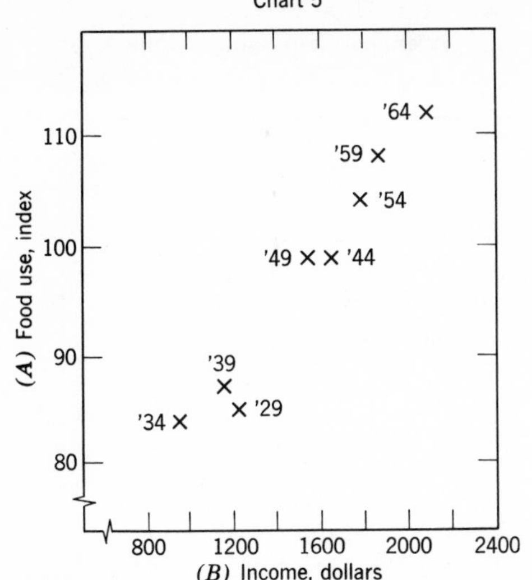

relocate any year number which may interfere with plotting later points.

Be sure that your chart has a title and that the scales are properly identified. Of course, the chart should have a number and identification of source of data, preferably in a footnote. It is also wise to put your name and date in the upper right-hand corner of the page.

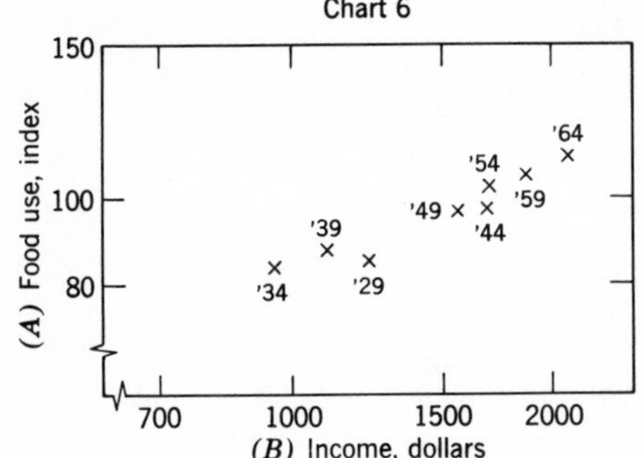

Instructions for Chart 6

Use the same data as for Chart 5, but lay out the chart on double log paper. You will find that you need two cycles on both axes. Refer to instructions for Chart 2 regarding setting up the logarithmic scales. Again, be sure to write a title, scale identifications, etc.

(2) To relate two variables at one point in time. Here we will draw Engel curves:

(*a*) Arithmetic paper

(*b*) Double log paper (2 cycles for each axis)

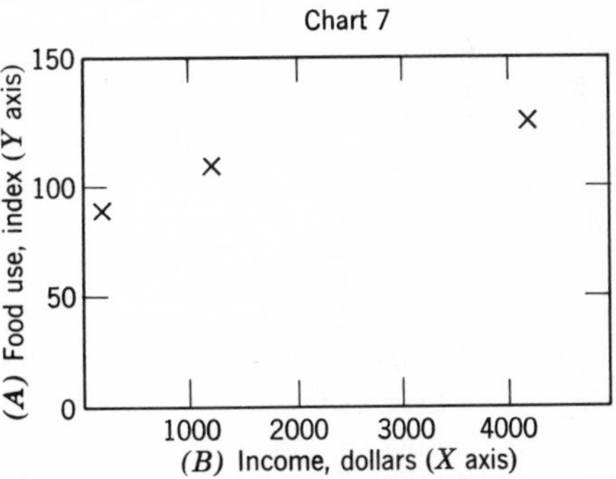

Instructions for Charts 7 and 8

For urban, rural nonfarm, and farm groups, use indexes of per person food use, purchased only (CFQ-lb) in spring 1955 for scale (A) from Table B.4 on Y axis and average money income per person from the same table for scale (B) on X axis. The charts will differ because one will be on arithmetic paper, the other on double log paper.

(3) To measure variability of consumption

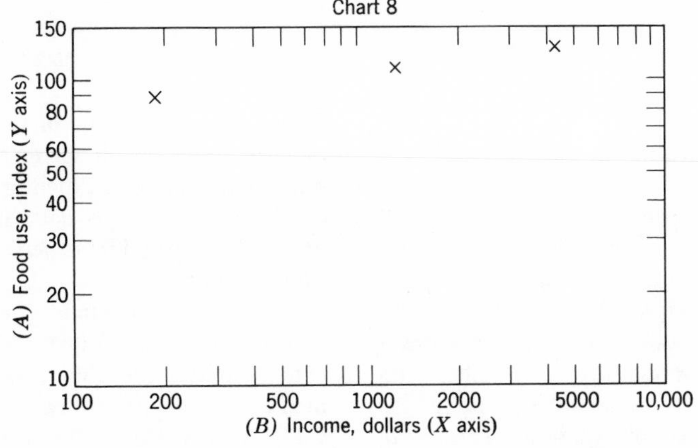

TABLE B.4 Cross-section Index of per Person Food Use—Purchased Only (CFQ-lb), United States, Spring 1955, and Average Disposable Money Income per Person in 1954[a]

1954 Disposable Money Income per Family	United States	Urban	Rural Nonfarm	Farm
	A—Per person food use—purchased only. Index numbers: United States average for all households = 100			
Under $1,000	57.1	89.6	58.1	43.6
$1,000– 2,000	75.0	92.4	73.0	52.5
2,000– 3,000	90.1	100.5	90.3	58.4
3,000– 4,000	97.1	105.7	92.9	60.6
4,000– 5,000	105.5	111.1	104.0	63.4
5,000– 6,000	111.5	118.3	106.6	70.7
6,000– 8,000	115.4	121.7	112.2	65.9
8,000–10,000	115.6	120.3	122.0	62.0
10,000 and over	127.1	131.2	114.3	88.6
Average for all households	100.0	112.8	95.2	56.8
	B—Per person income in 1954 in dollars			
Under $1,000	115	185	161	53
$1,000– 2,000	450	510	432	386
2,000– 3,000	703	766	652	612
3,000– 4,000	932	977	880	836
4,000– 5,000	1,196	1,233	1,156	1,023
5,000– 6,000	1,422	1,504	1,296	1,154
6,000– 8,000	1,811	1,869	1,752	1,404
8,000–10,000	2,267	2,350	2,151	1,758
10,000 and over	4,076	4,224	3,314	3,854
Average for all households	1,250	1,480	1,021	698

[a] Index matches concept of time-series index of per capita food use—purchased food (PFQ-lb); quantities of individual items converted to farm-weight equivalents and valued at average farm prices in 1947–1949. Data from Table 3.13 of *Measures and Procedures. . . .*

or expenditures with income, you can also use the method described in Section 4.2.3 and used in Chart 4.2 of *Measures and Procedures. . . .*

B.2.2 Arithmetic Methods

(1) Many significant findings can be derived from data such as those given in Table B.5. For example, by calculating percentages for changes in basic quantity and price series (e.g., items *a* and *c* of the table) and multiplying one percentage by the other, *p* times *q*, one obtains a first approximation of the expected change in value of per capita purchases of farm foods which serves as a check on the estimated change in expenditure, item *f*. Other combinations of the data in Table B.5 can provide enlightening experiences in consumption analysis.

(2) A more elaborate example of an analysis using sets of food quantity, price, and value data to determine the relative importance of major components of overall change in food value is provided in Section 4.5 of *Measures and Procedures. . . .*

TABLE B.5 Selected Data Pertinent to Changes in Food Value, Quantity, and Price, 1955 to 1965[1]

Item Letter	Description of Item	1955	1965	Ratio of 1965 to 1955, Percent
a.	Index of per capita food use of purchased farm foods (PFQ-1 b in *MP* Table 3.1, 1947–1949 = 100)	106	112	106
b.	Index of marketing services bought with domestic farm foods per capita (PFQ-7 in *MP* Table 3.2; 1947–1949 = 100)	106	115	108
c.	Index of farm value of market basket, approximating a farm level food price index (1955 = 100)[2]	100	110	110
d.	Index of marketing margin of the farm market basket, approximating a price index for marketing services (*MP* Table 3.8[2]; 1947–1949 = 100)	121	144[3]	119
e.	Per capita expenditures for domestic farm foods in current dollars. (Revised data matching PFV–13 b in *MP* Table 3.7)[3]	$\frac{\$51.0 \text{ bil.}}{162.3 \text{ mil.}}$ = $314	$\frac{\$75.4 \text{ bil.}}{191.9 \text{ mil.}}$ = $393	125
f.	Per capita farm value of domestic foods purchased, current dollars. (Revised USDA data matching TFV–1 in *MP* Table 3.3 divided by civilian population)	$\frac{\$18.7 \text{ bil.}}{162.3 \text{ mil.}}$ = $115	$\frac{\$25.5 \text{ bil.}}{191.9 \text{ mil.}}$ = $133	116
g.	Per capita marketing bill, current dollars (revised data matching TFV–15 b in *MP* Table 3.8 divided by the civilian population)[4]	= $199	$260	131

[1] Data for 1955 for 48 states from *Measures and Procedures . . .* (*MP*) except as noted. Data for 1965 for 50 states estimated by author from published data of U.S. Departments of Agriculture and Commerce in order to maintain series comparable with quantity series and U.S. Department of Commerce series for all foods.

[2] Data from *Marketing and Transportation Situation*, May 1966. 1965 estimated by author.

[3] Estimated by author. See note 1.

[4] Calculated as residual by subtracting farm value from expenditures.

B.2.3 Alternative Combinations of Consumption Rates and Population Distributions

(1) Effects of changes in one economic variable, such as income, on consumption rates when other elements are held constant can be calculated using a reweighting procedure and survey data on consumption rates, distributions of the population by size of family income, and distribution of the population among urbanization categories. (See *MP* Sections 4.3.1 and 4.3.3.)

(2) Simplified examples of the procedure:

$\text{Inc}_1 \times \text{Cons}_1 \times \text{Urb}_1 =$ average consumption in period 1

$\text{Inc}_2 \times \text{Cons}_2 \times \text{Urb}_2 =$ average consumption in period 2

Where Inc_1 = income–size distribution in period 1

Inc_2 = income–size distribution in period 2 (assuming same price level)

Cons_1 = consumption rate for beef per person at each income level within each urbanization category in period 1

Cons_2 = same for period 2

Urb_1 = percentage distribution of population in farm and nonfarm

TABLE B.6 Hypothetical Data on Distribution of Population by Size of Income and by Urbanization, and on Beef Consumption per Person in Each Income–Urbanization Category in Two Periods

	Percentage Distribution of Population, Percent				Per Person Consumption of Beef, Pound			
	Period 1		Period 2		Period 1		Period 2	
Income level	Farm	Nonfarm	Farm	Nonfarm	Farm	Nonfarm	Farm	Nonfarm
Under $3000	80	40	55	25	0.3	0.7	1.0	0.9
$3000 to 6000	15	40	30	50	0.5	1.0	1.4	1.3
$6000 and over	5	20	15	25	1.0	1.2	1.6	1.6
Urbanization average	100	100	100	100	—	—	—	—
United States average						—		—
Total change							—	
Percent of population by urbanization	20	80	10	90				

urbanization categories in period 1

Urb_2 = same for period 2

Problem: Work out at least one measure of effect of change in each of the elements in average consumption, using data given in Table B.6.

B.2.4 Regression Analysis

(1) The relationships among two or more variables are frequently studied by means of regression or correlation analyses. A graphic method is illustrated in Frederick V. Waugh's *Graphic Analysis* . . . (Agr. Handb. 326, pp. 40–47.) Pertinent mathematical methods are described in all statistical texts.

(2) For more advanced methods, see Richard J. Foote's *Analytical Tools for Studying Demand and Price Structures* (Agr. Handb. 146).

B.3 HOW TO ESTIMATE CONSUMPTION IN SUBAREAS

This procedure involves using the closest approximations of (*a*) income–size distributions, (*b*) the urbanization distributions, and (*c*) pertinent averages of consumption or expenditures for each income class within each regional urbanization category (such as North Central Region) to estimate comparable data for a subarea (e.g., State of Minnesota). The procedure is based on the idea that it is better to make informed guesses or approximations for each component than to go all out in guessing the overall average. Full description and an example are given in Section 4.3.4 of *Measures and Procedures*. . . .

B.4 HOW TO PROJECT TRENDS AND PATTERNS FOR THE UNITED STATES

B.4.1 Preliminary Steps

(1) Make graphic and/or statistical analysis of historical trends in supply, consumption, and price items being studied, in their substitutes and complements, and in related economic and social factors.

(2) Prepare graphic and/or statistical analysis of comparable cross-section data for two or more periods if at all possible.

(3) Do background reference work on economic and social changes in the last 30 years or so, and expectations for such changes in the next two or three decades.

B.4.2 Graphic Projections

(1) *First approximation.* Locate projected per capita income on historical semilog chart of per capita income—food consumption, for example, and use straight-line projection.

(2) *Second approximation.* Locate average income for each urbanization category in period of latest cross-section survey on chart of Engel curves. Then apply percentage change in income indicated by time-series income pro-

jection; read off the consumption rates for each urbanization at projected average income, combine these rates according to projected urbanization distribution to get United States average. The next step is to compare projected average with the observed United States average for the survey period, then to apply percentage change to matching time-series rate of consumption.

(3) *Third approximation.* If Engel curves have been shifting for known reasons, consider whether the shift is likely to continue. If so, adjust projected rates for each urbanization category, then follow the same procedure as in (2) by combining to get United States average.

(4) *Compare* second and third approximations with first and consider whether they adequately take into account major economic and social changes likely to occur.

(5) *Check results* for commodities by combining into all food average and comparing it with projection for all food.

B.4.3 Reweighting Procedure

The general procedure described in Section B.2.3 is applicable here. It requires projections for the distributions of the population by urbanization and income as well as a projection of changes in consumption rates. For full description, see Section 4.3.5 of *Measures and Procedures*. . . .

B.4.4 Regression Equations

(1) Calculate regression equations for a historical period (using pertinent time series of absolute data, not first differences or year to year changes) *after graphic analysis.*

(2) Insert projected income and other data for independent factors into regressions and solve the equations.

(3) Calculate regression equations for cross-section data matching factors in time-series regressions and compare coefficients.

(4) Do *not* develop equations involving substitution of cross-section coefficients in time-series analyses. By so doing, some economists confuse static and dynamic relationships.

(5) Adjust estimates for projected consumption rates derived in B.4.4.2 to take into account the curvature of the Engel curves or, better yet, compare estimates derived in B.4.4.2 with those developed with graphs and reweighting procedures.

Note: By now each student should be aware that making economic projections is an art, not a science.

B.4.5 More advanced statistical techniques are described in Foote's *Analytical Tools for Studying Demand and Price Structures,* USDA Agr. Handb. 146, but they will not necessarily yield more useful results. Sometimes, the more formal methods applied mechanically yield quite unrealistic results.

BIBLIOGRAPHY

BOOKS

Abrams, Charles. *Man's Struggle for Shelter in an Urbanizing World.* Cambridge, Massachusetts: M.I.T. Press, 1964.

Ackley, Gardner. *Macroeconomic Theory.* New York: The Macmillan Company, 1961.

Alderson, Wroe. *Marketing Behavior and Executive Action.* Homewood, Illinois: Richard D. Irwin, Inc., 1957.

Alevizos, John P. *Marketing Research.* Englewood Cliffs, New Jersey: Prentice-Hall, Inc., 1959.

Allport, Floyd H. *Theories of Perception and the Concept of Structure.* New York: John Wiley & Sons, Inc., 1955.

American Marketing Association. *The Technique of Marketing Research.* New York: McGraw-Hill Book Company, Inc., 1937.

Atkinson, J. W. *An Introduction to Motivation.* Princeton, New Jersey: D. Van Nostrand Company, Inc., 1964.

Backstrom, Charles H., and Hursh, Gerald B. *Survey Research.* Evanston, Illinois: Northwestern University Press, 1963.

Bandura, Albert, and Walters, Richard H. *Social Learning and Personality Development.* New York: Holt, Rinehart & Winston, Inc., 1963.

Bansil, P. C. *India's Food Resources and Population.* Bombay: Vora and Co., October 1958.

Barnett, H. G. *Innovation: The Basis of Cultural Change.* New York: McGraw-Hill Book Company, Inc., 1953.

Baumol, William J. *Economic Dynamics.* Second Edition. New York: The Macmillan Company, 1959.

Baumol, William J. *Economic Theory and Operations Analysis.* Second Edition. Englewood Cliffs, New Jersey: Prentice-Hall, Inc., 1965.

Berelson, Bernard, and Steiner, Gary A. *Human Behavior: An Inventory of Scientific Findings.* New York: Harcourt, Brace & World, Inc., 1964.

Blankenship, Albert B. *Consumer and Opinion Research.* New York: Harper & Brothers Publishers, 1943.

Bliss, Perry (Editor), *Marketing and the Behavioral Sciences.* Boston: Allyn & Bacon, Inc., 1963.

Brehm, Jack W., and Cohen, Arthur R. *Explorations in Cognitive Dissonance.* New York: John Wiley & Sons, Inc., 1962.

Brim, Orville G., Jr., Glass, David C., Lavin, David E., and Goodman, Norman. *Personality and Decision Process.* Stanford, California: Stanford University Press, 1962.

Britt, Steuart Henderson (Editor), *Consumer Behavior and the Behavioral Sciences.* New York: John Wiley & Sons, Inc., 1966.

Bruner, Jerome S., Goodnow, Jacqueline J., and Austin, George A. *A Study of Thinking.* New York: Science Editions, Inc., 1962.

Buchanan, K. M., and Pugh, J. C. *Land and People in Nigeria.* London: University of London Press, 1955.

Burk, Marguerite C. *Influence of Economic and Social Factors on U.S. Food Consumption.* Minneapolis, Minnesota: Burgess Publishing Co., 1961.

Cantril, Hadley. *The Pattern of Human Concerns.* New Brunswick, New Jersey: Rutgers University Press, 1965.

Caplovitz, David. *The Poor Pay More.* New York: The Free Press of Glencoe (A Division of the Macmillan Company), 1963.

Christensen, Harold T. (Editor), *Handbook of Marriage and the Family.* Chicago: Rand McNally & Co., 1964.

Clark, Lincoln H. (Editor), *Consumer Behavior: The Dynamics of Consumer Reaction.* Vol. I. New York: New York University Press, 1955.

Clark, Lincoln H. (Editor), *Consumer Behavior Vol. II: The Life Cycle and Consumer Behavior.* New York: New York University Press, 1955.

Clarkson, Geoffrey P. E. *The Theory of Consumer Demand: A Critical Appraisal.* Englewood Cliffs, New Jersey: Prentice-Hall, Inc., 1963.

Committee for Economic Development, Commission on Money and Credit. *Impacts of Monetary Policy.* Englewood Cliffs, New Jersey: Prentice-Hall, Inc., 1963.

Conference on Research in Income and Wealth. *Studies of Income and Wealth.* Vol. 10. New York: National Bureau of Economic Research, 1947.

Converse, Paul D., Huegy, Harvey W., and Mitchell, Robert V. *The Elements of Marketing.* Fifth Edition. Englewood Cliffs, New Jersey: Prentice-Hall, Inc., 1952.

Coons, Alvin E., and Glaze, Bert T. *Housing Market Analysis and Growth of Nonfarm Home*

Ownership. Bureau of Business Research Monograph No. 115. Columbus, Ohio: The Ohio State University, 1963.

Cox, Reavis, Alderson, Wroe, and Shapiro, Stanley J. (Editors), *Theory in Marketing*. Second Series. Homewood, Illinois: Richard D. Irwin, Inc., 1964.

Croxton, Frederick E., and Cowden, Dudley J. *Applied General Statistics*. Second Edition. Englewood Cliffs, New Jersey: Prentice-Hall, Inc., 1955.

David, Martin Heidenhain. *Family Composition and Consumption*. Amsterdam: North-Holland Publishing Company, 1962.

Dernburg, Thomas S., Rosette, Richard N., and Watts, Harold W. *Studies in Household Economic Behavior*. New Haven: Yale University Press, 1958.

Dewhurst, J. Frederic and Associates. *America's Needs and Resources: A New Survey*. New York: The Twentieth Century Fund, 1955.

Dolva, Wenzil K. (Editor), *Marketing Keys to Profits in the 1960's*. Chicago: American Marketing Association, 1960.

Duesenberry, James S. *Income, Saving and the Theory of Consumer Behavior*. Cambridge: Harvard University Press, 1949.

Duncan, Delbert J. (Editor), *Proceedings, Conference of Marketing Teachers from Far Western States*. Berkeley: University of California Press, 1958.

Duvall, Evelyn Millis. *Family Development*. Second Edition. Philadelphia: J. B. Lippincott Company, 1962.

Emberger, Meta Riley, and Hall, Marion Ross. *Scientific Writing*. New York: Harcourt, Brace & Co., 1955.

Faris, Robert E. L. (Editor), *Handbook of Modern Sociology*. Chicago: Rand McNally & Co., 1964.

Ferber, Robert. *Statistical Techniques in Market Research*, New York: McGraw-Hill Book Company, Inc., 1949.

Ferber, Robert, Blankertz, Donald F., and Hollander, Sidney, Jr. *Marketing Research*. New York: The Ronald Press Co., 1964.

Ferber, Robert, and Verdoorn, P. J. *Research Methods in Economics and Business*. New York: The Macmillan Company, 1962.

Ferber, Robert, and Wales, Hugh G. (Editors), *Motivation and Market Behavior*. Homewood, Illinois: Richard D. Irwin, Inc., 1958.

Festinger, Leon. *Conflict, Decision, and Dissonance*. Stanford, California: Stanford University Press, 1964.

Festinger, Leon, and Katz, Daniel (Editors), *Research Methods in the Behavioral Sciences*. New York: The Dryden Press, 1953.

Foote, Nelson N. (Editor), *Household Decision-Making*. New York: New York University Press, 1961.

Foote, Nelson N., Abu-Lughod, Janet, Foley, Mary Mix, and Winnick, Louis. *Housing Choices and Housing Constraints*. New York: McGraw-Hill Book Company, Inc., 1960.

Friedman, Milton. *A Theory of the Consumption Function*. Princeton, New Jersey: Princeton University Press, 1957.

Friend, Irwin, and Jones, Robert (Editors), *Consumption and Saving*. Proceedings of The Conference on: Study of Consumer Expenditures, Incomes, and Savings. Vols. I and II. Philadelphia: University of Pennsylvania, 1960.

Gage, N. L. (Editor), *Handbook of Research on Teaching*. Chicago: Rand McNally & Company, 1963.

Hagen, Everett E. *On the Theory of Social Change*. Homewood, Illinois: The Dorsey Press, Inc., 1962.

Hambidge, Gove (Editor), *Dynamics of Development*. New York: Frederick A. Praeger, 1964.

Hansen, Morris H., Hurwitz, William H., and Madow, William B. *Sample Survey Methods and Theory, Vol. I, Methods and Applications*. New York: John Wiley & Sons, Inc., 1953.

Henderson, James M., and Quandt, Richard E. *Microeconomic Theory*. New York: McGraw-Hill Book Company, Inc., 1958.

Hicks, J. R. *Value and Capital*. Oxford: The Clarendon Press, 1939.

Hilgard, Ernest E. (Editor), *Theories of Learning and Instruction*. 63rd Yearbook of the National Society for the Study of Education, Part I. Chicago: University of Chicago Press, 1964.

Holloway, Robert J., and Hancock, Robert S. (Editors), *The Environment of Marketing Behavior*. New York: John Wiley & Sons, Inc., 1964.

Houthakker, H. S., and Taylor, Lester D. *Consumer Demand in the United States, 1929–1970: Analyses and Projections*. Cambridge, Massachusetts: Harvard University Press, 1966.

Howard, John A. *Marketing Management: Analysis and Planning*. Revised Edition. Homewood, Illinois: Richard D. Irwin, Inc., 1963.

Howard, John A. *Marketing Theory*. Boston: Allyn and Bacon, Inc., 1965.

Hoyt, Elizabeth E., Reid, Margaret G., McConnell, Joseph L., and Hooks, Janet H. *American Income and Its Use*. First Edition. New York: Harper & Brothers, 1954.

Hubbell, George Shelton. *Writing Term Papers and Reports*. College Outline Series, No. 37. New York: Barnes & Noble, Inc., 1958.

Huff, Darrell. *How to Lie With Statistics*. New York: W. W. Norton & Company, Inc., 1954.

Hyman, Herbert. *Interviewing in Social Research*. Chicago: University of Chicago Press, 1954.

Hyman, Herbert. *Survey Design and Analysis*. Third Printing. Glencoe, Illinois: The Free Press, 1960.

Johnston, Bruce F. *The Staple Food Economies of Western Tropical Africa*. Stanford, California: Stanford University Press, 1958.

Kahn, Robert L., and Cannell, Charles F. *The Dynamics of Interviewing*. New York: John Wiley & Sons, Inc., 1957.

Katona, George. *The Powerful Consumer*. New York: McGraw-Hill Book Company, Inc., 1960.

Kemeny, John G. *A Philosopher Looks at Science*. New York: D. Van Nostrand & Co., Inc., 1959.

Keynes, John Maynard, *The General Theory of Employment, Interest, and Money*. New York: Harcourt, Brace & Company, 1936.

Klein, Lawrence R. (Editor), *Contributions of Survey Methods to Economics*. New York: Columbia University Press, 1954.

Klein, Lawrence R. *An Introduction to Econometrics*. Englewood Cliffs, New Jersey: Prentice-Hall, Inc., 1962.

Kosobud, Richard F., and Morgan, James N. (Editors), *Consumer Behavior of Individual Families over Two and Three Years*. Monograph No. 36. Ann Arbor, Michigan: Survey Research Center, Institute for Social Research, The University of Michigan, 1964.

Kyrk, Hazel. *A Theory of Consumption*. Boston and New York: Houghton Mifflin Co., 1923.

Lamale, Helen Humes. *Methodology of the Survey of Consumer Expenditures in 1950*, part of *Study of Consumer Expenditures, Incomes, and Savings*. Philadelphia, Pennsylvania: Wharton School of Finance and Commerce, University of Pennsylvania, 1959.

Lazarsfeld, Paul F., and Rosenberg, Morris (Editors), *The Language of Social Research*. Glencoe, Illinois: The Free Press of Glencoe, Inc., 1955.

Lorie, James H., and Roberts, Harry V. *Basic Methods of Marketing Research*. New York: McGraw-Hill Book Co., Inc., 1951.

Luck, David J., Wales, Hugh G., and Taylor, Donald A. *Marketing Research*. Second Edition. Englewood Cliffs, New Jersey: Prentice-Hall, Inc., 1961.

Matthews, John B., Jr., Buzzell, Robert D., Levitt, Theodore, and Frank, Ronald E. *Marketing: An Introductory Analysis*. New York: McGraw-Hill Book Co., 1964.

McClelland, David C. *The Achieving Society*. Princeton, New Jersey: D. Van Nostrand Company, Inc., 1961.

Mead, Margaret (Editor), *Cultural Patterns and Technical Change*. A manual prepared by The World Federation for Mental Health, United Nations Educational, Scientific, and Cultural Organization. New York: Mentor Book, 1955.

Merton, Robert K. *Social Theory and Social Structure*. Revised and Enlarged Edition. New York: The Free Press of Glencoe (A Division of the Macmillan Company), 1957.

Morgan, James N., David, Martin H., Cohen, Wilbur J., and Brazer, Harvey E. *Income and Welfare in the United States*. New York: McGraw-Hill Book Company, Inc., 1962.

Morgenstern, Oskar. *On the Accuracy of Economic Observations*. Second Edition. Princeton, New Jersey: Princeton University Press, 1963.

Newman, Joseph W. (Editor), *On Knowing the Consumer*. New York: John Wiley & Sons, Inc., 1966.

Nicosia, Francesco M. *Consumer Decision Processes*. Englewood Cliffs, New Jersey: Prentice-Hall, Inc., 1966.

Norris, Ruby Turner. *The Theory of Consumer's Demand*. New Haven, Connecticut: Yale University Press, 1941.

Orcutt, Guy H., Greenberger, Martin, Karbel, John, and Rivlin, Alice M. *Microanalysis of Socioeconomic Systems: A Simulation Study*. New York: Harper & Brothers, 1961.

Osgood, Charles E. *Method and Theory in Experimental Psychology*. New York: Oxford University Press, 1953.

Parsons, Talcott, and Shils, Edward A. (Editors), *Toward a General Theory of Action*. Cambridge, Massachusetts: Harvard University Press, 1951.

Parsons, Talcott, and Smelser, Neil J. *Economy and Society*. Paperback Edition. New York: The Free Press, 1965.

Parten, Mildred. *Surveys, Polls, and Samples*. New York: Harper & Brothers, 1950.

Richardson, Stephen A., Dohrenwend, Barbara Snell, and Klein, David. *Interviewing: Its Forms and Functions*. New York: Basic Books, Inc., 1965.

Robbins, Lionel. *An Essay on the Nature and Significance of Economic Science*. Second Edition. London: Macmillan and Co. Ltd., 1952.

Rogers, Everett M. *Diffusion of Innovations*. New York: The Free Press, 1962.

Rose, Arnold M. (Editor), *Human Behavior and Social Processes*. Boston: Houghton Mifflin Company, 1962.

Rose, Arnold M. *Theory and Method in the Social Sciences*. Minneapolis: The University of Minnesota Press, 1954.

Salter, Leonard A., Jr. *A Critical Review of Research in Land Economics*. Minneapolis: The University of Minnesota Press, 1948.

Samuelson, Paul A. *Economics: An Introductory Analysis*. Fifth Edition. New York: McGraw-Hill Book Company, Inc., 1961.

Schultz, Theodore W. *The Economic Value of*

Education. New York: Columbia University Press, 1963.

Schwartz, George (Editor), *Science in Marketing.* New York: John Wiley & Sons, Inc., 1965.

Seelye, Alfred L. (Editor), *Marketing in Transition.* New York: Harper & Brothers, 1958.

Selltiz, Claire, Jahoda, Marie, Deutsch, Morton, and Cook, Stuart W. *Research Methods in Social Relations.* Revised One-Volume Edition. New York: Holt, Rinehart, & Winston, Inc., 1962.

Smelser, Neil J. *The Sociology of Economic Life.* Englewood Cliffs, New Jersey: Prentice-Hall Inc., 1963.

Stigler, George J. *Essays in the History of Economics.* Chicago: The University of Chicago Press, 1965.

Theil, H. *Linear Aggregation of Economic Relations.* Amsterdam: North-Holland Publishing Company, 1954.

Thurston, Marjorie H. *The Preparation of Term Papers and Reports.* Fourth Edition. Minneapolis, Minnesota: Burgess Publishing Co., 1963.

U.S. Department of Agriculture. *Food,* The Yearbook of Agriculture, 1959. Washington, D.C.: U.S. Government Printing Office, 1959.

U.S. Department of Agriculture. *Marketing,* The Yearbook of Agriculture, 1954. Washington, D.C.: U.S. Government Printing Office, 1954.

Veblen, Thorstein. *The Theory of the Leisure Class.* New York: The Modern Library Inc., 1934.

Waite, Warren C., and Cassady, Ralph, Jr. *The Consumer and the Economic Order.* Second Edition. New York: McGraw-Hill Book Company, Inc., 1949.

Wales, Hugh G. (Editor), *Changing Perspectives in Marketing.* Urbana, Illinois: University of Illinois Press, 1951.

Wyand, Charles S. *Economics of Consumption.* New York: The Macmillan Company, 1938.

Zimmerman, Carle C. *Consumption and Standards of Living.* New York: D. Van Nostrand Co., Inc., 1936.

PERIODICALS

Adams, F. Gerard. "Consumer Attitudes, Buying Plans, and Purchases of Durable Goods: A Principal Components, Time Series Approach," *Review of Economics and Statistics* **XLVI:** 4:347–383, November 1964.

Alexander, R. S. "The Death and Burial of 'Sick' Products," *J. Marketing* **28:**2:1–7, April 1964.

American Dairy Assoication. *Dairy Promotion Topics,* published bimonthly by American Dairy Association, Chicago, Illinois.

Anderson, Lee K., Taylor, James R., and Holloway, Robert J. "The Consumer and His Alternatives: An Experimental Approach," *J. Marketing Research* **III:**1:62–67, February 1966.

Atkinson, L. Jay. "Factors Affecting the Purchase Value of New Houses," *Survey of Current Business* **46:**8:20–36, August 1966.

Atkinson, L. Jay. "Long-Term Influences Affecting the Volume of New Housing Units," *Survey of Current Business* **43:**11:8–19, November 1963.

Bayton, James A. "Contributions of Psychology to the Microeconomic Analysis of Consumer Demand for Food," *J. Farm Economics* **45:** 5:1430–1435, December 1963.

Bayton, James A. "Motivation, Cognition, Learning—Basic Factors in Consumer Behavior," *J. Marketing* **22:**3:282–289, January 1958.

Beckerman, Wilfred, and Bacon, Robert. "International Comparisons of Income Levels: A Suggested New Measure," *Economic Journal* **LXXVI:**303:519–536, September 1966.

Bilkey, Warren J. "A Psychological Approach to Consumer Behavior Analysis," *J. Marketing* **18:**1:18–25, July 1953.

Bird, Kermit. "Developing and Testing New Foods and Fibers," *The Marketing and Transportation Situation* **155:**35–41, November 1964.

Boulding, Elise. "Orientation Toward Achievement or Security in Relation to Consumer Behavior," *Human Relations* **13:**4:365–383, November 1960.

Brandt, Steven C. "Dissecting the Segmentation Syndrome," *J. Marketing* **30:**4:22–27, October 1966.

Brown, D. A., Buck, S. F., and Pyatt, F. G. "Improving the Sales Forecast for Consumer Durables," *J. Marketing Research* **II:**3:229–234, August 1965.

Brown, T. M. "Habit Persistence and Lags in Consumer Behaviour," *Econometrica* **20:**3:355–371, July 1952.

Burk, Marguerite C. "Can or Should the U.S. Fill the World Food Gap?" *AAUW Journal* **59:** 4:199–201, 214, May 1966.

Burk, Marguerite C. "Changes in the Demand for Food from 1941 to 1950," *J. Farm Economics* **XXXIII:**3:281–298, August 1951.

Burk, Marguerite C. "Development of a New Approach to Forecasting Demand," *J. Farm Economics* **46:**3:618–632, August 1964.

Burk, Marguerite C. "An Economic Appraisal of Changes in Rural Food Consumption," *J. Farm Economics* **XL:**3:572–590, August 1958.

Burk, Marguerite C. "Les Changements Qualitatifs dans l'Alimentation et leur Répercussions sur l'Agriculture: L'Expérience des États-Unis," *Economie Rurale* **66:**31–38, October–December. Also published in the German journal of agricultural economics as "Qualitative Veränderungen im Nahrungsmittelverbrauch und die Landwirtschaft-Erfahrungen in den USA," *Agrarwirtschaft* **15:**5:149–156, May 1966.

Burk, Marguerite C. "Ramifications of the Relationship Between Income and Food," *J. Farm Economics* **XLIV**: 1:115–125, February 1962.

Burk, Marguerite C. "The Study of Regional Food Consumption," *J. Farm Economics* **XLI**: 5:1040–1049, December 1959.

Burk, Marguerite C., and Lanahan, Thomas J., Jr. "Use of 1955 Food Survey Data for Research in Agricultural Economics," *Agricultural Economics Research* **X**:3:79–98, July 1958.

Business Week. "The Memo That Moved a Mountain," No. 1841, pp. 69, 72, 74, December 12, 1964.

Business Week. "Lenox Takes a Fast Boat for China," No. 1844, pp. 69–70, January 2, 1965.

Business Week. "Will It Go in Britain?" No. 1845, pp. 86–89, January 9, 1965.

Business Week. "Cotton's King Tills New Fields," No. 1847, pp. 138, 140, 142, January 23, 1965.

Business Week. "Still More Gold in California Land," No. 1847, pp. 112–114, January 23, 1965.

Business Week. "Hot Shoppes Adds to Its Menu," No. 1850, pp. 160, 162, February 13, 1965.

Business Week. "Young Blood Puts Life Into an Old Packer," No. 1850, pp. 142, 144, February 13, 1965.

Campbell, Carlos. "Commercial Canning—What Does the Future Hold?" *J. Marketing* **26**: 2:44–47, April 1962.

Chiang, Alpha C. "The 'Demonstration Effect' in a Dual Economy," *Am. J. Econ. and Soc.* **18**:2:249–258, April 1958.

Chinoy, Ely. "The Tradition of Opportunity and the Aspirations of Automobile Workers," *Am. J. Soc.* **LVII**:5:453–459, March 1952.

Consumers' Research, Inc. *Consumer Bulletin* (formerly Consumer's Research Bulletin), published monthly by Consumers' Research, Inc., Washington, New Jersey.

Consumers' Union, Inc. *Consumer Reports*, published by Consumers' Union, Inc., Mount Vernon, New York.

Daly, R. F., and Egbert, A. C. "A Look Ahead for Food and Agriculture," *Agricultural Economics Research* **XVIII**:1:1–9, January 1966.

Davis, Joseph S. "Standards and Content of Living," *Am. Econ. Rev.* **XXXV**:1:1–15, March 1945.

Demsetz, Harold. "The Effect of Consumer Experience on Brand Loyalty and the Structure of Market Demand," *Econometrica* **30**:1:22–33, January 1962.

Faltermayer, Edmund K. "It's a Spryer Singer," *Fortune* **LXVIII**:6:145–148, 154, December 1963.

Ferber, Robert. "Research on Household Behavior," *Am. Econ. Rev.* **LII**:1:19–63, March 1962.

Fisher, Janet A. "Consumer Durable Goods Expenditures, with Major Emphasis on the Role of Assets, Credit, and Intentions," *J. Am. Stat. Assn.* **58**:303:648–657, September 1963.

Form, William H., and Miller, Delbert C. "Occupational Career Pattern as a Sociological Instrument," *Am. J. Soc.* **LIV**:4:317–329, January 1949.

Fortune. "General Foods Is Five Billion Particulars," **LXIX**:3:115–117, 158, 160, 163, March 1964.

Friedman, Charles S. "Auto Ownership by Households in Mid-1964; Influences of Economic and Other Socioeconomic Factors," *Survey of Current Business* **46**:10:14–24, October 1966.

Goldberger, Arthur S., and Lee, Maw Lin. "Toward a Microanalytic Model of the Household Sector," *Am. Econ. Rev.* **LII**:2:241–251, May 1962.

Gorman, W. M. "The Empirical Implications of a Utility Tree: A Further Comment," *Econometrica* **27**:3:489, July 1959.

Gorman, W. M. "Separable Utility and Aggregation," *Econometrica* **27**:3:469–481, July 1959.

Gramm, Warren S. "Water Resource Analysis: Private Investment Criteria and Social Priorities," *J. Farm Economics* **45**:4:705–712, November 1963.

Halvorson, Harlow W., and Cook, Hugh L. "Pupil Response to Changes in School Milk Prices in Wisconsin," *J. Farm Economics* **XLII**:3:692–698, August 1960.

Hill, Reuben, and Hansen, Donald A. "The Identification of Conceptual Frameworks Utilized in Family Study," *Marriage and Family Living* **22**:4:299–311, November 1960.

Holloway, Robert J. "An Experiment on Consumer Dissonance," *J. Marketing* **31**:1:39–43, January 1967.

Houthakker, H. S. "The Present State of Consumption Theory," *Econometrica* **29**:4:704–740, October 1961.

Jacobi, John E., and Walters, S. George. "Dress Buying Behavior of Consumers," *J. Marketing* **23**:2:168–172, October 1958.

John, M. E. "Classification of Values that Serve as Motivators to Consumer Purchases," *J. Farm Economics* **XXXVIII**:4:956–963, November 1956.

Johnston, Bruce F., and Mellor, John W. "The Nature of Agriculture's Contributions to Economic Development," *Food Research Institute Studies* **I**:3:335–356, November 1960.

Kaneda, Hiromitsu, and Johnston, Bruce F. "Urban Food Expenditure Patterns in Tropical Africa," *Food Research Institute Studies* **II**:3:229–275, November 1961.

Keith, Robert J. "The Marketing Revolution," *J. Marketing* **24**:3:35–38, January 1960.

Kiehl, Elmer R., and Rhodes, V. James. "New Techniques in Consumer Preference Research,"

J. Farm Economics **XXXVIII**:5:1335–1345, December 1956.

Klein, L. R., and Lansing, J. B. "Decisions to Purchase Consumer Durable Goods," *J. Marketing* **XX**:2:108–132, October 1955.

Koppe, William A. "The Psychological Meanings of Housing and Furnishings," *Marriage and Family Living* **XVII**:2:129–132, May 1955.

Krugman, Herbert E., and Hartley, Eugene L. "The Learning of Tastes," *The Public Opinion Quarterly* **24**:4:621–631, Winter 1960.

Kuehn, Alfred A., and Day, Ralph L. "Strategy of Product Quality," *Harv. Bus. Rev.* **40**:6:100–110, November–December 1962.

Lamale, Helen H. "Workers' Wealth and Family Living Standards," *Monthly Labor Review* **86**:6:676–686, June 1963.

Lancaster, Kelvin J. "Change and Innovation in the Technology of Consumption," *Am. Econ. Rev.* **LVI**:2:14–23, May 1966.

Lancaster, Kelvin J. "A New Approach to Consumer Theory," *J. Pol. Econ.* **LXXIV**:2:132–157, April 1966.

Lansing, John B., and Kish, Leslie. "Family Life Cycle as an Independent Variable," *American Sociological Review* **22**:5:512–519, October 1957.

Lavell, Robert J. "Introduction of New Regional Indexes for Food Consumption Analysis," *National Food Situation* **89**:17–39, July 1959.

Letwin, William. "What's Wrong with Planning: The Case of India," *Fortune* **LXVII**:6:118–121, 144, 146, 148, 151, 152, June 1963.

Mainer, Robert, and Slater, Charles C. "Markets in Motion," *Harv. Bus. Rev.* **42**:2:75–82, March–April 1964.

Mann, W. S., and Nwankwo, J. C. O. "Case Study on Rural Food Consumption in Eastern Nigeria," *Agriculture Situation in India* **XX**:4:221–224, July 1965.

Martineau, Pierre. "Social Classes and Spending Behavior," *J. Marketing* **23**:2:121–130, October 1958.

Moore, Hugh L., and Hussey, Gorham. "Economic Implications of Market Orientation," *J. Farm Economics* **47**:2:421–427, May 1965.

Morgan, James N. "Housing and Ability to Pay," *Econometrica* **33**:2:289–306, April 1965.

Morgan, James N., and Sonquist, John A. "Problems in the Analysis of Survey Data, and a Proposal," *J. Am. Stat. Assn.* **58**:302:415–434, June 1963.

Newell, Allen, Shaw, J. C., and Simon, Herbert A. "Elements of a Theory of Human Problem Solving," *Psych. Review* **65**:3:151–166, May 1958.

Nicol, B. M. "The Calorie Requirements of Nigerian Peasant Farmers," *Br. J. of Nutrition* **13**:293–306, 1959.

Orcutt, Guy H. "Microanalytic Models of the United States Economy: Need and Development," *Am. Econ. Rev.* **LII**:2:229–240, May 1962.

Ostheimer, Richard H. "Who Buys What? *Life's* Study of Consumer Expenditures," *J. Marketing* **XXII**:3:260–272, January 1958.

Peryam, David R. "Discussion: Linear Programming Models for the Determination of Palatable Human Diets," *J. Farm Economics,* **XLI**:2:302–305, May 1959.

Poleman, Thomas T. "The Food Economies of Urban Middle Africa: The Case of Ghana," *Food Research Institute Studies* **II**:2:121–174, May 1961.

Reed, Vergil D., Parker, Katherine G., and Vitriol, Herbert A. "Selection, Training, and Supervision of Field Interviewers in Marketing Research," *J. Marketing* **XII**:3:365–378, January 1948.

Regan, William J. "The Service Revolution," *J. Marketing* **27**:3:57–62, July 1963.

Roseborough, Howard. "Some Sociological Dimensions of Consumer Spending." *Canadian Journal of Economics and Political Economy* **26**:3:452–464, August 1960.

Samuelson, Paul A. "Professor Samuelson on Theory and Realism: A Reply." *Am. Econ. Rev.* **LV**:5:1164–1172, December 1965.

Shaffer, James Duncan. "The Influence of 'Impulse Buying' on In-the-Store Decisions on Consumers' Food Purchases," *J. Farm Economics* **XLII**:2:317–324, May 1960.

Simon, Herbert A. "Theories of Decision-Making in Economics and Behavioral Science," *Am. Econ. Rev.* **XLIX**:3:253–283, June 1959.

Simon, Nancy W. "Personal Consumption Expenditures in the 1958 Input-Output Study," *Survey of Current Business* **45**:10:7–20, October 1965.

Sinha, R. P. "An Analysis of Food Expenditures in India," *J. Farm Economics* **48**:1:113–123, February 1966.

Smith, Richard Austin. "The Onrushing Auto Makers," *Fortune* **LXVIII**:2:96–101, August 1963.

Smith, Victor E. "Linear Programming Models for the Determination of Palatable Human Diets," *J. Farm Economics* **XLI**:2:272–283, May 1959.

Smith, Wendell R. "Product Differentiation and Market Segmentation as Alternative Marketing Strategies," *J. Marketing* **XXI**:1:3–8, July 1956.

Stigler, George J. "The Cost of Subsistence," *J. Farm Economics* **XXVII**:2:303–314, May 1945.

Stigler, George J. "The Early History of Empirical Studies of Consumer Behavior," *J. Pol. Econ.* **LXII**:2:95–113, April 1954.

Strotz, Robert H. "The Empirical Implications of

a Utility Tree," *Econometrica* **25**:2:269–280, April 1957.

Strotz, Robert H. "The Utility Tree—A Correction and Further Appraisal," *Econometrica* **27**: 3:482–488, July 1959.

Summers, Robert, Suits, Daniel B., and Dingle, Mona E. "Discussion," *Am. Econ. Rev.* **LII**: 2:252–258, May 1962.

Tibbets, Thomas R. "Expanding Ownership of Household Equipment," *Monthly Labor Review* **87**:10:1131–1137, October 1964.

Trier, Howard, Smith, Henry Clay, and Shaffer, James. "Differences in Food Buying Attitudes of Housewives," *J. Marketing* **25**:1:66–69, July 1960.

U.S. Department of Agriculture, Economic Research Service. Periodicals (usually issued quarterly)
The Dairy Situation
The Fats and Oils Situation
The Feed Situation
The Livestock and Meat Situation
The Marketing and Transportation Situation
The National Food Situation
The Wheat Situation

U.S. Department of Commerce, Office of Business Economics. *Survey of Current Business* (monthly).

Waldorf, William H. "The Demand for and Supply of Food Marketing Services: An Aggregate View," *J. Farm Economics* **48**:1:42–60, February 1966.

Weaver, Warren. "A Scientist Ponders Faith," *Saturday Review* **XLII**:1:8–10, 33, January 3, 1959.

Wolgast, Elizabeth. "Do Husbands or Wives Make the Purchasing Decisions?" *J. Marketing* **23**: 2:151–158, October 1958.

Woods, Walter A. "Psychological Dimensions of Consumer Decision," *J. Marketing* **24**:3:15–19, January 1960.

Yankelovich, Daniel. "New Criteria for Market Segmentation," *Harv. Bus. Rev.* **42**:2:83–90, March–April 1964.

Zajonc, Robert. "The Concepts of Balance, Congruity, and Dissonance," *Public Opinion Quarterly* **24**:3:280–296, Fall 1960.

Zwick, Charles J. "Discussion: Econometric Models in Agriculture," *J. Farm Economics* **XLI**: 2:306–308, May 1959.

REPORTS

Abel, Martin E., and Cochrane, Willard W. *Policies for Expanding the Demand for Farm Food Products in the United States*, Part II *Programs and Results*, University of Minnesota Agricultural Experiment Station Tech. Bul. No. 238, April 1961.

Alexis, Marcus, Simon, Leonard, and Smith, Kenneth. *Some Determinants of Food Buying Behavior* (Manuscript), College of Business Administration, University of Rochester, Rochester, New York, 1966.

American Marketing Association. *The Design of Research Investigations*, Mktg. Res. Tech. Series No. 1, Chicago: AMA, 1958.

American Marketing Association. *Sampling in Marketing Research*, Mktg. Res. Tech. Series No. 3, Chicago: AMA, 1958.

Bayton, James. "Conscious vs. Habit Purchases: Implications for Advertising," paper presented at the Association of National Advertisers, Inc. Workshop on Advertising Research, New York City, April 1, 1959, A.N.A. File Code No. 15, New York City: Assoc. National Advertisers, Inc.

Ben-David, Shaul, and Tomek, William G. *Allowing for Scope and Intercept Changes in Regression Analysis*, Cornell University, Department of Agricultural Economics, A. E. Res. 179, November 1965.

Beyer, Glenn H. *Housing and Personal Values*, Cornell University Agricultural Experiment Station Memoir 364, July 1959.

Bogue, Donald J. "The Prospects for World Population Control," paper presented at the Conference on Alternatives for Balancing Future World Food Production and Needs, Iowa State University, Center for Agricultural Economic Adjustment, Ames, Iowa, November 9, 1966.

Bourne, Francis S. "The Concept of Reference Group Influence," *Group Influence in Marketing and Public Relations*, a report of a 1956 seminar conducted for and published by the Foundation for Research on Human Behavior, Ann Arbor, Michigan, 1956.

Brew, Margaret L., O'Leary, Roxanne R., and Dean, Lucille C. *Family Clothing Inventories and Purchases*, U.S. Dept. Agr., Agr. Inf. Bul. 148, 1956.

Brown, Lester R. *Food Consumption and Expenditures: India, Japan, United States*, U.S. Dept. Agr., ERS Foreign–42, November 1962.

Burk, Marguerite C. *Consumption of Processed Farm Foods in the United States*, U.S. Dept. Agr., Marketing Research Report No. 409, June 1960.

Burk, Marguerite C. *Measures and Procedures for Analysis of U.S. Food Consumption*, U.S. Dept. Agr., Agr. Handb. 206, June 1961.

Burk, Marguerite C. *Trends and Patterns in U.S. Food Consumption*, U.S. Dept. Agr., Agr. Handb. 214, June 1961.

Calvin, Lyle D. "What Do Consumer Surveys Tell Us," in *Proceedings of the Conference on Consumer Studies and Meat Quality*, University of Missouri, Columbia, Missouri, September 10, 1957.

Christensen, Raymond P., Johnson, Sherman E.,

and Baumann, Ross V. *Production Prospects for Wheat, Feed, and Livestock, 1960–1965,* U.S. Dept. Agr., Agr. Res. Service, ARS 43–115, December 1959.

Clark, Faith, Murray, Janet, et al. *Food Consumption of Urban Families in the United States,* U.S. Dept. Agr., Agr. Inf. Bul. 132, 1954.

Clement, Wendell E. *Use and Promotion of Dairy Products in Public Eating Places,* U.S. Dept. Agr., Marketing Research Report No. 626, August 1963.

Cofer, Eloise, Grossman, Evelyn, and Clark, Faith. *Family Food Plans and Food Costs,* U.S. Dept. Agr., Home Economics Research Report No. 21, November 1962.

Coleman, John A., Murray, Edward, and Judson, C. H., Jr. *Tabulation: Elements of Planning and Techniques,* American Marketing Association, Mktg. Res. Tech. Series No. 5, Chicago: AMA, 1962.

Communauté Économique Européenne. *Le marché commun des produits agricoles: Perspectives "1970,"* Étude Serie Agriculture Nr. 10, Bruxelles, 1963.

Community Council of Greater New York, Research Department, The Budget Standard Service, *A Family Budget Standard,* New York: Community Council of Greater New York, 1963.

Compact Car Owners, a study made by R. L. Polk and Co. for *Redbook Magazine* (no date on publication).

Cowles Magazine and Broadcasting, Inc. *National Appliance Survey, 1963,* Vol. One: Major Appliances, New York: Cowles Magazine and Broadcasting, Inc., 1963.

Crespi, Irving. *Attitude Research,* American Marketing Association, Mktg. Res. Tech. Series No. 7, Chicago: AMA, 1965.

Culbertson, Viola, and Higgins, Marguerite. *Preparing Statistical Tables for Publication: A Guide to Usage in AMS,* U.S. Dept. Agr., Agr. Handb. 121, April 1957.

Daly, R. F. "Agriculture in the Years Ahead," talk presented at the Southern Agricultural Workers Conference, Atlanta, Georgia, February 3, 1964, issued by U.S. Dept. Agr., Economic Research Service.

Daly, Rex F. "Prospective Domestic Demands for Food and Fiber," paper submitted for hearings on Policy for Commercial Agriculture, Joint Economic Committee of the Congress, 85th Congress, 1st Session, November 22, 1957.

Dandekar, V. M. *The Demand for Food and Conditions Governing Food Aid During Development,* World Food Program Studies No. 1, UN Food and Agriculture Organization, Rome, 1965.

Denison, Edward F. *Sources of Economic Growth in the United States and the Alternatives Before Us,* Supplementary paper No. 13, New York: The Committee for Economic Development, 1962.

Dickins, Dorothy. *Food Purchases and Use Practices of Families of Gainfully Employed Homemakers,* Mississippi State Agricultural Experiment Station Bulletin 620, May 1961.

Dickins, Dorothy, and Johnston, Alvirda. *Children's Influence on Family Food Purchase Decisions,* Mississippi State University Agricultural Experiment Station Bulletin No. 671, September 1963.

Ferber, Robert. *Factors Influencing Durable Goods Purchases,* Bur. Econ. Bus. Res., University of Illinois Bulletin Series, No. 79, Urbana, Illinois, March 1955.

FitzGerald, D. A. *Operational and Administrative Problems of Food Aid,* World Food Program Studies No. 4, UN Food and Agricultural Organization, Rome, 1965.

Fliegel, Frederick C. *Food Habits and National Backgrounds,* Pennsylvania Agricultural Experiment Station Bulletin No. 684, October 1961.

Foote, Richard J. *Analytical Tools for Studying Demand and Price Structures,* U.S. Dept. Agr., Agr. Handb. 146, August 1958.

Ford Foundation, Agricultural Production Team, *Report on India's Food Crisis and Steps to Meet It,* New York: Ford Foundation, April 1959.

Gale, Hazen F. *The Farm Food Marketing Bill and Its Components,* U.S. Dept. Agr., Agr. Econ. Report No. 105, January 1967.

Gartner, Joseph, Kolmer, Lee, and Jones, Ethel B. *Consumer Decision Making.* Consumer Marketing Bulletin I, Iowa State University, Ames, Iowa, and the Cooperative Extension Service, November 1960.

Gunther, Edgar, and Goldstein, Frederick A. *Current Sources of Marketing Information, A Bibliography of Primary Marketing Data,* American Marketing Association Bibliography Series, Number 6, Chicago: AMA, 1960.

Holmes, Emma G. *Job-Related Expenditures and Management Practices of Gainfully Employed Wives in Four Georgia Cities,* U.S. Dept. Agr., Home Economics Research Report No. 15, February 1962.

Jackendoff, Ruth. *Consumer Apparel Expenditures:* An Analysis of Trends, Average 1935–39—1963, New York: Wool Bureau, March 1964.

Johnson, Stewart, Brinegar, George K., Howes, Richard R., Maina, James W., and Lundquist, Lynwood. *Economic Analysis of the U.S. Special Milk Program with Particular Reference to Connecticut,* University of Connecticut, College of Agriculture, Agricultural Experiment Station Bulletin No. 356, November 1960.

Koffsky, Nathan. "Potential Demand for Farm Products Over the Next Quarter Century," paper presented for the Seminar in Dynamics of Land Use at Iowa State University, May 3, 1960 (issued by U.S. Economic Research Service).

Le Bovit, Corinne, and Clark, Faith. *Household Practices in the Use of Foods*, Three Cities, 1953, U.S. Dept. Agr., Agr. Inf. Bul. 146, April 1956.

Levine, Daniel B. *Homemakers Appraise Cotton, Wool, and Other Fibers in Household Furnishings*, U.S. Dept. Agr., Marketing Research Report No. 279, November 1958.

Mann, Jitendar Singh. *The Contribution of United States Public Law 480 to Indian Economic Development*, unpublished Ph.D. Thesis, University of Minnesota, March 1966.

Maynes, E. Scott. "Consumer Attitudes and Buying Intentions: Retrospect and Prospect" (Manuscript), Buenos Aires, Argentina: Instituto Torcuato di Tella, Centro de Investigationes Económicas, September 1966.

Ministry of Food and Agriculture. *Review of the Food Situation*, New Delhi, India: Government of India, September 1964.

Murray, Janet, Blake, Ennis C., Dickins, Dorothy, and Moser, Ada M. *Collection Methods in Dietary Surveys: A Comparison of the Food List and Record in Two Farming Areas of the South*, Southern Cooperative Series Bulletin 23, April 1952 (obtainable from the Mississippi State Agr. Exp. Station).

Mushkin, Selma J. (Editor), *Economics of Higher Education*, U.S. Department of Health, Education, and Welfare, Office of Education, OE–50027, Bulletin No. 5, 1962.

National Commission on Food Marketing. (Publications distributed by the U.S. Government Printing Office.)

Food from Farmer to Consumer, Summary report, June 1966.

Organization and Competition in the Dairy Industry, Technical Study No. 3, June 1966.

Organization and Competition in the Milling and Baking Industries, Technical Study No. 5, June 1966.

National Council of Applied Economic Research (India). *Long Term Projections of Demand for and Supply of Selected Agricultural Commodities, 1960–61 to 1975–76*, New Delhi, India: National Council of Applied Economic Research, April 1962.

National Industrial Conference Board. *The Development of Marketing Objectives and Plans*, a Symposium of the Conference Board, Experiences in Marketing Management No. 3, New York: National Industrial Conference Board, 1963.

National Research Council. *Manual for the Study of Food Habits*, Bulletin 111, Washington, D.C.: National Research Council, National Academy of Sciences, January 1945.

National Research Council. *Nutrition Surveys: Their Techniques and Value*, Bulletin 117, Washington, D.C.: National Research Council, National Academy of Sciences, May 1949.

National Research Council, Report of the Committee on Food Habits, 1941–43, *The Problem of Changing Food Habits*, Bulletin No. 108, Washington, D.C.: National Academy of Sciences, National Research Council, October 1943.

National Sample Survey of India. *Report on Consumer Expenditure*, No. 20, published by Manager of Publications, Civil Lines, Delhi 8, Calcutta: Eka Press, 1959.

Newsweek. *Newsweek's 1963 Census of New Car Buyers*, third annual report, New York: *Newsweek*, 1963.

Nolan, Francena L. *Factors Associated with Preferences For Household Equipment and Furniture By 351 Rural Families*, Pennsylvania Agricultural Experiment Station Bulletin No. 591, January 1955.

Nolan, Francena L., and Levine, Daniel B. *Consumers' Concepts of Fabric*, U.S. Dept. Agr., Marketing Research Report No. 338, July 1959.

Outdoor Recreation Resources Review Commission (ORRRC). (Publications distributed by the U.S. Government Printing Office.)

Study Report 19. *National Recreation Survey*, by the Commission Staff, 1962.

Study Report 20. *Participation in Outdoor Recreation: Factors Affecting Demand Among American Adults*, by Eva Mueller and Gerald Gurin of the Survey Research Center, The University of Michigan, 1962.

Study Report 22. *Trends in American Living and Outdoor Recreation*, by Lawrence K. Frank, Herbert J. Gans, et al., 1962.

Study Report 24. *Economic Studies of Outdoor Recreation*, by the Commission Staff and Contributors, 1962.

Peryam, David R., Polemis, Bernice W., Kamen, Joseph M., Eindhoven, Jan, and Pilgrim, Francis J. *Food Preferences of Men in the U.S. Armed Forces*, report issued by the Department of the Army, Quartermaster Research and Engineering Command, January 1960.

Quackenbush, G. G., and Shaffer, J. D. *Collecting Food Purchase Data by Consumer Panel*—A Methodological Report on the MSU Consumer Panel, 1951–58, Michigan State University, Agricultural Experiment Station Tech. Bul. 279, August 1960.

Redstrom, Ruth A., Davenport, Elizabeth, and Murray, Janet. *Consumer Practices in the Handling and Storing of Commercially Frozen Foods, Two Cities, Two Seasons*, U.S. Dept.

Agr., Home Economics Research Report No. 23, September 1963.

Reh, Emma. *Manual on Household Food Consumption Surveys*, UN Food and Agriculture Organization, Nutrition Studies No. 18, Rome, 1962.

Sales Management Inc. *America's Lush Leisure Markets*, 1961.

Simmons, Will M. *Consumer Meat Purchases in Syracuse, New York, 1948 and Comparison with 1942*, Cornell University Agricultural Experiment Station Bulletin 869, June 1951.

Spencer, Vivian Eberle. *Raw Materials in the United States Economy, 1900–61*, U.S. Dept. of Commerce, Bureau of the Census, Working Paper No. 6, Washington, D.C., 1963.

Stallings, Dale G. *Long-Run Projections of Food Processing and Marketing in the West*, U.S. Dept. Agr., Agr. Econ. Report No. 78, June 1965.

Stanford Food Research Institute. *Summary Report of Food Research Institute Conference on Economic, Political and Human Aspects of Agricultural Development in Tropical Africa*, Stanford, California: Stanford University Press, 1959.

Stanton, B. F. *Table Talk*, Cornell University, Department of Agricultural Economics, A. E. Res. 98, December 1962.

Stevens, Robert D. *Elasticity of Food Consumption Associated With Changes in Income in Developing Countries*, U.S. Dept. Agr., Foreign Agricultural Economic Report No. 23, March 1965.

Stewart, Ian G., and Ogley, R. C. *Nigeria: Determinants of Projected Level of Demand, Supply, and Imports of Farm Products in 1965 and 1975*, U.S. Dept. Agr., ERS–Foreign–32, August 1962.

Stubbs, Alice C., and Blackstone, J. H. *Nutritional Knowledge and Consumer Use of Dairy Products in Urban Areas of the South*, Southern Cooperative Series Bulletin No. 87, July 1963 (obtainable from Southern Agricultural Experiment Stations).

United Nations. *Compendium of Social Statistics*, U.N. Series K, No. 2. New York: United Nations, 1963.

United Nations. *Handbook of Household Surveys*, A Practical Guide for Inquiries on Levels of Living, Studies in Methods Series F, No. 10. Provisional Edition, New York: United Nations, 1964.

United Nations. *Report on the World Social Situation*, New York: United Nations, 1963.

United Nations. *Yearbook of National Accounts Statistics*, New York: United Nations, 1965.

United Nations Food and Agriculture Organization. *State of Food and Agriculture* (annual), Rome: UN Food and Agriculture Organization, 1966.

United Nations Food and Agriculture Organization. *Third World Food Survey*, Freedom from Hunger Campaign Basic Study No. 11, Rome: UN Food and Agriculture Organization, 1963.

United Nations, Report of a Committee of Experts. *International Definition and Measurement of Standards and Levels of Living*, New York: United Nations, 1954.

United Nations, Social Committee, 14th Session. *Report of the Ad Hoc Group of Experts on Housing and Urban Development*, New York: United Nations, April 1962.

U.S. Department of Agriculture. *Agricultural Statistics* (Statistical Yearbook).

U.S. Department of Agriculture, Household Food Consumption Survey, 1955:

Report 1. *Food Consumption of Households in the United States*, December 1956.

Report 3. *Food Consumption of Households in the North Central Region*, December 1956.

Report 4. *Food Consumption of Households in the South*, December 1956.

Report 6. *Dietary Levels of Households in the United States*, March 1957.

Report 8. *Dietary Levels of Households in the North Central Region*, May 1957.

Report 9. *Dietary Levels of Households in the South*, May 1957.

Report 17. *Food Consumption and Dietary Levels of Households of Different Sizes, United States—by Region*, January 1963.

U.S. Department of Agriculture. *Major Statistical Series of the U.S. Department of Agriculture*, Volume 5, "Consumption and Utilization of Agricultural Products," U.S. Dept. Agr., Agr. Handb. 118, 1958.

U.S. Department of Agriculture, Agricultural Marketing Service. *Marketing Efficiency in a Changing Economy*, a Report of the National Workshop on Agricultural Marketing, June 17–24, 1955 at the University of Kentucky, AMS–60, September 1965.

U.S. Department of Agriculture, Agricultural Marketing Service. *Marketing Margins for White Bread*, U.S. Dept. Agr., Misc. Pub. 712, 1956.

U.S. Department of Agriculture, Agricultural Marketing Service. *Measuring the Supply and Utilization of Farm Commodities*, U.S. Dept. Agr., Agr. Handb. 91, 1955.

U.S. Department of Agriculture, Agricultural Marketing Service, Food Consumption Section. *Meat Consumption Trends and Patterns*, U.S. Dept. Agr., Agr. Handb. 187, July 1960.

U.S. Department of Agriculture, Agricultural Research Administration. *Market Demand and Product Quality*, a report of the Marketing

Research Workshop at Michigan State College, July 13–21, 1951.

U.S. Department of Agriculture, Agricultural Research Service. *Consumer Expenditures and Income: Rural Farm Population, North Central Region, 1961*, U.S. Dept. Agr., Cons. Exp. Survey Report No. 2, April 1965.

U.S. Department of Agriculture, Agricultural Research Service. *Consumer Expenditures and Income: Rural Farm Population, Southern Region, 1961*, U.S. Dept. Agr., Cons. Exp. Survey Report No. 3, April 1965.

U.S. Department of Agriculture, Agricultural Research Service. *Consumer Expenditures and Income: Rural Farm Population, United States, 1961*, U.S. Dept. Agr., Cons. Exp. Survey Report No. 5, April 1965.

U.S. Department of Agriculture, Agricultural Research Service. *Food Consumption and Dietary Levels of Households in the United States*, ARS 62–6, August 1957.

U.S. Department of Agriculture, Bureau of Agricultural Economics. *Consumption of Food in the United States, 1909–48*, U.S. Dept. Agr., Misc. Pub. 691, 1949 (superseded in 1953 by Agr. Handb. 62 and in 1965 by Statis. Bul. 364, *U.S. Consumption of Food*).

U.S. Department of Agriculture, Economic Research Service. *U.S. Food Consumption*, U.S. Dept. Agr., Statis. Bul. No. 364, June 1965.

U.S. Department of Agriculture, Economic Research Service, Foreign Development and Trade Division. *Changes in Agriculture in 26 Developing Nations, 1948 to 1963*, U.S. Dept. Agr., Foreign Agricultural Economic Report No. 27, November 1965.

U.S. Department of Agriculture, Economic Research Service, Foreign Regional Analysis Division. *The World Food Budget, 1970*, U.S. Dept. Agr., Foreign Agricultural Economic Report No. 19, October 1964.

U.S. Department of Agriculture, Economic Research Service, Marketing Economics Division. *Agricultural Markets in Change*, U.S. Dept. Agr., Agr. Econ. Report No. 95, July 1966.

U.S. Department of Agriculture, Foreign Agricultural Service. *Food Balances in Foreign Countries*, U.S. Dept. Agr., FAS–M–108, February 1961.

U.S. Department of Commerce. *Export Origin Study, State of Oregon*, 1962.

U.S. Department of Commerce, Bureau of the Census. *1963 Census of Business: Retail, Trade, Merchandise Line Sales*, 1965.

U.S. Department of Commerce, Bureau of the Census. *Historical Statistics of the United States, Colonial Times to 1957*, 1960.

U.S. Department of Commerce, Bureau of the Census. *Statistical Abstract of the United States* (published annually).

U.S. Department of Commerce, Office of Business Economics. *Business Statistics*, annual supplement to the *Survey of Current Business.*

U.S. Department of Commerce, Office of Business Economics. *The National Income and Product Accounts of the United States, 1929–1965*, Statistical Tables, a supplement to the *Survey of Current Business*, August 1966.

U.S. Department of Commerce, Office of Business Economics. *Personal Income by States*, a supplement to the *Survey of Current Business.*

U.S. Department of Commerce, Office of Business Economics. *U.S. Income and Output*, a supplement to the *Survey of Current Business*, 1958.

U.S. Department of Labor. *The American Worker's Stake in Foreign Trade*, 1962.

U.S. Department of Labor. *How American Buying Habits Change*, 1959.

U.S. Department of Labor, Bureau of Labor Statistics. *Workers' Budgets in the United States: City Families and Single Persons*, U.S. Bur. Labor Statis., Bul. No. 927, 1948.

U.S. Department of Labor, Bureau of Labor Statistics. *Family Spending and Saving in Wartime*, U.S. Bur. Labor Statis., Bul. No. 822, 1945.

U.S. Department of Labor, Bureau of Labor Statistics. Reports on Survey of Consumer Expenditures, 1960–61. *Consumer Expenditures and Income:*

Urban Places in the Northeastern Region, 1960–61, BLS Report No. 237–34, May 1964.

Urban Places in the North Central Region, 1960–61, BLS Report No. 237–35, May 1964.

Urban Places in the Southern Region, 1960–61, BLS Report No. 237–36, May 1964.

Urban Places in the Western Region, 1960–61, BLS Report No. 237–37, May 1964.

Urban United States, 1960–61, BLS Report No. 237–38, May 1964.

Rural Nonfarm Areas in the United States, 1961, BLS Report No. 237–88 (USDA Report CES–10), June 1964.

Total United States, Urban and Rural, 1960–61, BLS Report No. 237–93 (USDA Report CES–15), February 1965.

U.S. Senate, Select Committee on National Water Resources. *Water Resources Activities in the United States: Land and Water Potentials and Future Requirements for Water*, 86th Congress, First Session, Committee Print No. 12, Washington: U.S. Government Printing Office, 1960.

University of Pennsylvania, Wharton School of Finance and Commerce. *Study of Consumer Expenditures, Incomes and Savings*, Philadelphia: University of Pennsylvania, 18 Vols. 1956 and 1957 (contain data from 1950 survey by U.S. Bureau of Labor Statistics).

Van Dress, Michael G., and Freund, William H. *Survey of the Market for Food Away from Home:* A Preliminary Overview of Basic Tabulations From Phase I of the Survey, U.S. Dept. Agr., ERS–197, May 1967.

Waugh, Frederick V. *Graphic Analysis: Applications in Agricultural Economics,* U.S. Dept. Agr., Agr. Handb. 326, November 1966 (superseded Agr. Handb. 128).

Wetmore, John M., Abel, Martin E., Learn, Elmer W., and Cochrane, Willard W. *Policies for Expanding the Demand for Farm Food Products in the United States,* Part I *History and Potentials,* University of Minnesota Agricultural Experiment Station Tech. Bul. No. 231, April 1959.

Williams, Faith M., and Zimmerman, Carle C. *Studies of Family Living in the U.S. and Other Countries:* An Analysis of Material and Method, U.S. Dept. Agr., Misc. Pub. 223, December 1935.

NAME INDEX

SUBJECT INDEX